ARGUMENT!

What makes ARGUMENT! special?

Scholarship + Pedagogy = M-Series

ARGUMENT! offers instructors unmatched scholarship, content, and currency in a succinct magazine format that engages students.

3 56

362

What's Inside

Engaging pedagogy designed to be eye-catching and visually appealing can be found throughout the text. ARGUMENT! shows students how to read and think critically and respond to the arguments of others.

GOOD ADVICE

Good Advice offers practical and timely advice on topics that help students become better readers, thinkers, and writers.

Try It! asks students to think about what they have just read and apply it to the various types of exercises that include readings, writing, questions, and collaborative exercises.

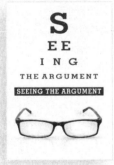

Seeing the Argument demonstrates how to acknowledge and respond to complex arguments that exist all around us—both visual and textual.

WHAT'S TO COME

What's to Come begins the chapter with important questions discussed in the chapter.

did you know

Did You Know? gives students additional information on topics that are discussed in the text.

connect

Connect gives students an opportunity to connect what they've learned with the real world—in groups or by themselves.

let's review

Let's Review summarizes the key points of each chapter in an easy-to-read format.

The McGraw·Hill Companies

Connect
Learn
Succeed™

ARGUMENT!

EXECUTIVE EDITOR: **CHRISTOPHER BENNEM**

MARKETING MANAGER: **KEVIN COLLEARY**

DEVELOPMENTAL EDITOR: **CRAIG LEONARD**

EDITORIAL COORDINATOR: **ZACHARY NORTON**

PRODUCTION EDITOR: **CAREY EISNER**

MANUSCRIPT EDITOR: **PATRICIA OHLENROTH**

DESIGN MANAGER: **JEANNE SCHREIBER**

TEXT DESIGNERS: **MAUREEN MCCUTCHEON AND LINDA ROBERTSON**

COVER DESIGNER: **SEAN LEE**

PHOTO RESEARCHER AND ART EDITOR: **SONIA BROWN**

BUYER: **LOUIS SWAIM**

TEXT PERMISSIONS COORDINATOR: **MARTY MOGA**

MEDIA PROJECT MANAGER: **JENNIFER BARRICK**

COMPOSITION: **10/12 SABON BY BILL SMITH GROUP**

PRINTING: **38# CONSOWEB GLOSS, QUAD/GRAPHICS**

VICE PRESIDENT EDITORIAL: **MICHAEL RYAN**

PUBLISHER: **DAVID PATTERSON**

DIRECTOR OF DEVELOPMENT: **DAWN GROUNDWATER**

COVER: © **MASTERFILE**; ICONS © **BUBAONE/ISTOCKPHOTO**.

CREDITS: THE CREDITS SECTION FOR THIS BOOK BEGINS ON PAGE 441 AND IS
CONSIDERED AN EXTENSION OF THE COPYRIGHT PAGE.

Brief Contents

PART ONE

[Understanding Arguments]

PART TWO

[Writing Arguments]

PART THREE

[Writing a Researched Argument]

PART FOUR

[An Anthology of Contemporary Arguments]

PART ONE

[Understanding Arguments]

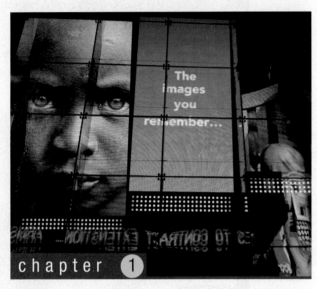

PART TWO

[Writing Arguments]

chapter 3

Writing Effective Arguments

chapter 4

More about Argument: Induction, Deduction, Analogy, and Logical Fallacies

chapter 5

Refuting an Argument

chapter 6

Taking a Position

chapter 7

Writing a Causal Analysis

chapter 8

Writing the Problem/Solution Essay

chapter 9

Writing a Rhetorical Analysis

PART THREE

[Writing a Researched Argument]

chapter 10

Reading, Analyzing, and Using Visuals and Statistics in Argument

chapter 11

Planning the Researched Argument

chapter 12

Evaluating and Utilizing Sources

chapter 13

Drafting and Revising the Researched Argument

chapter 14

Documenting Sources (MLA, APA, and More)

PART FOUR

[An Anthology of Contemporary Arguments]

chapter 15

The Myth and Reality of the Image in American Consumer Culture

chapter 16

The Challenges of Living in a High-Tech, Multimedia World

chapter 17

Violent Media or Violent Society?

chapter 21

Enduring Controversies in a New Age: Abortion, Animal Rights, Capital Punishment, and Health Care

chapter 22

Marriage and Gender Roles: Changing Attitudes vs. Traditional Values

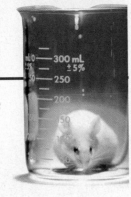

chapter 23

Arguing about Science and Religion: Policy, Politics, and Culture

chapter 24

Competing Perspectives on the American Economic and Financial Crisis

the basics
of argument

chapter 1

What Does an Argument Look Like?

Many everyday arguments are easy to spot. Most readers can sense when an author has intentionally chosen words and images to convince them to adopt a certain position or stance. This March 2010 *Vanity Fair* cover, for example, can clearly be seen as an argument. Critics have labeled this cover racist because it lacks diversity—no Asian, African American, or Hispanic actresses appear in the image.

Similarly, most readers would easily identify the words spoken by New Jersey Governor Chris Christie in early 2011 as an argument:

> The argument you heard most vociferously from the teachers' union was that this was the greatest assault on public education in the history of New Jersey. Now, do you really think that your child is now stressed out and unable to learn because they know that their poor teacher has to pay 1½ percent of their salary for their health care benefits? Have any of your children come home—any of them—and said, "Mom." Pause. "Dad." Another pause. "Please. Stop the madness."

From http://www.nytimes.com/2011/02/27/
magazine/27christie-t.html?_r=2&pagewanted=1

Although these examples seem rather straight-forward, other everyday arguments are harder to spot. Consider this example of "refrigerator" poetry. Is this an argument? You might claim that this poem was written primarily to entertain and to present one person's emotional perspective, not to present an argument. This is true—to a degree. However, this poet has made specific choices about what words to use, what visuals to use, the physical setting of the work, and about how his or her audience should read the material. Even writing primarily designed to entertain, such as a blog entry, a social networking post, or even highway graffiti, says to readers: Do it my way! Think about these ideas as I would! Believe what I believe!

Surely the argument made by this artist is more subtle than the one made by the editors of *Vanity Fair*. The ideas about life and experience that appear in works we label "expressive" are often more subtle than the points we meet head-on in an overt argument. Still, expressive writing gives us new ways of seeing the world. Perhaps, then, we need to recognize that writ-

This February 7, 2011, cover of *Time* magazine shows former U.S. President Ronald Reagan with his arm around President Barack Obama. Obama appears to be enjoying the company of Reagan, who held the president's office from 1981 until 1989 and who passed away in June 2004. However, Reagan, a Republican, adhered to a political philosophy presumably very opposed to that of Obama, a Democrat.

As you examine the *Time* cover, what do you notice? What ideas are suggested by the image of Presidents Reagan and Obama standing together? How do you think readers might view this cover? What makes this cover an argument? For what audience might this piece be targeted? How do you know?

ing strategies and purposes spread along a continuum; they often overlap and do not fit into neat categories. Oftentimes, one image or piece of writing has several different purposes. Typically, however, if you look hard enough, an argument of some sort is being made.

Recognizing Purpose in Everyday Arguments

Many pieces of communication that we do not think of as arguments still contain subtle elements of persuasion. For example, television personality Stephen Colbert's humorous book *I Am America (And So Can You!)* has the primary purpose of entertaining its readers, but we can also see this book as an attempt to make a more serious argument about how Americans see themselves and others in the global arena.

Although it may be fairly easy to identify a text's primary or general purpose (to entertain, to inform, to persuade), it is often more challenging to recognize the more subtle intentions of the author. Most texts have more than one purpose and most, in fact, attempt to persuade their readers to accept the positions and opinions of their authors. Much more about recognizing an argument's purpose will be covered in Chapter 3. For now, keep in mind that every piece of communication, whether written, visual, or even oral, has at least one clear and distinct purpose.

Understanding Audience in Everyday Arguments

Just as every argument has a clear purpose (to persuade its readers), so too does it have an intended audi-

ence. An author must understand the needs of his or her readers if he or she hopes to connect with them and persuade them to accept his or her position. An author who writes without considering his or her audience runs the risk of alienating and offending readers who are not ready to accept the proposed position, or wasting time and energy "preaching to the choir," or trying to convince readers who already agree with the proposed position.

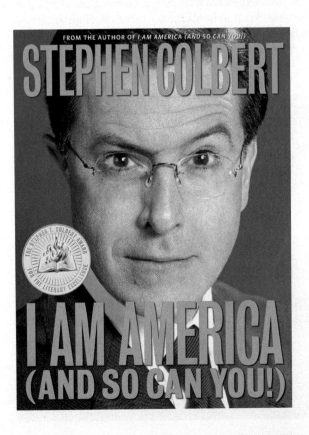

Can you think of other examples of texts with multiple purposes? Or can you think of something not typically considered an argument that actually is one? Find an everyday text, examine the continuum below, and decide where your piece might fall along it. Might your text actually include elements of all three purposes?

PRIMARY PURPOSE: EXPRESSIVE (to evoke feeling or provide humor)	**PRIMARY PURPOSE: EXPOSITORY** (to impart information)	**PRIMARY PURPOSE: PERSUASIVE** (to argue a position)
Author is expressing an emotional viewpoint, but guides the reader's experience by making specific choices about what is presented and how.	Author provides information but still has a distinct point of view on events, details, or facts that is evident in the choices he or she makes.	Author is taking an obvious position on an issue and wants the reader to come away thinking as he or she does.
Think poems, cell phone ringtones, Facebook pages, humorous books, or even T-shirt logos.	Think textbooks, newspaper articles, product labels, true-life crime books, or even the nightly news.	Think political speeches, television ads, newspaper editorials, sermons, or college research essays.

IMPLICIT ARGUMENT ← → EXPLICIT ARGUMENT

Much more about analyzing audience needs, values, and expectations will be covered in Chapter 3. For now, keep in mind that the success of an argument depends on the author's understanding of his or her audience.

Why You Need to Learn to Read and Write Arguments. Right Now.

Now that you've come to see the larger scope of argument and that it exists in practically every piece of communication, it's time to narrow our focus a bit. You can most likely expect that in your current course on argument you probably will not be asked to write a short story, personal narrative, poem, or T-shirt logo. You might, though, be asked to write a summary, critique, research essay, or analysis, so you will need to think about how those writing tasks connect to the world of argument. Regardless of what specific assignments your professor gives you, you can count on one thing: You will be asked to write!

Why work on your writing skills? Here are some good answers to this question:

1. The better writer you become, the better reader you will become and vice versa.

2. The more confident a writer you become, the more efficiently you will handle written assignments in all of your courses.

3. The more you write, the more you will learn about who you are and what really matters to you. More colleges and universities are design-

Communication and writing skills are *the most important abilities* sought by employers. As evidence, you may want to consider the following article from *The New York Times.*

The New York Times
August 26, 2007

Young Workers: U Nd 2 Improve Ur Writing Skills
PHYLLIS KORKKI

A generation ago, employers were still lamenting the poor technical abilities of their entry-level workers. Well, that's not much of an issue anymore, thanks to the omnipresence of computers, cellphones and the Internet.

In a survey of 100 human resources executives, only 5 percent said that recent college graduates lacked computer or technology skills, according to Challenger, Gray & Christmas, the outplacement firm.

The problem now is more basic. Nearly half the executives said that entry-level workers lacked writing skills, and 27 percent said that they were deficient in critical thinking.

It seems that some young employees are now guilty of the technological equivalent of wearing flip-flops: they are writing company e-mail as if they were texting cellphone messages with their thumbs.

In response, employers are sending a message of their own: When you're in the office, put on those dress shoes and start spelling your words correctly, and in full.

ing courses focused on critical thinking about personal values, ethics, and morals. Learning to write about your beliefs and to understand and accommodate the beliefs of others are great ways to be ready for future coursework in this area.

What You Can Expect from Your Writing Assignments

You are about to face a variety of writing assignments, each with its own specific audience and purpose. Pay close attention to each assignment sheet so that you will know what sort of writing your instructor expects. To help you learn the conventions of different types of writing for different audiences, this text includes a variety of argument forms: editorials, advertisements, articles from scholarly journals, photographs, book reviews, and of course, research essays.

While writing your own assignments, always think about what role you will play as the author and the expectations of that specific role. Are you expected to be a student demonstrating knowledge, a citizen arguing for tougher drunk-driving laws, or a scholar presenting the results of research? Any writer—including you—will take on different roles when writing for different audi-

ences and will use different strategies to reach each audience. There are many kinds of argument and many ways to argue successfully.

Why Read and Respond to the Work of Others?

If this is a text about *writing* arguments, why does it contain so many readings, you may wonder. There are good reasons for the collection of readings you find here:

1. College and the workplace will demand that you learn complex information and ideas through reading. This text will give you practice in reading more challenging works.

2. You will need to read to learn and to think critically about what you read. In the world of argument, your reading will serve as a basis for writing.

3. Your writing will be based in some way on one or more sources you have been assigned or that you have selected in response to an assignment. The focus of attention will shift from you to your subject, a subject others have debated before you. You will need to understand the issue,

think carefully about the views of others on the issue, and only then develop your own response.

Critical Reading and the Contexts of Argument

In some contexts, the word *critical* carries the idea of harsh judgment: "The manager was critical of her secretary's long phone conversations." In other contexts, though, the term means "to evaluate carefully." When we speak of the critical reader or critical thinker, we have in mind someone who reads actively, who thinks about issues, and who makes informed judgments. Here is a profile of the critical reader or thinker:

Traits of the Critical Reader/Thinker

- **Focused on the facts.** Give me the facts and show me that they are relevant to the issue.
- **Analytic.** What strategies has the writer/speaker used to develop the argument?
- **Open-minded.** Prepared to listen to different points of view, to learn from others.

- **Questioning/skeptical.** What other conclusions could be supported by the evidence presented? How thorough has the writer/speaker been?
- **Creative.** What are some different ways of looking at the issue or problem?
- **Intellectually active, not passive.** Willing to analyze logic and evidence. Willing to consider many possibilities. Willing, after careful evaluation, to reach a judgment, to take a stand on issues.

Active Reading: Use Your Mind!

Reading is not about looking at black marks on a page—or turning the pages as quickly as you can. Reading means constructing meaning from the marks on the page and getting a message. This concept is underscored by the term *active reading*. To be an active reader, not a passive page-turner, follow these guidelines:

- **Understand your purpose in reading.** Do not just start turning pages to complete an assignment. Think first about your purpose. Are you read-

GOOD ADVICE

You might be asking, "Won't my instructor be my audience?"

Yes, your instructor or TA is probably the actual audience for your paper. Your instructors read and grade your essays, and you want to keep their needs and perspectives in mind when you write. However, when you write an essay with only your instructor in mind, you might not say as much as you should or say it as clearly as you should, because you assume that your instructor knows more than you do and will fill in the gaps. This leaves it up to the instructor to decide what you are really saying, and she might decide that those gaps show that you don't understand the material. If you say to yourself, "I don't have to explain communism; my instructor knows more about that than I do," you could get back a paper that says something like "Shows no understanding of communism." That's an example of what can go awry when you think of your instructor as your only audience.

Thinking about your audience differently can improve your writing, especially in terms of how clearly you express your argument. The clearer your points are, the more likely you are to have a strong essay. Your instructor will say, "You really understand communism—you're able to explain it simply and clearly!" By treating your instructor *as an intelligent but uninformed audience*, you end up addressing her more effectively.

The Writing Center at UNC Chapel Hill, www.unc.edu/depts/wcweb/handouts/audience.html

ing for knowledge on which you will be tested? Focus on your purpose as you read, asking yourself, "What do I need to learn from this work?"

- **Reflect on the title before reading further.** Titles are the first words writers give us. Look for clues in the title that may reveal the work's subject and perhaps the writer's approach or attitude as well. The title "The Idiocy of Urban Life," for example, tells you both subject (urban or city living) and the author's position (urban living is idiotic).

- **Become part of the writer's audience.** Not all writers have you and me in mind when they write. As an active reader, you need to join a writer's audience by learning about the writer, about the time in which the piece was written, and about the writer's expected audience. For the readings in this text, you are aided by introductory notes; be sure to study them.

- **Predict what is coming.** Look for a writer's main idea or purpose statement. Study the work's organization. Then use this information to anticipate what is coming. For example, when you read "There are three good reasons for requiring a dress code in schools," you know the writer will list three reasons.

- **Concentrate.** Slow down and give your full attention to reading. Watch for transition and connecting words that show you how the parts of a text connect. Read an entire article or chapter at one time—or you will need to start over to make sense of the entire piece.

- **Annotate as you read.** The more senses you use, the more active your involvement. That means marking the text as you read (or taking notes if the material is not yours). Underline key sentences, such as the writer's thesis. Then, in the margin, indicate that it is the thesis. For a series of examples (or reasons), label them and number them. When you look up a word's definition, write the definition in the margin next to the word. Draw diagrams to illustrate concepts; draw arrows to connect example to idea. Studies have shown that students who annotate their texts get higher grades. Do what successful students do.

- **Keep a reading journal.** In addition to annotating what you read, you may want to develop the habit of writing regularly in a journal or creating a reading blog online. A reading blog gives you a place to note impressions and reflections on your reading, your initial reactions to assignments, and ideas you may use in your next writing.

Understanding the Arguments of Others

Readers expect accurate, fair, and sensitive uses of sources. An inaccurate summary does not serve its purpose. A passage that is misquoted or quoted out of context makes readers question your credibility. So, after reading and annotating, develop your understanding of each source and the author's argument by doing a preliminary analysis that answers the following questions:

1. **What is the work's primary purpose? Does it combine purposes?** Remember that texts can be classified as expressive (evoking feelings), expository (imparting information), or persuasive (arguing for a position). We can also distinguish between a serious purpose and a humorous one, although humor can be used to advance a serious topic. However, purposes shade into one another. Arguments appeal to emotions, and passionate fiction can teach us about human life and experience. You may assume that a textbook's primary purpose is to give information, but keep in mind that textbooks can take a position on various conflicts within their field.

Whether you are reading print material or online, be sure to create a quiet atmosphere in which you can concentrate.

2. **What is the thesis, or the main idea of the work?** Often the best way to understand a text's thesis is to first ask, What is the subject? Then ask, What does the author assert about that subject, or want me to understand about that subject? Stating the thesis as a complete sentence will help you move from subject to assertion. You may find one or two sentences that state the work's thesis, but keep in mind that sometimes the thesis is implied, not stated.

3. **How is the thesis developed and supported?** Does the writer present a series of examples to illustrate the main idea? Or blend reasons and evidence to develop an argument? Does the writer organize chronologically? Set up a contrast pattern or make an analogy? Explain causes? Observing both the type of support and its organization will help you see how the parts fit together. When you know what it says, you can write a summary or begin to analyze or judge the work.

try it!

Read the following selection from lehighvalleylive.com, noting the annotations that have been started for you. As you read, add your own annotations. Then write a journal or blog entry—four to five sentences at least—to capture your reactions to the following editorial.

Lehighvalleylive.com
Opinion
January 27, 2011
Find the Right Punishment for Teen-Age "Sexting"

This topic is timely and looks interesting.

I should find out more about the legislation in New Jersey and Pennsylvania as I conduct more research.

Legislators in New Jersey and Pennsylvania might want to double-back to their own teenage years as they consider bills to deal with the practice of sexting—teenagers sending nude photos of themselves to a boyfriend or girlfriend, friends sharing those photos with other friends, ex-friends posting compromising photos to get back at someone, etc.

Two adolescent truths we hold to be self-evident:

- For teenage boys, there can never, ever be enough images of the opposite sex unclothed.
- Anything worth sharing is worth hitting the cell-phone button to feed each others' curiosity as long as parents and teachers don't find out about it.

It's with a cautious nod to those forces of nature that legislators must make the case against sexting, acknowledging that a voluntary expression of intimacy can quickly become an unwanted invasion of privacy with the entire online world, and that such images can quickly become fodder for pedophiles and child pornographers. Some prosecutors have wielded a heavy club to go after teenagers in these circumstances, charging them with transmitting child pornography.

The lack of a clear-headed law is still a gaping problem. Last year, a federal judge in Pennsylvania ruled that girls who had e-mailed nude photos of themselves to friends could not be charged as child pornographers.

The Pennsylvania House of Representatives passed a bill last year, proposing a second-degree misdemeanor charge against minors "who intentionally or knowingly record, view, possess or transmit images of sexually explicit conduct involving a minor above age 13." It didn't go anywhere in the Senate.

A bill now moving through the New Jersey Assembly seems to strike the right balance. Assemblywoman Pamela Lampitt, D-Camden, has proposed an educational program for "sexters" as an alternative to criminal prosecution. The bill cleared the Judiciary Committee and now heads to the full Assembly.

"When our children are in many different places doing many different things, we need to find a means and a mechanism not to send them off to jail ... but to educate them," Lampitt said.

Sexting isn't always innocent; it can be a form of cyber-bullying and inflict real pain on young people. Under the bill, a juvenile court would assess whether a young offender would be harmed by prosecution and is unlikely to repeat the practice. Those who meet the criteria would be admitted to a program on the social consequences and potential criminal penalties of sexting. The programs would apply to teens, not adults, who would still face child pornography charges for such transmissions.

Given the rising tide of such incidents—a recent survey by The Associated Press and MTV found a quarter of American teenagers admitted to some form of sexting—it's only right to give first-timers a heavy dose of educating and lecturing. It wouldn't hurt to get parents involved, too. They should be laying down their own law, monitoring their kids' phones and suspending their privileges.

That's a lot more sensible than treating them as criminals.

http://www.lehighvalleylive.com/today/index.ssf/2011/01/opinion_find_the_right_punishm.html

Even everyday communications like Facebook profiles can be viewed as arguments.

Characteristics of Argument

When you begin to understand the basics of argument, you will start to look at the world around you in a new way. Facebook profiles, T-shirt logos, newspaper editorials, websites, and even junk mail all possess elements of persuasion. Have you ever considered how your own daily communications are actually arguments or attempts at persuading an audience? Look at any Facebook, MySpace, or similar web blog and think about what the author is trying to communicate to the world. Is there a purpose to the page? Is there an intended audience? If you can begin to look at even the most familiar forms of communication as arguments, you will soon begin to realize that arguments are everywhere.

Argument Is Conversation with a Goal

When you enter into an argument (as speaker, writer, or reader), you become a participant in an ongoing debate about an issue. Because you are probably not the first to address the issue, you need to be aware of the ways that the issue has been debated by others and then seek to advance the conversation, just as you would if you were having a casual conversation with friends about going to a movie. Once the time of the movie is set, the discussion turns to whose car to take or where to meet. If you were to just repeat the time of the movie, you would add nothing useful to the

GOOD ADVICE

In this section, we will explore the processes of thinking logically and analyzing issues to reach informed judgments. Mature people do not need to agree on all issues in order to respect one another's good sense, but they do have little patience with uninformed or illogical statements masquerading as argument. (Just ask Judge Judy how frustrating this can be.) As you learn to read, respond to, and write arguments, you will need to take other opinions and logical opposing points of view (often called counterarguments) into account. After all, there are always more than two sides to every argument!

Judge Judy, the famously impatient TV judge, has learned to recognize illogical arguments in her courtroom.

conversation. Also, if you were to change the subject to a movie you saw last week, you would annoy your friends by not offering useful information or showing that you valued the current conversation. Just as with a conversation about a movie, you want your argument to stay focused on the issue, to respect what others have already contributed, and to make a useful addition to everyone's understanding of the issue.

Argument Takes a Stand on an Arguable Issue

A meaningful argument focuses on a debatable issue. We usually do not argue about facts. "Professor Jones's American literature class meets at 10:00 on Mondays" is not arguable. It is either true or false. We can check the schedule of classes to find out. (Sometimes, however, the facts change; new facts replace old ones.) We also do not debate personal preferences for the simple reason that they are just that—personal. If the debate is about the appropriateness of boxing as a sport, for you to declare that you would rather play tennis is to fail to advance the conversation. You have expressed a personal preference, interesting perhaps, but not relevant to the debate.

Argument Uses Reasons and Evidence

Some arguments merely look right. That is, conclusions are drawn from facts, but the facts are not those that actually support the assertion, or the conclusion is not the only or the best explanation of those facts. To shape convincing arguments, we need more than an array of facts. We need to think critically, to analyze the issue, to see relationships, and to weigh evidence. We need to avoid the temptation to argue from emotion only, or to believe that just stating our opinion is the same thing as building a sound argument.

Argument Incorporates Values

Arguments are based not just on reason and evidence but also on the beliefs and values we hold and think that our audience may hold as well. In a reasoned debate, you want to make clear the values that you consider relevant to the argument. For example, many people disagree about whether boxing should be banned as a sport.

A writer against a ban on boxing might argue that boxing teaches children about the importance of discipline, persistence, and motivation in sports. The writer thinks these things are worthwhile, which gives us insights into the values he or she holds.

Arguments incorporate the values of their writers and try to appeal to the values of their readers. The famous "got milk?" campaign attempts to appeal to specific values both visually and with text. Look at the ads here. What values does the milk industry seem to believe are important to their customers? Do you think these two ads are targeted at different audiences? If so, what makes you think so?

S
EE
ING

THE ARGUMENT

SEEING THE ARGUMENT

A writer for a ban on boxing might argue that fighters are promoting vicious and injury-producing violence to children in order to make money. (These points give us insights into the things this writer values or believes worthwhile.)

Argument Recognizes the Topic's Complexity

Much false reasoning (the logical fallacies discussed in Chapter 4) results from a writer's oversimplifying an issue. A sound argument begins with an understanding that most issues are complicated. The wise person approaches ethical concerns such as abortion or euthanasia or public policy issues such as tax cuts or trade agreements with the understanding that there are many philosophical, moral, and political perspectives that complicate discussions of these topics. Recognizing an argument's complexity may also lead us to an understanding that there can be more than one "right" position. The thoughtful arguer respects the views of others, seeks common ground when possible, and often chooses a conciliatory approach.

The Shape of Argument

The Aristotelian Model

One of the best ways to understand the basics of argument is to reflect on what the Greek philosopher Aristotle describes as the three "players" in any argument:

- the writer (or speaker),
- the argument itself, and
- the reader (or audience).

Aristotle explained that we can use three different artistic proofs to support our arguments. These proofs are logos, pathos, and ethos.

GOOD ADVICE

Writing an essay with the following thesis statement would not lead to an effective argument:

The Office is my favorite show.

This statement is simply a personal preference and does not allow a rational reader to logically disagree with you. After all, what is the opposing position? This essay will most likely fall short of being an effective argument.

Even seemingly straightforward issues like vegetarianism can be complex and politically charged. Be sure that you understand the debate before you attempt to enter into it.

Does the author of this ad seem to understand and appreciate the complexity of this issue? Why or why not? Does this affect your reaction to this argument? Why do you think this author chose to handle the argument in this manner? What values does the author seem to hold?

Feeding kids meat is child abuse

FIGHT THE FAT • GO VEG *PeTA.org.uk*

Aristotle called the logic of the argument the *logos*—the assertion and the support for that assertion. A successful argument needs a logical and convincing logos. An argument also implies an audience, those whose views we want to influence. Aristotle called this part of argument *pathos*. Good arguers need to be alert to the values and attitudes of their audience and to appeal effectively to their emotions. However, Aristotle also explained that part of our appeal to an audience rests in the logos, our logic and evidence. An argument that is all emotional appeal will not move thoughtful audiences.

Finally (and for Aristotle the most important of the three players) is the writer/speaker, or *ethos*. No argument, Aristotle asserted, no matter how logical, no matter how appealing emotionally, will succeed if the audience rejects the arguer's credibility, the writer's "ethical" qualities. As members of the audience, we need to believe that the arguer is a person of knowledge, honesty, and goodwill.

We argue in a specific context of three interrelated parts. We present support for a concrete assertion, thesis, or claim to a specific audience whose demands, expectations, and character we have given thought to when shaping our argument. We also present ourselves as informed, competent, and reliable so that our audience will give

serious attention to our argument. Your audience evaluates *you* as a part of their evaluation of your argument. Lose your credibility and you lose your argument.

did you know **?**

Aristotle, one of the most famous of the Greek philosophers, a student of Plato and a teacher of Alexander the Great, was also one of the earliest to recognize the power of visuals in the creation of meaning.

In his famous work *De Anima*, or *On the Soul*, he states,

> "... the soul never thinks without an image."

http://classics.mit.edu/Aristotle/soul.3.iii.html

Read the following argument made by Steve Jobs, founder and CEO of Apple, during a speech to a senior team of a company. Does it successfully use all three of Aristotle's players? Does he possess credibility on this subject? Does his assertion seem logical? Does he understand to whom he is addressing his argument?

Killing bad ideas isn't that hard—lots of companies, even bad companies, are good at that. . . . What is really hard—and a hallmark of great companies—is that they kill a lot of good ideas. . . . For any single good idea to succeed, it needs a lot of resources, time, and attention, and so only a few ideas can be developed fully. Successful companies are tough enough to kill a lot of good ideas so those few that survive have a chance of reaching their full potential and being implemented properly.

http://blogs.bnet.com/bnet1/?p=680

Aristotle also explained that an argument can rely on *inartistic proofs*. Inartistic proofs include support for arguments that comes from outside sources. An attorney in a courtroom, for example, uses witness testimony to prove his or her case. Oftentimes, too, politicians employ statistical evidence in speeches to prove a point. A United States senator might cite a high unemployment rate of 10 percent as support for an argument in favor of expanding government jobs programs. Such statistics as well as citations from authorities, witnesses, and other fact-based evidence all constitute inartistic proof.

Topoi, or the common topics, provide another way we can construct arguments, according to Aristotle. An arguer can show *similarity and difference* (compare/contrast) to convince the audience that one option represents a superior choice over another. We see this approach applied in advertising all the time. Automobile commercials, for example, will acknowledge that Manufacturer A's car is similar in its features to Manufacturer B's model, but the commercial will quickly point out that Manufacturer A's car offers a superior feature that Manufacturer B's model does not. One could also argue the *division* of the parts: Manufacturer A, for example, could show how the separate and distinct features of the car make it a superior choice for consumers. In describing *cause and effect*, Manufacturer A could also argue that Manufacturer B's car has poor quality airbags that have failed to prevent fatalities on the road. Similarity and difference, division, and cause and effect represent three of a number of different common topics. These *topoi*—like the artistic and inartistic proofs—help us construct arguments and convince audiences of our positions.

The Toulmin Model

[handwritten: = evidence = assertion stated/implied]

British philosopher Stephen Toulmin added to what we have learned from Aristotle by focusing our attention on the basics of the argument itself. First, consider this definition of argument: An argument consists of evidence and/or reasons presented in support of an assertion or claim that is either stated or implied. Here are two examples:

CLAIM: We should not go skiing today

EVIDENCE: because it is too cold.

EVIDENCE: Because some laws are unjust,

CLAIM: civil disobedience is sometimes justified.

Toulmin explained that the basics of a complete argument are actually a bit more complex than these examples suggest. Each argument has a third part, which is not stated in the preceding examples. This third part is the glue that connects the support—the evidence and reasons—to the argument's claim and thus fulfills the logic of the argument. Toulmin called this glue an argument's *warrants*. These are the principles or assumptions that allow us to assert that our evidence or reasons—what Toulmin called the *grounds*—do indeed support our claim. Warrants represent a chain of reasoning linking claims with grounds. Look again at the sample arguments to see what warrants must be accepted to make each argument work:

CLAIM: We should not go skiing today.

EVIDENCE: It is too cold.

did you know ?

Despite the fact that rhetoricians have used his model as the basis for much of their work for decades, Stephen Toulmin (1922–2009) never intended to become one of the leading theorists in the field of rhetoric and writing.

In fact, he began his career as a philosopher and maintained a focus on ethics and moral reasoning for most of his career.

www.willamette.edu/cla/rhetoric/courses/argumentation/Toulmin.htm
www.giffordlectures.org/Author.asp?AuthorID=269
www.nytimes.com/2009/12/11/.../11toulmin.html

ASSUMPTIONS (WARRANTS): When it is too cold, skiing is not fun; the activity is not sufficient to keep one from becoming uncomfortable.

AND:

"Too cold" means whatever is too cold for me.

CLAIM: Civil disobedience is sometimes justified.

EVIDENCE: Some laws are unjust.

ASSUMPTIONS (WARRANTS): To get unjust laws changed, people need to be made aware of the injustice. Acts of civil disobedience will get people's attention and make them aware that the laws need changing.

Assumptions play an important role in any argument, so we need to be sure to understand what they are. Note, for instance, the second assumption operating in the first argument: The temperature the speaker considers uncomfortable will also be uncomfortable

try it!

Collaborative Exercise: Building Arguments

With your class partner or in small groups, examine each of the following claims. Select two, think of one statement that could serve as evidence for each claim, and then think of the underlying assumptions that complete each of the arguments.

1. Professor X is not a good instructor.
2. Americans need to reduce the fat in their diets.
3. Tiger Woods is a great golfer.
4. Physical education classes should be graded pass/fail.
5. College newspapers should be free of supervision by faculty or administrators.

for her companions—an uncertain assumption. In the second argument, the warrant is less debatable, for acts of civil disobedience usually get media coverage and thus dramatize the issue.

warrant = assumption

The Language of Claims and Support

What kinds of statements function as claims and as support? Philosopher Stephen Toulmin was particularly interested in the strength or probability of various arguments. Some kinds of arguments are stronger than others because of the language or logic they use. Other arguments must, necessarily, be heavily qualified for the claim to be supportable. Toulmin developed terminology to provide a strategy for analyzing the degree of probability in an argument and to remind us of the need to qualify some kinds of claims. You have already seen how the idea of warrants, or assumptions, helps us think about the glue that presumably makes an argument work. Additional terms and concepts from Toulmin help us analyze the arguments of others and prepare more convincing arguments of our own.

Types of Claims

claim = seeks to prove

A *claim* is what the argument asserts or seeks to prove. It answers the question, What is your point? In an argumentative speech or essay, the claim is the speaker's or writer's main idea or thesis. Although an argument's claim follows from reasons and evidence, we often present an argument—whether written or spoken—with the claim stated near the beginning. We can better understand an argument's claim by recognizing four types of claims: claims of fact, claims of value, claims of judgment, and claims of policy.

Claims of Fact

Although facts usually support claims, we do argue over some facts. Claims of fact state that a condition exists, did exist, or will exist. Historians and biographers may argue over what happened in the past, although they are more likely to argue over the significance of what happened. Scientists also argue over the facts, over how to classify an unearthed fossil, for example, or whether the fossil indicates that the animal had feathers.

CLAIM: The small, predatory dinosaur *Deinonychus* hunted its prey in packs.

This claim is supported by the discovery of several fossils of *Deinonychus* close together and with the fossil bones of a much larger dinosaur. Their teeth have also been found in or near the bones of dinosaurs that have died in a struggle.

As you will learn in Chapter 10, visual images (e.g., graphics, charts, and photographs) can make claims just like written essays and speeches. These two images both make claims with support. The first image, a billboard, makes a statement about the "War on Drugs," while the second shows homicide rates during both Prohibition in the early 1900s and about 30 years of fighting the "War on Drugs." With regard to the billboard, what do you see as its claim? Who is making it? How could the homicide statistics shown in the second image be used as support for the billboard's claim?

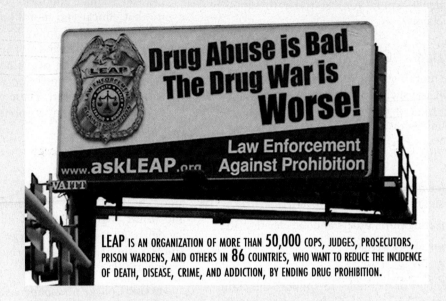

LEAP IS AN ORGANIZATION OF MORE THAN 50,000 COPS, JUDGES, PROSECUTORS, PRISON WARDENS, AND OTHERS IN 86 COUNTRIES, WHO WANT TO REDUCE THE INCIDENCE OF DEATH, DISEASE, CRIME, AND ADDICTION, BY ENDING DRUG PROHIBITION.

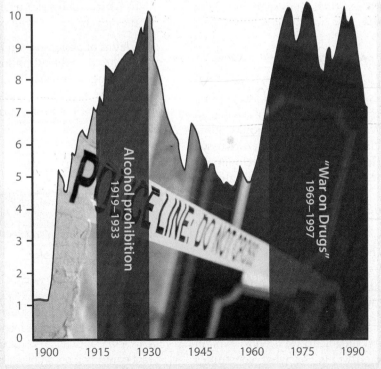

Drug War Facts, 6th ed., p. 21. www.drugwarfacts.org.

Assertions about what will happen are sometimes classified as claims of fact, but they can also be labeled as inferences supported by facts. Predictions about a future event may be classified as a claim of fact:

CLAIM: The United States will win the most gold medals at the 2014 Olympics.

CLAIM: I will get an A on tomorrow's psychology test.

What evidence would you use today to support each of these claims?

Claims of Value

These include moral, ethical, and aesthetic judgments. Assertions that use such words as *good* or *bad, better* or *worse,* and *right* or *wrong* are claims of value. The following are all claims of value:

CLAIM: *Family Guy* is a better show than *The Simpsons.*

CLAIM: *Adventures of Huckleberry Finn* is one of the most significant American novels.

CLAIM: Cheating hurts others and the cheater too.

CLAIM: Abortion is wrong.

Support for claims of value often include other value statements. For example, to support the claim that censorship is bad, arguers often assert that the free exchange of ideas is good and necessary in a democracy. The support is itself a value statement. The arguer may believe, probably correctly, that most people will more readily agree with the support (the free exchange of ideas is good) than with the claim (censorship is bad).

Claims of Judgment

Judgments are opinions based on values, beliefs, or philosophical concepts. In other words, claims of judgment argue principles without necessarily asking an authority (e.g., a government) to take action. Calling for action suggests a claim of policy, which is discussed in the next section. (Judgments also include opinions based on personal preferences, but we have already excluded these from argument.) Judgments concern right and wrong, good and bad, better or worse, and *should* or *should not:*

CLAIM: No more than twenty-six students should be enrolled in any English class.

CLAIM: Cigarette advertising should be eliminated, and the federal government should develop an antismoking campaign.

To support the first judgment, we need to explain what constitutes overcrowding, or what constitutes the best class size for effective teaching. If we can support our views on effective teaching, we may be able

to convince the college president that ordering more desks for Room 110 is not the best solution for the increased enrollment in English classes. The second judgment also offers a solution to a problem, in this case a national health problem. To reduce the number of deaths, we need to reduce the number of smokers, by encouraging smokers either to quit or not to start. The underlying assumption: Advertising does affect behavior.

As you evaluate and form your own judgments, be aware that ethical and moral judgments (those based on personal standards) may be more difficult to support because they depend not just on definitions and established criteria but on values and beliefs as well. If taking another person's life is wrong, why isn't it wrong in war? Or is it? These are difficult questions that require thoughtful responses rather than snap judgments.

Claims of Policy

Finally, claims of policy call for an action that a governing body should take. The words "should," "ought," and "must" signal these sorts of claims. Claims of policy debate, for example, college rules, state gun laws, and U.S. aid to Africans suffering from AIDS. The following are claims of policy:

CLAIM: College newspapers should not be controlled in any way by college authorities.

CLAIM: States should not have laws allowing people to carry concealed weapons.

CLAIM: The United States must provide more aid to African countries where 25 percent or more of the citizens have tested positive for HIV.

Claims of policy are often closely tied to judgments of morality or political philosophy, but they also need to be grounded in feasibility. That is, your claim needs to be doable, to be based on a thoughtful consideration of the real world and the complexities of public policy issues.

try it!

Exercise: Judgments

Go to your favorite website or pick up your favorite magazine. As you read through the content, compile a list of three claims of judgment. For each judgment listed, generate one statement of support, either a fact, an inference, or another judgment. Then state the warrant (underlying assumption) required to complete each argument.

The billboard shown here is an example of a claim of policy. But is simply making this claim enough to create an actual policy? The clear answer is no. In order to make a solid argument for a policy change, an audience member would expect this claim to be backed with evidence and convincing, logical support. What types of sources might this group use to support their claim that gay and lesbian couples should have equal protection, just as married couples do? Why do you think they used Coretta Scott King's quote here? Does it help their argument? If so, how?

Support for Claims ~~grounds~~ ~~evidence~~

Grounds (Reasons, Data, or Evidence)

The term *grounds* refers to the reasons and evidence provided in support of a claim. Although the words *data, reasons,* and *evidence* can also be used, *grounds* is the more general term because it includes logic as well as examples or statistics. We determine the grounds of an argument by asking, "Why do you think that?" or "How do you know that?" When writing your own arguments, you can ask yourself these questions and answer them by using a *because* clause:

CLAIM: Smoking should be banned in restaurants

GROUNDS: *because* secondhand smoke is a serious health hazard.

CLAIM: Pete Sampras was a better tennis player than Andre Agassi

GROUNDS: *because* (1) he was ranked number one longer than Agassi,

(2) he won more tournaments than Agassi, and

(3) he won more major tournaments than Agassi.

Let's consider what types of evidence are sometimes used as grounds for arguments and which are most effective and reliable.

Facts

Facts are statements that are verifiable. Factual statements refer to what can be counted, measured, or con-firmed by reasonable observers or trusted experts and are often used as grounds for researched arguments.

- There are 26 desks in Room 110.
- In the United States, about 400,000 people die each year as a result of smoking.

These are factual statements. We can verify the first by observation—by counting. The second fact comes from medical records. We rely on trusted record-keeping sources and medical experts for verification. By definition, we do not argue about the facts. Usually. Sometimes "facts" change, as we learn more about our world. For example, only in the last thirty years has convincing evidence been gathered to

GOOD ADV!CE

Get your facts from credible sources and critically analyze the information provided. Sometimes "facts" are false facts. These are statements that sound like facts but are incorrect. For example, if a writer were to report a source's claim that the war in Iraq is "the most expensive war in American history" based on dollars spent, he or she would be mistaken. Proper research would reveal that, taking inflation into account, World War II cost far more.

Read the following article and then complete the exercise that follows. This exercise tests both careful reading and your understanding of the differences among facts, inferences, and judgments.

Paradise Lost

Richard Morin

Richard Morin, a journalist with *The Washington Post*, writes a regular Sunday columfn titled "Unconventional Wisdom," a column presenting interesting new information from the social sciences. The following article was Morin's column for July 9, 2000.

Here's my fantasy vacation: Travel back in time to the 1700s, to some languid South Pacific island paradise where ripe fruit hangs heavy on the trees and the native islanders live in peace with nature and with each other.

Or at least that was my fantasy vacation until I talked to anthropologist Patrick Kirch, one of the country's leading authorities on the South Pacific and director of the Phoebe Hearst Museum of Anthropology at the University of California at Berkeley.

The South Seas islands painted by Paul Gauguin and celebrated by Robert Louis Stevenson were no Gardens of Eden, Kirch writes in his riveting new history of the South Pacific, *On the Road of the Winds*. Many of these islands witnessed episodes of environmental depredation, endemic warfare and bloody ritual long before seafaring Europeans first visited. "Most islands of the Pacific were densely populated by the time of European contact, and the human impact on the natural ecosystem was often disastrous—with wholesale decimation of species and loss of vast tracts of land," he said.

Kirch says we can blame the French for all the loose talk about a tropical nirvana. "French philosophers of the Enlightenment saw these islands, especially Tahiti, as the original natural society where people lived in a state of innocence and food fell from the trees," he said. "How wrong they were."

French explorer Louis Antoine de Bougainville visited Tahiti for two weeks in 1769 and thought he discovered a paradise awash in social tolerance and carefree sex. Bougainville's breathless description of Tahiti became the basis for Jean Jacques Rousseau's concept of *l'homme naturel*—the noble savage.

Savage, indeed. Even as Bougainville poked around their craggy volcanic island, Rousseau's "noble savages" were busy savaging each other. The Tahitians were in the midst of a bitter civil war, complete with ritual sacrifice to their bloodthirsty war god, Oro. On Mangaia in the Cook Islands, Kirch discovered ovens and pits filled with the charred bones of men, women, and even children.

And forget that free-love nonsense. Dating, mating, and reproduction were tricky business throughout the South Seas several hundred years ago. To keep the population in check, the residents of tiny Tikopia in the Santa Cruz Islands practiced infanticide. Abortion also was common. And to "concentrate" their bloodlines, Kirch said, members of the royal class in Hawaii married their brothers and sisters. If they only knew . . .

Not all South Seas islands were little cesspools. On some of the smaller islands, early Polynesians avoided cultural collapse by adopting strict population control measures, including enforced suicide. "Some young men were encouraged to go to sea and not return," he said.

Perhaps the best example of the havoc wrought by the indigenous peoples of the South Pacific is found on desolate Easter Island, home of the monolithic stone heads that have gazed out from the front of a thousand travel brochures. Until recently, researchers believed that Easter Island's open, grassy plains and barren knife-point volcanic ridges had always been, well, grassy plains and barren ridges.

Not true, says Kirch. The island was once covered with dense palm and hard-wood forests. But by the 1700s, when the first Europeans arrived, these forests had been burned by the islanders to clear land for agriculture, transforming lush groves into semi-tropical tundra. "On Easter Island, the ultimate extinction of the palm and other woody plants had a further consequence: the inability to move or erect the large stone statues" because there were no logs to use as rollers to move the giant heads from the quarries, Kirch writes.

The stone carvers' society collapsed, as did Easter Island culture. By the time Dutch explorer Jacob Roggeveen arrived on Easter Sunday in 1722, residents had taken to living in underground caves for protection from the social chaos that had enveloped their island home.

When viewed today, Kirch says, the monoliths remain an "imposing stone text that suggests a thousand human sagas." They also carry a lesson to our age, he argues—warning us "to achieve a sustainable relationship with our planet"—or else.

Label each of the following sentences as F (fact), FF (false fact), I (inference), or J (judgment).

_____ 1. In the 1700s native South Pacific islanders lived in peace and harmony.

_____ 2. It is foolish to romanticize life on South Sea islands.

_____ 3. French philosopher Rousseau based his idea of the noble savage on the Tahitians.

_____ 4. The stone statues on Easter Island suggest many stories.

_____ 5. In the past, noble Hawaiians married within their families.

_____ 6. Tahitians were savage people.

_____ 7. Some South Pacific islanders used to practice abortion and infanticide.

_____ 8. Easter Island has always had grassy plains and barren ridges.

_____ 9. Finding and using sustainable strategies will help preserve the environment.

_____ 10. People should not marry family members.

demonstrate the relationship between smoking and various illnesses of the heart and lungs.

Inferences

Inferences are opinions based on facts. Inferences are the conclusions we draw from an analysis of facts. If a proper and logical analysis is done, inferences can provide logical grounds for arguments.

- There will not be enough desks in Room 110 for upcoming fall-semester classes.

- Smoking is a serious health hazard.

Predictions of an increase in student enrollment for the coming semester lead to the inference that most English classes scheduled in Room 110 will have several more students than last year. The dean should order new desks. Similarly, we infer from the number of deaths that smoking is a health problem; statistics show more people dying from tobacco-related illnesses than from AIDS, murder, or car accidents, causes of death that get media coverage but do not produce nearly as many deaths.

Inferences vary in their closeness to the facts supporting them. That the sun will rise tomorrow is an inference, but we count on its happening, acting as if it is a fact. However, the first inference stated above is

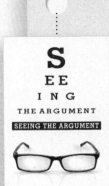
To create an effective argument, you need to assess the potential for acceptance of your warrants and backing. Is your audience likely to share your values, your religious beliefs, or your scientific approach to issues? If you are speaking to a group at your church, then backing based on the religious beliefs of that church may be effective. If you are preparing an argument for a general audience, then using specific religious assertions as warrants or backing probably will not result in an effective argument.

Consider this ad for Abercrombie & Fitch. What claims is the author making about the product (jeans)? Who is the target audience? Based on what you know about this target audience, are they likely to share the values and beliefs this ad demonstrates? What types of backing might this audience expect in support of this claim?

based not just on the fact of 26 desks but on another inference—a projected increase in student enrollment—and on two assumptions. The argument looks like this:

CLAIM: There will not be enough desks in Room 110 for upcoming fall-semester classes.

FACT: There are 26 desks in Room 110.

INFERENCE: There will be more first-year students next year.

ASSUMPTIONS:
1. English will remain a required course.
2. No additional classrooms are available for English classes.

This inference could be challenged by a different analysis of the facts supporting enrollment projections. Or if additional rooms can be found, the dean will not need to order new desks. Note that inferences can be part of the support of an argument, or they can be the claim of an argument.

Warrants

Why should we believe that your grounds do indeed support your claim?

Your argument's warrants answer this question. They explain why your evidence really is evidence. Sometimes warrants reside in language itself, in the meanings of the words we are using. If I am *younger* than my brother, then my brother must be *older* than I am.

In many arguments based on statistical data, the argument's warrant rests on complex analyses of the statistics—and on the conviction that the statistics have been developed without error.

In some philosophical arguments, the warrants are the logical structures (often shown mathematically) connecting a sequence of reasons. Still, without taking courses in statistics and logic, you can develop an alertness to the good sense of some arguments and the dubious sense of others. You know, for example, that good SAT scores are a predictor of success in college. Can you argue that you will do well in college because you have good SATs? No. We can determine only a statistical probability. We cannot turn probabilities about a group of people into a warrant about one person in the group. In addition, SAT scores are only one predictor. Another key variable is motivation.

Here is an example of how a claim, grounds (or evidence), and a warrant work together in forming a logical argument:

CLAIM: Pete Sampras was a better tennis player than Roger Federer.

GROUNDS:
- He had a streak of 31 straight wins at Wimbledon.
- Sampras won his first major tournament at 19, while Federer didn't win one until 21.
- Federer is $18 million and 24 titles shy of Sampras' career records.

WARRANT: It is appropriate to judge and rank tennis players on these kinds of statistics. That is, the better player is the one who has the higher winning streak at Wimbledon, who won a major tournament earlier in his career, and who has won more and earned more than the other.

Backing

good evidence?

Standing behind an argument's warrant may be additional support. Backing answers the question, How do we know that your evidence is good evidence?

You may answer this question by providing authoritative sources for the data (for example, the Census Bureau or the U.S. Tennis Association). Or you may explain in detail the methodology of the experiments performed or the surveys taken.

When scientists and social scientists present the results of their research, they anticipate the question of backing and automatically provide a detailed explanation of the process by which they acquired their evidence. In criminal trials, defense attorneys challenge the backing of the assumptions or warrants underlying the prosecution's argument. They question the handling of blood samples sent to labs for DNA testing, for instance. The defense attorneys want jury members to doubt the *quality* of the evidence, perhaps even to doubt the reliability of DNA testing altogether.

Qualifiers

Some arguments are absolute; they can be stated without qualification.

Having the ability to foresee and effectively rebut your audience's potential objections is a crucial part of crafting a successful argument. Candidates for political office, for example, anticipate their opponents' arguments and have a plan for refuting those arguments.

If I am younger than my brother, then he must be older than I am.

Most arguments, however, need some qualification; many, in fact, need precise limitations. If, when playing bridge, I am dealt eight spades, then my opponents and partner together must have five spade cards—because there are thirteen cards of each suit in a deck. My partner probably has one spade but could have no spades. My partner possibly has two or more spades, but I would be foolish to count on it. When bidding my hand, I must be controlled by the laws of probability.

Look again at the smoking ban claim made earlier. Observe the absolute nature of both the claim and its support. If secondhand smoke is indeed a health hazard, it will be that in all restaurants, not just in some. With each argument we have to assess the need of qualification that is appropriate to a successful argument.

Sweeping generalizations often come to us in the heat of a debate or when we first start to think about an issue.

UNQUALIFIED CLAIM: Gun control is wrong because it restricts individual rights.

But, on reflection, surely you would not want to argue against all forms of gun control. (An unqualified assertion is understood by your audience to be absolute.) Would you sell guns to felons in jail or to children on the way to school? Obviously not. So, let's try the claim again, this time with two important qualifiers:

QUALIFIED CLAIM: Adults without a criminal record should not be restricted in the purchase of guns.

Others may want this claim further qualified to eliminate particular types of guns or to limit the number purchased or to regulate the process for purchasing. The gun-control debate is not about absolutes; it is about which qualified claim is best.

Counterarguments and Rebuttals

Arguments can be challenged. Smart debaters assume that there are people who will disagree with them. They anticipate the ways that opponents can challenge their arguments. When you are planning an argument, you need to think about how you can counter or rebut the challenges you anticipate. Think of yourself as an attorney in a court case preparing your own argument and a defense against the other attorney's challenges to your argument. If you ignore the important role of rebuttals, you may not win the jury to your side.

Writers can handle counterarguments in several effective ways. You may, in fact, partially concede certain facts. For example, if your opponent points out that marriage has a long history of being between a man and a woman (and attempts to use this to counter

This, simply stated, is the argument that could be made against your position. Don't be fooled, however, into thinking a counterargument is simply the opposite of your position. Many counterarguments are subtle and more complex than you might first assume.

For example, the image here is designed to present a clear argument against drilling for oil in Alaska based on the claim that it would harm the natural habitat of animals. But is the counterargument simply that the drilling would not cause this harm? Or is it more complex than that? Might your opponent concede that some harm may come to the habitat of the polar bear, but that the increase in oil production is worth that sacrifice? Might she claim that not nearly as much harm will come to the native wildlife as many believe? Or might she even claim that this is simply a scare tactic created by those with an interest in maintaining our foreign oil dependence?

When considering potential objections to your argument, you need to analyze your opposition's position fully. What might he raise as potential questions or problems with your position? By fully understanding the complexity of your opponent's position, you will more effectively be able to refute or rebut his objections and ultimately strengthen your own argument.

your argument that gay marriage should be legalized), you can acknowledge that this is a true statement without undermining your own argument. You can rebut the assertion, however, that this fact somehow supports the notion that marriage should continue to be viewed in this manner.

You may also want to use support (evidence, facts, data) to completely repudiate your opponent's counterargument. By bringing potential objections to the forefront and effectively negating them, you will strengthen your own credibility with your audience and will ultimately create a stronger argument.

Using Toulmin's Terms to Analyze Arguments

Terms are never an end in themselves; we learn them when we recognize that they help us to organize our thinking about a subject. Toulmin's terms can aid your reading of the arguments of others. You can see what's going on in an argument if you analyze it, applying Toulmin's language to its parts. Not all terms will be useful for every analysis because, for example, some arguments do not have qualifiers or rebuttals. But to recognize that an argument is with-

out qualifiers is to learn something important about that argument.

First, here is a simple argument broken down into its parts using Toulmin's terms:

GROUNDS: Because Dr. Bradshaw has an attendance policy,

CLAIM: students who miss more than seven classes will

QUALIFIER: most likely (last year, Dr. Bradshaw did allow one student, in unusual circumstances, to continue in the class) be dropped from the course.

WARRANT: Dr. Bradshaw's syllabus explains her attendance policy,

BACKING: a policy consistent with the concept of a discussion class that depends on student participation and consistent with the attendance policies of most of her colleagues.

REBUTTAL: Although some students complain about an attendance policy of any kind, Dr. Bradshaw does explain her policy and her reasons for it the first day of class. She then reminds students that the syllabus is a contract between them; if they choose to stay, they agree to abide by the guidelines explained on the syllabus.

The argument in the example is brief and fairly simple. Let's see how Toulmin's terms can help us analyze a longer, more complex argument. Read actively and annotate the following essay while noting the existing annotations using Toulmin's terms. Then answer the questions that follow the article.

prereading } **What are some good reasons to have zoos? What**
questions } **are some problems associated with them?**

Let the Zoo's Elephants Go

Les Schobert

The author has spent more than 30 years working in zoos, primarily in care of elephants. He has been a curator of both the Los Angeles and North Carolina zoos. His argument was published October 16, 2005, in *The Washington Post*.

The Smithsonian Institution is a national treasure, but when it comes to elephants, its National Zoo is a national embarrassment.
Claim

In 2000 the zoo euthanized Nancy, an African elephant that was suffering from foot problems so painful that standing had become difficult for her. Five years later the zoo has announced that Toni, an Asian elephant, is suffering from arthritis so severe that she, too, may be euthanized.

The elephants' debilitating ailments are probably a result of the inadequate conditions in which they have been held. The same story is repeated in zoos across the country.
Grounds

When I began my zoo career 35 years ago, much less was known about elephants than is known today. We now understand that keeping elephants in tiny enclosures with unnatural surfaces destroys their legs and feet. We have learned that to breed naturally and rear their young, elephants must live in herds that meet their social requirements. And we have come to realize that controlling elephants through domination and the use of ankuses (sharply pointed devices used to inflict pain) can no longer be justified.
Backing

Zoos must change the concept of how elephants are kept in captivity, starting with how much space we allot them. Wild elephants may walk 30 miles a day.
Claim

A typical home range of a wild elephant is 1,000 square miles. At the National Zoo, Toni has access to a yard of less than an acre. Zoo industry standards allow the keeping of elephants in as little as 2,200 square feet, or about 5 percent of an acre.
Grounds

Some zoos have begun to reevaluate their ability to house elephants. After the death of two elephants in 2004, the San Francisco Zoo sent its surviving elephants to a sanctuary in California. This year the Detroit Zoo closed its elephant exhibit on ethical grounds, and its two surviving elephants now thrive at the California sanctuary as well.
Grounds

But attitudes at other zoos remain entrenched. To justify their outdated exhibits, some zoos have redefined elephant longevity and natural behavior. For example, National Zoo officials blame Toni's arthritis on old age. But elephants in the wild reproduce into their fifties, and female elephants live long after their reproductive cycles cease. Had she not been captured in Thailand at the age of 7 months, Toni, at age 39, could have had decades more of life as a mother and a grandmother. Instead, she faces an early death before her 40th birthday, is painfully thin and is crippled by arthritis.
Rebuttal to counter-argument

Claim qualified (options explained). Grounds
The National Zoo's other elephants face the same bleak future if changes are not made. A preserve of at least 2 square miles—1,280 acres, or almost eight times the size of the National Zoo—would be necessary to meet an elephant's physical and social needs. Since this is not feasible, the zoo should

continued

send its pachyderms to a sanctuary. One such facility, the Elephant Sanctuary in Tennessee, offers 2,700 acres of natural habitat over which elephants can roam and heal from the damage caused by zoo life. The sanctuary's soft soil, varied terrain, freedom of choice and freedom of movement have restored life to elephants that were suffering foot and joint diseases after decades in zoos and circuses.

The National Zoo has the opportunity to overcome its troubled animal-care history by joining progressive zoos in reevaluating its elephant program. The zoo should do right by its elephants, and the public should demand nothing less.

QUESTIONS FOR READING

1. What is the occasion that had led to the writing of this article?

2. What is Schobert's subject?

3. State his claim in a way that shows that it is a solution to a problem.

QUESTIONS FOR REASONING AND ANALYSIS

1. What type of evidence (grounds) does the author provide?

2. What are the nature and source of his backing?

3. What makes his opening effective?

4. What values does Schobert express? What assumption does he make about his readers?

QUESTIONS FOR REFLECTING AND WRITING

1. Are you surprised by any of the facts about elephants presented by Schobert? Do they make sense to you, upon reflection?

2. Should zoos close down their elephant houses? Why or why not?

3. Are there any alternatives to city zoos with small elephant houses besides elephant sanctuaries?

try it!

Using Toulmin's Terms to Structure Your Own Arguments

You have seen how Toulmin's terms can help you to analyze and see what writers are actually doing in their arguments. You have also observed from both the short and the longer argument that writers do not usually follow the terms in precise order. Indeed, you can find both grounds and backing in the same sentence, or claim and qualifiers in the same paragraph, and so on. Still, the terms can help you to sort out your thinking about a claim you want to support. The following exercises will provide practice in your use of these terms to plan an argument.

EXERCISES: USING TOULMIN'S TERMS TO PLAN ARGUMENTS

Select one of the following claims, or one of your own if your instructor approves, and plan an argument, listing as many grounds as you can and paying attention to pos-sible rebuttals of counterarguments. Expect your outline to be one to two pages.

   a. Professor X is (or is not) a good teacher.

   b. Colleges should (or should not) admit students only on the basis of academic merit.

   c. Americans need (or do not need) to reduce the fat in their diets.

   d. Physical education classes should (or should not) be graded pass/fail.

   e. Public schools should (or should not) have dress codes.

   f. Helmets for bicyclists should (or should not) be mandatory.

   g. Sales taxes on cigarettes should (or should not) be increased.

   h. All cigarette advertising should (or should not) be prohibited.

let's review

After reading Chapter 1, you should understand the following:

- An argument of some sort is usually being made in any type of writing.

- Many pieces of communication that we do not typically think of as arguments still contain subtle elements of persuasion.

- An author must understand the needs of readers if he or she hopes to connect with them and persuade them to accept his or her position.

- Any writer—including you—will take on different roles when writing for different audiences and will use different strategies to reach each audience. There are many kinds of argument and many ways to argue successfully.

- When we speak of the critical reader or critical thinker, we have in mind someone who reads actively, who thinks about issues, and who makes informed judgments.

- Arguments take a stand on a debatable issue. Ask yourself whether a logical audience member, after reading your thesis, could take an opposing position. If not, your essay will most likely fall short of being a sound and effective argument.

- Arguments are based not just on reason and evidence but also on the beliefs and values we hold and think that our audience may hold as well.

- Much false reasoning (the logical fallacies discussed in Chapter 4) results from a writer's over-simplifying an issue. A sound argument begins with an understanding that most issues are complicated.

- For an argument to be its most persuasive, it must use logos, ethos, and pathos. If one or more elements is lacking, the writer runs the risk that his or her readers will not find the argument convincing.

- The Toulmin model explains that an argument consists of evidence and/or reasons presented in support of an assertion or claim that is either stated or implied. It offers us a method by which to both read the arguments of others and construct our own logical arguments.

connect

Form a peer group and complete the exercise below, taking into account the characteristics of an argument, Aristotle's "players," and Toulmin's model.

Construct a claim of judgment regarding the problems caused by college students' drinking. Then support your claim using your knowledge and experience. You may also want to go online for some statistics about college drinking and health and safety risks. Drawing on both experience and data, can you effectively support your claim? What counterarguments might your opposition (those who disagree with your claim) assert? What might your rebuttals be? Develop an outline of your argument using the Toulmin terms. Be prepared to compare your outline to others in your class. Compare and evaluate the various types of claims and the sorts of support each group used to support their claims.

responding critically to the arguments of others

chapter 2

Responding to Arguments

To understand how critical thinkers may respond to the arguments of others, let's examine the Gettysburg Address, Abraham Lincoln's famous speech dedicating the Civil War battlefield—and quite possibly the best example of succinct persuasive argumentation in our history. We can use this document to see the various ways writers respond—in writing—to the writing of others.

Responding to Content: What Does It Say?

Instructors often ask students to *summarize* or *paraphrase* their reading of a complex chapter, a supplementary text, a difficult poem, or a series of journal articles on library reserve. Frequently, report or critique assignments specify that summary and evaluation be combined. Your purpose in writing a summary is to show your understanding of the work's main ideas and of the relationships among those ideas. If you can put what you have read into your own words and focus on the text's main points, then you have command of that material. Here is one student's restatement of the main argument in Lincoln's address:

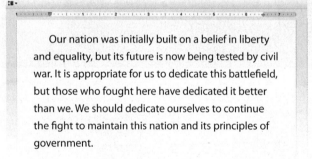

Our nation was initially built on a belief in liberty and equality, but its future is now being tested by civil war. It is appropriate for us to dedicate this battlefield, but those who fought here have dedicated it better than we. We should dedicate ourselves to continue the fight to maintain this nation and its principles of government.

Sometimes it is easier to recite or quote famous or difficult works than to state, more simply and in your own words, what has been written. The ability to summarize or paraphrase reflects both reading and writing skills.

Writing Summaries

Preparing a good summary is not always as easy as it looks. A *summary* briefly restates, in your own words, the main points of a work in a way that does not misrepresent or distort the original. A good summary shows your grasp of main ideas and your ability to

The Gettysburg Address

Abraham Lincoln

Four score and seven years ago our fathers brought forth on this continent a new nation, conceived in liberty and dedicated to the proposition that all men are created equal. Now we are engaged in a great civil war, testing whether that nation, or any nation so conceived and so dedicated, can long endure. We are met on a great battlefield of that war. We have come to dedicate a portion of that field as a final resting place for those who here gave their lives that that nation might live. It is altogether fitting and proper that we should do this. But, in a larger sense, we cannot dedicate—we cannot consecrate—we cannot hallow—this ground. The brave men, living and dead, who struggled here have consecrated it far above our poor power to add or to detract. The world will little note nor long remember what we say here, but it can never forget what they did here. It is for us, the living, rather to be dedicated here to the unfinished work which they who fought here have thus far so nobly advanced. It is rather for us to be here dedicated to the great task remaining before us—that from these honored dead we take increased devotion to that cause for which they gave the last full measure of devotion; that we here highly resolve that these dead shall not have died in vain; that this nation, under God, shall have a new birth of freedom; and that government of the people, by the people, for the people shall not perish from the earth.

express them clearly. You need to condense the original while giving all key ideas appropriate attention.

Students receive many occasions to summarize material. Examples include assignments to

- show that you have read and understood assigned works,

- complete a test question,

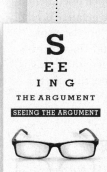
Many news sites and online newspapers use summaries to introduce articles or longer stories. You can easily identify these summaries because they are usually followed by a phrase such as "Read full story." Go online and find a summary of a current event. Does it follow the guidelines set up in this chapter? How and why might these summaries differ from the ones you will be asked to write for your college courses?

- have a record of what you have read for future study

- prepare for a class discussion, or

- explain the main ideas in a work that you will also examine in some other way, such as in a book review or a refutation essay.

Guidelines for Writing Summaries

No matter what assignment you receive, you can follow a few simple guidelines to prepare your summary. These guidelines offer a simple and concise means of showing what you know.

1. Write in a direct, objective style, using your own words. Use few, if any, direct quotations, probably none in a one-paragraph summary.

2. Begin with a reference to the writer (full name) and the title of the work and then state the writer's thesis. You may also want to include where and when the work was published.

3. Complete the summary by providing other key ideas. Show the reader how the main ideas connect and relate to one another.

4. Do not include specific examples, illustrations, or background sections.

5. Combine main ideas into fewer sentences than were used in the original.

6. Keep the parts of your summary in the same balance as you find in the original. If the author devotes about 30 percent of the essay to one idea, that idea should get about 30 percent of your summary.

7. Select precise, accurate verbs to show the author's relationship to ideas. Write "Jones argues," "Jones asserts," "Jones believes." Do not use

vague verbs that provide only a list of disconnected ideas. Do not write "Jones talks about," "Jones goes on to say."

8. Do not make any judgments about the writer's style or ideas. Do not include your personal reaction to the work.

Writing Paraphrases

Although the words *summary and paraphrase* are sometimes used interchangeably, they are not exact synonyms. Summaries and paraphrases are alike in that they are both written responses to sources. They differ in how they respond and why.

Like a summary, a paraphrase is an objective restatement of someone's writing. But the purpose of a paraphrase is to clarify a complex passage or to include material from a source in your own writing.

When using sources for research, you will incorporate some of their information and ideas in your own paper, in your own words, and with proper documentation. Usually each paraphrased passage is fairly brief and is blended into your own thinking on the topic. Paraphrasing clearly and accurately—and documenting correctly—takes some practice. Much more discussion, together with examples and opportunities for practice, can be found in the section on research (see pages 40–41).

Paraphrase of the Passage by Russell

All that we can do, before we lose our loved ones and then face our own death, is to place value on the important ideas that mark humans as special creatures and give meaning to our lives. We must reject any fear of dying that would make us slaves to Fate and instead be proud of what we have

try it!

Exercise: Paraphrase

When your purpose is to clarify a poem, a complex philosophical passage, or prose filled with figurative language, your paraphrase will be long, maybe longer than the original. Here is an example: first a passage from British philosopher Bertrand Russell's "A Free Man's Worship." As you read Russell's passage, underline words or phrases you find confusing. Then, as you read the paraphrase, look back to the original to see how the writer has restated Russell's ideas.

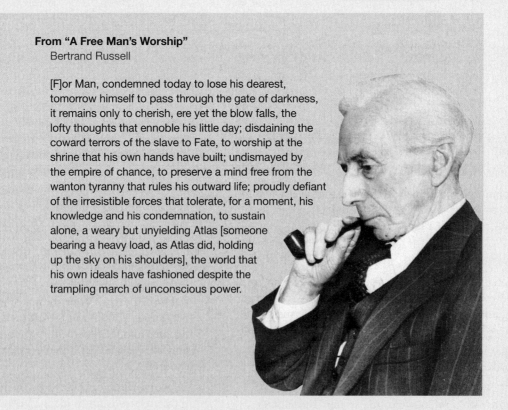

From "A Free Man's Worship"
Bertrand Russell

[F]or Man, condemned today to lose his dearest, tomorrow himself to pass through the gate of darkness, it remains only to cherish, ere yet the blow falls, the lofty thoughts that ennoble his little day; disdaining the coward terrors of the slave to Fate, to worship at the shrine that his own hands have built; undismayed by the empire of chance, to preserve a mind free from the wanton tyranny that rules his outward life; proudly defiant of the irresistible forces that tolerate, for a moment, his knowledge and his condemnation, to sustain alone, a weary but unyielding Atlas [someone bearing a heavy load, as Atlas did, holding up the sky on his shoulders], the world that his own ideals have fashioned despite the trampling march of unconscious power.

accomplished. We must not be distressed by the powers of chance or blind luck. We must not let their control over much that happens to us keep us from maintaining a mind that is free, a mind that we use to think for ourselves. Keeping our minds free and embracing knowledge are ways to defy the powers of the universe over which we have no control. And so, even though we may at times grow weary of battling the blind forces of the universe, we continue to find strength in the interior world that we have shaped by our ideals.

Note, first, that the paraphrase is longer than the original (on page 32). The goal is to clarify, not to highlight main ideas only. Second, the paraphrase clarifies the passage by turning Russell's one long sentence into several sentences and using simpler language. When you can state a writer's ideas in your own words, you have really understood the writer's ideas.

When you are asked the question "What does it say?" think about whether you need a summary or a paraphrase. When an instructor asks you to state in your own words the meaning of Lincoln's long concluding sentence in the Gettysburg Address, the instructor wants a paraphrase. When an instructor asks you what an assigned essay is about, the instructor wants a summary.

The Analytic Response: How Is It Written?

Although many assignments call for some measure of summary or paraphrasing, most of the time you will be expected to do something with what you have read, and to simply summarize or paraphrase will be insufficient. Frequently you will be asked to *analyze* a work—that is, to explain the elements of structure and style that a writer has chosen. You will want to examine sentence patterns, organization, metaphors, and other techniques selected by the writer to convey attitude and give force to ideas. Developing your skills in style analysis will make you both a better reader and a better writer.

Many writers have examined Lincoln's word choice, sentence structure, and choice of metaphors to make clear the sources of power in his Gettysburg Address. (See, for example, Gilbert Highet's essay "The Gettysburg Address" in *The Clerk of Oxenford: Essays on Literature and Life* [New York: Oxford UP, 1954].) Analyzing Lincoln's style, you might examine, among other elements, his effective use of *tricolon*: the threefold repetition of a grammatical structure, with the three points placed in ascending order of significance.

Lincoln uses two effective tricolons in his brief address. The first focuses on the occasion for his speech, the dedication of the battlefield: "we cannot dedicate—we cannot consecrate—we cannot hallow. . . ." The best that the living can do is formally dedicate; only those who died there for the principle of liberty are capable of making the battlefield holy. The second tricolon presents Lincoln's concept of democratic government, a government "of the people, by the people, for the people." The purpose of government—"for the people"—resides in the position of greatest significance.

A second type of analysis, a comparison of styles of two writers, is a frequent variation of the analytic assignment. By focusing on similarities and differences in writing styles, you can see more clearly the role of choice in writing, and you may also examine the degree to which differences in purpose affect style. One student, for example, produced a thoughtful and interesting study of Lincoln's style in contrast to that of Martin Luther King, Jr., as revealed in his "I have a dream" speech:

Although Lincoln's sentence structure is tighter than King's and King likes the rhythms created by repetition, both men reflect their familiarity with the King James Bible in their use of its cadences and expressions. Instead of saying "eighty-seven years ago," Lincoln, seeking solemnity, selects the biblical expression "four score and seven years ago." Similarly, King borrows from the Bible and echoes Lincoln when he writes "five score years ago."

Understanding Purpose and Audience in a Style Analysis

An analytic response helps you communicate the impact that the author's choice of style has on the text. In Chapter 9, "Writing a Rhetorical Analysis," you will learn more about how to write this kind of response.

A style analysis is not the place for challenging the ideas of the writer. A style analysis requires the discipline to see how a work has been put together even if you disagree with the writer's views. You do not have to agree with a writer to appreciate his or her skill in writing. A style analysis may imply, or even express, a positive evaluation of the author's writing—but that is not the same as agreeing or disagreeing with the author's ideas.

If you think about audience in the context of your purpose, you should conclude that a summary of content does not belong in a style analysis. Why? Because we write style analyses for people who have already

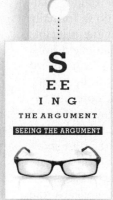
If instead of a piece of writing, you were asked to write a style analysis of a website like the one shown here, you might choose to organize your essay around use of color, design layout, font choice, and graphic elements. In each case, your goal is to analyze the author's style and tone based on the choices he or she made about how to write, design, and organize the piece.

read the work. Remember, though, that your reader may not know the work in the detail that you know it, so you will need to give examples to illustrate the points of your analysis.

Planning a Style Analysis

First, organize your analysis according to elements of style, not according to the organization of the work. Scrap any thoughts of hacking your way through the essay, commenting paragraph by paragraph. This approach invites summary rather than analysis. It also means that you have not selected an organization that supports your purpose in writing.

You need to select those techniques you think are most important in creating the writer's attitude and discuss them one at a time. Sentence patterns, organization, metaphors, and other elements of style can all give force to a writer's ideas. If you were asked to write an analysis of an essay by famous satirist Dave Barry, for example, you might select his use of italics and quotation marks, his use of hyperbole, and his use of irony. These are three techniques that stand out in Barry's writing.

Drafting a Style Analysis

If you were to select and analyze the three elements of style mentioned below as being characteristic of Dave Barry's writing (italics and quotation marks, hyperbole, and irony), your essay might have a structure like this:

Paragraph 1: Introduction
1. Attention-getter
2. Author, title, publication information of article/book
3. Brief explanation of author's subject
4. Your thesis—stating that you will be looking at Barry's style

Paragraph 2: First body paragraph
Analysis of italics and quotation marks.

Paragraph 3: Second body paragraph
1. Topic sentence that introduces analysis of hyperbole
2. Three or more examples of hyperbole
3. Explanation of how each example connects to the author's thesis—that is, how the example of hyperbole works to convey attitude. This is your analysis; don't forget it!

Paragraph 4: Third body paragraph
Analysis of irony—with same three parts as in paragraph 3.

Paragraph 5: Conclusion
Restate your thesis: We can understand the author's point through a study of these three elements of his style.

Revising a Style Analysis

As you revise your draft, use these questions to guide you in polishing your essay:

- Have I handled all titles correctly?
- Have I correctly referred to the author?
- Have I used quotation marks correctly when presenting examples of style?

- Do I have an accurate, clear presentation of the author's subject and thesis?
- Do I have enough examples of each element of style to show my readers that these elements are important?
- Have I connected examples to the author's thesis? That is, have I shown my readers how these techniques work to develop the author's attitude?

Of course, you can consider other questions than just those presented above, but at the very least, using such inquiries can help focus you on writing a style analysis. You will learn more about this kind of writing in Chapter 9, "Writing a Rhetorical Analysis."

try it!

To reinforce your understanding of style analysis, read the following essay by Ellen Goodman, answer the questions that follow, and then study the student essay that analyzes Goodman's style.

prereading questions What is Goodman's subject? Why is it incorrect to say that her subject is Thanksgiving?

CHOOSING OUR FAMILIES

Ellen Goodman

Author of Close to Home *(1979),* At Large *(1981), and* Keeping Touch *(1985), collections of her essays, Ellen Goodman has been a feature writer for* The Boston Globe *since 1967 and a syndicated columnist since 1976. She has won a Pulitzer Prize for distinguished commentary. The following column was published on November 24, 1988.*

BOSTON—They will celebrate Thanksgiving the way they always do, in the Oral Tradition. Equal parts of food and conversation. A cornucopia of family. These are not restrained people who choose their words and pick at their stuffing. These are people who have most of their meals in small chicken-sized households. But when they come together, they feast on the sounds as well as tastes of a turkey-sized family.

Indeed, their Thanksgiving celebrations are as crowded with stories as their tables are with chairs. Arms reach indelicately across each other for second helpings, voices interrupt to add relish to a story. And there are always leftovers too enormous to complete, that have to be wrapped up and preserved.

But what is it that makes this collection of people a family? How do we make a family these days? With blood? With marriage? With affection? I wonder about this when I hear the word *family* added to some politician's speech like gravy poured over the entire plate. The meaning is supposed to be obvious, self-evident. It is assumed that when we talk about family we are all talking about the same thing. That families are the same. But it's not that simple.

For the past eight years, the chief defender of the American family has lived in the White House. But Reagan's own family has always looked more like

continued

our contemporary reality than his traditional image. There has been marriage and divorce among the Reagans, adoption and blending, and more than one estrangement. There is a mother, this holiday season, who hasn't talked to her daughter for more than a year. The man who will take his place as head of this family ideology has wrapped himself in a grandfatherly image. Yet Bush's family is also extended in ways that are common but not always comforting to other Americans.

As young people, George and Barbara Bush left home again and again, setting up temporary quarters in 17 cities. Now they have five children scattered in an equal number of states: Texas and Florida, Colorado, Virginia and Connecticut. Theirs, like many of ours, do not live at home, but come home, for the holidays.

We hold onto a particular primal image of families—human beings created from the same genetic code, living in the same area code. We hold onto an image of the family as something rooted and stable. But that has always been rare in a country where freedom is another word for mobility, both emotional and physical.

In America, families are spliced and recombined in as many ways as DNA. Every year our Thanksgiving tables expand and contract, place settings are removed and added. A guest last year is a member this year. A member last year may be an awkward outsider this year. How many of our children travel between alienated halves of their heritage, between two sets of people who share custody of their holidays?

Even among those families we call stable or intact, the ride to the airport has become a holiday ritual as common as pumpkin pie. Many parents come from retirement homes, many children from college, many cousins from jobs in other zip codes. We retrieve these people, as if from a memory hole, for reunions.

What then makes a family, in the face of all this "freedom"? It is said that people don't choose their parents. Or their aunts and uncles. But in a sense Americans do choose to make a family out of these people. We make room for them in our lives, choose to be with them and preserve that choice through a ritual as simple as passing seconds at a table.

All real families are made over time and through tradition. The Oral Tradition. We create a shared treasure trove of history, memories, conversation. Equal parts of food and conversation. And a generous serving of pleasure in each other's company.

QUESTIONS FOR READING, REASONING, AND WRITING

1. What is Goodman's attitude toward families; that is, what does she assert about families in this column? Is there one sentence that states her thesis? If so, which one? If not, write a thesis for the essay.

2. Characterize Goodman's style. Analyze her word choice, metaphors, sentence structure, organization, and use of the Reagan and Bush families as examples. How does each contribute to our understanding of her point?

3. Why are Goodman's metaphors especially notable? Open up—or explain—three of her metaphors.

Student Essay—A Style Analysis

GOODMAN'S FEAST OF STYLE

Alan Peterson

Thanksgiving is a time for "families" to come together, eat a big meal, share their experiences and each other's company. In her November 24, 1988, article "Choosing Our Families," which appeared on Thanksgiving Day in *The Washington Post*, Ellen Goodman asks the question, Who makes up these families? By her definition, a family does not consist of just blood relatives; a family contains acquaintances, friends, relatives, people who are "chosen" to be in this year's "family." An examination of Goodman's essay reveals some of the elements of style she uses to effectively ask and answer her question.

Introduction includes author, title, and date of article

Student's thesis statement

Goodman's clever organization compels the reader to read on. She begins by focusing on a Thanksgiving dinner scene, referring to families and households in terms of food. After setting the table by evoking the reader's memories of Thanksgivings past, Goodman asks the central question of her essay: "[W]hat is it that makes this collection of people a family" (49)? Goodman argues that the modern meaning of *family* has evolved so much that the traditional definition of *family* is no longer the standard. To clarify modern definitions, she provides examples of famous families: First Families. After suggesting that the Reagans have been the "chief defender of the American family" (49) for the last eight years, she points out that the Reagans, with their divorces, their adoptions, their estrangements, are anything but the traditional family they wish to portray. Rather, the Reagans represent the human traits that define the "contemporary reality" (49) of today's families. Next, President Bush's family is examined. Goodman points out that the Bushes' five children live in five different states, and that Barbara and George Bush, as young people, set up "temporary quarters in 17 cities" (50). She develops an answer to her question in the ensuing paragraphs. She observes that families today are disjointed, nontraditional, different from one another. She refers to families that are considered "stable or intact" (50) and shows how even those families can be spread out all over the country. In her closing paragraphs she repeats the question "What then makes a family?" Then, after another reference to Thanksgiving dinner, she concludes the article by stating her main point: "All real families are made over time and through tradition" (50). Goodman's organization—a question, some examples, several answers, and strong confirmation—powerfully frames her thesis.

Analysis of Goodman's organization

In an essay written about a theme as homespun as family and Thanksgiving celebrations, a reader would not expect the language to be too formal. Choosing her words carefully, Goodman cultivates a familiar and descriptive, yet not overly informal style. Early in the essay, Goodman uses simple language to portray the Thanksgiving meal. She refers to voices interrupting, arms reaching, leftovers that have to be wrapped up. Another effective technique of diction Goodman employs is the repetition of words and sounds. She points out that the Bushes, as young people, "left home again and again" (50). She defines the image we have of families as that of people created from the same "genetic code," living in the same "area code," and of cousins in "other zip codes" (50). Then, characterizing the reality of the configuration of today's American families, Goodman states: "A guest last year is a member this year," while a "member last year may be an awkward outsider this year" (50). An additional example of repetition appears in the first and last paragraphs. Goodman repeats the sentence fragment "Equal parts of food and conversation" (50). This informal choice of words opens and closes her essay, cleverly setting the tone in the beginning and reiterating the theme at the end.

Analysis of Goodman's word choice and repetition

Perhaps the most prevalent element of style present in Goodman's piece, and a dominant characteristic of her essay style, is her use of metaphors. From the opening sentences all the way through to the end, this article is full of metaphors. Keeping with the general focus of the piece (the essay appeared on Thanksgiving Day), many of the metaphors liken food to family. Her references include "a cornucopia of family," "chicken-sized households" and a "turkey-sized family," people who "feast on the sounds as well as the tastes," and voices that "add relish to a story" (49).

Analysis of Goodman's metaphors

continued

She imparts that a politician can use the word *family* like "gravy poured over the entire plate" (49). Going to the airport to pick up members of these disjointed American families has become "a holiday ritual as common as pumpkin pie" (50). Goodman draws parallels between the process of "choosing" people to be with and the simple ritual of passing seconds at the table. Indeed, the essay's mood emphasizes the comparison of and inextricable bond between food and family.

Ellen Goodman's "Choosing Our Families" is a thought-provoking essay on the American family. She organizes the article so that readers are reminded of their own Thanksgiving experiences and consider who is included in their "families." After asking "What is it that makes this collection of people a family?" Goodman provides election-year examples of prominent American families, then an explanation of "family" that furnishes her with an answer. Her word choice and particularly the repetition of words and sounds make reading her essay a pleasure. The metaphors Goodman uses link in readers' minds the images of Thanksgiving food and the people with whom they spend the holiday. Her metaphors underscore the importance she places on having meals with the family, which is the one truly enduring tradition for all people. Perhaps the most important food-and-family metaphor comes in the last sentence: "a generous serving of pleasure in each other's company" (50).

Conclusion restates Goodman's position and student's thesis.

Works Cited

Goodman, Ellen. "Choosing Our Families." *Washington Post*. 24 Nov. 1988. Rpt. *Read, Reason, Write: An Argument Text and Reader*. 8th ed. Ed. Dorothy U. Seyler. New York: McGraw-Hill, 2008. 50–51.

The Evaluation Response: Does It Achieve Its Purpose?

Many critical responses to texts include some element of evaluation. Even when the stated purpose of an essay is "pure" analysis, the analysis implies a *judgment*. We analyze Lincoln's style because we recognize that the Gettysburg Address is a great piece of writing and we want to see how it achieves its power. On other occasions, judgment is the overtly stated purpose for close reading and analysis. The columnist who challenges a previously published editorial has analyzed the editorial and has found it flawed. The columnist may fault the editor's logic or lack of adequate or relevant support for the editorial's main idea. In each case, the columnist makes a negative judgment about the editorial, but that judgment is an informed one based on the columnist's knowledge of language and the principles of good argument.

Part of the ability to judge wisely lies in recognizing each writer's purpose and intended audience. It would be inappropriate, for example, to assert that Lincoln's address is weakened by its lack of facts about the battle. The historian's purpose might be to record the number killed or to analyze the generals' military tactics. Lincoln's purpose and audience were much different. Observe how one student evaluates Lincoln's speech in light of its intended purpose and audience:

As Lincoln reflected upon this young country's being torn apart by civil strife, he saw the dedication of the Gettysburg battlefield as an opportunity to challenge the country to fight for its survival and the principles upon which it was founded. The result was a brief but moving speech that appropriately examines the connection between the life and death of soldiers and the birth and survival of a nation.

These sentences establish a basis for an analysis of Lincoln's train of thought and use of metaphors, but this analysis, and its positive judgment, is grounded in an understanding of Lincoln's purpose, audience, and the context in which he spoke.

Combining Summary, Analysis, and Evaluation: The Critique or Review

Writing a good critique (or review) requires combining skills you have been working on: critical reading, accurate summary, analysis of style, and evaluation of the work—book, website, advertisement, essay, or

Movie reviews can be excellent examples of evaluative responses to the arguments of others. Take, for example, the following review of the movie *It's Kind of a Funny Story*. Reviewers typically attempt to establish and analyze relevant criteria (such as the quality of acting, for example) in order to evaluate how well the director or producers achieved their intended purpose for their intended audience. For the full text of this review, visit http://www.variety.com/review/VE1117943510?refcatid=31.

Discuss the review with your peers. Who is the intended audience for this review? Do you think the author does a good job of providing relevant and necessary information to his or her readers?

film—in the context of the writer's or director's subject and intended audience. Let's look again at steps in the writing process as they apply to writing a critique.

Knowing Your Audience

Try to imagine writing your critique for a larger audience, not just for your instructor. Try not to focus on this assignment as writing to be graded. Rather, think about why we turn to reviews: What do readers want to learn? They want to know if they should read the book or see the film. Your job is to help readers make that decision.

Understanding Your Purpose

Your purpose, then, is to provide clear, accurate information and a fair evaluation of both the material covered (or not covered) and the presentation of that material. Balance is important. You do not want most of your review to be summary, with just a few sentences of evaluation "stuck on" at the end. You also do not want a detailed summary of the work's beginning followed by skimpy coverage of the rest. This lack of balance may suggest to readers that you have not read or seen the entire work. Finally, when reviewing a novel or movie, make certain you do not explain the entire plot so that you do not give away the ending.

Establishing a General Plan

First, study the work carefully. Be sure that you can write a complete and accurate summary, even if you need to leave some of the plot details or main points out of your review. Second, the analysis part of your review or critique needs two elements: comment on the work's structure and special features plus discussion of the writer's (or director's) style.

As you study the work, consider these questions:

- How is the work put together?
- For a nonfiction book, how many chapters or sections are there, and what does each cover?
- Does the book contain visuals? An index?
- For a film, how does the story unfold? What actors are in the lead roles? What special effects are used?
- For an advertisement, how does the author use color or fonts to persuade the reader? What types of textual techniques are used?

Readers expect a reviewer to answer these kinds of questions. Your analysis of style needs to be connected to the work's intended audience. For example, if you are evaluating a biography, consider these questions:

- Is it informally written or heavily documented with notes and references?
- What is the level of formality of the book?
- What is the age level or knowledge level of the author's expected audience? Films are rated for age groups. Books can also be rated for age and level of knowledge of the subject. Websites might be targeted to a specific gender or audience.

Your summary and analysis can point the way to a fair and sensible evaluation. If, for example, you have many problems understanding a book aimed at a general audience, then it is fair to say that the author has failed to reach his or her audience. If, on the other hand, you selected a website to critique that was designed for specialists or for a group with a particular interest, then your reading challenge is irrelevant to a fair judgment. All it allows you to do is point out that the website is tough going for a nonspecialist (or that a movie sequel, for another example, is hard to follow in spots for those who did not see the original film). Your evaluation should include an assessment of content and presentation. Did the book or film fulfill its intended purpose? Was it as thorough as you expected in the light of other works on the same or a similar topic?

Drafting the Critique or Review

No simple formula exists for combining summary, analysis, and evaluation in a review or critique. Some instructors simplify the task by requiring a two-part review: summary first and then analysis and evaluation. If you are not so directed, then some blending of the three elements

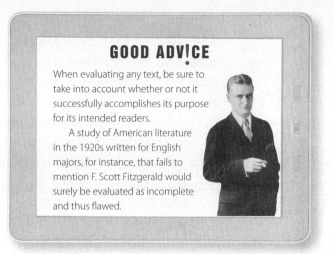

will be expected. Often reviews begin with an opening that is both an attention-getter and a broad statement of the work's subject or subject category. (This is a *biography* of Franklin; this is a *female action-hero* film.) An evaluation (in general terms) usually completes the opening paragraph. Then the reviewer uses a summary–analysis–evaluation pattern, providing details of content and presentation and then assessing the work.

The Research Response: How Does It Help Me Understand Other Works, Ideas, and Events?

Frequently, especially in your research writing courses, you will read not to analyze or evaluate but rather to use the source as part of learning about a particular subject. Lincoln's address is significant for the Civil War historian both as an event of that war and as an influence on our thinking about that war. The Gettysburg Address is also vital to the biographer's study of Lincoln's life and to the literary critic's study of famous speeches or of the Bible's influence on English writing styles. Thus Lincoln's brief speech is a valuable source for students in a variety of disciplines; it becomes part of their research process. Able researchers study it carefully; analyze it thoroughly; place it in its proper historical, literary, and personal contexts; and use it to develop their own arguments.

Arguments made by authors, especially experts in a particular field, can be valuable sources for students in a variety of disciplines. As you research for your own projects and papers, you will need to respond to the arguments of others as part of your research process. Able researchers study their sources carefully, analyze them thoroughly, place them in their proper historical, literary, and personal contexts, and then use them to develop their own arguments.

While writing research essays in future classes, for example, you will be asked to respond to the research and opinions of other writers. You will need to annotate the texts, make your own notes, and possibly even write short-response essays detailing and analyzing their perspectives, opinions, and assertions so that you can make good decisions about their usefulness to your own project.

try it!

Read the following article from MedicalNewsToday.com and consider how (or if) you might use this as a source for your own argument. Might this article be a useful research tool for certain topics or issues? Try to list any essay topics that come to mind as you read the article. Then make a note of what other types of sources you would try to find to assist with your research if you were writing an essay on each issue.

Medical News Today
May 29, 2007
Grim Warning for America's Fast Food Consumers Offered by "Supersize Me" Mice Research

It's research that may have you thinking twice before upgrading to the large size at your favorite fast food joint. Saint Louis University research presented in Washington, D.C., shows the dangers of high-fat food combined with high fructose corn syrup and a sedentary lifestyle—in other words, what may be becoming commonplace among Americans.

Brent Tetri, M.D., associate professor of internal medicine at Saint Louis University Liver Center, and colleagues studied the effects of a diet that was 40 percent fat and replete with high fructose corn syrup, a sweetener common in soda and some fruit juices. The research was presented at the Digestive Diseases Week meeting.

"We wanted to mirror the kind of diet many Americans subsist on, so the high fat content is about the same you'd find in a typical McDonald's meal, and the high fructose corn syrup translates to about eight cans of soda a day in a human diet, which is not far off with what some people consume," says Tetri, a leading researcher in nonalcoholic fatty liver disease, which can lead to cirrhosis and, ultimately, death. "But we were also keeping the mice sedentary, with a very limited amount of activity."

The study, which lasted for 16 weeks, had some curious results, says Tetri.

"We had a feeling we'd see evidence of fatty liver disease by the end of the study," he says. "But we were surprised to find how severe the damage was and how quickly it occurred. It took only four weeks for liver enzymes to increase and for glucose intolerance—the beginning of type II diabetes—to begin."

And unlike other studies, the mice were not forced to eat; rather, they were able to eat whenever they wanted—and eat they did. Tetri says there's evidence that suggests fructose actually suppresses your fullness, unlike fiber-rich foods, which make you feel full quickly.

The take-home message for humans is obvious, he says.

"A high-fat and sugar-sweetened diet compounded by a sedentary lifestyle will have severe repercussions for your liver and other vital organs," he says. "Fatty liver disease now affects about one of every eight children in this country. The good news is that it is somewhat reversible—but for some it will take major changes in diet and lifestyle."

Article adapted by Medical News Today from original press release.
www.medicalnewstoday.com/articles/71966.php

let's review

After reading Chapter 2, you should understand the following:

- There are multiple ways to respond to the writing of others, including responding to content (summaries and paraphrases); analyzing style; evaluating; and connecting to research.

- A good *summary* shows your grasp of main ideas and your ability to express them clearly. Like a summary, a *paraphrase* is an objective restatement of someone's writing, but the purpose of a paraphrase is to clarify a complex passage or to include material from a source in your own writing.

- Frequently you will be asked to *analyze* a work—that is, to explain the elements of structure and style that a writer has chosen. You will want to examine sentence patterns, organization, metaphors, and other techniques selected by the writer to convey attitude and give force to ideas.

- Many critical responses to texts include some element of evaluation. Even when the stated purpose of an essay is "pure" analysis, the analysis implies a judgment. You may be asked to combine summary, analysis, and evaluation while writing a critique.

- Frequently, especially in your research writing courses, you will read not to analyze or evaluate but rather to use sources as part of learning about a particular subject so that you can then incorporate sources into your own work.

connect

Read the article below and review the discussion questions that follow. Then form a peer group and discuss how you might respond to the piece. How might you respond to the content? How might you analyze the writer's style? How might you evaluate the piece? Might you use this as part of a larger research project? Write up notes about your discussion and be prepared to share your ideas with the class.

Communication Key to Egypt's Uprising

Hany Rashwan

ISSUE DATE: 2/14/11

It's been a few days now since the fall of Egypt's last pharaoh. While the days ahead are definitely both paramount and uncertain, this has been an outstanding first step and one that many hope will propel Egypt into fair democratic rule.

A month ago, if you were to tell any Egyptian (or Tunisian) that their ruler was easily disposable, that person would have looked at you as if you were crazy. Dictators do that; they almost always seem to have an apparently overwhelming power that stifles and cripples any potential opposition.

The mere fact that this revolution occurred is especially interesting and surprising. It's absolutely vital for us to analyze this uprising and study how something like this could have been caused. Surely the rampant corruption and poverty had to do with it, but as bad as things seem now, the Egyptian economy has largely been stagnant for the past few decades. Most citizens of that great nation have been struggling for years.

So why now? What's the catalyst for this sudden uprising?

I've been reading a lot of analysis on the events these past few days, but few words stuck with me more than what Wael Ghonim, the Middle-Eastern Google executive who created the Facebook group behind the initial protests, said: "If you want to liberate a government, give them the Internet."

Now that's just powerful. I remember getting goosebumps when I first read that. "If you want to liberate a government, give them the Internet."

What Ghonim is talking about is not the Internet itself; he's not referring specifically to the World Wide Web.

He's talking about what the Internet promises and delivers, namely the uninterrupted free flow of information. We use the Internet every day, but much like our other comforts in life, we seldom sit back and really relish how free we really are because of it.

Our web is the only platform on earth that gives anyone—regardless of age, gender, ethnicity or beliefs—full freedom in utilizing and contributing back to the Internet. No one checks your ID or badge; there's no security that you need to pass through. In many ways, the Internet is the world's greatest democracy: anyone's beliefs are allowed in, whether that's a Holocaust denial group on Facebook or an ACLU channel on YouTube, and the people get to collectively vote for what ultimately becomes more popular.

It is no surprise that the Egyptians managed to muster up the courage and get a huge number of people out to the rallies through simple things like Facebook pages and Twitter streams. What's even more beautiful about the whole thing is the awesome power of the web to bring people around the world together. Egypt has 80 million people; many more than that supported, helped, or followed the revolution online.

What the Internet does that's even far more remarkable is that it tends to lift our labels, bringing down a lot of walls that we typically build in the real world to separate us. When you click a link, you don't know who created it and frankly, you don't even care. Your link is just as good as my link; ultimately what the people choose will trump all.

All these walls have come down on the Internet. Perhaps the greatest example of this has been the use of the associated technologies assisting the revolution. Few have questioned or even brought up the fact that the top three technologies the protestors used—Google, Facebook and Twitter—have been started by Jewish entrepreneurs. When the Internet was taken down in Egypt, engineers at Google and Twitter worked extra hours on the weekend to come up with a way to enable Egyptians to get their tweets out via other ways, like phone calls.

That wasn't taken as a Western ploy or foreign interference; they were simply humans helping out their fellow humans. That's the beauty of the Internet. When you think about it that way, no wonder it was the Internet that the Egyptian government first tried to get rid of.

In 1971, John Lennon imagined a world with no borders or countries, only filled with co-existing humans living in peace. We're remarkably far from that in the real world and it's still largely impossible to achieve. Yet, I think we've largely removed such vain labels from our web ecosystem. It's not America's Internet or Europe's Internet; it's the World Wide Web.

That's an awesome power that we've yet to understand the true potential of, but today we've seen how it can unite us and cause true revolutions.

http://www.thelantern.com/opinion/communication-key-to-egypt-s-uprising-1.1978063

RESPONDING TO CONTENT

1. What is Rashwan's subject? What was Rashwan's purpose for writing?

2. What does Rashwan suggest as the catalyst for the uprising in Egypt?

3. How does Rashwan interpret Ghonim's statement about the Internet?

4. How might you summarize Rashwan's essay?

ANALYZING THE AUTHOR'S STYLE

1. What is Rashwan's attitude toward the uprising in Egypt? What examples and word choice help to convey that attitude?

2. Do you enjoy and appreciate the author's approach to the subject? If you appreciate it, what makes it clever? If you do not appreciate the approach, what bothers you?

EVALUATING

1. Do you think that this is an effective essay? Why or why not?

2. What criteria might you use to evaluate this piece?

RESEARCHING

1. Might you find this essay useful in writing a future research essay? Why or why not?

2. What information might you annotate as useful or interesting?

3. What types of sources might you try to find to further your research on this topic?

writing effective arguments

chapter 3

On January 21, 2010, U.S. Secretary of State Hillary Rodham Clinton gave a speech on Internet freedom at the Newseum in Washington, D.C. Many say that her speech has become important for Internet policy because it clearly established the U.S. stance on online global freedom. As you read the transcript of her speech, think about the characteristics of argument discussed in the previous two chapters. Do you think Clinton's speech is successful? Do you recognize specific strategies or tools she uses in her speech? You can watch Clinton's historic speech by accessing www.youtube.com and entering the search terms "Clinton Internet freedom."

Remarks on Internet Freedom

Hillary Rodham Clinton
Secretary of State
January 21, 2010

This is an important speech on a very important subject. But before I begin, I want to just speak briefly about Haiti, because during the last eight days, the people of Haiti and the people of the world have joined together to deal with a tragedy of staggering proportions. Our hemisphere has seen its share of hardship, but there are few precedents for the situation we're facing in Port-au-Prince. Communication networks have played a critical role in our response. They were, of course, decimated and in many places totally destroyed. And in the hours after the quake, we worked with partners in the private sector; first, to set up the text "HAITI" campaign so that mobile phone users in the United States could donate to relief efforts via text messages. That initiative has been a showcase for the generosity of the American people, and thus far, it's raised over $25 million for recovery efforts.

Information networks have also played a critical role on the ground. When I was with President Preval in Port-au-Prince on Saturday, one of his top priorities was to try to get communication up and going. The government [officials] couldn't talk to each other, . . . and NGOs, our civilian leadership, our military leadership were severely impacted. [As a result, the] technology community has set up interactive maps to help us identify needs and target resources. And on Monday, a seven-year-old girl and two women were pulled from the rubble of a collapsed supermarket by an American search-and-rescue team after they sent a text message calling for help. Now, these examples are manifestations of a much broader phenomenon.

The spread of information networks is forming a new nervous system for our planet. When something happens in Haiti or Hunan, the rest of us learn about it in real time—from real people. And we can respond in real time as well. Americans eager to help in the aftermath of a disaster and the girl trapped in the supermarket are connected in ways that were not even imagined a year ago, even a generation ago. That same principle applies to almost all of humanity today. As we sit here, any of you—or maybe more likely, any of our children—can take out the tools that many carry every day and transmit this discussion to billions across the world.

Now, in many respects, information has never been so free. There are more ways to spread more ideas to more people than at any moment in history. And even in authoritarian countries, information networks are helping people discover new facts and making governments more accountable.

During his visit to China in November, for example, President Obama held a town hall meeting with an online component to highlight the importance of the Internet. In response to a question that was sent in over the Internet, he defended the right of people to freely access information, and said that the more freely information flows, the stronger societies become. He spoke about how access to information helps citizens hold their own governments accountable, generates new ideas, encourages creativity and entrepreneurship. The United States belief in that ground truth is what brings me here today.

Because amid this unprecedented surge in connectivity, we must also recognize that these technologies are not an unmitigated blessing. These tools are also being exploited to undermine human progress and political rights. Just as steel can be used to build hospitals or machine guns, or nuclear power can either energize a city or destroy it, modern information networks and the technologies they support can be harnessed for good or for ill. The same networks that help organize movements for freedom also enable al-Qaida to spew hatred and incite violence against the innocent. And technologies with the potential to open up access to government and promote transparency can also be hijacked by governments to crush dissent and deny human rights.

In the last year, we've seen a spike in threats to the free flow of information. China, Tunisia, and Uzbekistan have stepped up their censorship of the Internet. In Vietnam, access to popular social networking sites has suddenly disappeared. And last Friday in Egypt, 30 bloggers and activists were detained. One member of this group, Bassem Samir, who is thankfully no longer in prison, is with us today. So while it is clear that the spread of these technologies is transforming our world, it is still unclear how that transformation will affect the human rights and the human welfare of the world's population.

On their own, new technologies do not take sides in the struggle for freedom and progress, but the United States does. We stand for a single Internet where all of humanity has equal access to knowledge and ideas. And we recognize that the world's information infrastructure will become what we and others make of it. Now, this challenge may be new, but our responsibility to help ensure the free exchange of ideas goes back to the birth of our republic. The words of the First Amendment to our Constitution

are carved in 50 tons of Tennessee marble on the front of this building. And every generation of Americans has worked to protect the values etched in that stone.

http://www.state.gov/secretary/rm/2010/01/135519.htm

The basics of good writing are much the same for works as different as the personal essay, the argument, the Web page, the Facebook Group post, and the researched essay. Good writing is focused, organized, and concrete. Effective essays are written in a style and tone that are suited to both the audience and the writer's purpose. These are sound principles, all well known to you. But how, exactly, do you achieve them when writing your own arguments? This chapter will help you answer that question.

Understand Your Writing Purpose

There are many kinds of arguments. As you consider possible topics, think about what you would want to do with each topic—beyond writing convincingly in defense of your claim. Different types of arguments require different approaches or different kinds of evidence. Here are some useful ways to classify arguments:

- **Inductive argument or investigative paper:** If you are given an assignment to collect evidence in an organized way to support a claim about a topic such as advertising strategies or violence in children's programming, then you will be writing an investigative paper, presenting evidence that you have gathered and analyzed to support your claim.

- **Claim of values or position paper:** If you are given the assignment to argue for your position on a topic such as euthanasia, trying juveniles as adults, or national identification cards, you need to recognize that this assignment calls for a claim of values. You will be writing a rather philosophical argument, presenting reasons in support of a complex, controversial issue. You will need to pay close attention to your warrants or assumptions.

- **A definition argument:** If you are asked to consider the qualities or traits we should look for in a president or professor, you are really being asked to define "a good president" or "a good professor." Some of your points may seem quite concrete—practical—to you, but your specifics are really tied to an ideal you imagine, and that ideal is best understood as a definition.

chapter 3 Writing effective arguments **49**

- **A problem/solution argument or claim of policy:** You are being asked to recommend solutions to a current problem, if you are asked to answer the broad question, What should we do about . . . ? What should we do about students' disruptive behavior? About gridlock on your town's streets? These kinds of questions ask for different types of answers than do questions about what traits make a good president or who are the greatest athletes.

- **A refutation or rebuttal of someone else's argument:** If you are given the assignment to find a letter to the editor, a newspaper editorial, or an essay in your textbook with which you disagree, you are being asked to prepare a refutation essay, a specific challenge to a specific argument. You will repeatedly refer to the work you are rebutting, so you will need to know that work thoroughly.

Understand at the beginning of your planning just what kind of argument you have chosen, and you will write more effectively.

Know Your Audience

Too often students plunge into writing without thinking much about audience. They wrongly assume that their audience is only the instructor who has given

SEEING THE ARGUMENT

What do you think the intended audience for this print ad values or believes? Understanding the values of your target readers can help you focus your argument and choose strategies that will be effective in persuading them to believe as you do.

the assignment, just as their purpose in writing is to complete the assignment and get a grade. These views of audience and purpose are likely to lead to poorly written arguments. First, if you are not thinking about readers who may disagree with you, you may not develop the best defense of your claim—which may need a rebuttal to possible counterarguments. Second, you may ignore your essay's needed introductory material on the assumption that the instructor, knowing the assignment, has a context for understanding your writing. To avoid these pitfalls, use the following questions to sharpen your understanding of audience.

Who Is My Audience?

If you are writing an essay for the student newspaper, your audience consists primarily of students, but do not forget that faculty and administrators also read the student newspaper. If you are preparing a letter-to-the-editor refutation of a recent column in your town's newspaper, your audience will be the readers of that newspaper—that is, adults in your town. Some instructors give assignments that identify an audience such as those just described so that you will practice writing with a specific audience in mind.

If you are not assigned a specific audience, imagine your classmates, as well as your instructor, as part of your audience. In other words, you are writing to many readers in the academic community. These readers are intelligent and thoughtful, expecting sound reasoning and convincing evidence. These readers also represent varied values and beliefs, as they are from diverse cultures and experiences. They may hold clear opinions about your topic, reject certain ideas based on value systems they were raised with, or automatically accept the validity of your claims based on their beliefs or experiences. Do not, however, confuse the shared expectations of writing conventions, sound reasoning, and accuracy in presenting data with shared beliefs. In order to identify and more clearly understand the values, positions, and beliefs of your intended readers, you may want to think about the following questions.

What Will My Audience Already Know about My Topic?

What can you expect a diverse group of readers to know? Whether you are writing on a current issue or a centuries-old debate, you must expect most readers to have some knowledge of the issues. Their knowledge does not free you from the responsibility of developing your support fully, though. In fact, their knowledge creates further demands. For example, most readers know the main arguments on both sides of the abortion issue. For you to write as if they do not—and thus to ignore the arguments of the opposition—is to

Most readers already know the main arguments on both sides of the abortion debate and realize that the issue is not as simple as this poster would have you believe. Ignoring the prior knowledge and experience of your readers can not only insult their intelligence, but can also work against your own credibility.

Is this poster convincing in presenting a pro-life position? Would it convince someone who has traditionally held a pro-choice point of view to change his or her position? Or would it be viewed as an oversimplification of a complex and important issue?

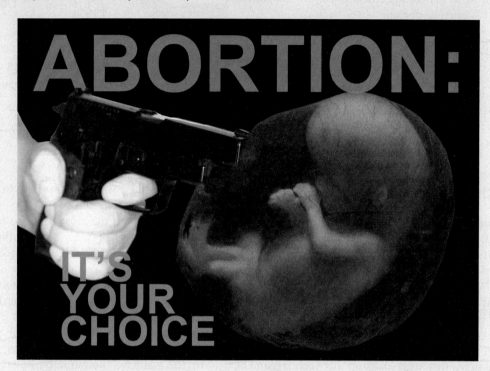

produce an argument that probably adds little to the debate on the subject.

On the other hand, what some readers "know" may be little more than an overview of the issues from TV news—or the emotional outbursts of a family member. Some readers may be misinformed or prejudiced, but they embrace their views enthusiastically nonetheless. So as you think about the ways to develop and support your argument, you will have to assess your readers' knowledge and sophistication. This assessment will, for example, help you decide how much background information to provide.

Where Does My Audience Stand on the Issue?

Expect readers to hold a range of views, even if you are writing to students on your campus or to an organization of which you are a member. It is not true, for instance, that all students want coed dorms or pass/fail grading. And if everyone already agrees with you,

you have no reason to write. An argument needs to be about a topic that is open to debate. So you will need to make these assumptions:

- Some of your audience will probably never agree with you but may offer you grudging respect if you compose an effective argument. If you know you hold an unpopular position, your best strategy will be a conciliatory approach (see page 56 for a discussion of the conciliatory argument).

- Some readers will not hold strong views on your topic and may be open to convincing if you present a good case.

- Those who share your views will still be looking for a strong argument in support of their position.

Your audience may cling not only to their positions on an issue, but also to their values, beliefs, and morals while reading your argument. In order to fully understand why your readers might hold their positions, you should attempt to uncover what they believe is important in the world. Oftentimes, these values are shaped by a reader's culture, personal experiences, and even religious beliefs. For example, many Americans have been raised to believe that patriotism is an extremely important value. If your argument attempts to challenge this value directly, like the political cartoon does, you will need to address the obvious disconnect or you will risk alienating your readers who do not believe as you do. If everyone already agrees with you, you have no reason to write. An argument needs to be about a topic that is open to debate.

As you read the cartoon, imagine how it might be received by various audiences—a soldier coming home from the war in Iraq, an anti-war protester on a college campus, a veteran's widow, and so on. Do you think every audience member would see the humor in this argument? Might some audience members feel that the author is failing to understand their values and beliefs? Does this cartoon make a compelling argument in your mind?

THE NEW AMERICAN PATRIOT

- Hasn't voted in 10 years.
- Doesn't know the name of his congressman.
- Has never read the entire U.S. Constitution.
- Doesn't question U.S. foreign policy.

Does have an American flag bumper sticker on his SUV.

russmo.com
11/01

www.russmo.com. Reprinted with permission.

How Should I Speak to My Audience?

Your audience will form an opinion of you based on how you write and how you reason. The image of argument—and the arguer—that we have been creating in this text's discussion is one of thoughtful claims defended with logic and evidence. However, the heated debate at yesterday's lunch does not resemble this image of argument. Sometimes the word *persuasion* is used to separate the emotionally charged debate from the calm, intellectual tone of the academic argument. Unfortunately, this neat division between argument and persuasion does not describe the real world of debate. The thoughtful arguer also wants to be persuasive, to win over the audience. And highly emotional presentations can contain relevant facts in support of

a sound idea. Instead of thinking of two separate categories—argument and persuasion—think instead of a continuum from the most rigorous logic at one end to extreme flights of fantasy on the other. Figure 3.1 suggests this continuum with different kinds of arguments placed along it.

Where should you place yourself along the continuum in the language you choose and the tone you create? You will have to answer this question with each specific writing context. Much of the time you will choose "thoughtful, restrained language" as expected by the academic community, but there may be times that you will use various persuasive strategies. Probably you will not select "strong appeals to emotion" for your college or workplace writing. Remember that you have different roles in your life, and you use dif-

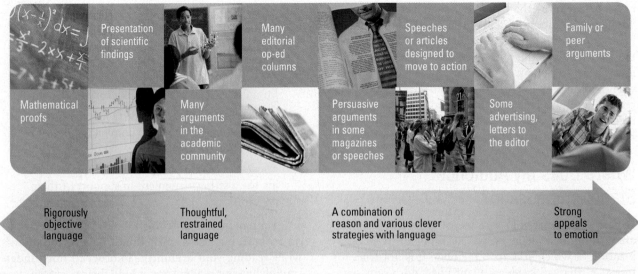

figure 3.1 A Continuum of Argumentative Language

Write the opening paragraph of a letter to each audience based on the following scenario. How might your letter differ based on these different potential lenders? Would you use different language? Include different details? Make different promises? Consider how the audience for your argument can completely change your strategy.

WHAT IF?

You decide that you need a new car. But you don't just want any car. You want a brand new, top-of-the-line hybrid. In order to borrow the money to purchase your dream ride, however, you must write a letter that argues why you want and need this vehicle rather than a less expensive model.

Your best friend, who doesn't own a car.

The local banker, whom you've never met.

Your mom, who worries about your safety.

Your uncle, who works for the Environmental Protection Agency.

GOOD ADVICE

Irony or Sarcasm?

As you learned in Chapter 2, irony is a useful rhetorical strategy for giving your words greater emphasis by writing the opposite of what you mean. Many writers use irony effectively to give punch to their arguments. Irony catches our attention, makes us think, and engages us with the text. Sarcasm is not quite the same as irony. Irony can cleverly focus attention on life's complexities; sarcasm is more often vicious than insightful, relying on harsh, negative word choice. Probably in most of your academic work, you will want to avoid sarcasm, and you will want to think carefully about the effect of any strongly worded appeal to your readers' emotions. Better to persuade your audience with the force of your reasons and evidence than to lose them because of the static of mean language. But the key, always, is to know your audience and understand how best to present a convincing argument to them.

Sarcasm and stupidity meet at the elevator.

ferent voices as appropriate to each role. Most of the time, for most of your arguments, you will want to use the serious voice you normally select for serious conversations with other adults. This is the voice that will help you establish your credibility, or your ethos (see Chapter 1).

Serious Conversation (handwritten margin note)

Move from Topic to Claim to Possible Support

When you write a letter to the editor of a newspaper, you have chosen to respond to someone else's argument that has bothered you. In this writing context, you already know your topic and probably your claim as well. You also know that your purpose will be to refute the article you have read. In composition classes, the context is not always so clearly established, but you will usually be given some guidelines with which to get started.

Selecting a Topic

Suppose that you are asked to write an argument that is in some way connected to First Amendment rights. Your instructor has limited and focused your topic choice and purpose. Start thinking about possible topics that relate to freedom of speech and censorship issues. To aid your topic search and selection, use one or more invention strategies:

general ideas topic (handwritten margin note)
reading research (handwritten margin note)
wording (handwritten margin note)

- **Map or cluster:** Connect ideas to the general topic in various spokes, a kind of visual brainstorming.

- **Brainstorm:** Make a list of ideas that come to mind. List absolutely everything and anything that crosses your mind.

- **Read:** In this case, look through the text for ideas, check out online chat rooms or Facebook groups, or conduct informal online research to learn about your topic.

- **Freewrite:** Write without stopping for 10 minutes. Do not edit yourself or correct errors. Just keep writing for the entire time.

Your invention strategies lead, let us suppose, to the following list of possible research questions or topics:

- Administrative restrictions on the college newspaper—should the administration have the right to tell reporters what they can or can't print?

- Hate speech restrictions or code—isn't hate speech exactly what the law was designed to protect?

- Deleting certain books from high school reading lists—can parents of underage students restrict their freedoms?

- Controls and limits on alcohol and cigarette advertising—if it's in the best interest of people, can speech be restricted?

- Restrictions on violent TV programming—should we restrict free speech in order to protect kids from violence?

All of the topics seem to have promise. Which one do you select?

Two considerations should guide you: interest and knowledge. First, your argument is likely to be more thoughtful and lively if you choose an issue that matters to you. You can also appreciate the usefulness of information and ideas on the topic. But unless you have time for study, you are wise to choose a topic about which you already have some information and ideas. To continue the example, let's suppose that you decide to write about television violence because you are concerned about violence in American society and you have given this issue some thought. It is time to phrase your topic as a tentative thesis or claim.

interest! knowledge (handwritten margin note)

Drafting a Claim or Thesis

Good claim (or thesis) statements will keep you focused in your writing—in addition to establishing your main idea for readers. Give thought, then, both to your position on the issue and to the wording of your claim. Here are some claim statements to avoid:

- Claims using vague words such as *good* or *bad*.

    VAGUE: TV violence is bad for us.

    BETTER: We need more restrictions on violent TV programming.

- Claims in loosely worded two-part sentences.

    UNFOCUSED: Campus rape is a serious problem, and we need to do something about it.

    BETTER: College administrators and students need to work together to reduce both the number of campus rapes and the fear of rape.

- Claims that are not appropriately qualified.

    OVERSTATED: Violence on television is making us a violent society.

    BETTER: TV violence is contributing to viewers' increased fear of violence and insensitivity to violence.

- Claims that do not help you focus on your purpose in writing.

    UNCLEAR PURPOSE: Not everyone agrees on what is meant by violent TV programming.

    (Perhaps this is true, but more importantly, this claim suggests that you will define violent programming. Such an approach would not keep you focused on a First Amendment issue.)

BETTER: Restrictions on violent TV programs can be justified.

(Now your claim directs you to the debate over restrictions of content.)

Listing Possible Grounds

As you learned in Chapter 1, you can generate grounds to support a claim by adding a *because* clause after a claim statement. You can start a list of grounds for the topic on violent TV programming by simply freewriting about your topic and thinking of all of the reasons you feel the way that you do. You can also collect images, graphs, and even statistics that you find while doing preliminary research or reading on your topic. The most important thing is to keep a log or journal of your ideas so that you can return to them when you begin to draft your essay.

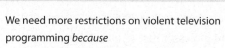

We need more restrictions on violent television programming *because*

1. many people, including children and teens, watch many hours of TV (I will need to get stats for this).
2. people are affected by the dominant activities/experiences in their lives.
3. there is a connection between violent programming and desensitizing and fear of violence and possibly more aggressive behavior in heavy viewers. (I will need to get detail of studies.) Maybe I could use this chart to help:

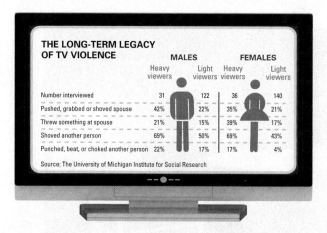

THE LONG-TERM LEGACY OF TV VIOLENCE

	MALES		FEMALES	
	Heavy viewers	Light viewers	Heavy viewers	Light viewers
Number interviewed	31	122	36	140
Pushed, grabbed or shoved spouse	42%	22%	35%	21%
Threw something at spouse	21%	15%	39%	17%
Shoved another person	69%	50%	69%	43%
Punched, beat, or choked another person	22%	17%	17%	4%

Source: The University of Michigan Institute for Social Research

4. society needs to protect young people. Everyone will agree with this, right?

You now have four good points to work on, a combination of reasons and inferences drawn from evidence, and even a potential visual for your essay.

Listing Grounds for the Other Side or Another Perspective

Remember that arguments generate counterarguments. Continue your exploration of this topic by considering possible rebuttals to your proposed grounds. How might someone who does not want to see restrictions placed on television programming respond to each of your points? Let's think about them one at a time:

We need more restrictions on violent television programming because

1. many people, including children and teens, watch many hours of TV.

   My opposition cannot really challenge this point on the facts, only on its relevance to restricting programming. The opposition might argue that if parents think their children are watching too much TV, they should turn it off. The restriction needs to be a family decision. How will I handle this?

2. people are affected by the dominant activities/experiences in their lives.

   It seems common sense to expect people to be influenced by dominant forces in their lives. My opposition might argue, though, that many people have the TV on for many hours but often are not watching it intently for all of that time. The more dominant forces in our lives are parents and teachers and peers, not the TV. The opposition might also argue that people seem to be influenced to such different degrees by television that it is not fair or logical to restrict everyone when perhaps only a few are influenced by their TV viewing to a harmful degree. Do I agree with any of these points? Should I concede any of them?

3. there is a connection between violent programming and desensitizing and fear of violence and possibly more aggressive behavior in heavy viewers.

   Some people are entirely convinced by studies showing these negative effects of violent TV programming, but others point to the less convincing studies or make the argument that if violence on TV were really so powerful an influence, most people would be violent or fearful or desensitized. Can I find studies from really reputable sources that will convince even the biggest skeptics? How can I best present my statistics? Can I create an easy-to-read chart or graph?

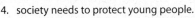

4. society needs to protect young people.

My opposition might choose to agree with me in theory on this point—and then turn again to the argument that parents should be doing the protecting. Government controls on programming restrict adults, as well as children, whereas it may only be some children who should watch fewer hours of TV and not watch adult cop shows at all. So what will my response be to this point?

Working through this process of considering opposing views can help you see

- where you may want to do some research for facts to provide backing for your grounds,
- how you can best develop your reasons to take account of typical counterarguments, and
- if you should qualify your claim in some ways.

Considering the Rogerian or Conciliatory Argument

Psychologist Carl Rogers asserts that the most successful arguments take a conciliatory approach. The characteristics of this approach include

- showing respect for the opposition in the language and tone of the argument,
- seeking common ground by indicating specific facts and values that both sides share, and
- qualifying the claim to bring opposing sides closer.

In their essay "Euthanasia—A Critique," Peter A. Singer and Mark Siegler provide a good example

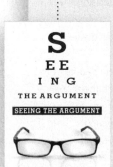

This photograph represents a good example of conciliatory argument. In July 2009, controversy ensued when the Cambridge, Massachusetts Police arrested Harvard professor Henry Louis Gates outside his home in response to a neighbor's complaint. A neighbor had previously reported that "two black males with backpacks" were trying to gain entrance to the home. When the police arrived and asked Professor Gates to step outside his residence, he became incensed and began shouting. Sergeant James Crowley arrested Professor Gates for disorderly conduct—a charge that was quickly dropped. Gates, however, threatened legal action against police for their treatment of him.

In an attempt to resolve this conflict, President Obama asked Gates and Crowley to the White House "for a beer." What is the issue here? And what are the two sides of this issue? What are people supposed to see in this image? What is President Obama attempting to accomplish by bringing Gates and Crowley together? Is it important that they are talking out their differences while drinking beer? Why or why not?

of a conciliatory approach. They begin by explaining and then rebutting the two main arguments in favor of euthanasia. After stating the two arguments in clear and neutral language, they write the following response to the first argument. The highlighted words "we agree" signal the authors' understanding of the argument. The words "we question, however," begin their refutation of it.

> We agree that the relief of pain and suffering is a crucial goal of medicine. We question, however, whether the care of dying patients cannot be improved without resorting to the drastic measure of euthanasia. Most physical pain can be relieved with the appropriate use of analgesic agents. Unfortunately, despite widespread agreement that dying patients must be provided with necessary analgesia, physicians continue to underuse analgesia in the care of dying patients because of concern about depressing respiratory drive or creating addiction. Such situations demand better management of pain, not euthanasia.

In this paragraph, Singer and Siegler accept the value of pain management among dying patients. They go even further and offer a solution to the problem of suffering among the terminally ill—better pain management by physicians. They remain thoughtful in their approach and tone throughout, while sticking to their position that legalizing euthanasia is not the solution.

Consider how you can use this conciliatory approach to write more effective arguments. It will help you avoid overheated language and maintain your focus on what is doable in a world of differing points of view. After reading these examples, do you agree with the old expression "You can catch more flies with honey than with vinegar"?

Planning Your Approach

Now that you have thought about arguments on the other side, you decide that you want to argue for a qualified claim that is also more precise.

My thesis:

To protect young viewers, we need restrictions on violence in children's programs and ratings for prime-time adult shows that clearly establish the degree of violence in those shows.

This qualified claim responds to two points of the rebuttals. You have not given in to the other side but have chosen to narrow the argument to emphasize the protection of children, an area of common ground.

Next, it's time to check some of the articles in your text, your library databases, or even go online to get some supporting data to develop Points 1 and 3. Your research might, for instance, help you find out that

- according to *USAToday,* "There are 2.73 TV sets in the typical home and 2.55 people" (www.usatoday.com/life/television/news/2006-09-21-homes-tv_x.htm)

- according to the American Academy of Child and Adolescent Psychiatry, by the time young people graduate from high school they have spent more time in front of the TV than in the classroom (www.aacap.org/cs/root/facts_for_families/children_and_watching_tv)

- according to the A. C. Nielsen Company, the average number of violent acts seen on TV by the time a child leaves elementary school is over 8,000 (www.csun.edu/science/health/docs/tv&health.html)

You may also find more images, charts, websites, or even videos that will help you illustrate and support your points more effectively.

Finally, how are you going to answer the point about parents controlling their children? You might counter that in theory this is the way it should be—but in reality not all parents are at home watching what their children are watching, and not all parents care enough to pay attention. Furthermore, all of us suffer from the consequences of those children who are influenced by violence on TV, and therefore we, as a society, have a responsibility to protect our citizens. After all, these children grow up to become adults we have to interact with, so the problem is one for the society as a whole to solve, not individual parents. If you had not disciplined yourself to go through the process of listing possible rebuttals, you may not have thought through this part of the debate.

Organizing and Drafting Your Argument

So how will you set up your argument? After you have planned your tentative thesis, your potential claims, your possible support, and your rebuttals to counterarguments, you then decide how you will organize your essay. You can choose from several approaches to argument organization. Your organizational plan should depend on what you think will be the most effective way of presenting your position to your audience. Will your reader expect you to immediately address obvious opposing points of view? Or should you lay out your entire position and present solid support before you refute your opponents' objections? Do you need to provide detailed background information about your topic before your reader can fully understand your position? These decisions, like all your writing choices, must be made by you according to your desired goals. Below are two possible organizations for the television violence essay. Which would you choose?

Plan 1: Organizing the Argument

Attention-getting opening (why the issue is important, current, etc.)

Claim statement (thesis)

Reasons and evidence in order from least important to most important

Challenge to potential rebuttals or counterarguments

Conclusion that reemphasizes claim

Plan 2: Organizing the Argument

Attention-getting opening

Claim statement (or possibly leave to the conclusion)

Arguments of opposing position, with my challenge to each

Conclusion that reemphasizes (or states for the first time) my claim

Now that you have chosen an organizational structure for your argument, it is time to get down to the work of actually composing, or drafting, your essay. Typically, writers follow a procedure that includes the following steps in the Good Advice box on page 59.

Writing the Introduction and the Conclusion

As you probably already know, your essay should have an effective opening and closing. Your introduction should gain the audience's attention and encourage them to take interest in your topic and your thesis. Your conclusion should present a clear summation of your overall claim.

In your introduction, a strong opening sentence becomes important. Sometimes, less experienced writers will begin with a weak sentence. A sentence may be weak in its focus, its content, or its mechanics. Consider this sample opening sentence for the topic on violence in television programming from the previous section:

"In today's society, violence is a major problem."

Not only does this sample opening sentence start with a clichéd comment ("In today's society"), it communicates little and does not relate well to the author's thesis. This kind of statement is labeled "rhetorical throat clearing" because it seems as though the writer used a sentence that did not say much simply because he or she did not know how to begin the paper.

Introductions should also clearly establish your argument or claim for the paper. Writers can state the claim *explicitly* or *implicitly*. For example, a writer might use the statement "TV violence is contributing to viewers' increased fear of violence and insensitivity to violence" as the claim or thesis of his or her essay. As an explicit claim, this exact statement will appear in the introduction. Conventionally, a writer can locate it near the end of the introduction. More experienced writers, on the other hand, will make their claims implicit; this means that their claim remains unstated yet clear.

In addition, an introduction will also establish the issues for the paper, and it can forecast or preview the overall structure of the paper. In other words, the writer can identify his or her major reasons in support of the claim in the introduction before developing each of those reasons separately in the body of the paper.

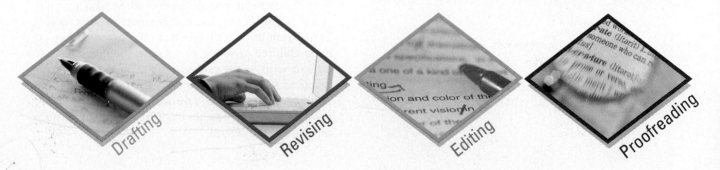

Drafting   Revising   Editing   Proofreading

Conclusions, on the other hand, summarize the importance of the issue the writer has addressed as well as reiterate the overall claim of the essay. However, the conclusion will not simply restate everything you have written about in the body of the essay. It will stress the uniqueness and significance of your point of view, and it might also call for the audience to take a specific action. A claim of policy, for example, will ask that government officials adopt legislation to improve a given situation.

Revising Your Draft

Begin your revision by looking at the total argument. Try not to look at the grammar or spelling at this point. You will not be ready to polish the writing until you are satisfied with the argument. If you have drafted your essay at the computer, you may want to print it out to look at it with a new perspective. Then remind yourself that revision is just that: re-vision. Your goal is to see your draft in a new way.

As you begin your revision, consider whether you have made a claim, provided support, and responded to possible counterarguments. Examine the order of your reasons and evidence. Do some of your points belong, logically, in a different place? Does the order

make the most powerful defense of your claim? Be willing to move whole paragraphs around to test the best organization. Also reflect on the argument itself. Have you avoided logical fallacies? Have you qualified statements when appropriate? Do you have enough support? The best support for your argument?

Consider development: Is your essay long enough to meet assignment requirements? Are points fully developed to satisfy the demands of readers? One key to development is the length of your paragraphs. If most of your paragraphs are only two or three sentences, you most likely have not developed the point of each paragraph satisfactorily. It is possible that some paragraphs need to be combined because they are really on the same subtopic. More typically, short paragraphs need further explanation of ideas or examples to illustrate ideas. Compare the following paragraphs for effectiveness:

First Draft of a Paragraph from an Essay on Gun Control

One popular argument used against the regulation of gun ownership is the need of citizens, especially in urban areas where the crime rate is higher, to possess a handgun for personal protection, either carried or kept in the home. Some citizens may not be aware of

GOOD ADVICE

Guidelines for Drafting

- Try to write a complete draft of an essay in one sitting, so that you can "see" the whole piece.

- If you can't think of a clever opening, state your claim and move on to the body of your essay. After you draft your reasons and evidence, a good opening may occur to you.

- If you find that you need something more in some parts of your essay, leave extra space as a reminder that you will need to return to those paragraphs later.

- Try to avoid using a dictionary or thesaurus while drafting. Your goal is to get the ideas down. You will polish later.

- Learn to draft at your computer. Revising is so easy on a computer that you will be more willing to make significant changes. If you are handwriting your draft, leave plenty of margin space for additions or for directions to shift parts around.

the dangers to themselves or their families when they purchase a gun. Others, more aware, may embrace the myth that "bad things only happen to other people."

Revised Version of the Paragraph with Statistics Added

One popular argument used against the regulation of gun ownership is the need of citizens, especially in urban areas where the crime rate is higher, to possess a handgun for personal protection, whether it is carried or kept in the home. Although some citizens may not be aware of the dangers to themselves or their families when they purchase a gun, they should be. According to the Center to Prevent Handgun Violence, from their Web page "Firearm Facts," "guns that are kept in the home for self-protection are 22 times more likely to kill a family member or friend than to kill in self-defense." The Center also reports that guns in the home make homicide three times more likely and suicide five times more likely. We are not thinking straight if we believe that these dangers only apply to others.

A quick trip to the Internet has provided this student with some facts to support his argument. The highlighted portion shows how he has referred informally but fully to the source of his information. (If your instructor requires formal MLA documentation in all essays, then you will need to add a Works Cited page and give a full reference to the Web page.)

Editing = mechanical errors

After you make your changes, you are ready to begin the editing process. Editing is different from revising. In revising, you are focused primarily on shaping your ideas. Editing, on the other hand, necessitates working toward improved sentence structure and better word choices, as well as proofreading for grammar and mechanical errors.

As you read through your essay, pay close attention to unity and coherence, to sentence patterns, and to word choice. Read each paragraph as a separate unit to be certain that everything is on the same subtopic. Then look at your use of transition and connecting words, both within and between paragraphs. Ask yourself, Have I guided the reader through the argument? Have I shown how the parts connect by using appropriate connectors such as *therefore, in addition, as a consequence,* and *also*?

Read again, focusing on each sentence, checking to see that you have varied sentence patterns and length. Read sentences aloud to let your ear help you find awkward constructions or unfinished thoughts. Strive as well for word choice that is concrete and specific, avoiding wordiness, clichés, trite expressions, and incorrect use of specialized terms. Observe how Samantha edited one paragraph in her essay "Balancing Work and Family":

Draft Version of Paragraph

Women have come a long way in equalizing themselves, but inequality within marriages do exist. One reason for this can be found in the media. Just last week America turned on their televisions to watch a grotesque dramatization of skewed priorities. On *The Bachelor*, a panel of women vied for the affections of a millionaire who would choose one of them to be his wife. This show said that women can be purchased. Also that men must provide and that money is worth the sacrifice of one's individuality. The show also suggests that physical attraction is more important than the building of a complete relationship. Finally, the show says that women's true value lies in their appearance. This is a dangerous message to send to both men and women viewers.

Edited Version of Paragraph

Although women have come a long way toward equality in the workplace, inequality within marriages can still be found. The media may be partly to blame for this continued inequality. Just last week Americans watched a grotesque dramatization of skewed priorities. On a popular television show called *The Bachelor*, a panel of women vied for the affections of a millionaire who would choose one of them to be his wife. Such displays teach us that women can be purchased, that men must be the providers, that the desire for money is worth the sacrifice of one's individuality, that physical attraction is more important than a complete relationship, and that women's true value lies in their appearance. These messages discourage marriages based on equality and mutual support.

Samantha's editing has eliminated wordiness and vague references and has combined ideas into one forceful sentence. If you have a good argument, you do not want to lose readers because you have not taken the time to polish your writing.

Word Choice and Tone

As discussed, careful examination of word choice can eliminate wordiness, vagueness, clichés, and so on. Here is a specific checklist of problems often found in student papers with some ways to fix the problems.

- **Eliminate clichés. Do** not write about "the fast-paced world we live in today" or the "rat race." First, do you know for sure that the pace of life for someone who has a demanding job is any faster than it was in the past? Using time effectively has always mattered. Second, clichés suggest that you are too lazy to find your own words.

- **Avoid jargon.** Specialists of any kind have their own language. That's one meaning of jargon, and if the audience is other specialists, it can be appropriate. However, some nonspecialists fill their writing with heavy-sounding terms to give the appearance of significance. Watch for any overuse of "scientific" terms such as *factor* or *aspect,* and other vague, awkward language.

- **Avoid language that is too informal for most of your writing contexts.** What do you mean when you write, *"Kids* today watch too much TV"? Alternatives include *children, teens, adolescents.* These words are both less slangy and more precise.

- **Avoid nasty attacks on the opposition.** Change "those jerks who are foolish enough to believe that TV violence has no impact on children" to language that explains your counterargument without attacking those who may disagree with you. After all, you want to change the thinking of your audience, not make them resent you for name-calling.

- **Avoid all discriminatory language.** In the academic community and the adult workplace, most people are bothered by language that belittles any one group. This includes language that is racist or sexist or reflects negatively on people because of age, disability, sexual orientation, or religious beliefs. Just don't use it!

Proofreading *punctuation*

You also do not want to lose the respect of readers because your paper is filled with "little" errors—errors in punctuation, mechanics, and word choice. Most readers will forgive one or two little errors but will become annoyed if these mistakes begin to pile up. So after you are finished rewriting and editing, print a copy of your paper and read it slowly, looking specifically at punctuation, at the handling of quotations and references to writers and titles, and at those pesky words that

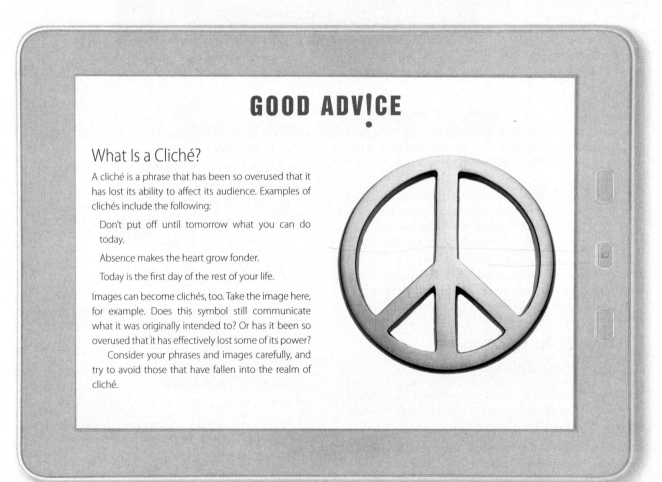

GOOD ADVICE

What Is a Cliché?

A cliché is a phrase that has been so overused that it has lost its ability to affect its audience. Examples of clichés include the following:

Don't put off until tomorrow what you can do today.

Absence makes the heart grow fonder.

Today is the first day of the rest of your life.

Images can become clichés, too. Take the image here, for example. Does this symbol still communicate what it was originally intended to? Or has it been so overused that it has effectively lost some of its power?

Consider your phrases and images carefully, and try to avoid those that have fallen into the realm of cliché.

Attack ads like these are used in political campaigns and on roadside billboards. Do you think these kinds of strategies are wise? What are the risks involved in attacking your opponent in this way?

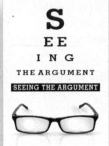

S
EE
ING
THE ARGUMENT
SEEING THE ARGUMENT

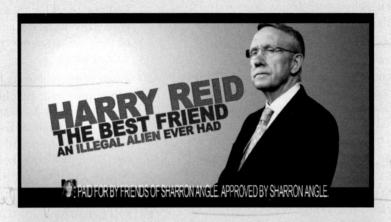

come in two or more versions: *to, too,* and *two; here* and *hear; their, there,* and *they're;* and so forth. Your computer spell checker cannot tell if the wrong version has been used.

If instructors have found these kinds of errors in your papers over the years, then focus your attention on the specific kinds of errors you have been known to make. Use a glossary of usage in a handbook for problems with homonyms (words that sound alike but have different meanings), and check a handbook for punctuation rules. Take pride in your work and present a paper that will be treated with respect.

A Checklist for Revision/ Editing/Proofreading

This checklist offers a review of questions to consider in writing a sound essay. Use this list to check whether parts of your essay need improvement.

- Have I selected an issue and purpose consistent with assignment guidelines?

- Have I stated a claim that is focused, appropriately qualified, and precise?

- Have I developed sound reasons and evidence in support of my claim?

- Have I used Toulmin terms to help me study the parts of my argument, including rebuttals to counterarguments?

- Have I taken advantage of a conciliatory approach and emphasized common ground with opponents?

- Have I found a clear and effective organization for presenting my argument?

- Have I edited my draft thoughtfully, concentrating on producing unified and coherent paragraphs and polished sentences?

- Have I eliminated wordiness, clichés, and jargon?

- Have I selected an appropriate tone for my purpose and audience?

- Have I used my word processor's spell checker and proofread a printed copy with great care?

let's review

After reading this chapter, you should understand the following points:

- Different types of arguments require different approaches or different kinds of evidence.

- Effective essays are written in a style and tone that are suited to both the audience and the writer's purpose.

- Your readers may hold very clear opinions about your topic, reject certain ideas based on their value systems, or automatically accept the validity of your claims based on their beliefs or experiences.

- Two considerations should guide your topic choice: interest and knowledge. Your argument is likely to be more thoughtful and lively if you choose an issue that matters to you.

- Good claim (or thesis) statements will keep you focused in your writing—in addition to establishing your main idea for readers.

- There are several approaches to argument organization. Your organizational plan should depend on what you think will be the most effective way of presenting your position to your audience.

- Revision is just that: re-vision. Your goal is to see your draft in a new way.

- Editing focuses on issues such as unity and coherence, sentence patterns, and word choice.

- Proofreading focuses on "little errors" such as errors in punctuation, mechanics, and word choice.

connect

Individually or in a small group, read the following essay by Deborah Tannen and answer the questions that follow.

prereading questions } **Should we avoid disagreements over politics for fear of offending someone? Or should we have serious debates that include disagreements?**

We Need Higher Quality Outrage

Deborah Tannen

University professor and professor of linguistics at Georgetown University, Deborah Tannen has written popular books on the use of language by ordinary people. Among her many books are You Just Don't Understand *(1990),* Talking from 9 to 5 *(1994),* I Only Say This Because I Love You *(2004), and* You're Wearing THAT? *(2006). The following article was published October 22, 2004, in the* Christian Science Monitor. *Even though it refers to former President Bush's campaign, think about its current political implications. Sarah Palin's recent reference to "blood libel" in early 2011, for instance, created controversy and alienated some members of the American public. In light of such occurrences, do Tannen's arguments still apply?*

We need to ratchet up the level of opposition in our public and private discourse.

This statement may seem surprising, coming from someone who wrote a book, *The Argument Culture*, claiming that the rise of opposition is endangering our civil life. Why do I now say we need more? The key is what I call "agonism": ritualized opposition, a knee-jerk, automatic use of warlike formats.

Agonism obliterates and obfuscates real opposition. When there's a ruckus in the street outside your home, you fling open the window and see what's happening. But if there's a row outside every night, you shut the window and try to block it out. That's what's happening in our public discourse. With all the shouting, we have less, rather than more, genuine opposition—the kind that is the bedrock on which democracy rests.

Agonism grows out of our conviction that opposition is the best, if not the only, path to truth. In this view, the best way to explore an idea is a debate that requires opponents to marshal facts and arguments for one side, and ignore, ridicule, or otherwise undermine facts and arguments that support the other side.

Many journalists prize two types of agonism: One is the value of attack over other modes of inquiry, such as analyzing, integrating, or simply informing. The other is a seemingly laudable search for "balance," which results in reporting accusations without examining their validity.

Legitimate opposition is quashed when dissension from public policy is branded "hate speech" or unpatriotic. True hate speech stirs passions against members of a group precisely because of their membership in that group. Expressing passionate opposition to—even hatred for—the policies of elected officials is a legitimate, necessary form of engagement in public life. Candidates and individuals may differ—indeed, must differ—on public policy, such as whether invading Iraq enhanced or hampered American security. But questioning the patriotism of those who believe the invasion was a mistake quashes legitimate debate.

We can know others' policies, but we cannot know their motives. Accusing opponents of venal motives makes it easy to dismiss valid criticism. One can decry the fact that many of the contracts for rebuilding Iraq were awarded to Halliburton without claiming that the war was undertaken in order to enrich the company the vice president once led. One can argue that having received medals for heroic deeds in the Vietnam war does not equip John Kerry to execute the war in Iraq without seeking to discredit not only his, but all, Purple Hearts. One can argue that the president is using the Sept. 11 attacks to bolster his public profile without going so far as to claim (as does a message circulating on the Internet) that he played a role in authorizing those attacks. And one can validly defend the way the war was conducted without accusing one's critics of undermining the war efforts.

Agonism leads to the conviction that fights are riveting to watch. Together with ever-diminishing budgets and corporate demands for ever-greater profits, this conviction tempts TV producers to quickly assemble shows by finding a spokesperson for each side—the more extreme, the better—and letting them slug it out. This format leaves no forum for the middle ground, where most viewers are. The result is that the extremes define the issues, problems seem insoluble, and citizens become alienated from the political process.

A single-minded devotion to "balance" also creates the illusion of equivalence where there is none. For example, as shown repeatedly by journalist Ross Gelbspan as well as in a recent article by Maxwell and Jules Boykoff in the academic journal *Global Environment Change*, news coverage of global warming actually ends up being biased because news reports of scientists' mounting concern typically also feature prominently one of the few "greenhouse skeptics" who declare the concern bogus. This "balanced" two-sides approach gives the impression that scientists are evenly divided, whereas in fact the vast majority agree that the dangers of global climate change are potentially grave.

Take, too, the current bemoaning of negativity in the presidential campaign. Given the devotion to "balance," reports tend to juxtapose negative statements from both sides. But negativity comes in many forms. Attacks on an opponent's character distract attention from the issues that will be decided in the election. Attacks on an opponent's proposed and past policies are appropriate; we need more of such attention to policy.

The preoccupation with balance plays a role here, too. If the goal is only ensuring balance, then journalists can feel their work is done when they have reported accusations flung from each side, abnegating the responsibility to examine the validity of the attacks.

Ironically, while the press is busy gauging who's ahead and who's behind in the contest, significant opposition is left out. Martin Walker, of United Press International, notes that when President Bush addressed the United Nations last month, newspapers in every country other than our own—including our British allies and papers such as the French *Le Figaro*, which supported the invasion of Iraq—reported the event as a duel, with President Bush on one side and UN Secretary-General Kofi Annan or the international community on the other. The American press, whether they are supportive or critical of the president's speech, ignored the oppositional context and reported on his speech alone.

This downplaying of genuine opposition is mirrored in our private conversations. In many European countries, heated political discussions are commonplace and enjoyed; most Americans regard such conversations as unseemly arguments, so they avoid talking politics—especially with anyone whose views differ, or are unknown, lest they inadvertently spark a conflict or offend someone who disagrees.

As a result, we aren't forced to articulate—and therefore examine—the logic of our views, nor are we exposed to the views of those with whom we disagree. And if young people don't hear adults having intense, animated political discussions, the impression that politics has no relevance to their lives is reinforced. Surely this contributes to the woefully low voter turnout among young Americans.

The Yugoslavian-born poet Charles Simic has said, "There are moments in life when true invective is called for, when it becomes an absolute necessity, out of a deep sense of justice, to denounce, mock, vituperate, lash out, in the strongest possible language."

We have come to such a moment. Leaving aside invective, vituperation, and mockery, I believe that we need space for peaceful yet passionate outrage. The challenges we face are monumental. Among them are the spread of nuclear weapons, the burgeoning number of individuals and groups who see the United States as a threat, and the question of how far to compromise our liberties and protections in the interest of security.

On the domestic side, the challenges include the impending insolvency of Medicare and social security, the rising number of working Americans with no health insurance, and the question of whether the checks and balances provided by the three branches of government should be strengthened or weakened.

In the face of challenges of these proportions, we can no longer afford to have voices of true opposition muted by the agonistic din.

QUESTIONS FOR READING

1. What is Tannen's subject? Be precise.

2. What does the term *agonism* mean? What is the typical response to agonism?

3. What are the two types of agonism embraced by journalists?

4. What are the characteristics of "attack" journalism? What are the consequences of this approach to the news? What is the problem with the "balanced" approach to reporting the news?

QUESTIONS FOR REASONING AND ANALYSIS

1. Examine Tannen's examples of attack journalism. What makes them effective?

2. Analyze her two examples of balanced journalism. What makes them effective? Observe that the author does not state a presidential preference. Is it possible to infer her preference?

3. Analyze the author's conclusion—her last four paragraphs. Study her lists of problems and her word choice. Is this an effective ending? Does she drive home her point and get the reader's attention focused on the problem she has examined? Why or why not?

QUESTIONS FOR REFLECTING AND WRITING

1. Look again at Tannen's list of problems at the conclusion of her argument. Would you make the same list of problems that we need to be debating? If not, what would you add? Delete? Why?

2. Does Tannen's objection to the balanced approach to reporting make sense to you? Agree or disagree and defend your choice.

3. Which form of agonism might most distort issues for the public? Why? Defend your choice.

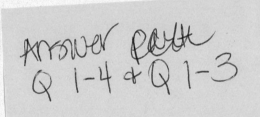

⚠ CAUTION

SLIPPERY
SLOPE

more about argument: induction, deduction, analogy, and logical fallacies

chapter 4

"Ozy and Millie"   www.ozyandmillie.org   ©2007 D.C. Simpson

Reprinted by permission of Dana Claire Simpson, OzyAndMillie.com.

You can build on your knowledge of the basics of argument, examined in Chapter 1, by understanding some traditional forms of argument: induction, deduction, and analogy. It is also important to recognize arguments, like the one in the cartoon here, that do not work due to a logical error or flaw.

Induction

Induction is the process by which we reach inferences—opinions based on facts or on a combination of facts and less-debatable inferences. The inductive process moves from particular to general, from support to assertion. We base our inferences on the facts we have gathered and studied. For this reason, scientists and lawyers use induction all the time. In general, the more evidence, the more convincing the argument. No one wants to debate tomorrow's sunrise; the evidence for counting on it is too convincing. Most inferences, though, are drawn from less evidence, so we need to examine inductive arguments closely to judge their reasonableness.

When we construct arguments based on experience or observation, we can use induction to reach our conclusion. This pattern is easy to understand if you imagine the following scenario:

> You have been assigned as the prosecuting attorney in a case against Mr. Jones. You are presented with his file which includes all of the evidence gathered against him. In court, you make the following argument:
>
> "Ladies and gentlemen of the jury, the EVIDENCE is as follows:
>
> - There is the dead body of Smith.
> - Smith was shot in his bedroom between the hours of 11:00 p.m. and 2:00 a.m., according to the coroner.
> - Jones was seen, by a neighbor, entering the Smith home at around 11:00 the night of Smith's death.
> - A coworker heard Smith and Jones arguing in Smith's office the morning of the day Smith died.

> - Smith was shot by a .32-caliber pistol.
> - The .32-caliber pistol left in the bedroom contains Jones's fingerprints.
>
> This evidence leads to a logical conclusion (CLAIM) that Jones killed Smith."

In this example, the prosecuting attorney has cited all the facts (i.e., the particulars) in order to establish the conclusion (i.e., the general) of the argument. The jury then infers that Jones is a murderer. Unless there is a confession or a trustworthy eyewitness, the conclusion is an inference, not a fact. This is the most logical explanation; that is, the conclusion meets the standards of simplicity and frequency while accounting for all of the known evidence.

As you write your own arguments, you may want to try to organize your points around an inductive pattern of reasoning. You can build your case by pointing to logical and sound evidence and then reaching a logical and well-supported conclusion.

try it!

Collaborative Exercise: Induction

With your class partner or in small groups, find evidence (make a list of facts or find images in magazines or online) that could be used to support each of the following inferences:

1. Whole-wheat bread is nutritious.

2. Fido must have escaped under the fence during the night.

3. Sue must be planning to go away for the weekend.

4. Students who do not hand in all essay assignments fail Dr. Bradshaw's English class.

5. The price of Florida oranges will go up in grocery stores next year.

Examine how the advertisement here uses inductive reasoning to make its argument. Consider how the author chooses images and the placement of those images to provide points of support that allow the reader to reach the logical conclusion that watching movies on Sony televisions is just like being there, amidst the action. Does this conclusion (or inference) seem justified by the images the author chooses to include? Does the author need to directly state this conclusion or does the audience simply reach it by examining the evidence presented? Think about how you might use images in your own arguments to provide points of support.

S
EE
I N G
THE ARGUMENT
SEEING THE ARGUMENT

Deduction

Although induction can be described as an argument that moves from particular to general, from facts (evidence) to inference (claim), deduction cannot necessarily be described as the reverse. Deductive arguments are more complex.

Deduction is the reasoning process that moves the reader from a set of premises (or ideas) to the logical conclusion that must be true if the premises are true.

In other words, your job in using deductive reasoning is to provide your readers with premises that they can assume to be true and then show how your conclusion must be true based on those premises.

For example, suppose, on the way out of American history class, you have the following conversation with your classmate:

Wow. I never realized that Nelson Mandela is such a great leader.

Why do you think he is a great leader?

Well, because he performed with courage and a clear purpose in a time of crisis!

Hmm . . . I guess it is true that people who perform that way in a time of crisis are great leaders. And we just learned about how Mandela did perform with courage and purpose, so I guess you're absolutely right—he IS a great leader!

Your explanation of your claim rests on the fact that your reader believes (1) that people who perform with courage and conviction in a time of crisis are great leaders and (2) that Nelson Mandela performed this way. If your reader believes that both of these statements are true, she must accept that Mandela is a great leader. You have convinced her using deductive reasoning!

The two reasons (or statements your reader must assume are true) are called *premises*. The broader one, called the *major premise*, is written first and the more specific one, the *minor premise*, comes next.

MAJOR PREMISE: All people who perform with courage and a clear purpose in a crisis are great leaders.

MINOR PREMISE: Nelson Mandela is a person who performed with courage and a clear purpose in a crisis.

CONCLUSION: Nelson Mandela is a great leader.

PENGUINS ARE BLACK AND WHITE.
SOME OLD TV SHOWS ARE BLACK AND WHITE.
THEREFORE, SOME PENGUINS ARE OLD TV SHOWS.

**Logic: another thing that
penguins aren't very good at.**

Reprinted by permission of Randy Glasbergen.

If these two premises are correctly, that is, logically, constructed, then the conclusion follows logically, and the deductive argument is *valid*.

But be careful! This does not mean that the conclusion is necessarily true. It does mean that if you accept the truth of the premises, then you must accept the truth of the conclusion, because in a valid argument the conclusion follows logically and necessarily.

When composing a deductive argument, your task will be to defend the truth of your premises. Then, if your argument is valid (logically constructed), readers will have no alternative but to agree with your conclusion. If your reader disagrees with your logically constructed argument, then he or she will need to show why one (or more) of your premises isn't true. In other words, your opponent's counterargument will seek to discredit one (or more) of your premises.

Generally, we can apply deductive reasoning when making arguments based on laws, rules, and other widely accepted principles, but reading and writing valid and true deductive arguments can be tricky. Some deductive arguments merely look right, but the two premises do not lead logically to the conclusion that is asserted. We must read each argument carefully to make certain that the conclusion follows from the premises.

Analogy

The *argument from analogy* is an argument based on comparison. Analogies assert that since A and B are alike in several ways, they must be alike in another way as well. An inference concludes the argument from analogy. An inference represents an assertion in which the arguer uses deductive reasoning to establish a significant similarity in the two items being compared.

GOOD ADV!CE

How Can a Conclusion Be Valid, But Not Necessarily True?

Remember that the only requirement for an argument to be valid is that the conclusion follows necessarily if the premises are true. If the connection between the premises and conclusion is logical, then the argument is valid.

But what if one or more of the premises isn't true? The connection between them and the conclusion may be valid, but the entire argument falls apart based on the fact that there is a flaw in the logic.

Consider this argument:

All mammals have hair.

Dogs are mammals.

If these premises are accepted as true by the reader, then the following conclusion must also be true and the argument is valid.

All dogs have hair.

But do all dogs really have hair? What about the hairless varieties? Where did this reasoning go wrong?

To learn more about logical fallacies and how they can affect your arguments, see pages 71–80.

Exercises: Completing and Evaluating Deductive Arguments

Here is an example of a valid and true argument:

PREMISE: All Jesuits are priests.
PREMISE: No women are priests.
CONCLUSION: No women are Jesuits.

The first premise is true by definition; the term *Jesuit* refers to an order of Roman Catholic priests. The second premise is true for the Roman Catholic Church, so if the term *priest* is used to refer only to people with a religious vocation in the Roman Catholic Church, then the second premise is also true by definition. And if both premises are true, the conclusion must logically and necessarily follow.

Turn each of the following statements into valid deductive arguments. (You have the conclusion and one premise, so you will have to determine the missing premise that would complete the argument.) Then decide which arguments have premises that could be supported. Note the kind of support that might be provided. Explain why you think some arguments have insupportable premises.

1. Mrs. Ferguson is a good teacher (**CONCLUSION**) because she can explain the subject matter clearly (**FIRST PREMISE**).

2. Segregated schools are unconstitutional because they are unequal.

3. Michael must be a good driver because he drives fast.

4. The media clearly have a liberal bias because they make fun of religious fundamentalists.

- Cats are pets, just like dogs.
- Cats live in residential communities, just like dogs.
- Cats can mess up other people's yards, just like dogs.
- Cats, if allowed to run free, can disturb the peace (fighting, howling at night), just like dogs.
- Therefore, cats should be required to walk on a leash, just like dogs.

Does it necessarily follow that cats should be required to walk on a leash, just like dogs? If such a county ordinance were passed, would it be enforceable? Have you ever tried to walk a cat on a leash? In spite of legitimate similarities brought out by the analogy, the conclusion does not logically follow because the arguer is overlooking a fundamental difference in the two animals' personalities. Dogs can be trained to a leash; most cats (Siamese are one exception) cannot be so trained. Such thinking will produce sulking cats and scratched owners. But the analogy, delivered passionately to the right audience, could lead community activists to lobby for a new law.

Observe that the problem with the cat-leash-law analogy is not in the similarities asserted about the items being compared but rather in the underlying assumption that the similarities logically support the argument's conclusion. A good analogy asserts many points of comparison and finds likenesses that are essential parts of the nature or purpose of the two items being compared. The best way to challenge another's analogy is to point out a fundamental difference in the nature or purpose of the compared items. For all of their similarities, when it comes to walking on a leash, cats are not like dogs.

The other similarities serve as evidence in support of the inference.

Although analogy is sometimes an effective approach because clever, imaginative comparisons are often moving, analogy is not as rigorously logical as either induction or deduction. Frequently an analogy is based on only one, two, or possibly three points of comparison, whereas a sound inductive argument likely presents many examples to support its conclusion. Further, to be convincing, the points of comparison must be fundamental to the two items being compared.

Observe one student's argument for a county leash law for cats developed by analogy with dogs. Does it seem logical? Or does it fall short of being a convincing and logical argument?

Arguments That Do Not Work: Logical Fallacies

As you can see, if one or more premises of an argument is shown to be untrue or illogical, the entire argument becomes suspect. Readers will not have faith in the conclusion you are reaching if your basic premises are not sound. A thorough study of argument needs to include a study of logical fallacies because so many arguments fail to meet standards of sound logic and good sense. Before examining specific types of arguments that do not work, let us consider briefly why people offer arguments that are not sensible.

SEEING THE ARGUMENT

This advertisement below is a good example of an analogy. It claims that choosing a sexual partner is like choosing which jack to plug your phone into. An analogy is being made between the two items, which provides support for the argument that choosing the right sexual partner and sticking with that person will help you avoid getting AIDS.

www.shibi.in

many options.
better choose **one** forever.

keep yourself away from A I D S

try it!

Exercises: Analogy

Analyze the following analogies. List the stated and implied points of comparison and the conclusion. Then judge each argument's logic and effectiveness as a persuasive technique. If the argument is not logical, state the fundamental difference in the two compared items. If the argument could be persuasive, describe the kind of audience that might be moved by it.

a. College newspapers should not be under the supervision or control of a faculty sponsor. Fortunately, no governmental sponsor controls *The New York Times,* or we would no longer have a free press in this country. We need a free college press, too, one that can attack college policies when they are wrong.

b. Let's recognize that college athletes are really professional and start paying them properly. College athletes get a free education, and spending money from boosters. They are required to attend practices and games, and—if they play football or basketball—they bring in huge revenues for their "organization." College coaches are also paid enormous salaries, just like professional coaches, and often college coaches are tapped to coach professional teams. The only difference: the poor college athletes don't get those big salaries and huge signing bonuses.

c. Just like any business, the federal government must be made to balance its budget. No company could continue to operate in the red as the government does and expect to be successful. A constitutional amendment requiring a balanced federal budget is long overdue.

Causes of Illogic

Ignorance

One frequent cause for illogical debate is a lack of knowledge of the subject. Some people have more information than others, either from formal study or from wide-ranging experiences. The younger you are, the less you can be expected to know about or understand complex issues. On the other hand, if you want to debate a complex or technical issue, then you cannot use ignorance as an excuse for producing a weak argument. Rather, you will need to conduct solid research in order to be fully educated about your topic.

Egos

Ego problems are another cause of weak arguments. Those with low self-esteem often have difficulty in

A third cause of irrationality is the collection of prejudices and biases that we carry around, having absorbed them ages ago from family and community. Prejudices range from the worst ethnic, religious, or sexist stereotypes to political views we have adopted uncritically (Democrats are all bleeding hearts; Republicans are all rich snobs), to perhaps less serious but equally insupportable notions (if it's in print, it must be right; if it's not meat and potatoes, it is not really dinner). People who see the world through distorted lenses cannot possibly assess facts intelligently and reason logically from them. For example, look at the sign on the left. Consider how this argument responds to deeply held prejudices about the issue of homosexuality. Might readers reject this author's point based on their own prejudiced point of view?

A Need for Answers

Finally, many bad arguments stem from a human need for answers—any answers—to the questions that deeply concern us. We want to control our world because that makes us feel secure, and having answers makes us feel in control. This need can lead to illogic from oversimplifying problems or refusing to settle for qualified answers to questions.

The causes of illogic lead us to a twofold classification of bad arguments: logical fallacies that result from (1) oversimplifying the issue or (2) ignoring the issue by substituting emotion for reason.

Fallacies That Result from Oversimplifying

Errors in Generalizing

Errors in generalizing include overstatement and hasty or faulty generalization. All have in common an error in the inductive pattern of argument. The inference drawn from the evidence is unwarranted, either because too broad a generalization is made or because the generalization is drawn from incomplete or incorrect evidence. *Overstatement* occurs when the argument's assertion is an unqualified generalization—that is, it refers to all members of a category or class, although the evidence justifies an assertion about only some of the class. Overstatements often result from stereotyping, giving the same traits to everyone in a group. Overstatements are frequently signaled by words such as *all, every, always, never,* and *none.* In addition, assertions such as "children love clowns" are understood to refer to all children, even though the word *all* does not appear in the sentence. It is the writer's task to qualify statements appropriately, using words such as *some, many,* or *frequently.* Overstatements are discredited by finding only one exception

debates because they attach themselves to their ideas and then feel personally attacked when someone disagrees with them. Usually the next step is a defense of their views with even greater emotion and irrationality, even though self-esteem is enhanced when others applaud our knowledge and thoughtfulness, not our irrationality. Try to remember that while good arguments often appeal to the emotions of the audience, they do not personally attack readers. You should be able to separate your (or your opponent's) argument from your own sense of worth or level of intelligence.

This poster attempts to make a case against teaching evolution. But is this argument grounded in a solid understanding of evolutionary theory? Might this argument be perceived by some readers as flawed due to the author's ignorance?

to disprove the assertion. One frightened child who starts to cry when the clown approaches will destroy the argument.

The following reading is another example, from LiveScience.com. See if you can find the generalizations that are being made.

Why Teens Are Lousy at Chores

LiveScience Staff
May 17, 2005

Finally researchers have come up with a reason other than pure laziness for why teenagers can't shower *and* brush their teeth or unload the dishwasher *and* wipe down the counter.

Blame it on "cognitive limitations." Their brains can't multitask as well as those of the taskmasters.

Trust, however, that they'll grow out of it.

The part of the brain responsible for multitasking continues to develop until late adolescence, with cells making connections even after some children are old enough to drive, according to a new study in the May/June issue of the journal *Child Development*.

The frontal cortex, which starts just behind the eyes and goes back almost to the ears, figures out (or doesn't) what to do when a person is asked to juggle multiple pieces of information. Imagine, then, how "make your bed and bring the laundry down" might befuddle a 13-year-old.

In one of the study's tests, subjects between ages 9 and 20 were given multiple pieces of information, then asked to re-order the information to formulate an accurate response to a question. In another of several tests, they were asked to find hidden items using a high degree of strategic thinking.

The ability to remember multiple bits of information developed through age 13 to 15, the study found. But strategic self-organized thinking, the type that demands a high level of multi-tasking skill, continues to develop until ages 16 to 17.

The notion is not entirely new. Brain imaging has suggested as much.

"Our findings lend behavioral support to that work and indicate that the frontal lobe is continuing to develop until late adolescence in a manner that depends upon the complexity of the task that is being demanded," said lead researcher Monica Luciana, an associate professor of psychology at the University of Minnesota.

Unfortunately the study did not reveal any solution to parents at their wits' end over the problem. But Luciana did offer this advice:

"We need to keep their cognitive limitations in mind, especially when adolescents are confronted with demanding situations in the classroom, at home, or in social gatherings."

Hasty or faulty generalizations may be qualified assertions, but they still oversimplify by arguing from insufficient evidence or by ignoring some relevant evidence. Here are examples:

- Lawyers are only interested in making money.

  (What about lawyers who work to protect consumers, or public defenders who take care of those unable to pay for a lawyer?)

- Political life must lead many to excessive drinking. In the last six months the paper has written about five members of Congress who either have confessed to alcoholism or have been arrested on DUI charges.

  (Five is not a large enough sample from which to generalize about *many* politicians. Also, the five in the newspaper are not a representative sample; they have made the news because of their drinking.)

Forced Hypothesis

The *forced hypothesis* is also an error in inductive reasoning. The explanation (hypothesis) offered to account for a particular situation is "forced," or illogical, because either (1) sufficient evidence does not exist to draw any conclusion or (2) the evidence can be explained more simply or more sensibly by a different hypothesis. This logical fallacy often results from failure to consider other possible explanations. You discredit a forced hypothesis by providing alternative conclusions that are more sensible or just as sensible as the one offered. Consider the following example:

- Professor Redding's students received either As or Bs last semester. He must be an excellent teacher.

  (The grades alone cannot support the conclusion. Professor Redding could be an excellent teacher; he could have started with excellent students; he could be an easy grader.)

Non Sequitur

The term *non sequitur,* meaning "it does not follow," could apply to all arguments that do not work, but the term is usually reserved for those arguments in which the conclusions are not logically connected to the reasons, those arguments with the glue missing. In a hasty generalization, for example, there is a connection between support (five politicians in the news) and conclusion (many politicians with drinking problems), just not a convincing connection. With the non sequitur there is no recognizable connection, because either (1) whatever connection the arguer sees is not made clear to others or (2) the evidence or reasons offered are irrelevant to the conclusion. For example:

- Donna will surely get a good grade in physics; she earned an A in her biology class.

  (Doing well in one course, even one science course, does not support the conclusion that the student will get a good grade in another course. If Donna is not good at math, she definitely will not do well in physics.)

Slippery Slope

The *slippery slope* argument asserts that we should not proceed with or permit A because, if we do, the terrible consequences X, Y, and Z will occur. This type of argument oversimplifies by assuming, without evidence and usually by ignoring historical examples, existing laws, or any reasonableness in people, that X, Y, and Z will follow inevitably from A. This kind of argument rests on the belief that most people will not want the final, awful Z to occur. The belief, however accurate, does not provide a sufficiently good reason for avoiding A. One of the best-known examples of slippery slope reasoning can be found in the gun-control debate:

- If we allow the government to register handguns, next it will register hunting rifles; then it will prohibit all citizen ownership of guns, thereby creating a police state or a world in which only outlaws have guns.

  (Surely no one wants the final dire consequences predicted in this argument. However, handgun registration does not mean that these consequences will follow. The United States has never been a police state, and its system of free elections guards against such a future. Also, citizens have registered cars, boats, and planes for years without any threat of these belongings being confiscated.)

False Dilemma

The *false dilemma* oversimplifies an issue by asserting only two alternatives when there are more than two. The either–or thinking of this kind of argument can be an effective tactic if undetected. If the arguer gives us only two choices and one of those is clearly unacceptable, then the arguer can push us toward the preferred choice. Here is an example:

- The Federal Reserve System must lower interest rates, or we will never pull out of the recession.

  (Clearly, staying in a recession is not much of a choice, but the alternative may not be the only or the best course of action to achieve a healthy economy. If interest rates go too low, inflation can be triggered. Other options include the government's creating new jobs and patiently letting market forces play themselves out.)

Politicians often try to use this fallacy to their advantage in their campaigns.

False Analogy

When examining the shape of analogy, we also considered the problems with this type of argument. Remember that you challenge a false analogy by noting many differences in the two items being compared or by noting a significant difference that has been ignored.

Post Hoc Fallacy

The term *post hoc,* from the Latin *post hoc, ergo propter hoc* (literally, "after this, therefore because of it") refers to a common error in arguments about cause. One oversimplifies causation by confusing a time rela-

This ad illustrates the slippery slope argument made by many anti-gun-control arguments. Can you see the logical fallacy? Do you find this argument against gun control compelling? Effective? Why or why not?

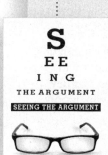
Look at the following classic slogan used fairly often by political groups. How is this slogan engaging in the false dilemma fallacy? Does it lead the reader to believe that there are only two choices? Is this necessarily a logical claim?

America
Love It Or Leave It!

tionship with cause. Reveal the illogic of post hoc arguments by pointing to other possible causes:

- We should throw out the entire city council. Since the members were elected, the city has gone into deficit spending.

  (Assuming that deficit spending in this situation is bad, was it caused by the current city council? Or did the current council inherit debts? Or is the entire region suffering from a recession?)

Fallacies That Result from Ignoring the Issue

There are many arguments that divert attention from the issue under debate. Of the six discussed here, the first three try to divert attention by introducing a separate issue or sliding by the actual issue; the following three seek diversion by appealing to the audience's emotions or prejudices. In the first three the arguer tries to give the impression of presenting an argument; in the last three the arguer charges forward on emotional manipulation alone.

Begging the Question

To assume that part of your argument is true without supporting it is to *beg the question*. Arguments seeking to pass off as proof statements that must themselves be supported are often introduced with such phrases as "the fact is" (to introduce opinion), "obviously," and "as we can see." Here is an example:

- Clearly, lowering grading standards would be bad for students, so a pass/fail system should not be adopted.

  (Does a pass/fail system lower standards? No evidence has been given. If so, is that necessarily bad for students?)

You are said to be "begging the question" when you simply state that you are right because you are right. Consider how you might avoid this illogical reasoning in your own arguments.

Red Herring

The *red herring* debater introduces a side issue or some point that is not relevant to the debate:

- The senator is an honest woman; she loves her children and gives to charities.

  (The children and charities are side issues; they do not demonstrate honesty.)

To further illustrate this fallacy, read the following article from *The Baltimore Sun*. Consider how the author brings the issue of a murder victim's family's

did you know?

The federal government's decision to raise the legal drinking age to 21 was, in the opinion of many, based at least partially on a post hoc fallacy. Read the following excerpt from President Reagan's statement that prompted most states to change their laws. Do you spot the logical fallacy?

> Now, raising that drinking age is not a fad or an experiment. It's a proven success.
> Nearly every state that has raised the drinking age to 21 has produced a significant drop in the teenage driving fatalities. In the state of New Jersey, whose governor made it a very personal crusade for himself, the rate dropped by 26 percent; in Illinois, it has fallen 23 percent; in Michigan, 31 percent. And when the Commission on Drunk Driving submitted its report, it forcefully recommended that all 50 States should make 21 the legal drinking age.

Source: President Ronald Reagan, 1984
www.madd.org/Parents/Parents/Research/View-Research
.aspx?research=22

Exercises: Fallacies That Result from Oversimplifying

1. Here is a list of the fallacies we have examined so far. Make up or collect from your reading, or from the Web, at least one textual or visual example of each fallacy.

   a. Overstatement
   b. Stereotyping
   c. Hasty generalization
   d. Forced hypothesis
   e. Non sequitur
   f. Slippery slope
   g. False dilemma
   h. False analogy
   i. Post hoc fallacy

2. Explain what is illogical about each of the following arguments. Then name the fallacy represented. (Sometimes an argument will fit into more than one category. In that case, name all appropriate terms.)

   a. Everybody agrees that we need stronger drunk-driving laws.

   b. The upsurge in crime on Sundays is the result of the reduced rate of church attendance in recent years.

   c. The government must create new jobs. A factory in Illinois has laid off half its workers.

   d. Steve has joined the country club. Golf must be one of his favorite sports.

   e. Blondes have more fun.

   f. You'll enjoy your Volvo; foreign cars never break down.

   g. Gary loves jokes. He would make a great comedian.

   h. The economy is in bad shape because of the Federal Reserve Board. Ever since it expanded the money supply, the stock market has been declining.

   i. Either we improve the city's street lighting, or we will fail to reduce crime.

   j. DNA research today is just like the study of nuclear fission. It seems important, but it's just another bomb that will one day explode on us. When will we learn that government must control research?

   k. To prohibit prayer in public schools is to limit religious practice solely to internal belief. The result is that an American is religiously "free" only in his own mind.

   l. Professor Johnson teaches in the political science department. I'll bet she's another socialist.

   m. Coming to the aid of any country engaged in civil war is a bad idea. Next we'll be sending American troops, and soon we'll be involved in another Vietnam.

   n. We must reject affirmative action in hiring or we'll have to settle for incompetent employees.

suffering to the forefront of his argument that the death penalty should exist. But consider the red herring here. Does the death of the murderer really put an end to the family's suffering? This appeal to the emotions of the reader acts as a distraction, or an effective red herring in this argument. Can you identify any other logical fallacies here that weaken this author's position?

To Murder Victims' Families, Executing Killers Is Justice

Gregory Kane
February 5, 2003

Frederick Anthony Romano remembers the night. More than 15 years later, he remembers it as if it happened within the last week. It was Sunday night, Nov. 1, 1987. Seventeen-year-old Romano had gone to bed. His mother, Betty Romano, was in the house with him and his father, Frederick Joseph Romano. Soon the father received a call from his son-in-law Keith Garvin, a Navy petty officer who had returned to his base in Oceana, Va. Garvin had called his wife, Dawn Garvin, to let her know he had arrived back safely. But there was no answer.

After two calls to his daughter's house, Frederick J. Romano headed to the newlywed couple's White Marsh apartment. He found his daughter beaten, tortured, mutilated and dead.

Frederick A. Romano remembers his mother's panic-filled voice as she talked to his father, of himself grabbing the phone only to hear his father tell him that his older sister had been hurt.

"But he knew she was dead," Frederick A. Romano said yesterday from his Harford County home. Yes, Frederick A. Romano—who prefers to be called just "Fred"—remembers it all. He remembers the man who murdered his sister and two other women—Patricia Antoinette Hirt and Lori Elizabeth Ward—and how he has waited for 15 years for one Steven Howard Oken to, in the younger Romano's words, "meet his maker."

Does the argument presented here highlight the complexity of and multiple perspectives on this important issue? Or does it attempt to divert attention to a more emotionally charged point?

"It's caused a lot of emotional problems for me and my mom and dad," Fred said. "They're on so many drugs to keep themselves calm, it's unbelievable."

That is a suffering death penalty opponents can't or won't understand. The pain of homicide victims' relatives never ends. It chips away at their souls and psyches year after depressing year. So what's the appropriate punishment for that? Death penalty opponents would have us believe that squirreling Oken away in a cell—where Frederick A. and Frederick J. Romano, Betty Romano and Keith Garvin would be among the taxpayers footing the bill for his housing and meals—is punishment enough. If the correctional system offered any college courses, the Romanos and Garvin would pay part of the cost if Oken wanted to take them.

Dawn Garvin never got to finish her education at Harford Community College. Capital punishment foes figure that's justice. Here's what death penalty advocates feel is justice. Execute Oken the week of March 17, as a Baltimore County judge ordered two weeks ago. After Oken is dead, death penalty advocates can then defy death penalty opponents to show us why and in what ways Oken's execution was not justice.

That's what it's about for Fred Romano. He doesn't buy into the closure argument some death penalty advocates make. (It's just as well. Death penalty opponents, ever noble with grief not their own, dismiss the notion of closure, too.) "It won't bring closure," Fred Romano said. "Dawn will never be back. I'm not looking for closure. That's a bad misconception on the part of some people. I want Oken to die for the murder of Dawn, Patricia Hurt and Lori Ward." This isn't even about revenge, another rallying cry of the anti-capital punishment crowd, who chide death penalty advocates for seeking vengeance. "It's justice," Fred Romano said. "It's not revenge." His wife, Vicki Romano, agreed, then elaborated. "Revenge would be going out and killing one of [the murderer's] family members," Vicki Romano said. "The death penalty isn't revenge. It's the law."

Fred Romano believes the man who's supposed to uphold that law, Maryland Attorney General J. Joseph Curran, has inserted himself squarely in the path of Oken's execution. Last week, Curran called for abolishing Maryland's death penalty. His reasons will appear in a separate column Saturday. Fred Romano called Curran after the announcement, to give the attorney general a piece of his mind. Curran, to his credit, called Fred Romano back and heard him out. Curran, Fred Romano said, asked him if he had a problem with a sentence of life without parole as opposed to the death penalty. His response was what you might expect from a guy who organized the Maryland Coalition for State Executions more than a year ago, and who's had the group's Web site (www.mc4se.org) up for two months. "My problem with it is that 10 years from now some other idiot will come along and say life without parole is too harsh," Fred Romano said. "Then they'll pass a bill granting them parole and then we'll have a bunch of murderers walking the streets." In Maryland's bleeding-heart liberal legislature, that's exactly what would happen.

Straw Man

The *straw man* argument attributes to opponents erroneous and usually ridiculous views that they do not hold so that their position can be easily attacked. We can challenge this illogic by demonstrating that the arguer's opponents do not hold those views or by demanding that the arguer provide some evidence that they do:

- Those who favor gun control just want to take all guns away from responsible citizens and put them in the hands of criminals.

  (The position attributed to proponents of gun control is not only inaccurate but actually the opposite of what is sought by gun-control proponents.)

Ad Hominem

One of the most frequent of all appeals to emotion masquerading as argument is the *ad hominem* argument (literally, argument "to the man"). Sometimes the debate turns into an attack on a supporter of the issue; other times, the illogic is found in name-calling. When someone says that "those crazy liberals at the ACLU just want all criminals to go free," or a pro-choice demonstrator screams at those "self-righteous fascists" on the other side, the best retort may be silence, or the calm assertion that such statements do not contribute to meaningful debate.

Common Practice or Bandwagon

To argue that an action should be taken or a position accepted because "everyone is doing it" is illogical. The majority is not always right. Peer pressure is a common use of this fallacy. Frequently when someone is defending an action as ethical on the grounds that everyone does it, the action is actually unethical and the defender knows it is unethical. The *bandwagon* argument is a desperate one. Here is an example:

- There's nothing wrong with fudging a bit on your income taxes. After all, the superrich don't pay any taxes, and the government expects everyone to cheat a little.

  (First, not everyone cheats on taxes; many pay to have their taxes done correctly. And if it is wrong, it is wrong regardless of the number who do it.)

Ad Populum

Another technique for arousing an audience's emotions and ignoring the issue is to appeal *ad populum*, or "to the people," to the audience's presumed shared values and beliefs. Every Fourth of July, politicians employ this tactic, appealing to God, mother, apple pie, and traditional family values. As with all emotional gim-

Savage Chickens by Doug Savage

www.savagechickens.com

Reprinted by permission of Doug Savage.

micks, we need to reject the argument as illogical. Here is an example:

- Good, law-abiding Americans must be sick of the violent crimes occurring in our once godly society. But we won't tolerate it anymore; put the criminals in jail and throw away the key.

  (This does not contribute to a thoughtful debate on criminal justice issues.)

SEEING THE ARGUMENT

How might the following cartoon illustrate logical fallacy? Which fallacy or fallacies are depicted here? How has the employee in the cartoon probably lost credibility with his boss by making these statements? Remember to be on the lookout for logical fallacies in everyday media. They are often effective because the reader is unaware of their presence. If, however, the reader understands what the author is attempting to do, the logic of the entire argument falls apart. In writing your own academic arguments, you should always try to avoid these fallacies and logical errors. Otherwise, you risk alienating your audience and losing your credibility as an author.

Dilbert © 2010 Scott Adams. Used by permission of Universal UClick. All rights reserved.

Exercises: Fallacies That Result from Ignoring the Issue

1. Here is a list of fallacies that result from ignoring the issue. Make up or collect from your reading (or from the Web) at least one example (either textual or visual) of each fallacy.

   a. Begging the question

   b. Red herring

   c. Straw man

   d. Ad hominem

   e. Common practice or bandwagon

   f. Ad populum

2. Explain what is illogical about each of the following arguments. Then name the fallacy represented.

   a. Gold's book doesn't deserve a Pulitzer Prize. She has been married four times.

   b. I wouldn't vote for him; many of his programs are basically socialist.

   c. Eight out of ten headache sufferers use Bayer to relieve headache pain. It will work for you, too.

   d. We shouldn't listen to Colman McCarthy's argument against liquor ads in college newspapers because he obviously thinks young people are ignorant and need guidance in everything.

   e. My roommate Joe does the craziest things; he must be neurotic.

   f. Since so many people obviously cheat the welfare system, it should be abolished.

   g. She isn't pretty enough to win the contest, and besides she had her nose "fixed" two years ago.

   h. Professors should chill out; everybody cheats on exams from time to time.

   i. The fact is that bilingual education is a mistake because it encourages students to use only their native language and that gives them an advantage over other students.

   j. Don't join those crazy liberals in support of the American Civil Liberties Union. They want all criminals to go free.

   k. Real Americans understand that free trade agreements are evil. Let your representatives know that we want American goods protected.

SEEING THE ARGUMENT

Consider the following article from the *New York* magazine. This reader is responding to a personal attack on Mariah Carey that was printed in the *New York Daily News*. It is clear that the ad hominem attack on Ms. Carey failed to succeed in persuading this reader and instead may have had the opposite effect by creating a sympathetic point of view. But does this writer himself engage in ad hominem attacks? Think about how these personal attacks on your opponent can hurt your credibility with your readers and ultimately weaken your argument.

Ad Hominem Attack on Mariah Carey in the 'Daily News'

3/18/08 at 12:45 PM | 3 Comments

Mariah Carey, hurting.
Photo: Getty Images

Dude, *News* editorial board, what's with this 63-word diatribe today?

Cultural note: We see that the warbler Mariah Carey, who has already tied Elvis Presley as the second-place holder of the most No. 1 records, will soon, if her new hit ditty goes to the top of the charts, tie the Beatles as the first-place holder of the most No. 1 records ever.

Man.

That's — that's just wrong.

On so many levels.

Why, exactly, is it wrong, you guys? Because you're a bunch of mostly white old people who don't understand R&B? If you'll recall, your parents thought Elvis and the Beatles were trashy, too. We won't defend Mariah Carey's cultural relevance in comparison to those musical giants — though we do love her. But from now on, you're no longer allowed to wonder why young people think your newspaper is irrelevant.

Off the Charts [NYDN]

http://nymag.com/daily/intel/2008/03/ad_hominem_attack_on_mariah_ca.html, March 18, 2008. Reprinted by permission of New York Magazine. Editorial © New York Daily News, L.P. used with permission. Photo: Getty Images.

let's review

After reading this chapter, you should understand the following:

- You can build on your knowledge of the basics of argument, examined in Chapter 1, by understanding some traditional forms of argument: induction, deduction, and analogy.

- It is also important to recognize arguments that do not work due to a logical error or flaw.

- The inductive process moves from particular to general, from support to assertion.

- Although induction can be described as an argument that moves from particular to general, from facts (or evidence) to inference (claim), deduction cannot accurately be described as the reverse. Deductive arguments are more complex. *Deduction* is the reasoning process that moves the reader from a set of premises (or ideas) to the logical conclusion that must be true if those premises are true.

- When composing a deductive argument, your task will be to defend the truth of your premises.

- The *argument from analogy* is an argument based on comparison. Analogies assert that since A and B are alike in several ways, they must be alike in another way as well.

- A thorough study of argument needs to include a study of logical fallacies because so many arguments fail to meet standards of sound logic and good sense, many for the following reasons:

  - a lack of knowledge of the subject;

  - attaching yourself to your ideas and then feeling personally attacked when someone disagrees with you;

  - having prejudices and biases that come out in your arguments;

  - wanting to control your world by having answers to important questions, leading to oversimplifying problems or refusing to settle for qualified answers to questions; and

  - diverting attention from the issue under debate.

connect

ANALYZING LOGICAL FALLACIES

Read the following piece from columnist Dave Barry. What fallacies do you see at work here? How do certain passages illustrate specific fallacies?

http://www.davebarry.com/natterings_files/daveHOWTOARGUE.pdf

How To Argue Effectively

Dave Barry

I argue very well. Ask any of my remaining friends. I can win an argument on any topic, against any opponent. People know this and steer clear of me at parties. Often, as a sign of their great respect, they don't even invite me. You too can win arguments. Simply follow these rules:

Drink Liquor.

Suppose you are at a party and some hotshot intellectual is expounding on the economy of Peru, a subject you know nothing about. If you're drinking some health-fanatic drink like grapefruit juice, you'll hang back, afraid to display your ignorance, while the hotshot enthralls your date. But if you drink several large martinis, you'll discover you have STRONG VIEWS about the Peruvian economy. You'll be a WEALTH of information. You'll argue forcefully, offering searing insights and possibly upsetting furniture. People will be impressed. Some may leave the room.

Make Things Up.

Suppose, in the Peruvian economy argument, you are trying to prove that Peruvians are underpaid, a position you base solely on the fact that YOU are underpaid, and you'll be damned if you're going to let a bunch of Peruvians be better off. DON'T say: "I think Peruvians are underpaid." Say instead: "The average Peruvian's salary in 1981 dollars adjusted for the revised tax base is $1,452.81 per annum, which is $836.07 below the mean gross poverty level."

NOTE: Always make up exact figures. If an opponent asks you where you got your information, make THAT up too. Say: "This information comes from Dr. Hovel T. Moon's study for the Buford Commission published on May 9, 1982. Didn't you read it?" Say this in the same tone of voice you would use to say, "You left your soiled underwear in my bathroom."

Use Meaningless But Weighty-Sounding Words and Phrases.

Memorize this list:

Let me put it this way
In terms of
Vis-a-vis
Per se
As it were
Qua
Ipso facto
Ergo
So to speak

You should also memorize some Latin abbreviations such as "Q.E.D.", "e.g.", and "i.e." These are all short for "I speak Latin, and you don't." Here's how to use these words and phrases. Suppose you want to say, "Peruvians would like to order appetizers more often, but they don't have enough money."

You never win arguments talking like that. But you WILL win if you say, "Let me put it this way. In terms of appetizers vis-a-vis Peruvians qua Peruvians, they would like to order them more often, so to speak, but they do not have enough money per se, as it were. Ergo, ipso facto, case closed. Q.E.D." Only a fool would challenge that statement.

Use Snappy and Irrelevant Comebacks.

You need an arsenal of all-purpose irrelevant phrases to fire back at your opponents when they make valid points. The best are:

You're begging the question.
You're being defensive.
Don't compare apples to oranges.
What are your parameters?

This last one is especially valuable. Nobody (other than engineers and policy wonks) has the vaguest idea what "parameters" means. Don't forget the classic: YOU'RE SO LINEAR. Here's how to use your comebacks:

YOU SAY: As Abraham Lincoln said in 1873 . . .

YOUR OPPONENT SAYS: Lincoln died in 1865.

YOU SAY: You're begging the question.

YOU SAY: Liberians, like most Asians . . .

YOUR OPPONENT SAYS: Liberia is in Africa.

YOU SAY: You're being defensive.

YOU SAY: Since the discovery of the incandescent light bulb . . .

YOUR OPPONENT SAYS: The light bulb is an invention.

YOU SAY: Well DUH!

Compare Your Opponent to Adolf Hitler.

This is your heavy artillery, for when your opponent is obviously right and you are spectacularly wrong. Bring Hitler up subtly. Say, "That sounds suspiciously like something Adolf Hitler might say," or "You certainly do remind me of Adolf Hitler."

So that's it. You now know how to out-argue anybody. Do not try to pull any of this on people who generally carry weapons.

Analyze the following letter to the editor published in the Minnesota State University *Mankato Reporter* on May 2, 2006, by a university student. How effectively does the author make his case? How convincing is the evidence that he presents? Do you find this argument effective? What do you think he should have included in the letter? What should he have done differently? Try to answer these questions in detail to be prepared for class discussion.

Letter: Better Things to Worry about Than Smoking

Miles Haefner, Student

Tanner, your sarcastic article on smoking was on par. For real, smoking isn't good for you? I never would have guessed outside of the Target Market commercials, the fresh laws banning smoking in every public space, the constant berating smokers get from others on how disgusting they are. Seriously, I am sick of it. I am not a smoker. My whole family smokes or is addicted to nicotine in some way or another. But me on the other hand is lucky enough to have dodged the black lung bullet and maintained the somewhat healthy life. But does this mean I can look down upon Marlboro Men with a snide comment? Of f—ing course not! Last time I checked, smoking was legal. We aren't selling marijuana in blunt form to 16-year-olds via a cartoon camel. The companies are marketing within the realm of legal to make a profit like every other company on the face of our capitalistic "money, money, money" country.

So who the hell are you to yell at the tobacco companies who are trying to increase their bottom line? You got a problem with tobacco? Then don't smoke and teach your kids not to either! Wow those beer commercials during halftime at the Super Bowl are entertaining and sure made me laugh before I was 21. Those male stiffy help ya outty keep ya boney pills that bombard the airways sure are good also. Dick you got a new sense of pride? Well I'll be damned, I want a little of that pride too! But hey, if the pride lasts for more than 4 hours con-sult your physician so he can perform emergency surgery. You getting my point MNSU? Our land has more to worry about than whether or not we are smoking. Our baby boomers are notorious smokers and our country seems to be doing alright now. Perhaps instead we should worry about the ridiculous no child left behind, or the fact that more young people (yeah you future leaders) would rather sit on Facebook than read the newspaper to pass the time.

Smoking is as old as the human race in one way or another. Hell, my grandpa used nicotine and lived to 92 years old. Let's quit arguing over tobacco use and start to worry about the real social, economic or political problems that face our country. Let smokers be free and enjoy it as they may. You don't like it? Then quit working at the bar, quit going to the bar, quit bitching about smoke and quit being such a pansy. I'm sorry to all the people with effects from smoke like certain incurable diseases, but what are smokers supposed to do? They don't start with the intent to harm others or themselves. So let people make their own decisions and let's get passed this juvenile argument of cigarettes. We have more to worry and debate about.

http://media.www.msureporter.com/media/storage/paper937/news/2006/05/02/EditorialOpinionletters/Letters.To.The.Editor-2021758.shtml

Top Riding Mowers Under $1600

Popular Mechanics

Jay Leno
Drives The World's
Biggest Pickup

TECHNOLOGY   SCIENCE   AUTOMOTIVE   HOME   OUTDOORS

DEBUNKING
9/11 LIES

Conspiracy Theories Can't Stand Up To The Hard Facts

A growi
chorus of frin
groups sa
a U.S. pl
brought dov
the towe
After
in-dep
investigatic
PM answe
with the trut

0   75470 08638   0

refuting an argument

WHAT'S TO COME

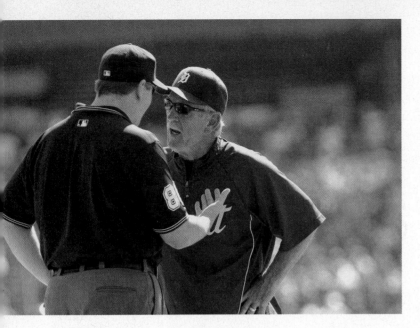

to challenge someone's argument rather than to present your own argument, you are writing a *refutation*. This is, in fact, an important skill when it comes to almost any type of argumentation. After all, any argument has at least two sides, right? In order to write a persuasive refutation argument, you will need to fully understand why your opponent may hold certain beliefs and construct a plan to show why those beliefs or reasons are wrong. However, you must remember that simply disagreeing with your opponent is not enough. Your reader will expect you to present logical, clear, and solid evidence that your opponent is wrong, misinformed, or not seeing things clearly.

A good refutation demonstrates, in an orderly and logical way, the weaknesses of logic or evidence in the argument, or it both analyzes weaknesses and builds a counterargument. Refutations can challenge a specific written argument, or they can challenge a prevailing attitude or belief that is, in the writer's view, contrary to the evidence. The sample refutation, "Gender Games" on page 87, shows the first purpose. It is annotated to show you how the author puts together his refutation. But first, let's look at the steps involved in preparing a good refutation essay.

What Is a Refutation Essay?

To refute something is to prove it wrong, illogical, or erroneous. When your primary purpose in writing is

---

GOOD ADV!CE

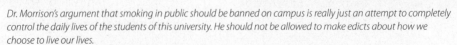

LOGICAL FALLACY ALERT!

As you write a refutation essay, you will want to take special care to avoid some of the logical fallacies (presented in Chapter 4) that can happen quite easily in the refutation essay. For example,

> **Ad Hominem Fallacy (Attacking the person instead of the argument.)**
>
> *Although Dr. Morrison's claim that smoking in public is rude is somewhat valid, he himself is often rude and has absolutely no room to talk.*

> **Straw Man Fallacy (Attributing and attacking a position that your opponent doesn't actually hold.)**

Dr. Morrison's argument that smoking in public should be banned on campus is really just an attempt to completely control the daily lives of the students of this university. He should not be allowed to make edicts about how we choose to live our lives.

The author of the argument on the billboard is obviously refuting the claim that Americans should have voted for Barack Obama in the 2008 election. Can you identify elements of both of these logical fallacies in this argument?

Guidelines for Writing a Refutation Essay

- **Read accurately.** Make certain that you have understood your opponent's argument. If you assume the writer holds views that he or she does not, you may commit the straw man fallacy, attributing and then attacking a position that the person does not hold. Look up terms and references you do not know, and examine the logic and evidence thoroughly.

- **Pinpoint the weaknesses in the original argument.** Analyze the argument to determine, specifically, what flaws the argument contains. If the argument contains logical fallacies, make a list of the ones you plan to discredit. Examine the evidence presented. Is it insufficient, unreliable, or irrelevant? Decide, before drafting your refutation, exactly which elements of the argument you intend to challenge.

- **Write a strong thesis.** After analyzing the argument and deciding on the weaknesses to challenge, write a thesis that establishes your disagreement with the writer's logic, assumptions, or evidence, or a combination of these.

- **Draft your essay, making sure to include all of the following elements in your organizational plan:**

  a. *The opponent's argument.* Usually, you should not assume that your reader has read or remembered the argument you are refuting. Therefore, toward the beginning of your essay, you need to state, accurately and fairly, the main points of the argument to be refuted.

  b. *Your thesis.* Make clear the nature of your disagreement with the argument you are refuting.

  c. *Your refutation.* The specifics of your counterargument will depend upon the nature of your disagreement. For example, if you are challenging the writer's evidence on the grounds that it is outdated, then you must present the more recent evidence to explain why the evidence used is unreliable or misleading. If you are challenging assumptions, then you must explain why each one does not hold up. If your thesis is that the piece is filled with logical fallacies, then you must present and explain each fallacy.

Read "Gender Games," study the annotations, and then answer the questions that follow.

Gender Games

David Sadker

A professor emeritus at American University and teaching at the University of Arizona, David Sadker has written extensively on educational issues, especially on the treatment of girls in the classroom. He is the author of *Still Failing at Fairness* (2009). "Gender Games" appeared in *The Washington Post* on July 31, 2000.

Remember when your elementary school teacher would announce the teams for the weekly spelling bee? "Boys against the girls!" There was nothing like a gender showdown to liven things up. Apparently, some writers never left this elementary level of intrigue. A spate of recent books and articles takes us back to the "boys versus girls" fray but this time, with much higher stakes. [Attention-getting opening]

May's *Atlantic Monthly* cover story, "Girls Rule," is a case in point. The magazine published an excerpt from *The War Against Boys* by Christina Hoff Sommers, a book advancing the notion that boys are the real victims of gender bias while girls are soaring in school. [Claim to be refuted]

Sommers and her supporters are correct in saying that girls and women have made significant educational progress in the past two decades. Females today make up more than 40 percent of medical and law school students, and more than half of college students. Girls continue to read sooner and write better than boys. And for as long as anyone can remember, girls have received higher grades than boys. [Concession: What's right about opponent's argument]

But there is more to these selected statistics than meets the eye. Although girls continue to receive higher report card grades than boys, their grades

continued

do not translate into higher test scores. The same girls who beat boys in the spelling bees score below boys on the tests that matter: the PSATs crucial for scholarships, the SATs and the ACTs needed for college acceptances, the GREs for graduate school and even the admission tests for law, business, and medical schools.

First point of refutation

Many believe that girls' higher grades may be more a reflection of their manageable classroom behavior than their intellectual accomplishment. Test scores are not influenced by quieter classroom behavior. Girls may in fact be trading their initiative and independence for peer approval and good grades, a trade-off that can have costly personal and economic consequences.

The increase in female college enrollment catches headlines because it heralds the first time that females have outnumbered males on college campuses. But even these enrollment figures are misleading. The female presence increases as the status of the college decreases. Female students are more likely to dominate two-year schools than the Ivy League. And wherever they are, they find themselves segregated and channeled into the least prestigious and least costly majors.

Second point of refutation

In today's world of e-success, more than 60 percent of computer science and business majors are male, about 70 percent of physics majors are males, and more than 80 percent of engineering students are male. But peek into language, psychology, nursing and humanities classrooms, and you will find a sea of female faces.

Higher female enrollment figures mask the "glass walls" that separate the sexes and channel females and males into very different careers, with very different paychecks. Today, despite all the progress, the five leading occupations of employed women are secretary, receptionist, bookkeeper, registered nurse, and hairdresser/cosmetologist.

Add this to the "glass ceiling" (about 3 percent of Fortune 500 top managers are women) and the persistence of a gender wage gap (women with advanced degrees still lag well behind their less-educated male counterparts) and the crippling impact of workplace and college stereotyping becomes evident.

Even within schools, where female teachers greatly outnumber male teachers, school management figures remind us that if there is a war on boys, women are not the generals. More than 85 percent of junior and senior high school principals are male, while 88 percent of school superintendents are male.

Third point of refutation

Despite sparkling advances of females on the athletic fields, two-thirds of athletic scholarships still go to males. In some areas, women have actually lost ground. When Title IX was enacted in 1972, women coached more than 90 percent of intercollegiate women's teams. Today women coach only 48 percent of women's teams and only 1 percent of men's teams.

Fourth point of refutation

If some adults are persuaded by the rhetoric in such books as *The War Against Boys*, be assured that children know the score. When more than 1,000 Michigan elementary school students were asked to describe what life would be like if they were born a member of the opposite sex, more than 40 percent of the girls saw positive advantages to being a boy: better jobs, more money and definitely more respect. Ninety-five percent of the boys saw no advantage to being a female.

Fifth point of refutation

The War Against Boys attempts to persuade the public to abandon support for educational initiatives designed to help girls and boys avoid crippling stereotypes. I hope the public and Congress will not be taken in by the book's misrepresentations. We have no time to wage a war on either our boys or our girls.

Author concludes by stating his claim (thesis)

QUESTIONS FOR READING

1. What work, specifically, is Sadker refuting? What is the claim presented by this work?
2. What facts about girls does Sadker grant to Sommers?
3. What facts about girls create a different story, according to Sadker?

QUESTIONS FOR REASONING AND ANALYSIS

1. What is Sadker's claim? What is he asserting about girls?
2. What does Sadker think about the whole idea of books such as Sommers's?

Read the following refutation piece from *The Chronicle of Higher Education*'s website. What do you think about the refutation made by this author? Is it effective? What elements of a good refutation essay does this piece exhibit? Annotate this piece, noting the specific strategies the author uses to attempt to persuade his reader. What might this author do to make this piece even more persuasive?

Dear Dr. Brottman,

Although, in reading your article "Goth's Wan Stamina," I found your thoughts on the goth subculture very interesting (I have always been interested in subcultures of all kinds), I was a bit disturbed by your treatment of punk and skin culture in this article. To say that "skinheads have come and gone" is to completely ignore the continued vitality of the skinhead subculture in the United States and the United Kingdom and such currently active Oi! bands such as The Business, The Dropkick Murphys, and The Cockney Rejects.

Furthermore, the claim that "punk didn't last" only has the slightest bit of validity if you choose to completely ignore the hardcore movement of the 1980s and its continued effect on a variety of punk genres. Not to mention it was this movement that imparted the punk subculture with, in my opinion, its most important feature: the DIY ethic.

I am a punk and a student at the University of Chicago, where I am part of the school's hardcore punk group UxCxHxC Trix. One only needs to come to one of the shows or lectures (affectionately referred to as "The Common 'Core'") to see that each member of the group, though each with his or her own specific knowledge of a subgenre of the music, still identifies himself or herself as "punk" and is continuing to listen to the music and practice the ideology every day.

I play in a ska-core band (which, if you're unfamiliar, is a blend of ska and hardcore influenced by bands such as The Clash, Operation Ivy, and Choking Victim) called Alleyway Sex in my home town of Champaign–Urbana, IL. We have been active for over two years, putting on our own shows in basements or renting out venues, and booking any touring band who wants to come through town. Although some shows are definitely better attended than others, one only needs to come to one of our shows to see the prominence of the punk subculture in the area. In fact, we recently released a DIY compilation called *C/U In The Streets* featuring 28 songs by 14 local bands, ranging in musical genre from thrash to folk to ska to hardcore to hip-hop, but all identifying as punks. I noticed from the article that you are writing from Baltimore, Maryland. Well, I would encourage you, if you would like to learn more about the prevailing punk subculture, to come out to the Sidebar Tavern on June 20th, where my band will be continuing its East Coast tour, playing with Baltimore locals The Twats.

Finally, I would like to disagree with the claim that, unlike goth, punk is only for the young. I am a punk now, and I will continue to be a punk for the rest of my life. It's not about the fashion. I personally don't really dress punk, have never dyed or gelled up my hair, but I still fiercely identify with the subculture, not only through the music, but also through the DIY ethic, as I mentioned before. Both I and my friends at the University of Chicago have incorporated this aspect of our lives into our schoolwork (in fact, one of my friends [guitarist for two UxCxHxC bands, f*** Your Face and Gun, With Occasional Music] gave a lecture at Yale on the affinity of straight-edge with hardcore music), and I have no reason to think that we will not continue to do so in our daily lives after college, both personal and professional. While goth is simply a fashion, punk (and especially hardcore) has a true ideology that rings true (or should ring true) for both young and old.

continued

Basically, I think you might find it of interest to re-examine the punk subculture here in America. If you have any questions, you can feel free to contact me via e-mail.

Up The Punks,
Mike Alleyway

http://chronicle.com/forums/index.php/topic,38949.0/prev_next,next.html#new. Posted on June 2007.

SEEING THE ARGUMENT

Consider this billboard as a refutation argument. Its purpose is clearly to refute a claim that is often used when arguing against legalizing gay marriage: that it is against God's wishes and is forbidden by the Christian Bible. However, another author has chosen to refute the billboard's claim by painting "LIE" on it. Is either refutation argument providing enough evidence to persuade its intended audience? Will either argument persuade viewers to alter their beliefs? Remember that attempting to refute deeply ingrained or commonly held beliefs can be particularly difficult.

Image by Jesus Metropolitan Community Church, www.JesusMCC.org

Using Research in Refutation Arguments

If you were writing a researched essay that was attempting to refute a deeply ingrained, highly controversial, and commonly held notion or a notion that challenged a popular belief, what types of sources, visuals, and organizational strategies might you choose to utilize? How would understanding your audience's values and beliefs help you as you conducted your research?

Consider the following editorial from *The New York Times*:

Flailing after Muslims

Bob Herbert
March 7, 2011

It has often been the case in America that specific religions, races and ethnic groups have been singled out for discrimination, demonization, incarceration and worse. But there have always been people willing to stand up boldly and courageously against such injustice. Their efforts are needed again now.

Representative Peter King, a Republican from Long Island, appears to harbor a fierce unhappiness with the Muslim community in the United States.

As the chairman of the powerful Homeland Security Committee, Congressman King has all the clout he needs to act on his displeasure. On Thursday, he plans to open the first of a series of committee hearings into the threat of homegrown Islamic terrorism and the bogus allegation that American Muslims have failed to cooperate with law enforcement efforts to foil terrorist plots.

"There is a real threat to the country from the Muslim community," he said, "and the only way to get to the bottom of it is to investigate what is happening."

That kind of sweeping statement from a major government official about a religious minority—soon to be backed up by the intimidating aura of Congressional hearings—can only serve to further demonize a group of Americans already being pummeled by bigotry and vicious stereotyping.

Rabbi Marc Schneier, the president of the Foundation for Ethnic Understanding, was among some 500 people at a rally in Times Square on Sunday that was called to protest Mr. King's hearings. "To single out Muslim-Americans as the source of homegrown terrorism," he said, "and not examine all forms of violence motivated by extremist belief—that, my friends, is an injustice."

To focus an investigative spotlight on an entire religious or ethnic community is a violation of everything America is supposed to stand for. But that does not seem to concern Mr. King. "The threat is coming from the Muslim community," he told The Times. "The radicalization attempts are directed at the Muslim community. Why should I investigate other communities?"

The great danger of these hearings, in addition to undermining fundamental American values, is that for no good reason—nearly a decade after the terrible attacks of Sept. 11, 2001—they will intensify the already overheated anti-Muslim feeling in the U.S. There is nothing wrong with the relentless investigation of terrorism. That's essential. But that is not the same as singling out, stereotyping and harassing an entire community.

On Monday, I spoke by phone with Colleen Kelly, a nurse practitioner from the Bronx whose brother, William Kelly Jr., was killed in the attack on the World Trade Center. She belongs to a group called September 11th Families for Peaceful Tomorrows and is opposed to Mr. King's hearings. "I was trying to figure out why he's doing this," she said, "and I haven't come up with a good answer."

She recalled how people were stigmatized in the early years of the AIDS epidemic and the way that stigmas become the focus of attention and get in the way of the efforts really needed to avert tragedy.

Mr. King's contention that Muslims are not cooperating with law enforcement is just wrong. According to the Triangle Center on Terrorism and Homeland Security, an independent research group affiliated with Duke University and the University of North Carolina, 48 of the 120 Muslims suspected of plotting terror attacks in the U.S. since Sept. 11, 2001, were turned in by fellow Muslims. In some cases, they were turned in by parents or other relatives.

What are we doing? Do we want to demonize innocent people and trample on America's precious freedom of religion? Or do we want to stop terrorism? There is no real rhyme or reason to Congressman King's incoherent flailing after Muslims. Witch hunts, after all, are about seeing what kind of ugliness might fortuitously turn up.

Mr. King was able to concoct the anti-Muslim ugliness in his 2004 novel, "Vale of Tears," in which New York is hit yet again by terrorists and, surprise, the hero of the piece is a congressman from Long Island. But this is real life, and the congressman's fantasies should not apply.

America should be better than this. We've had all the requisite lessons: Joe McCarthy, the House Un-American Activities Committee, the demonization of blacks and Jews, the internment of Japanese-Americans, and on and on and on. It's such a tired and ugly refrain.

When I asked Colleen Kelly why she spoke up, she said it was because of her great love for her country. "I love being an American, and I really try to be thankful for all the gifts that come with that," she said. But with gifts and privileges come responsibilities. The planned hearings into the Muslim community struck Ms. Kelly as something too far outside "the basic principles that I knew and felt to be important to me as a citizen of this country."

If you were given the task of refuting the claim in this editorial, how might you go about it?

> In response to Representative King, Herbert argues that investigating an entire religious or ethnic community violates American ideals. However, I want to refute Herbert's claim and persuade my readers that combating terrorism and protecting national security represent paramount concerns that necessitate we ask difficult questions about certain groups of people residing in this country.

As you write your researched essay refuting this common belief, you should consider the following questions:

- **What do my readers already know (or think that they know) about the American Muslim community?** Where are they primarily getting their information? From magazines? Scholarly journals? Billboards? Television advertisements? Print ads? Friends? Their churches? Personal experience? Their teachers? It is important to try to figure out what your readers' sources may have been and how reliable or credible those sources seem. For example, if the author's position about investigating the Muslim community is based on reading an article in *People* magazine, you could call that position into question based on a lack of credible research. He or she would not have enough evidence to make such a claim regarding the Muslim community.

- **What values most likely cause my readers to feel the way they do on this subject?** Oftentimes, people base their positions on the values they hold; that is, what they consider worthwhile and important in the world. Values can be formed early in life due to family members' opinions, religious affiliations, or even peer influence. If you try to understand why writers feel the way they do, you can often figure out why they hold certain positions. This can also point out flaws in their logic or places where they are relying purely on emotional or value-driven arguments rather than logical ones. If, for example, you discovered that this writer was actually an American Muslim, might that alter the way you viewed his claim? It might open up the possibility that he is arguing out of strong loyalty to his faith and may be ignoring important issues in the debate.

- **What types of evidence have informed the opinions of my readers?** Are there compelling statistics that support this belief? Are there visuals that have helped to create or perpetuate stereotypes or preconceived notions? Are there vocal experts who have influenced public opinion? This question means that you will need to enter into the debate in a very real way. You will need to find out the current trends regarding the subject, whether it has been in the news recently, who the leading experts may be, and how valid the current research seems. For example, what if a recent study had been published revealing that a large percentage of American Muslims had ties to extremist groups? Although the original author may not have cited this study, it would be relevant and could affect your ability to make a logical and informed refutation of her claim. You would need to somehow refute this study in order to be successful in your own essay. You cannot ignore expert opinions or

data simply because the original author did not mention them. To do so would only hurt your refutation essay's credibility.

- **What types of evidence could I present that would be persuasive to my readers, given all of the above?** Will statistics or case studies work? Should I incorporate visuals that will counter ones they may have already seen? Are there respected experts who disagree with the common belief? Remember that evidence is the key to any successful argument. You must be able to present sound, logical, and credible evidence that refutes your opponent's original argument. Statistics and visuals can be effective ways to do this, as can quotes from reputable sources.

- **Where can I find sources?** Should I start with my library databases? Are there journal articles that present a new perspective on this debate? Should I first conduct a general Internet search to get an overall sense of the debate? Will YouTube.com have videos that I can use? As with any research process, you will want to begin by surveying the current information on your issue. You will need to gather credible sources (whether from your library's database or some other online or print source) and try to determine which sources will help you the most. Do not ignore sources that seemingly disagree with you or that support the opposite position. These can be valuable in understanding the opposing point of view and ultimately how you can refute its assertions.

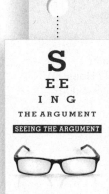

Consider this image of Jon Stewart from *The Daily Show* as a refutation argument against conservative commentator Glenn Beck. Although Stewart's primary purpose is to entertain, he is also making a serious point. Do you think Stewart's approach functions effectively as a refutation argument? Is it logically flawed in any way? Why or why not? You can watch the entire clip from which this still was taken at http://www.thedailyshow.com/watch/thu-november-18-2010/the-manchurian-lunatic.

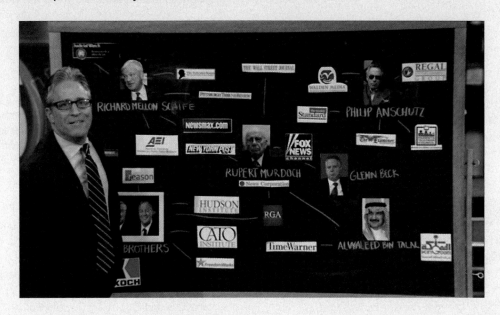

Mechanics making connections

let's review

After reading this chapter, you should understand:

- A good refutation demonstrates, in an orderly and logical way, the weaknesses of logic or evidence in the argument, or it both analyzes weaknesses and builds a counterargument.

- So that you can construct an effective refutation, you must read the original piece accurately in order to attempt to pinpoint its weaknesses.

- Your thesis should establish your disagreement with the writer's logical assumptions or evidence, or a combination of these.

- A typical refutation essay includes three parts: the opponent's argument, your thesis, and your support for your refutation.

- When using research to support your refutation, you should always consider what sources your readers may have already consulted about your issue and what attitudes and values they may bring to the table as a result.

- You should attempt to find sources and visuals that will be particularly persuasive to your readers given their probable values, beliefs, and attitudes toward your subject.

connect

Read the following refutation essay. Individually or in a small group, answer the questions that follow and be prepared to discuss you answers with the class.

prereading questions } Should police and airport security personnel use profiling to protect against terrorism? If profiling were used, would you be a suspect? Does how you answer the second question affect how you answer the first one?

You Can't Fight Terrorism with Racism

Colbert I. King

A native Washingtonian, Colbert King has held a number of positions in the government, including as special agent for the State Department, and in banking, including at the World Bank. King joined The Washington Post's *editorial board in 1990, began writing a weekly column in 1995, and became deputy editor of the editorial page in 2000. In 2003 he won a Pulitzer Prize for commentary. His column on fighting terrorism was published July 30, 2005.*

During my day job I work under the title of deputy editorial page editor. That entails paying more than passing attention to articles that appear on the op-ed page. Opinion writers, in my view, should have a wide range in which to roam, especially when it comes to edgy, thought-provoking pieces. Still, I wasn't quite ready for what appeared on the op-ed pages of Thursday's *New York Times* or Friday's *Post*.

A *New York Times* op-ed piece by Paul Sperry, a Hoover Institution media fellow ("It's the Age of Terror: What Would You Do?"), and a *Post* column by Charles Krauthammer ("Give Grandma a Pass: Politically Correct Screening Won't Catch Jihadists") endorsed the practice of using ethnicity, national origin, and religion as primary factors in deciding whom police should regard as possible terrorists—in other words, racial profiling. A second *Times* column, on Thursday, by Haim Watzman ("When You Have to Shoot First") argued that the London police officer who chased down and put seven bullets into the head of a Brazilian electrician without asking him any questions or giving him any warning "did the right thing."

The three articles blessed behavior that makes a mockery of the rights to which people in this country are entitled. Krauthammer blasted the random-bag-checks program adopted in the New York subway in response to the London bombings, calling it absurd and a waste of effort and resources. His answer: Security officials should concentrate on "young Muslim men of North African, Middle Eastern, and South Asian origin." Krauthammer doesn't say how authorities should go about identifying "Muslim men" or how to distinguish non-Muslim men from Muslim men entering a subway station. Probably just a small detail easily overlooked.

All you need to know is that the culprit who is going to blow you to bits, Krauthammer wrote, "traces his origins to the Islamic belt stretching from Mauritania to Indonesia." For the geographically challenged, Krauthammer's birthplace of the suicide bomber starts with countries in black Africa and stops somewhere in the Pacific Ocean. By his reckoning, the

rights and freedoms enjoyed by all should be limited to a select group. Krauthammer argued that authorities should work backward and "eliminate classes of people who are obviously not suspects." In the category of the innocent, Krauthammer would place children younger than 13, people older than 60 and "whole ethnic populations" starting with "Hispanics, Scandinavians and East Asians . . . and women," except "perhaps the most fidgety, sweaty, suspicious-looking, overcoat-wearing, knapsack-bearing young women."

Of course, by eliminating Scandinavians from his list of obvious terror suspects, Krauthammer would have authorities give a pass to all white people, since subway cops don't check passengers' passports for country of origin. As for sweaty, fidgety, knapsack-bearing, overcoat-wearing young women who happen to be black, brown, or yellow? Tough nuggies, in Krauthammer's book. The age-60 cutoff is meaningless, too, since subway cops aren't especially noted for accuracy in pinning down stages of life. In Krauthammer's worldview, it's all quite simple: Ignore him and his son; suspect me and mine.

Sperry also has his own proxy for suspicious characters. He warned security and subway commuters to be on the lookout for "young men praying to Allah and smelling of flower water." Keep your eyes open, he said, for a "shaved head or short haircut" or a recently shaved beard or moustache. Men who look like that, in his book, are "the most suspicious train passengers."

It appears to matter not to Sperry that his description also includes huge numbers of men of color, including my younger son, a brown-skinned occasional New York subway rider who shaves his head and moustache. He also happens to be a former federal prosecutor and until a few years ago was a homeland security official in Washington. Sperry's profile also ensnares my older brown-skinned son, who wears a very short haircut, may wear cologne at times, and has the complexion of many men I have seen in Africa and the Middle East. He happens to be a television executive. But what the hell, according to Sperry, "young Muslim men of Arab or South Asian origin" fit the terrorist profile. How, just by looking, can security personnel identify a Muslim male of Arab or South Asian origin goes unexplained.

Reportedly, after September 11, 2001, some good citizens of California took out after members of the Sikh community, mistaking them for Arabs. Oh, well, what's a little political incorrectness in the name of national security. Bang, bang— oops, he was Brazilian. Two young black guys were London bombers: one Jamaican, the other Somalian. Muslim, too. Ergo: Watch your back when around black men—they could be, ta-dum, Muslims.

So while advocates of racial profiling would have authorities subject men and women of black and brown hues to close scrutiny for criminal suspicions, they would look right past:

- White male Oklahoma bomber Timothy McVeigh, who killed 168 people, including 19 children, and damaged 220 buildings.

- White male Eric Rudolph, whose remote-controlled bomb killed a woman and an off-duty police officer at a clinic, whose Olympic Park pipe bomb killed a woman and injured more than 100, and whose bombs hit a gay club and woman's clinic.

- White male Dennis Rader, the "bind, torture, kill" (BTK) serial killer who terrorized Wichita for 31 years.

- D.C.–born and Silver Spring–raised white male John Walker Lindh, who converted to Islam and was captured in Afghanistan fighting for the Taliban.

- The IRA bombers who killed and wounded hundreds; the neo-fascist bombers who killed 80 people and injured nearly 300 in Bologna, Italy; and the truck bombings in Colombia by Pedro Escobar's gang.

But let's get really current. What about those non-Arab, non-South Asians without black or brown skins who are bombing apartment buildings, train stations, and theaters in Russia. They've taken down passenger jets, hijacked schools, and used female suicide bombers to a fare-thee-well, killing hundreds and wounding thousands. They are Muslims from Chechnya, and would pass the Krauthammer/Sperry eyeball test for terrorists with ease. After all, these folks hail from the Caucasus; you can't get any more Caucasian than that.

What the racial profilers are proposing is insulting, offensive and—by thought, word and deed, whether intentional or not—racist. You want estrangement? Start down that road of using ethnicity, national origin, and religion as a basis for police action and there's going to be a push-back unlike any seen in this country in many years.

QUESTIONS FOR READING

1. What are Krauthammer's views on random searches? Who should be targeted? Who ignored?

2. What are Sperry's views? Who would he profile?

QUESTIONS FOR REASONING AND ANALYSIS

1. What is King's claim? Where does he state it?

2. How does the author refute the arguments of Krauthammer and Sperry? List his points of rebuttal, both practical and value-based.

3. In paragraphs 10 and 11, King lists those who would not be stopped based on profiling. What is effective about the list? How might Krauthammer and Sperry respond to King's list?

4. Woven into the careful quoting and specific examples are lines that create a hard-edged tone to King's refutation. Find these lines and explain their effect.

QUESTIONS FOR REFLECTING AND WRITING

1. Has King effectively refuted Krauthammer and Sperry? Why or why not?

2. Do you see any opportunities for visual arguments in this article? Where and how might you add visual information or support?

3. If you were going to write a researched argument on this topic, what types of sources would you want to utilize? Do you see any points that could be made stronger through the use of source material?

taking a position

c h a p t e r 6

We have already seen that arguments are all around us. They appear throughout our daily lives, sometimes without even being noticed. However, some arguments are obvious. Taking-a-position or taking-a-stand arguments appear not only in academic settings as formal essays, but also as editorials in newspapers, flyers for causes or candidates, blog entries on the Web, and even magazine articles. Authors who have clear points of view and who wish to convince their readers to adopt those points of view often use this straightforward type of argument to accomplish their goals. While the position paper is often perceived as the easiest type of argument to write due to its clear purpose, in fact, it can actually be one of the most difficult argument assignments. Review the following characteristics of this kind of argument and consider why this might be so.

Characteristics of a Position Argument

- A position argument is often more general, abstract, or philosophical than other types of arguments. It may not always ask its readers to take a specific action, but it may instead ask them to change their belief systems or to examine their values.

- It makes a claim about what is right or wrong, good or bad for us as individuals or as a society. Topics can vary from the abolishment of the IRS to the legalization of prostitution to the best ways to protect endangered species.

- A position essay is developed in large part by a logical sequencing of reasons supported by reliable evidence.

- A successful position argument requires more than a forceful statement of personal beliefs and can often be weakened by appealing primarily to readers' emotions.

- In order to be successful, a position argument must take into account its readers' values, beliefs, and potential counterarguments or objections.

Writing a Position Essay

As you write a position essay, your primary goal will be to persuade your reader to accept your point of view as valid, worthwhile, and true. You are not simply explaining your opinion on a topic or issue. Rather, you are seeking a distinct and committed response from your audience. Even if your readers are already inclined to agree with you, you are still attempting to

solidify their current position. If your readers hold a different position on the issue, you are asking them to think about the issue in a new way or possibly even to abandon their position in favor of yours. Some position essays even go so far as to call for a specific action from the reader. None of these are easy tasks. You will need to carefully plan, draft, and revise your essay in order to be persuasive. You may also need to conduct research on your topic and use visual elements as ways to persuade your readers. In addition to the guidelines for writing solid and effective arguments presented in Chapter 3, you can use the advice specific to writing position papers presented throughout this chapter.

Planning and Organizing the Position Essay

Before you can begin drafting your essay, you will need to spend some time thinking about your topic, your audience, your specific purpose, and your strategy. The following questions can help you begin your prewriting and planning activities.

- **What claim, exactly, do you want to support?** What do you want your audience to think, believe, do, or feel after reading your essay?

- **Who is your audience?** Will you attempt to persuade those who clearly disagree with you? Those who agree with you on some points and not others? (Consider all of the questions concerning your readers' expectations and values from Chapter 3.)

- **What (if any) background information might your readers need on your topic?** Will you need to explain the controversy? Give them statistics? Tell a story? Consider how much your audience will already know about your issue and how much you will need to provide for them in the beginning of your essay.

- **What grounds (evidence) do you have or might you need to support your claim?** You may want to make a list of the reasons and facts you could use to defend your claim. Where might you find evidence or sources? Will you need to conduct interviews? Do library research? Conduct a survey? Recall your own experiences? Use visuals to illustrate your main points? Consider all the ways you can support your claims and which ones will be most persuasive to your particular audience.

- **What personal values do you and your audience members hold that inform your positions?** Study your list of possible grounds and recognize the assumptions (warrants) and backing for your grounds. Do you hold certain core beliefs that cause you to feel the way that you do? How might your readers view your values and beliefs? Will they automatically accept them as valid and

WHAT IS A VALUE?

A value is any principle, standard, or quality that we believe is worthwhile or important. People often form their positions based on their personal values and belief systems. This means that in order to write a persuasive position essay, you must understand not only your own values but also the values of your readers and how those values affect their position on your topic.

For example, in 2007, thousands of people filled the streets in a small Louisiana town to protest the arrests of six African American students charged with beating a white classmate after nooses were hung from a schoolyard tree. (For more information on the Jena 6, go to www.abc.net.au/news/stories/2007/09/21/2040080.htm.)

What do you think the protester in the photo values? What does he believe is important? How do you know? How might you attempt to convince him that even in the face of this racially charged act, the beating of the white student was not justified? Do you think it would be difficult to write a paper that would convince him to adopt this position?

true? Now make a list of the grounds most often used by those whose views oppose your claim and a list of the values these readers might hold. This second list will help you prepare rebuttals to your readers' possible counterarguments (opposing points), but first it will help you test your understanding of and commitment to your position. If you find the opposition's arguments persuasive and cannot think how you would rebut them, you may need to rethink your position. Ideally, your two lists will not only confirm your views but also increase your respect for opposing views.

Counterarguments and Finding Common Ground

Discovering the counterarguments to your position is an important part of the writing process. This will allow you not only to more fully understand the complexity of your issue, but also to more effectively defend your position in the face of opposition. Writing an effective rebuttal to your readers' counterargument is one of the trickiest and most delicate tasks you must undertake as you construct your position paper. It is not as simple as finding a directly opposing position and then claiming it is wrong. Rather, it means that you will need to identify and attempt to truly understand your potential readers, the positions they may hold, and the values that inform those positions. Then you will need to identify what logical strategies you can use to overcome their potential objections to your position.

First and foremost, your readers must believe that you fully understand their position and that you are presenting it in a fair and accurate way. But how can you do this without undermining your own (often directly opposing) position?

As you write a position essay, you will want to take special care to avoid the logical fallacies presented in Chapter 4 (Slippery Slope, Begging the Question, Bandwagon, Ad Populum) that can happen quite easily in this type of essay. Analyze the following visual arguments and see if you can match the logical fallacy to each.

circular reasoning works because

Slippery Slope Fallacy

Attention: Lunatic Atheists & their Lawyers
Anti-God is Anti-American
Anti-American is Treason
Traitors lead to Civil War
Rev. E. F. Briggs, PO Box 9066, Monongah, WV 26554

Begging the Question

LOVE IT
OR
LEAVE IT

Bandwagon Fallacy

McDonald's
OVER 99 BILLION SERVED
SAT 730 AM
COME HAVE BREAKFAST
WITH THE MUNCHKINS

Ad Populum Fallacy

The key to presenting your opponents' position is to always be fair but not to give their position any more weight than necessary. You should demonstrate that you understand the complexities of alternate positions and the reasons why readers may hold those views. You should never attack your opponents by insinuating that their position is ridiculous or unintelligent. Such insinuations will only turn off your readers before they have had a chance to consider your points.

One strategy that might help you is to use conciliatory language in an attempt to find common ground with your readers. Identifying points of agreement

(even if they are small) helps your readers feel open to your argument and will give you a chance to then rebut the points on which your opinions differ.

For example, you might present your counterargument by raising a potential objection using conciliatory language (in order to point to common ground), and then immediately rebutting the objection by using a transitional word or phrase:

<u>Admittedly</u>, there is evidence that mandatory vaccinations for children would help to eradicate specific diseases. <u>However</u>, when one considers all of the available statistics, the risks of these immunizations far outweigh any potential benefits.

The phrase *common ground* historically referred to the central place in many towns and villages made available to everyone and used for everything from trading or selling goods, to settling disagreements, to expressing opinions.

For example, one technique for anonymous trade between mutually suspicious parties was for the offerers to lay the goods (such as gold) in a clearing (the potential common ground), and then to hide in the forest with the gold in their plain sight, while armed with weapons in the event of treachery. Thus, the offers could be made to traders. The traders, who bore goods and who were also armed with weapons, would lay the trade goods in the clearing and take the gold back with them. This was a mechanism for trading between the Moors and the gold miners of Africa over a millennium ago, and also for trade with Sumatra (the isle of gold) and other islands of Southeast Asia. Now the term is typically used to mean a "foundation for mutual understanding."

Common ground definition from http://encyclopedia.thefreedictionary.com/common+ground+(communication+technique)

Consider how you might use a conciliatory approach as you present your position. When the issue is emotion-laden or highly controversial, or when your readers might hold values very different from your own, the conciliatory approach can be an effective strategy. Conciliatory arguments use

- nonthreatening language,
- a fair expression of opposing views, and
- a statement of the common ground shared by opposing sides.

You may want to use a conciliatory approach in the following instances:

1. You know your views will be unpopular with at least some members of your audience.

2. The issue is highly emotional and the sides are entrenched, so you are seeking some accommodations rather than dramatic changes of position.

3. You will need to interact with members of your audience in the future and want to maintain a respectful relationship.

GOOD ADVICE

Certain words and phrases can effectively set up a conciliatory rebuttal. Some words highlight specific points of agreement, while others point out the areas of opposition. These can be very effective in softening readers' attitude toward an argument that directly opposes their point of view. Try using these words as you construct your own counterarguments and rebuttal paragraphs.

Sample Conciliatory Words and Phrases to Introduce Counterarguments

Certainly	Obviously	Unquestionably
Assuredly	Admittedly	I will admit
I will concede the fact	Of course	Surely
While it is true	It seems clear	Without a doubt
Clearly	Undeniably	

Sample Transitional Words and Phrases to Introduce Rebuttals

However	Conversely	On the other hand
Nevertheless	Still	Yet
Even so	Regardless	Despite this fact

try it!

Draft a prewriting sheet or free-write a journal entry that answers each of the questions below. This will help you identify the potential counterarguments of your readers and will enable you to anticipate and effectively rebut those objections.

- What is my tentative thesis? What am I trying to convince my readers to do or believe?

- What specific beliefs, values, and experiences have helped to form my position on this issue? What do I believe is important regarding this issue?

- Who are my readers? What do they do? How old are they? Where do they live? Why do they care about this issue? What stake do they have in this debate? (Write down every characteristic you can think of regarding your potential audience.)

- What values and beliefs might my reader already hold that affect their current positions on this issue?

Why might they hold these values?

- What counterarguments or objections might my readers raise? Which of their points will be the most difficult to rebut? (Write down every possible objection and every possible rebuttal that you can think of—even if they sound far-fetched at this point.)

- Is there common ground between my readers' counterarguments and my own position? Are there things we can all agree on?

- Taking these counterarguments and points of common ground into account, how can I convince my readers to consider my points without offending them? Do I need to consider using a conciliatory approach?

Editorial Essay

The following sample essay illustrates a conciliatory approach. As you read, notice the highlighted elements of this approach. Does this writer do a good job of establishing common ground with the readers?

Editorial: Ultimately We Control Our Own Privacy Levels on Facebook
CT Editorial Board
February 19, 2009

Unbeknownst to many of the 175 million users worldwide, two weeks ago Facebook revised its terms of use, specifically giving itself permission to access users' account information even after they've deleted their accounts. This information included users' photos, wall posts, and personal information. When users caught wind of the changes in Facebook's terms, the backlash for Mark Zuckerberg was severe.

On Wednesday morning, Zuckerberg took to the Internet to clear up misconceptions among active users who were worried about the security of their information. On blog.facebook.com, Zuckerberg wrote that based on the feedback he had received regarding the changes, the Facebook team had decided to "return to our previous terms of use while we resolve the issues that people have raised."

While it's understandable that people are worried about their privacy and don't want people at Facebook to have access to their information—especially after their accounts have been deactivated—it is also ridiculous to assume that the information posted on Facebook on a daily basis is completely private, anyway.
Conciliatory language

Rebuttal

The Facebook team has always maintained that the users of Facebook own their information and control with whom they share it. And that is true, to a certain extent. However, whenever people access the Internet, they should always assume that they're taking a risk in regard to personal privacy and should accept whatever consequences arise as a result of personal decisions made on the Internet. It is up to us to decide what pictures we want to upload and have floating around the Internet. Similarly, the personal information we provide and the language we use to sign a friend's wall is also left to our discretion.
Conciliatory language

Transition to rebuttal

In a similar blog post from Monday evening, Zuckerberg attempted to better communicate to concerned users the idea behind Facebook's security. He calls out users, claiming that we want full ownership of our information so that we can control others' access to it at any given time, yet we also want to be able to use information that we receive from others, like phone numbers or e-mail addresses, for other services.

According to the blog, "There is no system today that enables me to share my e-mail address with you and then simultaneously lets me control who you share it with and also lets you control what services you share it with."

Facebook's decision to alter the terms of use understandably angered people because it made us feel like our privacy as users was being violated. However, rather than get hung up on specific wording, a more responsible option would be to closely monitor the information we upload and allow to be linked to us online. When signing up for Facebook a few years ago, few of us likely sat down and carefully read through the terms of use multiple times before deciding to become a member of the Web site. Few of us would have immediately noticed the difference between the original sentence in the terms of use reading, "Facebook could not claim any rights to original content that a user uploaded once the user closed his or her account," and the briefly updated version, "You may remove your User Content from the Site at any time. . . . [H]owever, you acknowledge that the Company may retain archived copies of your User Content." According to company spokesman Barry Schnitt's blog, within the next couple weeks, the Facebook team will be working on updating the terms of use in "simple language that defines Facebook's rights much more specifically."

This is good for users because in order to most responsibly take advantage of the Facebook applications, we need to know where we stand. We can't fully exercise our rights until we know what they are.

continued

It's safe to say that some of the people most upset about this are those who may not have used Facebook responsibly and are now concerned about the repercussions of that one picture from that one party that one night falling into the hands of someone who was never an intended viewer.

You've heard it time and time again. Be careful what you put online. We all want our privacy and that's understandable. It's one thing to obviously not want your information floating around out there freely, but don't be naive.

We should never count on technology to be 100 percent secure. It is a manmade resource, after all.

www.collegiatetimes.com/stories/13034

As you can see, this author anticipates the readers' values and counterarguments to the thesis "whenever people access the Internet, they should always assume that they're taking a risk in regard to personal privacy and should accept whatever consequences arise as a result of personal decisions made on the Internet." The author recognizes that readers place a high value on their privacy, may be highly upset at Facebook for sharing their information, and may claim that Facebook falsely led them to believe that users had control over their own information. Would the essay have been as effective if the author had not addressed these concerns and instead simply made the argument that people should take responsibility for their own information online?

Drafting the Position Essay

There are several strategies that you can use as you begin to organize and draft your essay:

- **Begin with an opening paragraph or two that introduces your topic in an interesting way.** Possibilities include a statement of the issue's seriousness or reasons why the issue is currently being debated— or why we should go back to reexamine it. Some writers are spurred by a recent event that receives media coverage; recounting such an event can produce an effective opening. You can also briefly summarize points of the opposition that you will challenge in supporting your claim.

- **Decide where to place your claim (thesis) statement.** Your best choices are either early in your essay (in order to capture your readers' attention and clarify your essay's purpose) or at the end of your essay, after you have made your case. The second approach can be an effective alternative to the more common pattern of stating the claim early if you are attempting to use deductive reasoning or lead your reader through your argument point by point, ultimately reaching a logical and necessary conclusion.

- **Avoiding Thesis Traps.** Writing a clear and engaging argumentative thesis statement can be difficult. Sometimes, students fall into one of the following traps that, more often than not, result in ineffective theses. Be sure that you clearly understand your purpose, your audience, and your writing situation as you construct your thesis statement, so as to avoid these traps.

  The Rhetorical Question Trap. If your thesis is a question, then it is not really an argumentative thesis because it doesn't assert a clear position. You can, of course, use a question to forecast an upcoming point you would like to make (for example, "Isn't making money the whole point of going to college?"), but this will not be suf-

To curb truancy, one Texas school system is requiring students to wear ankle monitors. If you were writing a position essay, would you support this program? What might be your opening line for your paper?

ficient to make clear your position. Do not make your reader guess where you stand.

The Obvious Fact Trap. If your thesis announces a commonly accepted fact (for example, "Dogs are popular pets" or "Building a fuel-efficient car is important"), you do not have an argument at all. Accepted facts do not stir up reactions or emotions. And in the rare event that someone might disagree with you, your argument will be lackluster and uninspired. You will leave your audience thinking, "I already knew that," and you surely don't want that reaction.

The Personal Response Trap. Your thesis (and your entire argument) depends on much more than your personal opinion. Your love of strawberry yogurt is not adequate support for the conclusion that it is the best flavor in the world. Be sure that your thesis doesn't simply make public your opinion on an event or issue ("I really liked the movie" or "My 1985 Toyota Corolla is my favorite car in the world"). You must approach your topic in a logical manner, and you must be able to provide clear and convincing support for your thesis. An academic argument cannot stand on the back of a personal opinion. It just can't.

The B-O-R-I-N-G Trap. You do not want your reader to put your essay down before they even get started, right? Your thesis is your chance to grab your readers' attention and excite them (or even fire them up) about your position. Do not blow this opportunity. Try to figure out how to use interesting and expressive nouns, adjectives, and verbs to express exactly what you want to say. Do not worry if you need two or even three sentences to state your thesis. Break the rules. Work it out.

Think about the differences between the following thesis statements. Which ones successfully avoid the thesis traps above?

- All kids should have chores.
- The overindulged and undermotivated teens of this give-it-to-me-now generation should be forced to put down their video game controllers, pick up the piles of stinking laundry on their bedroom floors, and actually contribute to society.
- All parents should require their teens to complete a lengthy list of chores before they are permitted any free time.
- I hated doing chores when I was growing up. Didn't you?

- **Organize evidence in an effective way.** Even if your thesis statement and main points are brilliant, your readers will not find your argument persuasive if they cannot follow it. If your essay seems jumbled or disorganized, or if you do not logically lead your reader from one point to the next, your essay will

not be successful. There are several ways to organize a position essay. What is important is to have a clear organization plan and to stick to it. Here are three typical organizations for a position essay:

- Move from the least important to the most important reasons, followed by rebuttals to potential counterarguments. This organizational plan allows readers to consider your most compelling points and your rebuttals to their objections last, which can increase their retention of these important points.

- Another possibility is to organize by the arguments of the opposition, explaining why each reason fails to hold up. As you rebut each of your opponent's main points, you will also assert and support your own arguments and show how they are more logical than those typically offered by the opposition. This strategy can be particularly effective if you are writing about a highly controversial issue or to a highly resistant audience. By fairly presenting and effectively refuting each opposing point, you leave your readers no choice but to consider your position on the issue.

- A third approach is to organize logically. That is, if some reasons require accepting other reasons, you want to begin with the necessary underpinnings and then move forward from those. This approach can be a bit difficult to plan, as many of your reasons will result from your presentation of other reasons. Use effective transitions between paragraphs (sometimes referred to as *metadiscourse*) to lead your reader from point to point. Be sure not to leave logical gaps or make sudden leaps from idea to idea.

- **Provide a logical defense of (or specifics in support of) each reason.** You have not finished your task by simply asserting several reasons for your claim. You also need to present facts or examples for (or a logical explanation of) each reason or rebuttal. For example, defending your views on capital punishment requires more than asserting that it is right or just to take the life of a murderer. Why is it right or just? Executing the murderer will not bring the victim back to life. Do two wrongs make a right? These are some of the questions skeptical readers may have unless you explain and justify your reasoning.

- **Provide adequate context for your relevant source materials.** Simply quoting another writer's opinion on your topic does not provide proof for your reasons. It merely shows that someone else agrees with you. Similarly, dropping quotations into your essay does not necessarily provide support for your ideas. In order to provide context for your quotes (as well as credible support for your argument), you should identify each quote's author,

GOOD ADV!CE

Conducting Research for Position Essays

Supporting your points with valid research is especially important when you are entering a debate about a highly controversial issue. Simply stating that you are right doesn't convince most readers. Consider conducting a basic keyword search in your library database as part of your prewriting process in order to learn what others are saying about your issue. From there, you can continue to search for relevant articles and even websites that will help you support your points. For example, if you are arguing that automated traffic control devices (ticket cameras) should not be legal, you could type the term "automated traffic ticket" into your library's database. Be sure, however, that you understand how your library database works. Unlike Google, which pulls up every possible lead related to all of the words in your search (and can often pull up completely useless material), most library databases use Boolean operators (AND, OR, NOT) to narrow searches to the most relevant and helpful materials. For example, if you type "state of iowa gay marriage legal" into Google, you will get hits, but if you type the same phrase into your library database, you may not (even if your library has many articles on your topic). This is because Boolean searches look for the exact phrase within the context of the articles. For a Boolean search, you would want to type "state of iowa AND gay marriage AND legal. For more information on Boolean operators and how they can affect your library searches, visit your campus library site or go to www.youtube.com/watch?v=vube-ZcJFk4.

George Boole is known as the inventor of Boolean logic, which is the basis of modern digital computer logic.

attempt to fully discuss the quote's significance, explain how it supports your claim, and then tie it back to your thesis. It is very important to put your sources (especially of direct quotes) into context for your readers so that they can fully understand the relationship between the author's words and your own. Read the following quote:

> I was called a terrorist yesterday.

If you were given nothing more than this, what guess would you make about the quote's author? Is he a good person? Is he a credible source? Difficult to tell, isn't it? Now read the full quote in the context of a student essay:

In an interview on *Larry King Live*, Nelson Mandela, who spent over 27 years in prison after fighting for civil rights in South Africa and who was elected that country's first Black president in 1994, stated, "I was called a terrorist yesterday, but when I came out of jail, many people embraced me, including my enemies, and that is what I normally tell other people who say

those who are struggling for liberation in their country are terrorists. I tell them that I was also a terrorist yesterday, but, today, I am admired by the very people who said I was one." The fact that Mandela, who is known as one of the most active civil rights advocates in the world could be called a terrorist by some supports my notion that terrorism, and in fact, the entire premise of "evil" is a subjective concept. After all, what is evil to one might just be necessary or even positive to another.

www.notable-quotes.com/t/terrorism_quotes.html

Does the quote make sense in this context? Would readers accept this as a credible and reliable source for an essay? Do you understand why this author chose this quote and how it supports his claim?

- **Use effective visuals to support your position.**
  - Oftentimes, a well-crafted or well-placed visual element can serve as excellent support for your argument. After all, people respond very dif-

ferently to visuals than they do to text, even in academic essays. Visuals can help to clarify statistics, provide evidence of your claims, or even make effective use of irony or satire. These tasks can be more difficult to accomplish with text alone. There is a good reason for the old expression "a picture is worth a thousand words." Let's examine some of the types of visuals you might want to use as you draft your position essay. *Note:* Be sure to provide captions for each of your visual elements to explain its significance for your argument and to properly provide attribution according to your instructor's documentation guidelines. Visuals, like all sources, need to be cited!

Top 10 Global Markets for Fast Food Consumption

Market	Percent of Adult Population That Eats Fast Food at Least Once a Week
Hong Kong	61%
Malaysia	59%
Philippines	54%
Singapore	50%
Thailand	44%
China	41%
India	37%
United States	35%
Australia	30%
New Zealand	29%

From *Consumers in Europe—Our Fast Food/Take Away Consumption Habits, 2nd Half, 2004.* ACNielsen, 2005. http://ie.nielsen.com/pubs/documents/EuroFastFood-Dec04.pdf. The Nielsen Company. Reprinted with permission.

- Charts, graphs, and tables can help you to clarify difficult concepts or statistics for your readers. Consider learning how to create your own tables or graphs in a spreadsheet or word-processing program. For example, if, while asserting that many Americans do not seem to care about their health, you presented the table in the left column showing that 35 percent of American adults eat fast food at least once a week, you would be providing solid support for your claim.

- Photographs can help to support your claims by actually showing rather than telling your reader that something is occurring or should be changed. For example, if you were writing an essay arguing that your environmental group should receive funding to clean up the local river, might a photograph like the one in the bottom left column and taken by you help support your claim?

- Stock images, while often not as compelling as personal photos, can make a big impact on a reader. They can help to introduce a controversy and show readers a side of an issue they may not have considered before. These can be especially useful at the beginning of an essay to grab the readers' attention and create interest in your topic. For example, if you were writing an essay about eating disorders, imagine using the stock photo below, in your introduction. Does it make an impact?

- **Maintain an appropriate level of seriousness for an argument of principle.** Of course, your word choice must be appropriate to a serious discussion, but in addition be sure your reasons are also appropriately serious. For example, if you are defending the claim that music CDs should not be subject to content labeling because such censorship is inconsistent with First Amendment rights, do not trivialize your argument by including the point that young people are tired of adults controlling their lives. (This is an issue for another paper.)

making connections

let's review

After reading this chapter, you should understand:

- Taking-a-position or taking-a-stand arguments appear not only in academic settings as formal essays, but also as editorials in newspapers, flyers for causes or candidates, blog entries on the Web, and even magazine articles.

- A position argument often makes a claim about what is right or wrong, good or bad for us as individuals or as a society. It may not always ask readers to take a specific action, but it may ask them to change their beliefs or to examine their values.

- A value is any principle, standard, or quality that we believe is worthwhile or important. People often form their positions based on their personal values and belief systems. This means that in order to write a persuasive position essay, you must understand not only your own values but also the values of your readers and how those values affect their position on your topic.

- Before you can begin drafting your essay, you will need to spend some time thinking about your topic, your audience, your specific purpose, and your strategy.

- Discovering the counterarguments to your position is an important part of the writing process. This will not only allow you to more fully understand the complexity of your issue, but also to more effectively defend your position in the face of opposition.

- The key to presenting your opponents' position is to always be fair but not to give their position any more weight than necessary. You should demonstrate that you understand the complexities of alternate positions and the reasons why your readers may hold those views.

- One strategy that might help you is to use conciliatory language in an attempt to find common ground with your reader.

- You will need to make important decisions about thesis placement, organization strategy, finding sources, and using visuals as you draft.

connect

Read the following position argument. Individually or with your classmates, analyze the argument being made. Use the questions at the end of the reading to guide your discussion.

Brain-Enhancing Drugs: Legalize 'Em, Scientists Say

Brandon Keim

December 10, 2008

If drugs can safely give your brain a boost, why not take them? And if you don't want to, why stop others?

In an era when attention-disorder drugs are regularly—and illegally—being used for off-label purposes by people seeking a better grade or year-end job review, these are timely ethical questions.

The latest answer comes from *Nature*, where seven prominent ethicists and neuroscientists recently published a paper entitled, "Towards a responsible use of cognitive-enhancing drugs by the healthy."

In short: Legalize 'em.

"Mentally competent adults," they write, "should be able to engage in cognitive enhancement using drugs."

Roughly seven percent of all college students, and up to 20 percent of scientists, have already used Ritalin or Adderall—originally intended to treat attention-deficit disorders—to improve their mental performance.

Some people argue that chemical cognition-enhancement is a form of cheating. Others say that it's unnatural. The *Nature* authors counter these charges: Brain boosters are only cheat-

ing, they say, if prohibited by the rules—which need not be the case. As for the drugs being unnatural, the authors argue, they're no more unnatural than medicine, education and housing.

In many ways, the arguments are compelling. Nobody rejects pasteurized milk or dental anesthesia or central heating because it's unnatural. And whether a brain is altered by drugs, education or healthy eating, it's being altered at the same neurobiological level. Making moral distinctions between them is arbitrary.

But if a few people use cognition-enhancing drugs, might everyone else be forced to follow, whether they want to or not?

If enough people improve their performance, then improvement becomes the status quo. Brain-boosting drug use could become a basic job requirement. Ritalin and Adderall, now ubiquitous as academic pick-me-ups, are merely the first generation of brain boosters. Next up is Provigil, a "wakefulness promoting agent" that lets people go for days without sleep, and improves memory to boot. More powerful drugs will follow. As the *Nature* authors write, "cognitive enhance-

continued

ments affect the most complex and important human organ and the risk of unintended side effects is therefore both high and consequential." But even if their safety could be assured, what happens when workers are expected to be capable of marathon bouts of high-functioning sleeplessness?

Most people I know already work 50 hours a week and struggle to find time for friends, family, and the demands of life. None wish to become fully robotic in order to keep their jobs. So I posed the question to Michael Gazzaniga, a University of California, Santa Barbara, psychobiologist and *Nature* article co-author.

"It is possible to do all of that now with existing drugs," he said. "One has to set their goals and know when to tell their boss to get lost!"

Which is not, perhaps, the most practical career advice these days. And University of Pennsylvania neuroethicist Martha Farah, another of the paper's authors, was a bit less sanguine.

"First the early adopters use the enhancements to get an edge. Then, as more people adopt them, those who don't, feel they must just to stay competitive with what is, in effect, a new higher standard," she said.

Citing the now-normal stresses produced by expectations of round-the-clock worker availability and inhuman powers of multitasking, Farah said, "There is definitely a risk of this dynamic repeating itself with cognition-enhancing drugs."

But people are already using them, she said. Some version of this scenario is inevitable—and the solution, she said, isn't to simply say that cognition enhancement is bad.

Instead we should develop better drugs, understand why people use them, promote alternatives and create sensible policies that minimize their harm.

As Gazzaniga also pointed out, "People might stop research on drugs that may well help memory loss in the elderly"—or cognition problems in the young—"because of concerns over misuse or abuse."

This would certainly be unfortunate collateral damage in the 21st-century theater of the War on Drugs—and the question of brain enhancement needs to be seen in the context of this costly and destructive war. As Schedule II substances, Ritalin and Adderall are legally equivalent in the United States to opium or cocaine.

"These laws," write the *Nature* authors, "should be adjusted to avoid making felons out of those who seek to use safe cognitive enhancements."

After all, according to the law's letter, 7 percent of college students and 20 percent of scientists should have done jail time—this journalist, too.

1. What is the writer's claim? Is it clear?

2. Is the claim qualified if necessary? Some claims of value are broad philosophical assertions: "Capital punishment is immoral and bad public policy." Others are qualified: "Capital punishment is acceptable only in crimes of treason."

3. What facts and sources are presented? Are they credible? Are they relevant to the claim's support?

4. What reasons are given in support of the claim? What assumptions are necessary to tie reasons to the claim? Make a list of reasons and assumptions and analyze the writer's logic. Do you find any fallacies?

5. Has the author considered the implications of his or her claim? For example, if you argue for the abolishment of a legal drinking age, you eliminate all underage drinking problems by definition. But what new problems may be created by this approach? Consider more car accidents and reduced productivity in school for openers.

6. Is the argument convincing? Does the evidence provide strong support for the claim? Has the writer demonstrated understanding of possible opposing positions? Has the writer effectively refuted or accommodated those positions without sacrificing his or her own position? Are you prepared to agree with the writer in whole or in part, or at the very least to consider the writer's position as valid?

writing a causal analysis

chapter 7

Autism Trend (1992–2005)
California Department of Education

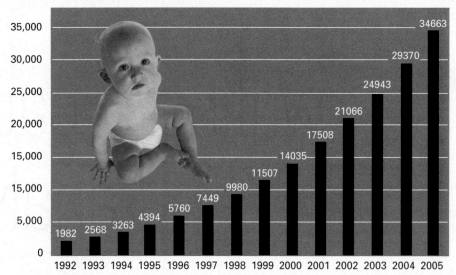

													34663
35,000												29370	
30,000											24943		
25,000										21066			
20,000								17508					
							14035						
15,000						11507							
					9980								
15,000				7449									
			5760										
5,000	1982 2568 3263 4394												
0													
	1992 1993 1994 1995 1996 1997 1998 1999 2000 2001 2002 2003 2004 2005												

Reprinted by permission from the California Department of Education, CDE Press, 1430 N Street, Suite 3207, Sacramento, CA 95814.

What Is a Causal Essay?

This graph demonstrates the increase in the number of autism cases reported in California between 1992 and 2005. Writing a causal argument can help you and your readers speculate about and possibly determine why such trends are occurring.

Because we want to know why things happen, arguments about cause abound. We want to understand past events (why did so many Americans buy houses in the early 2000s that they couldn't afford?). We want to explain current situations (why do some teenagers use drugs while others don't?). We want to predict the future (will the economy improve if taxes are cut?).

The answers to all three questions require causal arguments. In a causal essay, you will be expected to write an argument that asserts what you believe to be the main causes of the trend, event, or phenomenon and that supports your assertion with logical reasons and evidence.

Some specific terms related to the discussion of causation provide useful distinctions about why something has happened (or not happened). For example, a house fire is an **event**.

First, when looking for the cause of an event, we look for an **agent**—a person, a situation, another event that caused the event to take place. A lit cigarette dropped in a bed caused a house fire; the lit cigarette is the agent. But why, we ask, did someone drop a lit cigarette on a bed? The person, old and ill, took a sleeping pill and dropped the

cigarette when he fell asleep. Where do we stop in this chain of causes?

Second, we learn that most events do not occur in a vacuum with a single cause. There are **conditions** surrounding the event, making the assigning of only one cause often difficult. For example, the man's age and health are conditions.

Third, we can also speak of **influences**. The sleeping pill certainly influenced the man to drop the cigarette and cause the fire. Some conditions and influences may qualify as *remote causes*.

Proximate causes are more immediate, usually closer in time to the event or situation. The man's dozing off with a lighted cigarette is a proximate cause of the fire.

Finally, we come to the **precipitating cause,** the triggering event—for example, the cigarette's igniting the combustible mattress fabric. Isolating a precipitating cause is usually necessary to prevent events from recurring, but often we need to go further back to determine remote causes or conditions, especially if we are interested in assigning responsibility for what has occurred.

You encounter causal arguments all the time. Every scientific research project you will either write or read hypothesizes about a possible cause and then attempts to support or reject it. Investigative journalists often write articles that probe for potential causes of incidents or trends in their communities. And whenever a monumental event occurs (9/11 or the economic recession of 2008, for example), many newscasters, pundits, and even laypeople attempt to make sense of it by investigating its possible causes. This type of argument can lead not only to a better understanding of the world around us, but also to remedies that allow for positive change. We must, after all, understand what is causing something before we can make effective changes.

Characteristics of Causal Arguments

Assigning cause is tricky business. Perhaps that is the first and most important point to make. Here are some other points about causal arguments.

- Causal arguments are similar in their purpose but vary considerably in their subject matter and structure. Some causal arguments are about a particular situation; others seek explanations for a general state of affairs. However, in either case there may be one or there may be several causes.

- Because some complex situations have long chains of causes, arguers about cause need to decide on their focus—based on their purpose in writing. While it may be simpler to determine the causes of a specific event, sometimes it gets a bit more complicated to find the causes of a trend or an ongoing phenomenon. Suppose, for example, your concern is global warming. Cows contribute to global warming. Factories contribute to global warming. Car emissions contribute to global warming. But do all of these contribute

equally to the phenomenon? Your task as a writer is to determine which of all potential causes is the most likely or most plausible cause of the event, trend, or phenomenon. You do not need to present every potential cause. However, you must make it clear to your reader that while other possibilities exist, your chosen cause is the most likely or reasonable. This, in effect, allows you to deal with counterarguments (possible objections) to your claim. (For more on counterargument in causal arguments, see page 120, later in this chapter.)

Recognizing Relationships in Causal Arguments

It can be tricky to identify the cause-effect relationship between two events or issues. Just because one event follows another does not necessarily mean that the first caused the second. For example, imagine eating strawberry yogurt at every meal for three days. At the end of the third day, you get a severe migraine

try it!

From the following events or situations, select the one you know best and list as many conditions, influences, and causes—remote, proximate, precipitating—as you can think of. You may want to do this exercise with your class partner or in a small group. Be prepared to explain your causal pattern to the class.

1. Teen suicide

2. Decrease in the use of condoms by college students

3. Increase in the numbers of women elected to public office

4. High salaries of professional athletes

5. Increased interest in soccer in the United States

6. Comparatively low scores by U.S. students on international tests in math and science

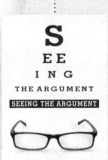
This billboard for AAA presents a causal argument. For what cause-and-effect relationship is the author attempting to argue? Do you think it is a valid causal relationship? How do you feel about the use of visuals in this argument? Do they serve as logical support or do they have a different purpose?

headache. Could you logically argue that the strawberry yogurt was the cause of the headache? Possibly. There may very well be a causal relationship between the two. On the other hand, there may be no relationship between the two events at all. It would be up to you to prove the relationship exists. Simply demonstrating that one followed the other would not be sufficient evidence for your readers. As you construct your own causal essay, you will need to pay special attention to causal relationships to ensure that you are not engaging in a post-hoc logical fallacy (see Chapter 4 for more on logical fallacies) or creating relationships that do not exist.

Mill's Methods for Investigating Causes

John Stuart Mill, a nineteenth-century British philosopher, explained some important ways of investigating and demonstrating causal relationships: commonality, difference, and process of elimination. We can benefit in our study of cause by understanding and using his methods.

1. **Commonality.** One way to isolate cause is to demonstrate that one agent is common to similar outcomes. For instance, 25 employees attend a company luncheon. Late in the day, 10 report to area hospitals, and another 4 complain the next day of having experienced vomiting the night before. Public health officials will soon want to know what these people ate for lunch. Different people during the same 12-hour period had similar physical symptoms of food poisoning. The common factor may well have been the tuna salad they ate for lunch.

2. **Difference.** Another way to isolate cause is to recognize one key difference. If two situations are alike in every way but one, and the situations result in different outcomes, then the one way they differ must have caused the different outcome. Studies in the social sciences are often based on the single-difference method. To test for the best teaching methods for math, an educator could set up an experiment with two classrooms similar in every way except that one class devotes 15 minutes three days a week to instruction by drill. If the class receiving the drill scores much higher on a standardized test given to both groups of students, the educator could argue that math drills make a measurable difference in learning math.

   But the educator should be prepared for skeptics to challenge the assertion of only one difference between the two classes. Could the teacher's attitude toward the drills also make a difference in student learning? If the differences in student scores are significant, the educator probably has a good argument, even though a teacher's attitude cannot be controlled in the experiment.

3. **Process of elimination.** You can develop a causal argument around a technique we all use for problem solving: the process of elimination. When something happens, we examine all possible causes and eliminate them, one by one, until we are satisfied that we have isolated the actual cause (or causes). When the Federal Aviation Administration investigates a plane crash, it uses this process, exploring possible causes such as mechanical failure, weather, human error, and terrorism. Sometimes the process points to more than one cause or to a likely cause without providing absolute proof.

Planning and Drafting a Causal Argument

Before you begin drafting your causal argument, you will want to spend a significant amount of time working through your ideas. This type of argument is tricky, and writers can easily be led astray and end up attempting to solve a problem (which is a different type of argument). Other pitfalls include focusing too heavily on one cause while ignoring other important possible causes, creating false or illogical cause-and-effect relationships between events, and simply stating a cause without providing sufficient evidence to support its effects. There are, however, specific strategies for writing causal arguments that you can use, in addition to the guidelines for writing arguments presented in Chapter 3.

Planning the Causal Argument

As with all effective arguments, organized and strategic planning is key to causal arguments. In order to plan your essay, you should begin by asking yourself the following questions:

- **What are the focus and limits of your causal argument?** Do you want to argue for one cause of an event or situation? Do you want to argue for several causes leading to an event or situation? Do you want to argue for a cause that others have overlooked? Do you want to show how one cause is common to several situations or events? Diagramming the relationship of cause to effect may help you see what to focus on. For example:

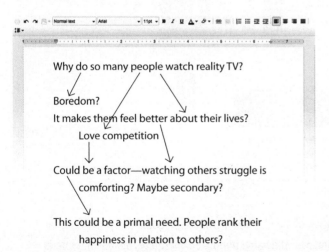

Why do so many people watch reality TV?

Boredom?

It makes them feel better about their lives?

Love competition

Could be a factor—watching others struggle is comforting? Maybe secondary?

This could be a primal need. People rank their happiness in relation to others?

- **What reasons and evidence do you have to support your tentative claim?** Consider what you already know that has led to your choice of topic. A brainstorming list may be helpful. You may also want to conduct some initial research in order to find out what others have said about your issue. For example:

What do I know?

All of my friends watch tons of reality shows.

It seems to be a trend over the past decade or so. There are lots more than there used to be.

Many of them include competition of some kind.

The producers make them very (maybe overly) dramatic.

Some of them are not real at all.

Many of them include love relationships.

What will I need to find out?

How many shows are there now as compared to a decade ago?

How many people watch these shows?

What do other researchers say is causing this trend?

Are there surveys that ask people why they watch?

What types of needs are these shows fulfilling? What do they do for them?

Are certain types of shows more successful than others? If so, why?

Where can I find these answers?

- **How, then, do you want to word your thesis?** As we have discussed, wording is crucial in causal arguments. Can you make a firm and definite claim about a direct cause-and-effect relationship? Or should you present several possible causes and then argue that one is more likely than the others? Or might you argue that several factors are contributing to the effect in combination? The key is to make your claim clear to your reader. Do not overstate or understate the relationship you are attempting to support.

- **What, if any, additional evidence do you need to develop a convincing argument?** You may need to do some library or online research to obtain data to strengthen your argument. Readers expect relevant, reliable, current statistics in most arguments about cause. Assess what you need and then think about what sources will provide the needed information.

- **What assumptions (warrants) are you making in your causal reasoning?** Do these assumptions hold up to logical scrutiny? Will readers be likely to agree with your assumptions, or will you need to defend them as part of the development of your argument? For example, one reason that heavy TV watching has an effect on viewers is the commonsense argument

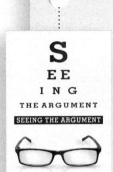

Consider the following options for integrating research into your causal argument. Which do you think would be more engaging, and ultimately more persuasive, to a reader? Why? What can visuals sometimes do more effectively for your argument than words?

OPTION A

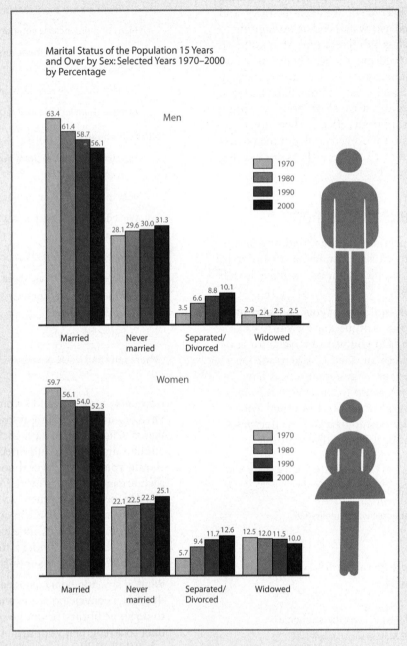

Marital Status of the Population 15 Years and Over by Sex: Selected Years 1970–2000 by Percentage

Men

	Married	Never married	Separated/Divorced	Widowed
1970	63.4	28.1	3.5	2.9
1980	61.4	29.6	6.6	2.4
1990	58.7	30.0	8.8	2.5
2000	56.1	31.3	10.1	2.5

Women

	Married	Never married	Separated/Divorced	Widowed
1970	59.7	22.1	5.7	12.5
1980	56.1	22.5	9.4	12.0
1990	54.0	22.8	11.7	11.5
2000	52.3	25.1	12.6	10.0

OPTION B

There were approximately 2,230,000 marriages in 2005—down from 2,279,000 the previous year, despite a total population increase of 2.9 million over the same period. Furthermore, the divorce rate in 2005 (per 1,000 people) was 3.6—the lowest rate since 1970, and down from 4.2 in 2000 and from 4.7 in 1990. (The peak was at 5.3 in 1981, according to the Associated Press.)

Jason Fields and Lynne M. Casper, America's Families and Living Arrangements: March 2000.
Current Population Reports, P20-537. Washington, DC: U.S. Census Bureau, Figure 4 (p. 10).
www.census.gov/prod/2001pubs/p20-537.pdf.

that what we devote considerable time to has a significant effect on our lives. Will your readers be prepared to accept this commonsense reasoning, or will they remain skeptical, looking for stronger evidence of a cause-effect relationship?

Using Visuals in the Causal Essay

Oftentimes, a causal analysis depends heavily on the presentation of research and statistical data. After all, you must demonstrate that the trend or phenomenon is actually occurring before you can defend a specific cause (or causes). Visual representations such as charts and graphs can be very helpful in causal essays. Visuals allow your readers to quickly and easily understand trends, statistics, and complex information about cause-effect relationships. (You will learn more about making arguments visually in Chapter 10.)

Drafting the Causal Argument

As you begin to draft your argument, keep the following points in mind:

- **Begin with an opening paragraph or two that introduces your topic in an interesting way.** Look at the way Gregg Easterbrook begins his essay (see Try It! on pages 121–123). Why does he present the controversy in this way rather than simply stating "I believe that television is a possible cause of autism"?

  This opening establishes the topic and Easterbrook's purpose in examining causes—that current research is supporting a hypothesis he made in the past. The statistics and research presented in these early paragraphs get the readers' attention. You may also want to use visuals in your introduction to grab your readers' interest and to present statistical data regarding your trend or phenomenon. Do not begin by announcing your subject. Avoid openers such as "In this essay I will explain the causes of teen vandalism."

- **Decide where to place your claim statement.** You can conclude your opening paragraph with it, or you can place it in your conclusion, after you have shown readers how best to understand the causes of the issue you are examining. Easterbrook uses a third technique—the implied claim—to his advantage. He makes it clear to his readers what his position is throughout the essay without actually stating it outright. Be careful when using this technique, however. It is usually much safer to explicitly state your claim at either the beginning or end of your essay.

- **Present reasons and evidence in an organized way.** There are several effective strategies for organizing a causal essay:

1. If you are examining a series of causes and begin with background conditions and early influences, then your basic plan will be time sequence. Readers need to see the chain of causes unfolding. Consider using appropriate terms and transitional words to guide readers through each stage in the causal pattern. Some transitional phrases that indicate a series of events include *at first, first of all, to begin with, in the first place, at the same time, for now, for the time being, the next step, in time, in turn, later on, meanwhile, next, then, soon, in the meantime, later, while, earlier, simultaneously, afterward, in conclusion, with this in mind.*

2. Or you may choose to organize your essay by refuting the validity of other potential causes. If you are arguing for an overlooked or less-than-popular cause, begin with the familiar causes and show the flaws in each one (in other words, rebut each potential counter-argument or alternate cause). Then present and defend your explanation of cause. This process-of-elimination structure works well when readers are likely to know what other causes have been offered in the past. You can also use one of Mill's other two approaches if one of them is relevant to your situation. That is, you can present the points of commonality or difference that show your explanation of cause to be valid.

3. Address the issue of correlation rather than cause, if appropriate. After presenting the results of a study of marriage that reveals many benefits (emotional, physical, financial) of marriage, you might wish to examine the question that skeptical readers may have: Does marriage cause the benefits, or is the relationship one of correlation only—that is, do the benefits of marriage just happen to come with being married instead of being caused by being married? As you try to determine the main cause of a trend or phenomenon, you will need to admit if there is a possibility for correlation. This demonstrates to your reader that you are a logical writer and creates credibility for your work.

4. Conclude by discussing the implications of the causal pattern you have argued for, if appropriate. If, for example, in explaining the causes of teen vandalism, you see one cause as "group behavior," a gang looking for something to do, it then follows that you can advise young readers to stay out of gangs. Often with arguments about cause, there are personal or public-policy implications in accepting

We've all waited for an elevator with someone who pushes the button repeatedly just prior to the doors opening. But does pushing the button repeatedly make the elevator come faster? The answer is clearly no. While there may be a correlation between the two events, the first does not cause the second. Watch for this common error while constructing your causal essay.

the causal explanation. Just be careful not to spend the majority of your essay on solutions rather than arguments for your claim.

Counterarguments in Causal Essays

Counterarguments play a very important role in the causal essay. They can help you eliminate alternate potential causes, which will help lead your reader to the conclusion that your cause is the most logical or acceptable. By refuting what others believe is causing the trend or phenomenon, you can build support for your own argument. But be careful! You do not have to completely dismiss the validity of every alternate cause. You can acknowledge their effects on the trend, while still building a case for your cause being the primary cause. For example, imagine writing a causal essay focusing on the state of the education system in America.

> Your writing purpose: Statistics suggest that America is falling far behind many other nations in producing well-educated and globally prepared citizens. What is the main cause of this trend?

> Tentative thesis: The central cause of the declining academic preparedness of American students is the lack of funding for public school systems that do not currently meet the "no child left behind" testing standards.

Imagine how this thesis might be received by your readers who believe that the "no child left behind" act is an effective program that promotes high standards. They may immediately reject your thesis (or your

entire essay) based on the fact that your focus seems to ignore the complexity of this issue. If your entire essay simply goes on to provide negative information about the "no child left behind" program and then concludes that this is the main cause of the problem, your essay will fail to persuade your skeptical readers.

Instead, you will need to address the complexity of the issue by pointing to other potential causes (counterarguments) and then addressing why they are not contributing to the problem as much as is your chosen cause (rebuttal). For example, if your thesis was revised to read

> Although many factors contribute to declining student preparedness in America, including poor teacher education and a lack of parental involvement, the primary cause of this disturbing trend is the lack of funding for public school systems that do not currently meet the "no child left behind" testing standards.

This thesis demonstrates the complexity of the issue and forecasts that you will present those alternate possibilities but will ultimately rebut the idea that they are the most likely or plausible causes of the trend. Including alternate causes and points of view demonstrates that you have a deep understanding of your issue and that you are a credible and thoughtful writer.

A Checklist for Revision

As you revise your causal essay, you will need to ask yourself the following questions. Read through your essay with these in mind:

- Do I have a clear statement of my claim? Is it appropriately qualified and focused?

- Have I organized my argument so that readers can see my pattern for examining cause?

- Have I used the language for discussing causes correctly, distinguishing among conditions and influences and remote and proximate causes? Have I selected the correct word—either *affect* or *effect*—as needed?

- Have I avoided the post hoc fallacy and the confusing of correlation and cause? Have I engaged in other logical fallacies? (See Chapter 4 for more on fallacies.)

- Have I carefully examined my assumptions and convinced myself that they are reasonable and can be defended? Have I defended them when necessary to clarify and thus strengthen my argument?

- Have I found relevant facts and examples to support and develop my argument? Do I need more research, statistics, or visuals to support my claims?

- Have I used the basic checklist for revision in Chapter 3 (see page 62)?

Many people are concerned about the state of America's educational system. In fact, a report by the Promise Alliance states that nearly 50 percent of students in America's largest cities fail to graduate from high school. A causal essay might argue that this is due to student apathy, poor teachers, a lack of funding for materials and curriculum development, or even a combination of all three. Can you think of other potential causes?

try it!

As you read the following excerpt from an article posted on Slate.com, see if you can identify how this author is using counterarguments to his advantage. Does he present alternate causes, but still manage to point to one as the most likely or plausible? Do you find his argument more compelling because of his use of counterargument? Why or why not? Is this author making a direct cause-and-effect claim? Or is his claim implied and more complicated than that? What do you think he believes causes autism? How do you know?

TV Really Might Cause Autism
A Slate exclusive: Findings from a new Cornell study
Gregg Easterbrook
Slate Magazine
October 16, 2006

Last month, I speculated in Slate that the mounting incidence of childhood autism may be related to increased television viewing among the very young. The autism rise began around 1980, about the same time cable television and VCRs became common, allowing children to watch television aimed at them any time. Since the brain is organizing during the first years of life and since human beings evolved responding to three-dimensional stimuli, I wondered if exposing toddlers to lots of colorful two-dimensional stimulation could be harmful to brain development. This was sheer speculation, since I knew of no researchers pursuing the question.

Today, Cornell University researchers are reporting what appears to be a statistically significant relationship between autism rates and television watching by children under the age of 3. The researchers studied autism incidence

continued

in California, Oregon, Pennsylvania, and Washington State. They found that as cable television became common in California and Pennsylvania beginning around 1980, childhood autism rose more in the counties that had cable than in the counties that did not. They further found that in all the western states, the more time toddlers spent in front of the television, the more likely they were to exhibit symptoms of autism disorders.

The Cornell study represents a potential bombshell in the autism debate. "We are not saying we have found the cause of autism, we're saying we have found a critical piece of evidence," Cornell researcher Michael Waldman told me. Because autism rates are increasing broadly across the country and across income and ethnic groups, it seems logical that the trigger is something to which children are broadly exposed. Vaccines were a leading suspect, but numerous studies have failed to show any definitive link between autism and vaccines, while the autism rise has continued since worrisome compounds in vaccines were banned. What if the malefactor is not a chemical? Studies suggest that American children now watch about four hours of television daily. Before 1980—the first kids-oriented channel, Nickelodeon, dates to 1979—the figure is believed to have been much lower.

[. . .]

But the fact that rising household access to cable television seems to associate with rising autism does not reveal anything about how viewing hours might link to the disorder. The Cornell team searched for some independent measure of increased television viewing. In recent years, leading behavioral economists such as Caroline Hoxby and Steven Levitt have used weather or geography to test assumptions about behavior. Bureau of Labor Statistics studies have found that when it rains or snows, television viewing by young children rises. So Waldman studied precipitation records for California, Oregon, and Washington State, which, because of climate and geography, experience big swings in precipitation levels both year-by-year and county-by-county. He found what appears to be a dramatic relationship between television viewing and autism onset. In counties or years when rain and snow were unusually high, and hence it is assumed children spent a lot of time watching television, autism rates shot up; in places or years of low precipitation, autism rates were low. Waldman [concludes] that "just under 40 percent of autism diagnoses in the three states studied is the result of television watching." Thus the study has two separate findings: that having cable television in the home increased autism rates in California and Pennsylvania somewhat, and that more hours of actually watching television increased autism in California, Oregon, and Washington by a lot.

[. . .]

There are many possible objections to the Cornell study. One is that time indoors, not television, may be the autism trigger. Generally, indoor air quality is much lower than outdoor air quality: Recently the Environmental Protection Agency warned, "Risks to health may be greater due to exposure to air pollution indoors than outdoors." Perhaps if rain and snow cause young children to spend more time indoors, added exposure to indoor air pollution harms them. It may be that families with children at risk for autism disorders are for some reason more likely to move to areas that get lots of rain and snow or to move to areas with high cable-television usage. Some other factor may explain what only appears to be a television-autism relationship.

[. . .]

Researchers might also turn new attention to study of the Amish. Autism is rare in Amish society, and the standing assumption has been that this is because most Amish refuse to vaccinate children. The Amish also do not watch television.

Gregg Easterbrook is a fellow at the Brookings Institution. His most recent book is The Progress Paradox: How Life Gets Better While People Feel Worse.

Guidelines for Analyzing Causal Arguments

When analyzing causal arguments, what should you look for? The basics of good argument apply to all arguments: a clear statement of claim, qualified if appropriate, a clear explanation of reasons and evidence, and enough relevant evidence to support the claim. How do we recognize these qualities in a causal argument? Use the following points as guides to analyzing:

- **Does the writer carefully distinguish among types of causes?** Word choice is crucial. Is the argument that A and A alone caused B, or that A was one of several contributing causes?

- **Does the writer recognize the complexity of causation and not rush to assert only one cause for a complex event or situation?** The credibility of an argument about cause is quickly lost if readers find the argument oversimplified.

- **Is the argument's claim clearly stated, with qualifications as appropriate?** If the writer wants to argue for one cause, not the only cause, of an event or situation, then the claim's wording must make this limited goal clear to readers. For example, one can perhaps build the case for heavy television viewing as one cause of stereotyping, loss of sensitivity to violence, and increased fearfulness. But we know that the home environment and neighborhood and school environments also do much to shape attitudes.

- **What reasons and evidence are given to support the argument?** Can you see the writer's pattern of development? Does the reasoning seem logical? Are the data relevant? Is the reasoning presented in a clear manner? Does the author use visuals to make statistical data easier to comprehend? This kind of analysis of the argument's support will help you evaluate it.

- **Does the argument demonstrate causality, not just a time relationship or correlation?** A causal argument needs to prove agency: A is the cause of B, not just something that happened before B

or something that is present when B is present. March precedes April, but March does not cause April to arrive.

- **Does the writer present believable and plausible causal agents, agents consistent with our knowledge of human behavior and scientific laws?** Most educated people do not believe that personalities are shaped by astrological signs or that scientific laws are suspended in the Bermuda Triangle, allowing planes and ships to vanish or enter a fourth dimension.

- **What are the implications for accepting the causal argument?** If A and B clearly are the causes of C, and we don't want C to occur, then we presumably must do something about A and B—or at least we must do something about either A or B and see if reducing or eliminating one of the causes significantly reduces the incidence of C.

- **Is the argument convincing?** After analyzing the argument and answering the preceding questions, you need to decide if, finally, the argument works.

did you know

Affect is used as a verb meaning "to influence."
   My fifth-grade teacher's love of history really affected me.
Effect is used as a noun and most typically means "result."
   The effect of the hail storm was a damaged roof.
Be sure you choose the correct word!

let's review

After reading this chapter, you should understand:

- How to write an argument that asserts what you believe to be the main causes of the trend, event, or phenomenon and that supports that assertion with logical reasons and evidence.

- This type of argument can not only lead to a better understanding of the world around us, but also to specific remedies that allow for positive change. We must, after all, understand what is causing something before we can make effective changes.

- Some causal arguments are about a particular situation; others seek explanations for a general state of affairs. However, in either case there may be one or several causes.

- It can often be tricky to identify the cause-effect relationship between two events or issues. Just because one event follows another, does not necessarily mean that the first caused the second.

- Before you begin drafting your causal argument, you will want to spend a significant amount of time working through your ideas.

- Oftentimes, causal essays depend heavily on the presentation of research and statistical data. Visual representations such as charts and graphs can be very helpful in causal essays. Visuals help readers quickly and easily understand trends, statistics, and complex information about cause-effect relationships.

- Counterarguments play a very important role in the causal essay. They can help you eliminate alternate potential causes, which will help lead your reader to the conclusion that your cause is the most logical or acceptable.

connect

Read and study the following annotated argument. See if you can recognize the features of a causal argument as you read. Answer the questions that follow and discuss your analysis with your class.

A Specious "Experiment"

Eugene Robinson

A graduate of the University of Michigan where he was the first black student to be co-editor-in-chief of the university's student newspaper, Eugene Robinson joined The Washington Post *in 1980. He has served as city reporter, foreign correspondent, and managing editor in charge of the paper's style section. He is now an associate editor and twice-weekly columnist. Robinson focuses on the mix of culture and politics as the following column, published October 4, 2005, reveals. In this piece, Robinson attempts to discover why William Bennett, a talk-radio host, made inflammatory comments on the air.*

There's no need to pillory William Bennett for his "thought experiment" about how aborting all black children would affect the crime rate. I believe him when he says he wasn't actually advocating genocide, just musing about it to make a point. Instead of going into high-dudgeon mode, let's put him on the couch.

Attention-getting opening. How the author will deal with the issue.

Bennett, the former education secretary and anti-drug czar who has found a new calling in talk radio, told his audience last week that "if you wanted to reduce crime, you could—if that were your sole purpose—you could abort every black baby in this country, and your crime rate would go down." He quickly added that

Explanation of the situation—what Bennett did and how he defended his actions.

doing so would be "impossible, ridiculous and morally reprehensible," which is certainly true.

So why would such a horrible idea even cross his mind? How could such an evil notion ever pass his lips?

Bennett was referring to research done by Steven D. Levitt, a University of Chicago economist and lead author of the best-selling book *Freakonomics*. The iconoclastic Levitt, something of an academic rock star, argues that the steep drop in crime in the United States over the past 15 years resulted in part from the *Roe v. Wade* decision legalizing abortion. In defending his words, Bennett has said he was citing *Freakonomics*. So why did his "thought experiment" refer only to black children?

Possible cause for Bennett's "experiment" and Robinson's rejection of this cause.

Levitt's thesis is essentially that unwanted children who grow up poor in single-parent households are more likely than other children to become criminals, and that *Roe v. Wade* resulted in fewer of these children being born. What he doesn't do in the book is single out black children.

Perhaps the ostentatiously intellectual Bennett went back and read Levitt's original 2001 paper on the subject, co-authored with John J. Donohue III. The authors do mention race briefly, in a discussion of the falling homicide rate, but attribute most of the decline to those race-neutral factors that Levitt later cited in *Freakonomics*. To bolster their argument, they cite research on abortion and lowered crime rates in Scandinavia and Eastern Europe—not places where you're likely to find a lot of black people.

If he was citing Levitt's work, Bennett could have said that to lower the crime rate "you could abort every white baby" or "you could abort every Hispanic baby" or "you could abort every Asian baby," since every group has unwanted, poor children being raised by single mothers.

Another possible cause for Bennett's "experiment" and Robinson's rejection of this cause.

So now that we have Bennett on the couch, shouldn't we conclude that he mentioned only black children because, perhaps on a subconscious level, he associates "black" with "criminal"?

That's what it sounds like to me. I grew up in the South in the days when we had to drink at "colored" water fountains and gas stations had separate "colored" restrooms; I know what a real racist is like, and Bennett certainly doesn't fit the description. But that's what's so troubling about his race-specific "thought experiment"—that such a smart, well-meaning opinion maker would so casually say something that translates, to African American ears, as "blacks are criminals."

Robinson's assertion of the "true" cause of Bennett's "thought experiment."

What makes it worse is that his words came in the context of abortion. That Bennett staunchly opposes abortion is beside the point. He should know enough history to understand why black Americans would react strongly when whites start imagining experiments to limit black reproduction. For hundreds of years, this country was obsessed with the supposed menace of black sexuality and fertility. Bennett's remarks have to make you wonder whether that obsession has really vanished or just been deemed off-limits in polite discourse.

Historical cause for the reactions of Blacks to Bennett's remarks.

I've heard people argue—mostly in discussions of affirmative action—that the nation's problem of racial discrimination has mostly been solved. The issue now is class, they say, not race. I'd like to believe that, but I don't.

Bennett is too intelligent not to understand why many of us would take his mental experiment as a glimpse behind the curtain—an indication that old assumptions, now unspoken, still survive. He ought to understand how his words would be taken as validation by the rapper Kanye West, who told a television audience that "George Bush doesn't care about black people," or by the New Orleans survivors who keep calling me with theories of how "they" dynamited selected levees to flood the poor, black Lower Ninth Ward and save the wealthy French Quarter and Garden District.

I have a thought experiment of my own: If we put our racial baggage on the table and talk about it, we'll begin to take care of a lot of unfinished business.

QUESTIONS FOR REFLECTING AND WRITING

1. What is Robinson's claim? What does he assert about Bennett? About America?

2. How does the author support his claim? What Mill strategy does he use?

3. How would you describe the essay's tone? How does the tone help Robinson with readers?

4. Can you think of any other reasonable cause for Bennett's "thought experiment"?

5. Evaluate the argument's effectiveness. Does it ultimately work? Why or why not?

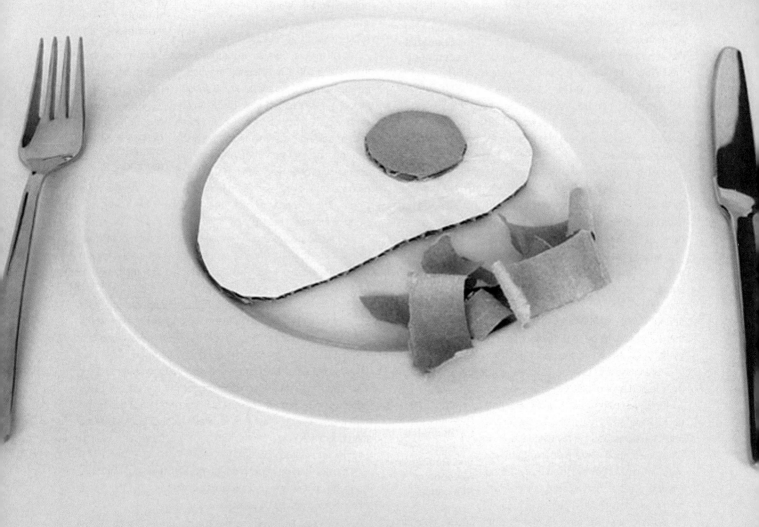

WITHOUT

writing the
problem/solution
essay

!

chapter 8

Problem/solution arguments are extremely common and can be seen throughout your daily life. Think about the last billboard you saw for a local charity, the last pamphlet you received in the mail regarding an election, or even the last television commercial you watched. It is almost certain that each of these mentioned some sort of problem or issue and offered a specific solution or remedy. In fact, most (if not all) advertisements and arguments about public policy can be understood as arguments that propose solutions to problems. This type of argument asks its readers to examine a current problem and accept the writer's solution (or solutions) as valid, feasible, and logical. It is very important, then, for the writer to clearly identify and explain the problem, state the proposed solution, and then to support the validity of that solution. Sometimes, the writer even encourages the reader to take specific action in order to implement the proposed solution. This type of argument hinges on a clear, workable, and feasible claim or thesis. For example, consider the following claim:

> Drunk drivers should receive mandatory two-year suspensions of their licenses.

This claim attempts to solve a specific problem—drunk driving. After all, fewer people will drink and drive (and potentially cause injury accidents) if they know they will lose their licenses. This statement also represents an ideal claim (or thesis) for a problem/solution argument.

Characteristics of Problem/ Solution Arguments

Problem/solution arguments are often easy to spot. They are typically straightforward in stating their claim and present clear suggestions for change. How-

Other examples of claims that attempt to solve problems include the following. See if you can identify the problem each is attempting to solve.

We need to spend whatever is necessary to stop the flow of drugs into this country.

The school year in the United States should be extended by at least thirty days.

All college textbooks should be made available online at half the cost of the printed versions.

All American citizens should be required to pass a citizenship test before they are permitted to vote in an election.

ever, even the most obvious arguments are carefully organized and contain elements of persuasion that readers may not immediately recognize. Consider the following strategies writers often use as they craft this type of argument.

- **Problem/solution arguments usually focus on the nature or definition of the problem, for the kind of problem has much to do with the kinds of solutions that are appropriate.** For example, some people are concerned about our ability to feed a growing world population. But many argue that the problem is not as much an agricultural one (how much food we can produce) as a political one (to whom will the food be distributed and at what cost). If the problem is agricultural, we need to worry about available farmland, water supply, and farming technology. If the problem is political, we need to worry about price supports,

SEEING THE ARGUMENT

Consider this box of Cheerios breakfast cereal and the problem/solution argument it presents. What is the problem it identifies? What is the solution? What is its claim (or thesis)? As you look at advertisements in magazines, on television, on billboards, and even on products themselves, begin to think about the problem/solution arguments they present and about the validity of the claims they assert.

This is an ad for a vegetarian restaurant. How does this ad define the problem it is offering a solution for? What might be the author's proposed solution?

distribution to poor countries, and grain embargoes imposed for political leverage. To support a solution claim, you will first need to define the problem for your readers.

- **How you define the problem also is related to what you think are the causes of the problem.** Cause is often a part of the debate and may need to be addressed, particularly if solutions are tied to eliminating what you consider to be the causes.

- **Successful problem/solution arguments present viable solutions to what can realistically be accomplished.** Consider Prohibition in the United States (1920–1933), for example. This was a solution to what many at the time perceived to be a huge social problem—alcohol abuse. This solution did not work and could not be enforced, however, because the majority of Americans would not accept the law as valid or fair.

- **Problem/solution arguments must be targeted to a specific and clearly defined audience.** Knowing your audience's expectations and preconceived notions plays a large role in determining what strategy you will use in your argument. Consider, for example, arguing for a smoking ban in order to solve the problem of illnesses related to secondhand smoke. Would your strategy change if you were presenting your solution to local bar owners as opposed to parents of small children in the community? Might you use different points of support? Different statistics or research? Knowing how your audience may react to your solution will help guide your argument.

This ad for Maredo's Steakhouse accurately identifies one of the causes of global warming. How is the proposed solution tied to the stated cause? Do you think this is an effective argument?

did you ? know

During Prohibition in the United States, illegal establishments called *speakeasies*, where patrons would order in soft voices in order to avoid suspicion, rapidly grew in popularity. Patrons typically brought their own alcohol in their coat pockets, purses, or even in their garters. The solution of completely outlawing alcohol in order to solve the problems associated with drinking was not plausible or workable. Be careful not to propose solutions to problems that will be unworkable or completely rejected by your audience. Can you think of a solution that may have been more workable than Prohibition? Why do you believe that your solution would be more viable?

Planning and Writing a Problem/ Solution Argument

As with any argument, having a clear plan is key. In addition to the guidelines for writing arguments presented in Chapter 3, use the following advice specific to problem/solution arguments as you think about and begin drafting your essay.

- **What should be the focus and limits of your argument?** There's a big difference between presenting solutions to the problem of physical abuse of women by men and presenting solutions to the problem of date rape on your college campus. Select a topic that you know something about and that you can realistically handle in your paper.

- **What reasons and evidence do you have to support your tentative claim?** Think through what you already know that has led you to select your particular topic. Suppose you decide to write on the issue of campus rapes. Is this choice due to a recent event on campus? Was this event the first in many years, or the latest in a trend? Where and when are they occurring? A brainstorming list may be helpful.

- **Is there additional evidence that you need to obtain to develop your argument?** If so, where can you look for this evidence? Does the library have past issues of the campus paper? Will the campus police grant you an interview?

- **What about the feasibility of each solution you plan to present?** Your readers will want to know that your solutions can be put into action. Are you thinking of one solution with several parts or several separate solutions, perhaps to be implemented by different people? Will coordination be necessary to achieve success? How will this be accomplished? For the problem of campus rape, you might want to consider several solutions as a package to be coordinated by the counseling service or an administrative vice president. Whatever solution or combination of solutions you present, make sure that they are doable and that your readers understand how they could be put into action.

Drafting

While there is no right or wrong organization for a problem/solution essay, you will want to make sure that you accomplish the following tasks as you write your argument:

- **Define the importance of the problem.** Begin by either reminding readers of an existing problem or arguing that a current situation should be recognized as a problem. Often, you can count on an audience who sees the world as you do and recognizes the problem you will address. But in some cases, your first task will be to convince readers that a problem exists that should worry them. If they are not concerned, they won't be interested in your solutions.

- **Define the problem.** Be sure, early in your essay, to define the problem—as you see it—for readers. Do not assume that they will necessarily accept your way of seeing the issue. You may need to defend your assessment of the nature of the problem before moving on to solutions.

- **Explain the causes of the problem (if appropriate).** If your proposed solution is tied to removing the cause or causes of the problem, then you need to

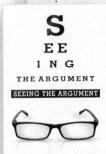
As you begin to look for a topic for your problem/solution essay, try surveying your local or state newspaper's website for current controversies in your area. You don't always have to take on large, global issues in order to have an impact. In fact, sometimes the most engaging and effective problem/solution arguments are about problems that are close to you. For example, look at the state newspaper site here. Do you see any potential issues or problems that you might attempt to solve? If so, what are some feasible and plausible solutions to these problems?

Reprinted by permission of The State News, Michigan State University. © Copyright 2009, The State News.

establish cause and prove it early in your argument. If cause is important, argue for it; if it is irrelevant, move to your solution.

- **Explain your solution.** If you have several solutions, think about how best to order them. If several need to be developed in a sequence, then present them in that sequence. If you are presenting a package of diverse actions that together will solve the problem, then consider presenting them from the simplest to the most complex.

- **Explain the process for achieving your solution.** If you have not thought through the political or legal steps necessary to implement your solution, then this step cannot be part of your purpose in writing. However, a skeptical audience is likely to ask, "How are we going to do that?" so you would be wise to have precise steps to offer. You might obtain an estimate of costs for new lighting on your campus and suggest specific paths that need the lights. You might investigate escort services at other colleges and spell out how such a service can be implemented on your campus.

Showing readers that you have thought about the next steps in the process and that you have answers to potential objections can be an effective method of persuasion.

- **Support the feasibility of your solution.** Be able to estimate costs. Show that you know who would be responsible for implementing the solution. Explain how your solution can be sold to people who may be unwilling to accommodate your proposals. All this information will strengthen your argument.

- **Show how your solution is better than others.** Anticipate challenges (or counterarguments) by including in your paper reasons for adopting your program rather than another program. Explain how your solution will be more easily adopted or more effective when implemented than other possibilities. Of course, a less practical but still viable defense is that your solution is the right thing to do. Whatever strategy you choose, be sure to acknowledge and address potential counterarguments your readers may have. Ignoring other solutions, especially those already publicly known, will hurt the credibility of your argument.

- **Use visuals to your advantage.** If you are attempting to demonstrate a serious problem and propose a solution, it might be useful to show the problem. If you are focusing on the problem of obesity in America, for example, think about including a chart or graph showing the rate of obesity or even a photograph that demonstrates the problem.

A Checklist for Revision

As you revise your essay, ask yourself the following questions:

- Do I have a clear statement of my policy claim? Is it appropriately qualified and focused?

- Have I clearly explained how the problem can be solved? If necessary, have I argued for seeing the problem that way?

- Have I presented my solutions—and argued for them—in a clear and logical structure? Have I explained how these solutions can be implemented and why they are better than other solutions that have been suggested?

- Have I used data that are relevant and current?

- Have I included visuals that are engaging and persuasive and that help support my claim?

- Have I used the basic checklist for revision in Chapter 3? (See page 62.)

Consider the following argument made by an editor of *The New York Times*. See if you can point to the elements of a problem/solution argument, including response to readers' possible counterarguments. Do you think this argument is ultimately successful? Why or why not?

The New York Times
Editorial
March 30, 2009
Reviewing Criminal Justice

America's criminal justice system needs repair. Prisons are overcrowded, sentencing policies are uneven and often unfair, ex-convicts are poorly integrated into society, and the growing problem of gang violence has not received the attention it deserves. For these and other reasons, a bill introduced last week by Senator Jim Webb, Democrat of Virginia, should be given high priority on the Congressional calendar.

The bill, which has strong bipartisan support, would establish a national commission to review the system from top to bottom. It is long overdue, and should be up and running as soon as possible.

The United States has the highest reported incarceration rate in the world. More than 1 in 100 adults are now behind bars, for the first time in history. The incarceration rate has been rising faster than the crime rate, driven by harsh sentencing policies like "three strikes and you're out," which impose long sentences that are often out of proportion to the seriousness of the offense.

Keeping people in prison who do not need to be there is not only unjust but also enormously expensive, which makes the problem a priority right now. Hard-pressed states and localities that reduce prison costs will have more money to help the unemployed, avert layoffs of teachers and police officers, and keep hospitals operating. In the last two decades, according to a Pew Charitable Trusts report, state corrections spending soared 127 percent, while spending on higher education increased only 21 percent.

Meanwhile, as governments waste money putting the wrong people behind bars, gang activity has been escalating, accounting for as much as 80 percent of the crime in some parts of the country.

The commission would be made up of recognized criminal justice experts, and charged with examining a range of policies that have emerged haphazardly across the country and recommending reforms. In addition to obvious problems like sentencing, the commission would bring much-needed scrutiny to issues like the special obstacles faced by the mentally ill in the system, as well as the shameful problem of prison violence.

Prison management and inmate treatment need special attention now that the Prison Litigation Reform Act has drastically scaled back prisoners' ability to vindicate their rights in court. Indeed, the commission should consider recommending that the law be modified or repealed.

Mr. Webb has enlisted the support of not only the Senate's top-ranking Democrats, including the majority leader, Harry Reid, but also influential Republicans like Arlen Specter, the ranking minority member on the Judiciary Committee, and Lindsey Graham, the ranking member of the crime and drugs subcommittee.

There is no companion bill in the House, and one needs to be written. Judging by the bipartisan support in the Senate, a national consensus has emerged that the criminal justice system is broken.

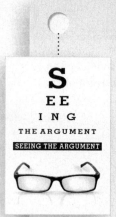
Consider the billboard here, which proposes a very clear solution to a problem. Some people might claim that the campaign in favor of abstinence in order to solve the problems of teen pregnancy and sexually transmitted disease is an oversimplified solution to a complicated problem and that it ignores many of the important issues that teens currently face. Do you agree? Why or why not?

Guidelines for Analyzing Problem/Solution Arguments

When analyzing problem/solution arguments, what should you look for? In addition to the basics of good argument, use the following points as guides to analyzing:

- **Is the writer's claim not only clear but also appropriately qualified and focused?** For example, if the school board in the writer's community is not doing a good job of communicating its goals for its funding proposal, the writer needs to focus on that particular school board, not on school boards in general.

- **Does the writer show an awareness of the complexity of most public policy issues?** There are many different kinds of problems with American schools and many more causes for those problems. A simple solution—a longer school year,

more money spent, vouchers—is not likely to solve the mixed bag of problems. Oversimplified arguments quickly lose credibility.

- **How does the writer define and explain the problem?** Is the problem stated clearly? Does it make sense to you? If the problem is defined differently than most people define it, has the writer argued convincingly for looking at the problem in this new way?

- **What reasons and evidence are given to support the writer's solutions?** Can you see how the writer develops the argument? Does the reasoning seem logical? Is the data relevant? This kind of analysis will help you evaluate the proposed solutions.

- **Does the writer address the feasibility of the proposed solutions?** Does the writer make a convincing case for the realistic possibility of achieving the proposed solutions?

- **Is the argument convincing?** Will the solutions solve the problem as it has been defined? Has the problem been defined accurately? Can the solutions be achieved?

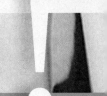

let's review

After reading this chapter, you should understand:

- Problem/solution arguments are extremely common and can be seen throughout daily life. This type of argument asks readers to examine a current problem and accept the writer's solution (or solutions) as valid, feasible, and logical.

- Problem/solution arguments usually focus on the nature or definition of the problem, for how we define a problem has much to do with the kinds of solutions that are appropriate.

- Successful problem/solution arguments present viable solutions, solutions that can realistically be accomplished.

- Problem/solution arguments must be targeted to a specific and clearly defined audience. Knowing your audience's expectations and preconceived notions will help you determine what strategy to use in your argument.

- While there is no right or wrong organization for a problem/solution essay, you should accomplish the following tasks as you write your argument:

  - Define the problem and its importance.
  - Explain the causes of the problem.
  - Explain your solutions fully.
  - Explain the process for achieving your solution.
  - Support the feasibility of your solution.
  - Show how your solution is better than others.
  - Use visuals to your advantage.

connect

Read and study the annotated argument below. Then analyze and respond to the essay by answering the questions that follow.

It's Time to Legalize Drugs

Peter Moskos and Stanford "Neill" Franklin

Monday, August 17, 2009

Undercover Baltimore police officer Dante Arthur was doing what he does well, arresting drug dealers, when he approached a group in January. What he didn't know was that one of the suspects knew from a previous arrest that Arthur was police. Arthur was shot twice in the face. In the gunfight that ensued, Arthur's partner returned fire and shot one of the suspects, three of whom were later arrested.

In many ways, Dante Arthur was lucky. He lived. Nationwide, a police officer dies on duty nearly every other day. Too

Moskos and Franklin help make the problem concrete and vivid for the reader by telling a story to illustrate its effects.

often a flag-draped casket is followed by miles of flashing red and blue lights. Even more officers are shot and wounded, too many fighting the war on drugs. The prohibition on drugs leads to unregulated, and often violent, public drug dealing. Perhaps counterintuitively, better police training and bigger guns are not the answer.

When it makes sense to deal drugs in public, a neighborhood becomes home to drug violence. For a low-level drug dealer, working the street means more money and fewer economic risks. If police come, and they will, some young kid

The authors suggest current measures to address the problem are inadequate.

will be left holding the bag while the dealer walks around the block. But if the dealer sells inside, one raid, by either police or robbers, can put him out of business for good. Only those virtually immune from arrests (much less imprisonment)—college students, the wealthy and those who never buy or sell from strangers—can deal indoors.

Six years ago one of us wrote a column on this page, "Victims of the War on Drugs." It discussed violence, poor community relations, overly aggressive policing and riots. It failed to mention one important harm: the drug war's clear and present danger toward men and women in blue.

Drug users generally aren't violent. Most simply want to be left alone to enjoy their high. It's the corner slinger who terrifies neighbors and invites rivals to attack. Public drug dealing creates an environment where disputes about money or respect are settled with guns.

> **The authors continue to detail the extent of the problem.**

In high-crime areas, police spend much of their time answering drug-related calls for service, clearing dealers off corners, responding to shootings and homicides, and making lots of drug-related arrests.

One of us (Franklin) was the commanding officer at the police academy when Arthur (as well as Moskos) graduated. We all learned similar lessons. Police officers are taught about the evils of the drug trade and given the knowledge and tools to inflict as much damage as possible upon the people who constitute the drug community. Policymakers tell us to fight this unwinnable war.

Only after years of witnessing the ineffectiveness of drug policies—and the disproportionate impact the drug war has on young black men—have we and other police officers begun to question the system.

Cities and states license beer and tobacco sellers to control where, when and to whom drugs are sold. Ending Prohibition saved lives because it took gangsters out of the game. Regulated alcohol doesn't work perfectly, but it works well enough. Prescription drugs are regulated, and while there is a huge problem with abuse, at least a system of distribution involving doctors and pharmacists works without violence and high-volume incarceration. Regulating drugs would work similarly: not a cure-all, but a vast improvement on the status quo.

Legalization would not create a drug free-for-all. In fact, regulation reins in the mess we already have. If prohibition decreased drug use and drug arrests acted as a deterrent, America would not lead the world in illegal drug use and incarceration for drug crimes.

Drug manufacturing and distribution is too dangerous to remain in the hands of unregulated criminals. Drug distribution needs to be the combined responsibility of doctors, the government, and a legal and regulated free market. This simple step would quickly eliminate the greatest threat of violence: street-corner drug dealing.

> **The authors argue that regulating alcohol has worked reasonably well to show that regulating drugs should also work reasonably well.**

> **Moskos and Franklin offer rebuttal to a possible counter-argument to their position.**

We simply urge the federal government to retreat. Let cities and states (and, while we're at it, other countries) decide their own drug policies. Many would continue prohibition, but some would try something new. California and its medical marijuana dispensaries provide a good working example, warts and all, that legalized drug distribution does not cause the sky to fall.

> **The authors cite a major advantage to their proposed solution.**

Having fought the war on drugs, we know that ending the drug war is the right thing to do—for all of us, especially taxpayers. While the financial benefits of drug legalization are not our main concern, they are substantial. In a July referendum, Oakland, Calif., voted to tax drug sales by a 4-to-1 margin. Harvard economist Jeffrey Miron estimates that ending the drug war would save $44 billion annually, with taxes bringing in an additional $33 billion.

Without the drug war, America's most decimated neighborhoods would have a chance to recover. Working people could sit on stoops, misguided youths wouldn't look up to criminals as role models, our overflowing prisons could hold real criminals, and—most important to us—more police officers wouldn't have to die.

QUESTIONS FOR REFLECTING AND WRITING

1. According to Moskos and Franklin, what is the major negative consequence of current attempts to wage the war on drugs?

2. What comparisons do the authors make to support the argument that drugs should be legalized?

3. Why do Moskos and Franklin say that "legalization would not create a drug free-for-all"? What are the authors attempting to do by making such a statement?

4. Why might legalizing drugs not represent a wise policy-making decision? Do you think the authors effectively address their opposition? Why or why not?

5. What gives these authors possibly a greater degree of credibility than someone else making the same argument?

6. Have Moskos and Franklin convinced you that drugs should be legalized? Why or why not?

writing a rhetorical analysis

chapter 9

What Is a Rhetorical Analysis?

In a rhetorical analysis, you do not merely summarize a text; you use your critical thinking skills to take apart a text. In other words, you focus on the way the writer chooses to compose the text rather than on the meaning he or she tries to convey.

By now, you know that writers adopt different strategies to achieve their goals. A rhetorical analysis, at least in part, seeks to uncover those strategies so that one can better understand the meaning and purpose of a text. To write a rhetorical analysis, you must analyze style and tone, but only after establishing the context for the piece. Context helps you understand content as well as a writer's stylistic choices.

Examining the Context of an Argument

A rhetorical analysis requires a process of critical reading, and reading critically requires preparation. Before analyzing the content and stylistic choices of the author, you must be able to answer the following four questions after your first read of the text.

Who Is the Author?

Key questions about the author include the following:

- **Does the author have a reputation for honesty, thoroughness, and fairness?** Read the biographical note, if there is one. Ask your instructor about the author. Learn about the author in a biographical dictionary or online. Try *Book Review Digest* (in your library or online) for reviews of the author's books.

- **Is the author writing within his or her area of expertise?** People can voice opinions on any subject, but they cannot transfer expertise from one subject area to another. A football player endorsing a political candidate is a citizen with an opinion, not an expert on politics.

- **Is the author identified with a particular group or set of beliefs?** Does the biography place the writer in a particular institution or organization? For example, a member of a Republican administration may be expected to favor a Republican president's policies. A Roman Catholic priest may be expected to take a stand against abortion. These kinds of details provide hints, but you should not assume what a writer's position is until you have

read the work with care. Be alert to reasonable expectations, but avoid stereotyping a writer.

Who Is the Audience?

Knowing the intended audience can give you a clue about the work's depth and sophistication and a possible bias or slant.

- **Does the writer expect a popular audience, a general but educated audience, or a specialized audience that shares professional expertise or cultural, political, or religious preferences?** Often you can judge the expected audience by noting the kind of publication in which an article appears or the publisher of the book. For example, *Reader's Digest* is written for a mass audience; *Psychology Today, Science,* and *Newsweek* aim for a general but more knowledgeable reader. By contrast, articles in the *New England Journal of Medicine* are written by medical doctors and research scientists for a specialized audience.

- **Does the writer expect readers who are likely to agree with the writer's views?** Some newspapers, magazines, and websites are usually liberal, whereas others are usually politically conservative. (Do you know the political leanings of your

Do you think this author is demonstrating bias? Why or why not? Will the intended audience accept this argument as credible or might the author risk losing credibility with his readers?

Exercises: Examining the Context

1. What can you judge about the reliability or bias of the following?

   Consider author, audience, and purpose.

   a. An article on the Republican administration written by a former campaign worker for the Democratic presidential candidate.

   b. A discussion, published in *The Boston Globe*, of the Patriots' hope for the next Super Bowl.

   c. A letter to the editor about conservation written by a member of the Sierra Club. (What is the Sierra Club? Study some of its publications or check out its website to respond to this topic.)

   d. A column in *Newsweek* on economics. (Look at the business section of *Newsweek*. Your library has the magazine.)

   e. A 1948 article in *Nutrition Today* on the best diets.

   f. A biography of Benjamin Franklin published by Oxford University Press.

   g. A *Family Circle* article about a special vegetarian diet written by a doctor. (Who is the audience for this magazine? Where is it sold?)

   h. A pamphlet by Jerry Lewis urging you to contribute to a fund to combat muscular dystrophy.

   i. A discussion of abortion in *Ms.* magazine.

   j. An editorial in your local newspaper titled "Stop the Highway Killing."

2. Analyze an issue of your favorite magazine. Look first at the editorial pages and articles written by the staff, then at articles contributed by other writers. Answer these questions:

   a. Who is the audience of both staff writers and contributors?

   b. What is the purpose of each of the articles and of the entire magazine?

   c. What type of article dominates the issue?

   d. Describe the style and tone of the articles. How appropriate are the style and tone?

3. Select one environmental website and study what it offers. The EnviroLink Network (www.envirolink.org) will lead you to many sites. Another possibility is the Nature Conservancy (www.tnc.org). Write down the name of the site you chose and its uniform resource locator (URL). Then answer these questions:

   a. Who is the intended audience?

   b. What seems to be the primary purpose or goal of the site?

   c. What type of material seems to dominate the site?

   d. For what kinds of writing assignments might you use material from the site?

Slanted? biased

local paper?) The particular interests of the *Christian Science Monitor* or *Ms.*, for example, should be considered when you read articles from them. Remember that all arguments are slanted or biased—that is, they take a stand. That's OK. You just need to read with an awareness of a writer's particular background and interests.

What Is the Author's Purpose?

Is the piece informative or persuasive in intent? Designed to entertain or to be inspiring? Think about the title; read a book's preface to learn of the author's goals; pay attention to tone as you read.

What Are the Writer's Sources of Information?

Some questions to ask about sources include these: Where was the information obtained? Is it still valid?

Are sources clearly identified? Be suspicious of writers who want us to believe that their unnamed "sources" are reliable. Pay close attention to dates. A biography of King George III published in 1940 may still be the best source; however, an article published in the 1980s urging the curtailing of county growth is no longer reliable.

Understanding an Author's Attitude and Tone

In a rhetorical analysis, you look for the implications of the text while being sensitive to tone and nuance. When you read, think about not just *what* is said but *how* it is said. Awareness of the author's attitude will be helpful as you attempt to analyze his or her overall approach and style. Consider the following excerpt:

What happened to the War on Drugs? Did Bush— the old man, not the son—think that we actually *won* that war? Or did he confuse the War on Drugs with the stupid Gulf War he's so proud of winning? Well, he never did understand "the vision thing."

First, we recognize that the writer's subject is the War on Drugs, an expression that refers to government programs to reduce drug use. Second, we understand that the writer does not believe that the war has been won; rather, we still have a drug problem that we need to address. We know this from the second sentence, the rhetorical question that suggests that Bush thought the drug problem had been solved, but the writer—like us—knows better.

What else do you observe in this passage? What is the writer's attitude toward George Bush? Note the writer's language. The former president is "the old man." He is proud of winning a "stupid" war. He, by implication, is stupid to think that he helped win the War on Drugs. And, finally, we are reminded of Bush's own words that he did not have a vision of what he wanted to do as president.

How would you rewrite the passage to make it more favorable to Bush? Here is one version that students wrote to give the passage a positive attitude toward Bush:

What has happened to the War on Drugs? Did some members of President George Bush's administration think that government policies had been successful in reducing drug use? Or did the administration change its focus to concentrate on winning the Gulf War? Perhaps, in retrospect, President Bush should have put more emphasis on the war against drugs.

The writers have not changed the assertion that the War on Drugs has not been won—yet they have greatly altered our outlook on the subject. This version suggests that the failure to win the drug war was the fault of Bush's administration, not of Bush himself, and that perhaps the failure is understandable given the need to focus attention on the Gulf War. In addition, references to the former president treat him with dignity. What is the difference in the two passages? Only the word choice.

Denotative and Connotative Word Choice

The students' ability to rewrite the passage on the War on Drugs to give it a positive slant tells us that, although some words may have similar meanings, they cannot always be substituted for one another without changing the message. Words with similar meanings have similar denotations. Often, though, words with similar denotations do not have the same connotations. A word's *connotation* is what the word suggests, what we associate the word with. The words *house and home,* for example, both refer to a building in which people live, but the word *home* suggests ideas—and feelings—of family and security. Thus the word *home* has a strong positive connotation. *House* by contrast brings to mind only a picture of a physical structure because the word does not carry any emotional baggage.

We learn the connotations of words the same way we learn their denotations—in context. Most of us living in the same culture share the same connotative associations of words. At times, the context in which a word is used will affect the word's connotation. For example, the word *buddy* usually has positive connotations. We may think of an old or trusted friend. But when an unfriendly person who thinks a man may have pushed in front of him says, "Better watch it, *buddy,*" the word has a negative connotation. Social, physical, and language contexts control the connotative significance of words. Become more alert to the connotative power of words by asking what words the writers could have used instead.

Recognizing Tone

Closely related to a writer's attitude is the writer's tone. We can describe a writer's attitude toward the subject as positive, negative, or (rarely) neutral. *Attitude* is the writer's position on, or feelings about, his or her subject. The way that attitude is expressed—the voice we hear and the feelings conveyed through that voice—is the writer's *tone.* Writers can choose to express attitude through a wide variety of tones. We may reinforce a negative attitude through an angry, somber, sad, mocking, peevish, sarcastic, or scornful tone. A positive attitude may be revealed through an enthusiastic, serious, sympathetic, jovial, light, or admiring tone.

Exercises: Connotation

1. For each of the following words or phrases, list at least two synonyms that have a more negative connotation than the given word:

   a. child
   b. persistent
   c. thin
   d. a large group
   e. scholarly
   f. trusting
   g. underachiever
   h. quiet

2. For each of the following words, list at least two synonyms that have a more positive connotation than the given word:

   a. notorious
   b. fat
   c. politician
   d. old (people)
   e. fanatic
   f. reckless
   g. sot
   h. cheap

3. Select one of the words listed below and explain, in a paragraph, what the word connotes to you personally. Be precise; illustrate your thoughts with details and examples.

   a. nature
   b. mother
   c. romantic
   d. nerd
   e. playboy
   f. artist

4. Read the following paragraph and decide how the writer feels about the activity described. Note the choice of details and the connotative language that make you aware of the writer's attitude.

> Needing to complete a missed assignment for my physical education class, I dragged myself down to the tennis courts on a gloomy afternoon. My task was to serve five balls in a row into the service box. Although I thought I had learned the correct service movements, I couldn't seem to translate that knowledge into a decent serve. I tossed up the first ball, jerked back my racket, swung up on the ball—clunk—I hit the ball on the frame. I threw up the second ball, brought back my racket, swung up on the ball—ping—I made contact with the strings, but the ball dribbled down on my side of the net. I trudged around the court, collecting my tennis balls; I had only two of them.

5. Write a paragraph describing an activity that you liked or disliked without saying how you felt. From your choice of details and use of connotative language, convey your attitude toward the activity. (The paragraph in Exercise 3 is your model.)

collaborative exercises

On Connotation

1. List all of the words you know for *human female* and for *human male*. Then classify them by connotation (positive, negative, neutral) and by level of usage (formal, informal, slang). Is there any connection between type of connotation and level of usage? Why are some words more appropriate in some social contexts than in others? Can you easily list more negative words used for one sex than for the other? Why?

2. Some words can be given a different connotation in different contexts. First, for each of the following words, label its connotation as positive, negative, or neutral. Then, for each word with a positive connotation, write a sentence in which the word would convey a more negative connotation. For each word with a negative connotation, write a sentence in which the word would suggest a more positive connotation.

   a. natural
   b. old
   c. committed
   d. free
   e. chemical
   f. lazy

3. Each of the following groups of words might appear together in a thesaurus, but the words actually vary in connotation. After looking up any words whose connotation you are unsure of, use one word in each group correctly in a sentence. Briefly explain why the other two words in the group would not work in that sentence.

   a. brittle, hard, fragile
   b. quiet, withdrawn, glum
   c. shrewd, clever, cunning
   d. strange, remarkable, bizarre
   e. thrifty, miserly, economical

did you know

One-third of 500,000 = 22? There are almost half a million words in our English language—the largest language on earth, incidentally—but a third of all our writing is made up of only twenty-two words.

www.readfaster.com/education_stats.asp#readingstatistics

We cannot be sure, however, that when a writer selects a light tone, the attitude must be positive. Humor columnists such as Dave Barry often choose a light tone to examine serious social and political issues. When we consider the subject, we recognize that the light and amusing tone actually conveys a negative attitude.

Analyzing an Author's Tone

We have begun the process of understanding attitude by becoming more aware of context and connotation and more alert to tone. Tone is created and attitude conveyed primarily through word choice and sentence structure but also through several other techniques. Sensitivity to such techniques becomes important when writing a rhetorical analysis.

Analyzing for Tone: Word Choice

In addition to responding to a writer's choice of connotative language, observe the *level of diction* used. Are the writer's words typical of conversational language or of a more formal style? Does the writer use slang words or technical words? Is the word choice concrete and vivid or abstract and intellectual? These differences help to shape tone and affect our response to what we read. A politician's word choice may be formal and abstract, using terms such as *commitment, sustainability,* and *economic recovery.* Another style, the technical, will be found in some articles in this text. The social scientist may write that "the child . . . is subjected to extremely punitive discipline," whereas a nonspecialist might write,

GOOD ADV!CE

In academic and professional writing, you should most often aim for a style informal enough to be inviting to readers but one that, in most cases, avoids contractions, the word *you,* and slang words. As with all writing tasks, the audience and purpose will dictate what is most appropriate and effective. Rules can be broken if you understand why you are breaking them!

more informally, that "the child is given beatings or other forms of punishment."

One way to create an informal style is to choose simple words: *given* instead of *subjected to.* To create greater informality, a writer can use contractions: *we'll* for *we will.*

Analyzing for Tone: Sentence Structure

The eighteenth-century satirist Jonathan Swift once said that writing well was a simple matter of putting "proper words in proper places." Writers need to think not just about the words they choose but also about their arrangement into sentence patterns. Studying a writer's sentence patterns will reveal how they affect style and tone. When analyzing these features, consider the following questions:

1. **Are the sentences generally long, or short, or varied in length?**

   Are the structures primarily

   • *Simple* (one independent clause)

   In 1900 empires dotted the world.

   • *Compound* (two or more independent clauses)

   Women make up only 37 percent of television characters, yet women make up more than half of the population.

   • *Complex* (at least one independent and one dependent clause)

   As nations grew wealthier, traditional freedom wasn't enough.

   Sentences that are both long and complex create a more formal style. Long

Jonathan Swift is most remembered for works such as *Gulliver's Travels,* "A Modest Proposal," and "An Argument against Abolishing Christianity."

compound sentences joined by *and* do not increase formality much because such sentences are really only two or more short, simple patterns hooked together. On the other hand, a long "simple" sentence with many modifiers will create a more formal style. The following example, from an essay on leadership by Michael Korda, is more complicated than the sample compound sentence above.

- *Expanded simple sentence:*

  [A] leader is like a mirror, reflecting back to us our own sense of purpose, putting into words our own dreams and hopes, transforming our needs and fears into coherent policies and programs.

Although many instructors struggle to rid student writing of fragments, professional writers know that the occasional fragment can be used effectively for emphasis. Science fiction writer Bruce Sterling, thinking about the "melancholic beauty" of a gadget no longer serving any purpose, writes:

Like Duchamp's bottle-rack, it becomes a found objet d'art. A metallic fossil of some lost human desire. A kind of involuntary poem.

The second and third sentences are, technically, fragments, but because they build on the structure of the first sentence, readers can add the missing words *It becomes* to complete each sentence. The brevity, repetition of structure, and involvement of the reader to "complete" the fragments all contribute to a strong conclusion to Sterling's paragraph.

2. **Does the writer seem to be using an overly simplistic style? If so, why?**
   Overly simplistic sentence patterns, just like overly simplistic words, can be used to show that the writer thinks the subject is silly or childish or insulting. In one of her columns, Ellen Goodman objects to society's oversimplifying of addictions and its need to believe in quick and lasting cures. She makes her point with reference to two well-known examples—but notice her technique:

   Hi, my name is Jane and I was once bulimic but now I am an exercise guru.

   Hi, my name is Oprah and I was a food addict but now I am a size 10.

   She uses a simplistic sentence style purposefully in order to make her point and her attitude clear for her reader.

3. **Does the writer use parallelism (coordination) or antithesis (contrast)?**

   When two phrases or clauses are parallel in structure, the message is that they are equally important. Look back at Korda's expanded simple sentence. He coordinates three phrases, asserting that a leader does these three things:

- reflects back our purpose
- puts into words our dreams
- transforms our needs and fears

Antithesis creates tension. A sentence using this structure says "not this" but "that." Abraham Lincoln, in the Gettysburg Address, uses both parallelism and antithesis in one striking sentence:

The world will little note nor long remember what we say here, but it [the world] can never forget what they did here.

Analyzing for Tone: Metaphors

When Korda writes that a leader is like a mirror, he is using a *simile*. When Lincoln writes that the world will not remember, he is using a *metaphor*—actually *personification*. Metaphors, whatever their form, make a comparison between two items that are not otherwise alike. The writer is making a figurative comparison, not a literal one. The writer wants us to think about some ways in which the items are similar. Metaphors state directly or imply the comparison; similes express the comparison using a connecting word; personification always compares a nonhuman item to humans. The exact label for a metaphor is not as important as

- recognizing the use of a figure of speech,
- identifying the two items being compared,

try it!

Exercise: Opening Up Metaphors

During World War II, E. B. White, the essayist and writer of children's books, defined the word *democracy* in one of his *New Yorker* columns. His definition contains a series of metaphors. Here is one in the series:

> [Democracy] is the hole in the stuffed shirt through which the sawdust slowly trickles.

We can open up or explain the metaphor this way: Just as one can punch a hole in a scarecrow's shirt and discover that there is only sawdust inside, nothing to be impressed by, so the idea of equality in a democracy punches a hole in the notion of an aristocratic ruling class and reveals that aristocrats are ordinary people, just like you and me.

Here are two more of White's metaphors on democracy. Open up each one in a few sentences.

> [Democracy is] the dent in the high hat.

> [Democracy is] the score at the beginning of the ninth.

- understanding the point of the comparison, and
- grasping the emotional impact of the figurative comparison.

Analyzing for Tone: Organization and Examples

Two other elements of writing, organization and choice of examples, also reveal attitude and help to shape the reader's response. When you study a work's organization, ask yourself questions about both placement and volume. Where are these ideas placed? At the beginning or end—the places of greatest emphasis—or in the middle, suggesting that they are less important? With regard to volume, ask yourself, What parts of the discussion are developed at length? What points are treated only briefly?

Analyzing for Tone: Repetition

Well-written, unified essays will contain some repetition of keywords and phrases. Some writers go beyond this basic strategy and use repetition to produce an effective cadence, like a drum beating in the background, keeping time to the speaker's fist pounding the lectern. In his repetition of the now-famous phrase "I have a dream," Martin Luther King, Jr., gives emphasis to his vision of an ideal America. (Visit www.youtube.com and use the search term "I have a dream" in order to watch this historic speech.)

In the following paragraph, a student tried her hand at repetition to give emphasis to her definition of liberty:

> Liberty is having the right to vote and not having other laws which restrict that right; it is having the right to apply to the university of your choice without being rejected because of race. Liberty exists when a gay man has the right to a teaching position and is not released from the position when the news of his orientation is disclosed. Liberty exists when a woman who has been offered a job does not have to decline for lack of access to day care for her children, or when a 16-year-old boy from a ghetto can get an education and is not instead compelled to go to work to support his needy family.

These examples suggest that repetition generally gives weight and seriousness to writing and thus is appropriate when serious issues are being discussed in a forceful style.

Analyzing for Tone: Hyperbole, Understatement, and Irony

Grace Lichtenstein chose *Playing for Money* as the title of her book on college sports. Now, college athletes do play, but presumably not for money. The title emphasizes that these games are serious business, not play, for the athletes, coaches, and colleges. The bringing together of words that do not usually go together—*play* and *money*—ironically underscores the problems in college athletics that Lichtenstein examines.

Hyperbole and understatement, on the other hand, represent two sides of the same coin. Hyperbole, or overstatement, makes a point through exaggerated statements or visual depictions for emphasis. Cartoons, for example, make use of hyperbole all the time, as the example on page 147 illustrates.

Sometimes, though, an argument can reflect understatement. In using understatement, a writer is making a situation or issue seem less serious to actually communicate its importance. Someone arguing for Bill Clinton's effectiveness as a president could say, for instance, "President Clinton only accomplished the small feat of balancing the budget."

Analyzing for Tone: Visuals

Several visual techniques can be used within text to give special attention to certain words or ideas and ultimately help create the author's tone:

- A writer can place a word or phrase in quotation marks and thereby question its validity or meaning in that context. Ellen Goodman writes, for example:

> What then makes a family, in the face of all this "freedom"?

Visual elements can also create irony in a text. Consider how this picture might communicate the same point that Grace Lichtenstein is making in her book *Playing for Money*. As you examine arguments around you, think about how visual elements play a role in communicating the author's tone.

Goodman suggests that *freedom* associated with the idea of family is paradoxical, and we know this immediately from her use of quotation marks.

- Italicizing a keyword or phrase also gives added emphasis.

Ellen Goodman, in her essay on page 35 in Chapter 2, uses italics for emphasis:

But what is it that makes this collection of people a family? How do we make a family these days? With blood? With marriage? With affection? I wonder about this when I hear the word *family* added to some politician's speech like gravy poured over the entire plate.

- Capitalizing words not normally capitalized has the same effect of giving emphasis. As with exclamation points, writers need to use italics or capitalization sparingly; otherwise, the emphasis sought through contrast will be lost.

We will discuss visual arguments in much greater detail in Chapter 10.

Italicizing
Capitalizing

SLOWPOKE

©Jen Sorensen

"Scenes from the Hyperbole Convention" © Jen Soreson. www.slowpokecomics.com

Along with these textual techniques, visual elements in the work can also add to the author's style. Pictures, boxes, headings, color choices, fonts, and even the layout of the piece are all important elements of tone. Consider, for example, the following visual argument:

What can you determine about the author's attitude toward the product by looking at the visual elements of the ad? Notice the colors, the positioning of the images, and the special effects that are utilized. Remember to look at how visuals affect your own emotional reaction to an argument and how they can give you clues about the author's intended tone.

try it!

1. Name the techniques used in each of the following passages. Then briefly explain the idea of each passage.

   a. We are becoming the tools of our tools. (Henry David Thoreau)

   b. The bias and therefore the business of television is to *move* information, not collect it. (Neil Postman)

   c. If guns are outlawed, only the government will have guns. Only the police, the secret police, the military. The hired servants of our rulers. Only the government—and a few outlaws. (Edward Abbey)

   d. Having read all the advice on how to live 900 years, what I think is that eating a tasty meal once again will surely doom me long before I reach 900 while not eating that same meal could very well kill me. It's enough to make you reach for a cigarette! (Russell Baker)

   e. If you are desperate for a quick fix, either legalize drugs or repress the user. If you want a civi-

   lized approach, mount a propaganda campaign against drugs. (Charles Krauthammer)

   f. Oddly enough, the greatest scoffers at the traditions of American etiquette, who scorn the rituals of their own society as stupid and stultifying, voice respect for the customs and folklore of Native Americans, less industrialized people, and other societies they find more "authentic" than their own. (Judith Martin)

   g. Text is story. Text is event, performance, special effect. Subtext is ideas. It's motive, suggestions, visual implications, subtle comparisons. (Stephen Hunter)

   h. This flashy vehicle [the school bus] was as punctual as death: seeing us waiting at the cold curb, it would sweep to a halt, open its mouth, suck the boy in, and spring away with an angry growl. (E. B. White)

Analyzing for Persuasive Appeals

In writing a rhetorical analysis, you might also choose to focus on an author's use of persuasive appeals, which you read about in Chapter 1. We can often point to how a writer has engaged his or her audience through the use of logos, pathos, and ethos.

Analyzing for Persuasive Appeals: Logos

Consider the use of logos in this persuasive appeal.

> Let us begin with a simple proposition: What democracy requires is public debate, not information. Of course it needs information too, but the kind of information it needs can be generated only by vigorous popular debate. We do not know what we need to know until we ask the right questions, and we can identify the right questions only by subjecting our ideas about the world to the test of public controversy. Information, usually seen as the precondition of debate, is better understood as its by-product. When we get into arguments that focus and fully engage our attention, we become avid seekers of relevant information. Otherwise, we take in information passively—if we take it in at all.
>
> Christopher Lasch, "The Lost Art of Political Argument"

This passage reflects Lasch's use of logical reasoning in making the claim "What democracy requires is public debate, not information." He then supports that claim with at least two major premises. His first premise basically asserts that members of a democratic society can only obtain information *after* public debate. In other words, public debate becomes a prerequisite for generating information. Lasch says that information only represents a by-product of public debate. His second premise in support of his claim is that a democratic society must "become avid seekers of relevant information" while subtly implying, in the last sentence of this passage, that taking in information passively only weakens democracy. By explaining the structure of Lasch's argument in this way, a writer can reveal how the author effectively uses the logos appeal.

Analyzing for Persuasive Appeals: Ethos

The following text offers an example of the ethos appeal.

> My Dear Fellow Clergymen:
>
> While confined here in Birmingham city jail, I came across your recent statement calling my present activities "unwise and untimely." . . . Since I feel that you are men of genuine good will and that your criticisms are sincerely set forth, I want to try to answer your statement in what I hope will be patient and reasonable in terms.
>
> I think I should indicate why I am here in Birmingham, since you have been influenced by the view which argues against "outsiders coming in." . . . I, along with several members of my staff, am here because I was invited here. I am here because I have organizational ties here.
>
> But more basically, I am in Birmingham because injustice is here. Just as the prophets of the eighth century B.C. left their villages and carried their "thus saith the Lord" far beyond the boundaries of their home towns, and just as the Apostle Paul left his village of Tarsus and carried the gospel of Jesus Christ to the far corners of the Greco-Roman world, so am I compelled to carry the gospel of freedom beyond my own home town. Like Paul, I must constantly respond to the Macedonian call for aid.
>
> Martin Luther King, Jr., "Letter from Birmingham Jail"

As Chapter 1 explains, the audience needs to see the arguer as a person of knowledge, honesty, and goodwill; in other words, they need to perceive he or she possesses credibility. Martin Luther King, Jr. establishes ethos in several ways. First, he acknowledges the sincerity of the clergy's criticisms in his opening remarks. Thus, he shows his audience that he has taken their positions into account. Second, in responding to allegations of his visit to Birmingham as "unwise and untimely," King notes that he and his staff visited there only upon invitation. Therefore, he suggests that his coming to Birmingham stemmed from a trust some members of the community had in his ability to aid them in their struggle. Finally, the last paragraph of the passage likens his carrying "the gospel of freedom" to Paul carrying "the gospel of Jesus Christ to the far corners of the Greco-Roman world." Given that King's audience represented members of the clergy, his comparison of his mission to Paul's mission would likely garner some favor and make him appear more credible in their eyes.

Analyzing for Persuasive Appeals: Pathos

This next text shows how a writer uses pathos to persuade his readers.

> For me, commentary on war zones at home and abroad begins and ends with personal reflections. A few years ago, while watching the news in Chicago, a local news story made a personal connection with me. The report concerned a teenager who had been shot because he had angered a group of his male peers. This act of violence caused me to recapture a memory from my own adolescence because of an instructive parallel in my own life with this boy who had been shot. When I was a teenager some thirty-five years ago in the New York metropolitan area, I wrote a regular column for my high school newspaper. One

week, I wrote a column in which I made fun of the fraternities in my high school. As a result, I elicited the anger of some of the most aggressive teenagers in my high school. A couple of nights later, a car pulled up in front of my house, and the angry teenagers in the car dumped garbage on the lawn of my house as an act of revenge and intimidation.

James Garbarino, "Children in a Violent World: A Metaphysical Perspective"

Garbarino shows empathy with the teenager who was shot in Chicago. His story relates a personal experience of victimization, and how he understands, at least to some degree, the teenager's suffering. In telling this story, Garbarino appeals to his audience's emotions, anticipating that they, too, will likely share similar feelings toward the teenager. His use of emotional appeal also works to persuade the audience of the seriousness of violent acts toward children.

Some Final Thoughts on Writing a Rhetorical Analysis

Like any other essay, your rhetorical analysis needs an effective thesis. Your thesis needs to make a point about the author's rhetorical choices as well as whether or not those choices result in a strong argument. After articulating your thesis, you should arrange the author's rhetorical strategies and choices in a logical way. You may have identified specific stylistic choices (e.g., diction, formal/informal language) and/or how tone is reflected in the piece. Regardless, you should effectively transition from analyzing one strategy to another while remaining focused on those strategies.

Perhaps most importantly, you should remember that you are *analyzing* and *evaluating* strategies, not merely *summarizing* the content of an author's work, although you will find yourself summarizing a bit to orient the reader to your analysis. You will also necessarily pay more attention to *how* the author wrote the essay rather than *what* he or she actually said. It is not, however, that you will totally ignore the "what," but your purpose in writing lies more with the choices the author made in conveying his or her message. Moreover, you need to keep in mind that you will ultimately explain *why* the author has chosen to write in a certain way.

The following example came from a student who chose to analyze author and scientist Jane Goodall's rhetorical strategies in an article titled "A Plea for the Chimpanzees." In reading the student's essay, pay particular attention to what she chose to analyze about Goodall's piece.

Essay: A Style Analysis

A PARAGON OF RHETORICAL PERSUASION

Claire Bruce

Mr. Fletcher

RHET 1302

6-October 2010

Ethos, logos, and pathos: these are the three rhetorical methods, as defined by the Greek philosopher Aristotle. The best and strongest arguments are those that twine all three of these together like a firm, unbreakable rope. The best strategy is to make use of the complimentary nature of these three methods, since heavy usage of one approach to the exclusion of the others invariably weakens any argument. The reason for this is that each of the three tactics aims for a different constituency of the audience. Animal rights activist Dame Jane Goodall's 1987 article, "A Plea for the Chimpanzees," deftly and movingly uses equal doses of all of these methods. Aiming for all of her audience, Goodall argues that the current state of treatment of the chimpanzees used in scientific experimentation is horrifying and unethical, and must be remedied. Her argument is balanced, logical, and fully supported by facts and evidence, while still drawing much of its rhetorical appeal from "pathos," or emotional reasoning.

In "A Plea for the Chimpanzees," Goodall asks, "Have you ever looked into the eyes of a person who, stressed beyond endurance, has given up, succumbed utterly to the crippling helplessness of despair?" This haunting question, with its emotional language and gripping mental image, is one of the appeals to pathos Goodall uses in her article. Pathos,

The student presents a thesis focused on *how* Goodall wrote her essay as opposed to *what* she actually wrote.

The student shows how Goodall's language and word choices reveal her use of pathos.

the rhetorical technique that calls out to the reader's emotions and sense of humanity, is the first of the three argument structures that comes to mind when we think of animal cruelty issues. Indeed, Goodall successfully calls out to our emotions, likening the chimpanzees that scientists test to three-year-old children, showing us the many similarities in genetic structure, mental capacity, behavioral predispositions, and thought structure. With this and several other arguments, she uses the issue to appeal to emotions in a way that pulls the reader close to the subject and makes him or her want to correct the problem and save the hurting animals.

The student shows how Goodall strategically uses pathos in making her argument.

Though this article contains a good amount of emotional appeal, it does not fall victim to a common flaw in many writings about animal cruelty: reliance on emotional reasoning rather than logic. This strategy fails to convince many readers, because the author misunderstands his audience. Pathos, though a legitimate form of rhetorical argument, has only surface appeal for most readers. It will interest the reader at first, and catch his attention, but it must be swiftly followed by logos and ethos to have any real significance. Goodall expertly avoids this mistake; though she does use emotional reasoning, it is with purpose. She shows that her emotional response to the problem of inhumane treatment was the incentive for the logical reasoning that led to her conclusion, not the reasoning itself.

The student also makes evaluative statements in noting Goodall's effective use of pathos.

She obviously realizes that she is speaking to a divided audience, half of which may be predisposed to agree with her while the other half may be predisposed to disagree. A significant portion of her audience is comprised of the very scientists whose scientific methods she questions in the article. For these readers, she provides specific, logical reasons for change. She explains to the reader how the physical functioning of depressed chimpanzees is different from that of healthy chimpanzees, making them more likely to develop illnesses and immune disorders. Dame Goodall then presents a simple list of improvements researchers could make in their practices to be more humane, and explains that though she knows these improvements are an extra expense, it is an expense she believes to be justified, and even necessary.

The student explains the composition of Goodall's audience.

Logos, though often accepted in scientific circles as a viable strategy on its own, cannot be blindly received in rhetorical compositions whose purpose is to convince readers to change their beliefs. The author must display proof of "ethos," which refers to the author's ethics, moral background, and previously acquired beliefs or biases. If the reader believes the author's beliefs are inflexible, no matter how much evidence is laid against them, the reader will be less likely to accept what the writer says. It is better for the author to leave personal bias out of the argument as much as possible, letting the reader believe him or her to be an impartial third-party observer. Because Goodall's research on chimpanzees is well known, it is unlikely that readers would believe her to be completely unbiased; however, she demonstrates that she approaches the issue less as an activist than as a thinking human. She prefaces her article by admonishing her readers to leave the issue of whether animal testing should even be a viable scientific experimentation method, indicating to those readers that she understands the importance of unbiased opinions. It is challenging to appeal to the emotions of the audience while also withholding one's own bias to maintain authorial credibility. Goodall accomplishes this by providing significant amounts of data and refraining from personal judgment in her descriptions of the horrors of chimpanzee captivity. By giving readers the facts and letting them make their own decisions, she inspires confidence in her informed opinion.

The student provides effective transition between paragraphs and areas of discussion. The opening sentence of this paragraph reflects good use of such transition.

The student connects the issue of bias with credibility to support her argument concerning Goodall's ethos.

Goodall may not be alone in her beliefs about animal treatment, but she is notable for the way she presents them. She presents her material in a way that appeals to her readers on all three of the classic rhetorical levels. With pathos she pulls her readers to the issue, uses logos to establish the credibility of her argument, and finally uses ethos to establish her own credibility, fully winning her audience over. The rhetorical structure of this article demonstrates an important fact: an argument can be made with any of the three argument strategies on its own, but in order to craft a truly sound and successful argument, all three strategies must be used in complement to one another.

Works Cited

Goodall, Jane. "A Plea for the Chimpanzees." American Scientist, Vol. 75 Issue 6 Nov. 1987: 574–77. Print.

let's review

After reading Chapter 9, you should understand the following:

- When we speak of the critical reader or critical thinker, we have in mind someone who reads actively, who thinks about issues, and who makes informed judgments.

- Writing a rhetorical analysis requires recognition and explanation of context (audience, purpose, and sources of information).

- Reading critically requires preparation. Instead of jumping into reading, begin by asking questions about the work's total context.

- When you read a piece you intend to rhetorically analyze, think about not just *what* is said but *how* it is said. This awareness of an author's attitude will be helpful as you attempt to analyze his or her overall approach and style.

- In writing a rhetorical analysis, be sensitive to issues of tone including diction, sentence structure, use of metaphor, organization, examples, and repetition as well as hyperbole, understatement, and irony.

- A writer engaged in rhetorical analysis can organize his or her essay around an author's use of rhetorical or persuasive appeals (logos, ethos, and pathos).

connect

With your class partner or in a small group, examine the following three paragraphs, which are different responses to the same event. First, decide on each writer's argument. Then describe, as precisely as possible, the tone of each paragraph, the writer's attitude, who you think the author might be, and within what context the paragraph might have been written. Discuss your conclusions with your classmates. What clues within the writing allowed you to draw these conclusions?

1. It is tragically inexcusable that this young athlete was not examined fully before he was allowed to join the varsity team. The physical examinations given were unbelievably sloppy. What were the coach and trainer thinking of not to insist that each youngster be examined while undergoing physical stress? Apparently they were not thinking about our boys at all. We can no longer trust our sons and our daughters to this inhumane system so bent on victory that it ignores the health—indeed the very lives—of our children.

2. It was learned last night, following the death of varsity fullback Jim Bresnick, that none of the players was given a stress test as part of his physical examination. The oversight was attributed to laxness by the coach and trainer, who are described today as being "distraught." It is the judgment of many that the entire physical education program must be reexamined with an eye to the safety and health of all students.

3. How can I express the loss I feel over the death of this wonderful boy? I want to blame someone, but who is to blame? The coaches, for not administering more rigorous physical checkups? Why should they have done more than other coaches have done before or than other coaches are doing at other schools? Jim, for not telling me that he felt funny after practice? His teammates, for not telling the coaches that Jim said he did not feel well? Myself, for not knowing that something was wrong? Who is to blame? All of us and none of us. But placing blame will not return Jim to me; I can only pray that other parents will not have to suffer so. Jimmy, we loved you.

reading, analyzing, and using visuals and statistics in argument

We live in a visual age. Many of us go to movies to appreciate and judge the film's visual effects. The Internet is awash in pictures and colorful icons. Perhaps the best symbol of our visual age is *USA Today,* a paper filled with color photos and many tables and other graphics as a primary way of presenting information. *USA Today* has forced the more traditional papers to add color to compete. We also live in a numerical age. We refer to the events of September 11, 2001, as 9/11—without any disrespect. This chapter brings together these markers of our times as they are used in argument—and as argument. Finding statistics and visuals used as part of argument, we also need to remember that cartoons and advertisements are arguments in and of themselves.

Responding to Visual Arguments

Many arguments bombard us today in visual forms. These include photos, political cartoons, and advertising. Most major newspapers have a political cartoonist whose drawings appear regularly on the editorial page. (Some comic strips are also political in nature, at least some of the time.) These cartoons are designed to make a political point in a visually clever and amusing way. (That is why they are both "cartoons" and "political" at the same time.) Their uses of irony and caricatures of known politicians make them among the most emotionally powerful, indeed stinging, of arguments.

Photographs accompany many newspaper and magazine articles, and they often tell a story. Indeed some photographers are famous for their ability to capture a personality or a newsworthy moment. So accustomed to these visuals today, we sometimes forget to study photographs. Be sure to examine each photo, remembering that authors and editors have selected each one for a reason.

Advertisements are among the most creative and powerful forms of argument today. Remember that ads are designed to take your time (for shopping) and your money. Their messages need to be powerful to motivate you to action. With some products (what most of us consider necessities), ads are designed to influence product choice, to get us to buy brand A instead of brand B. With other products, ones we really do not need or which may actually be harmful to us, ads need to be especially clever. Some ads do provide information (car X gets better gas mileage than car Y). Other ads (perfume ads, for example) take us into a fantasy land so that we will spend $50 on a small but pretty bottle. Another type of ad is the "image advertisement," an ad that assures us that a particular company

is top-notch. If we admire the company, we will buy its goods or services.

In Chapter 9, you learned techniques of rhetorical analysis that helped you focus more on *how* and *why* a writer said something than on *what* he or she actually said. You can use these same techniques when analyzing and responding to visuals. For example, you can analyze a visual for the persuasive appeals of logos, pathos, and ethos just as you would a written piece. Consider this image:

This particular image of a starving child in the Sudan definitely reflects use of the pathos appeal. The photograph appeals to an audience's sympathy by showing human suffering in an effort to get viewers to respond and react in some way.

Remember, too, that an image, just like a written piece, is never divorced from its context. The photograph of the starving child in Africa reflects the political turmoil in the Sudan and the consequences and effects of the genocide that took place there between 2003 and 2010. When analyzing the visual, you should understand an image's context before analyzing its message.

GOOD ADVICE

How Can You Read a Visual Argument with Insight?

READING PHOTOGRAPHS

- **Is a scene or situation depicted?** If so, study the details to identify the situation.
- **Identify each figure in the photo.**
- **What details of scene or person(s) carry significance?**
- **How does the photograph make you feel?**

READING POLITICAL CARTOONS

- **What scene is depicted?** Identify the situation.
- **Identify each of the figures in the cartoon.** Are they current politicians, figures from history or literature, the "person in the street," or symbolic representations?
- **Who speaks the lines in the cartoon?**
- **What is the cartoon's general subject?** What is the point of the cartoon, the claim of the cartoonist?

READING ADVERTISEMENTS

- **What product or service is being advertised?**
- **Who seems to be the targeted audience?**
- **What is the ad's primary strategy?** To provide information? To reinforce the product's or company's image? To appeal to particular needs or desires? For example, if an ad shows a group of young people having fun and drinking a particular beer, to what needs/desires is the ad appealing?
- **Does the ad use specific rhetorical strategies such as humor, understatement, or irony?**
- **What is the relation between the visual part of the ad (photo, drawing, typeface, etc.) and the print part (the text, or copy)?** Does the ad use a slogan or catchy phrase? Is there a company logo? Is the slogan or logo clever? Is it well known as a marker of the company? What may be the effect of these strategies on readers?
- **What is the ad's overall visual impression?** Consider both images and colors used.

try it!

Analyzing Photos, Cartoons, and Ads

1. Analyze the photo on page 158, using the guidelines previously listed.

2. Review the photos that open Chapters 1, 2, 6, 7, 8, and 9. Select the one you find most effective. Analyze it in detail to show why you think it is the best.

3. Analyze the cartoon on page 158 using the guidelines listed previously. You may want to jot down your answers to the questions to be well prepared for class discussion.

continued

4. Analyze the ad below and in the color insert, again using the guidelines listed above. After answering the guideline questions, consider these as well: Will this ad appeal effectively to its intended audience? If so, why? If not, why not?

Copyright © 2007 Mike Shelton.

the river of life

Retracing a historic journey to help fight malaria..

In 1858, Scottish missionary David Livingstone embarked on a historic journey along the Zambezi River in southern Africa. On that trip, malaria claimed the life of Livingstone's wife, Mary. Livingstone himself also later died from the disease.

Today, 150 years later, malaria remains a threat. Over one million people, mostly children and pregnant women, die from malaria each year. About 40% of the global population is vulnerable to the disease.

But an unprecedented global action–by governments and corporations, NGOs and health organisations–has been mobilised against malaria. And this combined effort is yielding results:

• Across Africa, people are receiving anti-malarial medications, as well as bed nets and insecticides that protect against the mosquitoes that transmit the disease.

• In Rwanda, malaria cases are down by 64%, and deaths by 66%. Similar results are seen in Ethiopia and Zambia. And in Mozambique, where 9 out of 10 children had been infected, that number is now 2 in 10.

• Scientists are expanding the pipeline of affordable, effective anti-malarial medicines, while also making progress on discovering a vaccine.

April 25 is World Malaria Day. As part of that event, a team of medical experts will retrace Livingstone's journey along the Zambezi - the "River of Life." They will travel 2400 kilometres in inflatable boats through Angola, Namibia, Botswana, Zambia, Zimbabwe and Mozambique.

By exposing the difficulties of delivering supplies to remote areas, the expedition will demonstrate that only a co-ordinated, cross-border action can beat back the disease, and turn the lifeline of southern Africa into a "River of Life" for those threatened by malaria.

ExxonMobil is the largest non-pharmaceutical private-sector contributor to the fight against malaria. But our support is more than financial. We are actively partnering with governments and agencies in affected countries, enabling them to combat malaria with the same disciplined, results-based business practices that ExxonMobil employs in its global operations.

Livingstone once said, "I am prepared to go anywhere, provided it be forward." The communities burdened by this disease cannot move forward until malaria is controlled and, someday, eradicated. We urge everyone to join in this global effort.

For more information, please visit zambeziexpedition.org and www.rollbackmalaria.org.

Photo by Helge Bendl

 Mobil

ExxonMobil
Taking on the world's toughest energy challenges.™

For more information, please visit exxonmobil.com/malaria

Reading Graphics

Graphics—photographs, diagrams, tables, charts, and graphs—present a good bit of information in a condensed but also visually engaging format. Graphics are everywhere: in textbooks, magazines, newspapers. It is a rare training session or board meeting that is conducted without the use of graphics to display information. So, you want to be able to read graphics and create them, when appropriate, in your own writing. To effectively use or read a graphic, you need to understand how graphics differ and how to interpret them.

Understanding How Graphics Differ

Each type of visual serves specific purposes. You cannot use a pie chart, for example, to explain a process; you need a diagram or a flowchart. So, when reading graphics, understand what each type can show you. When preparing your own visuals, select the graphic that will most clearly and effectively present the particular information you want to display. The Good Advice box below provides an overview of the different uses of various visuals.

Techniques for Interpreting Graphics

The following techniques offer general guidelines for interpreting graphics of all types. Each technique refers to Figure 10.1 or Figure 10.2 to illustrate its main point. Keep these techniques in mind whenever you need to interpret or create a graphic.

- **Locate the particular graphic to which the text refers and study it at that point in your reading.** Graphics may not always be placed on the same page as the text reference. Stop your reading to find and study the graphic; that's what the writer wants you to do. Find Figure 10.1 on the following page.

- **Read the title or heading of the graphic.** Every graphic is given a title. What is the subject of the graphic? What kind of information is provided? Figure 10.1 shows population growth from 1910 to 2010.

- **Read any notes, description, and the source information at the bottom of the graphic.** Figure 10.1 came from the U.S. Census Bureau for 2010. Critical questions: What is this figure showing me? Is the information coming from a reliable source? Is it current enough to still be meaningful?

GOOD ADVICE

Different graphics serve different purposes and perform different functions in a piece of writing. When choosing a graphic for an essay, you should consider what you are trying to accomplish with it as well as whether or not the graphic will clearly display the information. Consider the following types of graphics and the examples of each.

Type	Purpose	Example
Diagram	show details demonstrate process	drawing of knee tendons photosynthesis
Table	list numerical information	income of U.S. households
Bar chart	comparative amounts of related numbers	differences in suicide rates by age and race
Pie chart	relative portions of a whole	percentages of Americans by educational level
Flowchart	steps in a process	purification of water
Graph	relationship of two items	income increases over time
Map	information relative to a geographical area	locations of world's rain forests

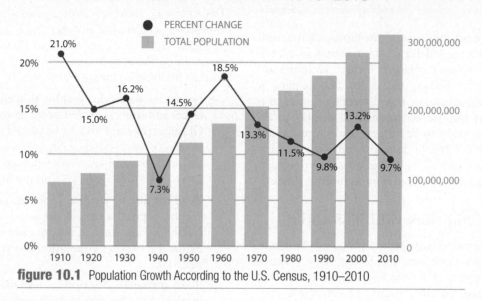

POPULATION GROWTH 1910–2010

- PERCENT CHANGE
- TOTAL POPULATION

21.0%
16.2%
15.0%
14.5%
18.5%
13.3%
11.5%
9.8%
13.2%
9.7%
7.3%

figure 10.1 Population Growth According to the U.S. Census, 1910–2010

- **Study the labels—and other words—that appear as part of the graphic.** You cannot draw useful conclusions unless you understand exactly what is being shown. Observe in Figure 10.1 that the bars (shown along the horizontal axis) represent the total population for every ten years beginning in 1910 and ending in 2010. You should also note that in Figure 10.2 different states are shaded as

blue, orange, or grey to show congressional seats gained or lost, or to reflect no change.

- **Study the information, making certain that you understand what the numbers represent.** Are the numerals whole numbers, numbers in hundreds or thousands, or percentages? In Figure 10.1, the red line shows the percentage change in popula-

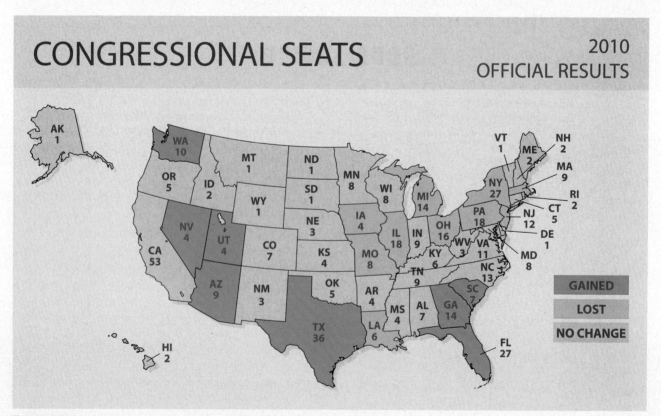

CONGRESSIONAL SEATS

2010
OFFICIAL RESULTS

AK 1
WA 10
OR 5
ID 2
MT 1
ND 1
MN 8
WI 8
MI 14
VT 1
ME 2
NH 2
NY 27
MA 9
RI 2
CT 5
NJ 12
DE 1
MD 8
WY 1
SD 1
NE 3
IA 4
IL 18
IN 9
OH 16
PA 18
WV 3
VA 11
NC 13
NV 4
UT 4
CO 7
KS 4
MO 8
KY 6
TN 9
CA 53
AZ 9
NM 3
OK 5
AR 4
MS 4
AL 7
GA 14
SC 7
TX 36
LA 6
HI 2
FL 27

GAINED
LOST
NO CHANGE

figure 10.2 Congressional Apportionment, 2010

tion for every ten years between 1910 and 2010. From this figure, you can see trends in population growth between each census.

- **Draw conclusions.** Think about the information in different ways. Critical questions: What does the author want to accomplish by including these figures? How are they significant? What conclusions can you draw from Figures 10.1 and 10.2? Answer the following questions to guide your thinking.

  - In Figure 10.1, which census saw the greatest percentage increase in population? Which saw the smallest percentage increase? What might account for these trends?

  - In Figure 10.2, what might account for a loss of population in certain states that also re-

sulted in a loss of congressional seats? On the other hand, what might account for an increase in population in some states that resulted in a gain of congressional seats?

- What can you conclude about these two graphics (Figures 10.1 and 10.2) in relationship to one another? In other words, does one help interpret the other and vice versa? Why or why not?

Graphics provide information, raise questions, explain processes, engage us emotionally, and make us think. Study the various graphics in the exercises that follow to become more expert in reading and responding critically to visuals.

Reading and Analyzing Graphics

1. Study the pie charts in Figure 10.3 and then answer the following questions.
   a. What is the subject of the charts?
   b. In addition to the information within the pie charts, what other information is provided?
   c. Which group increases by the greatest relative amount? How would you account for that increase?
   d. Which figure surprises you the most? Why?

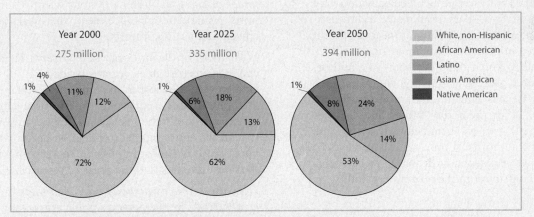

figure 10.3 The Shifting of U.S. Racial-Ethnic Mix Sources: U.S. Bureau of the Census. *Current Population Reports* P25:1130, 1996; James Henslin, *Sociology: A Down-to-Earth Approach*, 5th ed.

2. Study the table in Figure 10.4 and then answer the following questions.
   a. What is being presented and compared in this table?
   b. What, exactly, do the numerals in the second line represent? What, exactly, do the numerals in the third line represent? (Be sure that you understand what these numbers mean.)
   c. For the information given in lines 2, 3, 4, and 5, in which category have women made the greatest gains on men?

continued

d. See if you can complete the missing information in the last line. Where will you look to find out how many men and women were single parents in 2000?

e. Which figure surprises you the most? Why?

	1970		2000	
	MEN	WOMEN	MEN	WOMEN
Estimated life expectancy	67.1	74.1	74.24	79.9
% high school graduates	53	52	87	88
% of BAs awarded	57	43	45	55
% of MAs awarded	60	40	45	55
% of PhDs awarded	87	13	61	39
% in legal profession	95	5	70	30
Median earnings	$26,760	$14,232	$35,345	$25,862
Single parents	1.2 million	5.6 million	n/a	n/a

figure 10.4 Men and Women in a Changing Society Sources: for 1970: *1996 Statistical Abstract,* U.S. Dept. of Commerce, Economics and Statistics Administration, Bureau of the Census. 2000 data: National Center for Education Statistics http://nces.ed.gov/fastfacts

The Uses of Authority and Statistics

Most of the visuals you have just studied provide a way of presenting statistics—data that many today consider essential to defending a claim. One reason you check the source information accompanying graphics is that you need to know—and evaluate—the authority of that source. When a graphic's numbers have come from the Census Bureau, you know you have a reliable source. When the author writes that "studies have shown . . . ," you want immediately to become suspicious of the authority of the data. All elements of the arguments we read—and write—need to be evaluated. They all contribute to the writer's credibility, or lack thereof.

Judging Authorities

We know that movie stars and sports figures are not authorities on soft drinks and watches. But what about *real* authorities? When writers present the opinions or research findings of authorities as support for a claim, they are saying to readers that the authority is trustworthy and the opinions valuable. But what they are asserting is actually an assumption or warrant, part of the glue connecting evidence to claim. Remember: Warrants can be challenged. If the "authority" can be shown to lack authority, then the logic of the argument is destroyed. Use this checklist of questions to aid your evaluation of authorities.

- *Is the authority actually an authority on the topic under discussion?* When a famous scientist supports a candidate for office, he or she speaks as a citizen, not as an authority.

- *Is the work of the authority still current?* Times change; expertise does not always endure. Galileo would be lost in the universe of today's astrophysicists. Be particularly alert to the dates of information in the sciences in general, in genetics and the entire biomedical field, in health and nutrition. It is almost impossible to keep up with the latest findings in these areas of research.

- *Does the authority actually have legitimate credentials?* Are the person's publications in respected journals? Is he or she respected by others in the same field? *Just because it's in print does not mean it's a reliable source!*

- *Do experts in the field generally agree on the issue?* If there is widespread disagreement, then referring to one authority does not do much to support a claim. This is why you need to understand the many sides of a controversial topic before you write on it, and you need to bring knowledge of controversies and critical thinking skills to your reading of argument. This is also why writers often

Judging Authorities

1. Jane Goodall has received worldwide fame for her studies of chimpanzees in Gombe and for her books on those field studies. Goodall is a vegetarian. Should she be used as an authority in support of a claim for a vegetarian diet? Why or why not? Consider:

   a. Why might Goodall have chosen to become a vegetarian?

   b. For what arguments might Goodall be used as an authority?

   c. For what arguments might she be used effectively for emotional appeal?

2. Suppose a respected zoologist prepares a five-year study of U.S. zoos, compiling a complete list of all animals at each zoo. He then updates the list for each of the five years, adding births and deaths. When he examines his data, he finds that deaths are one and one-half times the number of births. He considers this loss alarming and writes a paper arguing for the abolishing of zoos on the grounds that too many animals are dying. Because of his reputation, his article is published in a popular science magazine. How would you evaluate his authority and his study?

   a. Should you trust the data? Why or why not?

   b. Should you accept his conclusions? Why or why not?

   c. Consider: What might be possible explanations for the birth/death ratio?

provide a source's credentials, not just a name, unless the authority is quite famous.

- *Is the authority's evidence reliable, so far as you can judge, but the interpretation of that evidence seems odd, or seems to be used to support strongly held beliefs?* Does the evidence actually connect to the claim? A respected authority's work can be stretched or manipulated in an attempt to support a claim that the authority's work simply does not support.

GOOD ADVICE

Evaluating Statistics

Study these questions to be alert to the ways data can be misleading in both the arguments you read and those you write.

- **Is the information current and therefore still relevant?** Crime rates in your city based on 1990 census data probably are no longer relevant, certainly not current enough to support an argument for increased (or decreased) police department spending.

- **If a sample was used, was it randomly selected and large enough to be significant?** Sometimes in medical research, the results of a small study are publicized to guide researchers to important new areas of study. When these results are reported in the press or on TV, however, the small size of the study is not always made clear. Thus one week we learn that coffee is bad for us, the next week that it is okay.

- **What information, exactly, has been provided?** When you read "Two out of three chose the Merit combination of low tar and good taste," you must ask yourself "Two-thirds of how many altogether?"

- **How have the numbers been presented?** And what is the effect of that presentation? Numbers can be presented as fractions, whole numbers, or percentages. Writers who want to emphasize budget increases will use whole numbers—billions of dollars. Writers who want to de-emphasize those increases select percentages. Writers who want their readers to respond to the numbers in a specific way add words to direct their thinking: "a *mere* 3 percent increase" or "the *enormous* $5 billion increase."

Understanding and Evaluating Statistics

There are two useful clichés to keep in mind: "Statistics don't lie, but people lie with statistics" and "There are lies, damned lies, and statistics." The second cliché is perhaps a bit cynical. We do not want to be naïve in our faith in numbers, but neither do we want to become so cynical that we refuse to believe any statistical evidence. What we do need to keep in mind is that when statistics are presented in an argument they are being used by someone interested in winning that argument.

Some writers use numbers without being aware that the numbers are incomplete or not representative. Some present only part of the relevant information. Some may not mean to distort, but they do choose to present the information in language that helps their cause. There are many ways, some more innocent than others, to distort reality with statistics. Use the guidelines from "Evaluating Statistics" on page 163 to evaluate the presentation of statistical information.

try it!

Reading Tables and Charts and Using Statistics

1. Table 1, a table from the U.S. Census Bureau, shows U.S. family income data from 1980 to 2005. Percentages and median income are given for all families and then, in turn, for white, black, Asian, and Hispanic families. Study the data and then complete the exercises that follow.

   a. In a paper assessing the advantages of a growing economy, you want to include a paragraph on family income growth to show that a booming economy helps everyone, that "a rising tide lifts all boats." Select data from the table that best support your claim. Write a paragraph beginning with a topic sentence and including your data as support. Think about how to present the numbers in the most persuasive form.

   b. Write a second paragraph with the following topic sentence: "Not all Americans have benefited from the boom years" or "a rising tide does not lift all boats." Select data from the table that best support this topic sentence and present the numbers in the most persuasive form.

   c. Exchange paragraphs with a classmate and evaluate each other's selection and presentation of evidence.

2. Table 2 (p. 165), another table from the U.S. Census Bureau, presents mean earnings by degree earned. First, be sure that you know the difference between mean and median (which is the number used in Table 1). Study the data and reflect on the conclusions you can draw from the statistics. Consider: Of the various groups represented, which group most benefits from obtaining a college degree—as opposed to having only a high school diploma?

Table 1 Money Income of Families—Percent Distribution by Income Level in Constant (2005) Dollars: 1980 to 2005

[Constant dollars based on CPI-U-RS deflator. Families as of March of the following year (60,309 represents 60,309,000). Based on Current Population Survey, Annual Social and Economic Supplement (ASEC): see text, Sections 1 and 13, and Appendix III. For data collection changes over time, see <http://www.census.gov/hhes/www/income/histinc/hstchg.html>. For definition of median, see Guide to Tabular Presentation]

Year	Number of families (1,000)	Percent distribution							Median income (dollars)
		Under $15,000	$15,000–$24,999	$25,000–$34,999	$35,000–$49,999	$50,000–$74,999	$75,000–$99,999	$100,000 and over	
ALL FAMILIES[1]									
1980	60,309	10.3	12.1	12.6	18.9	24.5	12.0	9.6	47,173
1990	66,322	10.2	10.6	11.3	16.8	22.6	13.4	15.2	51,202
2000[2]	73,778	8.1	9.7	10.7	15.0	20.7	14.3	21.5	57,508
2004[3]	76,866	9.2	10.3	10.6	14.5	20.4	13.6	21.4	55,869
2005	77,418	8.9	10.0	10.7	14.6	20.3	13.5	21.8	56,194
WHITE									
1980	52,710	8.4	11.3	12.5	19.2	25.6	12.7	10.3	49,150
1990	56,803	7.8	10.0	11.2	17.2	23.4	14.2	16.2	53,464
2000[2]	61,330	6.7	9.0	10.3	15.0	21.2	14.9	22.8	60,112
2004[3, 4, 5]	63,084	7.6	9.7	10.3	14.3	20.9	14.3	22.9	58,620
2005[4, 5]	63,414	7.2	9.3	10.5	14.7	21.0	14.1	23.2	59,317
BLACK									
1980	6,317	26.1	19.0	13.6	16.7	15.5	6.1	3.0	28,439
1990	7,471	27.0	15.1	13.1	14.4	16.9	7.0	6.4	31,027

Year	Number of families (1,000)	\$25,000	\$15,000–\$24,999	\$25,000–\$34,999	\$35,000–\$49,999	\$50,000–\$74,999	\$75,000–\$99,999	\$100,000 and over	Median income (dollars)
		Under \$15,000							
2000[2]	8,731	17.6	15.4	13.6	15.9	18.0	9.4	10.1	38,174
2004[3, 4, 6]	8,906	20.8	14.9	13.1	15.4	17.1	9.3	9.4	36,323
2005[4, 6]	9,051	20.5	15.6	13.3	14.7	16.4	9.2	10.2	35,464
ASIAN AND PACIFIC ISLANDER									
1990	1,536	8.7	9.0	8.0	12.8	23.4	15.2	22.7	61,185
2000[2]	2,982	6.9	6.9	8.1	12.6	18.9	16.0	30.6	70,981
2004[3, 4, 7]	3,142	6.2	7.5	8.3	13.1	20.4	13.7	30.8	67,608
2005[4, 7]	3,208	7.8	7.7	7.0	11.8	19.7	14.4	31.6	68,957
HISPANIC ORIGIN[8]									
1980	3,235	18.5	18.9	16.1	18.6	18.3	6.2	3.6	33,021
1990	4,981	19.9	17.0	14.8	17.3	17.4	7.3	6.2	33,935
2000[2]	8,017	14.5	16.1	14.3	17.8	18.8	9.5	8.9	39,043
2004[3]	9,521	15.4	17.6	15.0	16.7	17.5	8.3	9.5	36,625
2005	9,868	14.7	16.3	15.2	17.4	18.2	8.9	9.3	37,867

[1]Includes other races not shown separately. [2]Data reflect implementation of Census 2000-based population controls and a 28,000 household sample expansion to 78,000 households. [3]Data have been revised to reflect a correction to the weights in the 2005 ASEC. [4]Beginning with the 2003 Current Population Survey (CPS), the questionnaire allowed respondents to choose more than one race. For 2002 and later, data represent persons who selected this race group only and excludes persons reporting more than one race. The CPS in prior years allowed respondents to report only one race group. See also comments on race in the text for Section 1. [5]Data represent White alone, which refers to people who reported White and did not report any other race category. [6]Data represent Black alone, which refers to people who reported Black and did not report any other race category. [7]Data represent Asian alone, which refers to people who reported Asian and did not report any other race category. [8]People of Hispanic origin may be of any race.

U.S. Census Bureau, *Current Population Reports*, P60-231; and Internet sites <http://www.census.gov/prod/2006pubs/p60-231.pdf> (released August 2006) and <http://www.census.gov/hhes/www/income/histinc/f23.html>.

Table 2 Mean Earnings by Highest Degree Earned: 2005

[In dollars. For persons 18 years old and over with earnings. Persons as of March the following year. Based on Current Population Survey; see text, Section 1, and Appendix III. For definition of mean, see Guide to Tabular Presentation]

Characteristic	Total persons	Not a high school graduate	High school graduate only	Some college, no degree	Associate's	Bachelor's	Master's	Professional	Doctorate
All persons[1]	**39,579**	**19,915**	**29,448**	**31,421**	**37,990**	**54,689**	**67,898**	**119,009**	**92,863**
AGE									
25 to 34 years old	34,004	20,355	26,820	30,473	33,011	44,960	48,185	75,600	62,268
35 to 44 years old	45,373	22,516	32,637	39,124	41,110	60,297	72,098	126,520	97,109
45 to 54 years old	49,486	24,416	35,209	41,068	42,936	66,776	79,555	137,115	117,324
55 to 64 years old	46,561	25,071	33,424	41,005	42,532	56,142	69,981	129,956	87,125
65 years old and over	35,879	16,995	24,847	26,672	34,303	49,050	62,322	100,847	85,854
SEX									
Male	48,034	23,222	35,248	38,768	46,201	67,980	86,667	139,773	105,163
Female	26,897	14,294	22,208	24,086	30,912	40,684	49,573	82,268	66,411
WHITE[2]	40,717	20,264	30,569	32,191	38,788	55,785	69,112	122,975	93,412
Male	49,611	23,556	36,753	39,849	47,534	69,852	89,207	142,879	105,657
Female	30,125	14,086	22,590	24,248	31,005	40,344	49,281	84,125	66,728
BLACK[2]	30,472	17,216	23,904	27,291	33,198	47,101	56,057	100,030	79,087
Male	34,165	19,890	27,360	31,919	38,441	52,070	64,000	(B)	(B)
Female	27,314	14,300	20,449	23,798	29,722	43,516	50,831	76,298	(B)
HISPANIC[3]	27,760	19,294	25,659	28,539	33,053	45,933	62,449	83,239	99,774
Male	31,008	21,632	29,471	33,288	38,764	54,700	74,365	91,546	(B)
Female	22,887	14,365	19,864	23,073	27,673	37,003	50,314	(B)	(B)

B Base figure too small to meet statistical standards for reliability of a derived figure. [1]Includes other races, not shown separately. [2]For persons who selected this race group only. See footnote 2, Table 217. [3]Persons of Hispanic origin may be of any race.

U.S Census Bureau, Current Population Survey. See Internet site <http://www.census.gov/population/www/socdemo/educ-attn.html>.

GOOD ADVICE

A CHECKLIST FOR REVISION

In revising an essay in which you have used graphics, ask yourself the following questions:

- Have I stated a claim that is precise and appropriate to the data I have collected?

- Have I fully explained the methodology I used in collecting my data?

- Have I selected a clear and useful organization?

- Have I presented and discussed enough specifics to show readers how my data support my conclusions?

- Have I used graphics to present the data in an effective summary form?

- Have I revised, edited, and proofread my paper?

Sample Student Essay with Graphics

The following student paper illustrates how a writer can integrate different kinds of graphics into an essay. Graphics support the essay's argument just as the words on the page support that argument. Furthermore, the written discussion should explain and interpret the graphics. Read this student's paper paying particular attention to how he has integrated graphics with text in support of his claim.

BUYING TIME

Garrett Berger

Chances are you own at least one wristwatch. Watches allow us immediate access to the correct time. They are indispensable items in our modern world, where, as the saying is, time is money. Today the primary function of a wristwatch does not necessarily guide its design; like clothes, houses, and cars, watches have become fashion statements and a way to flaunt one's wealth.

Introduction connects to reader.

To learn how watches are being sold, I surveyed all of the full-page ads from the November issues of four magazines. The first two, *GQ* and *Vogue,* are well-known fashion magazines. *The Robb Report* is a rather new magazine that caters to the overclass. *Forbes* is of course a well-known financial magazine. I was rather surprised at the number of advertisements I found. After surveying 86 ads, marketing 59 brands, I have concluded that today watches are being sold through five main strategies: DESIGN/BRAND appeal, CRAFTSMANSHIP, ASSOCIATION, FASHION appeal, and EMOTIONAL appeal. The percentage of ads using each of these strategies is shown in Figure 1.

Student explains his methodology of collecting ads. Paragraph concludes with his thesis.

In most DESIGN/BRAND appeal ads, only a picture and the brand name are used. A subset of this category uses the same basic strategy with a slogan or phrases to emphasize something about the brand or product. A Mont Blanc ad shows a watch profile with a contorted metal link band, asking the question,

Discussion of first category.

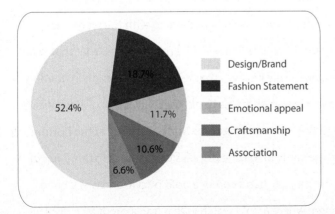

FIGURE 1 Percentage of Total Ads Using Each Strategy

- 52.4%
- 18.7%
- 11.7%
- 10.6%
- 6.6%

Design/Brand
Fashion Statement
Emotional appeal
Craftsmanship
Association

"Is that you?" The reputation of the name and the appeal of the design sell the watch. Rolex, perhaps the best-known name in high-end watches, advertises, in *Vogue,* its "Oyster Perpetual Lady-Datejust Pearlmaster." A close-up of the watch face showcases the white, mother-of-pearl dial, sapphire bezel, and diamond-set band. A smaller, more complete picture crouches underneath, showing the watch on its side. The model name is displayed along a gray band that runs near the bottom. The Rolex crest anchors the bottom of the page. Forty-five ads marketing 29 brands use the DESIGN/BRAND strategy. A large picture of the product centered on a solid background is the norm.

Discussion of second category.

CRAFTSMANSHIP, the second strategy, focuses on the maker, the horologer, and the technical sides of form and function. Brand heritage and a unique, hand-crafted design are major selling points. All of these ads are targeted at men, appearing in every magazine except *Vogue.* Collector pieces and limited editions were commonly sold using this strategy. The focus is on accuracy and technical excellence. Pictures of the inner works and cutaways, technical information, and explanations of movements and features are popular. Quality and exclusivity are all-important.

Detailed examples to illustrate second category.

A Cronoswiss ad from *The Robb Report* is a good example. The top third pictures a horologer, identified as "Gerd-R Lange, master watchmaker and founder of Cronoswiss in Munich," directly below. The middle third of the ad shows a watch, white-faced with a black leather band. The logo and slogan appear next to the watch. The bottom third contains copy beginning with the words: "My watches are a hundred years behind the times." The rest explains what that statement means. Mr. Lange apparently believes that technical perfection in horology has already been attained. He also offers his book, *The Fascination of Mechanics,* free of charge along with the "sole distributor for North America" at the bottom. A "Daniel Roth" ad from the same magazine displays the name across the top of a white page; towards the top, left-hand corner a gold buckle and black band lead your eye to the center, where a gold watch with a transparent face displays its inner works exquisitely. Above and to the right, copy explains the exclusive and unique design accomplished by inverting the movement, allowing it to be viewed from above.

The third strategy is to sell the watch by establishing an ASSOCIATION with an object, experience, or person, implying that its value and quality are beyond question. In the six ads I found using this approach, watches are associated with violins, pilots, astronauts, hot air balloons, and a hero of the free world. This is similar to the first strategy, but relies on a reputation other than that of the maker. The watch is presented as being desirable for the connections created in the ad.

Discussion of third category.

Parmigiani ran an ad in *The Robb Report* featuring a gold watch with a black face and band illuminated by some unseen source. A blue-tinted violin rises in the background; the rest of the page is black. The brief copy reads: "For those who think a Stradivarius is only a violin. The Parmigiani Toric Chronograph is only a wristwatch." "The Moon Watch" proclaims an Omega ad from *GQ*. Inset on a white background is a picture of an astronaut on the moon saluting the American flag. The silver watch with a black face lies across the lower part of the page. The caption reads: "Speedmaster Professional. The first and only watch worn on the moon." Omega's logo appears at the bottom. Figure 2 shows another Omega use of this strategy.

The fourth strategy is to present the watch simply as a FASHION statement. In this line of attack, the ads appeal to our need to be current, accepted, to fit in and be like everyone else, or to make a statement, setting us apart from others as hip and cool. The product is presented as a necessary part of our wardrobes. The watch is fashionable and will send the "right" message. Design and style are the foremost concerns; "the look" sells the watch.

Discussion of fourth category.

Techno Marine has an ad in *GQ* which shows a large close-up of a watch running down the entire length of the left side of the page. Two alternate color schemes are pictured on the right, separating small bits of copy. At the bottom

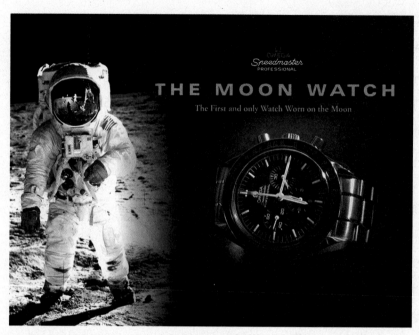

FIGURE 2 Example of Association Advertising

on the right are the name and logo. The first words at the top read: "Keeping time—you keep your closet up to the minute, why not your wrist? The latest addition to your watch wardrobe should be the AlphaSport." Longines uses a similar strategy in *Vogue*. Its ad is divided in half lengthwise. On the left is a black-and-white picture of Audrey Hepburn. The right side is white with the Longines' logo at the top and two ladies' watches in the center. Near the bottom is the phrase "Elegance is an Attitude." Retailers appear at the bottom. The same ad ran in *GQ*, but with a man's watch and a picture of Humphrey Bogart. A kind of association is made, but quality and value aren't the overriding concerns. The point is to have an elegant attitude like these fashionable stars did, one that these watches can provide and enhance.

Discussion of fifth category.

The fifth and final strategy is that of EMOTIONAL appeal. The ads using this approach strive to influence our emotional responses and allege to influence the emotions of others towards us. Their power and appeal are exerted through the feelings they evoke in us. Nine out of ten ads rely on a picture as the main device to trigger an emotional link between the product and the viewer. Copy is scant; words are used mainly to guide the viewer to the advertiser's desired conclusions.

A Frederique Constant ad pictures a man, wearing a watch, mulling over a chess game. Above his head are the words "Inner Passion." The man's gaze is odd; he is looking at something on the right side of the page, but a large picture of a watch superimposed over the picture hides whatever it is that he is looking at. So we are led to the watch. The bottom third is white and contains the maker's logo and the slogan "Live your Passion." An ad in *GQ* shows a man holding a woman. He leans against a rock; she reclines in his arms. Their eyes are closed, and both have peaceful, smiling expressions. He is wearing a Tommy Hilfiger watch. The ad spans two pages; a close-up of the watch is presented on the right half of the second page. The only words are the ones in the logo. This is perhaps one of those pictures that are worth a thousand words. The message is he got the girl because he's got the watch.

Even more than selling a particular watch, all of these ads focus on building the brand's image. I found many of the ads extremely effective at conveying their messages. Many of the better-known brands favor the comparatively simple DE-SIGN/BRAND appeal strategy, to reach a broader audience. Lesser-known, high-end makers contribute many of the more specialized strategies. We all count and mark the passing hours and minutes. And society places great importance on time, valuing punctuality. But these ads strive to convince us that having "the right time" means so much more than "the time."

Strong conclusion; the effect of watch ads.

let's review

After reading Chapter 10, you should understand the following:

- Arguments today inundate us in visual form. You need to learn to critically analyze these arguments as well as understand their context.

- Graphics require interpretation. To interpret a graphic, read its title, heading, and any notes or source information. You should also study its labels and the information in the graphic to make certain you understand what the numbers represent. Finally, draw conclusions about the graphic based on the information found within it.

- To ascertain the credibility of a visual, you need to judge the authority of the person or group presenting the visual. You should ask the following questions when judging authority:

  - Is the authority actually an authority on the topic under discussion?

  - Is the work of the authority still current?

  - Does the authority have legitimate credentials?

  - Do experts in the field generally agree on the issue?

  - Is the authority's evidence reliable, so far as you can judge, or does the interpretation of that evidence seem odd or seem to be used to support strongly held beliefs?

- Statistics are used by someone in an argument when he or she is interested in winning the argument. Upon seeing a statistic, you should ask the following questions:

  - Is the information current and therefore still relevant?

  - If a sample was used, was it randomly selected and large enough to be significant?

  - What information, exactly, has been provided?

  - How have the numbers been presented?

connect

Read and study the essay below. Then analyze and respond to the essay by answering the questions that follow.

prereading questions } **What does the term "counterintelligence" mean? How much attention do you give to body language messages from others?**

Every Body's Talking

Joe Navarro

Joe Navarro spent more than twenty-five years in the FBI, specializing in counterintelligence and profiling. He is recognized as an authority on nonverbal messages, especially given off by those who are lying, and he continues to consult to government and industry. He has also turned his expertise to poker and has published, with Marvin Karlines, Read 'Em and Reap (2006), a guide to reading the nonverbal messages from poker opponents. The following essay appeared in the Washington Post *on June 24, 2008.*

1   Picture this: I was sailing the Caribbean for three days with a group of friends and their spouses, and everything seemed perfect. The weather was beautiful, the ocean diaphanous blue, the food exquisite; our evenings together were full of laughter and good conversation.

2   Things were going so well that one friend said to the group, "Let's do this again next year." I happened to be across from him and his wife as he spoke those words. In the cacophony of resounding replies of "Yes!" and "Absolutely!" I noticed that my friend's wife made a fist under her chin as she grasped her

necklace. This behavior stood out to me as powerfully as if someone had shouted, "Danger!"

3   I watched the words and gestures of the other couples at the table, and everyone seemed ecstatic—everyone but one, that is. She continued to smile, but her smile was tense.

4   Her husband has treated me as a brother for more than 15 years, and I consider him the dearest of friends. At that moment I knew that things between him and his wife were turning for the worse. I did not pat myself on the back for making these observations. I was saddened.

5   For 25 years I worked as a paid observer. I was a special agent for the FBI specializing in counterintelligence—specifically, catching spies. For me, observing human behavior is like having software running in the background, doing its job—no conscious effort needed. And so on that wonderful cruise, I made a "thin-slice assessment" (that's what we call it) based on just a few significant behaviors. Unfortunately, it turned out to be right: Within six months of our return, my friend's wife filed for divorce, and her husband discovered painfully that she had been seeing someone else for quite a while.

6   When I am asked what is the most reliable means of determining the health of a relationship, I always say that words don't matter. It's all in the language of the body. The nonverbal behaviors we all transmit tell others, in real time, what we think, what we feel, what we yearn for or what we intend.

7   Now I am embarking on another cruise, wondering what insights I will have about my travel companions and their relationships. No matter what, this promises to be a fascinating trip, a journey for the mind and the soul. I am with a handful of dear friends and 3,800 strangers, all headed for Alaska; for an observer it does not get any better than this.

8   While lining up to board on our first day, I notice just ahead of me a couple who appear to be in their early 30s. They are obviously Americans (voice, weight and demeanor).

9   Not so obvious is their dysfunctional relationship. He is standing stoically, shoulders wide, looking straight ahead. She keeps whispering loudly to him, but she is not facing forward. She violates his space as she leans into him. Her face is tense and her lips are narrow slivers each time she engages him with what clearly appears to be a diatribe. He occasionally nods his head but avoids contact with her. He won't let his hips near her as they start to walk side by side. He reminds me of Bill and Hillary Clinton walking toward the Marine One helicopter immediately after the Monica Lewinsky affair: looking straight ahead, as much distance between them as possible.

10   I think everyone can decipher this one from afar because we have all seen situations like this. What most people will miss is something I have seen this young man do twice now, which portends poorly for both of them. Every time she looks away, he "disses" her. He smirks and rolls his eyes, even as she stands beside him. He performs his duties, pulling their luggage along; I suspect he likes to have her luggage nearby as a barrier between them. I won't witness the dissolution

of their marriage, but I know it will happen, for the research behind this is fairly robust. When two people in a relationship have contempt for each other, the marriage will not last.

11   When it comes to relationships and courtship behaviors, the list of useful cues is long. Most of these behaviors we learned early when interacting with our mothers. When we look at loving eyes, our own eyes get larger, our pupils dilate, our facial muscles relax, our lips become full and warm, our skin becomes more pliable, our heads tilt. These behaviors stay with us all of our lives.

12   I watched two lovers this morning in the dining room. Two young people, perhaps in their late 20s, mirror each other, staring intently into each other's eyes, chin on hand, head slightly tilted, nose flaring with each breath. They are trying to absorb each other visually and tactilely as they hold hands across the table.

13   Over time, those who remain truly in love will show even more indicators of mirroring. They may dress the same or even begin to look alike as they adopt each other's nonverbal expressions as a sign of synchrony and empathy. They will touch each other with kind hands that touch fully, not with the fingertips of the less caring.

14   They will mirror each other in ways that are almost imperceptible; they will have similar blink rates and breathing rates, and they will sit almost identically. They will look at the same scenery and not speak, merely look at each other and take a deep breath to reset their breathing synchrony. They don't have to talk. They are in harmony physically, mentally and emotionally, just as a baby is in exquisite synchrony with its mother who is tracing his every expression and smile.

15   As I walk through the ship on the first night, I can see the nonverbals of courtship. There is a beautiful woman, tall, slender, smoking a cigarette outside. Two men are talking to her, both muscular, handsome, interested. She has crossed her legs as she talks to them, an expression of her comfort. As she holds her cigarette, the inside of her wrist turns toward her newfound friends. Her interest and comfort with them resounds, but she is favoring one of them. As he speaks to her, she preens herself by playing with her hair. I am not sure he is getting the message that she prefers him; in the end, I am sure it will all get sorted out.

16   At the upscale lounge, a man is sitting at the bar talking animatedly to the woman next to him and looking at everyone who walks by. The woman has begun the process of ignoring him, but he does not get it. After he speaks to her a few times, she gathers her purse and places it on her lap. She has turned slightly away from him and now avoids eye contact. He has no clue; he thinks he is cool by commenting on the women who pass by. She is verbally and nonverbally indifferent.

17   The next night it is more of the same. This time, I see two people who just met talking gingerly. Gradually they lean more and more into each other. She is now dangling her sandal from her toes. I am not sure he knows it. Perhaps he sees it all in

TORSO	ARMS	HANDS AND FINGERS	FEET AND LEGS
LEANING AWAY FROM SOMEONE: Means we dislike or disagree with them. / **LEANING TOWARD SOMEONE:** Means we like or agree with them.	**FINGERTIPS SPREAD APART ON A SURFACE:** A display of confidence and authority.	**THUMBS UP:** A good indication of positive thoughts.	**JIGGLING/KICKING FOOT:** Indicates discomfort.
SPLAYING OUT: A sign of comfort becomes a territorial or dominance display when there are serious issues being discussed.	**ARMS AKIMBO:** Establishes dominance or communicates there are 'issues.'	**STEEPLING:** (FINGERTIP TO FINGERTIP) A powerful display of confidence.	**CROSSING LEGS:** Indicates we are comfortable.
CROSSED ARMS: Suddenly crossing arms tightly is a sign of discomfort.	**ARMS BEHIND THE BACK:** Says "don't draw near" —keeps people at bay.	**NECK TOUCHING:** Indicates emotional discomfort, doubt or insecurity.	**TOE POINTS UPWARD:** Signals a good mood.

Illustrations by Peter Arkle. Reprinted by permission.

her face, because she is smiling, laughing and relaxed. Communication is fluid, and neither wants the conversation to end. She is extremely interested.

18   All of these individuals are carrying on a dialogue in nonverbals. The socially adept will learn to read and interpret the signs accurately. Others will make false steps or pay a high price for not being observant. They may end up like my friend on the Caribbean cruise, who missed the clues of deceit and indifference.

This brings me back to my friend and his new wife, who are on this wonderful voyage. They have been on board for four days, and they are a delight individually and together. He lovingly looks at her; she stares at him with love and admiration. When she holds his hand at dinner, she massages it ever so gently. Theirs is a strong marriage. They don't have to tell me. I can sense it and observe it. I am happy for them and for myself. I can see cues of happiness, and they are unmistakable. You can't ask for more.

19

QUESTIONS FOR READING

1. What is Navarro's subject? (Do not answer "taking cruises"!)

2. What clues are offered to support the conclusion that the two cruise couples' relationships are about to dissolve?

3. What are the nonverbal messages that reveal loving relationships?

4. What nonverbal messages should the man in the lounge be observing?

QUESTIONS FOR REASONING AND ANALYSIS

1. What is Navarro's claim?

2. What kind of evidence does he provide?

3. How do the illustrations contribute to the argument? What is effective about the author's opening?

QUESTIONS FOR REFLECTING AND WRITING

1. Has the author convinced you that nonverbal language reveals our thoughts and feelings? Why or why not?

2. Can you "read" the nonverbal language of your instructors? Take some time to analyze each of your instructors. What have you learned? (You might also reflect on what messages you may be sending in class.)

planning the
researched
argument

chapter 11

We do research all the time. You would not select a college or buy a car without doing research: gathering relevant information, analyzing that information, and drawing conclusions from your study. You may already have done some research in this course: using sources in this text or finding data online to strengthen an argument—and then acknowledging your sources informally in your essay. And if your instructor has required formal documentation for even one source, then you have already explored this section for documentation guidelines.

When you are assigned a more formal research essay, you will need to use a number of sources and to document them according to a specific style. You may be required to produce a longer essay and to demonstrate skill in finding a variety of sources. Remember that you have been doing research, in some ways, all along, so use this section to guide you to success in the particular demands of your research essay assignment.

Before beginning a major argumentative researched essay, it is important to understand what tools, or argumentative strategies, are available to you. There are many different types of arguments that you might choose to make, each with its own distinct writing purpose and its own writing strategy. The essay types featured in Chapters 5–9 offer some suggestions for four types of arguments and strategies for writing each one. (See Figure 11.1.)

It is crucial that you understand your writing purpose before you begin your research, prewriting, or drafting. This writing purpose, along with clear ideas about your audience's needs and expectations, will guide every step of your writing process.

Finding a Workable and Manageable Topic

A major challenge as you begin a researched essay is to select and limit a topic. One key to success is finding a workable topic. After all, no matter how interesting or clever a topic may seem, it is not workable if it does not meet the guidelines of your assignment. Begin with a thorough understanding of the writing context created by the assignment. In considering the context for your assignment, you will want to fully analyze the following considerations.

Who Is My Audience?

If you are writing a research essay in a specific discipline, imagine your instructor as a representative of that field, a reader with knowledge of the subject area. If you are learning about the research process in a composition course, your instructor may advise you to write to a general reader, someone who reads newspapers or magazines but may not have the exact information and perspective you have. For a general reader, specialized terms and concepts may need to be defined. Within the category of general reader, you can identify specific traits, beliefs, values, and experiences that you imagine your reader might hold. For example, if you are writing on the topic of making birth control available in public schools, who might be the most likely readers for your essay? People who might be interested in the topic could include parents of teenagers, teenagers themselves, and even people who work for the local school district. Narrowing your audience in this way will help you figure out what information, types of sources, and approaches your readers will expect from you on your chosen topic. Remember, too, that you cannot address all potential audiences for any given topic. You will need to narrow your topic in order to specifically address your chosen audience.

figure 11.1 Argument Essay Types

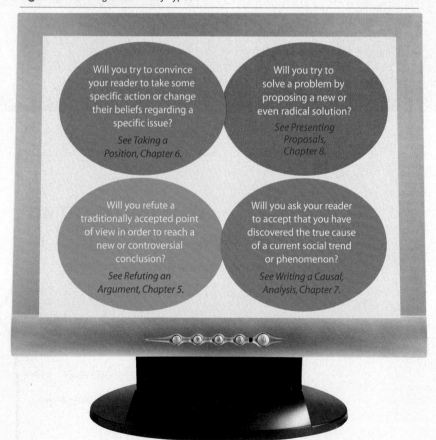

Will you try to convince your reader to take some specific action or change their beliefs regarding a specific issue?

See Taking a Position, Chapter 6.

Will you try to solve a problem by proposing a new or even radical solution?

See Presenting Proposals, Chapter 8.

Will you refute a traditionally accepted point of view in order to reach a new or controversial conclusion?

See Refuting an Argument, Chapter 5.

Will you ask your reader to accept that you have discovered the true cause of a current social trend or phenomenon?

See Writing a Causal, Analysis, Chapter 7.

Whether you are writing for a specialized, knowledgeable reader or a more general audience, you will need to consider the values those readers hold, what they already know about your subject, and what they will expect you to provide as convincing evidence for your thesis.

CONDOMS CAN CAUSE WRINKLES.

Who is the intended audience for this ad from Population Services International designed to increase AIDS awareness? Do you think the ad will appeal to its intended audience?

Remember that if after analyzing your audience's expectations, values, and needs, you decide that any of the following are true, you may want to consider changing your topic choice.

· **Your topic is so common or overly debated that your audience will view your essay as redundant or unnecessary.** If your readers can anticipate your main points and see your essay as a run-of-the-mill perspective on a heavily argued topic, you will most likely not succeed in gaining their attention or respect. If you are writing on a commonly debated topic, try to find a new or unique angle from which to approach it.

· **You do not have any authority on the subject.** This does not mean that you must be an expert on a topic in order to write about it. However, if you are attempting to persuade readers to accept your point of view as valid, you must have a thoughtful and well-informed opinion from which to start your writing process. Do not attempt to form your opinion on the subject as you write. Make sure you research your topic first and come to your writing with some measure of confidence and authority on your topic.

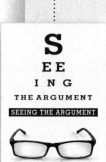

Analyze the intended audience for the advertisement here.

- Who do you think this author is trying to reach? How do you know?
- Do you think this audience will have preconceived ideas about this subject that might affect their attitude toward the author's position?
- Does this author attempt to approach this subject in a new way?
- Will readers accept PETA as a credible source on this issue?
- Do you think this ad ultimately does an effective job of reaching its intended audience with its message?

try it!

Consider the following issues that are typically considered overdone and run-of-the-mill. In a group or on your own, write a potential thesis statement that moves each topic in a new, engaging, and controversial direction. The first one has been done for you. Can you think of other overworked issues that might need to be moved in a new direction in order to become engaging research topics?

- Gun control

  Example: "Parents who keep guns in the house and whose children ultimately use those guns to commit a crime should receive a mandatory 10-year prison sentence."

- Television violence
- Teen pregnancy
- The drinking age
- Speed limits
- The death penalty
- Childhood obesity
- Prayer in public schools

Examine the billboard here. What argument is the author making? Would this be a good topic for a research essay aimed at parents of toddlers? Or might your readers simply agree with your main point that buckling up their children is a safe and wise choice? If your argument's claim (in this case, that children should use seat belts) will be accepted without question, you may want to search for a new topic.

Children are gifts. **Wrap them securely.**

Smart Choices Save Lives

- **Your readers will most likely agree with you.** This may seem like an odd statement, but if your chosen audience will most likely agree with every point you make, you may want to either choose a new topic or choose a new audience. After all, what is the point of working to persuade someone who values the same things you do and will automatically agree with every statement you make?

What Are the Assignment's Time and Length Constraints?

The required length of the paper, the time you have to complete the assignment, and the availability of sources are three constraints you must consider when selecting a research topic. Most instructors will establish guidelines regarding length. Knowing the expected length of the paper is crucial to selecting an appropriate topic, so if an instructor does not specify, be sure to ask.

Suppose, for example, that you must argue for solutions to either an educational or environmental problem. Your paper needs to be about six pages and is due in three weeks. Do you have the space or the time to explore solutions to all the problems caused by overpopulation? Definitely not. Limit your study to one issue such as coping with trash. You could further limit this topic by exploring waste management solutions for your particular city or county.

What Kinds of Topics Should I Avoid?

Here are several kinds of topics that are best avoided because they usually result in uninspired, irrelevant,

or disorganized essays, no matter how well researched they are.

1. **Topics that are irrelevant to your interests.** If you are not interested in your topic, you will not produce a lively, informative paper.

2. **Topics that are too broad.** These result in general surveys that lack appropriate detail and support. For example, it would be impossible to solve the issue of poverty in the space of eight pages. Be sure to narrow your topic sufficiently.

3. **Topics that can be fully researched with only one source.** You will produce a summary, not a research paper. For example, the issue of whether your neighbor should install a privacy fence would not sustain a fully documented research essay assignment. Topics can be too narrow, as well as too broad.

4. **Biographical studies.** Short undergraduate papers on a person's life usually turn out to be summaries of one or two major biographies.

5. **Topics that produce a strong emotional response in you.** If, in your mind, there is only one right answer to the abortion issue and you cannot accept counterarguments, don't choose to write on abortion. Probably most religious topics are also best avoided.

6. **Topics that are too technical for you at this point in your college work.** If you do not understand the complexities of the federal tax code, then arguing for a reduction in the capital gains tax may be an unwise topic choice.

Many online resources can help you choose and refine research essay topics or turn "overdone" issues into relevant and engaging paper topics.

Just be sure that the site you are using is a credible idea-generating site and not a site that sells or distributes plagiarized work from other authors. Plagiarism is a serious academic offense. Simply browsing websites for possible essay topics is not considered academically dishonest, however.

Try these sites for starters:

http://www.suite101.com/content/
    good-persuasive-essay-topics-a12517

www.goodessaytopics.com/argumentative-essay-
    topics.html

Choosing a topic from which you have a difficult time distancing your emotions can often be dangerous in a research essay. You must be able to understand and appreciate all the complexities of an issue if you are to conduct reliable research and write with authority and credibility. If you cannot do unbiased research, you may want to consider changing topics.

How Can I Select a Good Topic?

Choosing from Assigned Topics

At times, students are unhappy with topic restriction. Looked at another way, however, your instructor has eliminated a difficult step in the research process and has helped you avoid the problem of selecting an unworkable topic. If your professor gives you a list of possible topics, you will still have to choose well and develop your own claim and approach.

How Do I Get Started When There Are Few Restrictions?

When you are free to write on any course-related topic or any topic at all, you may need to use some strategies for topic selection. Here are some strategies to consider:

- Look through your text's table of contents or index for subject areas that can be narrowed or focused.
- Look over your class notes for topics that have particularly interested you.
- Consider college-based or local issues.
- Do a subject search in an electronic database to see how a large topic can be narrowed—for example, *dinosaur* may have subheadings such as *dinosaur behavior* and *dinosaur extinction*.
- To focus a broad topic, use one or more invention strategies:
    - Freewriting
    - Brainstorming
    - Asking questions about a broad subject, using the reporter's questions of who, what, where, when, and why.

Is My Topic Manageable?

Part of selecting a workable topic is making sure that the topic is sufficiently narrowed and focused. Students sometimes have trouble narrowing topics. Somehow it seems easier to write on a broad subject, such as education. You know there will be enough sources, all easy to find. But this line of thinking overlooks your purpose in doing research and what you know about good writing. Consider the following list of increasingly narrower topics about education:

1. Education

2. Problems in education today

3. Problems in K–12 education today

4. Problems with testing students

5. Why standardized tests are unfair for all students

The first three items are clearly too broad for a short research project. Do you recognize that topic 4 is also too broad? Remember that the more limited and focused your topic, the more concrete and detailed—and thus convincing and engaging—your research essay will be.

GOOD ADVICE

Oftentimes, you will find inspiration for your research essay topics by examining current issues on your campus or in your hometown or the city where you currently live. For example, the photo here shows a campus demonstration arguing for lower tuition rates. If you saw this image in your campus paper, it could be the start to forming an intriguing and relevant research essay topic. You could interview the participants in the rally, read local newspaper articles on the controversy, and then broaden your research to include national college tuition trends, student reactions, and governmental responses. You could then argue a position on this issue, propose possible solutions to the problem, and even speculate about the causes of the trend.

did you know?

A basic Google search for "No Child Left Behind Act" yields almost 1 million search results. A Google Scholar search for "No Child Left Behind Act failure rate public schools New York 2011" yields about 25,000 hits. While this is still far too many sources to use in a single research project, you can see that refining your search can significantly narrow the number of articles or websites you must consider on your way to finding the most effective and relevant sources.

Writing a Tentative Claim or Research Proposal

Once you have selected and narrowed a topic, you need to write a tentative claim, research question, or research proposal. Some instructors will ask to see a statement—

from one sentence to a paragraph long—to be approved before you proceed. Others may require as much as a one-page proposal that includes a tentative claim, a basic organizational plan, and a description of types of sources to be used. Even if your instructor does not require anything in writing, you need to write a plan for your own benefit—to direct your reading and thinking. Here are three student samples of research proposals, each of which takes a slightly different approach.

> **Subject:** Computers
>
> **Topic:** The impact of computers on the twentieth century
>
> **Claim:** Computers had the greatest impact of any technological development in the twentieth century.
>
> **Research Proposal:** I propose to show that computers had the greatest impact of any technological development in the twentieth century. I will show the influence of computers at work, in daily living, and in play to emphasize the breadth of influence. I will argue that other possibilities (such as cars) did not have the same impact as computers.

continued

> I will check the library's book catalog and databases for sources on technological developments and on computers specifically. I will also interview a family friend who works with computers at the Pentagon.

This example illustrates several key points. First, the initial subject, computers, is too broad and too unfocused. Second, the claim is more focused than the topic statement because it asserts a position, a claim the student must support. Third, the research proposal is more helpful than the claim only because it includes some thoughts on developing the thesis and finding sources.

Less sure of your topic? Then write a research question or a more open-ended research proposal. Take, for example, a history student studying the effects of Prohibition. She is not ready to write a thesis, but she can write a research proposal that suggests some possible approaches to the topic:

> **Topic:** The effect of Prohibition
>
> **Research Question:** What were the effects of Prohibition on the United States?
>
> **Research Proposal:** I will examine the effects of Prohibition on the United States in the 1920s (and possibly consider some long-term effects, depending on the amount of material on the topic). Specifically, I will look at the varying effects on urban and rural areas and on different classes in society. Ultimately, I would like to argue that Prohibition has had lasting negative effects on American society and that the lower socioeconomic classes feel these effects most profoundly.

Asking questions and working with fields of study (think of college departments) is a third approach. Suppose your assignment is to defend a position on a current social issue. You think you want to do something about television. Using an electronic database to search for a narrowed topic, you decide on the following:

> **Draft**
>
> **Topic:** Television and violence
>
> **Research Proposal:** I will explore the problem of violence on TV. I will read articles in current magazines and newspapers and see what's on the Internet.

Do you have a focused topic and a proposal that will guide your thinking and research? Not yet. Raise questions by field of study. This will help you narrow your focus and identify the direction you wish to take your research. For example, you may look at research questions raised in the following fields of study:

> **Literature/Humanities:** What kinds of violence are found on TV? Children's cartoons? Cop and mystery shows? The news? How are they alike? How are they different?
>
> **Sociology:** What are the consequences to our society of a continual and heavy dose of violence on television?
>
> **Psychology:** What are the effects of television violence on children? Why are we drawn to violent shows?
>
> **Politics/Government:** Should violence on TV be controlled in any way? If so, how?
>
> **Education:** What is the impact on the classroom when children grow up watching a lot of violence on TV? Does it impede social skills? learning?

Now your thinking is more focused. After reflecting, you choose a more specific topic:

> **Final draft—after conducting field-of-study preliminary research**
>
> **Topic:** The negative effects of television violence on children and some solutions
>
> **Research Proposal:** I will demonstrate that children suffer from their exposure to so much violence on TV and propose some solutions. Until I read more, I am not certain of the solutions I will propose; I want to read arguments for and against the V-chip and ratings and other possibilities.

Locating Effective Print and Online Sources

After you have refined your topic choice, identified your target audience, and written a tentative thesis or claim, it is time to begin your research. You will want to find relevant, up-to-date, and well-written sources so that you can learn what experts and other writers are saying about your issue, what counterarguments your readers might raise, and ultimately what you think about your issue. Research is a discovery process. It is not simply gathering quotes from experts who agree with you. It is part of the writing process and a way to think about your issue in new and interesting ways. The keys to conducting solid research are to target your searches effectively, to remain organized in collecting and citing your data, and to evaluate each source's relevance and importance to your writing goals. There are many effective strategies for finding, organizing, and evaluating your research, including the following.

Preparing a Working Bibliography

When you begin to gather important and relevant research for your topic, construct a working bibliography. This is a comprehensive list of all your potential sources, along with a brief note or explanation of why and how each source might help you in making your argument. By constructing a working bibliography,

you will come to see your topic and your argument more clearly. Once you begin to write your essay, you will also be able to easily find your sources and what they have to offer in support of your argument.

To begin this stage of your research, you need to have made three decisions:

1. **Your search strategy.** If you are writing on a course-related topic, your research may start with your textbook, looking for relevant sections and possible sources (if the text contains a bibliography). In this text, for example, you may find some potential sources among the readings. Think about what you already know or have in hand as you plan your search strategy.

2. **A method for recording bibliographic information.** You have two choices: the always-reliable 3 X 5 index cards or a bibliography file in your personal computer. You might simply start a Word document and keep a running list of your sources as you read them.

3. **The documentation format you will be using.** You may be assigned the Modern Language Association (MLA) format or perhaps given a choice

GOOD ADV!CE

You will discover that online article indexes rarely present information in MLA format. The screen shows an example of a source on animal rights found in an online database.

If you read the article in the journal itself, then the citation in MLA style would look like this:

> Vines, Gail. "Planet of the Free Apes?" *New Scientist* 5 June 1993: 39–42. Print.

However, if you obtain a full-text copy of the article from the electronic database, your citation will require additional information about the database. (See pages 190–193 for guidelines and examples.)

Do not be fooled into thinking that because the information is presented in a certain way on your computer screen, it will

be in the correct order for your citations page. Be sure to check your handbook or textbook for correct citation conventions as you move from your working bibliography to your formal citations.

between MLA and the American Psychological Association (APA) documentation styles. Once you select the documentation style, skim the appropriate pages in either your textbook or a college writing handbook to get an overview of both format and the information you will need about your sources.

A list of possible sources is called a *working bibliography* because you do not yet know which sources you will use. (Your final bibliography will include only those sources you cite—actually refer to—in your paper.) Remember that a working bibliography will help you see what is available on your topic and where to locate each source; it will also contain the information needed to document your paper. Whether you are using cards or computer files, follow these guidelines:

1. Check all reasonable catalogues and indexes for possible sources. (Use more than one reference source even if you locate enough information in the first one; you are looking for the best sources, not the first ones you find.)

2. Complete a card or prepare an entry for every potentially useful source. You won't know what to reject until you start a close reading of sources.

3. Copy (or download from an online catalogue) all information needed to complete a citation and to locate the source. (When using an index that does not give all needed information, leave a space to be filled in when you read the source.)

4. Put bibliographic information in the correct format for every possible source; you will save time and make fewer errors. Do not mix or blend styles. When searching for sources, have your text or handbook handy and use the model citations as guides.

5. Make a brief note about each source. Why did you choose it? What information might it contain that will help you as you write? Is the author an expert in a certain field? What point do you think it will support in your essay?

Using correct documentation as you keep track of your sources in your working bibliography will help you later in the writing process as you construct your Works Cited or References page.

The following brief guide to correct form will get you started. Guidelines are for MLA style only; use Chapter 14 if you have selected a different style.

Basic Form for Books

The basic MLA form for books includes the following information in this pattern:

1. The author's full name, last name first.
    Smith, James.

2. The title (and subtitle if there is one) of the book, italicized.
    The First of Many Improbable Questions.

3. The facts of publication: the city of publication (followed by a colon), the publisher (followed by a comma), the date of publication (followed by a period), and the medium of publication.
    London: Royal Press, 2008. Print.

Note that periods are placed after the author's name, after the title, after the year, and at the end of the citation. Other information, when appropriate (for example, the number of volumes), is added to this basic pattern. (See pages 236–239 for many sample citations.) In your working bibliography, include the book's classification number so that you can find it in the library.

Basic Form for Articles

This is the simplest form for magazine articles. Include the following information, in this pattern:

1. The author's full name, last name first.
    Morrell, Virginia.

2. The title of the article, in quotation marks.
    "A Cold, Hard Look at Dinosaurs."

3. The facts of publication: the title of the periodical (italicized), the volume number (if the article is from a scholarly journal), the date (followed by a colon), inclusive page numbers (followed by a period), and the medium of publication.
    Discover Dec. 1996: 98–108. Print.

Knowing Your Library

All libraries contain books and periodicals and a system for accessing them. A *book collection* contains the *general collection* (books that circulate), the *refer-*

as the book's International Standard Book Number (ISBN). When you go to your library's home screen and select the catalogue, you will come to the search screen. Usually, *keyword* is the default.

SEARCH: Gatsby

If you know the exact title, switch to *Title*, type in the title (without the initial article *a, an, the*), and click on Submit Search.

SEARCH: Great Gatsby

If you want a list of all of the library's books by a certain author (in this case, F. Scott Fitzgerald), click on *Author* and type in the author's last name.

SEARCH: Fitzgerald

Keep in mind:

- Use correct spelling. If you are unsure of a spelling, use a keyword search instead of an author or title search.
- If you are looking for a list of books on your subject, do a keyword or subject search.

ence collection (books of a general nature essential to research), and the *reserve book collection*. The library's *periodicals collection* consists of popular magazines, scholarly journals, and newspapers. Electronic databases with full texts of articles provide alternatives to the print periodicals collection.

Locating Books *Computer*

Your chief guide to the book (and audiovisual) collection is the catalogue, probably a computer database (see Figure 11.2 for an example).

In a catalogue there are at least three entries for each book: the author entry, the title entry, and one or more subject entries. Online catalogues use these same access points plus a keyword option and possibly others, such

Reading Entries: Brief and Long View Screens

If you do an author search by last name only, you will get a list of all the library's books written by writers with that last name. A keyword search will provide a list of all book titles containing your keyword. These "brief view" lists provide enough information to locate a book in the library: author, title, and classification number—the number by which the book is shelved.

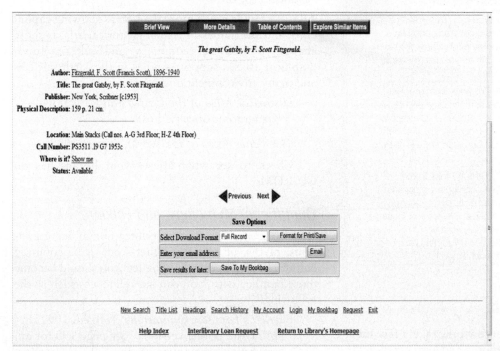

figure 11.2 Online Catalogue Entry—Long View of One Book

Catalog screen from University of Texas at Dallas Libraries, using the Voyager Integrated System from Ex Libris. Reprinted with permission.

For books that look promising for your research, click on View Record (or similar command icon) to obtain the "long view" screen. The screen, as shown in the example on page 187, provides additional information about the book, including its length, publication information, and status. For potentially useful books, copy all needed information into your working bibliography.

The book and periodicals collections are supplemented by audiovisual materials, including works on CD, tape, microfilm or microfiche, and online. Many libraries store back issues of periodicals on microfilm, so learn where the microfilm readers are and how to use them. In addition, articles from electronic databases and Internet sources can be printed or, in many cases, e-mailed directly to you.

Using the Reference Collection

The research process often begins with the reference collection. You will find atlases, dictionaries, encyclopedias, general histories, critical studies, and biographies. In addition, reference tools such as bibliographies and indexes are part of the reference collection.

Many tools in the reference collection once only in print form are now also online. Some are now only online. Yet online is not always the way to go. The table compares advantages of each of the formats.

Reasons to Use the Print Reference Collection	Reasons to Use Online Reference Materials
1. The reference tool is only in print—use it.	1. Online databases are likely to provide the most up-to-date information.
2. Only the print form covers the period you are studying. (Most online indexes and abstracts cover only from 1980 to the present.)	2. You can usually search all years covered at one time. (Some print references have separate volumes for each year.)
3. In a book, with a little scanning of pages, you can often find what you need without getting spelling or commands exactly right.	3. Full texts (with graphics) are sometimes available, as well as indexes with detailed summaries of articles. Both can be printed or e-mailed to you.
4. If you know the best reference source to use and are looking for only a few items, the print source can be faster than the online source.	4. Through links to the Internet, you have access to an amazing amount of material. (Unless you focus your keyword search, however, you may be overwhelmed.)
5. Your Internet connection is down—open a book!	

Before using any reference work, take a few minutes to check its date, purpose, and organization. If you are new to online searching, take a few minutes to learn about each reference tool by working through the online tutorial. (Go to the Help screen.) These strategies can supplement the following brief review of some key reference tools.

Basic Reference Tools

Use your library's reference collection for facts, for background information, and for indexes to possible sources.

Dictionaries

For the spelling of specialized words not in your computer's dictionary, consult an appropriate subject dictionary; for foreign words, the appropriate foreign-language dictionary. If you need a word's origin or its definition from an earlier time, use an unabridged dictionary. Here are two to know:

> *Webster's Encyclopedic Unabridged Dictionary of the English Language.* 1996.
>
> *The Oxford English Dictionary.* 20 volumes in print.

Both of these resources offer online subscriptions. This may be more convenient if you have access to the Internet as you write.

General Encyclopedias

Two multivolume encyclopedias to know are the *Encyclopedia Americana* and the *Encyclopedia Britannica.* The *Britannica,* the *World Book,* and other encyclopedias are available online as well as in print, which again, may be more convenient if you have access to the Internet as you write (see figure on page 189).

Atlases *Change in culture*

Atlases provide much more than maps showing capital cities and the names of rivers. Historical atlases show changes in politics, economics, and culture. Topographical atlases support studies in the earth sciences and many environmental issues.

> *Historical Atlas of the United States.* National Geographic Society, 1988.
>
> *The Times Atlas of the World,* 9th ed. 1992.

Check to see what atlases your library has on CD-ROM.

Quotations, Mythology, and Folklore

If in your research you encounter unfamiliar quotations, myths, or references that seem to be common cultural knowledge or that you feel you should become more familiar with, you can use references such as the following:

> *Bartlett's Familiar Quotations,* 16th ed. 1992. In print and online versions. (See page 190 for an example of the online version.)
>
> *Funk and Wagnall's Standard Dictionary of Folklore, Mythology, and Legend.*

Almanacs and Yearbooks *current events*

These annually published references answer all kinds of questions about current events and provide statistical information on many topics. Many of these works are both in print and online. Check to see which format your library offers.

> *Congressional Record.* 1873 to date. Issued daily during sessions. Online.
>
> *Facts on File.* 1940 to date. Digest of important news events. Online.
>
> *Statistical Abstract of the United States.* 1978 to date. Annual publication of the Bureau of the Census. Online.

Biographical Dictionaries

Most libraries have an array of biographical dictionaries, important tools for investigating authors with whom you are unfamiliar.

> *Contemporary Authors.* 1962 to date. A multivolume guide to current fiction and nonfiction writers and their books. Online.

> *International Who's Who.* 1935 to date. Brief biographies of important people from almost every country.
>
> *American Men and Women of Science.* Brief sketches of more than 150,000 scientists. Lists degrees held and fields of specialization. Regularly updated.
>
> *Who's Who.* 1849 to date. English men and women.
>
> *Who's Who in America.* 1899 to date.
>
> *Who's Who in American Women.* 1958 to date.

Using Indexes to Periodicals: In Print and Online

Periodicals (magazines, journals, and newspapers) are excellent sources for research projects, especially for projects on current issues. The best way to access articles on your topic is to use one or more periodical indexes. To be efficient, you want to select the most

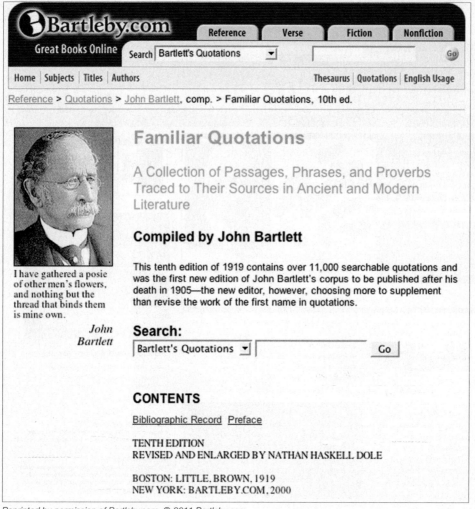

Reprinted by permission of Bartleby.com. © 2011 Bartleby.com.

useful indexes for your particular study. Your library will maintain some print indexes to popular magazines, some for scholarly journals, and some to newspapers. In addition, your library probably provides many online databases. Online databases are more likely than older print indexes to blend magazines, journals, and newspaper articles, and many online databases include full texts of the articles. Learn which of the indexes provide full texts and which indexes provide only lists of articles that you must then locate in your library's paper collection of periodicals.

The Readers' Guide to Periodical Literature

Probably the most-used paper and online index, *The Readers' Guide to Periodical Literature* (1900 to date) combines author and subject headings that guide users to articles in about 200 popular magazines. Most college libraries have access to this database on their sites. Check with your librarian to see if your school offers this service. As the sample entries in Figure 11.3 show, the information is heavily abbreviated. When using this index, study the explanation provided and check the list of periodicals found in the front of each volume for the complete title of each magazine. Use this index if you want articles written prior to 1980.

The New York Times Index

Newspapers are a good source of information about both contemporary topics and historical events and issues. Because it is one of the most thorough and respected newspapers, *The New York Times* is available in most libraries. So, when your topic warrants it, become familiar with *The New York Times Index*, for it can guide you to articles as far back as the mid-nineteenth century. (Back issues of the newspaper are on microfilm.) The print *NYT Index* is a subject index, cumulated and bound annually, with articles arranged chronologically under each subject heading. The *NYT Index* is also online, and articles in *The New York Times* are often indexed in other online databases.

Online Databases

You will probably access online databases by going to your library's home page and then clicking on the appropriate term or icon. (You may have found the book catalogue by clicking on Library Catalogue;

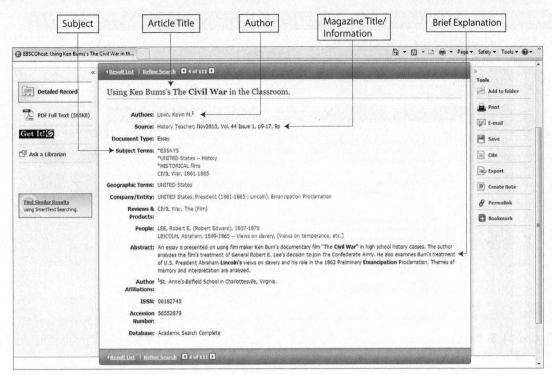

figure 11.3 Entry in *The Readers' Guide to Periodical Literature Online*

you may find the databases by clicking on Library Resources or some other descriptive label.)

You will need to choose a particular database and then type in your keyword for a basic search or select Advanced Search to limit your search by date or periodical or to search for articles by a specific author. Each library has somewhat different screens, but the basic process of selecting among choices provided and then typing in your search commands is the same.

Figure 11.4 below shows the first screen in response to a search for magazine and newspaper articles in the library's research databases. The list of databases on this screen is one that the librarians have noted as being useful for undergraduate research proj-

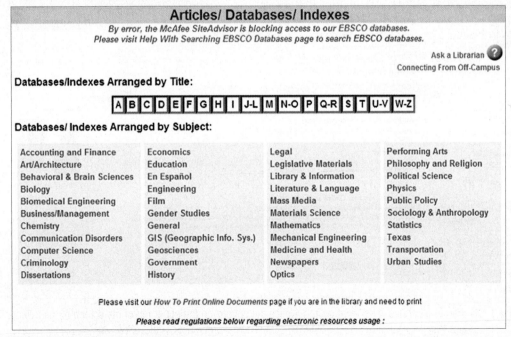

figure 11.4 Library search screen for online research databases

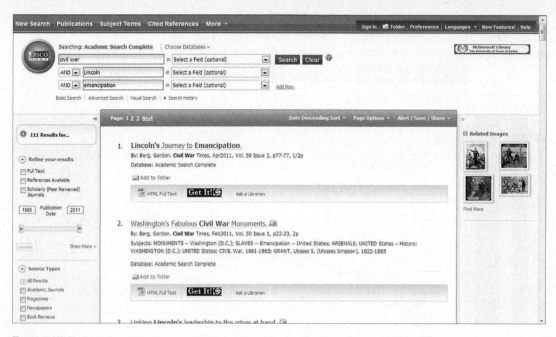

figure 11.5 Search screen in research database Academic Search Complete. Keyword search is the default for most online databases.

ects. If you know which database you would like to work with, you can click on the alphabetical list of databases or search by subject. If you do not already know which database might work for your research, you may want to scroll through the options and select the database that seems most useful for your topic.

Suppose, after looking over your options, you select Academic Search Complete (EBSCO Host). The first screen is shown next (see Figure 11.5). You can do a basic keyword search or modify your search in a number of ways.

A basic keyword search for "zoos and animal rights" yielded 113 articles. Figure 11.6 shows a partial list of those hits. You will want to try to narrow your search to a manageable number of hits. As a rule of thumb, if your keyword search returns more than 100

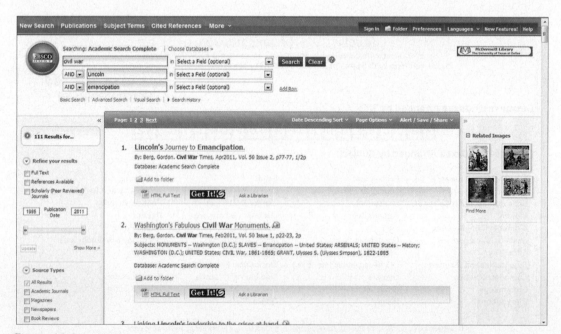

figure 11.6 Partial list of hits in keyword search. Notice the options on the upper left of the screen for narrowing this search. Notice also that the search results are listed in chronological order, not by relevance.

hits, you should try adding more keywords or using Boolean operators to narrow the search parameters. For more on how to effectively use Boolean operators in searches, see page 195 in this chapter.

Using Indexes to Academic Journals: In Print and Online

The indexes to magazines and newspapers just described provide many good articles for undergraduate research. At times, though, you may need to use articles from scholarly journals. Many of the indexes to specialized journals began as print indexes but are now online as well. The following is a brief list of some of the academic indexes students frequently use. Your reference librarian can recommend others appropriate to your study.

Applied Science and Technology Index. An index to periodicals covering engineering, data processing, earth sciences, space science, and more. Online through FirstSearch.

Book Review Digest. Begun in 1905, this index is arranged by author of the book reviewed. It contains brief reviews of both fiction and nonfiction works. Online.

Essay and General Literature Index. From 1900, this author and subject index includes references to both biographical and critical materials. Its chief focus is literary criticism.

Educational Research Information Center (ERIC). In its print form, there are two sections, Current Index to Journals in Education and Resources in Education, a collection of unpublished reports on educational issues. ERIC is also online.

The GPO Publications Reference File or GPO Access (on the Web). The former has been replaced by the regularly updated index on the Internet. You can reach GPO Access at www.access.gpo.gov/su_docs.

Humanities Index. This index lists articles on art, literature, philosophy, folklore, history, and related topics. Online.

MLA International Bibliography. The annual listing by the Modern Language Association of books, articles, and dissertations on language and literature. Online.

Public Affairs Information Service (PAIS). This index covers books, pamphlets, reports, and articles on economics, government, social issues, and public affairs. It is international in scope and emphasizes works that are strong on facts and statistics. Online.

GOOD ADVICE

Guidelines for Using Online Databases

Keep these points in mind as you use online databases:

- Although some online databases provide full texts of all articles, others provide full texts of only some of the articles indexed. The articles not in full text will have to be located in a print collection of periodicals.

- Articles not available in full text often come with a brief summary or abstract. This allows you to decide whether the article looks useful for your project. Do not treat the abstract as the article. Do not use material from it and cite the author. If you want to use the article, find it in your library's print collection or obtain it from another library.

- The database's information about an article is not in the correct format for any of the standard documentation styles (such as MLA or APA). You will have to reorder the information and use the correct style. If your instructor wants to see a list of possible sources in MLA format, do not hand in a printout of articles from an online database.

- Although some search engines, like Google, order their results by relevance to your search terms, most academic research databases do not. Articles may be ordered in chronological order, for example. Do not assume that the first article on the list is the most useful or relevant to your research needs.

- Because no single database covers all magazines, you may want to search several databases that seem relevant to your project.

Science Citation Index. An index of more than 3,000 journals in mathematics and the natural, physical, and behavioral sciences. It includes an index to articles, a subject index based on keywords appearing in titles of articles indexed, and a citation index arranged by author that reveals which articles are referred to by other authors in their papers. The online version is SciSearch or through Web of Science.

Social Sciences Citation Index. Like the *Science Citation Index*, this index includes a source index, a subject index by keywords, and a citation index. The online version is Social SciSearch or through Web of Science.

Searching the Internet

In addition to using the online databases to find sources, you can search the Internet directly. Keep in mind, however, these facts about the Internet:

- The Internet is both disorganized and huge, so you can waste time trying to find information that is easily obtained in a reference book in your library.

- The Internet is best at providing current information, such as news and movie reviews. It is also a great source of government information.

- Because anyone can create a website and put anything on it, you will have to be especially careful in evaluating Internet sources. Remember

that articles in magazines and journals have been selected by editors and are often peer reviewed as well, but no editor selects or rejects material on a personal website. (More on evaluating sources can be found in Chapter 12.)

If you are new to Internet searching, you may want to study online tutorials to be efficient in your search. Also, your college library may conduct workshops—check it out.

Access to the Internet provides information in a variety of ways, including:

- **E-mail.** E-mail can be used instead of a printed letter to request information from a government agency or company.

- **Mailing lists (listservs).** You can sign up to receive, via your e-mail, continually updated bulletins on a particular subject. Listservs are essentially organized mailing lists. If you find one relevant to your project, you can subscribe for a while and unsubscribe when you are no longer interested.

- **Newsgroups.** Newsgroups differ from listservs in that the discussions and exchanges are collected for you to retrieve; they are not sent to your e-mail address. Otherwise they are much the same: Both are a type of discussion group. To find newsgroups on a specific subject, go to http://groups.google.com, a research tool sponsored by the search engine Google, that surveys all Usenet newsgroups (see Figure 11.7).

- **World Wide Web.** To access the Web from your library terminal or on your own device through a hookup with your college library, you will, as

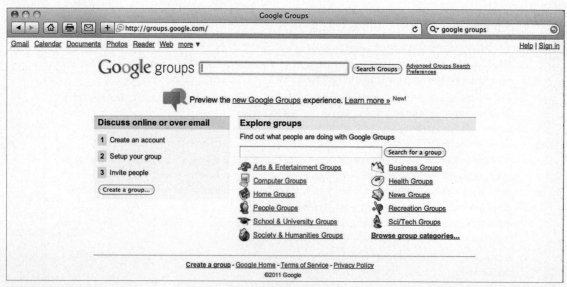

figure 11.7 Online newsgroups, like the ones on Google Groups, can be a useful tool in discovering what the current debates are in any given field of study. You can observe the conversation threads or even participate to gain a clearer understanding of your topic.

Google Brand Features are trademarks or distinctive brand features of Google Inc.

Guidelines for Searching the Internet

1. Bookmark sites you expect to use often so that you do not have to remember Web addresses (uniform resource locators, or URLs).

2. Make your search as precise as possible to avoid getting overwhelmed with hits.

3. If you are searching for a specific phrase, put quotation marks around it. This will reduce the number of hits and lead to sites more useful to your research; for example, "Environmental Protection Agency" or "civil disobedience."

4. Use Boolean connectors to make your search more precise.
   - AND: This connector limits results to sites that contain both terms; for example, "zoos AND animal rights."
   - OR: This connector extends the hits to include all sites that contain one or the other search term. So "zoos OR animal rights" will generate a list of sites containing either term.
   - NOT: This connector limits the search to only the first term and excludes the second. Thus, "animal rights NOT zoos" will give you sites about animal rights issues not involving zoos.

5. If you are not successful with one search engine, try a different one. Remember that each search engine searches only a part of the Internet.

6. To get the best sites for most college research projects, try a directory of evaluated sites or subject guides rather than, say, Yahoo! (Yahoo! is better for news, people searches, and commercial sites.) Some of the best academic subject guides are:
   - The University of California's Infomine (http://infomine.ucr.edu)
   - Internet Scout Project (http://scout.cs.wisc.edu)

7. Be certain to complete a bibliography card—including the date you accessed the material—for each site from which you take information. All sources must be documented, including Internet sources. (See pages 185–186 for documentation guidelines.)

with the catalogue and online databases, start at your library's home page. Usually selecting Search the Internet will take you to a menu of search engines and subject directories. Not all search engines are the same, and people differ on which are the best. Here are some sites to visit for help in selecting an appropriate search engine:

- *Librarians' Index to the Internet:* http://lii.org

- *Greg R. Notess's search engine comparison pages:* www.searchengineshowdown.com

- *Search Engine Watch:* www.searchenginewatch.com

Conducting Field Research

Field research (including conducting interviews, distributing surveys, and even firsthand observation of the issue) can enrich many projects. The following sections give some suggestions.

Federal, State, and Local Government Documents

In addition to federal documents you may obtain through *Public Affairs Information Services (PAIS)* or *GPO Access*, department and agency websites, or the Library of Congress's good legislative site, *Thomas* (http://thomas.loc.gov), consider state and county archives, maps, and other published materials. Instead of selecting a national or global topic, consider examining the debate over a controversial bill introduced in your state legislature. Use online databases to locate articles on the bill and the debate, and interview legislators and journalists who participated in or covered the debates or served on committees that worked with the bill.

You can also request specific documents on a topic from appropriate state or county agencies and nonprofit organizations. For example, one student, given the assignment of arguing for specific solutions to an ecological problem, decided to study the local problem of preserving the Chesapeake Bay. After visiting the website for the nonprofit group Chesapeake Bay Foundation (see Figure 11.8) and using the Contact Us link, she obtained issues of their newsletters and brochures advising homeowners about hazardous household waste materials that end up in the bay.

She was able to add bulletins on soil conservation and landscaping tips for improving the area's water quality to her sources. Local problems can lead to interesting research topics because they are current and relevant to you and because they involve uncovering different kinds of source materials.

Correspondence

Business and government officials are usually willing to respond to written requests for information. Make your letter brief and well written. Either include a self-addressed, stamped envelope for the person's convenience or e-mail your request. If you are not e-mailing, write as soon as you discover the need for information and be prepared to wait several weeks for a reply. It is appropriate to indicate your deadline and ask for a timely response. Whether you write or e-mail, consider these guidelines:

1. Explain precisely what information you need. Don't just ask, "Please send me anything you have on this topic." Busy professionals are more likely to respond to requests that are specific and reveal knowledge of the topic.

2. Do not request information that can be easily found in your library's reference collection.

3. Explain how you plan to use the information. Businesses are understandably concerned with their public image and will be disinclined to provide information that you intend to use in an attack on them.

Consult reference guides to companies and government agencies or their websites to obtain addresses and the person to whom your letter or e-mail should be addressed. For companies, address your request to the public information officer. For e-mail addresses, check the organization's homepage.

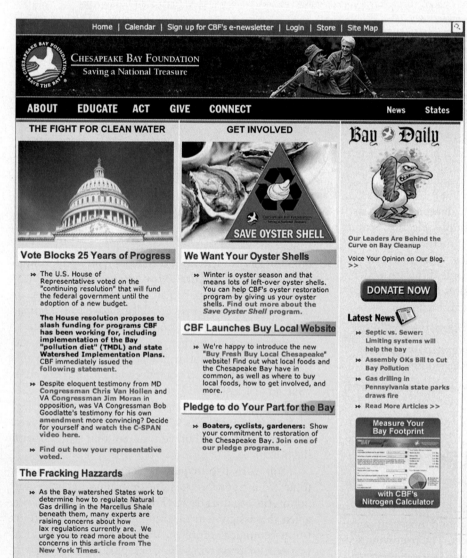

figure 11.8 Websites for nonprofit or government agencies can be useful sources of information on local topics and can often lead to interviews with those involved with the issues.

© Copyright 2011, Chesapeake Bay Foundation. Reprinted with permission.

Interviews

Some experts are available for personal interviews. Call or write for an appointment as soon as you recognize the value of an interview. Remember that you are more likely to be able to schedule an interview with state and local officials than with the president of General Motors. If you are studying a local problem, also consider leaders of civic associations with an interest in the issue. In many communities, the local historian or a librarian will be a storehouse of information about the community. Former teachers can be interviewed for papers on education. Interviews with doctors or nurses can add a special dimension to papers on medical issues.

If an interview is appropriate for your topic, follow these guidelines:

1. Prepare specific questions in advance.

2. Arrive on time, appropriately dressed, and behave in a polite, professional manner.

3. Take notes, asking the interviewee to repeat key statements so that your notes are accurate.

4. Take a tape recorder with you but ask permission to use it before taping.

5. If you quote any statements in your paper, quote accurately, eliminating only such minor speech habits as "you know" and "um." (See Chapter 14 for proper documentation of interviews.)

6. Direct the interview with your prepared questions, but also give the interviewee the chance to approach the topic in his or her own way. You may obtain information or views that had not occurred to you.

7. Do not get into a debate with the interviewee. You are there to learn, not to try to change the interviewee's thinking.

Lectures

Check the appropriate information sources at your school to learn about visiting speakers. If you are fortunate enough to attend a lecture relevant to a current project, take careful, detailed notes. Because a lecture is a source, use of information or ideas from it must be presented accurately and then documented. (See Chapter 14 for documentation format.)

Films, Tapes, Television, Online Multimedia Sources

Your library and the Internet will have audiovisual materials that provide good sources for some kinds of topics. For example, if you are studying *Death of a Salesman,* you might view a videotaped or online version of the play.

Also pay attention to documentaries on public television and to the many news and political talk shows on both public and commercial channels. In many cases, transcripts of shows can be obtained from the TV station. Alternatively, tape or DVR the program while watching it so that you can view it several times and obtain accurate quotes, if necessary. (The documentation format for such nonprint sources is illustrated in Chapter 14.)

Surveys, Questionnaires, and Original Research

Depending on your paper, you may want to conduct a simple survey or write and administer a questionnaire. Surveys can be used for many campus and local issues, for topics on behavior and attitudes of college students or faculty, and for topics on consumer habits. Prepare a brief list of questions with space for answers. Poll faculty through their mailboxes or e-mail and students individually on campus or in your classes. Be aware, however, that many universities and colleges require special approval for research studies involving human subjects. Be sure to ask your instructor about gaining subject approval or university approval prior to conducting any surveys.

When writing survey questions, keep these guidelines in mind:

• Use simple, clear language.

• Devise a series of short questions rather than only a few multipart questions. (You want to separate information for better analysis.)

• Phrase questions to avoid wording that seeks to control the answer. For example, do not ask, How did you survive the horrors of the Depression? Do not write, Did you perform your civic duty by voting in the last election? These are loaded questions that prejudge the respondent's answers.

In addition to surveys and questionnaires, you can incorporate some original research. As you read sources on your topic, be alert to reports of studies that you could redo and update in part or on a smaller scale. Many topics on advertising and television give opportunities for your own analysis. Local-issue topics may offer good opportunities for gathering information on your own, not just from your reading.

For example, one student, examining the controversy over a proposed new shopping mall on part of the Manassas Civil War Battlefield in Virginia, made the argument that the mall served no practical need in the community. He supported his position by describing existing malls, including the number and types of stores each contained and the number of miles each was from the proposed new mall. How did he obtain this information? He drove around the area, counting miles and stores. Sometimes a seemingly unglamorous approach to a topic turns out to be an imaginative one.

let's review

After reading this chapter, you should understand the following:

- Before beginning a major researched argumentative essay, it is important to understand what tools, or argumentative strategies, are available. The essay types featured in Chapters 5–9 offer some suggestions for four specific types of arguments and strategies for writing each.

- It is crucial that you understand your writing purpose before you begin your research, prewriting, or drafting. This writing purpose, along with clear ideas about your audience's needs and expectations, will guide every step of your writing process.

- One key to success is finding a workable topic. After all, no matter how interesting or clever a topic may seem, it is not workable if it does not meet the guidelines of your assignment. The required length of the paper, the time you have to complete the assignment, and the availability of sources are three constraints you must consider when selecting a workable research topic.

- Once you have selected and narrowed a topic, you need to write a tentative claim, research question, or research proposal.

- After you have refined your topic, identified your target audience, and written a tentative thesis or claim, it is time to begin your actual research. You will want to find the most relevant, up-to-date, and well-written sources available to you so that you can learn what experts and other writers are saying about your issue, what potential counterarguments your readers may raise, and ultimately what you think about your issue.

- One way to begin to gather important and relevant research for your topic is to construct a working bibliography. This is a list of all of your potential sources, along with a brief note or explanation of why and how each source will help you in making your argument.

- Your library is a valuable resource during your research process. There you can find books, articles, reference materials, newspapers, and access to online research databases.

- In addition to using the online databases to find sources, you can search the Internet directly. Keep in mind, however, that there are special challenges to searching for credible research sources online.

- Field research (including interviews, surveys, and even firsthand observation of the issue) can enrich many projects.

evaluating and
utilizing sources

c h a p t e r   12

In Chapter 11, you began the processes of finding a workable and manageable topic for your research essay and of finding appropriate and credible sources that support your thesis. The next step in this process involves two very important tasks: evaluating the sources you have found and figuring out where and how you will most effectively use them in your essay. After all, you will surely not be able to (or want to) use every single source you find regarding your topic, nor will every credible source fit with your particular argumentative strategy. Think, for example, of every article you might find on the topic of legalizing music downloading. Some might be written in favor of the idea, some might be opposed, some might be from noncredible sources, some might be too old to be relevant, some might be too technical, and some might be completely biased or full of logical fallacies. It is up to you as the researcher to figure out which sources will be credible, reliable, and useful to you as you construct your own argument. This is not an easy or quick task. It will involve careful research, reading and rereading your sources, evaluating each one as it relates to your thesis, and making an organized plan for where and how you will use each source. As you study your sources and your working bibliography, you will need to keep rethinking your purpose, audience, and approach. You should also test your research proposal or tentative claim against what you are learning. Remember: You can always change the direction and focus of your paper as new approaches occur to you, and you can even change your position as you reflect on what you are learning.

Finding Sources

You will work with sources more effectively if you keep in mind why you are using them. What you are looking for will depend on your topic and purpose, but you can use several basic approaches to finding sources:

1. **Acquiring information and viewpoints firsthand.** Suppose that you are concerned about the mistreatment of animals kept in zoos. You do not want to just read what others have to say on this issue. Visit a zoo and take notes on what you see. Before you go, arrange to interview at least one person on the zoo staff, preferably a veterinarian who can explain the zoo's guidelines for animal care. Only after gathering and thinking about these *primary sources* do you want to add to your knowledge by reading articles and books—*secondary sources*. Many kinds of topics require the use of both primary and secondary sources. If you want to study violence in children's TV shows, for example, you should first spend some time watching specific shows and taking notes.

2. **Acquiring new knowledge.** Suppose you are interested in breast cancer research and treatment, but you do not know much about the choices of treatment and, in general, where we are with this medical problem. You will need to turn to sources first to learn about the topic. You should begin with sources that will give you an overview, perhaps a historical perspective of how knowl-

[handwritten note: Make up your own ideas]

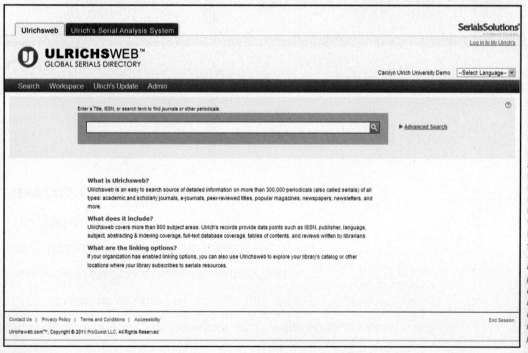

Ulrichsweb.com provides publisher information for more than 300,000 periodicals of all types— academic and scholarly journals, open access publications, peer-reviewed titles, popular magazines, newspapers, newsletters, and more— from around the world. It's a great starting point for finding sources.

GOOD ADV!CE

Buzzle.com is a dynamic network of authors and content contributors whom the site creators refer to as "Intelligent Life on the Web." As subject experts, these authors and content contributors create an informative, yet comfortable place for finding information about everything from animals to tourism. With current news in the What's the Buzz? section, thousands of interesting categories, an interactive online community, and thought-provoking polls, Buzzle .com offers a medium through which to share knowledge of the world. This would be an excellent place to search for a current and relevant topic or to begin your research process on your chosen issue. As with any online source, however, you will need to analyze and evaluate the credibility and authorship of each article. Be sure to click on the author's name in order to find out more about his or her specific qualifications, background, and organizational associations.

Reprinted by permission of Buzzle.com.

edge and treatment have progressed in the last 30 years. Similarly, if your topic is the effects of Prohibition in the 1920s, you will need to read first for knowledge but also with an eye to ways to focus the topic and organize your paper.

3. **Understanding the issues.** Suppose you think that you know your views on gun control or immigration, so you intend to read only to obtain some useful statistical information to support your argument. Should you scan sources quickly, looking for facts you can use? This approach may be too hasty. As explained in Chapter 3, good arguments rely on a writer's knowledge of counterarguments and opposing positions. You are wise to study sources presenting a variety of attitudes on your issue so that you understand—and can refute— the arguments of others.

With controversial issues, often the best argument is a conciliatory one that presents a middle ground and seeks to bring people together. In

[handwritten margin note: look at counter arguments]

order to fully understand all sides of your chosen issue, you may want to visit sites, read articles, or even collect survey responses in order to expose yourself to multiple points of view. This is a good way to educate yourself about the current debate so that you better understand your audience's values and potential counterarguments.

Evaluating Sources and Maintaining Credibility

When you use facts and opinions from sources, you are saying to readers that the facts are accurate and the ideas credible. If you do not evaluate your sources before using them, you risk losing your credibility as a writer. (Remember Aristotle's idea of *ethos*, or how your character is judged.) Just because they are in print

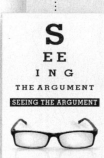
Online sources credited to authors with few or no credentials related to the subject matter, like the author of this blog, are not generally reliable for research essays. Although the information may seem accurate, it is best to try to find it in a source that comes from an author with credentials that relate to the information presented. Compare this blog to the article that follows. Based on authorship alone, which source seems more credible? Why? Which would you choose to use as a potential source for your research essay?

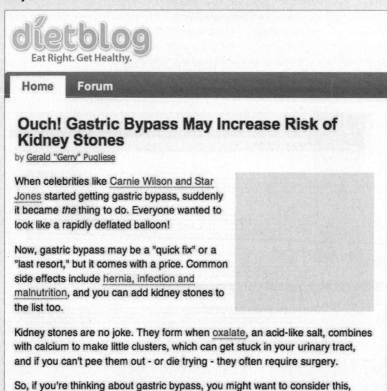

Medicinenet.com web page reprinted with permission, 2011.

GOOD ADV!CE

Although many online sources may not be excellent for research purposes, don't give up! You can find credible academic and journalistic articles online. Just be sure that the source is a reputable one and that the author supports his or her points with documented statistics, facts, and/ or noted authorities on the subject. In the web page shown here, for example, the author cites an expert in primatology in support of the article.

or online does not mean that a writer's "facts" are reliable or ideas worthwhile. Judging the usefulness and reliability of potential sources is an essential part of the research process.

Today, with access to so much material on the Internet, the need to evaluate is even more crucial. Here are some strategies for evaluating sources, with special attention to Internet sources:

- **Locate the author's credentials.** Periodicals often list their writers' degrees, current position, and other publications; books, similarly, contain an "about the author" section. If you do not see this information, check biographical dictionaries (such as *Biography Index, Contemporary Authors*) for information about the author. For articles on the Web, look for the author's e-mail address or a link to a homepage. Never use a Web source that does not identify the author or the organization responsible for the material. Critical question: Is this author qualified to write on this topic? How do I know?

- **Judge the credibility of the writing.** For books, read how reviewers evaluated the book when it was first published. For articles, judge the respectability of the magazine or journal. Study the author's use of documentation as one measure of credibility. Scholarly works cite sources. Well-researched and reliable pieces in quality popular magazines will also make clear the sources of any statistics used and the credentials of any authority who is quoted. One good rule: Never use undocumented or unreferenced statistical information. Another sign of credibility is the quality of writing. Do not use sources filled with grammatical and mechanical errors. For Web sources, find out what institution hosts the site. If you have not heard of the company or organization, find out more about it. The critical question to ask is, Why should I believe information/ideas from this source?

- **Select only sources that are at an appropriate level for your research.** Avoid works that are either too specialized or too elementary for college research. You may not understand the former (and thus could misrepresent them in your paper), and you gain nothing from the latter. The critical question to ask is, Will this source provide a sophisticated discussion for educated adults?

- **Understand the writer's purpose.** Consider the writer's intended audience. Be cautious using works that reinforce biases already shared by the intended audience. Is the work written to persuade

When evaluating your sources for an academic research essay, it is important to examine whether the piece is at the appropriate level (in both its writing and research) for an educated audience who has a serious investment in your argument. Consider this piece about eating disorders from *People* magazine. Would an academic audience accept this writer's writing style and research as credible and reliable? Would the visuals add to or detract from the perceived level of this article? Would you use this article as an academic source? Why or why not?

EXTREME MEASURES

Drastic thinness has become the reigning beauty ideal from runways to the red carpet—and it's having an alarming effect on girls everywhere

In interviews with PEOPLE at malls across the country, most teenage girls rejected Richie's body as "nasty" and "too skinny" but acknowledged that she and other stars serve as style role models. "Nicole's body is gross because her skeleton shows," says Kailey Koepplin, 17, of Eden Prairie, Minn. Other teens said they admire healthier-looking stars like Jessica Simpson ("She has cute clothes and she doesn't show too much"), Beyoncé and Jessica Alba ("She's tiny, but she's not too tiny").

rather than to inform and analyze? Examine the writing for emotionally charged language. For Internet sources, ask yourself why this person or institution decided to have a website or contribute to a newsgroup. Critical question: Can I trust the information from this source, given the apparent purpose of the work?

In general, choose current sources. Some studies published years ago remain classics, but many older works have become outdated. In scientific and technical fields, the "information revolution" has outdated some works published only five years ago. So look at publication dates (When was the website page last updated?) and pass over outdated sources in favor of current studies. Critical question: Is this information still accurate?

Documenting Sources to Avoid Plagiarism

Documenting sources accurately and fully is required of all researchers. Proper documentation distinguishes between the work of others and your ideas, shows readers the breadth of your research, and strengthens your credibility. In Western culture, copyright laws support the ethic that ideas, new information, and wording belong to their author. To borrow these without acknowledgment is against the law and has led to many celebrated lawsuits. For students who plagiarize, the consequences range from an F on the paper to suspension from college. Be certain, then, that you know the requirements for correct documentation; accidental plagiarism is still plagiarism and will be punished.

GOOD ADV!CE

While some sources can provide you with basic information about your topic, they may not always be appropriate to use as sources for your essay. The online source shown here, for example, is far too elementary and informal in its discussion of conspiracy theories and end-of-the-world scenarios. The tone of the website's author does not lend itself to serious academic writing. Be sure to fully evaluate the level of the author's research, his or her credentials, and the credibility of the writing before you use a source in your own essay.

Courtesy of HowStuffWorks.com.

Putting an author's ideas in your own words in a paraphrase or summary does not eliminate the requirement of documentation. To illustrate, compare the following excerpt from Thomas R. Schueler's report *Controlling Urban Runoff* (Washington Metropolitan Water Resources Planning Board, 1987: 3–4) and a student paragraph based on the report.

Original Source

The aquatic ecosystems in urban headwater streams are particularly susceptible to the impacts of urbanization. . . . Dietemann (1975), Ragan and Dietemann (1976), Klein (1979), and WMCOG (1982) have all tracked trends in fish diversity and abundance over time in local urbanizing streams. Each of the studies has shown that fish communities become less diverse and are composed of more tolerant species after the surrounding watershed is developed. Sensitive fish species either disappear or occur very rarely. In most cases, the total number of fish in urbanizing streams may also decline.

Similar trends have been noted among aquatic insects which are the major food resource for fish. . . . Higher post-development sediment and trace metals can interfere in their efforts to gather food. Changes in water temperature, oxygen levels, and substrate composition can further reduce the species diversity and abundance of the aquatic insect community.

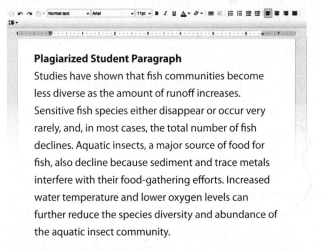

Plagiarized Student Paragraph

Studies have shown that fish communities become less diverse as the amount of runoff increases. Sensitive fish species either disappear or occur very rarely, and, in most cases, the total number of fish declines. Aquatic insects, a major source of food for fish, also decline because sediment and trace metals interfere with their food-gathering efforts. Increased water temperature and lower oxygen levels can further reduce the species diversity and abundance of the aquatic insect community.

The student's opening words establish a reader's expectation that the student has taken information from a source, as indeed the student has. But where is the documentation? The student's paraphrase is an obvious example of plagiarism: an unacknowledged paraphrase of borrowed information that even copies the source's exact wording in two places. For MLA style, the author's name and the page numbers are

Many students have heard of sites such as Turnitin.com, where instructors can check students' work against large databases in order to catch suspected plagiarists. But there are also sites such as WriteCheck (powered by the same technology as Turnitin) designed specifically for students to allow them to check their work in order to prevent accidental or unintentional plagiarism. For more information on WriteCheck, go to http://writecheck.turnitin.com

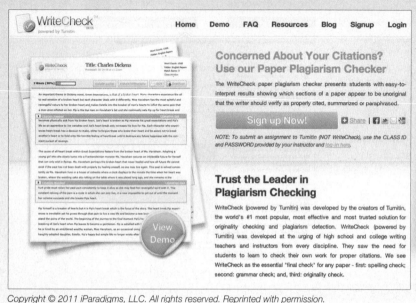

needed throughout the paragraph. Additionally, most of the first sentence and the final phrase must be put into the student's own words or be placed within quotation marks. The revised paragraph in Try It! shows appropriate acknowledgment of the source.

What Is Common Knowledge?

In general, common knowledge includes

- undisputed dates
- well-known facts
- generally known facts, terms, and concepts in the field of study in which you are writing

So do not cite a source for the dates of the American Revolution. If you are writing a paper for a psychology class, do not cite your text when using terms such as *ego* or *sublimation*. However, you must cite a historian who analyzes the causes of England's loss to the colonies or a psychologist who disputes Freud's ideas. Opinions about well-known facts must be documented. Discussions of debatable dates, terms, or concepts must be documented. When in doubt, defend your integrity and document.

try it!

Rewrite the plagiarized student paragraph to remove the plagiarism concern. Then check with the sample revision here to see how you did.

Revised Student Paragraph to Remove Plagiarism

In *Controlling Urban Runoff*, Thomas Schueler explains that studies have shown "that fish communities become less diverse as the amount of runoff increases" (3). Sensitive fish species either disappear or occur very rarely and, in most cases, the total number of fish declines. Aquatic insects, a major source of food for fish, also decline because sediment and trace metals interfere with their food-gathering efforts. Increased water temperature and lower oxygen levels, Schueler concludes, "can further reduce the species diversity and abundance of the aquatic insect community" (4).

GOOD ADVICE

Hints for Effective Note-Taking

ON CARDS

1. Use either 4 x 6 cards or half sheets of letter-size paper.

2. Write in ink.

3. Write only one item on each card. Each card should contain only one idea, piece of information, or group of related facts. The flexibility of cards is lost if you do not follow this procedure. You want to be able to group cards according to your outline when you are ready to draft the paper.

WITH A COMPUTER

1. Make a file titled "Notes" or make a separate file for each note.

2. Use clear headings and subheadings for notes so that you can find each note easily.

3. Consider printing copies of your notes and cutting them into separate "cards" for organizing prior to drafting. (When drafting, do not re-keyboard. Just use your printed notes as a guide to placement in the draft.) Use the Cut and Paste or Move features of your word processor to rearrange notes into the order you want.

ANNOTATING PHOTOCOPIES

1. Do not endlessly highlight your photocopies. Instead, carefully bracket the passages that contain information you want to use.

2. Write a note in the margin next to bracketed passages indicating how and where you think you want to use that material. Use the language of your informal outline to annotate marked passages (such as "causes," "effects," "rebuttal to counterargument," "solutions").

3. Keep in mind that you will have to paraphrase the marked passages before using the material in your draft.

Taking Notes on Sources

How are you going to keep track of information and ideas from your study? You have three possibilities: handwritten notes on cards, keyboarded notes in computer files, and annotations on photocopies of sources. How to choose? Most likely, your decision will be a matter of personal preference. However, if your instructor requires you to hand in notes, then you must use the first or second strategy. (Just print out your files and cut pages into separate "note cards.")

You will want to follow these guidelines as you begin to take notes on your potential sources. Remember that taking effective notes will help you remain organized as you later incorporate your sources into your research essay.

1. **Study first; take notes later.** First, do background reading. Second, skim what appear to be your chief sources. Prepare summary notes and annotate photocopies of sources. Read so that you can develop your preliminary outline. Learn what the writers on your topic consider to be important facts, issues, and arguments. Keep in mind that taking too many useless notes is a frustrating, time-wasting activity.

2. **Before preparing any note, identify the source of the note.** Write or type the author's name, a shortened title if necessary, and the page number from which the material comes. Remember: All borrowed information and ideas must be documented with precise page numbers if you are using MLA style—and for all direct quotations if you are using APA style.

3. **Type or write an identifying word or phrase for each note.** Identifying words or phrases will help you sort cards or find notes when you are ready to draft. Select words carefully to correspond to the sections of your preliminary outline.

4. **Record the information accurately and clearly.** Be sure to put all directly quoted passages within

quotation marks. To treat a direct quotation as a paraphrase in your paper is to plagiarize.

5. **Distinguish between fact and opinion.** Notes that contain opinion should be identified with such phrases as "Smith believes that" or "Smith asserts that." Or, label the note "opinion."

6. **Distinguish between information from sources and your own opinions, questions, and reactions to the recorded information.** Write notes to yourself so that you do not forget good ideas that come to you as you are reading. Just be certain to label your notes "my notes"—or draw (or type) a line between information from a source and your response.

Using "Tags" or "Signal Phrases" to Avoid Misleading Documentation

If you are an honest student, you do not want to submit a paper that is plagiarized, even though the plagiarism was unintentional. What leads to unintentional plagiarism?

- A researcher takes careless notes, neglecting to include precise page numbers on the notes, but uses the information anyway, without any documentation.

- A researcher works in material from sources in such a way that, even with page references, readers cannot tell what has been taken from the sources.

Good note-taking strategies will keep you from the first pitfall. Avoiding the second problem means becoming skilled in ways to include source material in your writing while still making your indebtedness to sources absolutely clear to readers. The way to do this: Give the author's name in the essay. You can also include, when appropriate, the author's credentials ("According to Dr. Hays, a geologist with the Department of Interior, . . .").

These introductory tags or signal phrases give readers a context for the borrowed material, as well as serving as part of the required documentation of sources. Putting a parenthetical page reference at the end of a paragraph is not sufficient if you have used the source throughout the paragraph. Use introductory tags or signal phrases to guide the reader through the material. Make sure that each tag clarifies rather than distorts an author's relationship to his or her ideas and your relationship to the source. Be aware, also, that simply introducing a source with a tag does not give your reader all of the information he or she may need about your source. Be sure to go on to explain the source's relevance to your argument, define key concepts or terms in the quote, or even explain the meaning of the source material if necessary.

Follow these guidelines to avoid misrepresenting borrowed material:

- **Pay attention to verb choice in tags.** When you vary such standard wording as "Smith says" or "Jones states," be careful that you do not select verbs that misrepresent Smith's or Jones's attitude toward his or her own work. Do not write "Jones wonders" when in fact Jones has strongly asserted her views.

- **Pay attention to the location of tags.** If you mention Jones after you have presented her views, be sure that your reader can tell precisely which ideas in the passage belong to Jones. If your entire paragraph is a paraphrase of Jones's work, you are plagiarizing if you conclude with "This idea is presented by Jones." Which of the several ideas in your paragraph comes from Jones? Your reader will assume that only the last idea comes from Jones.

- **Paraphrase properly.** Be sure that paraphrases are truly in your own words. To use Smith's words and sentence style in your writing is to plagiarize.

try it!

Acknowledging Sources

The following paragraph (from page 54 of Franklin E. Zimring's "Firearms, Violence and Public Policy" [*Scientific American*, Nov. 1991]) is the source material for the three student examples of adequate and inadequate acknowledgment of sources. After reading Zimring's paragraph, study the three examples and answer these questions:

(1) Which example represents adequate acknowledgment?

(2) Which examples do not represent adequate acknowledgment?

(3) In what ways is each plagiarized paragraph flawed?

ORIGINAL SOURCE

Although most citizens support such measures as owner screening, public opinion is sharply divided on laws that would restrict the ownership of handguns to persons with special needs. If the United States does not reduce handguns and current trends continue, it faces the prospect that the number of handguns in circulation will grow from 35 million to more than 50 million within 50 years. A national program limiting the availability of handguns would cost many billions of dollars and meet much resistance from citizens. These costs would likely be greatest in the early years of the program. The benefits of supply reduction would emerge slowly because efforts to diminish the availability of handguns would probably have a cumulative impact over time. [page 54]

STUDENT PARAGRAPH 1

One approach to the problem of handgun violence in America is to severely limit handgun ownership. If we don't restrict ownership and start the costly task of removing handguns from our society, we may end up with around 50 million handguns in the country by 2040. The benefits will not be apparent right away but will eventually appear. This idea is emphasized by Franklin Zimring (54).

STUDENT PARAGRAPH 2

One approach to the problem of handgun violence in America is to restrict the ownership of handguns except in special circumstances. If we do not begin to reduce the number of handguns in this country, the number will grow from 35 million to more than 50 million within 50 years. We can agree with Franklin Zimring that a program limiting handguns will cost billions and meet resistance from citizens (54).

STUDENT PARAGRAPH 3

According to law professor Franklin Zimring, the United States needs to severely limit handgun ownership or face the possibility of seeing handgun ownership increase "from 35 million to more than

continued

50 million within 50 years" (54). Zimring points out that Americans disagree significantly on restricting handguns and that enforcing such laws would be very expensive. He concludes that the benefits would not be seen immediately but that the restrictions "would probably have a cumulative impact over time" (54). Although Zimring paints a gloomy picture of high costs and little immediate relief from gun violence, he also presents the shocking possibility of 50 million guns by the year 2040. Can our society survive so much fire power?

Clearly, only the third student paragraph demonstrates adequate acknowledgment of the writer's indebtedness to Zimring. Notice that the placement of the last parenthetical page reference acts as a visual closure to the student's borrowing; then she turns to her response to Zimring and her own views on handguns.

making connections

let's review

- It is up to you as the researcher to figure out which sources will be credible, reliable, and useful to you as you construct your own argument. Making these determinations, however, is not an easy or quick task. It will involve careful research, reading and rereading your sources, evaluating each one as it relates to your thesis, and making an organized plan for where and how you will use each source.

- When you use facts and opinions from sources, you are saying to readers that the facts are accurate and the ideas credible. If you do not evaluate your sources before using them, you risk losing your credibility as a writer.

- Today, with access to so much material on the Internet, the need to evaluate is even more crucial. Effective strategies for evaluating sources include the following:

  - Locate the author's credentials.

  - Judge the credibility of the writing.

  - Select only sources that are at an appropriate level for your research.

  - Understand the writer's purpose.

  - In general, choose current sources.

- Documenting sources accurately and fully is required of all researchers. Proper documentation distinguishes between the work of others and your ideas, shows readers the breadth of your research, and strengthens your credibility.

- You do not need to document material that is common knowledge. In general, common knowledge includes

  - undisputed dates

  - well-known facts

  - generally known facts, terms, and concepts in the field of study in which you are writing

- The three basic possibilities for keeping track of information and ideas as you conduct your research are handwritten notes on cards, keyboarded notes in computer files, and annotations of photocopies of sources. The choice is most often a matter of personal preference.

- Using introductory tags or signal phrases gives readers a context for the borrowed material, as well as serving as part of the required documentation of sources. Make sure that each tag clarifies rather than distorts an author's relationship to his or her ideas and your relationship to the source.

connect

Evaluate the following online magazine article based on the criteria presented in the first part of this chapter. (See full article at www.time.com/time/health/article/0,8599,1889469,00.html.)

- Can you determine its authorship? Does the author and/or sponsoring organization seem reliable? How do you know?

- Does the author seem to have a particular bias? Does he ignore potential counterarguments or opposing positions?

- Does the article seem to be written at a level appropriate for educated audiences?

- Does the writing seem credible to you? Does the writer use credible sources and give proper attribution to those sources?

- Is the article current? How do you know?

Write a brief analysis of this source and explain why you would or would not use it as a source for an academic essay.

drafting and revising the researched argument

c h a p t e r   13

Now that you have chosen a workable topic and located sources that you think might be helpful in supporting your thesis, it is time to begin to construct your researched essay. As you organize and draft, keep in mind that your argument skills apply to the research paper as well. Do not let documenting of multiple sources distract you from your best use of critical thinking and writing skills.

Organizing the Paper

modify claim

To make decisions about your paper's organization, a good place to begin is with the identifying phrases at the top of your notes or the list of support you developed as you studied sources (see Chapters 11 and 12 for more on locating and taking notes on sources). These phrases represent subsections of your topic that emerged as you studied sources. They will now help you organize your paper, as well as figure out where and how sources may be synthesized with each other and with your own ideas. Here are some guidelines for getting organized to write:

themes

1. **Arrange notes by identifying phrases and read them through.** Read personal notes as well. Work all notes into one possible order as suggested by the identifying phrases or themes. In reading through all

notes at one time, you may discover that some now seem irrelevant. Set them aside, but do not throw them away yet. Some additional note-taking may be necessary to fill in gaps that have become apparent. You know your sources well enough by now to be able to find the additional material that you need.

2. **Re-examine your tentative claim or research proposal and the preliminary list that guided your research.** As a result of reading and reflection, do you need to alter or modify your claim in any way? Or if you began with a research question, what now is your answer to the question? What, for example, was the impact of Prohibition on the 1920s? Or is TV violence harmful to children? You need to decide. Remember that the final thesis or claim in a research argument cannot be a question. Rather, it must be your answer to the research question.

Central idea

3. **Decide on a final claim.** To produce a unified and coherent essay with a clear central idea and a reason for being, you need a claim that meets the following criteria:

   • *It is a complete sentence, not a topic or statement of purpose.*
     TOPIC: Rape on college campuses.
     CLAIM/THESIS: There are specific steps that both students and administrators should take to reduce incidents of campus rape.

GOOD ADVICE

It is sometimes helpful to use color to organize your notes according to the themes you identify. For example, consider how this student color-coded her notes according to themes surrounding her topic of mandatory living wills:

Burden on families
   Crisci & Crispi—family attitudes about not having a living will (p. 106)
   O'Mathuna—difficult decisions for families (p. 4)

Reduces costs
   A. Borthwick regarding costs of PVS (p. 42)
   B. O'Mathuna statistic on number of PVS cases in USA (p. 73)

Court/legal issues
   A. Jayson quote regarding Schiavo case (p. 53)
   B. CNN.com article regarding Schiavo case (online)

Objections to living wills
   A. Smith quote regarding torture of patients (p. 42)
   B. Gibbs quote regarding Schiavo case (p. 65)

Consider using colored markers for notecards or making a list on your word processor using the highlight feature. List your themes (which will become your possible points of support and counterarguments) and use a different color for each. Then highlight each source according to which theme it fits.

There are several websites dedicated to providing free help and advice for writers. The OWL (Online Writing Lab) at Purdue University is one of them. The site offers advice on how to outline and organize your research among other topics. Check it out!

did you know

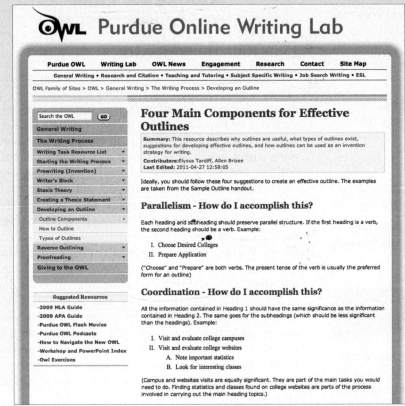

- *It is limited and focused.*
  UNFOCUSED AND NONLIMITED THESIS: Drunk driving violators should be punished.
  FOCUSED AND LIMITED THESIS: Drunk driving, even as a first offense, should be treated as an extremely serious criminal offense and should carry a mandatory sentence of five years in prison.

- *It can be supported by your research.*
  UNSUPPORTABLE THESIS: The mainstream media does not like Barack Obama.
  SUPPORTABLE THESIS: A study by George Mason University's Center for Media and Public Affairs reveals that anchors and reporters on the big three networks gave negative reports on the president 72 percent of the time.

- *It establishes a new or interesting approach to the topic that makes your research worthwhile.*
  NON-INVENTIVE THESIS: A regional shopping mall should not be built adjacent to the Manassas Battlefield.

INVENTIVE THESIS: Putting aside an appeal to our national heritage made by local historians, the building of a regional shopping mall adjacent to the Manassas Battlefield has no economic justification and should not be completed.

4. **Write down the organization revealed by the way you have grouped notes and compare this organization with your preliminary plan.** If you have deleted sections or reordered them, justify those changes in your own mind. Does the new, fuller plan now provide a complete and logical development of your claim?

The Formal Outline

Some instructors expect a formal outline with research essays. Preparing a formal outline requires that you think through the entire structure of your paper and *analyze* see the relationship of parts. Remember that the more you analyze your topic, the fuller and therefore more useful your outline will be. But do not expect more out of an outline than it can provide. A logical and clear organization does not result from a detailed outline; rather, a detailed outline results from a logical analysis of your topic.

Remember the following points as you construct your outline:

- The formal outline uses a combination of numbers and letters to show headings and subheadings.

- The parts of the paper indicated by the same types of numbers or letters should be equally important.

- Headings and subheadings indicated by the same types of numbers or letters should have the same structure (for example, A. Obtaining Good Equipment; B. Taking Lessons; C. Practicing).

- Headings that are subdivided must contain at least two subsections (that is, if there is a 1 under A, there has to be a 2). *5 days*

try it!

Consider this topical outline for a student's research essay. Then convert this outline into a full-sentence outline that allows you to clearly see the writer's direction and purpose. Compare your outline to a classmate's. Are they the same? Or do they differ?

What would be some potential benefits to a full-sentence outline as opposed to this brief topical outline? Be sure to check with your instructor regarding which type of outline is required for your course.

OUTLINE

Introduction	Introduce controversy and issue
Thesis:	A law should be created that makes having a living will mandatory
I. First point of support	Burden
II. Second point	Cost
III. Third point	Court
IV. Counterargument(s)	Might be torture
V. Rebuttal	But no feeling
VI. Conclusion	

- You can choose to write a full-sentence outline or a briefer, topical outline. Ask your instructor which is required.

Drafting the Paper

Plan Your Time *time management*

Effective time-management skills are crucial to any research essay project. Be sure you know your deadlines and leave yourself sufficient time to complete your tasks. One of the easiest ways to produce a poorly written research essay is to rush the process. Cramming weeks worth of work into a single night or two will not produce a thoughtful, well-crafted argument.

Consider how much time you will need to draft your essay. Working with notes and being careful about documentation make research paper writing more time-consuming than writing undocumented essays. You will probably need two or three afternoons or evenings to complete a draft. You should start writing, then, at least five days before your paper is due to allow time between drafting and revising. Do not throw away weeks of study by trying to draft, revise, and proof your paper in one day. The good news is that there are specific strategies that can help you and effectively utilize your time. The goal is to minimize the number of times you must revise by doing it right on your first draft.

Handle Documentation as You Draft

Although you may believe that stopping to include parenthetical documentation as you write will cramp your writing, you should not wait until you complete your draft to add the documentation. The risk of failing to document accurately is too great. Take the time to include parenthetical documentation as you compose. Then, when your paper is finished and you are preparing your list of works cited, go through your paper carefully to make certain that a work is listed for every parenthetical reference.

Choose and Maintain an Appropriate Writing Style

Specific suggestions for composing the parts of your paper will follow, but first here are some general guidelines for research paper style.

Use the Proper Person

Research papers are written primarily in the third person (*she, he, it, they*) to create objectivity and to direct attention to the content of the paper. You are not likely

3rd person

to use the second person (*you*) at all, for the second person often creates an informal and conversational tone that is inappropriate for research papers. The usual question is about the appropriateness of the first person (*I, we*). Although you want to avoid writing "as *you* can see," do not try to skirt around the use of *I* if you need to distinguish your position from the views of others. It is better to write "I" than "it is the opinion of this writer" or "the researcher learned" or "this project analyzed." On the other hand, avoid qualifiers such as "I think." Just state your ideas.

Use the Proper Tense

When you are writing about people, ideas, or events of the past, the appropriate tense is the past tense. When writing about current times, the appropriate tense is the present. Both may occur in the same paragraph, as the following paragraph illustrates.

Twenty-five years ago "personal" computers were all but unheard of. Computers were regarded as unknowable, building-sized, mechanized monsters that required a precise 68 degree air-conditioned environment and eggheaded technicians with thick glasses and white lab coats scurrying about to keep the temperamental and fragile egos of the electronic brains mollified. Today's generation of computers is accessible, affordable, commonplace, and much less mysterious. A computer that used to require two rooms to house is now smaller than a briefcase. A computer that cost hundreds of thousands of dollars twenty-five years ago now has a price tag in the hundreds. The astonishing progress made in computer technology in the last few years has made computers practical, attainable, and indispensable. Personal computers are here to stay.

In this example, when the student moves from computers in the past to computers in the present, he shifts tenses accurately.

When writing about sources, the convention is to use the present tense even for works or authors from the past. The idea is that the source, or the author, continues to make the point or use the technique into the present—that is, every time there is a reader. Use of the *historical present tense* requires that you write "Lincoln selects the biblical expression 'Fourscore and seven years ago'" and "King echoes Lincoln when he writes 'five score years ago.'"

Avoid Excessive Quoting

Many students use too many direct quotations. Plan to use your own words most of the time for these good reasons:

- Constantly shifting between your words and the language of your sources (not to mention all those quotation marks) makes reading your essay difficult.
- This is your paper and should sound like you.
- When you take a passage out of its larger context, you face the danger of misrepresenting the writer's views.
- When you quote endlessly, readers may begin to think either that you are lazy or that you don't really understand the issues well enough to put them in your own words. You don't want to present either image to your readers.
- You do not prove any point by quoting another person's opinion. All you indicate is that there is someone else who shares your views. Even if that person is an expert on the topic, your quoted material still represents the view of only one person. You support a claim with reasons and evidence, both of which can usually be presented in your own words.

When you must quote, keep the quotations brief, weave them carefully into your own sentences, and be sure to identify the author in a signal phrase. (For more on using direct quotations, see Chapter 12 or page 223 later in this chapter.)

Avoid Ineffective Openings

Chapter 3 discusses how writers sometimes create weak openings. The following rules offer some additional advice for avoiding openings that readers usually find ineffective or annoying:

1. **Do not restate the title** or use the title as the first sentence in paragraph 1. First, the title of the paper appears at the top of the first page of text. Second, it is a convention of writing to have the first paragraph stand independent of the title.

2. **Do not begin with "clever" visuals** such as artwork or fancy lettering.

3. **Do not begin with humor** unless it is part of your topic.

4. **Do not begin with a question that is just a gimmick, or one that a reader may answer in a way you do not intend.** Asking "What are the advantages of solar energy?" may lead a reader to answer "None that I can think of." However, a straightforward research question ("Is *Death of a Salesman* a tragedy?") is appropriate.

5. **Do not open with an unnecessary definition quoted from a dictionary.** "According to Webster, solar energy means . . ." is a tired, overworked beginning that does not engage readers.

6. **Do not start with a purpose statement:** "This paper will examine . . ." Although a statement of purpose

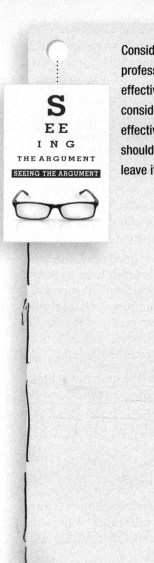
Consider the following opening for a student's research paper on mandatory drug testing for college professors. What tone is the author setting by using this particular font and visual? Do you find it effective? Do you think an educated audience will take this research argument seriously? Be sure to consider how your choice of visuals (especially in your opening paragraphs) can affect your essay's effectiveness. A good rule when using visuals is "just because you can, doesn't necessarily mean you should." Make sure that each visual has a clear purpose and helps to support your claim. Otherwise, leave it out.

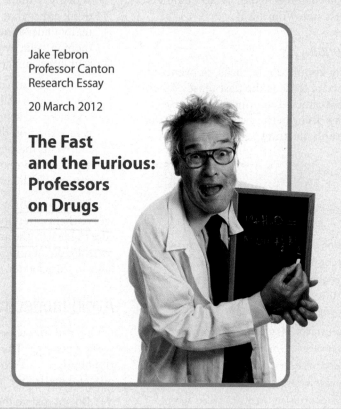

Jake Tebron
Professor Canton
Research Essay

20 March 2012

**The Fast
and the Furious:
Professors
on Drugs**

is necessary in a report of empirical research, the report still needs an interesting introduction.

Write Effective Openings

The best introduction is one that presents your subject in an interesting way to gain the reader's attention, states your claim, and gives the reader an indication of the scope and limits of your paper. In a short research essay, you may be able to combine an attention-getter, a statement of subject, and a claim in one paragraph. Typically in longer papers, the introduction will be two or three paragraphs. In the physical and social sciences, the claim may be withheld until the conclusion, but the opening introduces the subject and presents the researcher's hypothesis, often posed as a question. Since students sometimes have trouble with research paper introductions in spite of knowing these general guidelines, several approaches are illustrated in the following examples.

Begin with a brief example or anecdote to dramatize your topic. One student introduced her argument on the quality of America's nightly news with this attention-getter:

When I watched television in the first weeks after moving to the United States, I was delighted by the relaxing display of the news programs. It was different from what I was used to on German television, where one finds a stern-looking man reading the news without any emotion. Here the commentators laugh without showing distress; their tone with each other is amiable. Watching the news in this country was a new and entertaining experience for me initially, but as my English reading and speaking skills improved, I found that I was a bit disturbed by their ability to deliver negative, if not horrendous information with smiles on their faces. After reading Neil Postman's attack on television news shows in "Television News Narcosis," I was reminded of this odd disconnect. I wondered if American news programs were not somehow being irresponsible in their presentation of world events.

In the paragraph that follows this introductory paragraph, the student completes her introduction by explaining the procedures she used for analyzing network news programs and presents her thesis that American news programs are indeed being negligent in their duty to present accurate and important information to the masses.

In the opening to her study of car advertisements, a student, relating her topic to what readers know, reminds readers of the culture's concern with image:

Many Americans are highly image conscious. Because the right look is essential to a prosperous life, no detail is too small to overlook. Clichés about first impressions remind us that "you never get a second chance to make a first impression," so we obsessively watch our weight, firm our muscles, sculpt our hair, select our friends, find the perfect houses, and buy our automobiles. Realizing the importance of image, companies compete to make the "right" products, that is, those that will complete the "right" image. Then advertisers direct specific products to targeted groups of consumers. Although targeting may be labeled as stereotyping, it has been an effective strategy in advertising.

Challenge popular assumption

Challenging a popular attitude or assumption is an effective attention-getting opening. For a paper on the advantages of solar energy, a student began:

America's energy problems are serious, despite the popular belief that difficulties vanished with the end of the Arab oil embargo in 1974. Our problems remain because the world's supply of fossil fuels is not limitless.

Begin with a thought-provoking question. A student who was arguing that the media both reflect and shape reality started with these questions:

Do the media just reflect reality, or do they also shape our perceptions of reality? The answer to this seemingly chicken-and-egg question is: They do both.

Beginning with important, perhaps startling, facts, evidence, or statistics is an effective way to introduce a topic, provided the details are relevant to the topic. Observe the following example:

Teenagers are working again, but not on their homework. Over 40 percent of teenagers have jobs by the time they are juniors (Samuelson A22). And their jobs do not support academic learning since almost two-thirds of teenagers are employed in sales and service jobs that entail mostly carrying, cleaning, and wrapping (Greenberger and Steinberg 62–67), not reading, writing, and computing. Unfortunately, the negative effect on learning is not offset by improved opportunities for future careers.

Compose Solid, Unified Paragraphs

As you compose the body of your paper, keep in mind that you want to develop it effectively by (1) providing unity and coherence, (2) guiding readers clearly through source material, and (3) synthesizing source material and your own ideas. Do not settle for paragraphs in which facts from notes are just loosely strung together. Review the following discussion and study the examples to see how to craft effective body paragraphs.

Provide Unity and Coherence

You achieve paragraph unity when every sentence in a paragraph relates to and develops the paragraph's main idea. If you have a logical organization, composing unified paragraphs is not a problem. Unity, however, does not automatically produce coherence; that takes attention to wording. Coherence is achieved when readers can follow the connection between one sentence and another and between each sentence and the main idea. Strategies for achieving coherence

You might want to include in your introductory paragraph a compelling visual that helps to clarify your issue or provides background information for your reader. While cartoons or visuals meant simply to be eye-catching may not set the correct tone for a research essay, persuasive and informative visuals can be a great way to get your reader invested in your issue. Consider the following opening to a student essay on reforming the way in which animals are slaughtered in America. What does it provide for the reader that words might not? Do you think that this author is using an effective strategy by including this visual? Why or why not? Might it backfire in some way?

Emily Davis
Professor Yaska
Research Essay

12 March 2012

Cruelty to Feed the Masses

There is no easy answer to the question of whether slaughtering animals for food is right or wrong. There are clear arguments on both sides of the issue. However, one fact that is undeniable is that far too many animals are dying unnecessarily horrible and inhumane deaths in this process. Consider, for example, the chickens shown in Figure 1. These animals are dipped into boiling water (while still alive), then tied upside down for hours prior to slaughter while machines beat the feathers from their bodies, causing them excruciating pain before their throats are finally slashed.

Figure 1. Chickens being tortured before slaughter

include repetition of keywords, the use of pronouns that refer to those keywords, and the use of transition and connecting words and sentences (also called *meta-discourse*). The following student paragraph is unified (all of the sentences relate to the same topic), but it is not coherent. Compare the student's revision of the paragraph to provide better coherence or "flow."

Original "unified" paragraph

Many authors agree that blind obedience to authority is a bad thing. The most important difference between the ideas of Robinson and Biff is that Robinson only focuses on how blind obedience can devastate an individual's childhood and cause the child to become depressed and withdrawn. Biff discusses how he learned about adulthood—and entered adulthood—piecemeal and without support. This ultimately led him to a life filled with unquestioned obedience to poor authority figures. Both authors agree that when an individual is taught to follow direction without thinking critically about the situation, the outcome is usually a negative one.

Revised "unified and coherent" paragraph

Many authors agree on the basic fact that blind obedience to authority is a bad thing. Two such authors, Barry Robinson, a noted child psychologist, and Randall Biff, a best-selling author on the subject, provide slightly different perspectives on the issue, but ultimately arrive at the same notion: that teaching children to blindly "follow the leader" can be a dangerous practice. The most important difference between the ideas of Robinson and Biff, however, is that Robinson primarily focuses on how blind obedience can devastate an individual's childhood and cause the child to become depressed and withdrawn. Biff moves beyond the effects on the child, and discusses how he personally learned about adulthood—and entered adulthood—piecemeal and without support. This ultimately led him to a life filled with unquestioned obedience to poor authority figures, including his first "real" boss, who forced him to commit unethical acts as part of his job. While, clearly, these perspectives differ slightly, both authors agree that when an individual is taught to follow direction without thinking critically about the situation, the outcome is usually a negative one.

Note that, in order to create a more unified and coherent paragraph, the student has repeated keywords from one sentence in the following sentence. For example, the first sentence refers to "authors" and then again in the second sentence ("Two such authors"). Such techniques help create coherence. Coherence is needed not only within paragraphs, but also between paragraphs. You need to guide readers through your paper, connecting paragraphs and showing relationships by the use of transitions and effective metadiscourse. The following opening sentences of four paragraphs from a paper on solutions to rape on the college campus illustrate smooth transitions:

¶ 3 Specialists have provided a number of reasons why men rape.

¶ 4 Some of the causes of rape on the college campus originate with the colleges themselves and with how they handle the problem.

¶ 5 Just as there are a number of causes for campus rapes, there are also a number of ways to help solve the problem of these rapes.

¶ 6 If these seem like common-sense solutions, why, then, is it so difficult to significantly reduce the number of campus rapes?

Without awkwardly writing "Here are some of the causes" and "Here are some of the solutions," the student guides her readers through a discussion of causes for and solutions to the problem of campus rape.

Guide Readers through Source Material

To understand the importance of guiding readers through source material, consider first the following paragraph from a paper on the British coal strike in the 1970s:

The social status of the coal miners was far from good. The country blamed them for the dimmed lights and the three-day work week. They had been placed in the position of social outcasts and were beginning to "consider themselves another country." Some businesses and shops had even gone so far as to refuse service to coal miners (Jones 32).

The student has presented information and given Jones the credit for it. But who is Jones and how can we be sure that this information is reliable? Readers cannot begin to judge the validity of these assertions without some context provided by the writer. Most readers are put off by an unattached direct quotation or some startling observation that is documented correctly but given no context within the paper. Using introductory tags that identify the author of the source and, when useful, the author's credentials helps guide readers through the source material. The following revision of the paragraph above provides not only context but also sentence variety:

The social acceptance of coal miners, according to Peter Jones, British correspondent for *Newsweek*, was far from good. From interviews both in London shops and in pubs near Birmingham, Jones concluded that Britishers blamed the miners for the dimmed lights and three-day work week. Several striking miners, in a pub on the outskirts of Birmingham, asserted that some of their friends had been denied service by shopkeepers and that they "consider[ed] themselves another country" (32).

When you use introductory tags, try to vary both the words you use and their place in the sentence. Look, for example, at the first sentence in the sample paragraph above. The tag is placed in the middle of the sentence and is set off by commas. The sentence could have been written two other ways:

GOOD ADVICE

Whenever you provide a name and perhaps credentials for your source, you have three sentence patterns to choose from (as discussed on page 223) . Make a point to use all three options in your paper. Word choice can be varied as well. Instead of writing "Peter Jones says" throughout your paper, consider some of the many options you have:

Jones asserts	Jones contends	Jones attests to
Jones states	Jones thinks	Jones points out
Jones concludes	Jones stresses	Jones believes
Jones presents	Jones emphasizes	Jones agrees with
Jones argues	Jones confirms	Jones speculates

But be careful! Not all the words in this list are synonyms; you cannot substitute *confirms* for *believes*. First, select the term that most accurately conveys the writer's relationship to his or her material. Then, when appropriate, vary word choice as well as sentence structure.

Readers need to be told how they are to respond to the sources used. They need to know which sources you accept as reliable and with which you disagree, and they need to see you distinguish between fact and opinion. Ideas and opinions from sources need introductory tags and then some discussion from you.

The social acceptance of coal miners was far from good, according to Peter Jones, British correspondent for *Newsweek*.

OR

According to Peter Jones, British correspondent for *Newsweek*, the social acceptance of coal miners was far from good.

Synthesize Source Material and Your Own Ideas

As you write an academic researched argument, you will need to demonstrate the ability to synthesize, or smoothly combine, various authors' opinions, research findings, and quotations into your work. The ability to synthesize the ideas of others into your work requires much more than simply dropping quotations into your essay at appropriate points. It requires a critical understanding of your sources' meanings and how the ideas of other authors connect both to each other and to your own argument. Your goal is to develop the connections between your sources—to show how their ideas relate to each other and to the larger debate as a whole—and also to clarify for your reader how the ideas presented in your sources relate to your own thesis.

Synthesis is an exercise in both critical reading and critical thinking. It requires you to read, annotate, and fully understand each of your sources in order to find common themes, points of contention, or other connections that can be made with other readings on your topic.

A smooth synthesis of source material is aided by introductory tags and parenthetical documentation because they mark the beginning and ending of material taken from a source. But a complete synthesis requires something more: your ideas about the source and the topic. To illustrate, consider the following paragraph from a student's essay on the "skinny trend" in the media:

With television and magazines glamorizing skin and bones, it's no wonder that anorexia and bulimia are becoming problems with teenage girls. Author Jennifer Wulff states, "Surrounded by images of young celebrities who are painfully thin—or very slender with improbably large breasts—girls growing up can feel immense pressure to meet the same standard. Trying hard to look like their idols, some fall prey to eating disorders, and some abuse drugs to help them lose weight" (25). In another article, Dr. Helga Dittmar states, "Women and girls cannot help being exposed to ultra-thin models in advertising, whose body sizes are unrealistic and unhealthy. There is good evidence

This paragraph is a good example of random details strung together for no apparent purpose. How do we know that these sources are credible? And what purpose do these quotes serve in the paper's development? Note that the entire paragraph is developed with material from the two sources rather than from the author. This paragraph is weak for several reasons: (1) it lacks a controlling idea (topic sentence) to give it purpose and direction; (2) it relies for development entirely on its sources; (3) it lacks any discussion or analysis by the writer.

By contrast, the following paragraph demonstrates a successful synthesis:

Sample synthesis paragraph

(Editor screenshot, top left)

already that exposure to these unhealthy models leads a large proportion of women to feel dissatisfied with their own bodies" (16). Celebrities should take control and stop feeding this vicious cycle and instead start feeding themselves. Magazine editors should refuse to pander to this trend and should begin showing real women with healthy bodies.

(Annotations, left margin):

Source is fully introduced to lend credibility. Remember to use present tense when discussing quotes.

Synthesis connection is clear—shows how these sources are related to each other.

Author's discussion of how sources help her cause and support her main point. This explains to the reader why these sources were included in this essay.

(Main paragraph text):

With television and magazines glamorizing skin and bones, it's no wonder that anorexia and bulimia are becoming problems with teenage girls. Extremely thin celebrity "role models" are even driving young girls toward drugs like cocaine in order to shed the pounds. The results of this trend can be devastating. In an article in a leading women's magazine titled "Pressure to Be Perfect," author Jennifer Wulff states, "Surrounded by images of young celebrities who are painfully thin—or very slender with improbably large breasts—girls growing up can feel immense pressure to meet the same standard. Trying hard to look like their idols, some fall prey to eating disorders, and some abuse drugs to help them lose weight" (25). In another article titled "Research Backs Normal Size Models in Ads," Dr. Helga Dittmar of the University of Sussex expresses the same awareness of this dangerous trend. She conveys the message that young female fans feel extremely self-conscious about their bodies because of the images they constantly see being advertised as "normal." Dittmar states, "Women and girls cannot help being exposed to ultra-thin models in advertising, whose body sizes are unrealistic and unhealthy. There is good evidence already that exposure to these unhealthy models leads a large proportion of women to feel dissatisfied with their own bodies" (16). It is clear that current researchers and authors agree that ultra-thin celebrities and models are causing young girls to resort to eating disorders or drugs and to become insecure with their body image. More should be done to stop these images from permeating our media. Celebrities should take control and stop feeding this vicious cycle and instead start feeding themselves. Magazine editors should refuse to pander to this trend and should begin showing real women with healthy bodies.

(Annotations, right margin):

Paragraph begins with author's own voice and opinions. One reason these images are bad is that they can cause eating disorders/drug use.

Only page number is included since source was introduced before quote.

Gives brief explanation of how source connects to main idea.

Paragraph ends with a return to the main idea proposed in the topic sentence—eating disorders/drug use.

This paragraph's synthesis is accomplished by several strategies: (1) the paragraph has a controlling idea; (2) the paragraph combines information from several sources, but does not let it overwhelm the voice of the writer; (3) information from the different sources is clearly indicated to readers; and (4) the student explains and discusses the information.

You might have noticed the very different lengths of the two sample paragraphs just presented. Although the second paragraph is long, it is not unwieldy because it achieves unity and coherence. By contrast, body paragraphs of only three sentences are probably too short.

To sum up, good body paragraphs need

- a controlling idea,
- in most cases, information from more than one source, and
- analysis and discussion from the writer.

Avoid Ineffective Conclusions

In Chapter 3, you learned a little about writing weak conclusions. Follow these additional rules to avoid conclusions that most readers consider ineffective and annoying:

1. **Do not introduce a new idea.** If the point belongs in your paper, you should have introduced it earlier.

2. **Do not just stop or trail off,** even if you feel you have run out of steam. A simple, clear restatement of the claim is better than no conclusion.

3. **Do not tell your reader what you have accomplished:** "In this paper I have explained the advantages of solar energy by examining the costs . . ." If you have written well, your reader knows what you have accomplished.

4. **Do not offer apologies or expressions of hope.** "Although I wasn't able to find as much on this topic as I wanted, I have tried to explain the advantages of solar energy, and I hope that you will now understand why we need to use it more" is a disastrous ending.

5. **Do not end with a vague or confusing one- or two-sentence summary of complex ideas.** The following sentences make little sense: "These authors have similar and different attitudes and ideals concerning American desires. Faulkner writes with the concerns of man toward man whereas most of the other writers are more concerned with man toward money."

Write Effective Conclusions

Sometimes, ending a paper seems even more difficult than beginning one. You know you are not supposed to just stop, but every ending that comes to mind sounds corny, not clever. If you have trouble, try one of these types of endings:

1. Do not just repeat your claim exactly as it was stated in paragraph 1, but expand on the original wording and emphasize the claim's significance. Here is the conclusion of the solar energy paper:

> The idea of using solar energy is not as far-fetched as it seemed years ago. With the continued support of government plus the enthusiasm of research groups, environmentalists, and private industry, solar energy may become a household word quite soon. With the increasing cost of fossil fuel, the time could not be better for exploring this use of the sun.

2. End with a quotation that effectively summarizes and drives home the point of your paper. Researchers are not always lucky enough to find the ideal quotation for ending a paper. If you find a good one, use it. Better yet, present the quotation and then add your comment in a sentence or two. The conclusion to a paper on the dilemma of defective newborns is a good example:

> Dr. Joseph Fletcher is correct when he says that "every advance in medical capabilities is an increase in our moral responsibility" (48). In a world of many gray areas, one point is clear: From an ethical point of view, medicine is a victim of its own success.

3. If you have researched an issue or a problem, emphasize your proposed solutions in the concluding paragraph. The student opposing a mall adjacent to the Manassas Battlefield concluded with several solutions:

> Whether the proposed mall will be built is clearly in doubt at the moment. What are the solutions to this controversy? One approach is, of course, not to build the mall at all. To accomplish this solution, now, with the rezoning having been approved, probably requires an act of Congress to buy the land and make it part of the National Park. Another solution, one that would please the County and the developer and satisfy citizens objecting to traffic problems, is to build the needed roads before the mall is completed. A third approach is to allow the office park of the original plan to be built, but not the mall. The local preservationists had agreed to this original development proposal, but now that the issue has received national attention, they may no longer be willing to compromise. Whatever the future of the William Center, the present plan for a new regional mall is not acceptable.

Choose an Effective Title

Give some thought to your paper's title since that is what your reader sees first and what your work will be known by. A good title provides information and creates interest. Make your title informative by making it specific. If you can create interest through clever wording, so much the better. But do not confuse cutesiness with clever wording. Better to be just straightforward than to demean a serious effort with a cutesy title.

The Completed Paper

Your research paper should be double-spaced throughout (including the Works Cited page) with 1-inch margins on all sides. Your project will contain the following parts, in this order:

1. A title page, with the paper's title, your name, the course name or number, your instructor's name, and the date, centered, if an outline follows. If you do not include an outline, place this information at the top left of the first page. Check with your instructor regarding his or her preference.

2. An outline, or statement of purpose, if required.

3. The body or text of your paper. Number all pages consecutively, including pages of works cited, using arabic numerals. Place numbers in the upper right-hand corner of each page. Include your last name before each page number.

4. A list of works cited starting on a separate page after the text. Title the first page "Works Cited." (Do not use the title "Bibliography.")

Revising the Paper: A Checklist

After completing a first draft, catch your breath and then gear up for the next step in the writing process: revision. Revision involves three separate steps. *Revising*, Step 1, means rewriting—adding or deleting text, or moving parts of the draft around. Next comes *editing*, a rereading to correct errors from misspellings to incorrect documentation format. Finally, you need to *proofread* the typed copy. If you treat these as separate steps, you will do a more complete job of revision—and get a better grade on the completed paper!

GOOD ADVICE

While visuals can add clarity, background information, and even emotional power to your arguments, they typically are not as effective when used in your conclusion. If you have information to express to your reader, or want to grab their attention, do it early and throughout your essay rather than waiting until the end.

try it!

Review the following essay titles. Within each set, decide which one you would choose to use for your own essay. Discuss your results with your classmates. Why did you choose the one you chose? What about it seemed better or more effective than the other option?

A Perennial Issue Uncovered

The Perennial Issue of Press Freedom versus Press Responsibility Uncovered at Last!

Press Freedom versus Press Responsibility: The Perennial Issue

Earthquakes
The Need for Earthquake Prediction
Quake!!!!!!

Babes in Trouble
The Dilemma of Defective Newborns and What Can Be Done to Help
A Difficult Dilemma

A Call for Mercy: Euthanasia in America
Mercy for All
Euthanasia and Its Benefits

Revising

Read your draft through and make changes as a result of answering the following questions:

Purpose and Audience

- Is my draft long enough to meet assignment requirements and my purpose?
- Are terms defined and concepts explained appropriately for my audience?

Content

- Do I have a clearly stated thesis—the claim of my argument?
- Have I presented sufficient evidence to support my claim?
- Are there any irrelevant sections that should be deleted?

Structure

- Are paragraphs ordered to develop my topic logically?
- Does the content of each paragraph help develop my claim?

- Is everything in each paragraph on the same sub-topic to create paragraph unity?
- Do body paragraphs have a balance of information and analysis, of source material and my own ideas?
- Are there any paragraphs that should be combined? Are there any very long paragraphs that should be divided? (Check for unity.)

Editing

Make revisions guided by your responses to the questions, make a clean copy, and read again. This time, pay close attention to sentences, words, and documentation format. Use the following questions to guide revisions.

Coherence

- Have connecting words been used and key terms repeated to produce paragraph coherence?
- Have transitions been used to show connections between paragraphs?

Sources

- Have I paraphrased instead of quoted whenever possible?
- Have I used signal phrases to create a context for source material?
- Have I documented all borrowed material, whether quoted or paraphrased?

- Are parenthetical references properly placed after borrowed material?

Style

- Have I varied sentence length and structure?
- Have I used my own words instead of quotations whenever possible?
- Have I avoided long quotations?
- Do I have correct form for quotations? For titles?
- Is my language specific and descriptive?
- Have I avoided inappropriate shifts in tense or person?
- Have I removed any wordiness, trite expressions, and clichés?
- Have I used specialized terms correctly?
- Have I avoided contractions as too informal for most research papers?
- Have I maintained an appropriate style and tone for academic work?

Proofreading

When your editing is finished, prepare a completed draft of your paper according to the format described and illustrated at the end of this chapter. Then proofread the completed copy, making any corrections neatly in ink. If a page has several errors, print a corrected copy. Be sure to make a copy of the paper for yourself before submitting the original to your instructor.

proofread final copy in pen

making connections

let's review

After reading this chapter, you should know the following:

- To make decisions about your paper's organization, you need to begin with the identifying phrases at the top of your notes or the list of support you developed as you studied sources. They will now help you organize your paper as well as figure out where and how sources may be synthesized with each other and with your own ideas.

- To produce a unified and coherent essay with a clear central idea and a reason for being, you need a claim that meets the following criteria:

  - It is a complete sentence, not a topic or statement of purpose.
  - It is limited and focused.
  - It can be supported by your research.

- It establishes a new or interesting approach to the topic that makes your research worthwhile.

- Some instructors expect a formal outline with research essays. Preparing a formal outline requires you to think through the entire structure of your paper and see the relationship of parts. But do not expect more out of an outline than it can provide. A logical and clear organization does not result from a detailed outline; rather, a detailed outline results from a logical analysis of your topic.

- Effective time management skills are crucial to any research essay project. Be sure you know your deadlines and leave yourself sufficient time to complete your tasks.

- Take the time to include parenthetical documentation as you compose. Then, when your paper is finished and you are preparing your list of works cited, go through your paper carefully to make certain that there is a work listed for every parenthetical citation.

- The best introduction is one that presents your subject in an interesting way to gain the reader's attention, states your claim, and gives the reader an indication of the scope and limits of your paper.

- As you compose the body of your paper, keep in mind that you want to (1) maintain unity and coherence, (2) guide readers clearly through source material, and (3) synthesize source material and your own ideas.

- Coherence is needed not only within paragraphs but also between paragraphs. You need to guide readers through your paper, connecting paragraphs and showing relationships by the use of transitions and effective metadiscourse.

- Readers need to be told how they are to respond to the sources used. They need to know which sources you accept as reliable and which you disagree with, and they need to see you distinguish clearly between fact and opinion. Ideas and opinions from sources need introductory tags and then some discussion from you.

- As you write an academic researched argument, you will need to demonstrate the ability to synthesize, or smoothly combine, various authors' opinions, research findings, and quotations into your work. Your goal is to develop the connections between your sources—to show how their ideas relate to each other and to the larger debate as a whole—and also to clarify for your reader how the ideas presented in your sources relate to your own thesis.

connect

The following passages need additional revision and editing, particularly as related to style. If you were helping these writers improve these passages, what advice would you give? Would you eliminate some wordiness? Combine some sentences? Make changes to style and tone? Think about how you would revise, edit, and proofread the passages.

Passage A

As shadows filled the coach's office, the coach bent over his metal desk and cleaned out the bulging files. He was ready to dump an envelope when a photo caught his attention. The photo was fading from an earlier era. The young man's face was thin and determined, and his eyes hungered for a chance to play. The coach thought back and remembered something. He had pulled a sub off the bench and yelled instructions, but the lad had ignored them. The sub had faked to the baseline, twisted past his defender, and banked a shot off the glass. The sub had sent the crowd into ecstasy. (William Strong, *Sentence Combining: A Composing Book*, William Strong, 1994, page 7)

Passage B

Firstly, energy drinks can be a danger to our health, especially because our bodies are still growing and developing. These contain high amounts of caffeine, more than a regular cup of coffee. Caffeine raises the heart rate, makes the kidney work harder, and causes the brain vessels to narrow, and since our bodies aren't fully grown yet, the effects are worse. Some kids drink energy drinks before being active, like at a basketball game. Consuming caffeine while being physically active can be fatal because the heart rate would be raised three or four times as normal and result in a heart attack. Selling energy drinks on campus would promote the use of it and increase a student's health risk. (QuestionHub.com, uploaded 2010, downloaded 12-October 2010)

documenting sources (MLA, APA, and more)

chapter 14

Although the research process is much the same regardless of the area of study, documentation varies from one discipline to another. The common styles of documentation include MLA, author/year or APA style, and the footnote or endnote style.

MLA Style

The MLA style is favored by those in the humanities and is fully detailed in the *MLA Handbook for Writers of Research Papers* (7th edition, 2009). The following guidelines are drawn from this publication and provide an overview for in-text citations and Works Cited pages.

MLA In-Text (Parenthetical) Documentation

The most common form of parenthetical documentation in MLA style is parenthetical references to author and page number, or just to page number if the author has been mentioned in an introductory tag. Because a reference only to author and page number is an incomplete citation (readers could not find the source with such limited information), whatever is cited this way in the essay must refer to a specific source presented fully in a Works Cited list that follows the text of the paper. General guidelines for citing are given below, followed by examples and explanations of the required patterns of documentation.

Guidelines for Using Parenthetical Documentation

- The purpose of documentation is to make clear exactly what material in a passage has been borrowed and from what source the borrowed material has come.

GOOD ADVICE

You need a 100 percent correspondence between the sources listed on your Works Cited page(s) and the sources you cite (refer to) in your paper. Do not omit from your Works Cited any sources you refer to in your paper. Do not include in your Works Cited any sources not referred to in your paper.

- Parenthetical documentation requires specific page references for borrowed material.
- Parenthetical documentation is required for both quoted and paraphrased material.
- Parenthetical documentation provides as brief a citation as possible consistent with accuracy and clarity.

The Simplest Patterns of Parenthetical Documentation

The simplest parenthetical reference can be prepared in one of three ways:

1. Give the author's last name (full name in the first reference) in the text of your paper, and place the relevant page number(s) in parentheses following the borrowed material.

   > Frederick Lewis Allen observes that, during the 1920s, urban tastes spread to the country (146).

2. Place the author's last name and the relevant page number(s) in parentheses following the borrowed material.

   > During the 1920s, "not only the drinks were mixed, but the company as well" (Allen 82).

3. On the rare occasion that you cite an entire work rather than borrowing from a specific passage, give the author's name in the text and omit any page numbers.

   > Barbara Tuchman argues that there are significant parallels between the fourteenth century and our time.

Each one of these in-text references is complete *only* when the full citation is found in the Works Cited section of your paper.

> Allen, Frederick Lewis. *Only Yesterday: An Informal History of the Nineteen-Twenties*. New York: Harper, 1931. Print.
>
> Tuchman, Barbara W. *A Distant Mirror: The Calamitous 14th Century*. New York: Knopf, 1978. Print.

The three patterns just illustrated should be used in each of the following situations:

1. The work is not anonymous—the author is known.

2. The work is by one author.

3. The work cited is the only work used by that author.

4. No other author in your bibliography has the same last name.

Placement of Parenthetical Documentation

The simplest placing of a parenthetical reference is at the end of the appropriate sentence *before* the period, but, when you are quoting, *after* the quotation mark.

> During the 1920s, "not only the drinks were mixed, but the company as well" (Allen 82).

Do not put any punctuation between the author's name and the page number.

If the borrowed material ends before the end of your sentence, place the parenthetical reference at the first natural pause *after* the borrowed material and before any subsequent punctuation. This placement more accurately shows what is borrowed and what is your own work without interrupting the sentence.

> Sport, Allen observes about the 1920s, had developed into an obsession (66), another similarity between the 1920s and the 1980s.

If a quoted passage is long enough to require setting off in display form (block quotation), then place the parenthetical reference at the end of the passage, *after* the last period. (Remember that long quotations in display form do not have quotation marks.)

> It is hard to believe that when he writes about the influence of science, Allen is describing the 1920s, not the 1980s:
>
>> The prestige of science was colossal. The man in the street and the woman in the kitchen, confronted on every hand with new machines and devices which they owed to the laboratory, were ready to believe that science could accomplish almost anything. (164)

And to complete the documentation for all three examples:

Works Cited

Allen, Frederick Lewis. *Only Yesterday: An Informal History of the Nineteen-Twenties*. New York: Harper, 1931. Print.

Parenthetical Citations of Complex Sources

Not all sources can be cited in one of the three simplest forms described above, for not all meet the four criteria listed on page 234. Works by two or more authors, for example, will need somewhat fuller references. Each sample form of parenthetical documentation below would be completed with a full Works Cited reference, as illustrated above and in the next section of this chapter.

Two Authors, Mentioned in the Text

> Richard Herrnstein and Charles Murray contend that it is "consistently . . . advantageous to be smart" (25).

Two Authors, Not Mentioned in the Text

> The advantaged smart group form a "cognitive elite" in our society (Herrnstein and Murray 26–27).

A Book in Two or More Volumes

> Sewall analyzes the role of Judge Lord in Dickinson's life (2: 642–47).
>
> *OR*
>
> Judge Lord was also one of Dickinson's preceptors (Sewall 2: 642–47).

Note: The number before the colon always signifies the volume number: the number(s) after the colon represents the page number(s).

A Book or Article Listed by Title (Author Unknown)

> According to the *Concise Dictionary of American Biography*, William Jennings Bryan's 1896 campaign stressed social and sectional conflicts (117).
>
> The *Times*'s editors are not pleased with some of the changes in welfare programs ("Where Welfare Stands" 4:16).

Always cite the title of the article, not the title of the journal, if the author is unknown.

A Work by a Corporate Author

> According to the report of the Institute of Ecology's Global Ecological Problems Workshop, the civilization of the city can lull us into forgetting our relationship to the total ecological system on which we depend (13).

Although corporate authors may be cited with the page number within the parentheses, your presentation will be more graceful if corporate authors are introduced in the text. Then only page numbers go in parentheses.

Two or More Works by the Same Author

> During the 1920s, "not only the drinks were mixed, but the company as well" (Allen, *Only Yesterday* 82).
>
> According to Frederick Lewis Allen, the early 1900s were a period of complacency in America (*The Big Change* 4–5).
>
> In *The Big Change*, Allen asserts that the early 1900s were a period of complacency (4–5).

If your Works Cited list contains two or more works by the same author, the fullest parenthetical citation will include the author's last name, followed by a comma, the work's title, shortened if possible, and the page number(s). If the author's name appears in the text—or the author and title both, as in the third example above—omit these items from the parenthetical citation. When you have to include the title, it is best to simplify the citation by including the author's last name in the text.

Two or More Works in One Parenthetical Reference

> Several writers about the future agree that big changes will take place in work patterns (Toffler 384–87; Naisbitt 35–36).

Separate each author cited with a semicolon. But if the parenthetical citation would be disruptively long, cite the works in a "See also" note rather than in the text.

Complete Publication Information in Parenthetical Reference

Occasionally you may want to give complete information about a source within parentheses in the text of your paper. Then a Works Cited list is not used. Square brackets are used for parenthetical information within parentheses. This approach may be appropriate when you use only one or two sources, even if many references are made to those sources. Literary analyses are one type of paper for which this approach to citation may be a good choice. For example:

> Edith Wharton establishes the bleakness of her setting, Starkfield, not just through description of place but also through her main character, Ethan, who is described as "bleak and unapproachable" (*Ethan Frome* [New York: Scribner's, 1911; print] 3. All subsequent references are to this edition.). Later Wharton describes winter as "shut[ting] down on Starkfield" and negating life there (7).

Nonprint or Internet Sources

You may find yourself a little confused over how to cite electronic sources because they lack page numbers. However, you do not need to use parenthetical citations for these kinds of entries. Follow these guidelines for electronic or Internet sources:

- Include in the text the first item from the full citation in the Works Cited entry (e.g., author name, article name, website name, film name).
- Do not give paragraph numbers or page numbers based on your web browser's print preview function.
- Unless you must list the website name in the signal phrase or tagging (e.g., "According to Forbes.com, . . .") in order to get the reader to the appropriate entry, do not include URLs in-text. Only provide partial URLs, such as a domain name like CNN.com or Forbes.com, as opposed to writing out http://www.cnn.com or http://www.forbes.com.

An example of an Internet in-text citation is:

> Film critic Roger Ebert says that *The King's Speech* "is a superior historical drama and a powerful personal one."

Additional Information Footnotes or Endnotes

At times you may need to provide additional useful information, explanation, or commentary about your ideas or a source that is not central to the development of your paper. These additions belong in footnotes or endnotes. However, use these sparingly and never as a way of advancing your thesis. Some instructors object to content footnotes or endnotes and prefer only parenthetical citations in student papers.

> Chekhov's debt to Ibsen should be recognized, as should his debt to Maeterlinck and other playwrights of the 1890s who were concerned with the inner life of their characters.[1]

> 1. For further discussion of this point, see Bentley 330; Bruford 45; and Williams 126–29.

Preparing MLA Citations for a "Works Cited" Page

Parenthetical (in-text) citations are completed by a full reference to each source in a list presented at the end of the paper. To prepare your Works Cited page(s), alphabetize, by the author's last name, the sources you have cited and complete each citation according to the forms illustrated and explained in the following pages. The basic information for each citation includes the author, the title, publication information, and also the medium of the source (print, Web, DVD, etc.). The key is to find the appropriate model for each of your sources and then follow the model exactly.

Forms for Books: Citing the Complete Book

A Book by a Single Author

> Silver, Lee M. *Remaking Eden: Cloning and Beyond in a Brave New World*. New York: Avon, 1997. Print.

The subtitle is included, preceded by a colon, even if there is no colon on the book's title page.

A Book by Two or Three Authors

> Adkins, Lesley, and Ray Adkins. *The Keys of Egypt: The Race to Crack the Hieroglyph Code*. New York: HarperCollins, 2000. Print.

Second (and third) authors' names appear in signature form.

A Book with More Than Three Authors

> Baker, Susan P., et al. *The Injury Fact Book*. Oxford: Oxford UP, 1992. Print.

You may use the name of the first author listed on the title page, followed by "et al." (which means "and others"), or you may list all authors in the order their names appear on the title page. Shorten "University Press" to "UP."

Two or More Works by the Same Author

Goodall, Jane. *In the Shadow of Man*. Boston: Houghton, 1971. Print.

---. *Through a Window: My Thirty Years with the Chimpanzees of Gombe*. Boston: Houghton, 1990. Print.

Give the author's full name with the first entry. For the second (and additional works), begin the citation with three hyphens followed by a period. Alphabetize the entries by the books' titles.

A Book Written under a Pseudonym with Name Supplied

Wrighter, Carl P. [Paul Stevens]. *I Can Sell You Anything*. New York: Ballantine, 1972. Print.

Supply the author's name in square brackets.

An Anonymous Book

Beowulf: A New Verse Translation. Trans. Seamus Heaney. New York: Farrar, 2000. Print.

Do not use "anon." Alphabetize by the book's title.

An Edited Book

Hamilton, Alexander, James Madison, and John Jay. *The Federalist Papers*. Ed. Isaac Kramnick. New York: Viking-Penguin, 1987. Print.

Lynn, Kenneth S., ed. *Huckleberry Finn: Text, Sources, and Critics*. New York: Harcourt, 1961. Print.

If you cite the author's work, put the author's name first and the editor's name after the title, preceded by "Ed." If you cite the editor's work (an introduction or notes), then place the editor's name first, followed by a comma and "ed."

A Translation

Schulze, Hagen. *Germany: A New History*. Trans. Deborah Lucas Schneider. Cambridge: Harvard UP, 1998. Print.

Cornford, Francis MacDonald, trans. *The Republic of Plato*. New York: Oxford UP, 1945. Print.

Fagels, Robert, trans. *The Odyssey*. By Homer. New York: Viking, 1996. Print.

If the author's work is being cited, place the author's name first and the translator's name after the title, preceded by "Trans." If the translator's work is the important element, place the translator's name first, as in the second example above. If the author's name does not appear in the title, give it after the title, as in the third example.

A Book in Two or More Volumes

Spielvogel, Jackson J. *Western Civilization*. 2 vols. Minneapolis: West, 1991. Print.

Blotner, Joseph. *Faulkner: A Biography*. Vol. 2. New York: Random House, 1974. Print.

When using two or more volumes of a multivolume work, note the total number of volumes in the work after the title. But cite a specific volume when referring to only one of the volumes.

A Book within One Volume of a Multivolume Work

James, Henry. *The American*. New York: Scribner's, 1907. Print. Vol. 2 of *The Novels and Tales of Henry James*. 26 vols. 1907–17.

Cite the author and title of the single work used and the facts of publication for that work, then the volume number and title of the complete work. Then give the total number of volumes, followed by the inclusive publication dates for the work.

A Book in Its Second or Subsequent Edition

O'Brien, David M. *Storm Center: The Supreme Court and American Politics*. 2nd ed. New York: Norton, 1990. Print.

Sundquist, James L. *Dynamics of the Party System*. Rev. ed. Washington: Brookings, 1983. Print.

Always include the number of the edition you have used, abbreviated as shown, if it is not the first edition.

A Book in a Series

Parkinson, Richard. *The Rosetta Stone*. British Museum Objects in Focus. London: British Museum Press, 2005. Print.

The series title—and number, if there is one—follows the book's title but is not italicized.

A Reprint of an Earlier Work

Cuppy, Will. *How to Become Extinct*. 1941. Chicago: U of Chicago P, 1983. Print.

Twain, Mark. *Adventures of Huckleberry Finn*. 1885. Centennial Facsimile Edition. Introd. Hamlin Hill. New York: Harper, 1962. Print.

Faulkner, William. *As I Lay Dying*. 1930. New York: Vintage-Random, 1964. Print.

Since the date of a work is often important, cite the original date of publication as well as the facts of publication for the reprinted version. Indicate any new material that is part of the reprinted book, as in the second example. The third example shows how to cite a book reprinted, by the same publisher, in a paperback version. (Vintage is a paperback imprint of the publisher Random House.)

A Book with Two or More Publishers

Green, Mark J., James M. Fallows, and David R. Zwick. *Who Runs Congress?* Ralph Nader Congress Project. New York: Bantam; New York: Grossman, 1972. Print.

If the title page lists two or more publishers, give all as part of the facts of publication, placing a semicolon between them, as illustrated above.

A Corporate or Governmental Author

California State Department of Education. *American Indian Education Handbook*. Sacramento: California State Department of Education, Indian Education Unit, 1991. Print.

Hispanic Market Connections. *The National Hispanic Database: A Los Angeles Preview*. Los Altos, CA: Hispanic Market Connections, 1992. Print.

List the institution as the author even when it is also the publisher.

A Book in a Foreign Language

Blanchard, Gerard. *Images de la musique au cinéma*. Paris: Edilig, 1984. Print.

Capitalize only the first word of titles and subtitles and words normally capitalized in that language (e.g., proper nouns in French, all nouns in German). A translation in square brackets may be provided. Check your work carefully for spelling and accent marks.

The Bible

The Reader's Bible: A Narrative. Ed. with intro. Roland Mushat Frye. Princeton: Princeton UP, 1965. Print.

Although scriptural works such as the Bible, Talmud, or Koran are not italicized like other titles within the text of your paper, the versions of the works usually have specific names, which are italicized.

A Book with a Title in Its Title

Piper, Henry Dan, ed. *Fitzgerald's* The Great Gatsby: *The Novel, the Critics, the Background*. Scribner Research Anthologies. Ed. Martin Steinmann, Jr. New York: Scribner's, 1970. Print.

Forms for Books: Citing Part of a Book

A Preface, Introduction, Foreword, or Afterword

Sagan, Carl. Introduction. *A Brief History of Time: From the Big Bang to Black Holes*. By Stephen W. Hawking. New York: Bantam, 1988. ix–x. Print.

Use this form if you are citing the author of the preface, etc. Provide the appropriate identifying phrase after the author's name and give inclusive page numbers for the part of the book by that author at the end of the citation.

An Encyclopedia Article

Ostrom, John H. "Dinosaurs." *McGraw-Hill Encyclopedia of Science and Technology*. 1987 ed. Print.

"Benjamin Franklin." *Concise Dictionary of American Biography*. Ed. Joseph G. E. Hopkins. New York: Scribner's, 1964. Print.

When articles are signed or initialed, give the author's name. Complete the name of the author of an initialed article thus: K[enny], E[dward] J. Identify well-known encyclopedias and dictionaries by the year of the edition only. Give the complete facts of publication for less well-known works or those in only one edition.

A Work in an Anthology or Collection

Hurston, Zora Neale. "The First One." *Black Female Playwrights: An Anthology of Plays Before 1950*. Ed. Kathy A. Perkins. Bloomington: Indiana UP, 1989. 80–88. Print.

Comstock, George. "The Medium and the Society: The Role of Television in American Life." *Children and Television: Images in a Changing Sociocultural World*. Eds. Gordon L. Berry and Joy Keiko Asamen. Newbury Park, CA: Sage, 1993. 117–31. Print.

Cite the author and title of the work you have used. Then give the title, the editor(s), and the facts of publication of the anthology or collection. Conclude by providing inclusive page numbers for the work used and the publication medium.

An Article in a Collection, Casebook, or Sourcebook

Welsch, Roger. "The Cornstalk Fiddle." *Journal of American Folklore* 77.305 (1964): 262–63. Rpt. in *Readings in American Folklore*. Ed. Jan Harold Brunvand. New York: Norton, 1979. 106–07. Print.

MacKenzie, James J. "The Decline of Nuclear Power." *engage/social* April 1986. Rpt. as "America Does Not Need More Nuclear Power Plants" in *The Environmental Crisis: Opposing Viewpoints*. Eds. Julie S. Bach and Lynn Hall. Opposing Viewpoints Series. St. Paul: Greenhaven, 1986. 136–41. Print.

Most articles in collections have been previously published, so a complete citation needs to include the original facts of publication (excluding page numbers if they are unavailable) as well as the facts of publication for the collection. End the citation with inclusive page numbers for the article used and the publication medium.

Cross-References

If you are citing several articles from one collection, you can cite the collection and then provide only the author and title of specific articles used, with a cross-reference to the editor(s) of the collection:

> Head, Suzanne, and Robert Heinzman, eds. *Lessons of the Rainforest*. San Francisco: Sierra Club, 1990. Print.

> Bandyopadhyay, J., and Vandana Shiva. "Asia's Forest, Asia's Cultures." Head and Heinzman 66–77. Print.

> Head, Suzanne. "The Consumer Connection: Psychology and Politics." Head and Heinzman 156–67. Print.

Forms for Print Periodicals: Articles in Journals

Article in a Journal

> Truman, Dana M., David M. Tokar, and Ann R. Fischer. "Dimensions of Masculinity: Relations to Date Rape, Supportive Attitudes, and Sexual Aggression in Dating Situations." *Journal of Counseling and Development* 76 (1996): 555–62. Print.

Give the volume and issue number, separated by a period; followed by the year only, in parentheses; followed by a colon and inclusive page numbers; followed by the medium of publication.

Article in a Journal That Uses Issue Numbers Only

> Keen, Ralph. "Thomas More and Geometry." *Moreana* 86 (1985): 151–66. Print.

If the journal uses only issue numbers, not volume numbers, cite the issue number alone.

Forms for Print Periodicals: Articles in Magazines

Article in a Monthly Magazine

> Norell, Mark A., and Xu Xing. "The Varieties of Tyrannosaurs." *Natural History* May 2005: 35–39. Print.

Do not use volume or issue number. Instead, cite the month(s) and year after the title, followed by a colon and inclusive page numbers. If page numbers are not consecutive, cite the first page number followed by the plus sign. Abbreviate all months except May, June, and July.

Article in a Weekly Magazine

> Stein, Joel. "Eat This, Low Carbers." *Time* 15 Aug. 2005: 78. Print.

Provide the complete date, using the order of day, month, and year.

An Anonymous Article

> "Death of Perestroika." *Economist* 2 Feb. 1991: 12–13. Print.

The missing name indicates that the article is anonymous. Alphabetize under D.

A Published Interview

> Angier, Natalie. "Ernst Mayr at 93." Interview. *Natural History* May 1997: 8–11. Print.

Follow the pattern for a published article, but add the descriptive label "Interview" (followed by a period) after the article's title.

A Review

> Bardsley, Tim. "Eliciting Science's Best." Rev. of *Frontiers of Illusion: Science, Technology, and the Politics of Progress*, by Daniel Sarewitz. *Scientific American* June 1997: 142. Print.

> Shales, Tom. "A Chilling Stop in 'Nuremberg.'" Rev. of the movie *Nuremberg*, TNT 16 July 2000. *Washington Post* 16 July 2000: G1. Print.

If the review is signed, begin with the author's name, then the title of the review article. Give the title of the work being reviewed, a comma, and its author, preceded by "Rev. of." Alphabetize unsigned reviews by the title of the review. For reviews of art shows, videos, or computer software, provide place and date or descriptive label to make the citation clear.

Forms for Print Periodicals: Newspapers

An Article from a Newspaper

> Wilford, John Noble. "Astronauts Land on Plain; Collect Rocks, Plant Flag." *New York Times* 21 July 1969, late city ed.: 1. Print.

A newspaper's title should be cited as it appears on the masthead, excluding any initial article; thus *New York Times*, not *The New York Times*. If there is a specific edition listed in the masthead (late ed., nat'l ed.), include it after the date.

An Article from a Newspaper with Lettered Sections

> Diehl, Jackson. "Inhuman: Yes or No?" *Washington Post* 12 Sept. 2005: A19. Print.

Place the section letter immediately before the page number, without any spacing.

An Article from a Newspaper with Numbered Sections

> Roberts, Sam. "Another Kind of Middle-Class Squeeze." *New York Times* 18 May 1997, sec. 4: 1+. Print.

Place the section number after the date, preceded by a comma and the abbreviation "sec."

An Editorial

> "Japan's Two Nationalisms." Editorial. *Washington Post* 4 June 2000: B6. Print.

Add the descriptive label "Editorial" after the article title.

A Letter to the Editor

> Wiles, Yoko A. "Thoughts of a New Citizen." Letter. *Washington Post* 27 Dec. 1995: A22. Print.

If the letter is titled, use the descriptive label "Letter" after the title. If the letter is untitled, place "Letter" after the author's name.

Citing Other Print and Nonprint Sources

The materials in this section, although often important to research projects, do not always lend themselves to documentation by the forms illustrated above. Follow the basic order of author, title, facts, and medium of publication as much as possible, and add whatever information is needed to make the citation clear and useful to a reader.

Cartoons and Advertisements

> Schulz, Charles M. "Peanuts." Comic strip. *Washington Post* 10 Dec. 1985: D8. Print.

Give the cartoon title, if there is one; add the descriptive label such as "Cartoon"; then give the facts of publication. The pattern is similar for advertisements.

> Halleyscope. "Halleyscopes Are for Night Owls." Advertisement. *Natural History* Dec. 1985: 15. Print.

Computer Software

> "Aardvark." *The Oxford English Dictionary*. 2nd ed. Oxford: Oxford UP, 1992. CD-ROM.

Give author, title, edition or version, publisher, year of issue, and publication medium (CD-ROM or DVD-ROM).

Dissertation—Unpublished

> Brotton, Joyce D. "Illuminating the Present Through Literary Dialogism: From the Reformation Through Postmodernism." Diss. George Mason U, 2002. Print.

Dissertation—Published

> Brotton, Joyce D. *Illuminating the Present Through Literary Dialogism: From the Reformation Through Postmodernism*. Diss. George Mason U, 2002. Ann Arbor: UMI, 2002. Print.

Films or Videos

> Coen, Ethan, and Joel Coen, dir. *No Country for Old Men*. Perf. Javier Bardem, Josh Brolin, and Tommy Lee Jones. Miramax, 2008. DVD.

> *Slumdog Millionaire*. Dir. Danny Boyle. Perf. Dev Patel, Anil Dapoor, and Freida Pinto. Fox Searchlight Pictures, 2008. Film.

Begin a film or video entry with the title of the work, unless you are citing a particular individual's contribution. A title can be followed by relevant information like the director, screenwriter, and/or performers (unless already mentioned); then include the distributor, the release date, and the format. For video recordings, you may include the original film's release date before the distributor if pertinent.

Government Documents

> U.S. President. *Public Papers of the Presidents of the United States*. Washington: Office of the Federal Register, 1961. Print.

> United States. Senate. Committee on Energy and Natural Resources. Subcommittee on Energy Research and Development. *Advanced Reactor Development Program: Hearing*. 24 May 1988. Washington: GPO, 1988. Print.

> ---. Environmental Protection Agency. *The Challenge of the Environment: A Primer on EPA's Statutory Authority*. Washington: GPO, 1972. Print.

Observe the pattern illustrated here. If the author of the document is not given, cite the name of the government first followed by the name of the department or agency. If you cite more than one document published by the United States government, do not repeat the name but use the standard three hyphens followed by a period instead. If you cite a second document prepared by the Environmental Protection Agency, use the following pattern:

> United States. Cong. House. . . .

> ---. Environmental Protection Agency . . .

> ---.---. [second source from EPA]

If the author is known, follow this pattern:

Geller, William. *Deadly Force*. U.S. Dept. of Justice National Institute of Justice Crime File Study Guide. Washington: U.S. Dept. of Justice, n.d. Print.

If the document contains no date, use the abbreviation "n.d."

Hays, W. W., ed. *Facing Geologic and Hydrologic Hazards*. Geological Survey Professional Paper 1240-B. Washington: GPO, 1981. Print.

Abbreviate the U.S. Government Printing Office thus: GPO.

An Interview

Plum, Kenneth. Personal Interview. 5 Mar. 1995.

A Lecture, Reading, or Address

Whitman, Christine Todd, and Bill McKibben. "Containing Carbon: Markets, Morals, and Mobilization." Amherst College. Johnson Chapel, Amherst. 4 Feb. 2009. Address.

Legal Documents

U.S. Const. Art. 1, sec. 3.

The Constitution is referred to by article and section. Abbreviations are used; do not italicize.

Turner v. Arkansas. 407 U.S. 366. 1972. Print.

In citing a court case, give the name of the case (the plaintiff and defendant); the volume, name, and page of the report cited; and the date. The name of a court case is italicized in the text but not in the Works Cited.

Federal Highway Act, as amended. 23 U.S. Code 109. 1970. Print.

Labor Management Relations Act (Taft-Hartley Act). Statutes at Large. 61. 1947. Print.

34 U.S. Code. 1952. Print.

Citing laws is complicated, and lawyers use many abbreviations that may not be clear to nonexperts. Bills that become law are published annually in *Statutes at Large* (Stat.) and later in the *U.S. Code* (USC). Provide the title of the bill and the source, volume, and year. References to both *Statutes at Large* and the *U.S. Code* can be given as a convenience to readers.

Unpublished Letter/E-Mail

Usick, Patricia. Message to the author. 26 June 2005. E-mail.

Treat a published letter as a work in a collection.

Maps and Charts

Hampshire and Dorset. Map. Kent, Eng.: Geographers' A-Z Map, n.d. Print.

The format is similar to that for an anonymous book but add the appropriate descriptive label.

Plays or Concerts

Mourning Becomes Electra. By Eugene O'Neill. Shakespeare Theatre, Washington, DC. 16 May 1997. Performance.

Include title, author, theater, city, and date of performance. Principal actors, singers, musicians, and/or the director can be added as appropriate after the author.

Recordings

Holiday, Billie, perf. "All of You." By Cole Porter. Rec. 11 Mar. 1959. *Last Recording*. Cond. Ray Ellis. Polygram, 1990. CD.

The order of the entry depends upon the focus of the interest; composer, conductor, group, or performer may come first, followed by the title, the artists, or composer (if different from the first information), the manufacturer, the year, and the medium (CD, LP). You may also include the date of the recording.

A Report

Environment and Development: Breaking the Ideological Deadlock. Report of the Twenty-first United Nations Issues Conference, 23–25 Feb. 1990. Muscatine, Iowa: Stanley Foundation, n.d. Print.

Television or Radio Program

"The Wolf That Changed America." *Nature*. PBS. WNET, New York, 23 Nov. 2008. Television.

Additional information, such as directors, narrators, or performers, follow the title of the episode or the series, depending on which it describes.

Citing Web Publications

Remember that the purpose of a citation is to provide readers with the information they need to obtain the source you have used. Most sources on the Web have the same basic elements—author, title, and publication information—that print sources do. However, works on the Web can be changed or updated at any point, or they may be located in several places online. Citing Web sources requires that you provide more information than is usually needed for print sources in order to document the precise source you used. The citation formats for Web sources fall into three basic categories: sources with only Web publication infor-

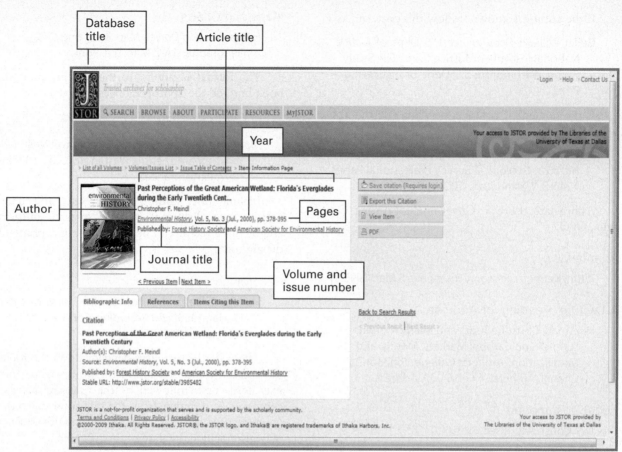

Writing a research paper will undoubtedly require that you use electronic databases. Such databases, like JSTOR, provide several key pieces of information necessary for your process of collecting research. Study the following diagram paying close attention to how you can locate the author's name, title of the journal, and so forth when using an electronic database.

mation, sources with additional print publication information, and sources retrieved through online databases.

Works from the Web

Articles cited with only Web publication information can include articles in online magazines, reference databases, professional websites, or homepages. The basic pattern for the citation includes:

1. Author (or editor or translator, as appropriate), if there is one

2. Title of the work, if there is a title separate from the larger page

3. Online publication information including title of the web page—italicized—the version used (if available), the publisher or sponsor (or n.p. if unavailable); the date of publication (or n.d. if unavailable); and the medium of publication (Web)

4. Date you accessed the source

   Coyne, Amanda. "Palin and the Wolves." *Newsweek .com.* Newsweek, 10 Apr. 2009. Web. 12 Apr. 2009.

   Rosner, Shmuel. "Too Busy to Save Darfur: The Obama Administration Has Very Few Options for Solving the Crisis in Sudan." *Slate.* Slate Magazine, 9 Apr. 2009. Web. 13 Apr. 2009.

   "Governor's Blue Ribbon Panel on Child Protection." *CNN.com.* Cable News Network, 27 May 2002. Web. 10 Apr. 2009.

   "Prohibition." *Encyclopedia Britannica Online.* Encyclopedia Britannica, 1998. Web. 24 Jan. 1998.

   Vachss, Andrew. "How Journalism Abuses Children." *The Zero—The Official Site of Andrew Vachss.* Ed. The Zero Collective, Aug. 1996. Web. 2 Aug. 2003.

Works from the Web with Previous Print Publication

For books, articles, poems, or other items that have been published previously and are also available online, you may include additional information about the original publication. Include the following information in your citation:

1. Citation for the original source: author, title, original publication information

2. Title of the website, italicized

3. Medium of publication

4. Date you accessed the source

"Failed States and Failed Policies: How to Stop the Drug Wars." *The Economist* 5 Mar. 2009. *Economist.com*. Web. 7 Apr. 2009.

Douglass, Frederick. *Life and Times of Frederick Douglass: His Early Life as a Slave, His Escape from Bondage, and His Complete History to the Present Time*. Hartford: Park Publishing, 1881. *Documenting the American South*. Web. 6 Apr. 2009.

Articles from Online Databases

To cite a journal article retrieved through a database, begin as you would if you had accessed the article in its print form, including the inclusive page numbers if possible (or n. pag. if unavailable). Then include the online access information.

1. Cite the source: author, title, journal, volume and issue, and page numbers
2. Title of the database
3. Medium of publication
4. Date you accessed the source

Adams, Terri M., and Douglas B. Fuller. "The Words Have Changed But the Ideology Remains the Same: Misogynistic Lyrics in Rap Music." *Journal of Black Studies* 36.6 (2006): 938–57. *CSA Illumina*. 6 Apr. 2009.

"The Bulls and Bears: A Tremendous Crash in the Wall Street Menagerie." *Washington Post* 22 Nov. 1879. *ProQuest*. Web. 10 Apr. 2009.

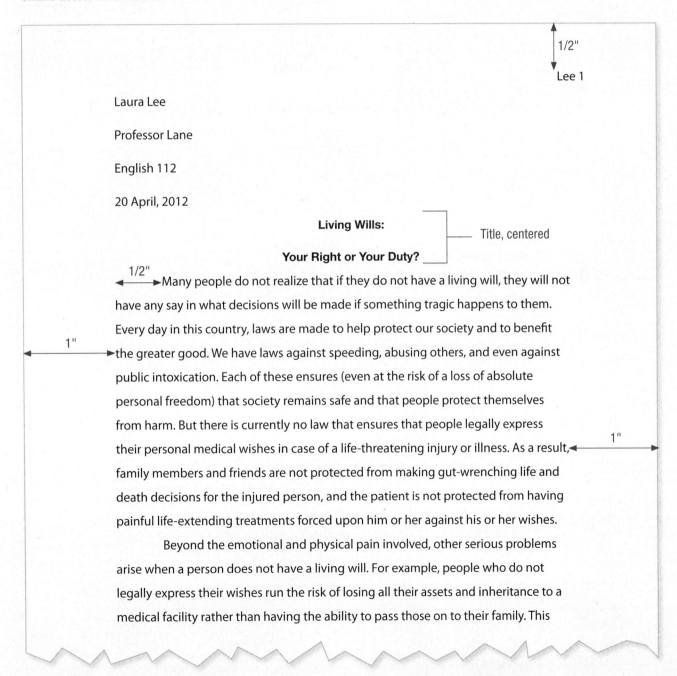

1/2"

Lee 1

Laura Lee

Professor Lane

English 112

20 April, 2012

Living Wills: ⎤

⎟ ——— Title, centered

Your Right or Your Duty? ⎦

1/2"

←——→ Many people do not realize that if they do not have a living will, they will not have any say in what decisions will be made if something tragic happens to them. Every day in this country, laws are made to help protect our society and to benefit

1"

←——————→ the greater good. We have laws against speeding, abusing others, and even against public intoxication. Each of these ensures (even at the risk of a loss of absolute personal freedom) that society remains safe and that people protect themselves from harm. But there is currently no law that ensures that people legally express

1"

their personal medical wishes in case of a life-threatening injury or illness. As a result, ←——————→ family members and friends are not protected from making gut-wrenching life and death decisions for the injured person, and the patient is not protected from having painful life-extending treatments forced upon him or her against his or her wishes.

Beyond the emotional and physical pain involved, other serious problems arise when a person does not have a living will. For example, people who do not legally express their wishes run the risk of losing all their assets and inheritance to a medical facility rather than having the ability to pass those on to their family. This

Sample Student Essay in MLA Style

The following paper illustrates MLA style of documentation for an argument that is developed using sources. The paper shows a separate title page and outline, though these may not be required by your instructor. Study how the student blends information and arguments from sources with her views on this issue to build her argument.

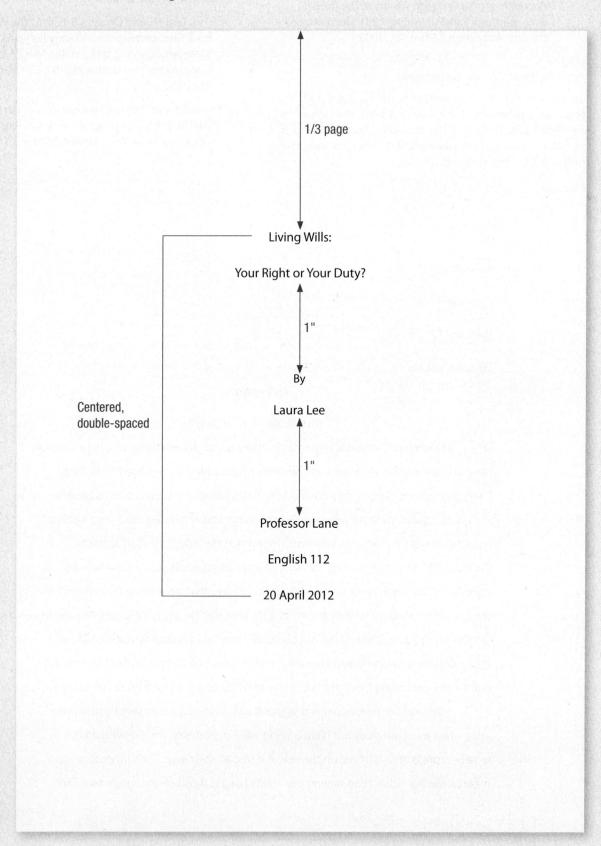

1/3 page

Living Wills:

Your Right or Your Duty?

1"

By

Centered,
double-spaced

Laura Lee

1"

Professor Lane

English 112

20 April 2012

Centered

Outline

Thesis: To alleviate all these problems, and despite arguments claiming that this type of law is a violation of civil rights, it is clear that a law should be created that makes having a living will mandatory for everyone over the age of eighteen in the United States.

I. What exactly is a living will?

II. One reason why a living will should be mandatory is so that patients in a persistent vegetative state (PVS) do not put a burden on their families and make them try to decide what would really be best for their loved one.

    A. Crisci and Crispi report that "[t]he relatives described their own quality of life as 'poor, miserable.'"

    B. O'Mathuna quote regarding difficult family decisions states that "[m]odern medicine has provided people with many great benefits, but it has also forced families to make difficult decisions."

III. A second reason as to why everyone over the age of eighteen should create their own living will is because it would help reduce some of the cost it would take to provide medical care for someone experiencing PVS.

    A. Borthwick article regarding costs of PVS gives estimate of the total annual costs in the United States for the care of adults and children in a persistent vegetative state to be $1 billion to $7 billion.

    B. O'Mathuna's statistic estimates that 10,000 to 25,000 adults and 4,000 to 10,000 children live in PVS in the United States.

IV. The final reason why those over the age of eighteen should be mandated to create their own living will is that if one was created, then a legal battle could easily be avoided.

    A. Jayson quote regarding Schiavo case states that "[t]he battle between Terri Schiavo's husband and parents is a call to action for the two-thirds of adult Americans who, like Schiavo, have not prepared living wills that help direct their care in terminal circumstances."

    B. CNN.com article regarding Schiavo case states, "Terri Schiavo did not leave anything in writing about what she would want if she ever became incapacitated. Over the years, courts have sided with her husband in more than a dozen cases."

1"

1"

Double-spaced

1"

1"

Living Wills:

Your Right or Your Duty?

      Many people do not realize that if they do not have a living will, they will

1"

not have any say in what decisions will be made if something tragic happens to

them. Every day in this country, laws are made to help protect our society and to

benefit the greater good. We have laws against speeding, abusing others, and even

against public intoxication. Each of these ensures (even at the risk of a loss of absolute

personal freedom) that society remains safe and that people protect themselves

from harm. But there is currently no law that ensures that people legally express their

personal medical wishes in case of a life-threatening injury or illness. As a result, family

1"

members and friends are not protected from making gut-wrenching life and death

decisions for the injured person, and the patient is not protected from having painful

life-extending treatments forced upon him or her against his or her wishes.

      Beyond the emotional and physical pain involved, other serious problems

arise when a person does not have a living will. For example, people who do not

legally express their wishes run the risk of losing all their assets and inheritance

to a medical facility rather than having the ability to pass those on to their family.

This situation also creates a financial burden on our government. For those who

cannot pay their medical bills, Medicaid (a last-resort program that picks up a

patient's medical costs at the expense of the taxpayers) must take over. To alleviate

all of these problems, and despite opponents' arguments that living wills amount

to a sort of assisted suicide (or even homicide), it is clear that a law should, in

fact, be created that makes a living will mandatory for everyone over the age of

eighteen in the United States. A mandatory living will statute will help eliminate

emotional controversies and legal battles, ease financial burdens on families and the

government, and will greatly benefit the American people.

      What exactly is a living will? A living will is simply a written document

defining a person's "right to die." Despite the negative image some have created for

the term, it is not a document that allows medical personnel or anyone else to "pull

the plug" or kill a patient against their wishes. Instead, it simply means that a person

gets to predetermine what happens in a medical emergency and has the right to die

1"

with dignity if he or she so chooses. The living will usually states to what extent he or she wishes to have his or her life artificially prolonged by all of the modern technology that hospitals now possess. Many people do not believe that it is desirable to be kept alive when there is no hope for curing them or for them to live normal lives. The living will instructs doctors whether or not a person wishes to die naturally, explains the patient's decisions regarding whether life-support equipment should be used, whether CPR should be administered, and about how much medicine should be used to relieve pain. It also typically names the person who is authorized to make all their care decisions for them when they are unable. In short, the living will is the document that can help to express a patient's personal, medical, and emotional or spiritual wishes.

One reason why a living will should be mandatory is so that patients' families do not bear the burden of making highly emotional decisions for their loved ones. If a person is in a persistent vegetative state (PVS), it is said that they do not experience any sensation or sentiment. According to some experts, "They are not even considered as persons [. . .] because their internal organs work automatically while their cortex is shut off, not engaged in even minimal social interaction" (Crisci and Crispi). Patients who are in a persistent vegetative state require a large amount of medical and nursing attention. As a result, complex family interactions and conflicts can occur. In one important study, several relatives of those who have a loved one in a PVS were asked what their attitudes and feelings were toward the situation. According to C. Crisci and F. Crispi, authors of the article "Patients in Persistent Vegetative State . . . and What of Their Relatives?" "The relatives described their own quality of life as poor, miserable. None of the relatives would ever clearly admit that death would have been better, but all admitted that this event would not have been more distressing than their present situation" (534). Dr. Donald O'Mathuna, a noted author on this subject, agrees with Crisci and Crispi that families often bear a huge burden in these situations, saying, "Modern medicine has provided people with many great benefits, but it has also forced families to make difficult decisions. People must now decide if and when they would want certain treatments withheld or withdrawn from themselves or others." It seems clear that if everyone over the age of eighteen were to create their

Brackets on either side of the ellipsis points indicates that the author of the paper has omitted words.

Ellipsis indicate that material has been omitted from the quote.

Since the author names are stated in the text, only a page number is needed here.

own living will, then the families of those in a PVS would not have to deal with the pressure of making the correct decisions for their loved ones. A living will would also help to clarify their loved ones' wishes and what, exactly, they want regarding their personal care, medication, and resuscitation, even if they are only temporarily unable to make their wishes known.

This benefit would be most applicable to families of patients who are unable to make decisions for themselves over long periods of time, that is, who are in a persistent vegetative state. Most relatives of those who are in a PVS understand the meaning of the illness, but often do not realize that the prognosis is generally poor. The relatives usually maintain hope for some months, praying that a miracle will happen and that their loved one will eventually respond. At four to six months after the beginning of PVS, however, the size of the group of relatives accepting involvement decreases and, typically, only one (usually the mother or a sister) remains as the "deputy of the family" to assist the patient (Crisci and Crispi). If a living will were mandatory for all of those over eighteen years of age, then the family of the loved one dealing with PVS would not ever have to face this awful situation. The strain of dealing with a situation like this can become very stressful to those involved and often can cause problems or even legal battles within the family. Creating a living will would help to eliminate all these problems, letting the family enjoy their last few moments with their loved one in peace instead of worrying about what decisions must be made.

Not only would a living-will mandate allow families to avoid difficult emotional decisions, it would also help to reduce some of the cost of medical care for someone in a PVS. Patients who are in a persistent vegetative state typically require intensive physical care, including respirators, feeding tubes, and round-the-clock supervision. The care given by a family member to someone who is in a persistent vegetative state is most often not enough. PVS patients must usually be either hospitalized or put in nursing homes for the constant care they must receive. According to Chris Borthwick, author of "The Permanent Vegetative State: Ethical Crux, Medical Fiction?" this type of care is extremely expensive:

> A previous survey of care costs for PVS patients that did at least refer to recorded costs in actual cases suggested a range from a low of $18,000

1/2"

to a high of $120,000 with an average of around $60,000. The Consensus Statement refers to a single case study to reach an estimate of cost of care for the PVS patient in a nursing facility as costing from $126,000 to $180,000 per year, on average two and a half times the previous estimate. A rough approximation of the total annual costs in the United States for the care of adults and children in a persistent vegetative state is $1 billion to $7 billion.

Donald O'Mathuna brings new light to these shocking figures by stating that "a review of the medical information concerning PVS was published in 1994 by the Multi-Society Task Force on PVS. They estimated that 10,000 to 25,000 adults and 4,000 to 10,000 children live in PVS in the United States." The figures presented by these authors, when taken in conjunction, show a shocking truth: there are large numbers of people in our country who are in a PVS and the cost is extremely high to keep those patients alive. The conditions of those who are considered long-term patients are more than likely never going to change. And inevitably, over time, the patient's resources and ability to pay run out. It then very often becomes either the family or the government that ends up paying these astoundingly high bills. Medicaid, funded by the U.S. taxpayers, will pay hundreds of thousands of dollars a year to keep a patient alive who may very well have wished to die given the option. And while cost alone is never a good reason to end a human life, it seems wrong to force families into bankruptcy or force taxpayers to foot the bill for care that the patient himself or herself would have chosen to refuse.

Finally, a living-will statute would prevent legal battles between family members, hospitals, and insurance companies. Often, when the patient's wishes cannot be determined and when different family members believe that they each "know" what the patient would want, a long, expensive, and emotional court battle ensues. Other times, hospitals and insurance companies must get involved in order to assert what medical professionals believe is appropriate care when family members refuse certain treatments. A perfect example of a fairly recent and very public legal battle over a patient's right to die is the Terri Schiavo case, which was waged in the nation's courts for several years until her feeding tube was ultimately removed in 2005. The battle between Terri Schiavo's husband and parents is evidence enough why a living will should be created by those over the age of eighteen. The CNN.com article "Schiavo's Feeding Tube Removed" provides some important background on this case:

> The disconnecting of the feeding tube was the latest step in a contentious family saga that began 15 years ago, when Terri Schiavo collapsed from heart failure that resulted in severe brain damage. [. . .] Michael Schiavo contends his wife would not want to be kept alive artificially. But her parents argue she had no such death wish and believe she could get better with rehabilitation. Terri Schiavo did not leave anything in writing about what she would want if she ever became incapacitated. Over the years, courts have sided with her husband in more than a dozen cases.

According to Sharon Jayson, who covered the story for *USA Today,* "The battle between Terri Schiavo's husband and parents is a call to action for the two-thirds of adult Americans who, like Schiavo, have not prepared living wills that help direct their care in terminal circumstances." The struggles involved in this case clearly support the idea of a mandatory living-will statute. If a patient has a living will, parents and loved ones will not have to make it a legal issue or get anyone other than family involved because they will already know the wishes of their loved one. If Terri Schiavo had had a living will, her family would have better understood what her wishes were and they would not have had to fight with her husband about what to do.

Many people don't fully understand the realities of having a living will. They often believe that it means that a person will be actively (and possibly painfully) killed in the event of an accident or injury. They may believe that when the feeding tube of someone in a persistent vegetative state is disconnected, the person will suffer and face a death that they should not have to face. Referencing the Terri Schiavo case, Wesley Smith seems to believe that this amounts to torture:

> Terri should be allowed reasonable rehabilitation attempts before Judge Greer (judge of the Sixth Judicial Circuit, in Clearwater, Florida) orders her dehydration to death. Refusing this clearly humane and merciful request would be to intentionally cause Terri harm. Some might even argue that refusing Terri any chance to live would be a non-voluntary euthanasia homicide.

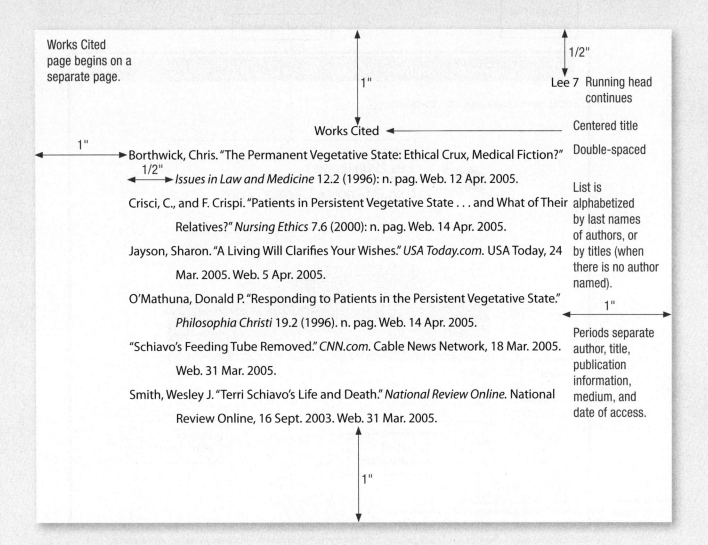

Works Cited page begins on a separate page.

1/2"

Lee 7   Running head continues

1"

Works Cited ◄─────────── Centered title

1"   Double-spaced

Borthwick, Chris. "The Permanent Vegetative State: Ethical Crux, Medical Fiction?"

1/2"   *Issues in Law and Medicine* 12.2 (1996): n. pag. Web. 12 Apr. 2005.

Crisci, C., and F. Crispi. "Patients in Persistent Vegetative State . . . and What of Their

Relatives?" *Nursing Ethics* 7.6 (2000): n. pag. Web. 14 Apr. 2005.

Jayson, Sharon. "A Living Will Clarifies Your Wishes." *USA Today.com*. USA Today, 24

Mar. 2005. Web. 5 Apr. 2005.

O'Mathuna, Donald P. "Responding to Patients in the Persistent Vegetative State."

Philosophia Christi 19.2 (1996). n. pag. Web. 14 Apr. 2005.

"Schiavo's Feeding Tube Removed." *CNN.com*. Cable News Network, 18 Mar. 2005.

Web. 31 Mar. 2005.

Smith, Wesley J. "Terri Schiavo's Life and Death." *National Review Online*. National

Review Online, 16 Sept. 2003. Web. 31 Mar. 2005.

List is alphabetized by last names of authors, or by titles (when there is no author named).

1"

Periods separate author, title, publication information, medium, and date of access.

1"

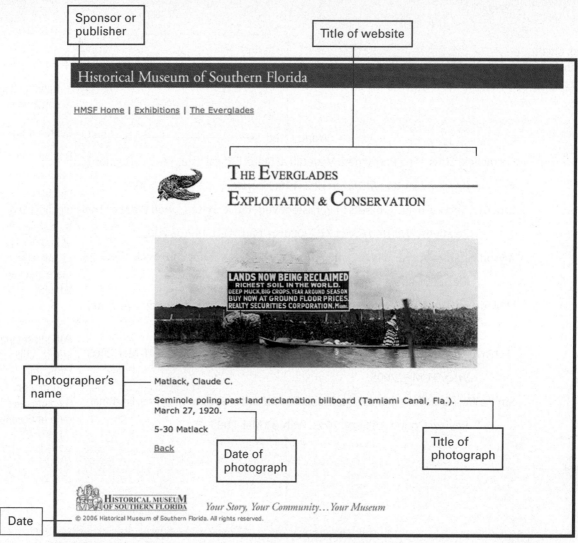

Sponsor or publisher

Title of website

Historical Museum of Southern Florida

HMSF Home | Exhibitions | The Everglades

THE EVERGLADES
EXPLOITATION & CONSERVATION

LANDS NOW BEING RECLAIMED
RICHEST SOIL IN THE WORLD.
DEEP MUCK, BIG CROPS, YEAR AROUND SEASON
BUY NOW AT GROUND FLOOR PRICES
REALTY SECURITIES CORPORATION, Miami

Photographer's name

Matlack, Claude C.

Seminole poling past land reclamation billboard (Tamiami Canal, Fla.). March 27, 1920.

5-30 Matlack

Back

Date of photograph

Title of photograph

HISTORICAL MUSEUM OF SOUTHERN FLORIDA *Your Story, Your Community...Your Museum*

Date

© 2006 Historical Museum of Southern Florida. All rights reserved.

When using websites as sources, you should pay particular attention to the publication information as well as other important identifiers.

Published with the permission of the Historical Museum of Southern Florida.

try it !

Presenting and Documenting Borrowed Information and Preparing Citations

Read the following passage and then the three plagiarized uses of the passage. Explain why each one is plagiarized and how it can be corrected.

Original Text: Stanley Karnow, *Vietnam, A History. The First Complete Account of Vietnam at War.* New York: Viking, 1983, 319.

Lyndon Baines Johnson, a consummate politician, was a kaleidoscopic personality, forever changing as he sought to dominate or persuade or placate or frighten his friends and foes. A gigantic figure whose extravagant moods matched his size, he could be cruel and kind, violent and gentle, petty, generous, cunning, naïve, crude, candid, and frankly dishonest. He commanded the blind loyalty of his aides, some of whom worshipped him, and he sparked bitter derision or fierce hatred that he never quite fathomed.

1. LBJ's vibrant and changing personality filled some people with adoration and others with bitter derision that he never quite fathomed (Karnow 319).

2. LBJ, a supreme politician, had a personality like a kaleidoscope, continually changing as he tried to control, sway, appease, or intimidate his enemies and supporters (Karnow 319).

3. Often, figures who have had great impact on America's history have been dynamic people with powerful personalities and vibrant physical presence. LBJ, for example, was a huge figure who polarized those who worked for and with him. "He commanded the blind loyalty of his aides, some of whom worshipped him, and he sparked bitter derision or fierce hatred" from many others (Karnow 319).

Read the following passage and then each of the four sample uses of the passage. Judge each of the uses for how well it avoids plagiarism and if it is documented correctly. Make corrections as needed.

Original Text: Stanley Karnow, *Vietnam, A History. The First Complete Account of Vietnam at War.* New York: Viking, 1983, 327.

On July 27, 1965, in a last-ditch attempt to change Johnson's mind, Mansfield and Russell were to press him again to "concentrate on finding a way out" of Vietnam—"a place where we ought not be," and where "the situation is rapidly going out of control." But the next day, Johnson announced his decision to add forty-four American combat battalions to the relatively small U.S. contingents already there. He had not been deaf to Mansfield's pleas, nor had he simply swallowed the Pentagon's plans. He had waffled and agonized during his nineteen months in the White House, but eventually this was his final judgment. As he would later explain: "There are many, many people who can recommend and advise, and a few of them consent. But there is only one who has been chosen by the American people to decide."

1. Karnow writes that Senators Mansfield and Russell continued to try to convince President Johnson to avoid further involvement in Vietnam, "a place where we ought not be" they felt. (327).

2. Though Johnson received advice from many, in particular Senators Mansfield and Russell, he believed the weight of the decision to become further engaged in Vietnam was solely his as the one " 'chosen by the American people to decide' " (Karnow 327).

3. On July 28, 1965, Johnson announced his decision to add forty-four battalions to the troops already in Vietnam, ending his waffling and agonizing of the past nineteen months of his presidency. (Karnow 357).

4. Karnow explains that LBJ took his responsibility to make decisions about Vietnam seriously (327). Although Johnson knew that many would offer suggestions, only he had " 'been chosen by the American people to decide' " (Karnow 327).

Turn the information printed in the right column into correct bibliographic citations for each of the works. Pay attention to the order of information, the handling of titles, and punctuation. Write each citation on a separate index card, or, if your instructor requests, prepare the citations as an alphabetical listing of works.

1. On July 14, 1997, Newsweek magazine printed Robert J. Samuelson's article titled Don't Hold Your Breath on page 40.

2. Richard B. Sewell's book The Life of Emily Dickinson was published in 1974. His book was published in two volumes by the New York City publisher Farrar, Straus, & Giroux.

3. Richard D. Heffner has edited an abridged version of Democracy in America by Alexis De Tocqueville. This is a Mentor Book paperback, a division of (New York City's) New American Library. The book was published in 1956.

4. The Object Stares Back: On the Nature of Seeing by James Elkins is reviewed in an article titled Vision Reviewed by Luciano da F. Costa. The review appeared on pages 124 and 125 in the March 1997 issue of Scientific American.

5. Arthur Whimbey wrote the article Something Better Than Binet for the Saturday Review on June 1, 1974. Joseph Rubinstein and Brent D. Slife reprinted the article on pages 102–108 in the third edition of the edited collection Taking Sides. Taking Sides was published in 1984 by the Dushkin Publishing Company located in Guilford, Connecticut.

6. The Discovery of Superconductivity appeared in Physics Today on pages 40–42. The author of the article is Jacobus de Nobel. The article appeared in the September 1996 issue, volume 49, number 9.

7. You used a biographical article, titled Marc Chagall (1887–1985), from Britannica Online which you found on the Internet September 25, 1999. You used the 1998 version, published by Encyclopaedia Britannica and available at <http://www.eb.com:180>.

8. An editorial appeared in the New York Times, on Sunday, September 7, 1997, with the title Protecting Children from Guns. The editorial could be found on page 16 of section 4.

9. Anthony Bozza's article "Moby Porn" appeared in the magazine Rolling Stone on June 26, 1977, on page 26. You obtained the text of the article from the September 1997 "edition" of General Periodicals Ondisc. The vendor is UMI-ProQuest.

10. A Letter to the Editor titled What Can We Do about Global Warming? appeared in the Washington Post on July 24, 1997. The letter was written by S. Fred Singer and printed on page A24.

APA Style

The *author/year system* identifies a source by placing the author's last name and the publication year of the source within parentheses at the point in the text where the source is cited. The in-text citations are supported by complete citations in a list of sources at the end of the paper. Most disciplines in the social sciences, biological sciences, and earth sciences use some version of the author/year style. Of the various style manuals presenting this style, the most frequently used is the *Publication Manual of the American Psychological Association* (6th ed., 2009), supplemented by the *APA Style Guide to Electronic References* (pdf, 2009).

APA Style: In-Text Citations

The simplest parenthetical reference can be presented in one of three ways:

1. Place the year of publication within parentheses immediately following the author's name in the text.

    In a typical study of preference for motherese, Fernald (1985) used an operant auditory preference procedure.

    Within the same paragraph, additional references to the source do not need to repeat the year, if the researcher clearly establishes that the same source is being cited.

    Because the speakers were unfamiliar subjects Fernald's work eliminates the possibility that it is the mother's voice per se that accounts for the preference.

2. If the author is not mentioned in the text, place the author's last name followed by a comma and the year of publication within parentheses after the borrowed information.

    The majority of working women are employed in jobs that are at least 75 percent female (Lawrence & Matsuda, 1997).

3. Cite a specific passage by providing the page, chapter, or figure number following the borrowed material. *Always* give specific page references for quoted material.

    *   A brief quotation:

    Deuzen-Smith (1988) believes that counselors must be involved with clients and "deeply interested in piecing the puzzle of life together" (p. 29).

    *   A quotation in display form:

    Bartlett (1932) explains the cyclic process of perception:

Suppose I am making a stroke in a quick game, such as tennis or cricket. How I make the stroke depends on the relating of certain new experiences, most of them visual, to other immediately preceding visual experiences, and to my posture, or balance of posture, at the moment. (p. 201)

Indent a block quotation of 40 words or more by 0.5″ from the left margin, do not use quotation marks, and double-space throughout. To show a new paragraph within the block quotation, indent the first line of the new paragraph an additional 0.5″. Note the placing of the year after the author's name and the page number at the end of the direct quotation.

If the author is not mentioned in the text, place the author's last name followed by a comma, the year followed by a comma, and the page number at the end of the direct quotation: (Bartlett, 1932, p. 201).

More complicated in-text citations should be handled as follows.

Two Authors, Mentioned in the Text

Kuhl and Meltzoff (1984) tested 4- to 5-month-olds in an experiment . . .

Two Authors, Not Mentioned in the Text

. . . but are unable to show preference in the presence of two mismatched modalities (e.g., a face and a voice; see Kuhl & Meltzoff, 1984).

Give both authors' last names each time you refer to the source. Connect their names with "and" in the text. Use an ampersand (&) in the parenthetical citation.

More Than Two Authors

For works coauthored by three, four, or five people, provide all last names in the first reference to the source. Thereafter, cite only the first author's name followed by "et al."

As Price-Williams, Gordon, and Ramirez have shown (1969), . . .

OR

Studies of these children have shown (Price-Williams, Gordon, & Ramirez, 1969) . . .

THEN

Price-Williams et al. (1969) also found that . . .

If a source has six or more authors, use only the first author's last name followed by "et al." every time the source is cited.

Corporate Authors

In general, spell out the name of a corporate author each time it is used. If a corporate author has well-known initials, the name can be abbreviated after the first citation.

FIRST IN-TEXT CITATION: (National Institutes of Health [NIH], 1989)

SUBSEQUENT CITATIONS: (NIH, 1989)

Two or More Works Within the Same Parentheses

When citing more than one work by the same author in a parenthetical reference, use the author's name only once and arrange the years mentioned in order, thus:

Several studies of ego identity formation (Marcia, 1966, 1983) . . .

When an author, or the same group of coauthors, has more than one work published in the same year, distinguish the works by adding the letters *a*, *b*, *c*, and so on, as needed, to the year. Give the last name only once, but repeat the year, each one with its identifying letters; thus:

Several studies (Smith, 1990a, 1990b, 1990c) . . .

When citing several works by different authors within the same parentheses, list the authors in the order in which they appear in the list of references. Separate authors or groups of coauthors with semicolons; thus:

Although many researchers (Archer & Waterman, 1983; Grotevant, 1983; Grotevant & Cooper, 1986; Sabatelli & Mazor, 1985) study identity formation . . .

APA Style: Preparing a List of References

Every source cited parenthetically in your paper needs a complete bibliographic citation. These complete citations are placed on a separate page (or pages) after the text of the paper and before any appendices included in the paper. Sources are arranged alphabetically by author's last name, and the first page is titled "References." Begin each source flush with the left margin and indent second and subsequent lines five spaces. Double-space throughout the list of references. Follow these rules for alphabetizing:

1. Organize two or more works by the same author, or the same group of coauthors, chronologically.

   Beck, A. T. (1991).

   Beck, A. T. (1993).

2. Place single-author entries before multiple-author entries when the first of the multiple authors is the same as the single author.

   Grotevant, H. D. (1983).

   Grotevant, H. D., & Cooper, C. R. (1986).

3. Organize multiple-author entries that have the same first author but different second or third authors alphabetically by the name of the second author or third and so on.

   Gerbner, G., & Gross, L.

   Gerbner, G., Gross, L., Jackson-Beeck, M., Jeffries-Fox, S., & Signorielli, N.

   Gerbner G., Gross, L., Morgan, M., & Signorielli, N.

4. Organize two or more works by the same author(s) published in the same year alphabetically by title and add a letter (*a*, *b*, *c*) to the year to distinguish each entry in your in-text citation.

Form for Books

A book citation contains these elements in this form:

Seligman, M. E. P. (1991). *Learned optimism*. New York: Knopf.

Weiner, B. (Ed.). (1974). *Achievement motivation and attribution theory*. Morristown, NJ: General Learning Press.

Authors

Give up to and including six authors' names, last name first, and initials. For more than seven authors, list the first six, three ellipses, and the final author. Separate authors with commas, use the ampersand (&) before the last author's name, and end with a period. For edited books, place the abbreviation "Ed." or "Eds." in parentheses following the last editor's name.

Date of Publication

Place the year of publication in parentheses followed by a period.

Title

Capitalize only the first word of the title and of the subtitle, if there is one, and any proper nouns. Italicize the title and end with a period. Place additional information such as number of volumes or an edition in parentheses after the title, before the period.

Butler, R., & Lewis, M. (1982). *Aging and mental health* (3rd ed.).

Publication Information

Cite the city of publication; add the state (using the Postal Service abbreviation) or country if necessary to avoid confusion; then give the publisher's name, after a colon, eliminating unnecessary terms such as *Publisher, Co.,* and *Inc.* End the citation with a period.

> Newton, D. E. (1996). *Violence and the media.* Santa Barbara: ABC-CLIO.
>
> Mitchell, J. V. (Ed.). (1985). *The ninth mental measurements yearbook.* Lincoln: University of Nebraska Press.
>
> National Institute of Drug Abuse. (1993, April 13). *Annual national high school senior survey.* Rockville, MD: Author.

Give a corporate author's name in full. When the organization is both author and publisher, place the word *Author* after the place of publication.

Form for Articles

An article citation contains these elements in this form:

> Changeaux, J-P. (1993). Chemical signaling in the brain. *Scientific American, 269,* 58–62.

Date of Publication

Place the year of publication for articles in scholarly journals in parentheses, followed by a period. For articles in newspapers and popular magazines, give the year followed by month and day (if appropriate).

> (1997, March).

See also example below.

Title of Article

Capitalize only the title's first word, the first word of any subtitle, and any proper nouns. Place any necessary descriptive information in square brackets immediately after the title.

> Scott, S. S. (1984, December 12). Smokers get a raw deal [Letter to the Editor].

Publication Information

Cite the title of the journal in full, capitalizing according to conventions for titles. Italicize the title and follow it with a comma. Give the volume number, italicized, followed by a comma, and then inclusive page numbers followed by a period. *If* a journal begins each issue with a new page 1, then also cite the issue number in parentheses immediately following the volume number. Do not use "p." or "pp." before page numbers when citing articles from scholarly journals and magazine articles; do use "p." or "pp." in citations to newspaper articles.

> Martin, C. L., Wood, C. H., & Little, J. K. (1990). The development of gender stereotype components. *Child Development, 61,* 1891–1904.
>
> Leakey, R. (2000, April–May). Extinctions past and present. *Time,* 35.

Form for an Article or Chapter in an Edited Book

> Goodall, J. (1993). Chimpanzees—Bridging the gap. In P. Cavalieri & P. Singer (Eds.), *The great ape project: Equality beyond humanity* (pp. 10–18). New York: St. Martin's.

Cite the author(s), date, and title of the article or chapter. Then cite the name(s) of the editor(s) in signature order after "In," followed by "Ed." or "Eds." in parentheses; the title of the book; the inclusive page numbers of the article or chapter, in parentheses, followed by a period. End with the place of publication and the publisher of the book.

A Report

> U.S. Merit Systems Protection Board. (1988). *Sexual harassment in the federal workplace: An update.* Washington, DC: U.S. Government Printing Office.

Electronic Sources

Many types of electronic sources are available on the Internet, and the variety can make documenting these sources complex. Generally, you should include the same information in the same order that you would for a print source; you replace the publication information, which no longer applies, with information on where to access the materials online. At minimum, an APA reference for any type of Internet source should include the following information: an author name, whenever possible; the date of publication or latest update (use n.d. for "no date" when a publication date is not available); a document title or description; and a Digital Object Identifier (DOI) or Internet address (URL).

The DOI is an alpha-numeric string that many scholarly publishers now assign to articles to connect them to their locations online. APA style uses this DOI instead of a URL whenever possible. Within your citation, do not place the DOI or URL in angle brackets (<>). Also, do not place a period at the end of a reference when the DOI or URL concludes it. If the DOI or URL falls across a line break, you should break the string or address before a punctuation mark.

Provide a retrieval date only for material that is likely to be moved or changed; otherwise, the DOI or URL is sufficient. Similarly, you should provide the database where you retrieved material only if the document has limited circulation and would be hard to find without the information. If you do include the database name, you do not need to include the URL. Finally, when a document is available only by subscription (like a journal article) or is available by search (like an entry in an online dictionary or an article on a magazine's website), you need give only the URL of the home or menu page for the document's source.

Journal Article with a DOI

Hussain, M. (2008). Freedom of speech and adolescent public school students. *Journal of the American Academy of Child & Adolescent Psychiatry, 47,* 614–618. doi: 10.1097/CHI.0b013e31816c42ac

Journal Article with No DOI

Michael, M. (2005). Is it natural to drive species to extinction? *Ethics and the Environment, 10*(1), 49–66. Retrieved from http://www.phil.uga.edu/eande

Electronic Daily Newspaper Article Available by Search

Schwartz, J. (2002, September 13). Air pollution con game. *Washington Times.* Retrieved from http://www.washtimes.com

U.S. Government Report on a Government Website

U.S. General Accounting Office. (2002, March). Identity theft: Prevalence and cost appear to be growing. Retrieved February 23, 2009, from http://www.gao.gov/new.items/d2363.pdf

Document from a Website

McDermott, M. (2009, February 26). Pedestrian-friendly improvements coming to NYC's Herald and Times Squares. [Online exclusive]. *Treehugger.* Retrieved February 26, 2009, from http://www.treehugger.com/files/2009/02/pedestrian-friendly-improvements-coming-to-new-york-city-herald-square-times-square.php

Cite information that has been archived and is available for retrieval, such as posts to newsgroups or electronic mailing lists, in the references lists. However, e-mails, like personal interviews or letters, should be cited as "personal communication" only in the essay and not in the list of references.

Sample Student Essay in APA Style

The following essay illustrates APA style. Use 1-inch margins and double-space throughout, including any block quotations. Block quotations should be indented *five spaces* or ½ inch from the left margin (in contrast to the ten spaces required by MLA style). The paper illustrates the following elements of papers in APA style: title page, running head, abstract, author/year in-text citations, subheadings within the text, and a list of references.

Sample title page for a paper in APA style.

Transracial Adoptions   1

Adoptions: An Issue of Love, Not Race

Connie Childress

Anthropology 314

Professor Murals

May 15, 2012

Abstract

Over 400,000 children are in foster care in the United States. The majority of these children are nonwhite. However, the majority of couples wanting to adopt children are white. While matching race or ethnic background when arranging adoptions may be the ideal, the mixing of race or ethnic background should not be avoided, or delayed, when the matching of race is not possible. Children need homes, and studies of racial adoptees show that they are as adjusted as adoptees with new parents of their own race or ethnicity. Legislation should support speedier adoptions of children, regardless of race or ethnic background.

Observe placement of running head and page number.

Papers in APA style usually begin with an abstract of the paper which should not exceed 150 to 200 words.

Student introduces her paper by referring to her adoption experience.

The first paragraph concludes with her thesis.

Observe form of author/year citations.

Adoption: An Issue of Love, Not Race

Nine years ago when my daughter, Ashley, was placed in my arms, it marked the happy ending to a long, exhausting, and, at times, heartbreaking journey through endless fertility treatments and the red tape of adoption procedures. Ironically, she had not been in our home a day before we received a call from another adoption agency that specialized in foreign adoptions. The agency stated that it was ready to begin our home study. As I look at Ashley, with her brown hair, hazel eyes, and fair complexion, I have trouble imagining not having her in my life. I know in my heart that I would have this feeling about my daughter whether she came to us from the domestic agency or the agency bringing us a child from a foreign country. To us the issue was only the child, not his or her race or ethnic background. The issue of race or ethnicity should be considered by adoptive parents along with all the other issues needing thought when they make the decision to adopt. But race or ethnicity alone should not be a roadblock to adoption. It is not society's place to decide for parents if they are capable of parenting a child of a different race or ethnic background.

Transracial adoptions are those adoptions involving a family and a child of a different race or ethnic background. Cultural differences occur when the family is of one racial or ethnic background and the adoptive child is of another. Amy Kuebelbeck (1996) reports that, according to the U.S. Department of Health and Human Services, "about 52 percent of children awaiting adoption through state placement services around the country are black." On average, Black children wait longer to be adopted than White, Asian, or Hispanic children. Why should it be more difficult for a White family to adopt an African American child than a child from China or Russia? Or a Hispanic American or mixed-race child? Any of these combinations still results in a mixed-race adoption.

Adoption Issues and Problems

Although interracial adoptions are "statistically rare in the United States," according to Robert S. Bausch and Richard T. Serpe (1997), who cite a 1990 study by Bachrach et al., the issue continues to receive attention from both social workers and the public (p. 137). A *New Republic* editorial (1994) lists several articles, including a cover story in *The Atlantic* in 1992, to illustrate the attention given to transracial adoptions. All of the popular-press articles as well as those in scholarly journals, the editors explain, describe the country's adoption and foster-care problems. While the great majority of families wanting to adopt are White, about half of the children in foster care waiting to be adopted are Black. Robert Jackson (1995) estimates that, in 1995, about 440,000 children are being cared for in foster families. The *New Republic* editorial reports on a 1993 study revealing that "a black child in California's foster care system is three times less likely to be adopted than a white child" (p. 6). In some cases minority children have been in a single foster home with parents of a different race their entire life. They have bonded as a family. Yet, often when the foster parents apply to adopt these children, their petitions are denied and the children are removed from their care. For example, Beverly and David Cox, a White couple in Wisconsin, were asked to be foster parents to two young sisters, both African American. The Coxes provided love and nurturing for five years, but when they petitioned to adopt the two girls, not only was their request denied, but the girls were removed from their home. Can removing the children from the only home they have ever known just because of their skin color really be in the best interest of the children? Cole, Drummond, and Epperson (1995) quote Hillary Clinton as saying that "skin color [should] not outweigh the more important gift of love that adoptive parents want to offer" (p. 50).

The argument against transracial adoption has rested on the concern that children adopted by parents of a different race or ethnic background will lose

> Page numbers must be given for direct quotations.

> Words added to a quotation for clarity are placed in square brackets.

their cultural heritage and racial identity, and that these losses may result in adjustment problems for the children (Bausch & Serpe, 1997). The loudest voice against mixed-race adoptions has been the National Association of Black Social Workers (NABSW), who passed a resolution in 1972 stating their "vehement opposition to the practice of placing Black children with white families" and reaffirmed their position in 1994 (Harnack, 1995, p. 188). Audrey T. Russell (1995), speaking at the 1972 conference, described White adoption of Black children as "a practice of genocide" (p. 189). Fortunately, for both children and families wanting to adopt, the NABSW has now reversed its position and concedes that placement in a home of a different race is far more beneficial to the child than keeping the child in foster care (Jackson, 1995). The NABSW's new position may have come in response to the passage of the Multiethnic Placement Act of 1994, legislation designed to facilitate the placement of minority children into adoptive homes. As Randall Kennedy (1995) explains, while this legislation continues to allow agencies to consider "the child's cultural, ethnic and racial background and the capacity of prospective foster or adoptive parents to meet the needs of a child of this background" (p. 44), it prohibits the delaying of an adoption solely for the purpose of racial matching. Kennedy objects to the law's allowing for even some consideration of race matching because he believes that this results in some children never being adopted, as agencies search for a race match. Sandra Haun (personal communication, Sept. 30, 1997), a social worker from Fairfax County, Virginia, said in an interview that she does not oppose transracial adoptions but that the best choice for a child is with a family of the same race, if the choice exists. Providing that both adoptive homes could offer the child the same environment in every aspect, then clearly the same-race home may be the best choice. More often than not, however, placing a child in a home of the same race is not an option. How can we worry about a child's cultural identity when the child doesn't have a home to call his or her own? In the cases of minority children who have been with a foster family of a different race for most of their young lives, the benefits of remaining in a stable home far outweigh the benefits of moving to a family of the same race.

The emotional effects of removing a child from a home that he or she has lived in for an extended period of time is well illustrated in the movie *Losing Isaiah.* In the film, a Black child is adopted by a White social worker and her husband after the child's birth mother has placed him in the garbage when he is three days old so that she can be free to search for drugs. When Isaiah is three, the courts return him to his birth mother, who is now off drugs. Is it fair to Isaiah for her reward to be at the expense of his emotional health? The attorney representing the adoptive parents sums up the plight of these children in one sentence: "The child is then wrenched from the only family they've ever known and turned over to strangers because of the color of their skin." In the end, Isaiah's birth mother realizes that this system is unfair to him. She appeals to his adoptive parents to assist him in his adjustment to his new home.

Good transition into discussion of movie.

Some Consequences of Negative Attitudes Toward Transracial Adoptions

Subheadings are often used in papers in the social sciences.

To protect themselves from heartbreaking situations such as the one depicted in *Losing Isaiah,* potential adoptive couples in this country are seeking other alternatives. We know that many couples seeking to adopt often adopt children from foreign countries. One of the reasons for this is the assumed shortage of children in the United States available for adoption. What may be less widely known is that many American children of mixed race or African American are placed with adoptive families overseas. One of the reasons for this situation is the continued unwillingness of social workers to place Black or mixed-race children with White couples. The NABSW's years of resistance to placing Black children with White parents has left its mark, although Edmund Blair Bolles (1984) speculates that the rare placing of Black—or American Indian—children with White couples may reflect racial prejudices rather than a great concern to preserve Black or Indian identities. Whatever the explanation, it is ironic that American babies are being "exported" to adoptive homes in other countries while babies from other countries are being "imported" to American adoptive homes. The child social services system needs to be overhauled to remove the stigmas or concerns that keep American children from being adopted in the country of their birth. If one of the arguments against transracial adoptions is the possible loss of cultural identity, how can we tolerate a system which appears to prefer placing African American children outside their own country—their own cultural heritage?

The argument that adopted children may lose their cultural identity is no longer a justifiable objection to transracial adoptions. As Randall Kennedy (1995) asserts, "there exists no credible empirical support that substantiates" the idea that "adults of the same race as the child will be better able to raise that child than adults of a different race" (p. 44). Bausch and Serpe (1997) cite four studies done between 1972 and 1992 that show that "most children of color adopted by white parents appear to be as well adjusted as children of color adopted by same-race parents" (p. 137). Perhaps the most important study is one conducted over twenty years by Rita Simon, American University sociologist. Davis (1995) reports that she studied 204 interracial adoptees over the twenty-year period and found that many of the adoptees supported transracial adoptions. Some did report that they felt isolated from other people of their own race, but we need to remember that those who participated in this study were adopted when adoptions were more secretive (and when races were more separated). At that time, most adoptees, regardless of race, may have felt isolated because of this lack of openness. Simon (1995), in her book (with Howard Altstein and Marygold S. Melli), draws these conclusions:

> Transracial adoptees do not lose their racial identities, they do not appear to be racially unaware of who they are, and they do not display negative or indifferent racial attitudes about themselves. On the contrary, . . . transracially placed children and their families have as high a success rate as all other adoptees and their families. (p. 204)

With open adoptions becoming increasingly popular, more adoptees today are aware of their adopted state and often have knowledge of one or both of their birth parents. It is not only possible, but probably easier, to provide opportunities for today's adoptee to learn about his or her racial and cultural background. The fact that the child is being raised by a family of a different race or ethnic background does not condemn that child to a life of ignorance concerning his or her own racial and cultural identity.

Conclusion

There can be only one logical solution to the issues surrounding mixed-race adoptions. Children and their adoptive parents should be united as a family because they have passed the background investigations and screening interviews that show they are emotionally and financially able to provide loving and nurturing environments for the children. To keep children needing homes and loving parents apart because they are of different races or ethnic backgrounds is not fair to the children or the adoptive parents. Preventing or delaying such adoptions is detrimental to each child's development. Children require a consistent home environment to flourish, to grow to be productive members of society. Legislation needs to support speedier adoptive placements for minority children to give them the same quality of life afforded other adoptees. Society needs to protect the right of adoptive parents by not denying transracial adoptions as an option for couples seeking to adopt.

Student restates her position in a concluding paragraph.

References

All in the family. (1994, January). *The New Republic, 210*(4), 6. Retrieved from
http://www.tnr.com

Bausch, R. S., and Serpe, R. T. (1997). Negative outcomes of interethnic adoptions of Mexican American children. *Social Work 42*(2), 136–143. Retrieved from http://naswpressonline.org

Bolles, E. B. (1984). *The Penguin adoption handbook: A guide to creating your
new family*. New York: Viking.

Cole, W., Drummond, T., & Epperson, S. E. (1995, August 14). Adoption in black
and white. *Time*. Retrieved from http://www.time.com

Davis, R. (1995, Apr. 13). Suits back interracial adoptions. *USA Today,* p. A3.
Retrieved from http://www.usatoday.com

Gyllenhaal, S. (Director). (1995). *Losing Isaiah* [Motion Picture]. United States:
Paramount Pictures.

Harnack, A. (Ed.). (1995). *Adoption: Opposing viewpoints*. San Diego: Greenhaven.

Jackson, R. L. (1995, April 25). U.S. stresses no race bias in adoptions. *Los Angeles Times*, p. A6. Retrieved from http://www.latimes.com

Kennedy, R., & Moseley-Braun, C. (1995). At issue: Interracial adoption—Is the
multiethnic placement act flawed? *ABA Journal, 81*, pp. 44–45. Retrieved
from http://abajournal.com

Kuebelbeck, A. (1996, December 31). Interracial adoption debated. *AP US
and World*. Retrieved October 10, 1999, from http://www.donet
.com/~brandyjc/p6at111.htm

Russell, A. T. (1995). Transracial adoptions should be forbidden. In A. Harnack
(Ed.), *Adoption: Opposing viewpoints* (pp. 189–96). San Diego: Greenhaven.

Simon, R. J., Altstein, H., & Melli, M. S. (1995). Transracial adoptions should
be encouraged. In A. Harnack (Ed.), *Adoption: Opposing viewpoints* (pp.
198–204). San Diego: Greenhaven.

Title the page
"References."

Double-space
throughout. In
each citation
indent all lines,
after the first,
five spaces.
Note APA style
placement
of date and
format for
titles.

Footnote or Endnote Style

Instructors in history, philosophy, and art history frequently prefer the footnote or endnote form of documentation to any pattern using parenthetical documentation. The chief guide for this pattern is the *Chicago Manual of Style* (16th ed., 2010). Chicago style states a preference for endnotes (citations placed at the end of the paper) rather than footnotes (citations placed at the bottom of appropriate pages), but some instructors may want to see footnotes, so always be sure to determine the precise guidelines for your assignment. Further learn your instructor's expectations with regard to a bibliography in addition to footnotes or endnotes. If the first footnote (or endnote) reference to a source contains complete bibliographic information, a list of works cited may not be necessary. Still, some instructors want both complete documentation notes and the alphabetized Bibliography following the text (with footnotes) or after the endnotes.

In-Text Citations

Notes can be easily made with the footnote or endnote function on a word processor. Use a raised (superscript, such as this [2]) arabic numeral immediately following all material from a source, whether the borrowed material is quoted or paraphrased. The number follows all punctuation except the dash, and it always follows material needing documentation at the end of a sentence or clause. Number footnotes or endnotes consecutively throughout the paper, beginning with "1." Use care to present material from sources with introductory tags and to place superscript numbers so that readers can tell where borrowed material begins and where it ends. Regularly placing citation numbers only at the ends of paragraphs will not result in accurate documentation.

Location and Presentation of Footnotes

1. Place footnotes on the same page as the borrowed material.

2. Begin the first footnote four lines (two double-spaces) below the last line of text.

3. Indent the first line of each footnote five spaces. Type the online, full-size numeral that corresponds to the superscript numeral in the text, followed by a period.

4. If a footnote runs to more than one line of text, single-space between lines and begin the second line flush with the left margin.

5. If more than one footnote appears on a page, double-space between notes.

Location and Presentation of Endnotes

1. Start endnotes on a new page titled "Notes." Endnotes follow the text and precede a list of works cited, if such a list is included.

2. List endnotes in consecutive order corresponding to the superscript numbers in the text.

3. Indent the first line of each endnote five spaces. Type the online number followed by a period, leave one space, and then type the reference.

4. If an endnote runs to more than one line, double-space between lines and begin the second line flush with the left margin.

5. Double-space between endnotes.

Footnote/Endnote Form: First (Primary) Reference

Each first reference to a source contains all the necessary author, title, and publication information that would be found in a list of works cited or list of references. Subsequent references to the same source use a shortened form. Prepare all first-reference notes according to the following guidelines.

Form for Books

1. Cite the author's full name in signature order, followed by a comma.

2. Cite the title of the book in italics. Include the complete subtitle, if there is one, unless a list of works cited is also provided. No punctuation follows the title.

3. Give the facts of publication in parentheses: city of publication followed by a colon, publisher followed by a comma, and year of publication.

4. Give the precise page reference. Do not use "p." or "pp." Place a comma after the closing parenthesis, before the page number. All notes end with a period.

> 1. Daniel J. Boorstin, *The Americans: The Colonial Experience* (New York: Vintage-Random, 1958), 46.

Form for Articles

1. Cite the author's full name in signature order, followed by a comma.

2. Cite the title of the article in quotation marks, and place a comma *inside* the closing quotation mark.

3. Give the facts of publication: the title of the journal, italicized; the volume in arabic numerals; the issue preceded by "no."; and the date followed by a colon. Citations of scholarly journals require the volume number followed by the date including month or season if desired in parentheses; citations of popular magazines and newspapers eliminate the volume number, giving the date only, not in parentheses. In the past, issue numbers have been required only when a journal paginates each issue separately rather than continuously throughout a volume. *The Chicago Manual of Style* now suggests including issue numbers whenever available to help locate a source. The month or season of an issue, sometimes given with the year, may also be included, but it is not required.

4. Provide a precise page reference following the colon, without using "p." or "pp." All notes end with a period.

> 2. Everard H. Smith, "Chambersburg: Anatomy of a Confederate Reprisal," *American Historical Review* 96, no. 2 (1991): 434.

Sample Footnotes/Endnotes

Additional information must be added as necessary. Some of the common variations are illustrated here. Note that the examples are presented as endnotes; that is, the lines of each note are double-spaced. Remember that footnotes are single-spaced *within* each note but double-spaced *between* notes. For materials that are accessed online, generally follow the guidelines given for print materials. Then, following a comma, provide a URL. If you retrieved the article through a subscription database (like LexisNexis or JSTOR), you may include the URL of the entry page only (http://jstor .org) rather than the entire URL.

A Work by Two or Three Authors

> 3. Charles A. Beard and Mary R. Beard, *The American Spirit* (New York: Macmillan, 1942), 63.

A Work by More Than Three Authors

> 4. Lester R. Brown et al., *State of the World 1990: A Worldwatch Institute Report on Progress Toward a Sustainable Society* (New York: Norton, 1990), 17.

(The phrase "and others" may be used in place of "et al.")

An Edited Work

> 5. *The Autobiography of Benjamin Franklin*, ed. Max Farrand (Berkeley: University of California Press, 1949), 6–8.

(Begin with the title—or the editor's name—if the author's name appears in the title.)

> 6. Bentley Glass, Owsei Temkin, and William L. Straus, Jr., eds., *Forerunners of Darwin: 1745–1859* (Baltimore: Johns Hopkins Press paperback edition, 1968), 326.

A Translation

> 7. Allan Gilbert, trans. and ed., *The Letters of Machiavelli* (New York: Capricorn Books, 1961), 120.

A Preface, Introduction, or Afterword

> 8. Ernest Barker, introduction to *The Politics of Aristotle* (New York: Oxford University Press, 1962), xiii.

A Book in Two or More Volumes

> 9. Paul Tillich, *Systematic Theology*, 3 vols. (Chicago: University of Chicago Press, 1951–63), 1:52.

(Make the page reference first to the volume number, followed by a colon, and then the page number.)

A Book in Its Second or Subsequent Edition

> 10. Frank J. Sorauf and Paul Allen Beck, *Party Politics in America*, 6th ed. (Glenview, IL: Scott, Foresman/Little, Brown, 1988), 326.

A Book in a Series

> 11. Charles L. Sanford, ed., *Benjamin Franklin and the American Character*, Problems in American Civilization (Lexington, MA: D.C. Heath, 1955), 4.

A Work in a Collection

> 12. George Washington, "Farewell Address, 1796," in *A Documentary History of the United States*, ed. Richard D. Heffner (New York: New American Library, 1965), 64–65.

An Encyclopedia Article

> 13. *The Concise Dictionary of American Biography*, 1964 ed., s.v. "Anthony, Susan Brownell."

(Do not cite a page number for reference works arranged alphabetically; rather, cite the entry in quotation marks after "s.v." [*sub verbo*—"under the word"]. The edition number or year is needed, but no other facts of publication are required for well-known reference works.)

An Article in a Scholarly Journal

14. Ellen Fitzpatrick, "Rethinking the Intellectual Origins of American Labor History," *American Historical Review* 96, no. 2 (1991): 426.

OR

14. Ellen Fitzpatrick, "Rethinking the Intellectual Origins of American Labor History," *American Historical Review* 96, no. 2 (1991): 426, http://www.proquest.com.

An Article in a Popular Magazine

15. Richard Leakey, "Extinctions Past and Present," *Time,* April 26, 2000: 35.

OR

15. Richard Leakey, "Extinctions Past and Present," *Time,* April 26, 2000, http://www.time.com/time/magazine/article/0,9171,996748,00.html.

An Editorial

16. "Means of Atonement," editorial, *Wall Street Journal,* 22 May 2000: A38.

OR

16. "Means of Atonement," editorial, *Wall Street Journal*, 22 May 2000: A38, http://www.lexis-nexis.com.

A Review

17. Gabriel P. Weisberg, "French Art Nouveau," review of *Art Nouveau in Fin-de-Siècle France: Politics, Psychology, and Style* by Deborah Silverman, *Art Journal* 49 (Winter 1990): 427.

OR

17. Gabriel P. Weisberg, "French Art Nouveau," review of *Art Nouveau in Fin-de-Siècle France: Politics, Psychology, and Style* by Deborah Silverman, *Art Journal* 49, no. 4 (1990): 427, http://www.jstor.org/stable/777145.

An Online News Service

18. Leslie Gevirtz, "US Leads 100-Year Game of Economic Development," *Reuters*, Nov./Dec. 1999, http://www.reuters.com/magazine.

An Article from a Reference Database

19. *Encyclopaedia Britannica Online*, s.v. "Prohibition," http://search.eb.com.

An Article from a Web Page

20. Alice C. Hudson, "Heading West: Mapping the Territory," Heading West: Touring West, The New York Public Library, http://www.nypl.org/west/hw_subhome.shtml.

A Document from a Website

21. Annie Page, Interview by Bernice Bowden, "Born in Slavery: Slave Narratives from the Federal Writers' Project 1936–1938," American Memory, Library of Congress, http://memory.loc.gov/cgi-bin/ampage?collId=mesn&fileName=025/mesn025.db&recNum=241&itemLink=D?mesnbib:1:./temp/~ammem_m1Zu:.

(Neither break a URL across a line after a hyphen, nor insert a hyphen to a URL to indicate a line break. You should make the break after a slash; before a tilde (~), a period, a comma, a hyphen, an underline (_), a question mark, a number sign, or a percent symbol; or before or after an equals sign or an ampersand.)

Footnote/Endnote Form: Short Forms

After the first full documentary footnote or endnote, subsequent references to the same source should be shortened forms. The simplest short form for any source with an author or editor is the author's or editor's last name followed by a comma and a precise page reference; thus: 20. Fitzgerald, 425. If there is no author cited, use a short title and page number. If two sources are written by authors with the same last name, then add first names or initials to distinguish between them.

21. Henry Adams, 16.
22. James T. Adams, 252.

If you use two or more sources by the same author, then add a short title to the note; thus:

23. Boorstin, *American Politics*, 167.
24. Boorstin, *The Americans*, 65–66.

The Latin abbreviations *loc. cit.* and *op. cit.* are no longer recommended, and ibid. is almost as obsolete, usually replaced now by the simple short form of author's last name and page number. Remember that ibid. can be used only to refer to the source cited in the immediately preceding note. The following footnotes, appearing at the bottom of a page from a history paper, illustrate the various short forms.

Sample Footnotes from a History Paper

While mid-twentieth-century historians may be more accurate, they may have lost the flavor of earlier American historians who had a clear ideology that shaped their writing.[20]

11. William Bradford, *Of Plymouth Plantation*, in *The American Puritans: Their Prose and Poetry,* ed. Perry Miller (New York: Anchor-Doubleday, 1956), 5.

12. Daniel J. Boorstin, *The Americans: The Colonial Experience* (New York: Vintage-Random, 1958), 16.

13. Ibid., 155.

14. James T. Adams, 136.

15. Henry Adams, *The Education of Henry Adams*, ed. D. W. Brogan (Boston: Houghton Mifflin, 1961), 342.

16. Boorstin, *American Politics,* 167.

17. Henry Adams, "The Tendency of History," 16.

18. Ibid., 71.

19. Henry Adams, *Education,* 408.

20. John Higham, "The Cult of the 'American Consensus': Homogenizing Our History," *Commentary* 27 (Feb. 1959): 94–96.

Sample Bibliography

A bibliography would include all cited works and may include additional works relevant to the paper's research or topic. The list is arranged in alphabetical order by the first word in the entry, usually the author's last name or the first significant word in a title. The first line of each entry begins at the far left, and additional lines are indented two or three spaces. Double-space the entire list. Bibliographies are not necessary in the note system since the notes contain complete bibliographic information. However, since they list all sources in one place, they provide a good overview of a paper's sources and may be required by an instructor. Entries in a bibliography differ from the information provided in the notes only in the inversion of the author's name (last name first), the use of periods instead of commas to separate elements in the entry, and the inclusion of the page range of articles rather than identifying the single page where a quotation or reference is located. Items from daily newspapers or reference books or databases are rarely given in the bibliography. Some of the common variations, based on earlier sample notes, are illustrated here.

Bibliography

Barker, Ernest. Introduction to *The Politics of Aristotle*. New York: Oxford University Press, 1962.

Beard, Charles A., and, Mary R. Beard. *The American Spirit*. New York: Macmillan, 1942.

Boorstin, Daniel J. *The Americans: The Colonial Experience*. New York: Vintage-Random, 1958.

Brown, Lester R., and others. *State of the World 1990: A Worldwatch Institute Report on Progress Toward a Sustainable Society*. New York: Norton, 1990.

Fitzpatrick, Ellen. "Rethinking the Intellectual Origins of American Labor History." *American Historical Review* 96, no. 2 (1991): 422–428. http://www.proquest.com.

Franklin, Benjamin. *The Autobiography of Benjamin Franklin*. Edited by Max Farrand. Berkeley: University of California Press, 1949.

Gilbert, Allan, trans. and ed. *The Letters of Machiavelli*. New York: Capricorn Books, 1961.

Glass, Bentley, Owsei Temkin, and William L. Straus, Jr., eds. *Forerunners of Darwin: 1745–1859*. Paperback. Baltimore: Johns Hopkins Press, 1968.

Hudson, Alice C. "Heading West: Mapping the Territory." Heading West: Touring West. The New York Public Library. http://www.nypl.org/west/hw_subhome.shtml.

Leakey, Richard. "Extinctions Past and Present." *Time* April 26, 2000: 35. http://www.time.com/time/magazine/article/0,9171,996748,00.html.

Page, Annie. Interview by Bernice Bowden. "Born in Slavery: Slave Narratives from the Federal Writers' Project 1936–1938." American Memory. Library of Congress. http://memory.loc.gov/cgi-bin/ampage?collId=mesn&fileName=025/mesn025.db&recNum=241&itemLink=D?mesnbib:1:./temp/~ammem_m1Zu:.

Sanford, Charles L., ed. *Benjamin Franklin and the American Character*. Problems in American Civilization. Lexington, MA: D. C. Heath, 1955.

Smith, Everard H. "Chambersburg: Anatomy of a Confederate Reprisal." *American Historical Review* 96, no. 2 (1991): 432–455.

Sorauf, Frank J., and Paul Allen Beck. *Party Politics in America*. 6th ed. Glenview, IL: Scott, Foresman/ Little, Brown, 1988.

Tillich, Paul. *Systematic Theology*. 3 vols. Chicago: University of Chicago Press, 1951–1963.

Washington, George. "Farewell Address, 1796." In *A Documentary History of the United States*, edited by Richard D. Heffner. New York: New American Library, 1965.

Weisberg, Gabriel P. "French Art." Review of *Art Nouveau in Fin-de-Siècle France: Politics, Psychology, and Style* by Deborah Silverman. *Art Journal* 49, no. 4 (1990): 426–429. http://www.jstor.org/stable/777145.

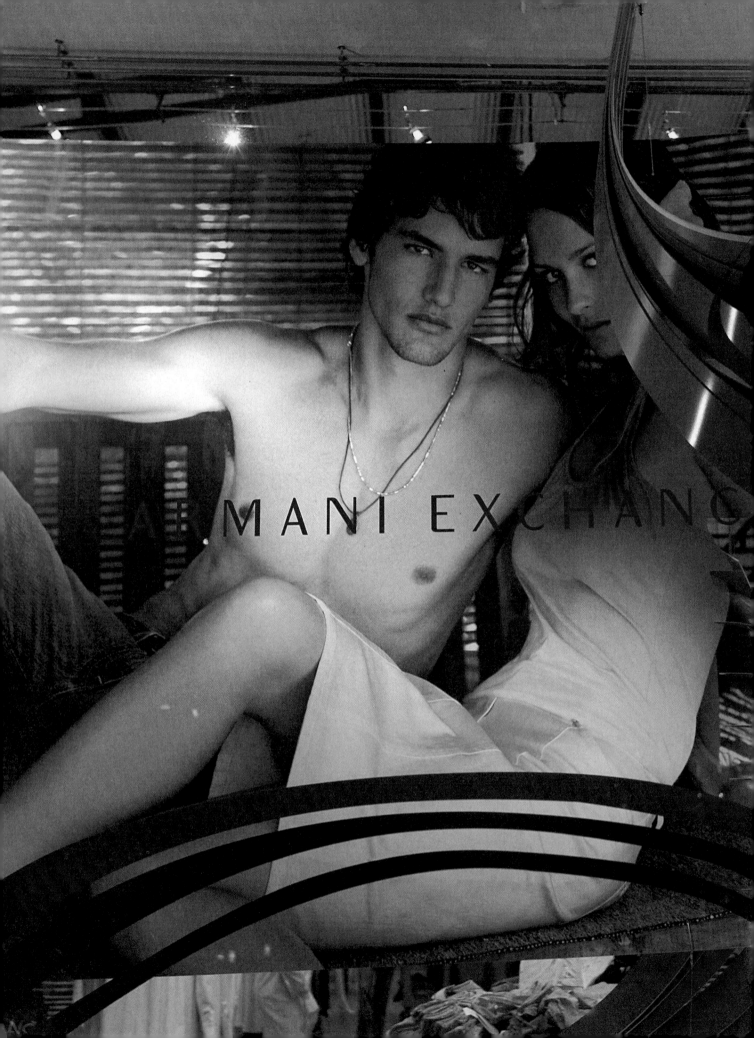

the myth and
reality of the
image in american
consumer culture

c h a p t e r   15

Media and advertising images bombard us all the time, pressuring us to buy a multitude of products and services. We encounter the omnipresent consumer culture whenever we watch television, go to the movies, play videogames, look at magazines, or even drive on an interstate highway. Advertising images from billboards, television commercials, and the World Wide Web are virtually inescapable. This chapter's selections address the impact of advertising images as part of consumer culture as well as the rise of product placement in videogames, popular television series, and big-budget films. The pervasiveness of images contributes significantly to creating a culture of consumerism, so it is important for us as citizens to understand the reality underlying the myths sometimes perpetuated by advertising and media.

prereading questions

1. How are new forms of media forcing changes in entertainment industry practices?
2. Do advertising images succeed in encouraging people to buy products? Why or why not?
3. How have companies become more concerned with marketing an image than marketing a product?
4. Product placement is becoming pervasive in movies, television shows, and videogames. Is this increasing pervasiveness a problem? Why or why not?

websites related to this chapter's topic

THE NADER PAGE
www.nader.org
Web page of consumer advocate Ralph Nader.

CENTER FOR MEDIA LITERACY
www.medialit.org
Website for the Center for Media Literacy offering several links and resources.

CAMPAIGN FOR A COMMERCIAL-FREE CHILDHOOD
www.commercialfreechildhood.org
Organization dedicated to minimizing the effect of commercials on children.

website essay

prereading question } What does it mean to "sell the sizzle and not the steak"?

The End of Consumer Culture?

Should designers work toward the end of aspirational consumer culture? Can the design industry, broadly defined, reposition and reinvent itself to provide value and sustainability while still creating desire?

Hugh Graham

Hugh Graham published this essay on his company's website on January 30, 2008. Hugh Graham Creative "provides design strategy, research, and storytelling for corporations, nonprofits, and community organizations" (Hugh Graham Creative website).

When I was at Northwestern, I took some classes from a professor of philosophy, David Michael Levin, who once asked us whether having a choice was important in our lives. Specifically, he was asking about the difference between choice and the appearance of choice. For instance, he asked, is it important to be able to choose between Crest and Colgate?

I think of Professor Levin from time to time, and often when I'm walking down the personal care aisle of the supermarket. Looking at all the variations of toothpaste and related products (Whitestrips, anyone?), I wonder whether it's possible that our society in general may have gone just a bit too far, and that the designers and product managers and marketers are spending too much of their creative resources on selling products with limited value and without any real differentiation.

I'm not arguing that there isn't valuable product innovation going on, but I tend to doubt the big change involves one of the 50 swirly paste/gel combos on every American supermarket aisle. Think of the improved efficiencies we"ll see just as soon as all the rest of you realize that Tom's of Maine Peppermint is plenty good enough for everyone.

Innovation, or Variation?

Okay, that's probably not going to be happening any time soon. And if there were only one kind of toothpaste, I"d likely never have gotten the chance to try out Tom's products, or the cool toothpaste that combines gel, paste, and some crazy sparkly bits. I do love the crazy sparkly bits.

I'm not recommending some sort of centralized control of the means of production; it wouldn't work anyhow, not in the fast-moving consumer goods market, and certainly not in the broader markets. But there's still something decadent and even unethical about the way we sell the aspirational in consumer goods.

Of course, if people didn't want it, we wouldn't sell it, and the invisible hand of the market will ultimately level everything out, right? Well, maybe.

The toothpaste reference is pretty trivial, but it points to a bigger question about designer culture. Designer culture is still about the aspirational, and it's well established in mainstream markets.

Rob Horning wrote an article on *PopMatters* called "The Design Imperative." In it, he considers both the historical underpinnings and the current nature of our consumer culture. Historically,

> the consumer revolution depended on the sudden availability of things, which allowed ordinary people to buy ready-made objects that once were inherited or self-produced.

And in our current world,

> We are consigned to communicating through design, but it's an impoverished language that can only say one thing: "That's cool." Design ceases to serve our needs, and the superficial qualities of useful things end up cannibalizing their functionality.

The problem ultimately is that all this consumption fills some sort of void in our lives, at least temporarily. And by feeding the void in our lives, designers are providing the stimulus that keeps the modern economy moving.

It's the Economy, Stupid

According to the news reports I've been reading, the economy of the United States has a pretty good chance of heading into a recession for most if not all of 2008. One of the primary causes, resulting in part from the rocking of the financial markets due to sub-prime lending, is decreased consumer spending. Consumer spending, which accounts for two thirds of economic activity, weakened in the month of December.

But for those of us who would like to see a decrease in consumption, is this necessarily bad news?

After the terrorist attacks in 2001, I remember being slightly horrified by Bush the 43rd admonishing the people of America to "go shopping" to fight back against terrorism. Of course, there was an important idea in there somewhere, that we shouldn't allow our lives to be controlled by a few fundamentalist wackos. But I found it hard to believe that a trip to Wal-mart was the best way to fight back against Osama bin Laden. It's a long way from the Victory Gardens our grandparents planted to help win World War II.

I was thinking about this when I came across an excellent article by Madeleine Bunting, published in the *Guardian*, called "Eat, drink and be miserable: The true cost of our addiction to shopping."

As Ms. Bunting points out:

We have a political system built on economic growth as measured by gross domestic product, and that is driven by ever-rising consumer spending. Economic growth is needed to service public debt and pay for the welfare state. If people stopped shopping, the economy would ultimately collapse. No wonder, then, that one of the politicians' tasks after a terrorist outrage is to reassure the public and urge them to keep shopping (as both George Bush and Ken Livingstone did). Advertising and marketing, huge sectors of the economy, are entirely devoted to ensuring that we keep shopping and that our children follow in our footsteps.

The question that I have been wrestling with regarding this question is how we can both decrease our rampant disposable consumerism while still continuing to have a reasonably robust economy. How am I supposed to continue pushing the economy forward while cutting my carbon footprint by 60 percent?

Happy Now?

In her article, Ms. Bunting discusses the work of Tim Kasser, an American psychologist concerned with materialism, values, and goals. Kasser has created an aspirational index which helps to distinguish between two types of goals:

Extrinsic, materialistic goals (e.g., financial success, image, popularity) are those focused on attaining rewards and praise, and are usually means to some other end. Intrinsic goals (e.g., personal growth, affiliation, community feeling) are, in contrast, more focused on pursuits that are supportive of intrinsic need satisfaction.

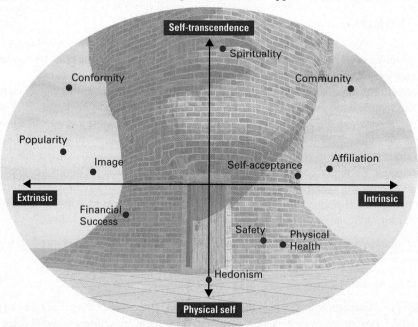

According to Kasser, he would like to "help individuals and society move away from materialism and consumerism and towards more intrinsically satisfying pursuits that promote personal well-being, social justice, and ecological sustainability."

Personally, I'm not quite sure where I fall on the Aspirational Index.

I try to be mindful of what I'm consuming, where it comes from, and where it ends up. Still, I have a couple pair of shoes that I bought on a whim, and a jacket I didn't wear more than a few times. I don't get a whole lot of joy out of going shopping, whether for clothes or anything else, but I'm sure there are many, many ways I could do more with less.

It occurs to me that there needs to be a new paradigm of consumption, one that will work for business, community, and environment. I don't know what form this new paradigm will take, but I believe it has something to do with learning to appreciate the real value of things and their place in our world.

Designers have an opportunity to engage in this paradigm shift. Part of the story lies in creating products that have intrinsic and lasting value, products that I like to call artisanal. And part of the story lies in better communicating the value of the artisanal. I believe that designers have an ethical duty to work toward the end of disposable culture. Of course, this isn't going to happen overnight, and it's not going to happen in vacuum. But it is going to happen, whether we choose to be a part of the process or not. Better to engage the future rather than have it thrust upon us.

Toward a Moral Equivalent of Consumerism

The subtitle of Madeleine Bunting's *Guardian* article is "Today it seems politically unpalatable, but soon the state will have to turn to rationing to halt hyper-frantic consumerism." She speaks to the inevitability of changing our behaviors, and believes that the change will not happen without intervention from the state. Whether it is rationing, or taxes, or other means, the change, ultimately, will have to come.

But change is never easy or simple. In *The Moral Equivalent of War* (1906), William James explained the difficulties of advocating pacifism:

> So far, war has been the only force that can discipline a whole community, and until an equivalent discipline is organized, I believe that war must have its way.

War, like consumer capitalism, offers a way of getting people motivated and organized. Adam Smith, in *The Wealth of Nations,* argues that "It is not from the benevolence of the butcher, the brewer, or the baker, that we expect our dinner, but from their regard to their own self-interest." Self-interest is a strong motivational force, and unless and until there is a "Moral Equivalent of Consumerism" it may well be impossible to create an alternative solution.

It will likely be necessary for government to engage in rationing or taxation to decrease our impact on the environment. But there is also an important component that should not be ignored, and one that can and should be engaged in by the designers of our products and communications. A new aspiration, perhaps focused on the intrinsic and self-transcendent as Tim Kasser explains. An aspiration toward what is valuable, an experience where less is truly more.

In *The Moral Equivalent of War,* James argues that:

> Great indeed is Fear; but it is not, as our military enthusiasts believe and try to make us believe, the only stimulus known for awakening the higher ranges of men's spiritual energy.

In seeking a moral equivalent of consumerism it is our challenge to use our capabilities to awaken the higher ranges of each person's spiritual energy, and to produce objects and communications that are filled with value.

Should designers work toward the end of aspirational consumer culture? Ultimately, I'm not sure there is any other choice.

http://hughgrahamcreative.com/2008/01/30/toward-a-moral-equivalent-of-consumerism

QUESTIONS FOR READING

1. What is "aspirational consumer culture"?
2. To what "bigger question" does the article's toothpaste example point?
3. What two types of goals does Tim Kasser's Aspirational Index distinguish between?

QUESTIONS FOR REASONING AND ANALYSIS

1. What is Graham's thesis? Is it explicit or implicit? If explicit, what sentence reflects his thesis? If implicit, how would you summarize his thesis in your own words?
2. Why does Graham include Kasser's Aspirational Index in his essay? What point does it support? Does providing the visual depiction of Kasser's index help support Graham's argument? Why or why not?
3. How does Graham define "artisanal" products? What problem will artisanal products address?
4. Who do you think is the primary audience for Graham's essay? Why does this group represent his primary audience?

QUESTIONS FOR REFLECTING AND WRITING

1. How do you view the impact of disposable consumerism or disposable culture? Do you agree with Graham regarding disposable consumerism? Why or why not?
2. With regard to your own buying habits, why do you purchase one product over another? Do you usually purchase a product based on its intrinsic value, the way Graham explains it, or because you prefer the color of the packaging, for instance?
3. How would you respond to Graham? Do you agree or disagree? Why or why not?

Capitalism, Consumerism, and Feminism

Nina Power

Nina Power is a senior lecturer in philosophy at Roehampton University in London. This article was first published on the website Newleftproject.org on February 25, 2010.

The gradual emancipation of women has been, without doubt, the greatest social revolution of the past few hundred years. The widespread acceptance of women's entry into the workplace, together with the admission that there is no "natural" role for women has thoroughly transformed economic, political and social relations. But even as the number of women in the U.S. workforce overtake men for the first time, there is a widespread sense that some of the aims and ambitions of feminism, particularly in its second "wave", have been profoundly undermined by capitalism and a capitalist culture that has proved to be singularly adept at turning revolutionary and radical impulses into their very opposite. In a recent piece for the *New Left Review*, Nancy Fraser worries that: "The diffusion of cultural attitudes born out of the second wave has been part and parcel of another social transformation, unanticipated and unintended by feminist activists—a transformation in the social organization of postwar capitalism. This possibility can be formulated more sharply: the cultural changes jump-started by the second wave, salutary in themselves, have served to legitimate a structural transformation of capitalist society that runs directly counter to feminist visions of a just society." Elsewhere, too, there are serious worries about the unwitting complicity of some of the aims of feminism with a pernicious and demoralising consumerism. Natasha Walter in her new book, *Living Dolls: The Return of Sexism* is incredibly critical of earlier, more positive models of feminism, including her own in her earlier *The New Feminism* (1998). She writes in *Living Dolls*: "I believed that we only had to put in place the conditions for equality for the remnants of old-fashioned sexism in our culture to wither away. I am ready to admit I was entirely wrong . . . The rise of a hypersexual culture is not proof that we have reached full equality; rather, it has reflected and exaggerated the deeper imbalances of power in our society."

It is clear, even without reading Walter and Co., that the "sexual revolution" in which men and women would freely express their desires without the old worries about pregnancy and conservative objections has today become the commodification of a narrow version of sexuality which perversely fuses a porn aesthetic with a regressive fetish for the domestic couple: it is perfectly possible for both men and women to be as hedonistic as humanly possible in their teens and twenties before settling down with "the one" in a humdrum bill-sharing and mortgage-splitting "partnership." This goes for gay couples as well as straight (albeit with a minimally persistent lack of parity to appease residual conservatism on the part of voters): what matters is that the couple is the apex of sexual identity and human achievement, even if you might end up in several such couplings over the course of a lifetime. Early discussions of the civil partnership bill (passed in 2004) mooted the idea that couples not sexually involved could become partners, but ultimately bottled out of passing the legislation. Thus two sisters could potentially leave everything to one another (as the famous failed test-case attempted to do), or two friends, or a carer and his or her ward. More radical suggestions for civil partnerships proposed that such an arrangement could allow for multiple partners on the same contract—thus a household of friends could "marry" one another, or three brothers, or a student household, and so on. It is easy to laugh at such desires for collective admissions of affection and care, but only, perhaps, because we have been taught to laugh at their supposed utopianism. But why has the image of the two, the sexualized couple, come to dominate our understanding of the limits of modern love? Culturally, we are aware of a longstanding paradox in the way we deal with sex and the couple: we are thunderously puritanical when it comes to the infidelity of celebrities, at the same time as we are utterly prurient about these same sex lives. We have a culture that pushes free-flowing, loveless sex at every opportunity yet chastizes those that would take this one-sided emancipation at face-value. The same goes for the sexualization of children: the excessive protection of "innocents" and the hysteria surrounding the figure of the pedophile (even at the same time as we know that most violence, and sexual violence, is carried out by someone known to the child) goes hand-in-hand with the hyper-sexualization of children, particularly girls, who inexorably come to see themselves as princesses before tomboys and flirts before scholars.

On a recent episode of *The Review Show*, Kirsty Wark held up a padded bra for an 9-year-old as evidence of the decadence of our sexualized childhood culture in the same way that anti-feminists might once have held a picture of a woman in trousers: something has gone terribly awry with the way we picture little girls, and the women they will all-too-soon become. It is incredibly easy to be moralistic about this early sexualization, and, indeed, this was the avenue precisely taken by the guests on the show. Novelist and sister of London's mayor, Rachel Johnson, took the bra to be the sign of a specifically working-class kind of problem: "I don't see middle-class mothers going to Primark and buying padded bras or thongs for their nine-year-olds."

Walter in *Living Dolls* makes similar, if slightly more refined, use of the same kind of middle-class aesthetic-moral hand-wringing: "'Me-time' for a young home-maker now can include dressing as a Playboy bunny; breaking into a respectable career that would make your mum proud can start with stripping for nothing in a crowded nightclub." However, merely feeling appalled at the supposed barbarism of the proles is not an explanation, nor could it ever be one. Besides, it is very clearly untrue that flashing flesh is the province of the supposedly amoral working class, threatening town centres like some sort of slutty Hogarthian vision and upsetting upright girls and their parents: "nice" middle-class girls are just as frequently likely to be flashing their breasts in student union bars, or wearing very little outside clubs in the freezing cold, or sleeping around. It's just that we mind less, because somehow they have more independence, and grade 8 violin, and some money behind them. Thus the rise of the self-aware "I'm not a slut, I just like sex" woman, the sex-blogger, the high-class call girl who does it "because she wants to," not because she has to (which, to be fair to Walter, she is equally critical of in *Living Dolls*). On the same *Review Show*, Zoe Margolis, author of the blog and the book *Girl with a One-Track Mind*, could very easily agree with Walter's rather prudish demolition of the sexualization of contemporary culture, despite extolling the virtues of string-free sex, because she shares the middle-class assumption that working-class girls and women are "not free" to choose their own sexuality, either through their own stupidity or their dire economic circumstances. But class-based, aesthetic and/or moral disapproval of the way in which people buy into their own narrow sexualization is not the point. It explains nothing, and promulgates the faulty idea that somehow there is "their" culture and "ours": drunken, promiscuous working-class ladettes versus refined, thoughtful middle-class ladies who may sleep around a bit, but will ultimately settle down with someone nice from the home counties. If our culture is increasingly sexualized, and it is, then it is for everyone, and we should begin from this admission, rather than disapprove of those we think are doing it distastefully.

But what explains this hyper-sexualization? What purpose does it serve to get women to see themselves as constantly on display? I think that this kind of self-advertising has to be understood in the context of work, and a kind of ambient pressure to "sell oneself" on the job-market in an age of enforced precariousness and the rise of temporary employment. I continue to think that this dimension of the argument—a kind of economic-cultural approach—is lacking in the recent despair over the premature sexualization of young women. What Walter and others miss is the fact that the old categories we used to try to explain the oppression of women: misogyny, patriarchy, objectification and so on, do not exactly capture the more complex logic of self-exploitation. Men are not "to blame" for the rise in "raunch culture," to quote Ariel Levy, even as structurally they are paid more, in better positions, and so on: if only it were so simple! We have to look at the bigger picture: what kinds of workers do companies need? How little can they get away with paying people? How much work can it expect men and women to do that it doesn't need to reward? Women are increasingly useful in an economy that replaces manual labor with service jobs, whether they involve caring, speaking, e-mailing, cleaning or waitressing. The dimension of "flexibility" that has always been part of women's relation to work, mainly due to the pressures of childcare, has now been repackaged as a virtue for all workers, regardless of their gender. The idea of a job for life, of state-provided childcare, of the ability of a family to live on a single wage has now been so enervated it seems absurd to think that it was ever the norm: women's entry into the workforce has corresponded with the depressing of men's wages—thus the couple, in order to have any sort of stability at all, however minimal, must both work all the time, even if there are children to look after. Capitalism and the state have somehow managed to dump all responsibility for the reproduction of the workforce on the couple, so that the very idea of discussing any sort of collective response to child-rearing is greeted with a kind of dystopian horror: what is this, the sixties? Similarly, the young woman that sells herself, using whatever means she has, is merely behaving rationally in a world where jobs are scarce, where

continued

employment is "flexible" to the point of insanity and where another perky young thing is just around the corner to take your position.

It seems to me not implausible that the techniques that women might have used in a similarly pragmatic vein to "get a man" and thus secure some sort of economic stability are now used, in a rather more limitless way, to "get a job." The sexualization of contemporary women, from which men are of course not exempt from either, reflects less a freely-chosen desire to express oneself as a fully-rounded sensual being and far more the desperate, yet eminently comprehensible, desire to insert oneself in whatever way possible into a cruel economic structure that will selectively use and value the "assets" of its workers whenever it needs to. We should not be "blaming" women for their complicity in such a logic, as if blame were ever a useful political category, but try better to understand it. The hyper-real sexuality of today's culture has as little to do with real libidinal emancipation as contemporary "flexible" work has to do with true human fulfillment. Feminism must restore its links to an understanding of economic shifts and the cunning of capitalism if it is to remain relevant: less hand-wringing and despair, more structural analysis!

http://www.newleftproject.org/index.php/site/article_comments/capitalism_consumerism_and_feminism

QUESTIONS FOR READING

1. What is the "longstanding paradox" to which the author refers?
2. What does Power mean by "sexualization"?
3. According to Power, what must feminism do to remain relevant?

QUESTIONS FOR REASONING AND ANALYSIS

1. How would you describe or characterize Power's thesis in this article?
2. What is the link Power establishes between feminism and capitalism?

QUESTIONS FOR REFLECTING AND WRITING

1. Do you agree with Power's argument? Why or why not?
2. Power states that the "sexualized couple" has come to dominate our understanding of love. Should we recognize other types of unions that are not based on a sexual relationship? Why or why not?

advertisement

prereading question } Does advertising succeed in encouraging people to buy products?

Kia Advertisements

QUESTIONS FOR REASONING AND ANALYSIS

1. Do these advertisements for Kia perpetuate ethnic stereotypes? Why or why not?
2. How would you describe the comparison that the ads make between the Kia and other kinds of cars?
3. Why do you think the advertisers chose the hamster as opposed to some other animal?
4. Does a relationship exist between the name for this model of the Kia (i.e., the Soul) and the approach of these ads? Why or why not?

QUESTIONS FOR REFLECTING AND WRITING

1. The Kia advertisements make use of anthropomorphism or assigning human characteristics to nonhuman animals or nonliving things. Is this approach effective in persuading the audience to buy a Kia Soul? Why or why not?
2. Do you think advertising succeeds in encouraging people to buy products? Why or why not?
3. Is it ethical for advertisers to encourage people to buy products they do not necessarily need? Should advertisers emphasize only positive aspects of a product without mentioning any negative attributes? Why or why not?

Consumerism Is "Eating the Future"

Andy Coghlan

Andy Coghlan writes for Newscientist.com. This article appeared on August 7, 2009.

We're a gloomy lot, with many of us insisting that there's nothing we can do personally about global warming, or that the human race is over-running the planet like a plague.

But according to leading ecologists speaking this week in Albuquerque at the annual meeting of the Ecological Society of America, few of us realize that the main cause of the current environmental crisis is human nature.

More specifically, all we're doing is what all other creatures have ever done to survive, expanding into whatever territory is available and using up whatever resources are available, just like a bacterial culture growing in a Petri dish till all the nutrients are used up. What happens then, of course, is that the bugs then die in a sea of their own waste.

One speaker in Albuquerque, epidemiologist Warren Hern of the University of Colorado at Boulder, even likened the expansion of human cities to the growth and spread of cancer, predicting "death" of the Earth in about 2025. He points out that like the accelerated growth of a cancer, the human population has quadrupled in the past 100 years, and at this rate will reach a size in 2025 that leads to global collapse and catastrophe.

But there's worse. Not only are we simply doing what all creatures do: we're doing it better. In recent times we're doing it even faster because of changes in society that encourage and celebrate conspicuous and excessive consumption.

"Biologists have shown that it's a natural tendency of living creatures to fill up all available habitat and use up all available resources," says William Rees of the University of British Columbia in Vancouver, Canada. "That's what underlies Darwinian evolution, and species that do it best are the ones that survive, but we do it better than any other species," he told me prior to the conference.

Spreading Humans

Although we like to think of ourselves as civilized thinkers, we're subconsciously still driven by an impulse for survival, domination and expansion. This is an impulse which now finds expression in the idea that inexorable economic growth is the answer to everything, and, given time, will redress all the world's existing inequalities.

The problem with that, according to Rees and Hern, is that it fails to recognize that the physical resources to fuel this growth are finite. "We're still driven by growing and expanding, so we will use up all the oil, we will use up all the coal, and we will keep going till we fill the Petri dish and pollute ourselves out of existence," he says.

But there's another, more recent factor that's making things even worse, and it's an invention of human culture rather than an evolved trait. According to Rees, the change took place after the second world war in the United States, when factories previously producing weapons lay idle, and soldiers were returning with no jobs to go to.

American economists and the government of the day decided to revive economic activity by creating a culture in which people were encouraged to accumulate and show off material wealth, to the point where it defined their status in society and their self-image.

Rees quotes economist Victor Lebow as saying in 1955: "Our enormously productive economy demands that we make consumption our way of life, that we convert the buying and use of goods into rituals, that we seek our spiritual satisfaction and our ego satisfaction in consumption. We need things consumed, burned up, worn out, replaced and discarded at an ever-increasing rate."

Insecure Society

In today's world, such rhetoric seems beyond belief. Yet the consumer spree carries on regardless, and few of us are aware that we're still willing slaves to a completely artificial injunction to consume, and to define ourselves by what we consume.

"Lebow and his cronies got together to 'create' the modern advertising industry, which plays to primitive beliefs," says Rees. "It makes you feel insecure, because the advertising industry turned our sense of self-worth into a symbolic presentation of the possessions we have," he told me. "We've turned consumption into a necessity, and how we define ourselves."

The result is a world in which rampant consumption in rich countries is rapidly outstripping the resources in the world needed to satisfy demand.

For evidence, Rees developed in 1992 a process called ecological footprint analysis (EFA). Produced by combining national consumption statistics with calculations of the resources needed to meet reported consumption patterns, EFA generates figures that conveniently demonstrate where consumption is least sustainable, and how fast finite material resources are being used up (calculate your own here).

Big Footprints

Rees cited latest figures, taken from the WWF's study Living Planet Report 2008, showing that, globally, we're already in "overshoot," consuming 30 per cent more material than is sustainable from the world's resources. At present, 85 countries exceed their domestic "bio-capacities," compensating for their lack of local material by depleting stocks elsewhere, in countries that have "surpluses" because they're not consuming as much.

Perhaps not surprisingly, given the encouragement from Lebow, North Americans are the most consumptive, eating resources equivalent to 9.2 global average hectares per capita.

The world can only supply 2.1 global average hectares per person, so already, Americans are consuming four times what the Earth can sustainably supply. "North Americans should be taking steps to lower their eco-footprints by almost 80 per cent, to free up the "ecological space" for justifiable growth in the developing world," says Rees.

The worrying thing is that if everyone on Earth adopted American lifestyles overnight, we would need four extra worlds to supply their needs, says Rees.

We haven't yet mentioned climate change or global warming. What's to be done? Marc Pratarelli of Colorado State University at Pueblo believes we need to snap out of our sleepwalking and begin to take real steps to cut consumption. "We have our heads in the sand, and are in a state of denial," he says. "People think: 'It won't happen to me, or be in my lifetime, or be that bad, so what's the point of change.'"

What to Do?

But there is hope, however slim, according to Rees, both from the top down and the bottom up. The hope from above is that governments will finally realize that never-ending economic growth is incompatible with the finite material resources Earth has to offer, and begin to manage those resources more fairly and equitably through some kind of world government.

Without global management, destruction will continue, producing food and energy "crunches" that make the credit crunch look like a tea party.

"We need to learn to live within the means of nature," says Rees. "That means sharing and redistribution of wealth, and for that we need leadership at the highest level to understand that the competitive instinct and the drive for power and more resources is mutually destructive, so governments must act in our collective interest."

From the bottom up, there are the glimmers of global grassroots organizations campaigning for global justice and global solutions, such as the Internet-based justice organization Avaaz, which collects e-mail votes for petitions on issues of international or personal justice.

Desire to Acquire

Solving the other problem—the advertising that feeds our desire to acquire—might be more tricky. In an ideal world, it would be a counter-advertising campaign to make conspicuous consumption shameful.

"Advertising is an instrument for construction of people's everyday reality, so we could use the same media to construct a cultural paradigm in which conspicuous consumption is despised," he says. "We've got to make people ashamed to be seen as a "future eater.'"

Whether we're capable of such a counter-revolution is doubtful, both because of our state of personal denial and because of the huge power of industry to continue seducing us.

"In effect, globalism and consumerism have succeeded in banishing moderation and sanctifying greed, thereby liberating Homo economicus from any moral or ethical constraints on consumption," says Rees.

Pararelli is even more pessimistic. The only hope, he says, is a disaster of immense scale that jolts us out of our denial. "My sense is that only when the brown stuff really hits the fan will we finally start to do something."

http://www.newscientist.com/article/dn17569-consumerism-is-eating-the-future.html?full=true

1. According to Coghlan, what is the main cause of the current environmental crisis?
2. What is the problem with economic growth?
3. Why does Coghlan say we are so compelled to consume?
4. What is Coghlan's solution to the problem?

QUESTIONS FOR REASONING AND ANALYSIS

1. What organizational pattern does Coghlan's essay basically follow?
2. What is Coghlan's thesis?
3. Do the causes Coghlan cites for earth's eventual destruction make sense to you? Why or why not?

QUESTIONS FOR REFLECTING AND WRITING

1. Do you agree that consumerism and consumption pose detrimental effects for earth's resources? Why or why not?
2. Do you see population growth and rampant consumerism as problems that require a solution? If so, why? If not, what global problems do you think need a more immediate solution?

---

blog post

prereading question } **Why do fast food restaurants give toys to children?**

McDonald's Hit by Happy Meal Toy Ban

Carla Fried

Carla Fried made this post on November 4, 2010 to The Daily Money, a blog that is part of CBS's MoneyWatch.com website. Fried is a freelance writer who has published articles for *The New York Times* and *Kiplinger*.

Come 2012, kids in San Francisco will not be getting a free toy with their McDonald's Happy Meal. The San Francisco's Board of Supervisors voted earlier this week to ban McDonald's and all fast food restaurants from plying kids with free toy giveaways on meals that are deemed to be too full of calories, fat, and sodium. Before you crank up the "only in San Francisco" chants, though, take note that S.F. is not the first region to cut off toy marketing by fast food restaurants. This past spring, California's Santa Clara County—which encompasses Silicon Valley—passed a similar Happy Meals toy ban ordinance.

Moreover, if the Center for Science in the Public Interest has its way, the toy ban could go national. It is getting ready to sue McDonald's over its practice of throwing in a free toy along with an order of fries and Chicken McNuggets. "McDonald's use of toys undercuts parental authority and exploits young children's developmental immaturity—all this to induce children to prefer foods that may harm their health. It's a creepy and predatory practice that warrants an injunction," says CSPI litigation director Stephen Gardner. But just how valid are these claims, particularly when weighed against consumers" rights to choose what they want to eat and buy?

Big Brother Lording over Parents . . .

Plenty of parents don't seem exactly thrilled with government stepping in and trying to do their job. Cries of "nanny state" and "leave the parenting to the parents" dominate the comments to the Happy Meals ban report at the San Francisco Chronicle's website. Outgoing S.F. Mayor Gavin Newsom (outgoing in that he was elected the state's next lieutenant governor in Tuesday's election) is also on record as saying that he is against the Happy Meals ban, citing business, not nutritional concerns. "I don't think you can regulate how people market products without going down a dangerous path," Newsom has said. "This is a whole ['nother] role of government I am not supporting." Even if Newsom had remained in charge, though, the Board of Supervisors"

8-3 vote would have been enough to override a mayoral veto.

. . . Or a Smart Health Initiative?

According to the Centers for Disease Control, childhood obesity has tripled over the past 30 years. More specifically:

- Among pre-school age children 2 to 5 years of age, obesity increased from 5 percent to 10.4 percent over the same time period.
- Among children ages 6 to 11, obesity increased from 6.5 percent in 1980 to 19.6 percent in 2008.
- Among adolescents aged 12 to 19, obesity increased from 5.0 percent to 18.1 percent.

And unhealthy kids have a habit of growing into unhealthy adults. (To wit, a Brazilian court recently sided with a former McDonald's manager who sued the firm after gaining 65 pounds on the job.) Banning toys served up with a fat-laden and sodium-soaked fast food meal won't solve the problem. Maybe it doesn't even make a sizable dent. But as BNET's Melanie Warner points out, sometimes symbolic gestures are the start of more substantive change.

Plus, there are the financial costs to consider. According to a recent study, being obese costs women an estimated $4,879 a year and men $2,646 due to factors such as having to take more sick days and reduced productivity. And all of us are paying a price in terms of the cost to our health care system. A new study out of Cornell estimates that the annual cost of treating obesity in the U.S. is $168 billion, representing about 16.5 percent of our national medical care costs. That's some food for thought next time you're wondering what can be done to rein in your ever-rising health insurance costs, as well as our national tab for Medicare.

http://moneywatch.bnet.com/economic-news/blog/daily-money/mcdonalds-hit-by-happy-meal-toy-ban/1510

QUESTIONS FOR REASONING AND ANALYSIS

1. How would you respond to Fried's question from her post: "But just how valid are these claims, particularly when weighed against consumers" rights to choose what they want to eat and buy?"

2. Which arguments supporting the toy ban do you find most compelling? Least compelling? Why?

QUESTIONS FOR REFLECTING AND WRITING

1. Can you think of other instances in which corporations may be undercutting parental authority and exploiting a child's developmental immaturity? How might they be doing so? Is it cause for concern? Why or why not?

2. Is fast food a major factor in childhood as well as adult obesity? Why or why not? What other factors contribute to obesity? How do those factors contribute?

prereading questions } How are new forms of media bringing about changes in music industry practices? How will new media continue to affect the way people purchase and consume music?

Why the Music Industry Hates *Guitar Hero*

Jeff Howe

This essay, by contributing editor Jeff Howe, appeared in *Wired* magazine on February 23, 2009. Mr. Howe is also the author of *Crowdsourcing: Why the Power of the Crowd Is Driving the Future of Business*, published in 2008.

Nobody expected the number-one-with-a-bullet rise of the music videogame—least of all the music industry. Armed with little more than crappy graphics, plastic guitars, and epic hooks, play-along titles like *Guitar Hero* and *Rock Band* have become an industry in their own right, raking in more than $2.3 billion over the past three years. Album sales fell 19 percent this past holiday season, but the thrill isn't gone—it just moved to a different platform.

The success of these games is good news for the music biz. They're breathing new life into old bands (Weezer, anyone?) and helping popularize new ones. They're even becoming a significant distribution outlet for new releases. So the record labels ought to be ecstatic, right? Nope. They're whining over licensing fees.

"The amount being paid to the music industry, even though [these] games are entirely dependent on the content we own and control, is far too small," Warner Music Group CEO Edgar Bronfman told analysts last summer. The money Warner receives for the use of its songs is "paltry," he said, and if the gamemakers don't pony up more cash, "we will not license to those games." In response, *Rock Band* publisher MTV Games is now boycotting Warner artists, according to a source close to the negotiations.

This is a fight no one can win. Putting the brakes on music gaming would hurt everyone in the ailing music industry. Instead of demanding greater profit participation, Warner should be angling for creative participation. Thirty years ago, Hollywood took a similar threat—the VCR—and turned it into a new source of revenue, building customer loyalty in the process. The music industry could use new games the same way—but its track record suggests that it won't.

How does this play out? Gamemakers could respond by using cover versions of songs from the Warner catalog, but Bronfman already has that move blocked. He also runs the giant music publisher Warner/Chappell, and he could deny the game companies access there, too. From Bronfman's perspective, the record labels got ripped off when MTV was sold in 1985 for $690 mil-

lion ($1.4 billion in today's dollars) on the strength of videos it received for free, and then ripped off again when Apple initially denied the labels control over pricing on iTunes. He won't get fooled again.

To be fair, Bronfman has a point. Game publishers generally sign low-cost synchronization licenses—as if the music were being used incidentally, in the background. Compare this to Electronic Arts' *Madden NFL* franchise, from which the football league collects some 30 percent of gross revenue, and you can begin to feel his pain.

But there's better money to be made by playing together. Music games are proven earners—Aerosmith has reportedly earned more from *Guitar Hero: Aerosmith* than from *any single album* in the band's history. The labels ought to push for more such titles and integrate them into their promotional strategies. They might not maximize profit on the licensing, but who cares? With more entries to come in the play-along genre, and networked hardware to play them on, the games themselves could even become an online music retail channel to rival iTunes. Or what about a game for turntable artists? Labels could provide the stem tracks for songs (in which each instrument's recording is isolated) and let players mix their own versions. Users could vote for their favorites through online services like Xbox Live, and Warner could sell the winning mixes back to customers using the very platform on which they were created. Call it Wii-Mix.

If the company wants a case study, it need look no further than Universal Music Group. Rather than cavil over licensing fees, Universal parent company Vivendi simply bought *Guitar Hero's* publisher, Activision. Look, the labels know that recorded music is in irreversible decline. Warner has actually led the industry with a policy of signing bands to so-called 360 deals, in which artists give the label a cut of everything they sell, be it ringtones, merchandise, or concert tickets. On the strength of such foresight, Bronfman has styled himself as the man who will reinvent the music industry. But part of that reinvention must be an end to petty haggling over fees. Going PvP [player versus player] against gamemakers isn't going to solve the industry's problems. At this point, Bronfman still seems intent on dragging his business kicking and screaming back to the 20th century.

www.wired.com/culture/culturereviews/
magazine/17–03/st_essay

QUESTIONS FOR READING

1. What are record labels "whining over," according to Howe?
2. How should record labels, like Warner, use music videogames to their advantage?

3. What does Howe suggest record labels should do to offset declining revenues?

QUESTIONS FOR REASONING AND ANALYSIS

1. How does Howe organize his article like a problem-solution essay? What is the problem as he defines it? What is Howe's solution?
2. The photograph preceding the essay shows someone holding a deflated electric guitar. What does this image suggest? Why do you think the *Wired* editors chose this image to introduce Howe's piece?

3. Howe suggests "Wii-Mix" as one possible answer to the music industry's declining revenues. What is "Wii-Mix"? Do you agree that "Wii-Mix" represents a plausible solution for the music industry? Why or why not?
4. Howe's last sentence suggests Bronfman, the Warner Music Group CEO, refuses to adapt to a changing business environment. How do you think Howe conceives of doing business in the twenty-first century?

QUESTIONS FOR REFLECTING AND WRITING

1. What does the future hold for music consumers? Will the sale of CDs, for example, eventually become a thing of the past? Why or why not?
2. Do you think record labels are entitled to more money from companies using music tracks in other media (such as music videogames)? Why or why not?

3. Have you considered another compromise solution different from "Wii-Mix"? If so, what is your solution?

the challenges of living in a high-tech, multimedia world

chapter 16

Every day, we find ourselves increasingly immersed in a media environment and constantly engaged in use of new and innovative communication and digital technologies. Media is literally everywhere; we cannot even walk into some fast-food restaurants without encountering a digital television mounted to the wall of a dining area. News updates from CNN, MSNBC, or Fox News resonate while restaurant patrons feast on hamburgers and french fries. We have become so accustomed to our high-tech and multimedia world that some of us may find it difficult to remember a time when media was somewhat less pervasive. Some authors of this chapter's selections, however, are less than optimistic concerning the ubiquity of technology, media, and information. They cite potential problems with diminished social relations and threats to privacy that people should take very seriously.

prereading questions

1. Even though we are all now a part of the global economy, that seems an abstract concept to many people. How does technology affect your life in more immediate ways? Try listing the ways that technology affects our daily lives.

2. Do you miss any of the "older" ways of doing things? If so, what? If not, why not?

3. How do you envision technology and media affecting your life in the next 20 years? In the next 50 years? Will the effects be good or bad—or both? Why?

4. Are you concerned about your privacy online or as a member of a social networking site like Facebook? Why or why not?

websites related to this chapter's topic

WIRED NEWS
www.wired.com
Site for *Wired* magazine as well as links to other technology and media resources.

SOCIAL NETWORKING SITES: SAFETY TIPS FOR TWEENS AND TEENS
www.ftc.gov/bcp/edu/pubs/consumer/tech/tec14.shtm
Federal Trade Commission's "Facts for Consumers" site providing information concerning online safety.

PRESIDENT OBAMA'S AGENDA FOR TECHNOLOGY
www.whitehouse.gov/issues/technology
White House site explaining the Obama Administration's agenda for technology.

Maps of Facebook, Internet, and Cell Penetration in North Africa and Middle East

These maps appeared on CNN.com in 2011 after a wave of protests and civil unrest in the Middle East and North Africa.

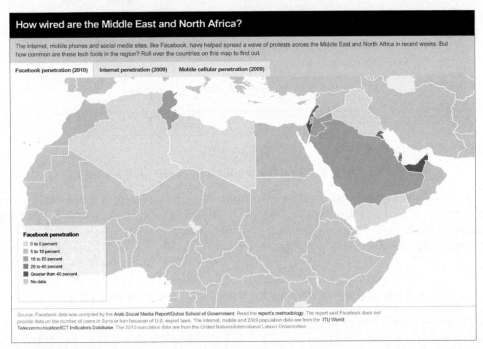

Reprinted with permission from CNN.com.

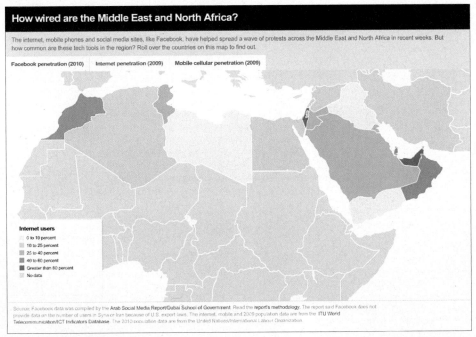

Reprinted with permission from CNN.com.

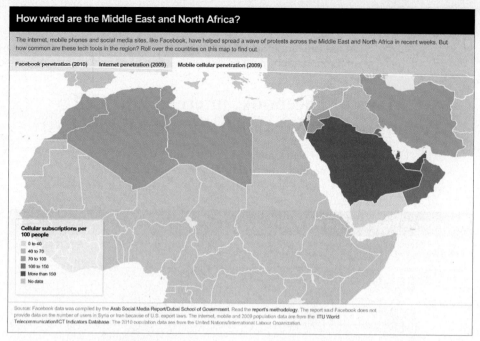

How wired are the Middle East and North Africa?

The internet, mobile phones and social media sites, like Facebook, have helped spread a wave of protests across the Middle East and North Africa in recent weeks. But how common are these tech tools in the region? Roll over the countries on this map to find out.

Facebook penetration (2010)   Internet penetration (2009)   Mobile cellular penetration (2009)

Cellular subscriptions per 100 people
- 0 to 40
- 40 to 70
- 70 to 100
- 100 to 150
- More than 150
- No data

Source: Facebook data was compiled by the Arab Social Media Report/Dubai School of Government. Read the report's methodology. The report said Facebook does not provide data on the number of users in Syria or Iran because of U.S. export laws. The internet, mobile and 2009 population data are from the ITU World Telecommunication/ICT Indicators Database. The 2010 population data are from the United Nations/International Labour Organization.

Reprinted with permission from CNN.com.

QUESTIONS FOR REASONING AND ANALYSIS

1. Overall, the maps show that mobile cellular technology has penetrated the Middle East and North Africa more so than Facebook or the Internet. What are some possible reasons for greater mobile cellular use in these regions?

2. Facebook penetration appears to be greater in the Middle East than in North Africa. What might be the reason?

QUESTIONS FOR REFLECTING AND WRITING

1. How do social networking sites, the Internet, and mobile cellular phones help spread protests in regions like the Middle East and North Africa? Do you think these technologies contributed to the success of protests in, for example, Egypt? Why or why not?

2. Do you think communication technologies (e.g., Facebook, mobile phones) can help bring about democracy in nations currently governed by more autocratic regimes? Will communication technologies change the way people participate in the democratic process in the future? Why or why not?

Five Years Later, The Huffington Post (And Online Media) Are Coming Of Age

Henry Blodget

Henry Blodget is the CEO and Editor-in-Chief of Business Insider. This piece appeared on May 18, 2010. Sometime after Blodget wrote this piece, The Huffington Post sold for $315 million.

Controversy

The Huffington Post is now five years old.

Subject

In those five years, the site has gone from a tiny blog featuring posts from famous friends of founders Arianna Huffington and Ken Lerer to one of the largest independent news sites in the world.

In another five years, the Huffington Post will likely have blown past the few remaining news sites that are still bigger than it is—the New York Times and CNN, for example—and become the largest independent news site in the world. Don't believe it? Let's go to the numbers.

continued

Two-and-a-half years ago, according to Comscore, the Huffington Post was visited by 1.2 million uniques a month. That compared to 11.1 million at the main site of the New York Times, 5.8 million at the Washington Post, 2.8 million at the Wall Street Journal, and 2.6 million at the LA Times.

Now, again according to Comscore, Huffington Post has 12.3 million uniques, way ahead of the main sites for Wapo (green line), the WSJ (purple line), and the LAT, which have stagnated. The Huffington Post (red line) still lags the New York Times (blue line), but not by much—and not for long.

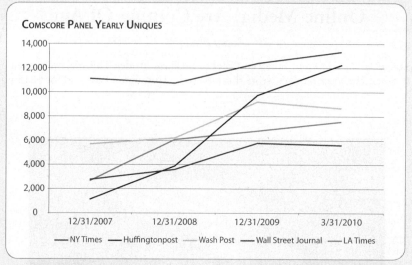

COMSCORE PANEL YEARLY UNIQUES

Legend: NY Times — Huffingtonpost — Wash Post — Wall Street Journal — LA Times

Huffington Post traffic in red (monthly uniques)

(The numbers from Compete show a bigger gap between HuffPo and the NYT, but the trend is the same. The numbers from Quantcast, meanwhile, show Huffpo already ahead of the NYT).

As those who work at the leapfrogged sites and the NYT will be quick to point out, of course, traffic is not the same as revenue. But traffic does lead to revenue. And here, too, the Huffington Post is coming of age.

The Huffington Post booked about $15 million of revenue last year. Sales boss Greg Coleman thinks the company can double revenue this year to $30 million and double it again next year, to $60 million. And from there, as long as the site's traffic keeps growing, it's just a hop, skip, and jump to $100+ million.

(Where is all this revenue coming from? In part, from new, brand-name advertisers. Among those that have recently bought campaigns, says a Huffington Post source, are Amex, IBM, GE, Johnson & Johnson, Mercedes, Chevrolet, HBO, AMC, Toyota, Paramount Pictures, Sony, AT&T, Coke, Pepsi, Google, Microsoft, Yahoo, CNN, Colgate, Bulgari, Ford, Discovery, and PBS. This is what hiring Yahoo's ex sales boss and 10 new reps so far this year gets you.)

Now, $100+ million is not the $1 billion or so of revenue of the New York Times. But most of the $1 billion or so of the New York Times revenue is going away (its paper-based ads and subscriptions). What will be left, eventually, when the NYT's paper-based distribution finally collapses, are the online revenues. And those, for now, are in the neighborhood of $150 million.

So, by the end of this year, Huffington Post should be bigger than the New York Times in terms of online traffic. By 2012, Huffington Post should have vastly more traffic than the New York Times. AND by 2012 Huffington Post could also be within spitting distance of the NYT in terms of online revenue.

And a few years after that?

It seems reasonable to think that Huffington Post could eventually just be bigger than the New York Times, online and offline.

But, but, but . . . !

"But Huffington Post isn't anywhere near as good as the New York Times!" the traditionalists will scream. The Huffington Post is a blog. The Huffington Post is an aggregator. The Huffington Post is written by ranting lefties padding around their bedrooms in their underwear!

Yes, to some extent, that's true. Some of the Huffington Post is a blog. Some of it is an aggregator. And some of it is written by ranting lefties, wherever they may be. But there are now 19 other content verticals on the Huffington Post in addition to politics, and politics contributes only about a quarter of the site's traffic. (Here's a recent snapshot of what people are reading on Huffington Post: Only a small portion of it is politics.)

The New York Times, meanwhile, is, well, the *New York Times*. It's the paper of record! It's the paragon of quality journalism. It's...

Yes, for now.

For now, advertisers are willing to pay a lot more for New York Times inventory than they'll pay for Huffington Post inventory (2+ times). Over time, however, that may begin to change. Much of the New York Times's online advertising is sold in conjunction with the paper's print advertising, and it's hard to separate the value of the two. If the Huffington Post eventually builds vastly more inventory than the New York Times, moreover, the per-page revenue-per-thousand won't matter.

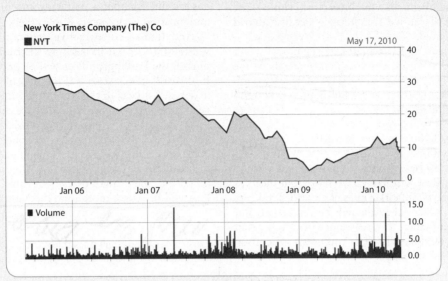

New York Times Company (The) Co
■ NYT   May 17, 2010

It hasn't been a great 5 years for the New York Times…

Reproduced with permission of Yahoo! Inc. © 2011 Yahoo! Inc. YAHOO! and the YAHOO! logo are registered trademarks of Yahoo! Inc.

And before you invest a lot of time arguing about the relative quality of a New York Times page and a Huffington Post page, don't lose sight of what's really going on here.

The Huffington Post, like Gawker Media, TechCrunch, dozens of blog networks, the Drudge Report, and other next-generation media properties (including the one you're reading—I'm talking my own book), is what is known as a "disruptive technology."

Clayton Christensen's "Disruption" Strikes Again

Now, when most people think of disruptive technologies, they think of technologies that are immediately and obviously superior to the technologies they are rendering obsolete. But in the nomenclature of Clayton Christensen, the Harvard professor who first laid out the concept of disruption, immediately superior technologies actually aren't disruptive technologies. Those are called sustaining technologies. Those technologies will often be acquired or otherwise co-opted by the incumbent leaders (the New York Times, in this case) and used to make their product lines better.

Disruptive technologies, meanwhile, are emphatically NOT better than incumbent technologies—at least not at the beginning. Disruptive technologies are often worse than incumbent technologies. Their advantage—the reason people begin to adopt them—is that they're also simpler, cheaper, and more convenient.

The Huffington Post provides a simple service for its readers and contributors: It aggregates thousands of news sources into a single location, and it serves as a powerful distribution engine for thousands of content creators. It does this in a manner that strikes many as chaotic and messy (in addition to politically biased). But in a world with hundreds of thousands of sources, it's also necessary and effective (and, in the manner Huffpo does it, fun—don't underestimate the value of that). The Huffington Post is also free, which the paper-based version of the NYT isn't.

In Clay Christensen's words, the Huffington Post meets the needs of more than 10 million uniques not because it's "better" but because it's "good enough."

And, like other disruptive technologies, it's getting better all the time.

This, after all, is the typical pattern with disruptive technologies. The disruptor enters at the low end of the market, providing a simple service that is cheaper and more convenient than incumbent alternatives and "good enough." The low end of the market adopts the technology—and the incumbent players, which serve the profitable middle and high-end of the market—snigger and point out that their products are "better."

But then the disruptor improves its product, the way the Huffington Post has improved its product for the last few years. And soon the disruptive product is useful to the middle of the market as well—and it's still simpler and more convenient. Soon, the incumbent player, under attack from below, is forced to migrate to the higher end of the market, seeking to preserve its huge profit margins. Eventually, the disruptor takes over

continued

the middle of the market, and the incumbent player collapses.

The other common feature of disruptive technologies, one that certainly is at play here, is that the new market they create is often much smaller (in terms of revenue and profit) than the one they disrupt. This is one reason incumbents like the New York Times resist embracing the disruptive technology—because they'd go broke if they did.

But just because the Huffington Post's model won't sustain the high salaries, pensions, and benefits of the 1,100 folks who still work in the NYT's newsroom, doesn't mean that it won't let the Huffington Post build a very nice business.

How nice?

Most likely, $100+ million in revenue and 30%+ profit margin within a few years.

As it grows, and as it seeks to improve its product, the Huffington Post will likely hire more and more of the folks that the New York Times can't afford to keep, so much of its potential profit will be reinvested. But over the long haul, there's no reason it can't enjoy profit margins that would have made even the last generation of newspaper barons happy.

respond

Welcome to Adolescence

So, the Huffington Post is 5 years old. It's still an adolescent, so it's not surprising that it often looks and behaves like an adolescent (don't we all). But the Huffington Post is a huge, powerful, and rapidly growing adolescent, one that is maturing into one of the biggest and most powerful news sites in the world.

And thanks to attractive economics (those thousands of contributors seeking distribution don't cost much), the Huffington Post will be profitable this year. It also still has at least $15 million of the $25 million it raised last year in the bank. Over the next couple of years, the company will likely figure out how to put at least some of that money to good use.

And then it will probably go public.

And one day, we suspect, through a combination of the reduction in value of the old line newspaper businesses and the growth of its own value, the Huffington Post will be worth more than the New York Times.

http://www.businessinsider.com/huffington-post-comes-of-age-2010-5

QUESTIONS FOR READING

1. What does the author mean when he says that The Huffington Post should be bigger than The New York Times?

2. What does Blodget mean by "disruptive technology"?
3. According to the author, why will The Huffington Post continue to be profitable?

QUESTIONS FOR REASONING AND ANALYSIS

1. Do the graphs Blodget uses aid him in making a convincing argument? Why or why not?

2. What is Blodget's thesis? Do you agree or disagree with his argument? Why or why not?

3. Do you agree with Blodget's analysis of "disruptive technologies"? Why or why not?

QUESTIONS FOR REFLECTING AND WRITING

1. What are some other examples of "disruptive technologies" besides The Huffington Post and similar such sites? Why are these technologies "disruptive," in your view?

2. Will print-based journalism eventually become a thing of the past? Write an argument supporting the premise that print-based journalism will eventually disappear or an argument supporting the premise that it will remain and coexist alongside digitally based journalism.

Save the Internet

The SavetheInternet.com Coalition is a collective of people who
have come together to protect Internet freedom.

Reprinted with permission of Free Press, www.freepress.net.

Reprinted with permission of Free Press, www.freepress.net.

continued

Reprinted with permission of Free Press, www.freepress.net.

QUESTIONS FOR REASONING AND ANALYSIS

1. How does this website make an argument? What does it use for support?

2. The site uses a quote from President Obama, in part to establish credibility or ethos. In what other ways does the site establish ethos with its audience?

3. Who is the audience for this site?

QUESTIONS FOR REFLECTING AND WRITING

1. Research the major arguments in favor of and in opposition to "Net Neutrality." Which arguments do you find most compelling? Why?

2. What are some possible consequences of restricting the Internet too much? Do even minor restrictions inhibit freedom too much? Why or why not?

Defending Video Games: Breeding Evil?

There's no solid evidence that video games are bad for people, and they may be positively good

This article appeared on Economist.com on August 4, 2005.

Big Statement

"IT IS an evil influence on the youth of our country." A politician condemning video gaming? Actually, a clergyman denouncing rock and roll 50 years ago. But the sentiment could just as easily have been voiced by Hillary Clinton in the past few weeks, as she blamed video games for "a silent epidemic of media desensitization" and "stealing the innocence of our children."

The gaming furor centers on "Grand Theft Auto: San Andreas," a popular and notoriously violent cops and robbers game that turned out to contain hidden sex scenes that could be unlocked using a patch downloaded from the Internet. The resulting outcry (mostly from Democratic politicians playing to the center) caused the game's rating in America to be changed from "mature," which means you have to be 17 to buy it, to "adults only," which means you have to be 18, but also means that big retailers such as Wal-Mart will not stock it. As a result the game has been banned in Australia; and, this autumn, America's Federal Trade Commission will investigate the complaints. That will give gaming's opponents an opportunity to vent their wrath on the industry.

Scepticism of new media is a tradition with deep roots, going back at least as far as Socrates' objections to written texts, outlined in Plato's Phaedrus. Socrates worried that relying on written texts, rather than the oral tradition, would "create forgetfulness in the learners' souls, because they will not use their memories; they will trust to the external written characters and not remember of themselves." (He also objected that a written version of a speech was no substitute for the ability to interrogate the speaker, since, when questioned, the text "always gives one unvarying answer." His objection, in short, was that books were not interactive. Perhaps Socrates would have thought more highly of video games.)

Novels were once considered too low-brow for university literature courses, but eventually the disapproving professors retired. Waltz music and dancing were condemned in the 19th century; all that twirling was thought to be "intoxicating" and "depraved," and the music was outlawed in some places. Today it is hard to imagine what the fuss was about. And rock and roll was thought to encourage violence, promiscuity and satanism; but today even grannies buy Coldplay albums.

Joystick Junkies

The opposition to gaming springs largely from the neophobia that has pitted the old against the entertainments of the young for centuries. Most gamers are under 40, and most critics are non-games-playing over-40s. But what of the specific complaints—that games foster addiction and encourage violence?

There's no good evidence for either. On addiction, if the worry is about a generally excessive use of screen-based entertainment, critics should surely concern themselves about television rather than games: American teenage boys play video games for around 13 hours a week (girls for only five hours), yet watch television for around 25 hours a week. As to the minority who seriously overdo it, research suggests that they display addictive behavior in other ways too. The problem, in other words, is with them, not with the games.

TV could be more of a problem

Most of the research on whether video games encourage violence is unsatisfactory, focusing primarily on short-term effects. In the best study so far, frequent playing of a violent game sustained over a month had no effect on participants' level of aggression. And, during the period in which gaming has become widespread in America, violent crime has fallen by half. If games really did make people violent, this tendency might be expected to show up in the figures, given that half of Americans play computer and video games. Perhaps, as some observers have suggested, gaming actually makes people less violent, by acting as a safety valve.

Neophobes Unite

So are games good, rather than bad, for people? Good ones probably are. Games are widely used as educational tools, not just for pilots, soldiers and surgeons, but also in schools and businesses. Every game has its own interface and controls, so that anyone who has learned to play a handful of games can generally figure out how to operate almost any high-tech device. Games require players to construct hypotheses, solve problems, develop strategies, learn the rules of the in-game world through trial and error. Gamers must also be able to juggle several different tasks, evaluate risks and make quick decisions. One game, set in 1930s Europe, requires the player to prevent the outbreak of the second world war; other games teach everything from algebra to derivatives trading. Playing games is, thus, an ideal form of preparation for the workplace of the 21st century, as some forward-thinking firms are already starting to realize.

Pointing all this out makes little difference, though, because the controversy over gaming, as with rock and roll, is more than anything else the consequence of a generational divide. Can the disagreements between old and young over new forms of media ever be resolved? Sometimes attitudes can change relatively quickly, as happened with the Internet. Once condemned as a cesspool of depravity, it is now recognized as a valuable new medium, albeit one where (as with films, TV and, yes, video games) children's access should be limited and supervised. The benefits of a broadband connection are now acknowledged, and politicians worry about extending access to the have-nots. Attitudes changed because critics of the Internet had to start using it for work, and then realized that, like any medium, it could be used for good purposes as well as bad. They have no such incentive to take up gaming, however.

Eventually, objections to new media resolve themselves, as the young grow up and the old die out. As today's gamers grow older—the average age of gamers is already 30—video games will ultimately become just another medium, alongside books, music and films. And soon the greying gamers will start tut-tutting about some new evil threatening to destroy the younger generation's moral fiber.

http://www.economist.com/node/4247084

QUESTIONS FOR READING

1. What comparisons does the author make between video games and other forms of media from history?
2. What does the author say about the evidence supporting the claim that video games encourage violence?
3. According to the author, how are video games good for people?

QUESTIONS FOR REASONING AND ANALYSIS

1. Describe the ways in which this author refutes the arguments that video games foster addiction and encourage violent behavior. Does the author effectively answer the opposition's argument? Why or why not?
2. How would you describe the tone of this article? As neutral and detached? As skeptical? As condescending? Why would you describe the author's tone in a certain way?

QUESTIONS FOR REFLECTING AND WRITING

1. Can video games cause people playing those games to become desensitized to violence? Why or why not?
2. At the end of the article, the author states that video games will eventually become just another medium, like films and television. However, some still claim that films and television perpetuate and encourage violent behavior. Should those in the entertainment industry exercise more responsibility in the media they produce? Why or why not?

If Technology Is Making Us Stupid,
It's Not Technology's Fault

David Theo Goldberg

David Theo Goldberg is the Director of the University of California Humanities Research Institute. He publishes on issues ranging from political theory to law and society to digital humanities. Goldberg made this post to dmlcentral.net on August 16, 2010.

There has been growing concern that computers have failed to live up to the promise of improving learning for school kids. The *New York Times*, the *Washington Post*, and PBS have all done stories recently calling into question the benefits of computers in schools. When computers fail kids, it's too easy to blame the technology. And it's disingenuous simply to cast aspersions on the kids. Those are responses that do little if anything to account for what is a much more layered set of conditions. Computers don't define how they are taken up socially, people do. Guardians, or extended families more largely, are a key constituent in the conditions for productive, participatory learning engagements with technology. But they are not the only players, by far. Teachers, policymakers, even gaming corporations share responsibility to fashion the sort of robust, attractive learning ecologies, instruments, and products to maximize the vast potential computing technologies and the Internet hold for engaged and indeed lifelong learning experiences.

Recent empirical research has shown decreased reading and math skills for middle school children after adoption of computers at home and school. Media observers and political commentators have made much of these apparent trends. Nicholas Carr's widely read book, *The Shallows: What the Internet Is Doing to Our Brains* (rooted in his *Atlantic* article, "Is Google Making Us Stupid?"), and his blog posts at Rough Type have stressed the negative data in well-publicized empirical research by the likes of Jacob Vigdor and Helen Ladd of Duke University.

Blaming the Computer and the Internet

In a five-year study of North Carolina middle school kids, Vigdor and Ladd found that introduction of computers in homes led to children spending less time on homework and more time on recreational games, resulting in somewhat deflated reading and math skills

as conventionally tested. The effects were more acute for black youth than for white. In a *New York Times* op ed piece, David Brooks stressed a related finding from another study. Schoolchildren who were sent home for the summer with 12 library books increased their reading capability and put the brakes on the traditional summer slide in reading skill. Brooks links the summer reading findings to the Vigdor/Ladd results and Carr's book, arguing that reading the classics cultivates respect and longstanding wisdom, while the Internet experience "smashes hierarchy," undermining respect for longstanding values and deference to the "wisdom" of history and knowledge of "lasting import."

The Duke researchers do acknowledge improved computing skills—the capacity to negotiate software and to find their way around the Internet—that are useful for future employability in the contemporary economy. But these findings are overshadowed by the stress on what they identify as the computer related failings. And it is these failings that social critics are quick to take up. While none link these findings and arguments to the pejorative dismissal of Mark Bauerlein's purposely incendiary "dumbest generation," their skepticism about the benefits of computer enabled learning reinforces the skepticism identified with vocal critics, skeptical politicians, and a reinforcing public distrustful of the new.

Playing to Longstanding Social Fears

Vigdor and Ladd's findings should hardly surprise us. Computers and the Internet are no different than other socially transforming technologies like television and automobiles. When television became socially widespread in the 1950s the concern was that it would undermine learning. And that no doubt has been part of its effect, as the culture of the couch potato took hold of kids emulating adults. But the stereotype of the empty-headed

continued

television generation overlooks the extraordinary impact television also had on learning from creative programs such as *Sesame Street* and the Discovery and History Channels.

Likewise, when the possibility of driving became a reality for teenagers it produced a profound cultural shift, prompting discussion among anxious parents and policymakers alike, not to mention considerable cultural commentary, about the impacts and effects of teenage access to a technology that wasn't just potentially dangerous but educationally subversive. Give the car keys to an unsupervised teenager and . . . there goes the neighborhood! James Dean is so yesterday?

Unlike television, and perhaps more like automobiles, computers are far from passive consumptive technologies. They enable, if not encourage, interactive engagement, creativity, and participatory interaction with others. The interaction can assume various forms, not all productive. Yet like the appealing impacts of both television and automobile access for youth, the productive and creative capacities of computing technology for ordinary users are staggering. The question then is not the false dilemma between unqualified good and evil, but how best to enable the productive learning possibilities of new digital technologies.

Deconstructing False Dilemmas

What the skeptical media commentators always seem to do is push for a single explanation for a multidimensional and multi-determined condition. Stirring trouble creates readership, and a following. But the underlying assumptions are misleading at best, pernicious at worst. They seem to expect everyone to learn in the same way, subject to the same conditions, with the same resources. One can only be cultivated by reading Shakespeare and the like. British poet and cultural critic Matthew Arnold was making this argument 130 years ago: this is the best that has been thought and taught—and one can add written and read. So everyone needs to buckle down and do it. All well to get the lesson of putting together a library, so long as my library is just like your library—and it better be on wooden shelves in a room with pages gathering dust.

The French philosopher Jacques Derrida was once asked on camera by a young person interviewing him amazed at his vast library whether he had read all those books (every professor has had a version of this question). His response was delicious. No, he said, I have read only four. But I have read them very well. The Internet makes available a vast array of reading materials, including books. Poll any 100 pairs of American parents about what four they would have their own kids read well, and you are bound to get at least 150 responses. Proliferate the number of parental source countries and you are unlikely to get universal consensus on any one book at all.

So there are things wrong with the premises, things wrong with generalizations, and things wrong with the assessment regimes promoted by the technology skeptics. First, they presume not just that one model should or does fit all but that model presupposes at least a solidly middle class environment. Not everyone is interested in Jane Austen, as good as she was. The writing may be technically superb, but the world she writes about is just not that interesting to those not drawn in some way to emergent bourgeois romance. Houston Baker has long argued that if you can't make Shakespeare into a hip hopper no amount of insisting will make hip hoppers into Shakespeareans. Purists may balk at the Maori cinematic Merchant of Venice or at the township film of Bizet's opera, U-Carmen eKayelitsha, but they bring to life iconic European cultural contributions for audiences well outside their range of reference, at once shifting the meaning and significance of those works for all of us.

Answers Tend to Depend on What a Person's Looking for

Second, it remains an open question whether or how far reading skills have in fact deteriorated. The answers will depend in part on where one looks. There is emerging evidence that those youth who are, for whatever reason, reluctant to read in conventional school settings, including testing, are quite able readers when negotiating the Internet for personal or perceived social needs, like multi-player game interaction or gleaning information they deem relevant to their cultural needs and communication. Extensive ethnographic research has revealed the complex ways "hanging out, messing around, and geeking out" translate into productive participatory learning experiences largely opaque to conventional learning advocates.

Environments for hanging out, messing around and geeking out have to include not just creative schools such as Quest2Learn, a New York City public school the curriculum for which is designed around gaming for pretty much all subjects. They must incorporate into networks with creative schools, inviting after school programs, library spaces, museums and science centers, computer clubs, and yes, sitting rooms at home.

Books Versus the Internet—Why Frame It This Way?

Just as television has offered a range of viewing experiences, some terrifically productive for learning, so the Internet offers a huge array of reading possibilities, including online versions of many of the European classics. David Brooks begrudgingly admits as much when he says that "Already, more 'old-fashioned' outposts are opening up across the Web. It could be that the real debate will not be books versus the Internet but how to build an Internet counterculture that will better attract people to serious learning." Why, but for the likes of Brooks, was the debate ever about books versus the Internet? He and those for whom he writes need also to open up to different conceptions of what "serious learning" amounts to. That, too, is part of what is at issue here, without the usual pejorative dismissal of "lowering standards." Learning what, and for what, when, and under what conditions—those are the questions.

This is not to deny concerns over diminishing scores, only to portray the concerns within a more varied and nuanced set of contexts. Where scores have declined, does it have to do with the fact that wealth inequities have widened dramatically over the same period? That perhaps the supposedly dumbest generation wallowing in the murky shallows is a product of teachers constantly forced to worry about almost nothing else than responses to standardized testing? We know all too well that different kids learn in sometimes dramatically different ways, at different paces, in different temporalities of skill development, and so on. If reading has become shallower, is it just because the Internet makes us read quicker or are there many other factors at work—that there is so much to read, so many more books and magazines, electronic media aside—that to get a sense of any good portion we have to skim; that life, and earning money to support a family, and even school, that going and getting about is so complex and time-consuming and quick-paced, that the time for leisurely reading is no longer so readily available?

But the premise here too may be wrong. There are plenty of deep works that plenty of people, including youth, seem to be reading. Harry Potter is to this generation what the Hardy Boys or Enid Blyton was to the British 1950s. Freshlyground is the South African girl group playing back up to Shakira for the Waka Waka World Cup theme song. In explaining the meaning of "The Big Man" on their own new cd, Radio Africa, recorded in New York, one of the group leaders made reference to Wizard of the Crow, the award winning novel by Kenyan writer Ngugi wa Thiongo, now teaching at the University of California, critical of the role of powerful male politicians in postcolonial Africa. We simply live in different times. It was never the case that everyone read everything, or all the same things, or had time to.

A Call to Action

Carr writes that the "The Net is making us smarter, in other words, only if we define intelligence by the Net's own standards." Well, perhaps he should apply that standard to his own argument, and Brooks to his: we are only better read, or cultivated, if we take as the criteria of assessment the ways of reading and being cultivated to which the likes of Carr and Brooks ascribe. The criteria of assessment have a significant impact on who registers as well-read or cultivated on the scale.

The media mega-critics so ready to diss the learning legacy of the digital, it turns out, can themselves be selective in their citing of the central study from which they wish to draw their conclusions. Vigdor and Ladd are more subtle in their prognosis than those so readily taking up their cause. In a completely ignored passage, they caution that, "One interpretation of these findings is that home computer technology is put to more productive use in households with more effective parental monitoring, or in households where parents can serve as more effective instructors in the productive use of online resources. We find evidence consistent with this interpretation."

The point is crucial, but should be generalized. Vigdor and Ladd are to be applauded for emphasizing that it is not the technology, but the social conditions of their use that are the most compelling concerns in play here.

http://dmlcentral.net/blog/3655

1. What were the results of the Vigdor and Ladd study?
2. How does Goldberg distinguish computers from television as technologies?

3. How does Goldberg answer the argument that kids' reading skills have deteriorated?
4. According to the author, what questions should we be asking when it comes to "serious learning"?

QUESTIONS FOR REASONING AND ANALYSIS

1. How would you express the author's thesis?
2. What types of evidence (e.g., statistics, studies, quotations) does Goldberg use in support of his argument? Has he used evidence effectively to make a compelling argument? Why or why not?

3. Are the author's comparisons between television and computers effective in making his argument? Why or why not?

QUESTIONS FOR REFLECTING AND WRITING

1. Are computers helping students learn more effectively or hindering their intellectual development? Write a short essay defending one of those positions.

2. Does the Internet encourage kids to read more or less? How so?

---

newspaper column

prereading question } **Should people exercise more caution when revealing information about themselves on social networking sites?**

On Facebook, Biggest Threat to Your Private Data May Be You

Jacquielynn Floyd

Jacquielynn Floyd has written for the *Dallas Morning News* since 1990. This article appeared in the February 21, 2009 edition of that newspaper.

Don't friend me! I mean it.

While we're talking about this, I don't want to be Twittered, blasted, poked or super-poked, either. Kindly refrain from telling me What You're Doing Right Now, and I'll return the favor. Don't confide that you have two spleens or that you threw up at your junior prom, and I won't burden you with my secret passion for the late Paul Henreid.

It's not that I don't like you. It's just that, if I want you to know that stuff, maybe it would be nicer to tell you in person over a glass of wine than to send out a buckshot bulletin to 200 people online.

Look, there's not a thing wrong with Facebook. But all this hysteria and hand-wringing over privacy could readily be sidestepped by not posting private information on the Internet.

The big alarm went off this week when alert bloggers noted a change in the micro-print "terms of service" agreement that goes with signing up for the ubiquitous social-network site. "Facebook *owns* you!" angry critics howled.

Opinions seem divided over whether the change in language actually constitutes a threat. Some saw a resurgence of the company's ill-fated "Beacon" experiment, when it devised the idea of essentially alerting everybody you know every time you buy something.

Others say it was nothing more than standard, self-protecting legal language. No matter: The bad-publicity deluge put Facebook's CEO (How old is that guy, anyway? Seventeen?) on the defensive, and the change was—for the moment—abandoned.

But people are surely fooling themselves if they depend on a company—any company—to guarantee privacy for information voluntarily posted in a place that, by definition, is extremely public.

Face this: You are your own front line of defense in maintaining your privacy. This extends to vetting personal information on the Internet. In the same way, it means exercising discretion over allowing people to take hilarious party pictures of you that might wind up being published as the Bong Hit Heard 'Round the World.

Sites like Facebook work from an oddly inverted social premise of starting with the whole of cyberspace and winnowing your way down, through a series of blocks and filters. Don't want that creepy guy from the mailroom to be your "friend"? You have to reject him. Don't want embarrassing pictures of you posted to your "wall"? Make sure you trust your friends.

Some people seem to plant the flag with a minimum of information: no picture, no bio, no recitation of favorite bands or (God help us) astrological sign. They bypass the rather juvenile, one-size-fits-all personality template the site provides.

But others "share" in an odd stream-of-consciousness broadcast about what they wore today, how they feel, what time they need to be at the dentist, and leave it to their friends to sift through the information for what's relevant. Their friends do the same to them—there's no boundary between what goes on inside and outside their skulls.

And that's what's really, deeply, seriously frightening.

What if, in our addiction to the temporary rush of joy that we all experience in talking about ourselves, we lose the ability to distinguish between our public and our private selves?

If we don't have enough sense not to "friend" somebody we haven't seen in 20 years and we didn't really know that well in the first place, what business do we have getting all huffy over Facebook's terms of service?

How can we expect somebody we don't know to safeguard our privacy if we think so little of it ourselves?

Sure, Facebook has an obligation to its users. But long before that, users have obligations to themselves.

Dallas Morning News, February 21, 2009. Reprinted with permission of *The Dallas Morning News*.

QUESTIONS FOR READING

1. What is the answer to the "hand-wringing over privacy," according to Floyd?
2. What recent event had angered Facebook users?
3. What ability does Floyd think is dangerous to lose?

QUESTIONS FOR REASONING AND ANALYSIS

1. What is Floyd's thesis or major claim? Do you agree or disagree? Why or why not?
2. How does Floyd defend her argument? Through evidence? Through reasons and logic? Has she effectively substantiated her claims? Why or why not?
3. Should Facebook users exercise greater discretion with regard to how much they reveal about themselves? Why or why not? Do you agree with Floyd that losing the ability to distinguish between our public and private selves is a serious concern? Why or why not?

QUESTIONS FOR REFLECTING AND WRITING

1. What kinds of information have you divulged about yourself on LinkedIn, Facebook, or Twitter? Are you concerned that you have made too much information available—even to your friends and people you know well? Why or why not? If you have never joined one or more of these social networking sites (SNS), then why have you chosen not to do so?

2. What are the possible consequences of revealing too much about oneself on an SNS? Are you concerned about such consequences? Why or why not?
3. How can a person best determine what information to make publicly available and what information to keep private?

All Watched over by Machines of Loving Grace

Richard Brautigan

Richard Gary Brautigan was a twentieth-century poet and novelist. He published this poem in 1963.

I like to think (and
the sooner the better!)
of a cybernetic meadow
where mammals and computers
live together in mutually
programming harmony
like pure water
touching clear sky.

I like to think
(right now, please!)
of a cybernetic forest
filled with pines and electronics
where deer stroll peacefully
past computers
as if they were flowers
with spinning blossoms.

I like to think
(it has to be!)
of a cybernetic ecology
where we are free of our labors
and joined back to nature,
returned to our mammal
brothers and sisters,
and all watched over
by machines of loving grace.

Richard Brautigan, www.jamesshuggins
.com/h/tek1/rememberwhen.htm.

QUESTIONS FOR REASONING AND ANALYSIS

1. How would you describe the tone of this poem's speaker?

2. How is the speaker making an argument in the poem? What is the speaker's thesis?

3. Why do you think the poet includes the statement in parentheses "and the sooner the better!" in the first stanza?

QUESTIONS FOR REFLECTING AND WRITING

1. Can we ever achieve a balance between the natural and the technological? Why or why not?

2. Does technological advancement occur at the expense of our natural environment? Do we risk completely destroying the natural environment for the sake of innovation? Why or why not?

POLICE LINE DO NOT CROSS

violent media or violent society?

Many people see societal violence as a problem growing rapidly out of control in this country. In recent years, for example, we have seen a dramatic increase in incidents of school violence on both high school and college campuses. Several experts believe that violence as depicted in videogames and in popular television programs and movies encourages young people to commit heinous acts. They hold media responsible as the major cause for violence in society. Others, however, argue that Americans' love affair with guns fosters a violent culture. In this chapter, readings as well as visual rhetoric examples capture not only the debate over causes of societal violence but also the debate over solutions—solutions that may mean greater restrictions for some individuals and groups.

prereading questions

1. Are people concerned about the influence of media violence overreacting, or should we be worried?

2. What is your position on gun control? Do you think other people share your interpretation of what "gun control" means?

3. What sources have influenced your thinking about guns and violence? Is it primarily friends, family, religion, or your own reading on the topic? How willing are you to listen to someone whose views differ from yours?

websites related to this chapter's topic

BABY BAG
www.babybag.com/articles/amaviol.htm
Facts about media violence directed to parents but useful for others as well.

BRADY CAMPAIGN TO PREVENT GUN VIOLENCE
www.bradycampaign.org
Large nonpartisan, grassroots campaign dedicated to preventing gun violence.

NATIONAL RIFLE ASSOCIATION
www.nra.org
This large gun lobby provides commentary and news updates on gun control issues.

website essay

prereading question } **What is the answer to the immigration problem?**

Arizona Immigration Law Could Lead to Surge in Violent Crime

America's Voice

This article and graph were published on July 12, 2010, by America's Voice Research on Immigration Reform.

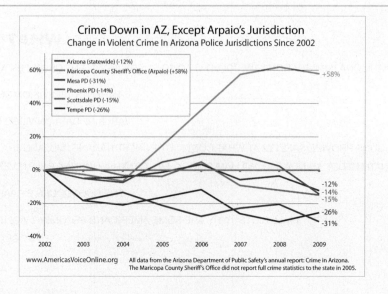

Crime Down in AZ, Except Arpaio's Jurisdiction
Change in Violent Crime In Arizona Police Jurisdictions Since 2002

- Arizona (statewide) (-12%)
- Maricopa County Sheriff's Office (Arpaio) (+58%)
- Mesa PD (-31%)
- Phoenix PD (-14%)
- Scottsdale PD (-15%)
- Tempe PD (-26%)

www.AmericasVoiceOnline.org   All data from the Arizona Department of Public Safety's annual report: Crime in Arizona. The Maricopa County Sheriff's Office did not report full crime statistics to the state in 2005.

Unfortunately, the evidence shows that the Arpaio approach is a proven failure at reducing crime. From 2002 to 2009, the crime rate in Maricopa County has increased 58 percent, while the state as a whole averaged a 12 percent decrease. Compare that 58 percent crime increase to other localities of Arizona that did not use the immigrant-targeting approach. In that same time period, Phoenix enjoyed a 14 percent decrease; Tempe, a 26 percent decrease; and Mesa, a 31 percent decrease.

SB 1070 mandates that this proven failure spread statewide, forcing every police jurisdiction in Arizona reverse years of successful trust building between law enforcement and the communities they serve. Police will now have to spend precious time and squander community trust checking the status of anyone they apprehend who they have "reasonable suspicion" is undocumented. And if law enforcement officials don't adopt Arpaio's priorities and put enforcing immigration law "to its fullest extent" at the top of the agenda, they could get sued.

Under the direction of Sheriff Joe Arpaio, Maricopa County's law enforcement regularly sweeps Latino neighborhoods and pulls over Latino drivers while felony warrants go unaddressed. Arpaio's department is under Federal investigation, his jails have had their health certification revoked and police chiefs around the nation have decried his tactics. Sheriff Arpaio takes pride in his anti-immigrant reputation, openly admitting to arresting "very few non-Hispanics."

http://americasvoiceonline.org/research/
entry/arizona_immigration_law_could_
lead_to_surge_in_violent_crime

QUESTIONS FOR REASONING AND ANALYSIS

1. The graph shows a significant increase in violent crime in Maricopa County over the other counties in Arizona. The authors of this website argue that "immigrant-targeting" has contributed to this significant increase. Is their claim valid? Why or why not? What other factors might have contributed to an increase in violent crime in Maricopa County?

2. What does the last paragraph on this page suggest or imply about Sheriff Arpaio's attitude toward Hispanics?

3. According to the authors, what are the negative effects of SB 1070 as well as Sheriff Arpaio's tactics? Do you think SB 1070 and Arpaio's tactics actually cause these effects? Why or why not?

QUESTIONS FOR REFLECTING AND WRITING

1. Conduct additional research on Arizona's SB 1070. After learning more about it, do you think SB 1070 represents good legislation? Why or why not?

2. How might you go about refuting the argument made by America's Voice Research on Immigration Reform?

What arguments would you make in response? How might you support those arguments? Write an essay refuting their claim using good support and sound reasoning.

website

prereading question } Should parents do more to monitor what their children see on television and in the movies?

Parents Television Council

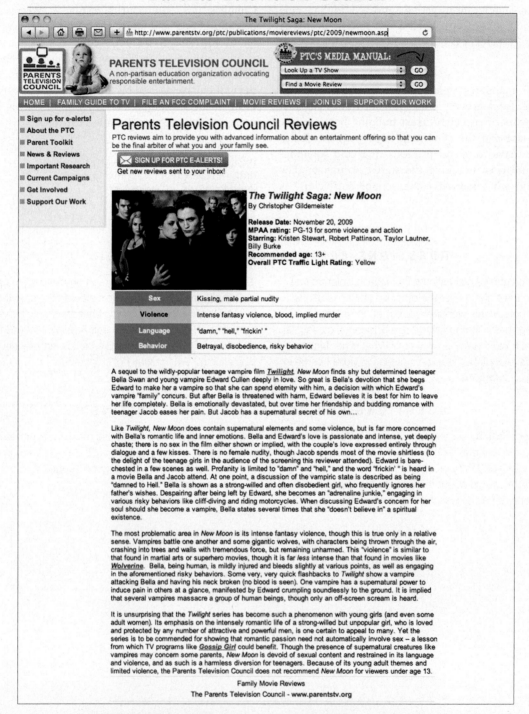

http://www.parentstv.org/ptc/publications/moviereviews/ptc/2009/newmoon.asp

PARENTS TELEVISION COUNCIL
A non-partisan education organization advocating responsible entertainment.

PTC'S MEDIA MANUAL:
Look Up a TV Show   GO
Find a Movie Review   GO

HOME | FAMILY GUIDE TO TV | FILE AN FCC COMPLAINT | MOVIE REVIEWS | JOIN US | SUPPORT OUR WORK

- Sign up for e-alerts!
- About the PTC
- Parent Toolkit
- News & Reviews
- Important Research
- Current Campaigns
- Get Involved
- Support Our Work

Parents Television Council Reviews

PTC reviews aim to provide you with advanced information about an entertainment offering so that you can be the final arbiter of what you and your family see.

SIGN UP FOR PTC E-ALERTS!
Get new reviews sent to your inbox!

The Twilight Saga: New Moon
By Christopher Gildemeister

Release Date: November 20, 2009
MPAA rating: PG-13 for some violence and action
Starring: Kristen Stewart, Robert Pattinson, Taylor Lautner, Billy Burke
Recommended age: 13+
Overall PTC Traffic Light Rating: Yellow

Sex	Kissing, male partial nudity
Violence	Intense fantasy violence, blood, implied murder
Language	"damn," "hell," "frickin' "
Behavior	Betrayal, disobedience, risky behavior

A sequel to the wildly-popular teenage vampire film *Twilight*, *New Moon* finds shy but determined teenager Bella Swan and young vampire Edward Cullen deeply in love. So great is Bella's devotion that she begs Edward to make her a vampire so that she can spend eternity with him, a decision with which Edward's vampire "family" concurs. But after Bella is threatened with harm, Edward believes it is best for him to leave her life completely. Bella is emotionally devastated, but over time her friendship and budding romance with teenager Jacob eases her pain. But Jacob has a supernatural secret of his own...

Like *Twilight*, *New Moon* does contain supernatural elements and some violence, but is far more concerned with Bella's romantic life and inner emotions. Bella and Edward's love is passionate and intense, yet deeply chaste; there is no sex in the film either shown or implied, with the couple's love expressed entirely through dialogue and a few kisses. There is no female nudity, though Jacob spends most of the movie shirtless (to the delight of the teenage girls in the audience of the screening this reviewer attended). Edward is bare-chested in a few scenes as well. Profanity is limited to "damn" and "hell," and the word 'frickin' " is heard in a movie Bella and Jacob attend. At one point, a discussion of the vampiric state is described as being "damned to Hell." Bella is shown as a strong-willed and often disobedient girl, who frequently ignores her father's wishes. Despairing after being left by Edward, she becomes an "adrenaline junkie," engaging in various risky behaviors like cliff-diving and riding motorcycles. When discussing Edward's concern for her soul should she become a vampire, Bella states several times that she "doesn't believe in" a spiritual existence.

The most problematic area in *New Moon* is its intense fantasy violence, though this is true only in a relative sense. Vampires battle one another and some gigantic wolves, with characters being thrown through the air, crashing into trees and walls with tremendous force, but remaining unharmed. This "violence" is similar to that found in martial arts or superhero movies, though it is far *less* intense than that found in movies like *Wolverine*. Bella, being human, is mildly injured and bleeds slightly at various points, as well as engaging in the aforementioned risky behaviors. Some very, very quick flashbacks to *Twilight* show a vampire attacking Bella and having his neck broken (no blood is seen). One vampire has a supernatural power to induce pain in others at a glance, manifested by Edward crumpling soundlessly to the ground. It is implied that several vampires massacre a group of human beings, though only an off-screen scream is heard.

It is unsurprising that the *Twilight* series has become such a phenomenon with young girls (and even some adult women). Its emphasis on the intensely romantic life of a strong-willed but unpopular girl, who is loved and protected by any number of attractive and powerful men, is one certain to appeal to many. Yet the series is to be commended for showing that romantic passion need not automatically involve sex – a lesson from which TV programs like *Gossip Girl* could benefit. Though the presence of supernatural creatures like vampires may concern some parents, *New Moon* is devoid of sexual content and restrained in its language and violence, and as such is a harmless diversion for teenagers. Because of its young adult themes and limited violence, the Parents Television Council does not recommend *New Moon* for viewers under age 13.

Family Movie Reviews
The Parents Television Council - www.parentstv.org

QUESTIONS FOR REASONING AND ANALYSIS

1. The author voices some concern over the "fantasy violence" in *New Moon*. In your view, can children readily distinguish between fantasy and real violence or any other aspect of a movie? Why or why not?

2. Reviews on this website assess movie or television content based on four different categories: sex, violence, language, and behavior. Do you agree with the use of these categories? Would you omit one or more of these categories? Would you add categories? Why or why not?

3. Based on the reasons given, do you agree with the reviewer's recommendation in the last paragraph? Why or why not?

1. Is monitoring what a child views on TV or in the movies a matter of parental responsibility or should government do more to restrict and regulate content? Why should it be one or the other?
2. Do you think people—and children, specifically—mimic or "copycat" what they see on TV and in movies in a way that becomes detrimental or unhealthy? Why or why not?
3. Peruse the other features of the Parents Television Council website. What is your reaction to its content? Do you agree or disagree with what the site is attempting to do? Why or why not?

statistical graphic

prereading question } **Does a causal relation exist between playing violent video games and exhibiting antisocial behaviors?**

Table of Data on Video Game Violence

This information appeared on the website of Procon.org, a nonprofit organization with no government affiliation. Procon.org provides resources for critical thinking and education.

Problem Behaviors and M-Rated Game Preferences: Boys

PROBLEM AREA	TYPE OF BEHAVIOR PREVIOUS 12 MONTHS	OVERALL PERCENTAGE OF BOYS INVOLVED IN BEHAVIOR	PERCENTAGE OF M-GAMERS	PERCENTAGE OF NON-M-GAMERS
AGGRESSION AND BULLYING	Been in a physical fight	44.4%	51%	28%**
	Hit or beat up someone	53.2%	60%	39%**
	Took part in bullying another student†	9.2%	10%	8%
DELINQUENT BEHAVIORS	Damaged property just for fun	18.6%	23%	10%**
	Got into trouble with the police	4.9%	6%	2%
	Stole something from a store	10.5%	13%	6%*
SCHOOL PROBLEMS	Got poor grades on a report card	31.6%	35%	23%**
	Skipped classes or school without an excuse	11.2%	13%	8%
	Got into trouble with teacher or principal	52.9%	60%	39%**
	Got suspended from school	20.1%	22%	15%
VICTIMIZATION	Been threatened or injured with a weapon	12.6%	15%	6%**
	Been bullied at school†	10.2%	8%	15%*

*Statistically significant difference within gender between m-gamers and non-m-gamers at the P<.05 level.

**Statistically significant difference within gender between m-gamers and non-m-gamers at the P<.01 level.

†This bullying occurred at school at least two to three times per month over the past few months: Olweus bully/victim questionnaire definitions.

Problem Behaviors and M-Rated Game Preferences: Girls

PROBLEM AREA	TYPE OF BEHAVIOR PREVIOUS 12 MONTHS	OVERALL PERCENTAGE OF GIRLS INVOLVED IN BEHAVIOR	PERCENTAGE OF M-GAMERS	PERCENTAGE OF NON-M-GAMERS
AGGRESSION AND BULLYING	Been in a physical fight	20.9%	40%	14%**
	Hit or beat up someone	34.5%	49%	29%**
	Took part in bullying another student†	4.4%	6%	4%
DELINQUENT BEHAVIORS	Damaged property just for fun	7.9%	15%	5%**
	Got into trouble with the police	1.8%	2%	2%
	Stole something from a store	9.8%	14%	8%
SCHOOL PROBLEMS	Got poor grades on a report card	23.7%	37%	20%**
	Skipped classes or school without an excuse	10.8%	20%	7%**
	Got into trouble with teacher or principal	35.5%	49%	31%**
	Got suspended from school	8.4%	16%	5%**
VICTIMIZATION	Been threatened or injured with a weapon	9.0%	14%	7%*
	Been bullied at school†	6.9%	8%	6%

*Statistically significant difference within gender between m-gamers and non-m-gamers at the P<.05 level.

**Statistically significant difference within gender between m-gamers and non-m-gamers at the P<.01 level.

†This bullying occurred at school at least two to three times per month over the past few months: Olweus bully/victim questionnaire definitions.

Lawrence Kutner, PhD, and Cheryl K. Olsen, ScD, *Grand Theft Childhood: The Surprising Truth about Violent Video Games and What Parents Can Do*, 2008. Courtesy of Cheryl K. Olson, ScD and Lawrence Kutner, PhD.

QUESTIONS FOR REASONING AND ANALYSIS

1. Do you see a significant difference between the results for boys and those for girls who play violent video games? If so, what are those differences and what might account for them? If not, then what might account for the lack of difference in the results?

2. Do you think all of these results are worth presenting? If so, why? If not, which results are not worth reporting upon and why?

3. Do you see any problems with the wording of categories (e.g., "Problem Area," "Type of Behavior")? Are some categories, for instance, worded in an overly vague or general way? If so, which ones? Do the categories accurately depict the type of behavior or problem area? Why or why not?

QUESTIONS FOR REFLECTING AND WRITING

1. The source from which this information was taken (Kutner and Olsen, 2008) clearly seeks to establish a causal relationship between violent video games and antisocial and/or violent behaviors. Do you agree that a causal relationship exists between the two? Why or why not?

2. If violent video games do not encourage violent behavior, then what are some other possible causes of such behavior in children and adolescents? What do you think society can do to address these causes?

Do Guns Provide Safety? At What Cost?

Puneet Narang, MD; Anubha Paladugu, MD; Sainath Reddy Manda, MD; William Smock, MD; Cynthia Gosnay, RN; Steven Lippmann, MD

The authors are members of the Department of Psychiatry, Hennepin County Medical Center and the Departments of Psychiatry and Emergency Medicine at the University of Louisville School of Medicine. This article appeared on Medscape.com on March 3, 2010.

Abstract and Introduction

ABSTRACT

Many people feel that having a gun provides greater safety for them and their family. Actually, having a firearm in the home escalates the risk for death or injury, while using it to shoot someone who endangers the household is much less common. The resultant injuries, deaths, emotional turmoil, and/or disabilities lead to greater utilization of health care and legal/police services. Payment for these expenses is provided by higher insurance premiums and tax rates. This financial aspect has become a part of our country's current political concern over firearm ownership rights, gun violence or regulation, health care costs, the economy, and taxes.

INTRODUCTION

Many Americans say, "I need a gun to protect my family and myself." But does owning a firearm really provide safety? Does the prevalence of firearms in the United States have any association with the fact that our health care system is the most expensive in the world?

There is controversy about whether gun possession actually enhances personal safety. There is also discussion about the degree to which gun violence is a factor in increased medical expenses. Cutting health care costs is a current national agenda; less gun-related violence should result in some savings. With medical insurance, taxes, and the economy being active political issues, a review of firearm-related violence and its costs is relevant.

DO GUNS PROVIDE SAFETY?

Gun use and regulations controlling them are important current issues. The Second Amendment to our Constitution states that, "A well regulated militia, being necessary to the security of a free state, the right of the people to keep and bear arms, shall not be infringed"; this remains a matter of active political debate. Some people think that this Amendment constitutes a citizen's right to gun ownership in America, while others believe that it does not guarantee easy firearm access to private individuals. Among some people there is a feeling that having a gun should diminish criminal activity since potential perpetrators are deterred from committing crimes when targeted victims may be armed. Others contend that they need weapons to protect themselves from the excesses of the government.

Access to guns affects the risk of death and firearm-related domestic violence.[1,2] The presence of such weapons have been associated in America with high rates of suicide, accidental injury, homicide, and domestic violence.[1] Suicide is the leading cause of death among gun owners in the initial years of acquisition. [3] Out of 395 fatalities occurring at a family home where a gun was present, suicide accounted for 333 cases (84%); 41 were domestic violence homicides, and 12 were accidents, while only nine were shootings of an intruder.[4] Presence of a firearm in the home reportedly results in death or injury to household members or visitors over 12 times more often than to an intruder. [5] Trauma centers receive many people with gunshot wounds said to be "accidents," but the circumstances in some of these cases seem to indicate that many of them initially were stress-related shootings, done originally with an intent to die.

Self-inflicted gunshot suicides outnumber both homicides and fatal accidents combined, and are the most common method of committing suicide.[1] According to the Kentucky Violent Death Reporting System (http://www.kvdrs.uky.edu), there were 541 gun-violence deaths in Kentucky during 2005. Gun shot suicides accounted for 375 (69%), homicides for 143, accidents for 11, police shootings for 9, and 3 were undetermined. In Kentucky, suicide continued in 2006 and 2007 to occur over twice as frequently as homicide and all other shooting deaths combined. Household firearm ownership is associated with elevated rates of shooting oneself.[6] This risk escalates not only for the owner, but also for suicides by family members or other people in the home.[7] Many of these shootings are impulsive acts; pre-existing psychopathology is not a consistently present cause.[8]

continued

DO GUNS MAKE OTHERS SAFE?

While there is a saying that, "guns don't kill, people do," firearms are the most commonly used weapon in domestic homicides, accounting for about 65% of all such deaths.[9] They increase the risk of intimate partner homicide by fivefold.[10,11] Having a gun in the home results in loss of life to women by suicide three times more often than where no such weapon was available.[11] In 2005, it was documented that 5,285 US children were killed by gunshots according to data collected over a full year time period by the Centers for Disease Control; compare this to none in Japan, 19 for Great Britain, 57 in Germany, 109 in France, and 153 in Canada.[12] During 2002, the Children's Defense Fund with the National Center for Health Statistics reported that 3,012 American children were killed in shootings and many more were injured.[12] Other sources agree, indicating that approximately 15 children or adolescents die from firearm-related causes every day in the United States.[13] Although, Child Access Prevention laws exist, they are not uniformly enacted; the intent is to require parents to store firearms safely and deny access to children, while maintaining adult availability.[14] Cases of domestic gun violence go beyond the actual event; as people who witness such tragedy exhibit higher levels of prolonged personal grief and dysfunction and higher suicidal risks than their peers.[15]

The consequences of gun-related violence, death, injury, disability, and/or dysfunction have a powerful impact on our society and health care system. Socially, it includes loss of loved ones, economic hardship, and psychological trauma to survivors. Bereavement compromises the quality of life after a shooting. This is especially true for children, even if they remain physically unharmed. Long-term adjustment problems often follow such traumas. When violent incidents occur in the community or if people generally feel threatened by consistent danger, it affects the whole population, thereby spreading the emotional pain. When young people repeatedly witness guns being used to deal with conflict, they adopt this form of problem solving. Medical expenses are affected as well, and this burden extends to the general population, governments, and the health care delivery system.

Guns have been utilized in assassinations of famous people, including several presidents. In America, guns are frequently used weapons in attacks on large numbers of people. The mass shooting at Virginia Tech in 2007 was initiated by a student who killed 32 individuals, wounded 24, and then committed suicide. This pattern of easy gun access, shooting others, and then oneself is tragically recurrent in our society. Easy access to firearms is well illustrated by the Virginia Tech incident. The shooter had a record which might not have passed the background check; according to the official report, he ordered his weapon over the Internet and picked it up at a pawn shop.[16] Beyond this, there are also fatalities during gang violence, criminal activities, drug procurements, interpersonal disagreements, law enforcement actions, or even random and accidental shootings. The sniper attacks in the Washington D.C. area during 2002 and the mass shootings of 2009 at Fort Hood, Texas are examples of the ongoing risk.

WHAT IS THE COST?

In 2005, approximately 30,000 Americans died of gunshots and nearly 70,000 received emergency treatment for nonfatal wounds.[17] Emergency facilities are constantly burdened by the services required in such traumatic events. Medical care for these patients costs up to $4 billion per year.[17] The overall economic cost due to these injuries in America, including health care, disability, unemployment, and other intangibles is about $100 billion per year.[17]

The case-to-fatality rate for gunshot trauma is 30%, which is much higher than for other injuries; for example, death occurs following a shooting 18 times more often than from motorcycle accidents.[17] Typically, hospital stays for firearm-injured people are in the range of nearly two weeks' duration and disability averages approximately half a year.[17] At a major Kentucky trauma center, medical care for gunshot victims in 2008 cost over $18 million, and charges for those needing admission averaged $43,000 per patient.[18] In Louisville, Kentucky, expenses for the uninsured gun-injury victims alone exceeded the allotment of moneys allocated for all indigent care medical costs for the entire community. Similar concerns occur throughout our country. Death has a lower monetary impact. Disabilities, secondary illness, grief, and prolonged dysfunction add to the societal costs. Even these high numbers do not account for family losses and reduced social or personal productivity.

Taxpayers often bear a large percentage of these financial burdens; thus this matter is a hot political topic nationally. In Kentucky in 2008, 73% of gunshot victims were uninsured, 10% were covered by governmental plans, and 17% were insured.[18] Nationally, data reported in 2001 documented that government programs pay for about 49% of this amount, 18% is covered by private insurance, and 33% by all other sources.[19] Past medical bills are reflected in future insurance rates.[2]

Gun violence costs about 2.4 billion dollars annually to the criminal justice system in America, which is almost equal to all other crimes put together.[19] Each homicide results in approximately $244,000 of incarceration expenses for our taxpayers. Indirect costs are high as well; for example, local governments across our country spend up to $100 million each year just on bulletproof vests.[19] Most of these bills are then passed on to the taxpayers.

REFERENCES

Centers for Disease Control and Prevention; National Center for Injury Prevention and Control. Web-based injury statistics query and reporting system (WISQARS) [online]. (2006) [cited February 8, 2006]. Available at: www.cdc.gov/ncipc/wisqars. Accessed July 24, 2009.

Lemaire J. The cost of firearm deaths in the United States: reduced life expectancy and increased insurance costs. J Risk Insur 2005;72:359–374.

Miller M, Hemenway D. Guns and suicide in the United States. N Engl J Med 2008;359:989–991.

Kellermann A. Guns for safety? Dream on Scalia. The Washington Post. June 29, 2008. Page B02. Available at: http://www.washingtonpost.com/wp-dyn/content/article/2008/06/27/AR2008062702864.html. Accessed July 24, 2009.

Kellermann A, Heron S. Firearms and family violence. Emerg Med Clin North Am 1999;17:699–716.

Miller M, Lippmann S, Azrael D, et al. Household firearm ownership and rates of suicide across the 50 United States. J Trauma 2007;62:1029–1035.

Wintemute J. Guns, fear, the constitution, and the public health. N Engl J Med 2008;358:1421–1424.

Miller M, Barber C, Azrael D, et al. Recent psychopathology, suicidal thoughts and suicide attempts in households with and without firearms: findings from the National Comorbidity Study Replication. Inj Prev 2009;15:183–187.

Karch D, Lubell K, Friday J, et al. Surveillance for violent death reporting system, 16 states, 2005. MMWR (mortality and morbidity weekly report): surveillance summaries. April 11, 2008;57(SS03):1–43, 45. Available at: http://www.cdc.gov/mmwr/preview/mmwrhtml/ss5703a1.htm. Accessed July 23, 2009.

Campbell J, Webster D, Koziol-McLain J, et al. Risk factors for femicide in abusive relationships: results from a multisite case control study. Am J Public Health 2003;93:1089–1097.

Bailey J, Kellermann A, Somes G, et al. Risk factors for violent death of women in the home. Arch Intern Med 1997;157:777–782.

Available at: http://www.neahin.org/programs/schoolsafety/gunsafety/State%20Fact%20Sheets/Kentucky.pdf. Accessed July 23, 2009.

Powell E, Sheehan K, Christoffel K. Firearm violence among youth: public health strategies for prevention. Ann Emerg Med 1996;28:204–212.

McClurg A. Child access prevention laws: a common sense approach to gun control. Presented at the St. Louis University Public Law Review Gun Control Symposium, St. Louis University, Missouri, 1999, pp 47.

Jouriles E, McDonald R, Norwood W, et al. Knives, guns, and interparent violence: relations with child behavior problems. J Fam Psychol 1998;12:178–194.

Giduck J, Chi W; Archangel Group, Ltd. An Evaluation and Assessment of the Law Enforcement Tactical Response to the Virginia Tech University Shootings of Monday, April 16, 2007. Colorado: Archangel Group 2008.

Cook P, Lawrence B, Ludwig J, et al. The medical costs of gunshot injuries in the United States. JAMA 1999;282:447–454.

University of Louisville School of Medicine. Gun Shot Wound Registry. Louisville, Kentucky, Department of Emergency Medicine, University of Louisville School of Medicine, 2008.

Cook P, Ludwig J. Gun violence: the real costs. JAMA 2001;286:605–607.

Davis K. Slowing the growth of health care costs—learning from international experience. N Engl J Med 2008;359:1751–1755.

http://www.medscape.com/viewarticle/717278

QUESTIONS FOR READING

1. According to the authors, what is the leading cause of death among gun owners in the initial years of acquisition?
2. What is the most commonly used weapon in domestic homicides?
3. Why do the authors say that Child Access Prevention laws fail to effectively protect children from gun violence?
4. According to the authors, how do guns, or access to guns, result in higher medical care costs?

QUESTIONS FOR REASONING AND ANALYSIS

1. What is the authors' overall claim or thesis? Do you agree with their claim? Why or why not?
2. Under the heading "What is the Cost?," a substantial amount of the authors' evidence includes statistics about gun violence and health care costs in the state of Kentucky. Would their argument become more compelling, and perhaps more credible, if their statistics were more nationally based? Why or why not?
3. Do you see these authors as credible? Why or why not? In what ways do they establish their ethos in this article?

QUESTIONS FOR REFLECTING AND WRITING

1. In light of the authors' argument, should U.S. citizens still be allowed to purchase and own guns? Why or why not?
2. What are some other likely causes of rising health care costs? Write an essay exploring other contributing factors to the rising cost of health care in the United States.

The Boondocks

Aaron McGruder

QUESTIONS FOR REASONING AND ANALYSIS

1. The boy in the second frame asks why "they" do not "go after gun manufacturers and gun dealers instead of people who make video games?" The character claims it does not make sense. What is the cartoonist saying in this frame about the causes of violent behavior?

2. What is the other character—in the third frame of this comic strip—implying when he says, "Who would you rather start a beef with—some nerd who makes video games or some dude with a warehouse full of AK-47s?" In a different sense, what is the cartoonist implying?

3. How would you explain the claim or thesis of this comic strip? In other words, what is the cartoonist attempting to argue?

QUESTIONS FOR REFLECTING AND WRITING

1. In your view, do media-related activities, like watching movies or playing videogames, contribute to the causes of violent behavior in society? Why or why not?

2. Those arguing that violent videogames contribute to violence in society basically assume that some people will most likely mimic behaviors they have seen acted out on screen (that is, "copycat" behavior). Is this warrant (implicit assumption) in their argument valid? Why or why not?

3. Do violent videogames contribute to any societal ills at all? Are videogames completely innocuous? Why or why not?

prereading question } Is American society suffering from an overall lack of civility?

Mall Riots: Why Are Some Americans Becoming Violent Shoppers?

Americans used to protest in the streets; now some have resorted to fighting each other in shopping malls. What happened?

Seth Sandronsky

Seth Sandronsky writes for Alternet.org, an online community and news magazine. This article was posted on February 11, 2010.

On Dec. 23 of last year, police narrowly averted a consumer uprising in suburban Sacramento, California, where over 1,000 people had gathered at a shopping mall and nearly sparked a riot. The cause of all this unrest was a pair of shoes. Every member of the angry horde was after the latest line of Nike Air Jordans, complete with a $175 price tag.

What is turning Americans into such violent consumers?

Al Sandine's new book, *The Taming of the American Crowd: From Stamp Riots to Shopping Sprees*, unpacks some of the history and sociology embedded in these bizarre modern consumer gatherings. Sandine focuses on three factors that spawned the U.S. shopping craze: Cars, freeways and suburbs. None of these economic touchstones rose to prominence without the others, and together, they laid the foundation for the wild U.S. culture of consumption we know today. And what a unique way of living it is: "Americans spend more time shopping than anyone else, three or four times as much as Europeans," Sandine writes.

Shopping is an activity we undertake alone amid throngs of strangers, an experience very similar to freeway driving, where we motor alongside hundreds of other unknown drivers. Both driving and shopping tend to be anti-cooperative. Each can foster aggression. Mall shopping induces behavior that Sandine dubs "competitive consumption," in which a "hard-won purchase becomes a trophy for valor in combat." It's easy to imagine the exultation of those rebuffed Sacramento shoppers returning a few days later to buy a pair of new Air Jordans. Sweet victory!

As with road rage, competitive shopping can be lethal. During the Black Friday shopping rush in 2008, a horde of Long Island, N.Y. Wal-Mart shoppers trampled security guard Jdimytai Damour to death in their rush to spend, spend, spend.

Throughout U.S. history, citizens used the street as a public space for ordinary people to express their grievances to the powers-that-be. But where is that public street as a site of class struggle now? The street has become a private thoroughfare, linking people to cars and roads. This nexus isolates citizens as atomized shoppers making their way to and from sprawling malls. The public space has become a realm of private aggression.

Wal-Mart and other major corporate importers of foreign-made goods reflect a trend in the U.S. workforce that contributes to our bizarre consumer culture. Over the past few decades, American employers have shifted much manufacturing work overseas. The reasons are simple: the "strong dollar" makes it cheaper for companies to pay workers in other countries, and weaker environmental and labor rules abroad help cut corporate expenses. Nike, which makes the Air Jordans that caused the Sacramento hubbub, was formerly a poster child for exploiting workers in nations like Indonesia. In the meantime, in the minds of Americans, the human labor that actually makes the products that stock the shelves of Wal-Mart and other U.S. retailers become faceless and nameless workers in far-off nations. What were once products that Americans associated with work and creativity have become mere units of consumption.

But trade policy is not the only factor that has changed U.S. consumption culture in the last 50 years. Today's crowds of consumers stand in stark contrast to mass gatherings from previous eras, when citizens gathered as agents of social change to protest injustice. Sandine mines this relevant past of often riotous behavior, from the Whiskey Rebellion to the Vietnam-era antiwar movement.

In the first decade of the 21st century, only a trickle of that activist crowd history remains. The nonviolent "Day Without Immigrants" saw migrant and native workers boycott and march on May Day 2006, taking to the streets to demand fair treatment of immi-

continued

grants. More recently, the Tea Party movement has held rallies in opposition to political threats both real and imagined. But the race-baiting and conspiracy theorizing that dominate Tea Party gatherings underscore the fringe nature of today's political crowds. Mobilized political activism is not mainstream behavior.

With the decline of protesting crowds, public space for Americans to gather and voice their collective aspirations has narrowed. In its place we see incidents like the thwarted rush to be the first to buy the newest new Air Jordans in Sacramento. That scene reveals a radical break with America's past, away from a cultural heritage spanning all the way from the raucous crowds of the colonial era through the turbulent 1960s.

Amid widespread job-destruction, the question of what it will take to make consuming crowds give way to protesting crowds looms large. This is more than an academic query. In 2010, market failure is our economy's new normal. Unemployment has doubled since the Great Recession began, but even as the labor market fails to provide employment opportunities to workers, Americans are not collectively demanding jobs as they did during the 1930s. Instead, today's labor force

is fighting amongst itself to be the first in line to purchase overpriced athletic shoes with an NBA superstar's brand.

For Sandine, intensifying economic inequality is putting U.S. democracy under serious pressure. Workers' real wages (what they can buy with their pay) have been stagnant for more than 30 years. At the same time, their economic productivity (output per-person for each labor hour) has boomed. But they have not reaped the benefits of their productivity gains. The problem has a solution, and it begins with individuals—but it doesn't end there.

"For the long and necessary struggle ahead to succeed, we will have to overcome the dispersive impulses of consumerism," Sandine writes. "Among other things, we will need to rehabilitate a tradition in which the physical assembly—again, the crowd—is not just an obstacle to the pursuit of private objectives but an agency of protest and much-needed change."

http://www.alternet.org/story/145614/mall_riots:_why_are_some_americans_becoming_violent_shoppers?page=entire

QUESTIONS FOR READING

1. What are the factors that created the U.S. shopping craze? According to the author, how did these factors create this craze?

2. How has the decline of "public space" contributed to Americans becoming violent consumers?

3. In citing Sandine, what problem does Sandronsky say is putting U.S. democracy under "serious pressure"?

QUESTIONS FOR REASONING AND ANALYSIS

1. What is Sandronsky's thesis? Do you agree or disagree with his argument? Why or why not?

2. What is the relationship between the "three factors that spawned the U.S. shopping craze" and consumerism? Have other factors contributed to consumerism? If so, what are those factors?

3. Why does Sandronsky use the Tea Party rallies and May Day 2006 examples in this article? What is he trying to show through use of these events?

QUESTIONS FOR REFLECTING AND WRITING

1. Reread and reflect upon the Sandine quotation that ends Sandronsky's piece. What is Sandine saying? In your own words, explain the quote from Sandine.

2. Do you agree that rampant consumerism represents a societal problem? Why or why not? Write an essay defending your position.

arguing about politics: the good, the bad, and the ugly

c h a p t e r 18

In early January 2011, a shooting in Tucson left six dead and several others severely wounded, including U.S. Representative Gabrielle Giffords of Arizona. The tragedy prompted some politicians and political pundits to question whether or not anti-immigration rhetoric had fueled this violence. The selections in this chapter address "the good, the bad, and the ugly" of American politics while exploring, in many instances, whether or not political discourse and rhetoric has come to lack civility–or even become "violent," as at least two authors describe it.

prereading questions

1. Has discourse in American politics become less civil in recent years?
2. Can rhetoric become "violent"? If so, in what way?
3. How do comic books reflect contemporary American politics?
4. What is the future of American politics?

websites related to this chapter's topic

PUBLIC DISCOURSE: ETHICS, LAW, AND THE COMMON GOOD (THE WITHERSPOON INSTITUTE)
www.thepublicdiscourse.com

AMERICAN RHETORIC
www.americanrhetoric.com

POLITIFACT.COM OF THE ST. PETERSBURG TIMES
www.politifact.com

magazine essay

prereading question } Does illegal immigration contribute to violent crime, particularly in the border regions?

Violent Rhetoric and Arizona Politics

Nathan Thornburgh

Nathan Thornburgh writes for *Time* magazine. This piece appeared on January 8, 2011.

Sometimes, rumors of violence beget actual violence. Saturday's mass shooting at a Safeway on North Oracle Road in Tucson, which killed six and left Democratic Congresswoman Gabrielle Giffords and others gravely wounded, may well be one of those occasions.

It's impossible to know this early what the motivations for the attack were. Was the alleged shooter—who has been identified as 22-year-old Tucsonan Jared Loughner—angry about immigration? Or perhaps another hot-button issue? YouTube videos ascribed to him bore the mark of mental illness—they were conspiratorial, unintelligible, espousing no particular cause—but no matter his mental state, his crime took place in an overheated political environment. Last March, at the height of the health care reform battle, Giffords' office was vandalized. She mentioned in an MSNBC interview that a Sarah Palin graphic had depicted her district in the crosshair of a gun sight. "They've got to

realize there are consequences to that," she said. "The rhetoric is incredibly heated." The corner next to her office had also become, she said, a popular spot for Tea Party protests.

As Pima County Sheriff Clarence Dupnik put it in an extraordinary and melancholic press conference after the shooting, "we have become the Mecca for prejudice and bigotry." He added that he's "not aware of any public officials who are not receiving threats."

Another shooting victim, a federal judge named John Roll, had been placed under 24-hour security in 2009 after ruling in favor of illegal immigrants in a high-profile case. It's unclear why he was at the supermarket event. But for almost a year now, Arizona's leaders have been grappling with anti-immigration sentiments, inflamed by reports of crossborder violence. National media attention, with its attendant voices of hysteria, only added to the churn. Pundits spoke gravely about a wave of violence, born in Mexico and now flooding Arizona. Arizona's two most famous politicians fueled the fury. Republican Senator John McCain, facing an unexpected reelection challenge from the right, ran a campaign obsessed with crossborder crime. And GOP Governor Jan Brewer, who invited the national spotlight by championing strict anti-illegal immigrant legislation, talked of beheadings in the desert.

The only problem with all this talk about a massive crossborder crime wave is that it wasn't true. Phoenix had not become one of the world's kidnapping capitals. Crime rates in Arizona had been steady or even fallen in some areas. There had been no beheadings in the desert. There were plenty of deaths there, but they were pathetic and meek tragedies: impoverished bordercrossers, abandoned by their heartless guides, dying of exposure and dehydration.

But the idea of a state under siege took hold. When I was on the border last year reporting on the murder of rancher Rob Krentz, I talked to many who sincerely believed that they were under attack. Krentz's murder was a terrible event, but it was an isolated event. The relatively small number of home invasions, holdups and other crimes deeply disturbed border communities, but only because they had been living in such calm for so long. Their crime rates still don't match most cities in the states.

The supermarket meet-and-greet where Giffords was shot was actually a testimony to just how safe southern Arizona is. As a press release from her office last week put it, "'Congress on Your Corner' allows residents of Arizona's 8th Congressional District to meet their congresswoman one-on-one and discuss with her any issue, concern or problem involving the federal government."

Not exactly the kind of event a politician would hold in a war zone.

It's true that Giffords was not a fan of the state's anti-immigration bill SB1070, but there were higher-profile opponents, such as her fellow Congressional Representative in Tuscon, Raul Grijalva. Yet the idea that Arizona is under attack has been pushed hard enough that it's very possible that the coward who shot her (in the head, according to a Tucson paper) believed that the 40-year-old Democrat, who had been tarred by some as soft on immigration because she didn't support SB1070, was contributing to larger-scale violence against Arizonans.

If that is the case, it would only add to the tragedy. The fact is, that among all the overwrought promises and all the panic I heard last summer in Arizona, I found that Giffords was one of the few politicians offering concrete law enforcement steps that would actually work against the drug cartels and other smugglers. It's not just that she fought for more money and police for border protection, although she did that. She cosponsored legislation last year with a California Republican that aimed to give law enforcement important new tools in cracking down on the cash cards that were a favored method of money-laundering. It was one of the many sensible, pragmatic ideas she had for cracking down on crime.

Whatever dark fantasies drove someone to try to take her life, Giffords is a sensible politician who was likely shot because she dealt with Arizona's reality, not its rumors.

http://www.time.com/time/nation/article/0,8599,2041408,00.html

QUESTIONS FOR READING

1. How did YouTube videos depict Jared Loughner?
2. According to the author, what was the problem with talk about a massive crossborder crime wave?
3. What legislation did Giffords cosponsor with a California Republican?

QUESTIONS FOR REASONING AND ANALYSIS

1. What question is Thornburgh asking in this piece? How is he using this question to argue a thesis?
2. Why do you think Thornburgh mentions the murder of Rob Krentz? How is the author refuting an argument by citing this incident?
3. What does Thornburgh mean by the last sentence of this article?

QUESTIONS FOR REFLECTING AND WRITING

1. Do you agree or disagree with Thornburgh's arguments in the article? Write an essay either defending Thornburgh's position or refuting his stance on the immigration issue in Arizona.
2. Does illegal immigration contribute to violent crime? Why or why not? Conduct research on the Internet and/or in the library to learn more about the relationship between illegal immigration and violent crime in the United States.
3. How should the United States address the immigration issue? Should the government do even more to curb illegal immigration? Why or why not?

Conservatives for America

This picture appeared in 2011 on a web page of the Conservatives for America, an Internet site devoted to politically conservative themes.

QUESTIONS FOR REASONING AND ANALYSIS

1. What point is being made by this image?
2. Why do you think the three stooges were chosen to characterize President Obama, Representative Feinstein, and Senator Reid?

3. Do you think it is fair to depict these political leaders in this way? Why or why not?

QUESTIONS FOR REFLECTING AND WRITING

1. Write a response to this image. Do you agree or disagree with its premise? Why or why not?

2. Has the U.S. government been engaged in effective policy-making in recent years? Why or why not?

What is "Violent Rhetoric"?

Scott Eric Kaufman

Scott Eric Kaufman made this post to the Lawyersgunsmoney blog on January 10, 2011. Kaufman earned a PhD in English from the University of California at Irvine in 2008.

As someone who teaches rhetoric, I can only say that I've been profoundly disappointed in the quality of the conversation about the assassination attempt on Gabrielle Giffords. Despite all the condemnation of everyone else's "violent rhetoric," I've yet to see one post in which the term itself is defined. It seems to mean, in the current political vernacular, anything said by someone else that involves anything even remotely violent. Katrina Trinko's attempt to *tu quoque* Keith Olbermann is particularly enlightening, as it describes a number of angry statements by Olbermann that are neither violent nor rhetorical, *e.g.*

> In 2007, Olbermann called rival network Fox News "worse than al-Qaeda ... for our society" and said the channel was "as dangerous as the Ku Klux Klan ever was."

Neither of those statements are rhetorical because neither of them attempts to call its audience to action. For them to be rhetorical, as per Aristotle in *On Rhetoric*, they would need to be intended to *persuade*. Moreover, they would need to be intended to persuade *a particular audience* to undertake a particular action. This is the rhetorical triangle:

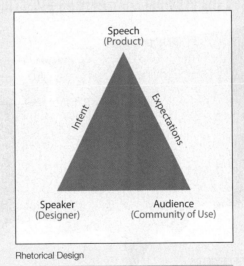

Rhetorical Design

Note the interconnectedness of the speaker and audience. The general problem with discussing rhetoric in the current media environment is that the particularity of the audience is absent. Anyone can read or watch or listen to anything without regard for their relation to the intended audience and without reference to the action whose commission the rhetor intends. In such a situation, it is not surprising when the mode of persuasion favored by speakers is the one that is most effectively general. To quote Aristotle again:

> The first [mode of persuasion] depends on the personal character of the speaker [*ethos*]; the second on putting the audience into a certain frame of mind [*pathos*]; the third on the proof, or apparent proof, provided by the words of the speech itself [*logos*].

continued

Though *pathos* is typically translated as an "appeal to emotion," it is better understood as an "appeal to imagination." Anything that stokes the imagination, be it an image or a narrative, fits the bill. It goes without saying that the majority of political rhetoric in America is, in this technical sense, pathetic. This is simply because most politicians have questionable *ethos* and very few have speechwriters sufficiently talented to produce persuasive *logos*. But it is also because most Americans are too suspicious of political motives to allow politicians to establish an ethos and too untrained in the literary arts to understand an appeal to *logos*.

Typically, then, we are left in a situation in which politicians, as rhetors, design speeches whose *pathos* is general enough to appeal to as wide an audience as possible. It stands to reason that if we want to understand what "violent rhetoric" entails, we must focus on whose images and stories are stoking whose imaginations and *to what effect*. Pointing out that Keith Olbermann associated Fox News with terrorist organizations foreign and domestic does nothing of the sort because the audience and intended effect of his statements is unclear. How unclear?

If we posit his intended audience is liberals and leftists who believe President Obama is a centrist—which strikes me as a fairly accurate assessment—then we need to ask what the intended effect *on that particular audience* of associating Fox News with al-Qaeda would be. Keeping in mind that we are currently at war with al-Qaeda, are we to believe that Olbermann is encouraging liberals and leftists to join a military-like organization and wage an Afghanistan-type offensive against Fox News? Given that his audience is composed of people who are, generally speaking, opposed to war, does that make any sense? Or is it more likely that he is simply attempting to create an association of like-with-like in which the likeness is supremely unflattering? His rhetoric here is pathetic and inflammatory, but from the perspective of what it is intended to persuade its audience, it is also incoherent. It can't be considered "violent" because it in no way encourages its audience to have its imagination stoked by reference to violence.

Consider a slightly more infamous example:

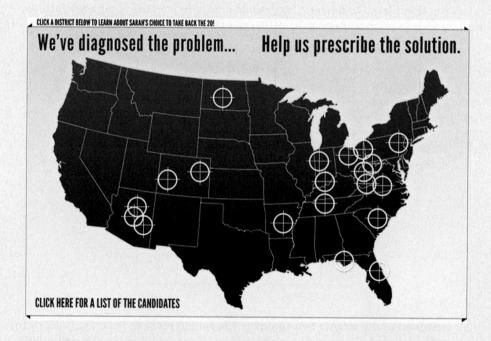

Here the intended audience is those who believe President Obama is a radical leftist and associates itself with the center-right. Unlike the audience of liberals and leftists, who oppose war and favor a restrictive interpretation of the Second Amendment, this audience is more hawkish and more likely to support an expansive interpretation of the Second Amendment. I would contend that this is an example of "violent rhetoric" not because it contains crosshairs aimed at "the candidates" who represent "the problem" in need of "solution," and despite the fact that talking about "solving" human beings has a rather untoward history, but because its violence is a product of whose imaginations are being stoked and how it is being done.

The intended effect of this image is *not* to encourage the assassination of candidates; however, the pathetic appeal being made to this particular audience is certainly intended to stoke their imaginations in ways related to their ideological belief in an expansive interpretation of the Second Amendment. This rhetoric is violent, then, because it was intended to appeal to an audience whose imaginations would be stoked by a reference to shooting things. The same cannot be said of this similar map:

Why not? Are bullseye that different from crosshairs? Of course not. However, the intended audience is: the imaginations of liberals and leftists who support a restrictive interpretation of the Second Amendment are not stoked by images of bullseyes. They generally have no pathetic investment in crossbows and so appeals of this sort are less likely to be effective than those like the one above. In terms of rhetoric, then, only the first of these two maps can be designated as "violent" because only it attempts to persuade its audience into action by stoking imaginations by referencing shooting things.*

So now that we have something resembling a proper working definition of "violent rhetoric," the next question is whether "violent rhetoric" like Palin's is responsible for the assassination attempt on Gifford. The answer is that I'm not convinced.** From what I've read, he never expressed interest in guns until last November, so the likelihood of ads like hers stoking his imagination is slim. The more pernicious rhetoric here is the conspiratorial variety being mainstreamed by the likes of Glenn Beck: rabid and ahistorical anti-federalism feeds into the beliefs of those who believe they're being persecuted by vast faceless conspiracies.

---

*I suppose one possible objection is that shooting is not, in and of itself, a violent act, but given that it specifically links the crosshairs to candidates, I think that would be a difficult argument to make here.

**That said, I do believe whichever party was responsible for the dismantling of the mental health system—generally in the 1980s and more recently in Arizona—and consistently lobbies for fewer restrictions on the purchasing of powerful weaponry is partly culpable for what happened on Saturday.

http://www.lawyersgunsmoneyblog.com/2011/01/what-is-violent-rhetoric

QUESTIONS FOR READING

1. According to Kaufman, why are Keith Olbermann's statements not rhetorical?
2. How does the author characterize most political rhetoric in America?

3. According to Kaufman, how is the crosshairs map an example of "violent rhetoric"?
4. Who does Kaufman say is "partly culpable" for the tragedy in Arizona?

QUESTIONS FOR REASONING AND ANALYSIS

1. What role does "imagination" play in political rhetoric?
2. Does Kaufman's use of visuals aid him in making an effective written argument? Why or why not?

3. What major examples does Kaufman use in making his argument? Does Kaufman choose good examples to illustrate his point? Why or why not?

1. Do you agree with Kaufman's claim that American political rhetoric is "pathetic"? Why or why not?
2. How would you improve the quality of political rhetoric in America? Write an essay explaining what steps you would take to improve rhetoric and political discourse in this country.

drawing/illustration

prereading question } **Do visual arguments like these contribute to good political discourse?**

The first image on the left appeared as part of The Sundries Shack, a blog managed by Jimmie Bise, Jr., on August 3, 2009. The other set of images was shown on The Contemporary Condition, a blog that addresses current political issues, on January 13, 2011.

QUESTIONS FOR REASONING AND ANALYSIS

1. What does the image of President Obama communicate? What do the respective images of Glenn Beck, Sarah Palin, and Bill O'Reilly communicate?
2. Why do you think these particular color patterns were chosen for the images (shades of red, blue, and black)?
3. Why were the words "fear," "ignorance," and "intimidation" chosen for Beck, Palin, and O'Reilly respectively?

QUESTIONS FOR REFLECTING AND WRITING

1. What do these images suggest about the nature of American political discourse? Do you agree or disagree with the approach? Why or why not?
2. Has American political discourse become too dumbed down? Why or why not?

Text of President Obama's Tucson Memorial Speech

Posted by CBS Interactive staff

On January 12, 2011, President Obama gave the following remarks during the memorial service for those who died in the Tucson shooting. CBS News posted the speech on its website.

To the families of those we've lost; to all who called them friends; to the students of this university, the public servants gathered tonight, and the people of Tucson and Arizona: I have come here tonight as an American who, like all Americans, kneels to pray with you today, and will stand by you tomorrow.

There is nothing I can say that will fill the sudden hole torn in your hearts. But know this: the hopes of a nation are here tonight. We mourn with you for the fallen. We join you in your grief. And we add our faith to yours that Representative Gabrielle Giffords and the other living victims of this tragedy pull through.

As Scripture tells us:

There is a river whose streams make glad the city
*   of God,*
the holy place where the Most High dwells.
God is within her, she will not fall;
God will help her at break of day.

On Saturday morning, Gabby, her staff, and many of her constituents gathered outside a supermarket to exercise their right to peaceful assembly and free speech. They were fulfilling a central tenet of the democracy envisioned by our founders—representatives of the people answering to their constituents, so as to carry their concerns to our nation's capital. Gabby called it "Congress on Your Corner"—just an updated version of government of and by and for the people.

That is the quintessentially American scene that was shattered by a gunman's bullets. And the six people who lost their lives on Saturday—they too represented what is best in America.

Judge John Roll served our legal system for nearly 40 years. A graduate of this university and its law school, Judge Roll was recommended for the federal bench by John McCain twenty years ago, appointed by President George H.W. Bush, and rose to become Arizona's chief federal judge. His colleagues described him as the hardest-working judge within the Ninth Circuit. He was on his way back from attending Mass, as he did every day, when he decided to stop by and say hi to his Representative. John is survived by his loving wife, Maureen, his three sons, and his five grandchildren.

George and Dorothy Morris—"Dot" to her friends—were high school sweethearts who got married and had two daughters. They did everything together, traveling the open road in their RV, enjoying what their friends called a 50-year honeymoon. Saturday morning, they went by the Safeway to hear what their Congresswoman had to say. When gunfire rang out, George, a former Marine, instinctively tried to shield his wife. Both were shot. Dot passed away.

A New Jersey native, Phyllis Schneck retired to Tucson to beat the snow. But in the summer, she would return East, where her world revolved around her 3 children, 7 grandchildren, and 2 year-old great-granddaughter. A gifted quilter, she'd often work under her favorite tree, or sometimes sew aprons with the logos of the Jets and the Giants to give out at the church where she volunteered. A Republican, she took a liking to Gabby, and wanted to get to know her better.

Dorwan and Mavy Stoddard grew up in Tucson together—about seventy years ago. They moved apart and started their own respective families, but after both were widowed they found their way back here, to, as one of Mavy's daughters put it, "be boyfriend and girlfriend again." When they weren't out on the road in their motor home, you could find them just up the road, helping folks in need at the Mountain Avenue Church of Christ. A retired construction worker, Dorwan spent his spare time fixing up the church along with their dog, Tux. His final act of selflessness was to dive on top of his wife, sacrificing his life for hers.

Everything Gabe Zimmerman did, he did with passion—but his true passion was people. As Gabby's outreach director, he made the cares of thousands of her constituents his own, seeing to it that seniors got the Medicare benefits they had earned, that veterans got the medals and care they deserved, that government was working for ordinary folks. He died doing what he loved—talking with people and seeing how he could help. Gabe is survived by his parents, Ross and Emily, his brother, Ben, and his fiancé, Kelly, who he planned to marry next year.

And then there is nine year-old Christina Taylor Green. Christina was an A student, a dancer, a gymnast,

continued

and a swimmer. She often proclaimed that she wanted to be the first woman to play in the major leagues, and as the only girl on her Little League team, no one put it past her. She showed an appreciation for life uncommon for a girl her age, and would remind her mother, "We are so blessed. We have the best life." And she'd pay those blessings back by participating in a charity that helped children who were less fortunate.

Our hearts are broken by their sudden passing. Our hearts are broken—and yet, our hearts also have reason for fullness.

Our hearts are full of hope and thanks for the 13 Americans who survived the shooting, including the congresswoman many of them went to see on Saturday. I have just come from the University Medical Center, just a mile from here, where our friend Gabby courageously fights to recover even as we speak. And I can tell you this—she knows we're here and she knows we love her and she knows that we will be rooting for her throughout what will be a difficult journey.

And our hearts are full of gratitude for those who saved others. We are grateful for Daniel Hernandez, a volunteer in Gabby's office who ran through the chaos to minister to his boss, tending to her wounds to keep her alive. We are grateful for the men who tackled the gunman as he stopped to reload. We are grateful for a petite 61 year-old, Patricia Maisch, who wrestled away the killer's ammunition, undoubtedly saving some lives. And we are grateful for the doctors and nurses and emergency medics who worked wonders to heal those who'd been hurt.

These men and women remind us that heroism is found not only on the fields of battle. They remind us that heroism does not require special training or physical strength. Heroism is here, all around us, in the hearts of so many of our fellow citizens, just waiting to be summoned—as it was on Saturday morning.

Their actions, their selflessness, also pose a challenge to each of us. It raises the question of what, beyond the prayers and expressions of concern, is required of us going forward. How can we honor the fallen? How can we be true to their memory?

You see, when a tragedy like this strikes, it is part of our nature to demand explanations—to try to impose some order on the chaos, and make sense out of that which seems senseless. Already we've seen a national conversation commence, not only about the motivations behind these killings, but about everything from the merits of gun safety laws to the adequacy of our mental health systems. Much of this process, of debating what might be done to prevent such tragedies in the future, is an essential ingredient in our exercise of self-government.

But at a time when our discourse has become so sharply polarized—at a time when we are far too eager to lay the blame for all that ails the world at the feet of those who think differently than we do—it's important for us to pause for a moment and make sure that we are talking with each other in a way that heals, not a way that wounds.

Scripture tells us that there is evil in the world, and that terrible things happen for reasons that defy human understanding. In the words of Job, "when I looked for light, then came darkness." Bad things happen, and we must guard against simple explanations in the aftermath.

For the truth is that none of us can know exactly what triggered this vicious attack. None of us can know with any certainty what might have stopped those shots from being fired, or what thoughts lurked in the inner recesses of a violent man's mind.

So yes, we must examine all the facts behind this tragedy. We cannot and will not be passive in the face of such violence. We should be willing to challenge old assumptions in order to lessen the prospects of violence in the future.

But what we can't do is use this tragedy as one more occasion to turn on one another. As we discuss these issues, let each of us do so with a good dose of humility. Rather than pointing fingers or assigning blame, let us use this occasion to expand our moral imaginations, to listen to each other more carefully, to sharpen our instincts for empathy, and remind ourselves of all the ways our hopes and dreams are bound together.

After all, that's what most of us do when we lose someone in our family—especially if the loss is unexpected. We're shaken from our routines, and forced to look inward. We reflect on the past. Did we spend enough time with an aging parent, we wonder. Did we express our gratitude for all the sacrifices they made for us? Did we tell a spouse just how desperately we loved them, not just once in awhile but every single day?

So sudden loss causes us to look backward—but it also forces us to look forward, to reflect on the present and the future, on the manner in which we live our lives and nurture our relationships with those who are still with us. We may ask ourselves if we've shown enough kindness and generosity and compassion to the people in our lives. Perhaps we question whether we are doing right by our children, or our community, and whether our priorities are in order. We recognize our own mortality, and are reminded that in the fleeting time we have on this earth, what matters is not wealth, or status, or power, or fame—but rather, how well we have loved, and what small part we have played in bettering the lives of others.

That process of reflection, of making sure we align our values with our actions—that, I believe, is what a tragedy like this requires. For those who were harmed, those who were killed—they are part of our family, an American family 300 million strong. We may not have known them personally, but we surely see ourselves in them. In George and Dot, in Dorwan and Mavy, we sense the abiding love we have for our own husbands, our own wives, our own life partners. Phyllis—she's our mom or grandma; Gabe our brother or son. In Judge Roll, we recognize not only a man who prized his family and doing his job well, but also a man who embodied America's fidelity to the law. In Gabby, we see a reflection of our public spiritedness, that desire to participate in that sometimes frustrating, sometimes contentious, but always necessary and never-ending process to form a more perfect union.

And in Christina…in Christina we see all of our children. So curious, so trusting, so energetic and full of magic.

So deserving of our love.

And so deserving of our good example. If this tragedy prompts reflection and debate, as it should, let's make sure it's worthy of those we have lost. Let's make sure it's not on the usual plane of politics and point scoring and pettiness that drifts away with the next news cycle.

The loss of these wonderful people should make everyone of us strive to be better in our private lives—to be better friends and neighbors, co-workers and parents. And if, as has been discussed in recent days, their deaths help usher in more civility in our public discourse, let's remember that it is not because a simple lack of civility caused this tragedy, but rather because only a more civil and honest public discourse can help us face up to our challenges as a nation, in a way that would make them proud. It should be because we want to live up to the example of public servants like John Roll and Gabby Giffords, who knew first and foremost that we are all Americans, and that we can question each other's ideas without questioning each other's love of country, and that our task, working together, is to constantly widen the circle of our concern so that we bequeath the American dream to future generations.

I believe we can be better. Those who died here, those who saved lives here—they help me believe. We may not be able to stop all evil in the world, but I know that how we treat one another is entirely up to us. I believe that for all our imperfections, we are full of decency and goodness, and that the forces that divide us are not as strong as those that unite us.

That's what I believe, in part because that's what a child like Christina Taylor Green believed. Imagine: here was a young girl who was just becoming aware of our democracy; just beginning to understand the obligations of citizenship; just starting to glimpse the fact that someday she too might play a part in shaping her nation's future. She had been elected to her student council; she saw public service as something exciting, something hopeful. She was off to meet her congresswoman, someone she was sure was good and important and might be a role model. She saw all this through the eyes of a child, undimmed by the cynicism or vitriol that we adults all too often just take for granted.

I want us to live up to her expectations. I want our democracy to be as good as she imagined it. All of us—we should do everything we can to make sure this country lives up to our children's expectations.

Christina was given to us on September 11th, 2001, one of 50 babies born that day to be pictured in a book called "Faces of Hope." On either side of her photo in that book were simple wishes for a child's life. "I hope you help those in need," read one. "I hope you know all of the words to the National Anthem and sing it with your hand over your heart. I hope you jump in rain puddles."

If there are rain puddles in heaven, Christina is jumping in them today. And here on Earth, we place our hands over our hearts, and commit ourselves as Americans to forging a country that is forever worthy of her gentle, happy spirit.

May God bless and keep those we've lost in restful and eternal peace. May He love and watch over the survivors. And may He bless the United States of America.

QUESTIONS FOR READING

1. How does President Obama characterize those who lost their lives?

2. What does Obama say about the way in which Americans should talk to each other about this tragedy?

3. According to Obama, what can a more civil and honest public discourse achieve?

QUESTIONS FOR REASONING AND ANALYSIS

1. How would you explain the thesis of Obama's speech?

2. How is debating what might be done to prevent future tragedies an "essential ingredient in our exercise of self-government"?

3. Which of Obama's words or stylistic choices are particularly noteworthy for you? Why?

1. If you were asked to give remarks at this service, would you choose the same themes as Obama? Why or why not? If not, which themes would you highlight?
2. One could say that Obama's speech calls for civility in public discourse, but it also represents an example of such discourse. What is civil public discourse? How can Americans achieve such discourse?

website essay

prereading question } Do comic-book movies reveal something about the twenty-first-century political landscape?

The Politics of Superheroes

Want a map of the debates of the early 21st century? Watch a comic-book movie.

Jesse Walker

Jesse Walker is the managing editor of Reason.com and the author of *Rebels on the Air: An Alternative History of Radio in America* from NYU Press. This article was taken from the May 2009 issue of Reason.com.

On April 28, 2005, Spider-Man, Captain America, and Defense Secretary Donald Rumsfeld flexed their muscles onstage at the Pentagon. The trio was promoting *The New Avengers*, a comic book being sent to soldiers around the world. The effort was part of America Supports You, a program that in time would be exposed for misspending its money on self-promotion rather than boosting morale, with at least $9.2 million "inappropriately transferred."

The stench of the scandal stuck to several former Pentagon employees, but the superheroes emerged unscathed. In the January issue of *The Amazing Spider-Man*, Spidey and Barack Obama teamed up to defeat a supervillain's Inauguration Day plot. At the end, the incoming president called the webslinger "partner" and gave him a friendly fist bump, with nary a reference to Peter Parker's previous work with the Bush administration.

Future historians can offer a more complete account of how costumed crusaders came to dominate Hollywood in the early 21st century. But one factor that has to be acknowledged is the superhero film's philosophical flexibility. As comic-book crimefighters found a mass audience at the multiplex, they displayed an almost unerring ability to invoke important issues without clearly coming down on one side or the other. There are many reasons why Peter Parker's alter ego can both strike poses with Rumsfeld and bump fists with Obama. But surely one of them is that Republicans and Democrats alike see their worldviews reflected onscreen when Spider-Man—and Batman, and Iron Man, and others—battle bad guys.

A decade ago, most of those Republicans and Democrats wouldn't have cared. In the 1990s, superhero films weren't just fewer. They were aimed, with only a handful of exceptions, at a cult audience. A movie like Mark Dippé's *Spawn* (1997) might do fairly well commercially, making nearly $55 million at home and over $87 million around the world, but it was easy for the average American not to notice it. Today, by contrast, it's hard to avoid contact with Batman or Spider-Man, or even with more obscure vigilantes, such as the hero of James McTeigue's *V for Vendetta* (2006).

In three of the last seven years, the most popular picture in America has centered around a superhero. In the other four years, at least one specimen of the genre made the box office top 10. Several of those movies, notably Sam Raimi's *Spider-Man 2* (2004) and Christopher Nolan's *The Dark Knight* (2008), have been critical as well as commercial successes, and even widely derided efforts such as Ang Lee's *Hulk* (2003) and Tim Story's *Fantastic Four* (2005) attracted some highbrow defenders. The trend is mature enough to have unleashed a new wave of hybrids and parodies, from the relationship comedy *My Super Ex-Girlfriend* (2006) to the *Airplane!*-style farce *Superhero Movie* (2008). A popular 40-minute Internet video, *Dr. Horrible's Sing-Along Blog* (2008), manages to combine the conventions of the superhero film, the romantic comedy, the classical tragedy, the musical, and the vlog.

Not all of these movies are ambivalent about their worldviews. *V for Vendetta*, for example, turned a politically charged comic with a deliberately enigmatic outlook into a straightforwardly sympathetic tale of a rebellion against a right-wing regime. More often, though, the opposite occurs: A film genre that critics frequently deride for seeing the world in black and white is actually ambiguous about war, privacy, empire, and state power. It took this form as Americans, often derided for the exact same reason, grew increasingly ambivalent about the very same subjects.

The boom arguably began with Bryan Singer's *X-Men*, a surprise hit in the summer of 2000. But it reached its present resonance with the first major superhero film to appear after 9/11, Sam Raimi's *Spider-Man* (2002). This was not, at first glance, a particularly political picture. The movie's most obvious metaphor involves masturbation, not the Middle East. (The adolescent Peter Parker finds his body changing in mysterious ways, including the ability to eject a gooey substance with his hands.) Still, *Spider-Man*'s message, borrowed directly from the original comic and enunciated by Parker's doomed Uncle Ben, had ideological overtones: "With great power comes great responsibility." That was enough for several hawks to declare the webslinger a spiritual cousin. The conservative cultural critic Mark Steyn would eventually argue that Spidey's first film "makes a very good case for the Bush pre-emption doctrine" because "the men who killed his Uncle Ben were small-time crooks Peter could have stopped earlier but chose not to."

Spider-Man was mostly made before 9/11, with the producers withdrawing a trailer right after the attacks because it featured the World Trade Center. If the narrative echoed our wartime debates, that was probably an accident. But when *Spider-Man 2* appeared in 2004, its political elements were more deliberate and more conspicuous. They were also more complicated—or, if you prefer, more confused.

This time around, Parker attempts to retire from vigilantism. Crime jumps, the press that had been denouncing Spider-Man as a criminal starts wailing that he's nowhere to be found, and every hawk in the audience nods his head with recognition: Why, Spider-Man is just like America! Writing in *The Spectator*, Steyn called the movie an "antidote to the stunted paranoia of *Fahrenheit 9/11*," noting that "Peter recognizes that the bad stuff doesn't go away just because you refuse to acknowledge it." In *National Review*, David Frum pronounced the picture "the great pro-Bush movie of the summer."

And they were right, sort of, except that the story also included the tale of Doctor Octopus, a scientist whose well-intentioned mucking about nearly destroys New York. He can't face the fact that he has miscalculated, so he plunges back into the same destructive project. If you come to the cinema searching for symbols, it's hard to escape the idea that Doc Ock's dangerous fusion generator represents empire and the mechanical arms that come to control him are a stand-in for the military-industrial complex. Hard to escape it, that is, unless the movie's other allegories have transfixed you. (Steyn, for example, merely notes that Spidey's antagonist is "a peace-loving man of science." Viewers not obsessed with politics were probably still fixated on the semen symbolism: This time around, when Parker starts to feel impotent, he loses the ability to shoot webs.)

Spider-Man 3 (2007), also directed by Raimi, introduces two more villains to the series. One is Venom, an alien that initially appears as a crude black liquid. The other is a figure called the Sandman. Of all the characters the writers could recycle from the comics, they picked the embodiments of oil and sand.

For a while, the oil infects Parker, who consequently becomes arrogant, homicidal, and driven by revenge—a motive, his Aunt May sagely informs us, that can "turn us into something that we're not." To save himself, he has to shake the addiction and forgive his enemies. A more leftist fable can hardly be imagined, except that Spidey then goes to war against an oil-and-sand alliance, pausing briefly before an enormous American flag before swinging in to save the day. And then, just when you're hoping the politics would resolve themselves one way or the other, everything collapses in a heap of Christ imagery. Our metaphors have gotten muddled again.

Of all the superhero movies released since 9/11, Jon Favreau's *Iron Man* (2008) engages American foreign policy most directly. In its very first scene, soldiers ferry Tony Stark, an engineering genius and wealthy munitions manufacturer, through Afghanistan. Terrorists attack the convoy and kidnap Stark. The last thing he sees before he passes out is one of the weapons used in the assault. It has a Stark Industries logo on it.

After escaping, Stark announces that he cannot abide the thought that his output is being used against U.S. soldiers, and he pledges to shut down weapons production. As the company's stock plunges, Stark starts work on a secret new project built around a compact and powerful reactor. You might initially suspect he's working on a way to, say, bring cheap energy to the world. Nope: He's building an Iron Man costume, which he promptly uses on a secret rescue mission in Afghanistan. Eventually we learn that his father's old business partner, Obadiah Stane, has been selling Stark's weapons to the enemy, allowing Iron Man to take out the traitor and return to his previous partnership with the American government.

continued

In *Human Events*, the conservative writer Martin Sieff certified the story as "a celebration of what's great about American capitalism" and suggested that the flick has "done more in two weeks for America's image around the world than seven and a half years of plodding, hapless bureaucratic bungling by the Bush administration." *New York*, on the other hand, presented the movie as "an action magnet for liberals," with critic David Edelstein describing a plot in which "the military-industrial complex ravages the Third World." The most perceptive comment on the picture's politics came from Sonny Bunch in *The Weekly Standard*, who called Favreau's feature "the film equivalent of a Rorschach test. If you go into *Iron Man* seeking right-wing imagery, you'll find it: Tony Stark is a patriot, pro-military, and likes unilateral intervention. If you go into *Iron Man* looking for left-wing imagery, you'll find that, too: The true villain here is Stane, representing an out-of-control military-industrial complex."

If anything, Bunch understates what an inkblot this picture is. When Tony Stark is captured by terrorists using his own weapons, it's a concise artistic depiction of blowback, the idea that American power exercised abroad boomerangs back against Americans. Even the Iron Man outfit, a smart weapon that allows Stark to target the enemy while leaving innocent bystanders standing, grows dangerous when it inspires Obadiah Stane to build a similar suit of his own. (Both *Iron Man* and *Spider-Man 3* climax with the heroes battling villains who are, in effect, evil versions of themselves.) On the other hand, fixing the system seems to be a simple matter of eliminating one well-placed crook. Without Stane in the picture, the film gives us no reason to suspect that our power will ever backfire or that our weapons will end up in the wrong people's hands. It's an outlook that lends itself to either a liberal Obama fantasy, in which reform is a simple matter of changing the people in charge, or an equally dubious conservative narrative in which it is only treason on the home front that thwarts our victory abroad.

And if that's hard to parse, look at what Bruce Wayne's been up to.

Batman Begins (2005), directed and co-written by the ex-arthouse auteur Christopher Nolan, is an epic of ambiguity. The Spider-Man and Iron Man films sometimes feel like their creators were reaching for resonant images and ideas without pondering just how they fit together. Nolan's pictures, by contrast, never seem to escape their creator's control. They give every impression of making a coherent argument, just not one easily reducible to one side in a rerun of *Crossfire*.

If you're making a vigilante movie, it's a fair bet that some critic is going to describe it as "fascist." That's harder to do where *Batman Begins* is concerned, since the villains here are fascists themselves—or, more exactly, they espouse the fascist doctrine that societies must be violently cleansed of decadence. (The actual operation of a totalitarian state is beyond their interests.) Their secret society, the League of Shadows, trains Wayne in the Japanese art of Ninja warfare in a hidden camp located, confusingly, in China.

Like many of the major superheroes, Wayne is an orphan. The film paints his father as a liberal urban leader whose vision for Gotham City bears little resemblance to the crime and disorder that have settled in instead. The senior Wayne's signature accomplishment was an elevated train system—in his words, "a new, cheap public transportation system to unite the city. And at the center, Wayne Tower." As Bruce Wayne becomes Batman, the movie puts him at an exact midpoint between the semi-fascist misanthropy of the League and the liberal optimism of his father. Batman is a product of both and a duplicate of neither; his very existence suggests that two seemingly opposed worldviews might actually have something in common. The idea is symbolically reinforced at the end of the film: To kill the villain, the hero must also destroy the physical embodiment of his father's idealism, the elevated train.

The sequel, last year's *The Dark Knight*, sets up an even more complex system of opposites that sometimes seem to be doubles and doubles that sometimes seem to be opposites. Along with Wayne's costumed hero, we have copycat Batmen who share neither his skills nor his scruples. Wayne himself wants to retire from vigilantism, and he puts his hopes in Harvey Dent, a crusading straight-arrow district attorney; Dent later loses his mind and becomes Two-Face, a villain with a visage that's half handsome, half deformed. The film's chief antagonist, the Joker, sets out to prove that everyone can be corrupted, driving Dent to madness and provoking Batman to create an elaborate surveillance system covering the entire city—a temporary, necessary evil, the hero insists.

In a film filled with hard moral decisions, the harshest one arrives when the Joker wires two ferries with explosives. One is filled with convicts, the other with ordinary travelers; each is given the power to destroy the other ship; each is told that if they don't detonate the other boat before midnight, the Joker will destroy both vessels. In a film where neither public official nor superhero can completely resist the abuse of power, the people on those ferries, criminals included, find themselves unable to kill even to save their own lives. It's the closest *The Dark Knight* comes to optimism, and it's the real rebuttal to the Joker's claim that everyone is always corruptible.

That barely begins to scratch the surface of the movie's moral nuances. Nearly every decision in the story is a tragic choice, with unfortunate effects either way. Nonetheless, several critics praised or damned *The Dark Knight* as a simple brief for Bushism. In a notorious *Wall Street Journal* essay, the crime novelist Andrew

Klavan declared: "Like W, Batman is vilified and despised for confronting terrorists in the only terms they understand. Like W, Batman sometimes has to push the boundaries of civil rights to deal with an emergency, certain that he will re-establish those boundaries when the emergency is past." In one bizarre passage, Klavan complains that in other films, "the good guys become indistinguishable from the bad guys, and we end up denigrating the very heroes who defend us"—as though *The Dark Knight* doesn't beat us over the head with the idea that men attempting to do good are capable of unleashing evil. Klavan's take has caught on among some critics, but you could as easily come away from the movie agreeing with the liberal blogger Dymaxion-WorldJohn, who argued that "Batman has, in many ways, been a disaster for Gotham, and what Gotham needs isn't a hero in tights but better law enforcement." Or if not better law enforcement, then more chances for people like the civilians on the ferries to let their inner decency overcome their inner decay.

As the Bush years give way to the Obama era, there will be no shortage of superheroes at the cineplex. Both *Iron Man 2* and *Spider-Man 4* are in the works, and an-other Batman picture will surely appear as well. There will be more sequels starring the X-Men and the Hulk, and there will be new franchises featuring Captain Marvel and the Sub-Mariner. With *Watchmen*, Zack Snyder's adaptation of Alan Moore's acclaimed graphic novel, we've already seen one major superhero movie on Obama's watch. The film is overstylized and under-satisfying, but it preserves its source's central theme of the limits and dangers of power. It is also, like the comic that inspired it, open to more than one political reading.

No one knows how the genre will adapt to the changes in Washington. But despite the comic-book Spidey's easy partnership with the president, you shouldn't expect Hollywood's superheroes simply to fall in behind the new guy. It didn't take long for public doubts about Bush to be reflected on screen, and there was a time when the 43rd president was more popular than Obama is now. Superhero stories may have begun as power fantasies, but it is our ambivalence about power that keeps the modern genre thriving.

http://reason.com/archives/2009/05/05/the-politics-of-superheroes

QUESTIONS FOR READING

1. In what comic book did President Obama appear?
2. According to Walker, why would Republicans and Democrats not have cared about comic-book movies a decade ago?
3. Which comic-book movie engages American foreign policy most directly?
4. How does *The Dark Knight* set up a "complex system of opposites," according to Walker?

QUESTIONS FOR REASONING AND ANALYSIS

1. Why do you think Walker begins with the story about the America Supports You scandal?
2. What does Walker mean by the last statement of his article: "Superhero stories may have begun as power fantasies, but it is our ambivalence about power that keeps the modern genre thriving"?
3. How would you describe Walker's attitude toward Andrew Klavan's take on *The Dark Knight*? Why would you describe it in this way?

QUESTIONS FOR REFLECTING AND WRITING

1. Choose one or two scenes from one of your favorite comic-book movies and write an analysis. Why do you see these scenes as significant?
2. Do you agree with Walker's notion that comic-book movies reflect the contemporary political climate or current political debates? Why or why not?
3. Why do you think American culture has become so focused on superheroes in recent years?

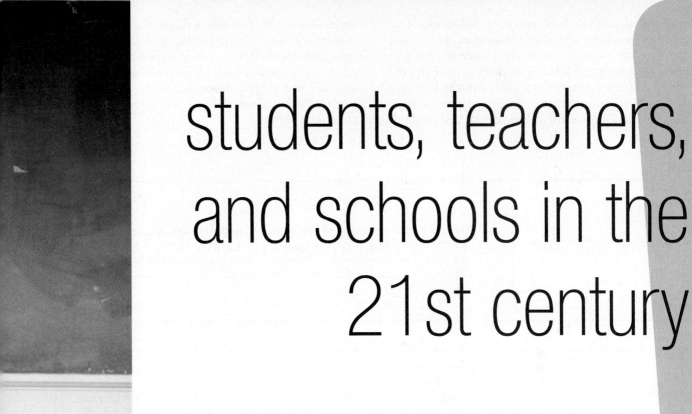

students, teachers, and schools in the 21st century

chapter 19

Issues in education reflect numerous and serious concerns for teachers, school administrators, politicians, and, last but not least, parents and students. The federal government and state legislatures as well as local school districts constantly struggle with the best way to finance schools and educational programs and, at the same time, constantly deliberate the best methods for evaluating teacher job performance and assessing student learning. The examples in this chapter highlight those challenges, revealing different sides of arguments over quality and fairness of our educational system. On a slightly different note, however, the last two readings address the new and connected issue of the digital library.

prereading question

> The topics of these selections are connected to one another and to the questions about U.S. education in general. Think about each author's particular argument, but also reflect on the ways that each one contributes to the larger debate about quality and fairness in America's schools.

websites related to this chapter's topic

U.S. DEPARTMENT OF EDUCATION
www.ed.gov
This government site contains links to many resources on educational issues.

AMERICAN FEDERATION OF TEACHERS
www.aft.org
This union's site contains many resources and links. Go to their higher education page for resources on college issues, including distance learning.

PRESIDENT OBAMA'S AGENDA FOR EDUCATION
www.whitehouse.gov/issues/education
This web page explains President Barack Obama's agenda for education.

website

prereading question } **What do you think is the most significant problem U.S. education faces today?**

National Education Association

The National Education Association (NEA) boasts a membership of 3.2 million with affiliate organizations in every state and in over 14,000 communities across the United States. Its major goal is to advance public education at every level (preschool through graduate education).

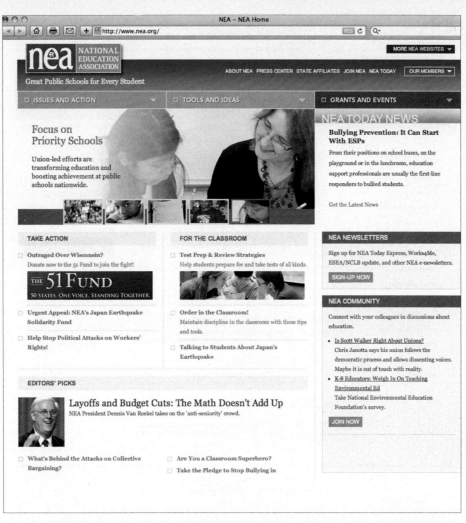

© Copyright 2002–2009 National Education Association. Reprinted with permission from nea.org.

QUESTIONS FOR REASONING AND ANALYSIS

1. What do you find persuasive and compelling about the NEA home page? Why do you find certain features more compelling than others?

2. Under the "Take Action on NCLB" page, what is the major argument or claim? Are adequate reasons given to support the claim? Why or why not? If so, what are those reasons?

3. Overall, do you think the site (these layers, specifically) depends more upon emotional or logical appeal? Why? How has the association attempted to establish credibility for audiences?

QUESTIONS FOR REFLECTING AND WRITING

1. Conduct some additional research on the No Child Left Behind (NCLB) Act. What are the provisions of this legislation? In your view, is the NCLB Act a solid piece of legislation? Why or why not?

2. What should be the priorities of the U.S. educational system? Why should the system set these priorities as priorities per se?

3. How would you improve education in your home state? What actions would you take and why?

Daryl Caglel

This cartoon originally appeared on MSNBC.com.

© 2007 Daryl Cagle and PoliticalCartoons.com.

QUESTIONS FOR REASONING AND ANALYSIS

1. In your view, what is the cartoonist's point?
2. How would you describe the character applying for the job? Is it significant that the cartoonist has depicted the character in a certain way? Why or why not?

3. Would the cartoon communicate the point more effectively if a college admissions officer was interviewing the high school graduate? How so? If not, why not?

QUESTIONS FOR REFLECTING AND WRITING

1. Many claim that high school teachers are required all too often to "teach to the test." As a person who recently graduated from high school, do you see that claim as valid? Why?
2. If high school teachers do "teach to the test," then why is their doing so problematic, assuming that

standardized tests effectively assess a student's basic skills and competencies? Are standardized tests an accurate measure, in your view? Why or why not?

3. How would you assess and evaluate students' mastery of skills and concepts in high school? Why would you choose one particular assessment over another?

Gary Varvel

This cartoon appeared in the Union Leader.com on May 2, 2006 ("State of Education" section).

By permission of Gary Varvel and Creators Syndicate, Inc.

QUESTIONS FOR REASONING AND ANALYSIS

1. In your own words, what is the cartoonist's thesis or claim?
2. With whom are the parents in the cartoon meeting? A teacher or a principal? What evidence suggests one over the other? Is the identity of the character important? Why or why not?
3. The cartoonist suggests something about emphasis on athletics, but more specifically, do you think the cartoonist is suggesting something about funding for schools? If so, what is the cartoonist trying to say? What evidence or reasoning from the cartoon supports the idea that the cartoonist is making a statement about the allocation of funds in schools (that is, the way schools and school districts spend money)?

QUESTIONS FOR REFLECTING AND WRITING

1. Is a strong emphasis on athletics in public schools contrary to a school's academic mission? Do you agree with what this cartoon implies about the relationship between the two? Why or why not?
2. In many instances, public school teachers must express a willingness to coach athletics to fulfill job expectations regardless of whether or not they wish to do so. Does it make sense to hire teachers more for their ability or willingness to coach athletics rather than for their ability or willingness to teach a subject? Why or why not?
3. How might schools achieve a better balance between supporting athletic programs and stressing academics?

prereading question } **What can be done to improve math and science education in the United States?**

America's Failing Education System

Michael Chang

Michael Chang is a contributor for Splice Today, a "web magazine featuring idiosyncratic writing and visual presentation on topics of interest and concern to an audience that values perspective over popularity" (Splice Today website). This article was posted on July 22, 2010.

Is the problem in fact poor teacher training in math and science?

Take a step back in time to your high school days. Whether feathered hair and Led Zeppelin albums characterized your adolescence or it was American Idol and the Dave Matthews Band, we can all remember the long locker-lined hallways buzzing with hormone-induced teen drama. It's a relatively carefree time where we begin to form identities and engage in culture and society: what's to hate, right? However, our national curriculum has become outdated, and the inadequacies in the secondary school system have had long-run adverse effects on our workforce.

The United States has long been known for the highest skilled workers earning the highest wages in the world. This is a legacy that finds it[s] roots in the embedded free-market ideal that lies at the core of the American system, but it's burdened by the inevitable stress and anxiety of capitalist competition. Most recently, this stress has taken the form of job insecurity due to outsourcing and the rapid technological advance that has taken place in the past 20 years. That hardworking Americans fear losing their job to outsourcing is not an indication that domestic corporations are foreign biased, but rather reflects an inability of our workforce to adapt to the needs of an ever-advancing workplace.

A study carried out in 2003 showed that American students placed well above the world average on standardized testing coming out of the fourth grade, but by the end of eighth grade they had fallen to the average, and by high school graduation were well below this point. What is happening in the years before graduation that causes our students to perform poorly compared to their international competition? The answer lies in the arcane way that we train teachers, especially in math and science.

In the past two decades, the American system has become strained; reflecting an inability of our workforce to fully meet the increasing skill requirements of an economy whose GDP is becoming more conceptual. The inability to compete in the global environment is a result of the complacency that has gripped our education system. Math and basic computing skills are a practical requirement in order to operate productively in the modern computer-driven service sector, but our students seem to be lacking in both these analytical areas.

Almost 40 percent of high school math teachers have neither a college major nor minor in math. This problem stems from the dilemma most math scholars face when graduating college; there are many lucrative opportunities for workers with math and computing skills, but far fewer opportunities of similar payoff for those versed in the humanities. This creates a shortage of qualified math teachers because many choose to pursue a higher-paying job rather than teach, an opportunity that is much harder to come by for a history or English major. The ultimate result is that American children learn math from unqualified teachers, hindering their ability to get a job in the new global market.

The manner in which we educate our students is hurting the productive potential of workers, but it has also caused one of the greatest concentrations of wealth at the upper rungs of the income ladder that this country has seen in the past century. For the past 20 years the incomes of skilled workers have risen more than the average, whereas increases in unskilled incomes were flat. This is due to the surplus of less skilled workers that our secondary schools are producing.

The modern workplace has seen the creation of a privileged native-born elite of skilled workers whose inflated incomes are supported by both immigration quotas on skilled labor and the inability of schools to produce a competitive environment. Corporate managers identify the lack of skilled workers as a huge problem and are willing to bid up pay packages in order to acquire them. If we are to continue to maintain our position as global arbiter, we will either have to open barriers to foreign skilled workers in order to stimulate wage competition at the top of the income ladder, or undertake education reform on a large scale.

http://www.splicetoday.com/on-campus/america-s-failing-education-system

QUESTIONS FOR READING

1. What problem does Chang explain in the first paragraph?
2. According to Chang, what results from the stress and anxiety of capitalist competition?
3. What has caused students to perform poorly in math and science as compared to their international competition?

QUESTIONS FOR REASONING AND ANALYSIS

1. What is Chang's thesis?
2. How does Chang's piece reflect a problem-solution organizational pattern?
3. Why do you think Chang chose to begin this essay by asking the audience to "take a step back in time" to their high school days? Was this approach an effective one for opening the essay? Why or why not?
4. What does Chang mean by the term "arcane" at the end of the third paragraph?
5. Overall, do you agree or disagree with his argument? Why or why not?

QUESTIONS FOR REFLECTING AND WRITING

1. How can the United States educate and train a more skilled workforce for the twenty-first century? Write an essay exploring the different ways in which this country might better educate students to compete in a global economy.
2. Think back to your own high-school experience. Did you receive a good education in science and math? A good education overall? Why or why not?
3. Do teachers today lack necessary qualifications to be in the classroom? How so? If not, what would you do to train teachers more effectively?

---

newspaper editorial

prereading question } **Does a weakening education system detrimentally affect national security?**

America's Security Put in Peril by Our Failing Education System

Michael Reagan

Michael Reagan is the son of Ronald Reagan, president of the United States from 1981 until 1989. The *San Francisco Examiner* published this editorial on March 14, 2010.

Today, Washington is so focused on expanding the size and influence of our federal government at the expense of taxpayers that they are overlooking one of the greatest security risks facing our nation—our failing education system.

Our broken education system is failing America's children while countries around the world, our own global competitors, are making dramatic strides in educating their future work forces.

The consequences to this failure cannot be underestimated. A 2007 study from Columbia University revealed the scope of the consequences of simply failing to earn a high school diploma.

High school graduates are healthier and more productive. They are far less likely to be dependent on government social services. In tax dollars alone, a high school diploma translates into upwards of $150,000 in the lifetime contribution of one person.

Looking at the results coming out of our current education system, I cannot help but be deeply alarmed. As detailed in the *New York Times*, Congress heard testimony this week from education experts on the state, national, and international level as part of the culmination of a yearlong effort by state leaders to establish new academic standards.

The personal and economic benefits from a strong education system are clear. The moment we can no longer keep up, we will have surrendered our national prosperity and security.

Our country now faces a decision regarding the proposed standards, which encompass achievement goals in English and math from kindergarten through 12th grade. I am pleased that governors and local educators took the lead on his project, but we must walk a careful line as we move forward in establishing protocols for our education.

So long as federal taxpayer money goes to schools across the country, the government is right to demand accountability. But when federal control threatens to stifle the creativity and productivity of our local schools, we must step back and return power to our communities.

Our children's future, our country's future, must never be a political pawn in the government's all-too-familiar gambit for more control.

http://www.sfexaminer.com/node/85911

QUESTIONS FOR READING

1. What did the 2007 Columbia University study reveal?
2. According to Reagan, what must the federal government not threaten to stifle?
3. What is Reagan's ultimate concern by the end of the piece?

QUESTIONS FOR REASONING AND ANALYSIS

1. Do you agree or disagree with Reagan's argument? Why or why not?
2. Does Reagan ever really say how the United States surrenders its "national prosperity and security" by failing to strengthen its educational system? How might a weakening educational system hinder prosperity and security?

QUESTIONS FOR REFLECTING AND WRITING

1. What entity should exercise the most control over education and education reform? The federal government, the states, or the local school districts? Why one over the other two?
2. Research and review the "proposed standards" that Reagan mentions in this editorial. What is your opinion of these standards? Do they represent effective measures? Why or why not?

---

magazine essay

prereading question } **How should we fund education in the United States?**

Education Funding: Follow the Money
How tax deals short schools, and what you can do about it.

Cynthia Kopkowski McCabe

Cynthia Kopkowski McCabe writes for the *NEA Today*. This article appeared in the January/February 2009 issue of that publication.

Every day in this country, big businesses are getting a sweetheart deal paid for by our public school children. And no, we're not talking high-interest lunch money loans.

It's common practice in most states and municipalities to let businesses off the hook for paying taxes, in the vague hope of stimulating economic development. But that practice regularly shortchanges the schools where you work and send your children. Maybe *shortchanges* isn't the best term, actually. Try *shortbillions*. Over the past 20 years, the percentage of profits corporations paid in state and local taxes dropped 50 percent. Have your taxes gone down 50 percent in the last 20 years? Didn't think so.

Yet, after decades of watching such incentives weaken the financial footing of the nation's schools, many peo-

continued

ple still don't understand the relationship between tax breaks and things like class size and salaries. "We have a wonderful antenna that goes up when we hear a politician talk about public schools and testing and pay and pensions," says NEA Vice President Lily Eskelsen. "We need that same antenna to start vibrating when we hear a politician talk about economic development."

Here's how it works: A large corporation comes to state legislators, county commissioners, or city council members and offers to set up shop in their area, creating jobs and boosting the local economy. In exchange, they ask for tax breaks. Lots of them. Well-meaning government officials agree, seeing the business's arrival as the quickest way to spur development in the area. The problem is that many of these deals spell years of lost tax revenues.

"People don't see the other side of it," says Bruce Nissen, the director of research at the Center for Labor Research and Studies at Florida International University. "Tax cuts mean cuts to necessary services from government." Taxes not paid by the corporation can hit local residents twice: Their local schools are shorted and, on top of that, local governments are forced to shift the tax obligation to residents to stanch the bleeding.

Add this to the growing list of things about which educators now have to be concerned, knowledgeable, and energized. But what's the solution to this tax break bonanza? That would be "TEF," an economic theory whose acronym is shorthand for tax structure, economic development policies, and funding for schools. Essentially, TEF is a call for fair taxation—both personal and corporate—and economic development that invests in education, rather than cripples it.

Right now, the nation's schools are at the mercy of misguided policies around these three elements, says Associate Project Director Michael Kahn of NEA Research. "Unfortunately, these things have been going in the wrong direction for the last 30 years." (If you're wondering about the multi-billion-dollar bailouts for the banking and credit industries, that's a separate issue, says Dawn Addy, director of the Center for Labor Research and Studies. "We're talking about money that goes directly into the community and certainly that's different from giving buyouts to the big guys.")

Let's look at personal taxation first. American workers on average pay $12 in taxes for every $100 they earn. Anyone making more than $1 million annually pays only $5 out of every $100. "We can't achieve adequate schools if the tax responsibility is being shifted to those who have the least amount of money," says Kahn.

Unfair economic development is just as troublesome. Consider Sykes Enterprises, Inc., a call center company. In 1999, the company located in Pikeville, Kentucky, after the local government gave it a multimillion-dollar package that included a five-year pass on property tax, which would have helped fund schools. In 2004, the company shuttered the facility and eliminated 324 jobs.

Similar stories come from Colorado, Oregon, North Dakota, Kansas, Nebraska, Minnesota, and Florida. Nationwide, state tax subsidies, cuts, incentives, and abatements offered to businesses and corporations have an annual price tag of more than $50 billion. Michigan alone estimates its state and local giveaways hover around $929 million annually. Decades ago, education activists didn't pay much attention to these tax breaks, NEA's Eskelsen says. "Now we've all seen what can happen to school dollars when some slick snake oil salesman with a PowerPoint presentation talks about economic development," she says. (Oddly enough, these companies examine the quality of the local schools—the same schools that any tax breaks they might get would end up hurting—as they mull whether to locate their employees there.)

And nowhere are the current failed system's misplaced priorities more apparent than school funding. In recent years, District of Columbia taxpayers footed a $611 million bill for a new stadium for the Washington Nationals baseball team. That amount of money could have built 61 brand new elementary schools, 36 middle schools, or 32 high schools, or refurbished hundreds of crumbling facilities in the District.

As the country's economy continues to stumble, TEF proponents want local and state leaders to understand that a country's fiscal health is directly related to a fair and equitable tax system, a level economic development playing field for large and small businesses, and adequate and equitable funding for public education. The underlying premise is simple: In the new global, knowledge-based economy, investing in public education—our human capital—provides a greater return on investment than tax cuts and subsidies for big business and sports stadiums.

Included in these TEF proponents are members of the Mississippi Association of Educators. After watching for years as businesses came into the state and received deals that let them escape local taxes for as long as a decade in some cases, state and local Association leaders began fighting back. Why? Cuts to school supplies and equipment, eroding facilities that had no relief coming in the form of repairs or renovations, ballooning class sizes, stagnant salaries, and staff layoffs. When it was finally time for the corporations to start paying their taxes, "they would up and leave," says Frank Yates, the Association's executive director. Nobody is anti-business, Yates says. "The idea here now is that yes, we want the local governments to recruit economic development, but they need to pay their fair share of taxes, otherwise the local citizens have to have their taxes raised," to pay for essential services like schools and educator salaries and pensions, he says.

With the help of NEA, the Mississippi affiliate trained 25 members and UniServ directors to talk to colleagues, parents, and others about the importance of supporting fair taxation and economic development, and increased school funding. They're heading out into their communities, holding forums and giving people "a true picture of our economic future," says Yates.

David Odom, a high school algebra teacher in DeSoto County, Mississippi, is a member of that team. He travels the state in his free time, explaining in cafeterias and church halls how, in some cases, educators pay a higher percentage of their salaries in taxes than big businesses do. Adding insult to injury, they're then forced to dig into their own pockets to pay for essential supplies when schools don't get the money they need. "If these businesses were paying their fair share, we wouldn't have that problem," Odom says. "Most people don't realize what is actually going on. You get mad when you do."

There is hope on the horizon. Efforts like Odom's and similar ones in other states are paying off as con-cern about corporate tax breaks is starting to take root among the general public. A study this fall by the Wisconsin Education Association Council found that nearly seven out of 10 voters think changes are needed in school funding, and a majority strongly favor eliminating corporate tax loopholes. "Public opinion is very much in tune with our beliefs," says Council President Mary Bell. "We need a better school funding system—one that is accountable to the people who pay for it and depend on it."

But it can't be just a handful of states that tackle big business opportunism and the legislators who enable it. Grassroots activists are needed across the country to point out how educators and students are being hurt by unfair taxes, underfunded schools, and corrosive economic development. And there's no better spokesperson to talk with parents, community members, and legislators about the damage being done in schools than the very people on the frontlines. "In order for TEF to work," says Odom, "everyone needs to get on the bandwagon."

www.nea.org/home/20750.htm

QUESTIONS FOR READING

1. How much have corporate taxes on profits dropped in the last 20 years?

2. According to McCabe, what is the overall effect on schools of corporate tax breaks or cuts?

3. What is TEF? What are its goals?

QUESTIONS FOR REASONING AND ANALYSIS

1. How would you summarize McCabe's thesis or claim in this article?

2. Consider the argument McCabe makes in these sentences: "Let's look at personal taxation first. American workers on average pay $12 in taxes for every $100 they earn. Anyone making more than $1 million annually pays only $5 out of every $100. 'We can't achieve adequate schools if the tax responsibility is being shifted to those who have the least amount of money,' says Kahn." What is the warrant, or implicit assumption, linking her evidence to the claim here?

3. What are some examples of logical appeal from this article? Why are these appeals logical rather than emotional?

4. How might McCabe's essay reflect a problem-solution argument?

5. Has McCabe made a convincing case? Why or why not?

QUESTIONS FOR REFLECTING AND WRITING

1. If you were to post a comment in response to McCabe, what would you say? Would you defend corporate tax breaks? Why or why not?

2. In one paragraph, McCabe claims that the District of Columbia spent $611 million of taxpayer money to build a new baseball stadium. She argues that a trade-off occurred; in other words, the District could have spent that money on infrastructure for schools. What argument can one make in response? What reasons might defend the District's decision to build a new baseball stadium?

3. What is your answer to the problem of funding public education? Higher corporate taxes? Measures to encourage economic development? Budget cuts for other programs?

Standards-Based Accountability's High Stakes

Ronald A. Wolk

Ronald A. Wolk is the founder and former editor of *Education Week* and the author of *Wasting Minds: Why Our Education System Is Failing and What We Can Do About It*. This article appeared March 9, 2011, in *Education Week*.

Through the 1980s and 1990s, the mantra of the school reform movement was "all children can learn." This sentiment was in perfect harmony with our nation's long-standing commitment to universal education—the promise that every child would have the opportunity to be educated to the level of his or her ability.

By any measure, our education system has failed to keep that promise. Although the evidence is abundant and well known, and so need not be detailed here, consider three indisputable facts that capture the essence of the system's failure.

First: The National Assessment of Educational Progress, or NAEP, has reported for decades that an average of three out of 10 seniors score "proficient" or above in reading, writing, math, and science, and their scores generally decline as they move from the 4th grade to the 12th grade.

Second: Of every 100 students who start the 9th grade, about 30 drop out, and, according to recent studies, another 35 or so graduate without being adequately prepared either for college or the modern workplace. That means that about 65 percent of the nation's young people are not being adequately educated.

Third: The brunt of the failure falls on poor and minority children, who are on the wrong side of an unyielding achievement gap. It is no coincidence that the gap is between white and most minority students. More than half of all African-American, Hispanic, and Native American students reach the 9th grade without being able to score proficient on reading and math tests. These students are more likely to fail the high-stakes tests and to drop out. They are least likely to attend college, and, if they do, they are most likely to leave without a degree.

To assume that these students fail because of "the soft bigotry of low expectations," as President George W. Bush suggested in making the case for the No Child Left Behind Act, is preposterous. Their failure is due to the hard bigotry that generations of these kids have suffered. And high common standards won't rectify that. Indeed, they divert attention away from the real problem by creating the illusion that things will improve if students and teachers are held to even higher standards.

If that were even close to being true, how do we explain that nearly 30 years of unprecedented effort and enormous expenditures has not improved student performance, reduced the dropout rate, or closed the achievement gap?

I am convinced we have made little or no progress in improving education because we misdiagnosed the problem at the outset and, consequently, our efforts to improve student performance have been seriously off course.

That misdiagnosis arrived in April 1983 with the publication of *A Nation at Risk*, the report of a federal commission that stunned the nation. Its major assumption was that our schools were essentially sound and that student performance had declined because we lowered our standards. To improve, we would need to raise academic standards and establish more-rigorous requirements for high school graduation and college admission. That recommendation placed the highest priority on standards and testing.

"Why is it necessary to increase the use of testing when we know from years of previous testing what the results will be?"

After a flurry of publicity, most federal commission reports vanish with little or no lasting effect. Not this one. The reform movement's course was set. And standards-based accountability has been the dominant strategy of the school reform movement ever since.

But the strategy produced few gains. And now the response of the states is to adopt common-core curricular standards that are to be aligned with common tests being created with $362 million in federal grants.

Why is it necessary to increase the use of testing when we know from years of previous testing what the results will be? Why make standards more rigorous when experience has consistently shown that student performance does not improve much? The new common standards appear to be better than most state standards, but experience suggests that they will increase only standardization, not student learning.

More standardization is not what our schools need. As the Harvard business professor Clayton Christensen puts it in his book *Disrupting Class*, applying his ideas about "disruptive innovation" to education: "If the nation is serious about leaving no child behind, it cannot be done by standardized methods. Today's system was designed at a time when standardization was seen as a virtue. It is an intricately interdependent system. Only an administrator suffering from virulent masochism would attempt to teach each student in the way his or her brain is wired to learn within this monolithic batch system. Schools need a new system."

Personalized education would be the engine of that new system. This change in approach would be rational and would shape virtually every aspect of schooling:

- Schools would be of human scale because students and teachers need to know each other well if education is to be personalized.

- Preschool education would be universal. The primary years would focus intensely on literacy and numeracy, using the arts and other subject matter as the context for learning reading and math.

- Beginning in middle school, multiple educational pathways would lead to college and other post-secondary programs to prepare young people for work in a complex and changing world. A student could choose a pathway reflecting his or her interests and aspirations. Each student would play a significant role in designing the curriculum, which would be anchored in the real world, not in the abstractions of most classrooms.

- There would be no "traditional" core curriculum with typical academic courses and rigid schedules in middle and high school.

- Traditional classroom instruction would be minimal. Teachers would become advisers who guide students in educating themselves. They would tutor students and help them manage their time and energy.

- Technology would largely replace textbooks and worksheets. It would be used innovatively to individualize education and extend the student's reach.

- Student learning would be assessed on the basis of portfolios, exhibitions, special projects and experiments, and recitals and performances—real accomplishments, not abstract test scores.

- Standardized tests would be used at transitional levels of schooling only to monitor student achievement and school performance for accountability purposes commensurate with public funding.

Some will see this approach as lowering standards even further and substituting "touchy-feely" for rigor and content. I would take that charge more seriously if the rigorous content-and-standards approach were solving the problem today, but it is not.

Yes, standards are an integral part of education; without them, schools are unacceptable. Assessments are also essential to make sure students are learning to read for comprehension, write clearly, and understand basic math. These skills are key to fulfilling the fundamental purposes of schooling: learning to reason and solve problems; and developing habits of mind and behavior to be good citizens, productive workers, and decent human beings.

Used properly, assessment is a tool that helps teachers see where students need help. It can be personalized to reflect the particular needs, talents, and aspirations of students and accommodate how they learn and at what rate. A new system would have high expectations for students as well as for school administrators, teachers, policymakers, and parents. Those expectations would take into account the enormous diversity of our children and the circumstances that shape their lives; they would also reflect the values of the family and society and not simply the archaic academic demands of college admission offices. Students would evaluate their own work to heighten their sense of responsibility for their own education and their awareness of what is expected of them and why.

In fairness, *A Nation at Risk* addressed the importance of attracting the best and the brightest teachers—who, nearly everybody agrees, are at the heart of successful education—including preparing them well, offering them a career track, and improving their compensation. I believe we would have made real gains by now if we had been as aggressive in promoting these goals for our educators as we've been for promoting standards and tests.

But that course correction would be costly. It would require universities and colleges to finally redesign teacher education, and, most of all, would require transforming schools into professional workplaces.

Going forward, it would be unwise and unnecessary to bet everything on standards-based accountability. The stakes in such a gamble are so enormous that we are morally obliged to consider, simultaneously, the second course I've described and embark on a parallel strategy of creating a new, innovative system.

http://www.edweek.org/ew/articles/
2011/03/09/23wolk_ep.h30.html?qs=wolk

1. What was the mantra of the school reform movement in the 1980s and 1990s?
2. What are the three "indisputable facts" Wolk cites?
3. According to Wolk, why do students fail?

4. What is the "engine" of the new system schools need?
5. What should expectations take into account, according to the author?

QUESTIONS FOR REASONING AND ANALYSIS

1. What is Wolk's thesis? Does one statement from the article express his thesis? If so, what is that statement?
2. How does Wolk's essay reflect a problem-solution organizational pattern? How does Wolk also refute an argument?
3. Why does Wolk begin by referencing the "mantra" from the 1980s and 1990s? Is making this reference an

effective approach for opening the essay? Why or why not?
4. How would you explain Wolk's criticism of standards-based accountability? Why does he take such issue with it?

QUESTIONS FOR REFLECTING AND WRITING

1. Conduct additional research on standards-based accountability and assessment. Do you think standards-based accountability represents good policy for schools? Why or why not?
2. Reread and reflect upon Wolk's eight bullet points for creating personalized education. Do you agree with some or all of these points? Why or why not?

3. In your view, how should schools conduct educational assessments? Write an essay defending your approach.

---

newspaper column

prereading question } **What can the United States do to curb growing unemployment?**

Educated, Unemployed, and Frustrated

Matthew C. Klein

The New York Times published this opinion piece by Matthew C. Klein on March 21, 2011. Klein is a research associate at the Council on Foreign Relations.

We all enjoy speculating about which Arab regime will be toppled next, but maybe we should be looking closer to home. High unemployment? Check. Out-of-touch elites? Check. Frustrated young people? As a 24-year-old American, I can testify that this rich democracy has plenty of those too.

About one-fourth of Egyptian workers under 25 are unemployed, a statistic that is often cited as a reason for the revolution there. In the United States, the Bureau of Labor Statistics reported in January an official unemployment rate of 21 percent for workers ages 16 to 24.

My generation was taught that all we needed to succeed was an education and hard work. Tell that to my friend from high school who studied Chinese and international relations at a top-tier college. He had the mis-

fortune to graduate in the class of 2009, and could find paid work only as a lifeguard and a personal trainer. Unpaid internships at research institutes led to nothing. After more than a year he moved back in with his parents.

Millions of college graduates in rich nations could tell similar stories. In Italy, Portugal and Spain, about one-fourth of college graduates under the age of 25 are unemployed. In the United States, the official unemployment rate for this group is 11.2 percent, but for college graduates 25 and over it is only 4.5 percent.

The true unemployment rate for young graduates is most likely even higher because it fails to account for those who went to graduate school in an attempt to ride out the economic storm or fled the country to teach

English overseas. It would be higher still if it accounted for all of those young graduates who have given up looking for full-time work, and are working part time for lack of any alternative.

The cost of youth unemployment is not only financial, but also emotional. Having a job is supposed to be the reward for hours of SAT prep, evenings spent on homework instead of with friends and countless all-nighters writing papers. The millions of young people who cannot get jobs or who take work that does not require a college education are in danger of losing their faith in the future. They are indefinitely postponing the life they wanted and prepared for; all that matters is finding rent money. Even if the job market becomes as robust as it was in 2007—something economists say could take more than a decade—my generation will have lost years of career-building experience.

It was simple to blame Hosni Mubarak for the frustrations of Egypt's young people—he had been in power longer than they had been alive. Barack Obama is not such an easy target; besides his democratic legitimacy, he is far from the only one responsible for the weakness of the recovery. In the absence of someone specific to blame, the frustration simply builds.

As governments across the developed world balance their budgets, I fear that the young will bear the brunt of the pain: taxes on workers will be raised and spending on education will be cut while mortgage subsidies and entitlements for the elderly are untouchable. At least the Saudis and Kuwaitis are trying to bribe their younger subjects.

The uprisings in the Middle East and North Africa are a warning for the developed world. Even if an Egyptian-style revolution breaking out in a rich democracy is unthinkable, it is easy to recognize the frustration of a generation that lacks opportunity. Indeed, the "desperate generation" in Portugal got tens of thousands of people to participate in nationwide protests on March 12. How much longer until the rest of the rich world follows their lead?

QUESTIONS FOR READING

1. What country's unemployment rate does Klein use for comparison?
2. According to Klein, what are the impacts of youth unemployment?
3. What are the potential negative effects, according to the author, of governments balancing their budgets?

QUESTIONS FOR REASONING AND ANALYSIS

1. What is Klein's claim?
2. How is Klein's essay a causal essay?
3. Why does Klein use the country of Egypt throughout the essay for purposes of comparison? Is this approach effective? Why or why not?

QUESTIONS FOR REFLECTING AND WRITING

1. Is the problem of unemployment among college graduates under the age of 25 as severe as Klein describes? Should the United States take more serious steps to help new college graduates find good jobs after graduation? Why or why not?
2. Is the United States in danger of suffering political turmoil due to high unemployment? Why or why not?
3. Think about your own job prospects after you graduate college. Are you enthusiastic or discouraged about your employment prospects? Are you willing to wait a few years to find that "ideal" position? Why or why not?

freedom of expression in the 21st century

chapter 20

This chapter explores controversies over First Amendment rights as related to privacy, censorship, obscenity, and freedom of speech on college campuses. Essays, websites, political cartoons, and photographs make arguments in favor of unequivocally supporting First Amendment rights, or they make arguments that certain forms of expression (pornography, for instance) are not protected under the Constitution. The themes and issues here remain timely and controversial, particularly considering that the U.S. Supreme Court continues to hand down rulings that shape interpretations of the First Amendment.

prereading questions

1. Have you considered positions between the extremes of absolutely no censorship of published materials (in any medium) and of laws prohibiting the publication of obscene, pornographic, or treasonable works or hate speech? What are some possible restrictions that may be agreed upon by most people?

2. What are some ways to control what is published (in any medium) without always resorting to legal restrictions? Are any of these possibilities feasible?

websites related to this chapter's topic

NATIONAL COALITION AGAINST CENSORSHIP (NCAC)
www.ncac.org
Organization promoting free speech. Site contains articles and news alerts.

NATIONAL FREEDOM OF SPEECH WEEK
www.freespeechweek.org
Site promoting the annual National Freedom of Speech Week.

WE WILL STAND
www.wwstand.org
Nondenominational Christian organization that opposes pornography.

magazine essay

prereading question } Should school officials ever be able to censor a student's speech?

The Schools Are Destroying Freedom of Speech

John W. Whitehead

Constitutional attorney John W. Whitehead is founder and president of The Rutherford Institute. His most recent book, *The Change Manifesto*, was published in 2008 by Sourcebooks, Inc. This editorial appeared on *Right Side News* in March 2009.

"The Constitution makes clear there can be no religious test for holding office, and it is just as clear there can be no religious test for individual expression of free speech—or censorship thereof, including at a high school graduation."—*Nat Hentoff, author and journalist*

Looking at America's public schools, it is difficult to imagine that they were once considered the hope of freedom and democracy.

That dream is no longer true. The majority of students today have little knowledge of the freedoms they possess in the Constitution and, specifically, in the Bill of Rights.

For example, a national survey of high school students reveals that only 2% can identify the Chief Justice of the Supreme Court; 35% know the first three words of the U.S. Constitution; 1.8% know that James Madison is considered the father of the U.S. Constitution; and 25% know that the Fifth Amendment protects against double jeopardy and self incrimination, among other legal rights. Clearly, high school civics classes are failing to teach the importance of our constitutional liberties.

Public educators do not fare much better in understanding and implementing the Constitution in the classroom. A study conducted by the University of Connecticut found that while public educators seem to support First Amendment rights in principle, they are reluctant to apply such rights in the schools. Consequently, the few students who do know and exercise their rights are forced to deal with school officials who, more often than not, fail to respect those rights.

Unfortunately, instead of being the guardians of freedom, the courts increasingly are upholding acts of censorship by government officials. As a result, the horrific lesson being taught to our young people is that the government has absolute power over its citizens and young people have very little freedom. Two incidents come to mind to illustrate this sad state of affairs, both having to do with school officials heavy-handedly silencing student expression at high school graduation ceremonies.

The first incident involves Nicholas Noel, the senior class president of his graduating class at Grand Rapids Union High School in Michigan. With more than 1,000 people in the audience listening to Noel deliver his commencement address, school officials turned off the microphone when he strayed from his approved speech and referred to the high school as a "prison." Noel said he described the school as a "prison" because it stressed conformity and students were "expected to act alike." His message was that high school paints an incomplete picture of life for students. "The colors of life are yet to come," Noel said. "It was really nice, nothing in bad taste. I tried to be different, and I was punished." Adding insult to injury, school officials even initially refused to award him his diploma.

The second incident, strikingly similar to Noel's, also involves a student whose microphone was cut off during her graduation speech simply because she voiced her personal convictions. Brittany McComb, the graduating valedictorian at Foothill High School in Nevada, was instructed by school officials to reflect over past experiences and lessons learned, say things that came from her heart and inject hope into her speech. Brittany adhered to the school's guidelines and wrote about the true meaning of success in her life—her religious beliefs. However, when she submitted her speech in advance to school administrators, they censored it, deleting several Bible verses and references to "the Lord" and one mention of "Christ."

Believing that the district's censorship amounted to a violation of her right to free speech, McComb attempted to deliver the original version of her speech at graduation. The moment school officials realized that she was straying from the approved text, they *unplugged* her microphone. The move drew extended jeers from the audience, with some people screaming, "Let her speak!"

School officials justified their actions by claiming that McComb's speech amounted to proselytizing. McComb disagrees. "I was telling my story," she said. "And if what I said was proselytizing, it was no more so than every other speaker who espoused his or her personal moral viewpoint about success. We're talking about life here: opinions about the means of success in life, from whatever source, are indeed forms of individual religious expression. It's also hard for me to believe that anyone at graduation could think I or any other speaker was speaking on behalf of the school system."

McComb filed a First Amendment lawsuit in federal court. But on March 19, 2009, a federal appeals court held that school officials did not violate her First Amendment rights by censoring her speech and unplugging the microphone. McComb, who is majoring in journalism at Biola University, plans to appeal to the U.S. Supreme Court.

She should not expect much help from the ACLU. Despite being a longtime champion of student expression, the ACLU actually condoned the school's act of censorship. As ACLU lawyer Allen Lichtenstein remarked about the case, "It's important for people to understand that a student was given a school-sponsored forum by a school and therefore, in essence, it was a school-sponsored speech."

Frankly, if the ACLU applied this logic consistently, then nowhere in the schools would students have the right to say anything that wasn't approved by their teachers or high-level school officials since every area in a public school is controlled and sponsored by the school.

Unfortunately, the trend in the federal courts is to agree with this type of skewed reasoning. However, this type of logic will only succeed in eradicating free expression by students in schools, and the ramifications are far-reaching. Eventually, it will mean that government officials can pull the plug on microphones when they disagree with whatever any citizen has to say. Yet the lessons of history are clear: every authoritarian regime from Hitler to Saddam Hussein has not only unplugged citizens' microphones but stopped those with whom the government disapproved from speaking.

Civil libertarians and the courts have long held that the First Amendment right to free speech applies to everyone, whatever their beliefs. This includes what many people consider offensive or deplorable speech. It also includes speech that persuades, as well as religious speech, non-religious speech or pointedly atheistic speech. Thus, unless we want free speech to end up in a totalitarian graveyard, no one, no matter their viewpoint or ideology, should be censored in any state institution.

QUESTIONS FOR READING

1. What were the findings of the University of Connecticut study?
2. According to Whitehead, what "horrific lesson" are students learning?
3. Why did school officials unplug McComb's microphone, effectually censoring her graduation speech?

QUESTIONS FOR REASONING AND ANALYSIS

1. What is Whitehead's claim? What evidence does Whitehead marshal in support of his claim?
2. Does Whitehead rely more on emotional or logical appeal? How does he rely more on one than the other?
3. Why does Whitehead think that the ACLU, in supporting the school against McComb, has used faulty logic in support of its position? Do you agree with Whitehead? Why or why not?

QUESTIONS FOR REFLECTING AND WRITING

1. Should school officials ever restrict or censor a student's speech? Why or why not? If school officials are justified in sometimes censoring students, then under what circumstances should they do so?
2. Whitehead does not explain the federal appeals court's justification for ruling against McComb. Does this omission hurt his credibility or weaken his argument? Why or why not?
3. In relating the McComb example, Whitehead never mentions the possible objection to her actions based on the constitutional separation of church and state. How might someone argue that McComb's actions violated the separation of church and state? Should Whitehead have explicitly addressed the church and state issue? Why or why not?

---

scholarly journal essay

prereading questions } Should the government control content on the Internet?
Does the First Amendment protect flag burning?

Why the First Amendment (and Journalism) Might Be in Trouble

Ken Dautrich and John Bare

Ken Dautrich, chair of the Department of Public Policy at the University of Connecticut, directed the study *The Future of the First Amendment* with colleague David Yalof. They are coauthors of the book *The First Amendment and the Media in the Court of Public Opinion* (2002). John Bare, Dautrich's coauthor for this article, is vice president for strategic planning and evaluation at the Arthur M. Blank Family Foundation in Atlanta. Their article appeared in the Summer 2005 issue of *Nieman Reports*, published by Harvard University.

Our first-of-its-kind exploration of the future of the First Amendment among American high school students—a highly visible study of 112,000 students and 8,000 teachers in over 300 high schools—suggests a fragile future for key constitutional freedoms while also pointing us to potential remedies. This study, *The Future of the First Amendment*, which was released earlier this year, arrived at a timely moment in American history, on the heels of a national election and amid a war the President is using, by his account, to spread democratic freedoms. The results drew remarkable media attention, which tended to focus on one of the more fearful statistics to emerge from the study: Only 51 percent of 9th to 12th graders agree that newspapers should be allowed to publish freely without government approval of stories—in other words, nearly half entertain the idea of newspaper censorship.

Beyond that flashpoint finding, the study allows for a more thorough understanding of today's high school students and can point us to potential remedies. The research also suggests ways to improve support for the First Amendment. While many of the findings raise concern, some are not so bad. Some are even encouraging. Most of all, the results should be viewed within the context of the history of the First Amendment, which faced challenges—some would say it was compromised—as soon as it was adopted.

First Amendment Challenges

One of the first acts of the first Congress in 1789 was to append a bill of rights to the U.S. Constitution, which, among other things, explicitly denied Congress the ability to tamper with Americans' rights of free expression. Indeed, through the course of our history, Americans and their leaders have proclaimed a commitment to freedom and liberty. Most recently, President Bush, in his second inaugural address, justified the Iraqi and Afghani military operations as a vehicle to spread freedom and liberty throughout the world.

Despite a long history of veneration to these values, freedom of expression has met with a number of challenges. Not long after adoption of the First Amendment, President John Adams and the Federalist Congress passed the Alien and Sedition Acts, severely thwarting the freedom to speak out against government. Abraham Lincoln's suspension of habeas corpus, the internment of Japanese Americans during Franklin Roosevelt's administration after Pearl Harbor, Senator Joseph McCarthy's "red scare," and Attorney General John Ashcroft's aggressive implementation of the USA Patriot Act represent just a few of the more notable breaches to liberty in America.

Like any value in our society, the health and vitality of freedom and liberty are largely dependent upon the public's attention to, appreciation for, and support of them. When Americans are willing to compromise freedom of expression in return for a sense of being more secure, then government officials can more readily take action to curtail freedom. Public fear of Communism allowed McCarthy to tread on people's liberty, just as fear of terrorism allowed Ashcroft to curb freedoms.

The real protection of free expression rights lies not in the words of the First Amendment. Rather, it lies in the people's willingness to appreciate and support those rights. That idea led the Freedom Forum's First Amendment Center to commission an annual survey on public knowledge, appreciation and support for free expression rights since 1997 to gauge the health and well-being of the First Amendment.

If public opinion is a good measure of the First Amendment's well-being, then its annual checkup has been fraught with health problems.

- While more than 9 in 10 agree that "people should be allowed to express unpopular opinions," a paltry 4 in 10 believe that high school students should be able to report on controversial issues in school newspapers without the consent of school officials.
- More than one-third say the press has too much freedom.
- Fewer than 6 in 10 say that musicians should be able to sing songs with lyrics that may be offensive to some.

These annual checkups have shown over time that half of adults think that flag burning as a method of protest should not be tolerated. In general, the surveys have revealed that the public holds low support for, a lack of appreciation for, and dangerously low levels of knowledge of free expression rights. Is it no wonder, then, that the suspension of liberty in this land of freedom has been so readily accomplished by its leaders from time to time?

It was these rather anemic annual checkups that convinced the John S. and James L. Knight Foundation to commission this unique survey of American high school students and to begin a wider discussion about how to strengthen the polity's commitment to the democratic ideal of freedom and liberty.

What follows are some findings from the Knight Foundation survey of high school students that explain, in part, why Americans should be concerned about the First Amendment's future.

- Thirty-six percent of high school students openly admit that they take their First Amendment rights for granted and another 37 percent say they never thought enough about this to have an opinion.
- Seventy-five percent incorrectly believe that it is illegal to burn the flag as a means of political protest, and 49 percent wrongly think that government has the right to restrict indecent material on the Internet.
- A source of the lack of support for free press rights might be due to the fact that only four percent of students trust journalists to tell the truth all of the time.
- Thirty-five percent say the First Amendment goes too far in the rights it guarantees, and 32 percent think the press has too much freedom to do what it wants.

Proposing Some Remedies

This is a bleak picture of what may be in store for the First Amendment as this group matures into adulthood. More importantly, however, a number of findings from the study suggest policies or actions that might better prepare students to value and use their constitutional freedoms. While the suggestions below grow out of findings that are based on correlations, not causation, the logic of the policy ideas holds up against both our experience and our understanding of the data.

1. Instruction on the First Amendment matters. Education works! Students who have taken classes that deal with journalism, the role of the media in society, and the First Amendment exhibit higher levels of knowledge and support for free expression rights than those who haven't. The problem, of course, is that the strong trend toward math and science and "teaching to the standardized test" has

continued

crowded out instruction that could help students develop good citizenship skills. The less the schools focus on developing strong citizens, the weaker our democracy becomes. The positive lesson to learn from this is that through enhancements to the high school curriculum, students can become better prepared to value and use their freedoms.

2. Use leads to greater appreciation. When students are given an opportunity to use their freedoms, they develop a better appreciation for them. The Knight project found that students who are engaged in extracurricular student media (such as school newspaper, Internet sites, etc.) are more aware and much more supportive of free expression rights.

3. School leaders need lessons, too. Most high school principals need to be reminded of the value of experiential learning and its implications for the future of the First Amendment. While 80 percent of principals agree that "newspapers should be allowed to publish freely without government approval of a story," only 39 percent say their students should be afforded the same rights for publishing in the school newspaper. Granted, principals have many issues to deal with (like parents and school board members calling and asking how they could have ever allowed a story to be printed in a school paper). But if we are to expect students to mature into responsible democratic citizens, they should be given the freedom to express themselves and act responsibly while in school.

4. Place the issues in the context of their daily lives. The project suggests that, as with most people, when issues affecting one's freedom are brought close to home, students are best able to discern the true meaning and value of freedom. When asked if they agreed or disagreed with this statement— "Musicians should be allowed to sing songs with lyrics that might be offensive to others"—70 percent agreed (only 43 percent of principals and 57 percent of adults agree with this). Music matters to many young people. When this form of free expression is challenged, most students come to its defense. The lesson, of course, is that in teaching students about the virtues of free expression, showing how it relates to things important to them will best instill in students why it is so important to the life of a democracy.

The future of the First Amendment is, at best, tenuous. As the current group of high school students takes on their important role as citizens in our democracy, their lack of appreciation and support for free expression rights will provide a ripe atmosphere for government to further intrude on these freedoms. Many institutions in society should shoulder part of the responsibility to ensure good citizenship skills for our youth. Parents, religious institutions, the media, as well as leadership from public officials, just to name a few. But the public schools play an especially important role in socializing youngsters in how to be responsible citizens, and through the schools the future health and vitality of the First Amendment might be restored.

QUESTIONS FOR READING

1. What is the occasion for the authors' article? What was the purpose of the study?

2. What is the primary source of protection for free expression? For what reason do Americans allow free expression to be restricted?

3. What views revealed in the nation's "annual checkup" put First Amendment rights at risk, according to the authors? What did the study reveal about high school students' views?

4. State the four remedies proposed by the authors in your own words.

QUESTIONS FOR REASONING AND ANALYSIS

1. What, specifically, is the essay's topic? What is the authors' claim?

2. What assumption about freedom is part of this argument?

3. Analyze the four proposals. Do they seem logical remedies to you? Do some seem more likely to produce change than others?

QUESTIONS FOR REFLECTING AND WRITING

1. What statistic is most surprising to you? Why?

2. Do you share the authors' concerns for the tenuous state of free speech in the United States? If you disagree, how would you rebut them?

3. Can democracy survive without First Amendment rights? Be prepared to debate this issue.

Matt Wuerker

This cartoon by Matt Wuerker was originally posted to Politico.com. It speaks to a 2010 landmark United Supreme Court decision, *Citizens United v. F.E.C.*, that corporate funding of independent political broadcasts could not be limited because doing so would infringe upon First Amendment rights.

Copyright © 2010 Matt Wuerker. Reprinted by permission of Cartoonist Group.

QUESTIONS FOR REASONING AND ANALYSIS

1. What argument is this cartoon making? Do you agree or disagree? Why or why not?

2. Is it significant that the *Citizens United v. F.E.C.* is placed on top of the U.S. Constitution? Why or why not?

3. Why is it important that only five of the nine U.S. Supreme Court justices are depicted in this cartoon?

QUESTIONS FOR REFLECTING AND WRITING

1. Are corporations granted greater rights of free speech and expression than individuals? Why or why not? Write an essay defending your position.

2. Conduct additional research on *Citizens United v. F.E.C.* Do you find yourself in agreement with the majority decision? Why or why not?

A Little Civility, Please

Mark Davis

Mark Davis, a Texas native and graduate of the University of Maryland, is a popular radio talk show host (the *Mark Davis Show*) for WBAP Dallas-Fort Worth and has been writing for the *Dallas Morning News* since 2004. The following column was posted on Star-Telegram.com on March 5, 2003.

Try something for me.

Send your teenager to school wearing a T-shirt that says "Martin Luther King Jr. Was Evil" or "Jews Lie: There Was No Holocaust."

Then wait for supporters to suggest that your child was not engaged in the spread of hate but rather in the sparking of vigorous debates.

First, your kid would have been yanked from school so fast that his eyeballs would have popped out.

But just let him (or you) argue that all this does is get people talking about the civil rights era or anti-Semitism, and the shock will be replaced by laughter.

That is exactly the argument made by defenders of Bretton Barber, a Michigan high school junior. The intellectual opening salvo he offered in his school on February 17 was a T-shirt bearing the face of President Bush, framed by the words "International Terrorist."

A regular William F. Buckley, this kid. His intent was obviously not to start a constructive discussion. Conversely, the school did not seek to squelch debate by ordering young Barber to turn the shirt inside out or go home.

If his T-shirt was more generalized and less hateful, with a slogan such as "No War" or even the famous Steve Nash shirt, "Shoot for Peace," I'd say the school should relax.

In the 1960s, students wearing black armbands to protest the Vietnam War won U.S. Supreme Court approval. In the case of *Tinker v. Des Moines*, the court ruled that students "did not shed their constitutional rights to freedom of expression at the schoolhouse gate."

Well, not all of them, anyway. In the years since, we have properly learned that schools do indeed have the right to establish dress guidelines. Most people have shed the absurd notion that an 11th-grader in a public school has the exact same First Amendment rights as an adult in the outside world.

The student newspaper can be barred from calling for the principal's ouster. Student assemblies can be squelched if they feature racial or religious bigotry.

And T-shirts can be nixed if they are—here's the tough word—disruptive. Well, how exactly does a T-shirt disrupt? Do the words on the fabric leap from the wearer's chest and block the students' view of the teacher and blackboard?

No, but an atmosphere that fails to preserve a sense of order and decorum sends the message that various other behavioral extremes might also be tolerated. That is bad.

An armband is one thing. Hate speech, even under the guise of political discourse, is quite another.

How bizarre is it that most who would stand up for Barber's hamhanded "protest" condemning the president would recoil in shock if a kid wore a logo for Marlboro cigarettes or a Confederate flag emblem?

Gosh, wouldn't these be lost opportunities to discuss tobacco and the Civil War?

Passionate debate on controversial issues is good for students and should be encouraged. But within that exercise must be rules of decorous speech and behavior.

This should have nothing to do with whether we agree or disagree with the sentiment expressed. A student wearing a "Clinton Is a Pervert" shirt around 1999 or so would have received no argument from me with regard to content, but I would have supported any school banning it.

The *Star-Telegram* is not the only newspaper to stick up for Bretton Barber. I would expect a certain First Amendment zeal from journalists, and I am not immune to it myself.

But his scolding is not, as an editorial stated, a missed opportunity for discussion. It is an opportunity far too rarely claimed, namely to teach a kid what is and is not permissible within the borders of civilized debate.

Young Barber should be welcome to suggest and participate in vigorous discussions on important issues on his own time or in an appropriate class.

1. What is Davis's occasion for writing? That is, what student action has received media attention?
2. What are some of the controls that the courts have given to K–12 schools since the 1960s? What, specifically, can lead to a prohibiting of T-shirts?

3. What is Davis's newspaper's position on Bretton Barber? Why is Davis not surprised by his paper's position?

QUESTIONS FOR REASONING AND ANALYSIS

1. What is Davis's claim? Where does he state it?
2. What is Davis's evidence? How does he defend his position?
3. How does he rebut the potential counterargument that students should be encouraged to debate controversial issues?

4. Study the examples Davis gives of T-shirt slogans that would quickly be squelched. What do they have in common? What is Davis's point in using those examples?
5. What strategy does Davis use in paragraphs 7 and 18?

QUESTIONS FOR REFLECTING AND WRITING

1. Do you agree with Davis's position on T-shirt slogans? If so, why? If not, how would you rebut his argument?
2. Why have the courts defended the right of K–12 schools to limit the First Amendment rights of students? Is this

different from the issue of controlling access to certain websites through a college server? (See Robert O'Neil, pages 363–365.) Should it be different? Why or why not?

---

newspaper column

prereading questions }
Should pornography be restricted on the Internet? Should access to pornography be restricted at the office? Do you have a position on these issues?

What Limits Should Campus Networks Place on Pornography?

Robert O'Neil

A former president of the University of Wisconsin system and the University of Virginia, Robert O'Neil holds a law degree from Harvard University and currently teaches constitutional and commercial law at the University of Virginia. He is also the founding director of the Thomas Jefferson Center for the Protection of Free Expression and an authority on First Amendment issues. His article was published in the *Chronicle of Higher Education* on March 21, 2003.

What if you were about to present a PowerPoint lecture to a large undergraduate class, but found instead on your computer a series of sexually explicit ads and material from pornographic Web sites? That's essentially what happened recently to Mary Pedersen, a nutrition-science professor at California Polytechnic State University at San Luis Obispo. That incident and the increasing presence of such imagery at Cal Poly have led to a novel, although undoubtedly predictable, struggle over computer content—one that is quite likely to be replicated at countless campuses in the coming months.

A concerned faculty group at Cal Poly has announced its intention to bring before the Academic Senate,

sometime this spring, a Resolution to Enhance Civility and Promote a Diversity-Friendly Campus Climate. Specifically, the measure would prohibit using the university's computers or network to access or download digital material generally described as "pornography." The resolution would also forbid the "transmission" of hate literature and obscenity on the Cal Poly network.

The sponsoring faculty members have offered several reasons for proposing such drastic action. First and foremost, they contend that the ready availability of sexually explicit imagery can create occasional but deeply disturbing encounters like Pedersen's discovery of unwelcome and unexpected material on her class-

continued

room computer. The pervasive presence of such images, proponents of the resolution argue, is inherently demeaning to female faculty members, administrators, and students.

Indeed, they suggest that the university might even be legally liable for creating and maintaining a "hostile workplace environment" if it fails to take steps to check the spread of such offensive material. That concern has been heightened by a putative link to a growing number of sexual assaults in the environs of the university.

Those who call for tighter regulation cite several other factors to support anti-pornography measures. In their view, a college or university must maintain the highest of standards, not only in regard to the integrity of scholarship and relations between teachers and students, but also in the range of material to which it provides electronic access. The clear implication is that the ready availability of sexually explicit and deeply offensive imagery falls below "the ethical standards that the university claims to uphold."

Critics of easy access to such material also claim that it can divert time, talent, and resources from the university's primary mission. Kimberly Daniels, a local lawyer who is advising the resolution's sponsors, told the student newspaper that "it is offensive that Cal Poly is taking the position that it is acceptable for professors to view pornography during work hours in their work office." That risk is not entirely conjectural. In fact, one professor left the institution last year after being convicted on misdemeanor charges for misusing a state-owned computer, specifically for the purpose of downloading in his office thousands of sexually explicit images. Local newspapers have also reported that the FBI is investigating another former Cal Poly professor who allegedly used a campus computer to view child pornography.

Finally, the concerned faculty group insists that the free flow of pornographic materials may expose the Cal Poly computer network to a greater risk of virus infection. They cite a student's recent experience in opening a salacious virus-bearing attachment that the student mistakenly believed had been sent by one of his professors.

The proposed Academic Senate resolution has touched off an intense debate. The university's existing computer-use policy presumes that access and choice of material are broadly protected, although it adds that "in exceptional cases, the university may decide that such material directed at individuals presents such a hostile environment under the law that certain restrictive actions are warranted." The new proposal would focus more sharply on sexually explicit imagery, and would require those who wish to view such material through the campus network to obtain the express permission of the university's president.

Defenders of the current approach, including the senior staff of the university's office of information technology, insist that a public university may not banish from its system material that is offensive, but legal, without violating First Amendment rights. Those familiar with the operations of such systems also cite practical difficulties in the enforcement of any such restrictions, given the immense volume of digital communications that circulate around the clock at such a complex institution.

The debate at Cal Poly echoes what occurred some six years ago in Virginia. The General Assembly enacted what remains as the nation's only ban on public employees' use of state-owned or state-leased computers to access sexually explicit material—at least without express permission of a "superior" for a "bona fide research purpose." Six state university professors immediately challenged the law on First Amendment grounds. A district judge struck down the statute, but the U.S. Court of Appeals for the Fourth Circuit reversed that ruling. The law had been modified before that judgment, and many Virginia professors have since received exemptions or dispensations, but the precedent created by the appeals-court decision remains troubling for advocates of free and open electronic communications.

The Virginia ruling complicates the Cal Poly situation. The First Amendment challenge of those who oppose the Academic Senate resolution is less clear than it might at first appear. Two premises underlying that resolution—the need to protect government-owned hardware and the imperative to combat sexual hostility in the public workplace—contributed both to the passage of the Virginia ban, and to its eventual success in the federal courts. What's more, the U.S. Equal Employment Opportunity Commission some months ago gave its blessing to a hostile-workplace complaint filed by Minneapolis Public Library staff members who were offended by persistent display of graphic sexual images on reading-room terminals.

Thus, there is more than a superficial basis for the claims of Cal Poly's porn-banishers that (in the words of one faculty member) "the First Amendment doesn't protect . . . subjecting others to inappropriate material in the workplace." Even the information-technology consultant who has championed the current computer-use policy at the university has conceded that access to controversial material is fully protected only "as long as it isn't offending others."

Although the desire to reduce the potential for offense and affront to other users of a campus computer network seems unobjectionable, its implications deserve careful scrutiny. In the analogous situation of public terminals in a library reading room, it is one thing to ask a patron who wishes to access and display sexually explicit material—or racially hateful material, for that matter—to use a terminal facing away from other users and staff members. It is quite another matter to deny access to such material altogether on the plausible premise that, if it can be obtained at all, there is a palpable risk that its visible display will offend others. To invoke an analogy that is now before the U.S. Supreme Court in a challenge to the Children's Internet Protection Act: It is one thing for a library to provide—even be compelled to provide—filtered access for parents who wish it for their children, but quite another to deny all adult patrons any unfiltered access.

What Cal Poly should seek to do, without impairing free expression, is to protect people from being gratuitously assaulted by digital material that may be deeply offensive, without unduly restricting access of those who, for whatever reason, may wish to access and view such material without bothering others. The proposal in the resolution that permission may be obtained from the university's president, for bona-fide research purposes, is far too narrow. Among other flaws, such a precondition might well deter sensitive or conscientious scholars, whether faculty members or students, who are understandably reluctant to reveal publicly their reasons for wishing to access sexually explicit images or hate literature.

A responsible university, seeking to balance contending interests of a high order, might first revisit and make more explicit its policies that govern acceptable computer use and access, by which all campus users are presumably bound. Such policies could condemn the flaunting of thoughtless dissemination of sexually explicit material and digital hate literature, expressing institutional abhorrence of such postings, without seeking to ban either type of material. The computer network might also establish a better warning system through which to alert sensitive users to the occasional and inevitable presence of material that may offend. Finally, a broader disclaimer might be in order, recognizing the limited practical capacity of a university server to control (or even enable users to avoid) troubling material.

What is needed is a reasonable balance that avoids, as Justice William O. Douglas warned a half-century ago, "burning down the house to roast the pig." That aphorism has special felicity here; in the offensive flaunting of sexually explicit imagery, there is a "pig" that doubtless deserves to be roasted. But there is also a house of intellect that must remain free and open, even to those with aberrant tastes and interests.

QUESTIONS FOR READING

1. What is the occasion for O'Neil's article? What is he responding to?
2. What is the resolution some Cal Poly faculty want passed by their Academic Senate? How do they want to limit access?
3. List the arguments for their resolution in your own words.
4. What are the arguments of those supporting the current Cal Poly Internet guidelines?
5. What arguments were used to support the Virginia ban?
6. How do these First Amendment debates affect terminals in public libraries? What is the current ruling on public libraries?

QUESTIONS FOR REASONING AND ANALYSIS

1. What is O'Neil's claim? Where does he state it? What, specifically, does he think that a university's position or strategy should be regarding "offensive" materials obtained through the university's server?
2. What organizational pattern does O'Neil use in the development of his argument? (Note where he states his claim.) What does he gain by his approach?
3. Where, essentially, does the author stand on censorship versus First Amendment freedoms?
4. Examine O'Neil's conclusion. How does he use Justice Douglas's metaphor to conclude his argument effectively?

QUESTIONS FOR REFLECTING AND WRITING

1. Evaluate O'Neil's argument. Is he clear and thorough in his analysis of the conflicting positions in this debate? Does he, in your view, have the stronger argument? If so, why? If not, why not?
2. Analyze the author's use of a conciliatory approach. Where does he acknowledge the merits of the opponents' views? How does his claim seek common ground? What might you conclude about the effectiveness of the conciliatory approach when engaged in First Amendment issues?

A Perfect Storm
Privacy. Neutrality. Free Expression.

Rick Santorum

Former U.S. Senator Rick Santorum (R-PA) worked as a senior fellow for the Ethics and Public Policy Center until 2011, when he became a Republican candidate for the 2012 presidential election. "A Perfect Storm" is an excerpt from *It Takes a Family: Conservatism and the Common Good* (Intercollegiate Studies Institute, 2005).

> EDITOR'S NOTE: This is the fourth in a series of five excerpts from *It Takes a Family*, by Sen. Rick Santorum. Together they comprise Chapter 23, "The Rule of Judges."

I could go further and discuss the cases that touch on pornography and obscenity, also part of our moral ecology. For decades, communities in America have tried to shore up common decency, have tried to guard their collective moral capital, by regulating *smut*. Congress has likewise responded to Americans' moral sensibilities by attempting to regulate broadcast media and the Internet. But time and again over the past generation America's communities and Congress have run up against a Supreme Court intent to side *against* the American people and *with* the pornographers. The Court's doctrine has been that virtually all efforts to regulate smut run afoul of the First Amendment, which the Court says protects all individuals' "freedom of expression."

But let's look for a minute at what that First Amendment actually says about our freedoms: "Congress shall make no law . . . abridging freedom of speech. . . ." Since this amendment goes on to discuss the people's right to assemble and to petition the government, as well as freedom of the press, it is clear that the "speech" in question concerns, in the first instance, *political* speech—arguments about the public good. At the time this amendment was passed, the English Crown could and did regulate what could be published and said about sensitive political questions; in America, things would be different.

But you may have noticed that in pornography the words aren't really the point, are they? *Speech* implies words, rationally intelligible discussion and argument, *communication*. Pictures also can be "worth a thousand words," of course: Sometimes images are central

to a political or social cause. But America's huge porn industry is not about political debate; it is not about the communication of ideas. It's about the commercial production of objects of titillation for profit. Based on the text of the Constitution, the courts should have recognized a hierarchy of protected "speech," with political speech and writing receiving the greatest constitutional protection, commercial speech less protection, and mere titillation the least of all. Yet in the topsy-turvy world of the new court-approved morality, limits on political speech like the recently passed McCain-Feingold campaign finance bill are just fine, but congressional restrictions on Internet pornographers are seen as violating the First Amendment and are therefore struck down.

Privacy. Neutrality. Free Expression. None of these terms is in the Constitution. They "look like" terms that actually are there. Freedom from "unreasonable searches and seizures": That's in the Fifth Amendment. "Equal protection of the laws": That's in the Fourteenth Amendment. "Freedom of speech": That's in the First Amendment. That is why liberals believe what they are doing is merely refining the intentions of our founders, making explicit the underlying philosophical tenets of our Constitution. The problem is that these "philosophical" tenets are pure abstractions, fit only for those great abstractions, "liberal individuals." But the U.S. Constitution was the fruit of long experience in the great complexity and wisdom of English common law.

As Harvard's Mary Ann Glendon has written,

> [T]he peculiar excellence of the Anglo-American common-law tradition over centuries, that which distinguished it from continental "legal science," was its rejection of simplifying abstractions, its close attention to facts and patterns of facts. . . . It was this unique combination of common sense and modest . . . theory that enabled England and the United States to develop and maintain a legal order possessing the toughness to

weather political and social upheavals. . . . When legal scholars distance themselves from those ways of thinking, they repudiate much of what is best in their professional tradition.

The Supreme Court of the United States in the past half-century has been a bad steward of its own jurisprudential traditions, preferring instead the neat abstractions of the latest "theories."

Privacy. Neutrality. Free Expression. These three abstractions together make for a perfect storm, a jurisprudential hurricane for wreaking havoc on a moral ecosystem. Together they make of our Constitution not a document for democratic self-governance, but instead describe a pure liberal society of isolated individuals each doing their own thing within the politically correct boundaries carefully crafted and enforced by the village elders.

The irony is that the tradition of common law had made marriage and family exactly a *privileged* institu-

tion; Supreme Court decisions originally based on this traditional conception (*Griswold*) eventually undermined that privileged status in the name of abstract privacy. Similarly, as Justice O'Connor observed, on its face the U.S. Constitution is not neutral between religion and irreligion. Religion is a specially protected category in the actual text of the Constitution: It gets a special mention as the "first freedom" of the First Amendment. Religion and the family were the two main agents for *moralizing* society, for generating new moral capital. The Court's decisions have undermined these institutions, creating in their place a society of atomized and de-moralized individuals, shielded by the village elders from the natural moral influences of faith and family.

National Review Online, June 21, 2005. www.nationalreview.com/comment/ santorum200507210812.asp

QUESTIONS FOR READING

1. How does Santorum define "political speech"?
2. If not about "speech," what is pornography really about, according to Santorum?
3. What "philosophical tenets" does Santorum label "pure abstractions"?

4. In the last paragraph, what accusation does Santorum make of the U.S. Supreme Court?

QUESTIONS FOR REASONING AND ANALYSIS

1. What is Santorum's thesis?
2. Santorum uses the terms *privacy, neutrality,* and *free expression* to begin two paragraphs of this essay. He simply states the terms in sequence without using the terms in an actual sentence. What is the rhetorical effect of doing so? How does using the terms in this way become a strategy for organizing the essay?
3. Why does Santorum use textual evidence from Harvard professor Mary Ann Glendon? What point is he trying to support with use of her statement?

4. At the beginning of the piece, Santorum references "moral ecology," and near the end, he mentions the "moral ecosystem." What is he suggesting through use of such references? How do these references function as metaphors? How does the comparison support his thesis?

QUESTIONS FOR REFLECTING AND WRITING

1. Do you agree with the way Santorum defines "free speech" or "free expression" in this essay? Why or why not?
2. "A Perfect Storm" appeared in the *National Review Online,* a far-right and conservative publication. In your view, does its appearance in *NRO* suggest bias? If an author arguing the opposite point of view published

his or her article in *New Republic,* a far-left and liberal magazine, would its appearance there also suggest bias? Why or why not?
3. Does pornography indeed harm the institutions of marriage and family? If so, how so? Do you agree with what Santorum suggests by the end of the essay?

The Power of Information: A Critique of Privacy, Wikileaks, and Recent Events

This article appeared on the Security Generation website, which features news, articles, and forums covering a variety of security topics. This piece was posted on December 28, 2010.

The recent explosion of Wikileaks and Cablegate has yet again brought the unique power of information to the forefront of the world's attention. What makes this different from the usual "knowledge is power" debate, is that it highlights the sensitive balance between those wishing to reveal information to the world, and those who, for whatever reason, want to prevent that from happening. Historically it was the role of investigative journalists to look into the activities of companies and governments, however due to the high costs of long-term investigative stories, political affiliations, the chance of government gag orders, and the threat of lawsuits, these have been in decline. It is not only massive government-focused leaks that have been gagged in the past, smaller journalists and even individuals have been prevented from legally reporting or capturing an event.

A real-world, non-digital example of this ongoing battle is one regularly fought by photographers around the world. Photos and videos have the ability to capture and convey information unlike any other medium, and in most cases can be understood by anyone irrespective of language or education. A single image, unlike written articles which must be read and understood, can tell the viewer what they need to know in a single glance. This is why the Collateral Murder (video) leak of a U.S. Apache helicopter killing innocent Iraqis was so effective at spreading across the world. A purely written account of that incident could have gone unnoticed.

It's for this reason that law-abiding photographers and videographers are harassed on a regular basis by authorities—it's the fear that they will capture something they don't want shared with the rest of the world. I posted about one incident a few months back about two photojournalists being thrown out of the Miami metro for legally taking photos and video footage. The police have gotten involved for even more mundane situations. In most developed countries any photographer, registered or not, has the right to take and distribute photographs that are taken on public property (taking into account local laws), and it helps to know those

rights and stand up for them.

Clearly Wikileaks' leaked videos and cables are not public property, and whether you are pro-disclosure or not, the underlying issue remains the same. Wikileaks is releasing information that the U.S. government does not want the world to see. Now, instead of photographers' rights, people are talking about journalists' rights which are fairly well protected around the world. The U.S. seems to think that Wikileaks' Editor-in-Chief, Julian Assange, has broken Espionage laws by publishing this information, however these claims would place the rest of the media and journalistic field into hot water as well, as they rely on the same rights when publishing controversial content. Many people are calling it shameful that the mainstream media has done such a poor job of outing the lies and coverups of governments around the world. This is possibly because mainstream media almost always has a stake in politics these days. We've also seen the likes of Amazon, MasterCard and Bank of America shut out Wikileaks based on what they say is a conflict with their terms of service—yet they continue to provide service for far shadier groups. The result? Groups such as Anonymous have sprung up in the defence of Wikileaks, in the name of freedom of information and transparency, going as far as carrying out vigilante-style DDoS attacks on those opposing Wikileaks and Assange.

So why all the fuss all of a sudden? Privacy is a fragile thing, and over the past five years there has been an increasing amount of advocates, myself included, warning of the microscopic but relentless erosion of privacy due to the evolution of technology, the monetization of personal data, information-based online services, and governments seeking to further monitor and control the population (under the pretext of "Terrorism"). Everyone talks of the UK becoming a Big Brother-style surveillance society thanks to the seemingly rabbit-like reproduction of CCTV cameras, and privacy-busting legislation such as RIPA. The U.S. has also been pushing the envelope with things like the Patriot Act, more domestic and international wiretapping, confiscating computers and copying information at the borders, and now the much maligned bodyscanners.

It was most unclear what individuals could do to protect themselves from the encroachment on their civil liberties and, in reality, many people simply didn't care yet. It seems as though the ice has begun to crack, and we're starting to see the tip of the iceberg (no pun intended), of the upcoming backlash from the people. First a (belated) outcry about the use of bodyscanners, and now waves of supporters defending Wikileaks and *what it stands for*. Note that I italicized those words, as there are some who may question Wikileaks' methods in distributing this material, yet understand that a significant battle is being waged around the freedom of information, and of the individual. What we're seeing is actually a synergetic amalgamation of people with two distinct mindsets, pro-privacy and pro-information, and this is what makes the current movement so powerful.

The unfortunate target in this case is the U.S. government, who is having its own privacy shattered, and dirty laundry aired for all to see (in the name of freedom of information). Although there has been an outcry—particularly from politicians (who are essentially under attack), pro-government outlets (that have a stake in the current government), and some Americans who are concerned that this information may endanger the country and its troops—there has been far more support for Wikileaks' cause. Some of that support comes not from people who care about the information being released, but from *those who object to the techniques being employed in an attempt to shut it down*: an international man-hunt, calls for assassination, pressure on American and international companies, and even foreign governments.

In my opinion, a couple of things could now happen. Either the U.S. government somehow succeeds at making Julian Assange the scapegoat and convicts him of espionage (or otherwise eliminates him), changing the face of journalism and freedom of speech/information—or—Wikileaks will prevail, and we'll enter a new era where governments (and companies) are aware that "the people" will hold them accountable for their actions, and responsible whistleblowing will become more accepted. Note that in the first scenario the balance of power moves, even further, onto the side of the government and large corporations. In the second, that balance is evened out somewhat. In no scenario do we end up in a society where the people have the power. None of this restores our individual privacy, but it does send out the message that principled individuals and the population are willing to keep an eye on the governments of the world, and have the right to hold them accountable for unlawful or immoral actions.

"The Power of Information: A Critique of Privacy, Wikileaks and Recent Events" by Sebastion Jeanquier. http://www.security-generation.com/privacy/the-power-of-information-a-critique-of-privacy-wikileaks-and-recent-events

QUESTIONS FOR READING

1. According to the author, who in the nondigital world fights an ongoing battle to release information?
2. What is the "underlying issue" as the author sees it?
3. According to the author, what will be the two likely outcomes of the Wikileaks scandal?

QUESTIONS FOR REASONING AND ANALYSIS

1. How would you express the author's thesis or main claim?
2. Why does the author compare Wikileaks and Cablegate to the experiences of photographers and videographers? Is it an effective technique? Why or why not?
3. What does the author mean by "synergetic amalgamation" at the end of the sixth paragraph?
4. Could this essay be considered a causal argument? Why or why not? If not, what kind of argument is it?

QUESTIONS FOR REFLECTING AND WRITING

1. Should the government restrict the release of information under certain circumstances? If so, under what circumstances and why? If not, why not?
2. Conduct some additional research on the Second Amendment to the U.S. Constitution. Can you think of other instances in which limits were placed on free expression? Was it justified to do so in those situations? Why or why not?

prereading question } Should sensitive national security information be made available to the general public?

A Defense of Wikileaks

How it could actually improve U.S. foreign policy

John B. Judis

John B. Judis is a senior editor and author of opinion pieces for *The New Republic*. This particular piece posted on December 1, 2010.

The Obama administration has condemned Wikileaks for its second release within a year of classified foreign policy documents. And some liberal commentators have backed up the administration's complaints. And I am not going to argue that the administration doesn't have a case. Governments rely on candid assessments from their diplomats; and if Americans in overseas embassies have to assume that they are writing for the general public and not for their superiors back home, they are not likely to be very candid. But there is also something to be said in defense of Wikileaks. Or to put it in the most minimal terms, there is a reason why, outside of Washington, most people, and much of the respectable press, have focused on the contents of these leaks rather than on the manner in which they were leaked.

Many of the cables consist of high-level gossip, or educated but not necessarily insightful opinion, with little bearing on policy. Yet those that do deal with policy reveal contradictions between what the Bush or Obama administrations have been telling the public and what was known inside the State Department and White House. For instance, while the White House was warning Congress that Iran was arming the Taliban in Afghanistan, Secretary of Defense Robert Gates was assuring the Italian foreign minister that "there was little lethal material crossing the Afghanistan-Iranian border."

Other revelations bear upon what the administration knew or thought it knew about other countries, but was not telling the public. Some of the most significant concern China. The State Department believed that the Chinese government was behind the global computer hacking that affected not only Google in China, but American Defense Department computers. The Chinese have also rebuffed American pleas to stop exporting militarily sensitive equipment to Iran and North Korea. Should this kind of information be known to the public? The administration says it should not. Referring to the leak about China and proliferation, a "senior administration official" told the *Washington Post*, "Clearly, you don't want any information like this leaked illegally and disseminated to the public." But I

beg to differ. I think the public has a right to know about China's willingness to arm Iran and North Korea. And I applaud Wikileaks for making *this* kind of material public. I would feel the same way if an enterprising reporter unearthed the relevant documents and published them in *The New York Times*. If Wikileaks is doing a disservice by indiscriminately airing classified dirty laundry, the U.S. government is doing its public a disservice by keeping this kind of information about China or Iran or about Afghanistan's government secret.

There is another consideration—one that bears on the history of these kind of leaks. These Wikileaks revelations are the third major episode of this type which occurred during the past century. The first was the new Bolshevik government's release in 1917 of secret treaties signed by Great Britain, France, and Czarist Russia during World War I. The second was the Pentagon Papers in 1971. They have something in common. Each was—and I use the word advisedly, and will explain how—a protest against great power imperialism.

On November 26, 1917, the new Bolshevik government of Russia released copies of the secret wartime agreements between Russia, France, and Great Britain. The most sensational of these was the Sykes-Picot agreement of 1916 to divide up the Ottoman Middle East after World War I. The revelations were shocking in the Middle East, but also in the United States, where many blamed European imperial ambitions for the onset of the Great War.

The Pentagon Papers, which Daniel Ellsberg released to *The New York Times*, laid bare the secret history of the Vietnam war. It revealed that the Kennedy and Johnson administrations had consistently lied to the public about the aims and scope of American intervention, which, it turned out, had little to do with professed aim of spreading or protecting democracy in Southeast Asia. The Wikileaks have primarily been concerned with exposing American intervention in the Middle East and neighboring Afghanistan.

Imperialism? Many Americans hoped that World War I would end the age of imperialism that had led to much of Asia and Africa being divvied up into colonies, protectorates and spheres of influence. But as Lenin would correctly note in his wartime polemic, *Imperialism*, the conflict was in fact a war of imperial redivision. And the Sykes-Picot agreement and what happened after the war proved that to be the case.

After the war, the great powers resorted to various subterfuges (for instance, League of Nations mandates) to maintain their hold over new or former colonies; or they adopted a neo-imperial strategy pioneered by the British in Egypt of fostering client states staffed by locals, but under the quiet control of their embassies. If the locals didn't do as they were told, the troops were brought in. It wasn't imperialism in the sense that the word began to be used in the 1880s, but it was a continuation of the age of empire.

These forms of great power intervention lingered in Latin America, Asia, and Africa, as well as Eastern Europe, in the decades after World War II, but they disappeared by the end of cold war, except in the Middle East, where they endured due to the importance of oil to the world economy and to national militaries. When the United States became the principal outside power in the region after the British announced their withdrawal in February 1947, it also assumed a version of the British neo-imperial strategy.

The United States does not have colonies in the region, but it does have client states, or protectorates, whose governments it defends and sometimes sustains in exchange for access to their oil, or in exchange for their acquiescence to American objectives in the region.

As the United States demonstrated in January 1991, it will go to war to protect these states. Or as it demonstrated in 2003, it will go to war to punish nations that defy it. American relations with these states, most of which have autocratic regimes, has largely had to be conducted in secret for fear of inflaming the regime's subjects, many of whom resent their control. So in this respect, secret diplomacy has remained endemic. And the Wikileaks revelations are in the spirit of past attempts to expose the older imperialism and its newer variations.

Is this kind of intervention a worthy target for these kind of leaks—the way that the Sykes-Picot agreement or the war in Vietnam was? After World War II, the United States justified its interventionism on the grounds of cold war necessity; and recently it has invoked the threat of radical Islamic terror. Radical Islam and its war against the United States can in turn be traced to American support for oil autocracies—Al Qaeda was borne out of opposition to American bases on Saudi soil—and America's extensive support for Israel. Does America need to create client states in Iraq and Afghanistan in order to protect its citizens from Al Qaeda? Or from other threats? I am not going to get into these questions, but the fact that they are questions indicates why so many people around the world have been more focused on the Wikileaks rather than the Wikileaker.

http://www.tnr.com/article/politics/79526/in-defense-wikileaks-iraq-iran-china-foreign-policy?page=0,0

QUESTIONS FOR READING

1. What does Judis think the public has a right to know about China? Why does he feel this way?
2. According to Judis, what do the three major episodes in the last 100 years involving leaks represent?
3. What was the Sykes-Picot Agreement of 1916?
4. What were the Pentagon Papers?

QUESTIONS FOR REASONING AND ANALYSIS

1. What is Judis's thesis or main claim?
2. Why do you think the author focuses so much on imperialism as the pivotal issue associated with the three major leaks of the last century? Is he right to do so? Why or why not?
3. The subtitle of this essay states that Wikileaks "could actually improve U.S. foreign policy." Does the article adequately support this statement? Why or why not?

QUESTIONS FOR REFLECTING AND WRITING

1. Conduct additional research on the Sykes-Picot Agreement of 1916 and the Pentagon Papers of 1971. In your view, is the Wikileaks incident comparable to the controversies surrounding Sykes-Picot and the Pentagon Papers? Why or why not?
2. Would Wikileaks actually improve United States foreign policy? Why or why not? Write an essay defending your position.
3. How would you answer these two questions that Judis poses in the last paragraph of his article: Does America need to create client states in Iraq and Afghanistan in order to protect its citizens from Al Qaeda? Or from other threats? Write an essay addressing these two questions.

website essay

prereading question } How important is trust between people and their government?

Special Report: Could Wikileaks Cause World War III or the End of the World?

David Gewirtz

David Gewirtz is the executive director of the U.S. Strategic Perspective Institute and author of such books as *Reawakening the American Dream* and *Where Have All The Emails Gone?*. This article was posted to ZD Net Government on November 28, 2010.

Trust.

It's a simple, one syllable word. If you think about it, trust is all that stands between us and terrible circumstance, whether that's the breakup of a family or total, nuclear Armageddon.

Trust is vitally important to the operations of nations and governments, as well. Not everyone, for example, is entrusted with America's nuclear codes. Not everyone is entrusted with the command of virtually independent nuclear ballistic missile submarines. And not everyone is entrusted with secret government documents.

For many things, trust has to be selective. It's not a good idea, as an example, to put controlling nuclear weapons on the honor system. My friends worry enough when I get around a good fireworks store or wax poetic about plasma torches—they wouldn't feel comfortable if I had nukes.

Yet, we have to trust *some* people. It's not possible to do everything yourself. Working parents must trust *someone* to watch their newborn. Bosses who can't do everything themselves, or be in multiple places at once *must* put some trust in their employees.

Because the United States is a large nation with many interests all over the world, our military and diplomatic leadership *must* put some trust into the lower-level men and women who move and analyze tremendous amounts of information the world over. Even if they're only 22.

And so it came to be that the great nation of the United States of America entrusted Bradley Manning—a young Private First Class of the U.S. 10th Mountain Division in Iraq, a former school dropout and pizza greeter—with handling message traffic considered confidential and not for foreign eyes.

While most American soldiers are more than worthy of our trust, respect, and thanks, young Bradley was not. Manning, without any formal training or education in geopolitical affairs, without the ability to see all the national security ramifications, and without the ability to understand (or possibly even care) about the lives that would inevitably be lost, took it upon himself to betray the sacred trust granted him by the United States military.

There are always people willing to take advantage of naive young people in positions of trust. So it came to pass that Manning's betrayal had an outlet, in the person of an ambitious foreign narcissist named Julian Assange, a man so amoral he tried to blackmail Amnesty International.

But naivety and audience can't act alone.

There must also be opportunity. Beyond the need to entrust our diplomatic security to 22-year-old dropouts—we have another serious security flaw. We allow removable media, iPods, smartphones, and thumb drives behind the firewall.

I have been banging on this drum for years now. Over and over, I have told politicians, military leaders, homeland security professionals*, and the American people that these tiny handheld devices pose a tremendous security risk.

For a while, it seemed like the Pentagon, at least, was going to take some action. They put a ban on USB drives in the military. But then, after only a year, they substantially reduced the ban's effectiveness.

I'm telling you this because, according to *The Guardian*, Manning stole more than 250,000 confidential diplomatic cables (all of 1.6 gigabytes of data) by smuggling a thumb drive and a re-writable CD labeled "Lady Gaga" into work, filled them, and then forwarded them to a waiting Assange.

While it's not clear whether or not Manning's betrayal could have been prevented by better security procedures, it certainly could have been made more difficult. Even so, now we're left with the fallout.

I'm not going to recount the sordid details of what was contained in those not-for-foreign-eyes diplomatic cables. First, I don't believe they should be public and, second, many other publications, including *The New York Times*, are publishing the leaks.

I'm also not going to tell you that nothing contained in those cables was disturbing. Instead, I'll tell you why we (and every other nation) keep some information to ourselves, or release information only in carefully controlled circumstances.

International diplomacy is a precise dance.

Although some nations are vastly larger and vastly wealthier than others, it is a facade of diplomatic protocol that all nations and all leaders are treated as equals—at least in public. Many nations (and the U.S., in particular) maintain protocol offices to make sure that every diplomatic interaction goes according to plan, stays on message, and doesn't offend (unless, of course, it's time to not be nice).

Internal national politics, on the other hand, is a gutter fight.

Nations must communicate with other nations according to an established protocol, but the leaders who make that national policy must always answer to their constituents. If the leaders can't seem to maintain an upper hand, can't demand respect, and aren't seen to be getting things done, those leaders are usually replaced.

The challenge is that diplomacy is always a give-and-take sort of thing. When nations bargain with other nations, sometimes it goes smoothly, sometimes there's horse-trading, and sometimes there's pressure to be applied. Whenever two leaders negotiate, each wants to come back to his or her country and brag about how he won the negotiation. Neither wants to lose face.

As we all know, people will do incredibly idiotic things to protect their honor. So will leaders.

I've written previously about how the documents leaked by Wikileaks could cause people to die. Wikileaks hasn't redacted the information about confidential informants, and it's likely that these informants—in large numbers—will be executed by their factions over the coming weeks and months.

That's bad enough. But many national leaders would prefer to project bravado, send people to war, and engage in years-long conflicts with other nations rather than lose face or admit a mistake.

Here is where the Wikileaks risk is extreme. Manning and Assange "outed" confidential negotiations (and, yes, pressure) about nuclear defense issues. They "outed" defensive tactics America was taking against cyberwarfare advances by certain other nations. They "outed" the procedures we're going through to find "homes" for Guantanamo prisoners. They "outed" discussions about protecting Americans from terrorists.

Each of these disclosures will likely cause leaders to do damage control. Because diplomacy always involves more than one player, the damage control will be different from nation to nation. Nations that were in some level of agreement (whether coerced or not) will now find that, for political reasons, they must agree to not agree.

For some nations, the fact that this information is now public will prevent them from being able to compromise. For some nations, the fact that this information is now public will prevent them from being able to trust.

Trust.

If you think about it, trust can be all that stands between us and terrible circumstance, whether that's the breakup of a family or total, nuclear Armageddon.

http://www.zdnet.com/blog/government/special-report-could-wikileaks-cause-world-war-iii-or-the-end-of-the-world/9696?tag=mantle_skin;content

---

QUESTIONS FOR READING

1. With what did the United States entrust Bradley Manning?
2. Besides entrusting Manning, what is the other "serious security flaw" Gewirtz mentions?
3. What does Gewirtz think is a "facade of diplomatic protocol"?

4. At the end of the piece, Gewirtz explains what consequence for some nations now that sensitive information has been made public?

QUESTIONS FOR REASONING AND ANALYSIS

1. Gewirtz begins and ends with the word *trust*. What do you think is the intended effect of doing so?
2. What is Gewirtz's thesis? Do you agree or disagree with his argument? Why or why not?

3. How does Gewirtz support his argument? Does he use good evidence and reasoning? Why or why not?

1. In your view, how important is "trust" in diplomatic relations and in making foreign policy? Write an essay explaining your position on "trust" related to these matters.

2. Consider Gewirtz's argument in relation to Judis's position on Wikileaks. With which author do you most agree? Why?

3. What, for you, is the most critical factor in international relations with other countries? Write an essay explaining why that factor is so important.

opinion column

prereading question } Should classic books undergo revision to better accommodate the current sociocultural and/or political climate?

Huckleberry Finn Revision: Pro

Jessica Peterson

At the time of publication in early 2011, Jessica Peterson was a sophomore criminal justice and psychology major at Texas Christian University.

Producing a new version of "The Adventures of Huckleberry Finn" that replaces the "N-word" with the word "slave" allows the book to continue to reach into the lives of generations to come.

In a society where change and progress are valued, removing offensive terms allows for a more comfortable read.

In classes, students learn equality alongside peers of every race and background. However, confusion swirls when the teacher assigns a highly praised and beloved book for the class and students find racial slurs embedded throughout the text.

Literature in its original form definitely has a place in the world and is important to preserve. But who is to say that a changing society does not create a demand for modified accounts?

Parents who love the story of Huck Finn can now willingly give the book to their children and not have conflicting thoughts on what is or isn't appropriate. The story's plot is unchanged and the historical differences remain intact, but the potentially harmful terms are gone.

Children of a new age and upbringing can indulge in the stories of their parents' and grandparents' childhoods without learning or developing socially inappropriate language.

Public education is continually changing in order to keep up with modern times and guide children in the right direction.

A major goal in modern society is to encourage colorblindness in school, careers and relationships. This modified version of a classic story aids in furthering that idea.

The new version of "Huckleberry Finn" is purely a new edition, not a complete replacement of the old. Books are continually produced in new forms, and classic novels now include "interpretations" alongside the original text. This version is simply another form as well. Those who prefer to read the original text are free to do so, and producing new versions does not mean that all prior versions will be destroyed and never mentioned again.

This is another tool for parenting, if nothing else, that allows parents to censor what their children read if they so choose.

Generating a more sensitive version of the story may even bring more readers to "outdated" books such as this one.

Keeping literature alive in various communities is an important objective, and contemporary revisions such as this can help achieve that goal. If literature continues to play an active role in society, education and the spread of knowledge, will prevail.

http://www.tcudailyskiff.com/opinion/huckleberry-finn-revision-pro-1.2435427

Huckleberry Finn Revision: Con

Wyatt Kanyer

At the time of publication in early 2011, Wyatt Kanyer was a journalism major and also a student at Texas Christian University.

Monday marked the 25th anniversary of Martin Luther King Jr. Day, which meant it was the 25th time Americans came together across the nation to serve in honor of perhaps the greatest civil rights activist in U.S. history. In the midst of this positivity, however, loomed the negativity of ignorance.

NewSouth Books, an Alabama-based publisher that, according to its website, "gravitate[s] to material which enhances our understanding of who we are and which asks us to stretch in our understanding of others," will release a rewrite of Mark Twain's American classic "The Adventures of Huckleberry Finn" next month that will feature a replacement for a historically controversial word in American history: the "N-word."

The decision came after Auburn University professor and Mark Twain scholar Alan Gribben suggested the change be made in order to make the book more accommodating to teachers who were reluctant to use a book with such language.

While NewSouth is striving to uphold its principles in doing so, this rewrite eliminates Twain's original intent in including the word in his work.

According to an opinion piece in The Huffington Post by Craig Hotchkiss, education program manager at the Mark Twain House and Museum, Twain grew up in Missouri using the N-word and seeing black people as inferior to whites. As he grew in age and knowledge, however, Twain realized the bigoted nature of the word, at which point he became more tolerant.

Huckleberry Finn is, among other things, a representation of Twain's transformation of racial awareness, Hotchkiss writes.

"[Twain] used his story of the boy Huckleberry Finn to illustrate his own epiphany about American racism and to offer a cautionary tale at a time when American society was receding back into the same depravity that had earlier torn the nation apart in the Civil War," he writes.

Hotchkiss' piece demonstrates the fact that the rewrite not only ignores the clear racial barriers that existed at that point in history but also that it eliminates the reason why the book was written in the first place: because of Twain's personal growth in understanding.

While those issues need to be addressed, experts and common citizens alike must also recognize the degree to which Twain's creative license and personal experience is being ignored.

Furthermore, one must also consider whether the publisher is making an attempt to make amends for centuries of racial inequality.

NewSouth is based in Alabama, a state that has been a center for racial inequality throughout U.S. history.

The company's aforementioned goal is admirable; however, there is no quick fix for centuries of racial pain and suffering experienced by black people nationwide.

Lastly, the rewrite will feature the use of "slave" instead of the N-word.

This word choice only further damages Twain's original intent. Slavery was only one example of racial inequality in the U.S.

Even after the days of slavery, there were severe, clear racial divisions generations later in the segregated South, divisions which Dr. King and others fought to defeat.

This racial tension was due in large part to Jim Crow laws and Black Codes, which were in place for almost 90 years. It would be irrational and illegal if history books were printed without mention of the Crow laws, so it is inappropriate for NewSouth to print a historic work without demonstrating the laws' effects.

Also, modern-day racism does not feature the use of the word slave. More times than not, it features the N-word.

It seems, then, that using slave instead of the N-word is a close-minded decision by NewSouth, as it only highlights a chapter in the history of American racism.

Ignoring racism would, in essence, ignore the positive impact of brave leaders like Dr. King and remove a substantial amount of history that defines the advances the U.S. has made in accepting diversity.

Stretching our understanding of each other should not include eliminating the realities of history, no matter how gruesome those realities may be.

http://www.tcudailyskiff.com/opinion/columnists/huckleberry-finn-revision-con-1.2435256

QUESTIONS FOR READING

1. According to Peterson, what represents a "tool for parenting"?
2. What goal does Peterson say contemporary revisions can help achieve?

3. What change does Kanyer say NewSouth Books made to *Huckleberry Finn*?
4. Why does Kanyer favor leaving the N-word in *Huckleberry Finn*?

QUESTIONS FOR REASONING AND ANALYSIS

1. Do the authors use good reasoning and provide good support for their claims? Why or why not?
2. On what assumption does Peterson's thesis or main argument rest?

3. Kanyer argues that changing the N-word to "slave" damages Twain's original intent. What does he mean by this statement?

QUESTIONS FOR REFLECTING AND WRITING

1. Whose point of view do you agree with more and why? Do you see a compromise position between the two? If so, what is that position?
2. As a student, which version of *Huckleberry Finn* would you want to read? Why? If you were, or possibly are, a parent, then what version would you want your child to read? Why?

enduring controversies in a new age

Abortion, Animal Rights, Capital Punishment, and Health Care

chapter 21

Since 2000, people have continued to debate some of the same issues people debated in the 1970s, 1980s, and 1990s. Abortion, animal rights, capital punishment, and health care issues still evoke very strong emotions. Health care, for instance, is one of the most enduring crises because costs have spiraled seemingly out of control, with a number of people—particularly those living below the poverty line—finding them-selves unable to receive adequate treatment because they cannot afford it. Selections in this chapter represent opposing viewpoints about such serious problems as funding for international organizations supporting abortion rights, the use of animals in medical and scientific research, the administration of the death penalty, and universal health care coverage.

prereading questions

1. Should the U.S. government fund organizations in other countries that perform abortions or provide counseling to women considering the option?

2. Do advances in medical research ever outweigh the cruelty associated with the use of animals to achieve those advances?

3. What are the current laws on the use of capital punishment? In capital cases, what kinds of evidence should be presented to decide on guilt beyond a reasonable doubt?

4. Is health care a right or a responsibility—an entitlement or the moral obligation of government to provide?

5. Should the free market determine the cost of health care? If not, should the government establish price controls to keep costs down?

6. If you wanted to change any of the current laws on these issues to make them reflect your views, how would you go about trying to get the laws changed?

websites related to this chapter's topic

CORNELL LAW SCHOOL—CORNELL DEATH PENALTY PROJECT
http://library2.lawschool.cornell.edu/death
Information on court decisions and results of relevant studies.

ASSOCIATION OF THE BRITISH PHARMACEUTICAL INDUSTRY
www.abpi.org.uk/amric/amric.asp
Site of an association that supports the use of animals in medical research.

RELIGIOUS TOLERANCE.ORG, MEXICO CITY POLICY
www.religioustolerance.org/abo_wrld.htm
Site that explains the history of this policy as well as arguments for and against it.

PRESIDENT OBAMA'S AGENDA FOR HEALTH CARE
www.whitehouse.gov/issues/health_care
White House website that explains the Obama-Biden plan for health care.

NATIONAL INSTITUTES OF HEALTH
www.nih.gov
Information from U.S. government agency and links to other resources on health issues and health research.

Sharron Angle Reveals Controversial Abortion Views

Senate nominee says that "two wrongs don't make a right"
in cases of rape and incest.

Ravi Somaiya

Ravi Somaiya wrote this article, which appeared on July 8, 2010, for Newsweek.com.

Sharron Angle, the GOP nominee for Senate in Nevada, is maintaining her reputation for uncompromising conservative policies. In a radio interview from late June uncovered by the Huffington Post, Angle addresses the issue of abortion in the case of rape and incest. Angle told conservative radio host Alan Stock that she would counsel a (hypothetical) 13-year-old girl, raped and impregnated by her father, that "two wrongs don't make a right," and that it is possible to make "a lemon situation into lemonade."

It is the latest in a series of very right-wing positions Angle has revealed. She has also said she wants to abolish the Department of Education, the Energy Department, the Environmental Protection Agency, and huge swaths of the Internal Revenue Service. She wants to take the U.S. out of the U.N. because the latter "has been captured by the far left," phase out Social Security, and perhaps ban alcohol. She has backed a Scientology-based drug-rehab program and called for armed revolution against the very political body she seeks to join.

Her strategy, since winning the Republican primary and beginning a campaign against Senate Majority Leader Harry Reid, has been to avoid the press except conservative outlets—an attempt, it seems, to avoid questioning of her more outside-the-mainstream ideas. That seems, in this case, to have backfired.

Here's the full transcript of the exchange between Angle and Stock.

STOCK: Let me bring up one other topic that I rarely talk about here, because it's one of those topics that's a lose-lose, but we've got to talk about it because it was brought up in your TV interview. And that has to do with the issue of abortion, and whether or not abortion should be available in the case of rape or incest. The question to you at the time by the interviewer was that do you want the government to go and tell a 13-year-old child who has been raped by her father that she has to have that baby. And of course you responded, "I didn't say that, I always say that I value life." Where do you stand on the issue of abortion, a consensual abortion, from a person who is raped or is pregnant as a result of incest?

ANGLE: Well, right now our law permits that. My own personal feelings, and that is always what I express, my personal feeling is that we need to err on the side of life. There is a plan and a purpose, a value to every life no matter what its location, age, gender, or disability. So whenever we talk about government and government's role, government's role is to protect life, and that's what our Founding Fathers said, that we have the right to life, liberty, and the pursuit of happiness.

STOCK: What do you say, then, to a young girl—I am going to place it as he said it—when a young girl is raped by her father, let's say, and she is pregnant. How do you explain this to her in terms of wanting her to go through the process of having the baby?

ANGLE: I think that two wrongs don't make a right. And I have been in the situation of counseling young girls, not 13 but 15, who have had very at-risk, difficult pregnancies. And my counsel was to look for some alternatives, which they did. And they found that they had made what was really a lemon situation into lemonade. Well, one girl in particular moved in with the adoptive parents of her child, and they both were adopted. Both of them grew up—one graduated from high school, the other had parents that loved her and she also graduated from high school. And I'll tell you, the little girl who was born from that very poor situation came to me when she was 13 and said, "I know what you did. Thank you for saving my life." So it is meaningful to me to err on the side of life.

QUESTIONS FOR READING

1. What is Angle's position on abortion in cases of rape and incest?

2. What other controversial positions does Angle hold?

QUESTIONS FOR REASONING AND ANALYSIS

1. What is your reaction to Angle's position on abortion? Do you agree or disagree? Why or why not?

2. What evidence does Angle use in support of her position? What persuasive appeal does she rely upon by supporting her argument in this way?

QUESTIONS FOR REFLECTING AND WRITING

1. What is your own position on abortion? Pro-life? Pro-choice? Why do you adhere to one particular position over another?

2. How would you respond to Angle's story about the 13-year-old girl who gave birth to a child as a result of incest?

3. Are current laws and policies related to abortion justified? Why or why not?

photo

prereading question } **Is animal research absolutely necessary for improving human health?**

A newly formed "pro-test" group marched in Oxford, England, in February 2006. The group was responding to an animal rights group that had targeted an Oxford University laboratory—a facility which at the time was still under construction.

QUESTIONS FOR REASONING AND ANALYSIS

1. The sign the person holds in this photograph makes a clear argument. In your own words, what is that argument?

2. What is the premise supporting the claim of the protest sign? In other words, what is the major reason why animal testing should receive support—as expressed by the protest sign, that is?

3. Why do you think the protesters have written the word *human* in red?

4. How would you explain the warrant, or implicit assumption, that links the claim and the reasoning offered by this protest sign?

1. Is animal testing the only method for achieving advances in medical science? If not, what other methods exist? Are animal testing methods superior? Why or why not?

2. Assume for a moment that you stand opposed to animal testing for medical research purposes. (Understandably, you may already oppose animal testing, but take the opposite point of view in this instance.) If medical scientists, for example, argued that the *only* way to achieve a cure for cancer was through animal testing, would you then support such testing? Why or why not?

3. Should animals have rights per se? Why or why not?

website

prereading question } **What steps, if any, should be taken to protect animal rights?**

People for the Ethical Treatment of Animals

The following is the website for People for the Ethical Treatment of Animals, or PETA. This organization focuses on protecting the rights of animals and on preventing their mistreatment.

Image courtesy of PETA; www.peta.org.

QUESTIONS FOR REASONING AND ANALYSIS

1. What audiences is the website attempting to reach? Is it just animal rights activists? What indications suggest that this group is trying to communicate with other audiences besides animal rights activists?
2. What is the major purpose of this site? What are its creators trying to accomplish by communicating with audiences this way?

3. In what ways does this website establish credibility—or ethos—with audiences?

QUESTIONS FOR REFLECTING AND WRITING

1. Do animals have "rights" per se? Why or why not?
2. Conduct additional research related to one of the issues highlighted on this site. What is your position on the issue? What are your reasons for taking a particular stance on the issue?

3. Are you a vegetarian or a vegan? What are your reasons for choosing a vegetarian or vegan lifestyle? If you choose to eat meat, what are your reasons for doing so?

drawing/illustration

prereading questions } Is the death penalty a suitable punishment for some crimes? If so, which ones?

Scott Stantis

This political cartoon by Chicago cartoonist Scott Stantis appeared in a 2010 issue of *The Chicago Tribune.*

QUESTIONS FOR REASONING AND ANALYSIS

1. What does the tall figure pointing a finger represent?
2. What does the Grim Reaper represent? Is it significant that the cartoonist chose the Grim Reaper over another image? Why or why not?
3. What argument is the cartoon making?

QUESTIONS FOR REFLECTING AND WRITING

1. What are the arguments and reasons opposing the death penalty? Do you find those arguments compelling? Why or why not?
2. Are you opposed to or in favor of the death penalty? For what reasons do you oppose or support the death penalty?
3. Conduct additional research on the death penalty in Illinois. What are the issues surrounding the death penalty controversy in that state? What is your assessment of the debate over the death penalty there?

---

political cartoon

prereading question } **Is administration of the death penalty racially biased?**

Khalil Bendib

The following political cartoon appeared alongside an unsigned entry in *The Black Sentinel* on August 9, 2007, a blog devoted to issues facing African Americans (http://theblacksentinel.word-press.com). The cartoonist, Khalil Bendib, was born in North Africa and now lives in Berkeley, California. His cartoons appear in newspapers and online publications. This one first appeared in December 2005.

Reprinted by permission of Khalil Bendib. www.bendib.com.

1. In your own words, how would you summarize the thesis or claim of this cartoon?
2. What do the two major images (blind justice and the grim reaper) represent?
3. What does the cartoon imply or suggest about justice for accused people of different races?
4. Does the cartoon rely more on logical or emotional appeal? Why does it rely more on one than the other?

1. The cartoon makes a very controversial statement in a very bold way. In your view, is the statement accurate? Do you agree or disagree? Why?
2. Many experts cite statistics showing that African American inmates outnumber Caucasians in U.S. prisons by a large margin. This cartoon, however, suggests, albeit implicitly, that more blacks await execution on death row than whites. If one accepts this condition as true, then why might this condition exist? Why might more blacks receive the death penalty instead of a life sentence?
3. Some people remain opposed to the death penalty because they believe the judicial system fails to apply it fairly and equitably. Assuming the validity of their belief, would making changes to ensure fairness in sentencing make the death penalty a more effective punishment? Why or why not?

Viguerie and Bozell: Support Is Waning for Death Penalty

Richard A. Viguerie and L. Brent Bozell III

Richard A. Viguerie is chairman of ConservativeHQ.com, and Brent Bozell III is founder and president of the Media Research Center. This essay was posted to the Timesdispatch.com on October 5, 2010.

WASHINGTON We lifelong conservatives and Tea Party supporters recently urged the death sentence for Teresa Lewis in Virginia be commuted to life in prison without parole instead.

We are among a growing number of conservatives who have questions and reservations about the death penalty, believe it is no longer a necessary form of punishment based on either Lockean or biblical principles, or oppose it outright.

Around the country death sentences are dropping, and support for the death penalty is waning. This trend is not limited to bleeding-heart liberals and criminal coddlers.

We urge our fellow conservatives to at least consider some issues when contemplating the death penalty.

The Old Testament required the death penalty for certain sins and a litany of offenses. In John 8 of the New Testament, the Pharisees confronted Jesus about a woman ready to be stoned for adultery. Jesus, sensing a trap they laid on a conflict between the Old Testament and Roman law, said: Let him who is without sin cast the first stone.

We believe John 8 of the New Testament shows that Jesus did not consider the death penalty mandatory punishment for sins, and certainly not unless the process complied with God's law. Deuteronomy 17:6 requires more than one witness to convict.

We also believe conservative Lockean principles do not compel the death penalty.

John Locke's Second Treatise on Government offers a justification of the State's taking the life of someone who is guilty of a heinous crime. Locke, on whose principles conservatism is built, believed the death penalty was a justifiable punishment for two reasons: protecting society (self-preservation) and deterrence.

Locke described the social compact of society as much like the notion: Do unto others as you'd have done to you. Some people commit acts so despicable they no longer merit the protections of that social compact. They may be so dangerous that they are a threat to us.

Therefore, like we may kill a wild animal that threatens us, the death penalty was an acceptable form of punishment even under Locke's view of limited government power.

We now, however, have maximum security prisons that were incapable of being built in Locke's time. Society may protect itself without putting a human to death as it would a wild animal. Since we believe each person has a soul, and is capable of achieving salvation, life in prison is now an alternative to the death penalty.

Under Locke's other reason, deterrence, punishment should be severe enough to discourage criminal acts. We certainly agree. However, some data show the death penalty does not act as deterrence.

In fact, the data seem to indicate murder and other heinous crimes may be lower in jurisdictions that do not have the death penalty. That's not proof, of course, but we believe death penalty proponents bear the burden of proof that the ultimate punishment is in fact a deterrence.

From our conservative perspective, there are other reasons we oppose the death penalty. It is an expensive government program with the power to kill people.

Conservatives don't trust the government is always capable, competent, or fair with far lighter tasks.

When it comes to life and death, mistakes are made, or perhaps worse, bad decisions are made. States have wrongly convicted people based on false confessions and inaccurate eyewitness identification. In some of these cases, the real perpetrator was identified decades after the crime occurred. Since DNA evidence is not available in the majority of murder cases, other wrongful convictions based on similar types of evidence may never come to light.

We know our opinion is not held by all conservatives. Surely, however, there are many questions about the death penalty's accuracy, fairness, and financial efficiency that should be addressed.

We urge those who ascribe to the Old Testament to consider whether the Virginia death penalty system reflects God's law. We also ask Christians to contemplate the meaning of John 8.

http://www2.timesdispatch.com/news/2010/oct/05/ed-gopcap05-ar-542103

QUESTIONS FOR READING

1. According to the authors, John 8 reveals what about Jesus's perspective on the death penalty?
2. Under Locke's view, what two reasons justify the death penalty?
3. What is Viguerie and Bozell's response to Locke's view of the death penalty?
4. What other reasons do the authors cite for their opposition to the death penalty?

QUESTIONS FOR REASONING AND ANALYSIS

1. Why do the authors choose the specific examples from the Bible and John Locke in making their argument?
2. Because Viguerie and Bozell are political and social conservatives, does their making a traditionally "liberal" argument against the death penalty give them greater credibility or ethos? Why or why not?
3. How does the authors' essay reflect a refutation argument?

QUESTIONS FOR REFLECTING AND WRITING

1. Some have claimed that a relatively large percentage of death row inmates are actually innocent of the crimes that resulted in their executions. Viguerie and Bozell, in fact, make mention of this problem in their essay. Are you sensitive to this concern? Why or why not?
2. The Eighth Amendment of the United States Constitution says, "Excessive bail shall not be required, nor excessive fines imposed, nor cruel and unusual punishments inflicted." Some opponents of the death penalty argue that it represents a form of cruel and unusual punishment, thereby making the death penalty unconstitutional. Why might one consider the death penalty "cruel and unusual"? Why do you agree or disagree with this argument?

prereading question } Are the concerns over universal health care coverage founded?

School of Glock

Gail Collins

Gail Collins has worked as a columnist and member of the editorial board for *The New York Times* since 1995. This article was published in *The New York Times* on March 9, 2011.

It's been nearly nine weeks since that tragic shooting in Tucson, and you may be wondering whether there's been any gun legislation proposed in the aftermath.

Well, in Florida, a state representative has introduced a bill that would impose fines of up to $5 million on any doctor who asks a patient whether he or she owns a gun. This is certainly a new and interesting concept, but I don't think we can classify it as a response to Tucson. Jason Brodeur, the Republican who thought it up, says it's a response to the health care reform act.

A sizable chunk of this country seems to feel as though there is nothing so secure that it can't be endangered by Obamacare. It's only a matter of time before somebody discovers that giving everyone access to health insurance poses a terrible threat to the armed forces, or the soybean crop, or poodles.

Brodeur's is one of many, many gun bills floating around state legislatures these days. Virtually all of them seem to be based on the proposition that one of the really big problems we have in this country is a lack of weaponry. His nightmare scenario is that thanks to the "overreaching federal government," insurance companies would learn who has guns from the doctors and use the information to raise the owners' rates.

However, it turns out that the health care law has a provision that specifically prohibits insurers from reducing any coverage or benefits because of gun ownership. A *St. Petersburg Times* reporter, Aaron Sharockman, looked this up. I had no idea, did you? Apparently Senate Majority Leader Harry Reid himself stuck this in to make the gun-lobby folks happy.

Which they really aren't. The gun lobby will never be happy, unless the health care law specifically requires every American to have a pistol on his or her person at all times.

Great idea! thought State Representative Hal Wick of South Dakota, who tossed in a bill this year requiring every adult citizen to purchase a gun. Actually, even Wick admitted this one wasn't going anywhere. It was mainly a symbolic protest against the you-know-what law.

Actual responses to the Tucson shooting—that is, something that might actually stop similar tragedies in the future or reduce the carnage—seem to be limited to a proposal in Congress to ban the sale of the kind of ammunition clip that allowed the gunman to fire 31 shots in 15 seconds. That bill is stalled at the gate. Perhaps Congress has been too busy repeatedly voting on bills to repeal the health care law to think about anything else. But, so far, the gun-clip ban has zero Republican supporters, which is a problem given the matter of the Republicans being in the House majority.

Meanwhile in the states, legislation to get more guns in more places (public libraries, college campuses) is getting a more enthusiastic reception.

The nation's state legislators seem to be troubled by a shortage of things they can do to make the National Rifle Association happy. Once you've voted to allow people to carry guns into bars (Georgia), eliminated the need for getting a permit to carry a concealed weapon (Arizona) and designated your own official state gun (Utah—awaiting the governor's signature), it gets hard to come up with new ideas.

This may be why so many states are now considering laws that would prohibit colleges and universities from barring guns on campus.

"It's about people having the right to personal protection," said Daniel Crocker, the southwest regional director for Students for Concealed Carry on Campus.

Concealed Carry on Campus is a national organization of students dedicated to opening up schools to more weaponry. Every spring it holds a national Empty Holster Protest "symbolizing that disarming all law-abiding citizens creates defense-free zones, which are attractive targets for criminals."

And you thought the youth of America had lost its idealism. Hang your head.

The core of the great national gun divide comes down to this: On one side, people's sense of public safety goes up as the number of guns goes down; the other side responds to every gun tragedy by reflecting that this might have been averted if only more legally armed citizens had been on the scene.

I am on the first side simply because I believe that in a time of crisis, there is no such thing as a good shot.

"Police, on average, for every 10 rounds fired, I think, actually strike something once or twice, and they are highly trained," said Bill Bratton, the former New York City police commissioner.

Concealed Carry on Campus envisions a female student being saved from an armed assailant by a freshman with a concealed weapon permit. I see a well-intentioned kid with a pistol trying to intervene in a scary situation and accidentally shooting the victim.

And, somehow, it'll all turn out to be the health care reform law's fault.

QUESTIONS FOR READING

1. What did the state representative in Florida introduce?
2. What is the provision associated with gun ownership in the health care law?
3. According to Collins, what does the core of the great national gun divide come down to?

QUESTIONS FOR REASONING AND ANALYSIS

1. What is Collins's thesis?
2. What is the objection that Collins voices in this essay? Do you think it is a legitimate one? Why or why not?
3. How would you describe the tone of Collins's article? Why would you describe it in this way?

QUESTIONS FOR REFLECTING AND WRITING

1. Although Collins frames her argument around gun legislation, she is actually pointing to a perhaps greater concern over proposed health care legislation. What is that concern? Do you share her sentiments? Why or why not? Write an essay defending your position.
2. Collins mentions "concealed carry" laws that would permit students to bring firearms on college campuses. What is your position on this issue? Should students be allowed to carry firearms to class? Why or why not?
3. Conduct some additional research on the arguments for and against recent health care proposals and legislation. Which arguments do you find most compelling? Why?

opinion column

prereading questions } How do you conceive of "rights"? What rights constitute human rights, civil rights, and so forth? Is universal health care a right?

Everyone Prospers Under Health Law

Kathleen Sebelius

Kathleen Sebelius is the secretary of health and human services in the Obama administration. This article was published to Politico.com on March 14, 2011.

Just 12 months after the Patient Protection and Affordable Care Act became law, the American people are enjoying new protections, greater freedoms and lower costs.

Children are now protected from being turned away by insurers because of a pre-existing condition. Seniors enrolled in Medicare now have the freedom to get preventive care—such as mammograms and colonoscopies—for free. A Patient's Bill of Rights is freeing families from some of the worst abuses of insurance companies, including canceling coverage when you get sick because of a paperwork error.

Early signs show that, after years of decline, the number of small businesses offering coverage to employees is increasing.

Perhaps less widely recognized, but no less significant, has been the way the law is demanding transparency and accountability from the insurance industry to bring down premiums.

For too long, it's been common for people to receive a letter from an insurer announcing a premium increase of 20 percent to 25 percent, with little explanation and no recourse. That's already changing.

continued

During the past year, our department has provided states with almost $250 million in funding to strengthen their ability to review, revise or reject unreasonable rate hikes. New proposed rules would force many insurers to justify big increases and post explanations on the Web. States from California to Connecticut have already shown that vigorous oversight can be effective in stopping unjustified premium increases.

And for the first time, insurers are being held accountable for the way they spend consumer premiums. New rules require insurers to pay out 80 percent to 85 percent of premium dollars on health care and quality improvement efforts—rather than marketing and executive bonuses. Those who don't meet this standard will have two choices: reduce rates or send customers rebates.

By holding insurance companies accountable, we are making sure families and small-business owners get the best value for their premium dollars.

We also know that individuals and small businesses have often had to pay significantly more for health insurance than big businesses, which can use their size to negotiate lower premiums. But in 2014, individuals and small businesses will be able to pool their purchasing power through new state-based health insurance exchanges to bring down their rates. Millions of people will be eligible for tax credits, based on need, to help them afford health coverage.

Today, Americans also have a new Web-based tool that allows them to comparison shop for the best insurance options available in their zip codes. Go to www.healthcare.gov to check it out.

These efforts are helping to make the health care marketplace more competitive. When consumers have the information they need to easily compare plans, insurance companies will no longer be able to hide behind fine print. If they want to compete, they'll have to provide quality coverage at an affordable price.

When you add together all these improvements under the Affordable Care Act, projections based on data from the nonpartisan Congressional Budget Office show that a family of four, making $55,000, could save more than $6,000 a year on health insurance in 2014. For a family making $33,000, those savings will be nearly $10,000 annually. For many American families, this means that health insurance will be within reach for the first time.

Ultimately, we know that the biggest factor driving up premiums is the soaring cost of care. So, as part of the health care law, we have invested in preventive care, and innovative programs aimed at slowing that growth of premiums. By testing and implementing new ideas to coordinate care, improve patient safety, and reduce waste, fraud and abuse, the law will create additional savings for decades to come. Analysts predict that by 2019, these efforts could save an additional $2,000 for a family policy for employer-based coverage.

President Barack Obama has made clear that his administration is willing to work with anyone to improve the law and fix what needs fixing. That's why, after hearing from governors, providers and patients, the president recently announced his support for legislation that allows states to pursue innovative alternatives to the law, provided they can achieve the same results as the Affordable Care Act—including relief from skyrocketing costs.

What we can't afford to do is take away these benefits, cancel these rights, and return to the days when insurance companies got between you and your doctor. If we want to relieve the burden of rising health care costs on families, businesses, and government, we need to move forward not back.

http://www.politico.com/news/stories/0311/51205.html

QUESTIONS FOR READING

1. According to Sebelius, what are the benefits of the Patient's Bill of Rights?
2. According to the author, how does the law benefit small businesses?
3. For what are insurers now being held accountable?
4. What is the "biggest factor" driving up premiums?

QUESTIONS FOR REASONING AND ANALYSIS

1. What is Sebelius's thesis or main argument? How does her essay represent an argument taking a position?
2. Sebelius refers to health care as a "right" in this essay. How do you think she conceives of "right"? In other words, how might she define "right" or "rights"?
3. Which of Sebelius's arguments do you see as the strongest? Which arguments do you find less compelling? Why?

1. Conduct additional research on the Patient's Bill of Rights. What does the Patient's Bill of Rights stipulate? Would you oppose any aspect of it? Why or why not?
2. Is universal health care coverage a "right"? How do you conceive of "rights"? Do you view a distinction between "right" and "responsibility"? If so, what is the distinction?
3. Should the United States government make sure that everyone receives health care coverage? Why or why not?

opinion column

prereading question } Is "Obamacare" good law or legislation?

Why I Voted to Repeal Health Reform

Rep. Dan Boren

Representative Dan Boren (D-Oklahoma), a member of the Blue Dog Coalition, serves on the Natural Resources Committee and the Permanent Select Committee on Intelligence. This essay was published to Politico.com on March 16, 2011.

We are one year removed from the passage of the Affordable Care Act and nearly two months past a vote in the House to repeal it. Since that first vote was cast, my constituents remind me at every town hall meeting I hold that they are overwhelmingly opposed to this law. That is why I supported repeal.

They are aware, as am I, that we have many uninsured Oklahomans who need assistance. Many voters also agree that reforms are needed to address the issue of rising health insurance premiums, the staggering number of medical bankruptcies and the burden that health care costs have on small-business growth and job creation. But as the debate for health care reform moved along in the summer of 2009, the sheer size and scope of what the Obama administration had proposed were more than enough to convince me—and a significant majority of my constituents—that this was not the solution to America's health care problems.

In fact, a survey conducted by Public Policy Polling in my district in March 2010, just weeks after Congress voted on final passage of this legislation, showed that just 17 percent of my constituents supported the law.

The most disappointing aspect of the health care reform debate is the fact that a majority of Americans support several reforms that Congress could have addressed in a bipartisan and incremental way. Provisions such as preventing companies from denying coverage to individuals with pre-existing conditions, allowing children to stay on their parents' insurance until age 26 and making it illegal to cancel insurance coverage when a person becomes sick are all common-sense reforms that share a broad level of support among a majority of Americans.

Rather than taking a bipartisan approach and tackling these issues incrementally, Congress and President Barack Obama produced a 2,000-page bill that dramatically expanded the federal government's role in the private sector, placed burdensome mandates on small businesses and individuals and increased taxes during an economic downturn.

I have said many times since the economic collapse in fall 2008 that the No. 1 priority for Congress should be job creation and economic expansion. Unfortunately, the leadership in Washington got sidetracked from this priority and, in turn, lost the confidence of the American people.

While many have advocated for a full repeal—which I voted for last month—the president's veto pen will very likely prevent it. That leaves Congress with the option of trying to improve the legislation—which we have already started to do.

Just two weeks ago, the House repealed the 1099 reporting requirement that many small businesses in my district, and across the nation, have found alarming. This was a solid first step.

We are also beginning to address the unpopular mandates on individuals and businesses found throughout the law.

Last week, Rep. Mike Rogers (R-Mich.) and I introduced the Health Care Waiver Fairness Act. This legislation will allow every small-business owner or average American the opportunity to apply for a waiver from the new health care law if they so desire. The basics of this bill are that if you like the health care reform law, you can take advantage of it. If you want no part of it, you can opt out.

Finally, tort reform should be addressed in a meaningful way. Without tort reform, the cost of insuring health care providers is likely to continue to be a significant drag on our ability to provide quality and, most important, affordable care.

We can all agree that the health care reform debate was incredibly divisive on both sides of the aisle. But there is still a real opportunity to improve this law in a bipartisan manner.

http://www.politico.com/news/stories/0311/51343.html

QUESTIONS FOR READING

1. Why did Boren become convinced that the Obama administration's proposal was not the solution to the health care problem?
2. According to Boren, what is the most disappointing aspect of the health care reform debate?
3. What should be the "No. 1 priority" for Congress in Boren's view?

QUESTIONS FOR REASONING AND ANALYSIS

1. What is Boren's thesis or main argument? Do you agree or disagree? Why or why not?
2. Why do you think Boren mentions the legislation he coauthored with Representative Mike Rogers (R-Michigan)? Does doing so bolster his credibility or help him establish ethos? Why or why not?
3. Who do you think is Boren's primary audience? Why do you see this group as his main audience?

QUESTIONS FOR REFLECTING AND WRITING

1. If you were to post a response to Boren, what would you say? Would you agree with some of his arguments while disagreeing on other points? Why or why not? Write a response to Boren, giving equal consideration to all the points he makes in the essay.
2. Do you believe that mandating universal health care coverage is overly burdensome for small businesses and individuals? Why or why not?
3. Is free market capitalism the answer to the health care crisis? What problems might emerge in a completely free market health care system? What problems can you see with a totally government-operated health care system (i.e., socialized medicine)?

marriage and gender roles

Changing Attitudes vs. Traditional Values

c h a p t e r 22

WHAT'S TO COME

The selections in this chapter represent two different sides of a controversial issue. Some argue vehemently in favor of permitting same-sex marriage and allowing for changing gender roles in subsequent family arrangements; others, however, argue passionately against the acceptance of same-sex marriage. In 2008, the controversy over Proposition 8 in California brought this issue to the forefront, with California voters passing the measure and thereby supporting a change in the state's constitution to recognize marriage as only between a man and a woman. Although a 1996 federal law known as DOMA, or the Defense of Marriage Act, essentially forbids gay marriage, six states now allow people of the same sex to marry, while several other states permit civil unions. As events of the twenty-first century continue to unfold, will we see more states legalize gay marriage?

prereading questions

1. What role, if any, should the government and the courts have in defining marriage?
2. What has been meant by the "traditional family"? How has it changed in the past thirty years?
3. Do you have a position on gay marriage? On partnership recognition and rights? If you have a position, what is it, and what is its source?
4. Is there anything that you can learn from arguments presenting opposing views on gay rights or acceptance of gay marriage? Why or why not?

websites related to this chapter's topic

THE WHITE HOUSE
www.whitehouse.gov/agenda/civil_rights
President Obama's agenda for civil rights.

YAHOO NEWS
http://fullcoverage.yahoo.com/fc/us/same_sex_marriage
This Yahoo Full Coverage site contains news, opinions, and useful links.

THE HUFFINGTON POST
www.huffingtonpost.com/news/gay-marriage
News site about gay marriage.

blog post

prereading question } Should children be raised by only heterosexual couples in more traditional marriages?

Top Medical Journal Publishes Study of Lesbian Families

Nan Hunter

Nan Hunter is a professor of law and associate dean for graduate programs at the Georgetown University School of Law. She made this blog post on June 10, 2010.

Pediatrics, the official peer-reviewed journal of the American Academy of Pediatrics, has published online a groundbreaking study from a research project that has measured the psychological health from conception to adolescence of children raised in a cohort of lesbian families. It is the largest and longest running longitudinal study of the children of lesbian parents, and will continue until the children reach adulthood. In US National Longitudinal Lesbian Family Study: Psychological Adjustment of 17-year-old Adolescents, lead author Nanette Gartrell and co-author Henny Bos report that the children in the study were rated significantly higher (using a standardized survey instrument) than an age-matched national sample on the following measures: social, school/academic and total competence. In addition, they were rated significantly lower in social problems, rule-breaking, and aggressive and externalizing problem behavior.

Dr. Gartrell told *Time* magazine that she had expected to find no difference in psychological development between children in the study and those in the control group. She believes that the results are likely due to the extent to which the lesbian moms were actively involved in their children's lives, with significant engagement by both mothers continuing in many instances after 56% of the original couples broke up. The cohort consists solely of children born after the mothers had come out; unlike the majority of children with lesbian moms, none of these children were born to parents in a heterosexual relationship that ended in divorce, followed by the mother's coming out. In this cohort, the children of partners who had separated did as well on the standardized measurements as those of partners who were still together.

The study specifically addresses the question of the children's experience of, and reaction to, stigma. It found that 41% of the children reported having endured some teasing, ostracism or discrimination related to their being raised by same-sex parents. According to

the *Time* interview of Dr. Gartrell, at age 10, the children who reported discrimination exhibited more signs of psychological stress than their peers, but by age 17, the harmful effects had decreased.

Dr. Gartrell is an Associate Clinical Professor of Psychiatry at the University of California, San Francisco and a Williams Institute Distinguished Scholar. Her co-investigator is Henny Bos, Ph.D., of the Graduate School of Pedagogical and Educational Sciences at the University of Amsterdam.

http://hunterforjustice.typepad.com/
hunter_of_justice/social_science/page/2

QUESTIONS FOR READING

1. What were the results of the U.S. National Longitudinal Lesbian Family Study?
2. What did Gartrell expect to find in her research?

3. What question did this study specifically address? What did the researchers find in response to this question?

QUESTIONS FOR REASONING AND ANALYSIS

1. Does the fact that Hunter has omitted the total number of research subjects raise any questions about the validity of the results? Why or why not?
2. Why do you think that the harmful effects of discrimination decreased for these children between the ages of 10 and 17?

3. Gartrell believes, according to Hunter, that these children perform better socially and do better in school because they have two actively engaged mothers. Do you think this reason accounts for the results? Why or why not?

QUESTIONS FOR REFLECTING AND WRITING

1. Should only heterosexual couples in traditional marriages raise children? Why or why not?
2. Do you think the results of this study would be different if the children of male homosexual couples comprised the

cohort groups? Why or why not? How might the results be different?

---

blog post

prereading question } **Should the government legislate who a person can and cannot marry?**

Maryland Gay Marriage Debacle Reveals Cowards and Civil Rights Myopia

Jonathan Capehart

Jonathan Capehart is a member of *The Washington Post* editorial board and a regular contributor to the PostPartisan blog. He made this post on March 15, 2011.

Today's *Post* editorial on the marriage-equality debacle in Maryland wisely takes the long view. "The trend in public opinion continues in favor of equal rights for gays in general and same-sex marriage in particular," the editorial board points out. "The direction of the debate seems clear enough; the pace is frustrating."

A pace not helped at all by cowards in the state legislature who talked out of both sides of their mouths

to the gay community and who refused to heed the call of leadership. Or by African Americans who can't or refuse to see that one's civil rights should not be encumbered by race or sexual orientation.

Y'all saw me open a vein on the treachery of Del. Sam Arora. He's the first-term Montgomery County Democrat who raised a ton of cash from the gay community and progressives based on his stance on marriage equal-

continued

ity. He was a proud co-sponsor of the same-sex marriage bill. But when it came time, Arora disgracefully wavered after getting push-back from some of his constituents. That he voted for it in the Judiciary Committee and would have voted for his marriage-equality bill on the floor was completely undercut by his newfound support for civil unions and for a voter referendum on the bill. A referendum that most everyone agrees would render same-sex marriage illegal in Maryland.

And then there was that other spineless profile in courage, Del. Tiffany T. Alston (D-Prince George's). She, too, was a co-sponsor of the marriage-equality bill. But when it came time to vote in the Judiciary Committee, she literally fled the House. Alston, her chief of staff and Del. Jill P. Carter (D-Baltimore) rode around for 15 minutes to avoid casting votes. Alston said she would have voted no.

I feel really strongly that people who love each other should be able to get married, no matter what their gender. But I also realize that that's not my function here. I'm here to represent the 110,000 people back home, many of whom had called and e-mailed and said, "We don't want that bill." . . . We send our soldiers off, sometimes to die, to tell people that ours is the best damn government in the world, so we can't bastardize that by not letting the people have their say.

Alston and others who use that lame argument should contemplate what would have happened if "the people" had their say back in the 1950s and 1960s on questions of integration, voting rights and discrimination. Putting the civil rights of a minority up for a popular vote is never a good idea. As we have learned

so many times in this nation's history, sometimes "the people" need to be led by public officials with the guts to do the right thing even when their constituents are not (and may never be) supportive. The most notable example were Senate Republicans who bucked their party to vote in favor of the repeal of the ban on gay men and lesbians serving openly in the military.

What I find even more troubling is the wedge being driven between African Americans and gays. After the marriage-equality bill was tabled, the Family Research Council gave "particular thanks" to black preachers, their churches and legislators "who spoke out against the attempted hijacking of the concept of 'civil rights.'" Del. Emmett Burns (D-Baltimore County) is one of those who found the linkage offensive. "The civil-rights movement as I knew it . . . had nothing to do with same-sex marriage," he said. "And those who decide to ride on our coattails are historically incorrect."

Fine, don't listen to the gays. Listen to Rep. John Lewis (D-Ga.), an architect of the famed 1963 March on Washington who was beaten at the Edmund Pettus Bridge on "Bloody Sunday," one of many beatings he suffered. "I have fought too hard and too long against discrimination based on race and color not to stand up against discrimination based on sexual orientation," wrote Lewis back in 2003. "I've heard the reasons for opposing civil marriage for same-sex couples. Cut through the distractions, and they stink of the same fear, hatred and intolerance I have known in racism and in bigotry."

Here—once again—is what Lewis said in 1996 before casting a vote against the so-called Defense of Marriage Act.

You Tube | john lewis you cannot tell people youtube | Search

John Lewis - You Cannot Tell People They Cannot Fall In Love
absentpresence 1 video ⌄ Subscribe

Watch the video at: http://www.youtube.com/watch?feature=player_embedded&v=Y4rj_mUhlYQ

The last part of Del. Burns's otherwise wrong-headed quote is actually true. "The civil-rights movement was about putting teeth into the Declaration of Independence." It still is. The struggle for civil rights and equality is part of a continuum. As Dr. Martin Luther King often said, "The arc of the moral universe is long, but it bends toward justice." African Americans neither own that arc nor have exclusive right to it. Gay men and lesbians have every right to follow it until it bends toward justice for them.

QUESTIONS FOR READING

1. What is Capehart's criticism of Del. Sam Arora of Maryland?
2. What does Capehart find an "even more troubling" aspect of the debate?
3. With what part of Del. Burns's quote does Capehart agree?

QUESTIONS FOR REASONING AND ANALYSIS

1. What is Capehart's thesis?
2. On what assumption or assumptions does Capehart's argument rest?
3. Capehart labels certain members of the Maryland state legislature "cowards." Do you think this label is appropriate? Why or why not?

QUESTIONS FOR REFLECTING AND WRITING

1. Does a strong parallel exist between the civil rights movement of the 1960s and the gay marriage movement? Why or why not? Write an essay defending your position.
2. If you were to make a post in response to Capehart, what would you say? Would you agree or disagree with him? Why would you agree or disagree?

website

prereading question } **Is same-sex marriage threatening to children and, more broadly, the institution of marriage?**

Protect Marriage: Vote "Yes" on Proposition 8

Protect Marriage: Vote "Yes" on Proposition 8 is a website that campaigned for passage of this measure in California. *Protectmarriage.com* is a project of a group calling itself California Renewal.

QUESTIONS FOR REASONING AND ANALYSIS

1. On the home page, what actions does California Renewal want its supporters to take? Which actions do you think the audience would most likely take? Why?

2. What is the argument under "Why Marriage Matters"? How has this organization attempted to support that argument?

3. View the two short advertisements expressing opposition to legalizing gay marriage (see http://protectmarriage.com/video/view/7 and http://protectmarriage.com/video/view/8). What is the major argument made in both these videos? What evidence is cited in support of this major argument? Are the assumptions behind the argument valid? Why or why not?

4. Do the videos rely more on logical or emotional appeal? How might the videos rely on one more than another?

QUESTIONS FOR REFLECTING AND WRITING

1. Evaluate the Protect Marriage website as an argument. Does it achieve its purpose and communicate effectively with its intended audience? Why or why not? Are some arguments stronger than others? Weaker? If so, which ones? Overall, how could the site become more effective in persuading audiences and solidifying a support base for Proposition 8?

2. Do you agree or disagree that same-sex marriage poses a threat to children? If so, what is that threat? What is the ultimate consequence to children if persons of the same sex are permitted to marry? If you disagree, why is this concern over children misplaced?

3. Does same-sex marriage pose a threat to the institution of marriage? If so, what is that threat? If not, then why not?

prereading question } Are children hindered emotionally or developmentally when raised by two same-sex parents?

My Daughters Have No Mother

Max Mutchnick

Max Mutchnick was the co-creator of the television show *Will and Grace*, which aired on NBC from 1998 until 2006. A writer and producer in Hollywood, Mutchnick lives with his partner and their two daughters. He posted this argument on February 27, 2009, to The Huffington Post blog.

Some of you were annoyed. You didn't like that I referred to my daughters' surrogate as an oven. Truly I meant no disrespect. I love and admire the generous soul that carried my daughters for thirty-seven weeks. She went into labor as I sat in a theatre watching a preview of *9 to 5: The Musical*. I always wondered if she went into labor because she had sympathy pains for me. I have friends involved so I'll keep my review simple: Cute . . . with kinks. Mostly it brought back my repressed desire to own a silk work kimono like the one Lily Tomlin wore in the movie version.

Honey, I'm leaving for the office. Just gonna pour myself a cup of ambition, grab my purple work kimono and I'm out the door . . .

But I digress. Back to the oven, I mean, the surrogate. Here's what it's all about: It takes a village to make a *gaybie* (not my word). When a gay man realizes he wants to have a child, it forces him to face his own queerness, in the true sense of the word. And it's contrary to his life-long mantra: "I'm normal. I'm just like everyone else." So like it or not, it's back to the village. You're going to need everyone; especially the villagers with vaginas. You'll also need: money, support systems, time, lawyers, fertility specialists, location, and cashmere (don't ask). Homosexuals are not as fortunate as our heterosexual counterparts. We certainly don't have the luck on our side like, say, a Jamie Lynn Spears or a Palin daughter. Making children the gay way is like building a yacht.

Somewhere along the line I started to feel guilty or less than. As a result, I built up some defenses. You must want it so badly that you literally have to reach out your hand to virtual strangers for assistance. Of course they become real in the fullness of time, but when you're introduced at a Marie Callender's to the woman that's going to carry your children, it's impossible to think:

You're mommy.

So with key players, I found myself doing this thing I call "distance regulating." So much intimacy. So much vulnerability. So much need from others. I must save myself the only way I know how. Nicknames. Less eye-contact. Jokey banter. Let's keep it light . . . because it's *so not light*. And then there's the egg donor. You never even get to meet her.

It's hitting me now. My daughters have no mother.

So listen to this part. You log onto a secured website. (Octomom, if you're reading this, please skip to the next paragraph.) Page after page of girls—not women, girls. A headshot, a small video testimonial, and an extensive medical history. That's all you get. Fifty percent of my babies' DNA would be purchased online. Something about it depressed me. I must distance regulate.

Want a mom? She's three clicks away!

We quickly learned about the dearth of desirable donors. They're like diamonds; it's all good on the surface, but when you take a loupe to them, the difference between a flawless stone and an occluded one seems small, but looms large. Take the "Diamond" out of Lou Diamond Phillips and you're just stuck with a guy called Lou Phillips. (That almost makes sense.) I learned everything I know about diamonds from Suzanne Pleshette, may she rest in peace. She wore ten carats on her finger to work every day. A gift from a man, she told me.

Wow, that's quite a ring, Suzanne.

It's a piece of shit. You couldn't even cut the cheese with it. A zircon costs more.

So if and when you see a donor you like, it's a BUY NOW situation. Turn your head for a second and donors get scooped up by other gay couples competing from the same pool. We decided to go with V139K2 (not her real name). There was something very exciting and scary about it once the decision was made. We'll never know her. Our daughters will never kiss her. She is everything . . . and nothing. Oh my god, my daughters have no mother!

See that's what it is. I have to call our surrogate an oven because I can't call her their mother and I can't call V139K2 (not her real name) their mother. And it drives me crazy. I can't tell you how it drives me crazy.

But this is what saves me . . .

continued

Here's a list of what they do have:

doting grandparents
lots of cousins
fifty gay uncles
two gay aunts
clean sheets
bubble baths
kisses from morning 'til night
walks in the park
laughter
dogs that lick their feet

and two adoring fathers.

And that's enough. And that's our family. And that's everything.

The Huffington Post, February 27, 2009. © 2009 Max Mutchnick. Reprinted with permission. www.huffingtonpost.com/max-mutchnick/ my-daughters-have-no-moth_b_170614 .html

QUESTIONS FOR REASONING AND ANALYSIS

1. What do you think Mutchnick means when he says, "Making children the gay way is like building a yacht"? In a latter passage, he refers to "distance regulating." What is he suggesting by using this term?

2. What is Mutchnick saying when he compares "desirable donors" to diamonds? He then proceeds to disparage "diamonds" (Suzanne Pleshette's ring, specifically). Why?

3. How would you describe the tone of Mutchnick's post? Is it playful, sarcastic, serious, or somber? Why is it one and not the other?

4. What argument is Mutchnick making by providing a list at the close of his post?

5. How would you summarize the thesis or claim of Mutchnick's post?

QUESTIONS FOR REFLECTING AND WRITING

1. Consider the opposing argument to Mutchnick's position. How would you express that opposing argument? What reasons or evidence would support that argument?

2. Can society dictate who can and cannot raise children? Why or why not? Under what circumstances might an authority prevent a person or couple from taking custody of and raising a child? Can such circumstances pertain to same-sex couples? If so, why?

3. Evaluate Mutchnick's claim in "My Daughters Have No Mother." Has he effectively made his argument? Are parts of his argument stronger than others? Weaker? If so, which ones? Regardless of whether or not you agree or disagree, do you take issue with any of his statements? Why or why not?

prereading question } Are racial discrimination and discrimination against someone for their sexual orientation the same thing?

Darrin Bell

This political cartoon appeared on Robyn Ochs's website (www.robynochs.com). Ochs is a professional author and public speaker.

Reprinted by permission of Darrin Bell. www.candorville.com.

QUESTIONS FOR REASONING AND ANALYSIS

1. How would you explain the thesis or claim of this cartoon?
2. What does it mean to "protect the sanctity of marriage"? What does the word *sanctity* mean?
3. What do you think of the portrayal of the male characters? What is the cartoonist attempting to say through this portrayal?

4. Is prohibiting gay marriage the same as prohibiting interracial marriage? Why or why not?

QUESTIONS FOR REFLECTING AND WRITING

1. What is the difference between marriage and legally recognized civil unions, life partnerships, and domestic partnerships? Do you oppose gay marriage but support civil unions? Why?

2. If you oppose gay marriage, why? If you support gay marriage, why?
3. Why do you think gay marriage has become such a controversial issue?

The Best Argument Against Gay Marriage: And Why It Fails

Kenji Yoshino

New York University Law Professor Kenji Yoshino wrote the following piece as a response to an article in the *Harvard Journal of Law and Public Policy* that was published on Slate.com on December 13, 2010. The authors of that article—Robert P. George, Ryan T. Anderson, and Sherif Girgis—responded to Yoshino in turn.

In last week's arguments in Perry v. Schwarzenegger, the California same-sex marriage case, it was clear that the main secular argument for limiting marriage to opposite-sex couples is the "common procreation" rationale. The idea is that marriage is properly limited to opposite-sex couples because they, and only they, can engage in procreation within their union. The lawyers defending California's gay marriage ban, Proposition 8, did not fully elaborate the argument—the *New York Times* editorial page called it a "tired, and thoroughly specious, assertion."

Now conservative blogs are celebrating—as "one of the best arguments" and "outstanding work"—the more fulsome defense of the common procreation argument made in a forthcoming article by Sherif Girgis, Robert P. George, and Ryan T. Anderson. Yet the article's more comprehensive elaboration of the argument reveals why the Proposition 8 defenders were right not to shine too bright a light on it. Closely examined, the common-procreation argument denigrates not only same-sex couples but several kinds of married opposite-sex couples.

Princeton professor Robert George is a conservative heavyweight in debates over same-sex marriage. With two graduate student co-authors, he claims to have revealed the true nature of marriage. The article argues for common procreation as the sole basis for a "real" or "conjugal" marriage by asserting that only a man and a woman can create a "comprehensive union." In defining that special status, the authors begin by drawing a distinction between "sexual" exclusivity and "tennis" exclusivity: "Suppose that Michael and Michelle build their relationship not on sexual exclusivity, but on tennis exclusivity. They pledge to play tennis with each other, and only with each other, until death do them part. Are they thereby married? No." While the purpose of this distinction is initially mystifying, the authors are making a serious point. They are contending that sexual activity has been privileged over other kinds of bonding activities in determining who gets to marry.

George and his co-authors continue, however, to observe that not all sexual activity counts as a basis for marriage—what is required is sexual activity capable of producing a child. The article infers this requirement from the physical makeup of men and women. Because same-sex couples cannot create this child-producing combination by themselves, their relationship is a recreational activity more like tennis than like marriage.

But mark the sequel—if a prerequisite of marriage is procreative capacity, then are the marriages of infertile opposite-sex couples not called into question? George and his co-authors are quick to reassure with another sports analogy: "A baseball team has its characteristic structure largely because of its orientation to winning games; it involves developing and sharing one's athletic skills in the way best suited for honorably winning. . . . But such development and sharing are possible and inherently valuable for teammates even when they lose their games." In other words, infertile couples are still playing ball, even if they never win a game. They are the Phillies, except that they have no hope of ever improving.

I suspect it will be cold comfort to many infertile opposite-sex couples to hear that while their marriage is still "real," it is a "losing" marriage as opposed to a "winning" one. Ideally, most of them view their marriages as something more than honorable defeats and would despise the contention that they had not fulfilled the central purpose of the institution. Moreover, the article says nothing of straight people who choose not to procreate. It is unclear why they would have "true marriages," as they are not even trying to win.

George's second argument for the centrality of common procreation to marriage is the special link that parents have to children. He and his co-authors rely on the research institution Child Trends for the proposition that "it is not simply the presence of two parents . . . but the presence of *two biological parents* that seems to support children's development." This source, like

continued

many cited by the opponents of same-sex marriage, does not compare the children raised by two biological parents with the children raised by two same-sex parents. Instead, the research compares children raised by two biological parents with children raised by single parents, divorced couples, and cohabiting straight couples. The study simply has nothing to do with gay adoption. And the research comparing the kids of gay adoptive parents to the kids of straight birth parents shows that the first group fares just as well as the second. On this basis, the American Psychiatric Association, the American Psychological Association, and the National Association for Social Workers all support same-sex parenting—and marriage.

From the point of view of straight couples, however, the salient aspect of the contention that two biological parents are best for a child lies in how it demeans anyone who has chosen to adopt or to use reproductive technologies (such as an egg or sperm donor) to create a family. In the view of George and his co-authors, such couples apparently are not really parents: "Children . . . can have only two parents—a biological mother and father."

We all know that the common-procreation argument declares war on all same-sex marriages. But it is worth reviewing just how demeaning it is to opposite-sex couples who do not produce their own offspring. They are like losing baseball teams. They are not the real parents of their children. True, their status is not directly on the line in the gay marriage debate—George and his co-authors are not coming after their marriage licenses. But if common procreation were to be accepted as the central basis of marriage, it would necessarily treat their marriages as inferior. In its broad and unforgiving sweep, this argument is self-destructively over-inclusive. It succeeds only in diminishing the institution of marriage itself.

http://www.slate.com/id/2277781

The Argument Against Gay Marriage: And Why It Doesn't Fail

A Response to NYU Law Professor Kenji Yoshino

Robert P. George, Ryan T. Anderson, and Sherif Girgis

The response to Yoshino's article from George, Anderson, and Girgis appeared in *Public Discourse: Ethics, Law, and the Common Good* on December 17, 2010. Robert P. George is McCormick Professor of Jurisprudence at Princeton University. In late 2010, Ryan T. Anderson was a PhD candidate in political science at the University of Notre Dame. Sherif Girgis was a PhD candidate in philosophy at Princeton University.

Last week we released our *Harvard Journal of Law and Public Policy* article, "What is Marriage?" It offers a robust defense of the conjugal view of marriage as the union of husband and wife, and issues specific intellectual challenges to those who propose to redefine civil marriage to accommodate same-sex partnerships.

Kenji Yoshino of NYU Law School, a prominent and influential gay rights legal scholar, has posted on *Slate* a response to our article under the title "The Best Argument Against Gay Marriage," proposing to show "why it fails." Although we are glad that our efforts have attracted the critical attention of an important advocate of redefining marriage, Professor Yoshino's response is long on rhetoric designed to stigmatize a position he opposes, and short on arguments that might actually cast doubt on its soundness.

Indeed, Yoshino's posting brings to mind points developed in a recent paper by Yoshino's colleague at NYU, Professor Jeremy Waldron—one of the world's most eminent legal philosophers. Waldron observes that it "infuriat[es]" many of his fellow liberals that some intellectuals remain determined, in Waldron's words, "to actually argue on matters that many secular liberals think should be beyond argument, matters that we think should be determined by shared sentiment or conviction." In particular, Waldron laments, "many who are convinced by the gay rights position are upset" that others "refuse to take the liberal position for granted."

The central argument of our article is that equality and justice are indeed crucial to the debate over civil marriage law, but that to settle it—to determine what equality and justice demand—one must answer the question: what is marriage? So this is what the debate is ultimately about. In making our case for conjugal marriage, we consider the nature of human embodiedness; how this makes comprehensive interpersonal union sealed in conjugal acts possible; and how such union and its intrinsic connection to children give marriage its distinctive norms of monogamy, exclusivity, and permanence.

Our article offers detailed responses to the most significant objections to our view: that it has no principled grounds for recognizing infertile couples' marriages, ignores the needs of same-sex attracted people, is morally similar to support for anti-miscegenation laws, assumes the mutability of sexual desire, relies on religious belief, or fails to show the concrete harm in redefining civil marriage.

We also show that those who would redefine civil marriage, to eliminate sexual complementarity as an essential element, can give no principled account of why marriage should be (1) a sexual partnership as opposed to a partnership distinguished by exclusivity with respect to other activities (including non-sexual relationships, as between cohabiting adult brothers); or (2) an exclusive union of only two persons (rather than three or more in a polyamorous arrangement). Nor can they give robust reasons for making marriage (3) a legally recognized and regulated relationship in the first place (since, after all, we don't legally recognize or closely regulate most other forms of friendships).

We were explicit in framing these as *challenges* to proponents of gay civil marriage. And if anyone is capable of meeting them, surely it is Professor Yoshino. So his decision to pass over those challenges in perfect silence confirms and reinforces our belief (also amply defended in our article) that only the conjugal view can answer them.

If even that much of our article's argument is right, then the case against conjugal marriage laws as it is now being made in the courts collapses—and Yoshino knows it. If the logic of recognizing same-sex partnerships as marriages undermines the rational basis of the very idea of marriage as a sexually exclusive and monogamous union, then all but the most extreme sexual liberationists will draw back from his position. And if the same argument for radically reforming marriage policy also undercuts the point of legally regulating marriage at all, then it is self-defeating.

Instead of addressing these points, Yoshino grossly misrepresents two analogies we made as if they were identities. He thus represents us as holding what we do not hold and neither said nor implied (e.g., that infertile couples are just like losers in a baseball game; or that adoptive parents are not real parents).

But this exchange would be fruitless if we responded in kind. Instead, we will attempt to answer the concrete objections that seemed to motivate Professor Yoshino's essay.

At one point, Yoshino concedes that we have a "serious point," but he distorts it in a manner that works to the advantage of his own critique: "They are contending that sexual activity has been privileged over other kinds of bonding activities in determining who gets to marry." Notice the question-begging implication of the phrase "who gets to marry." Yoshino assumes (and assumes that we assume) that the institution of marriage *inherently* has nothing to do with sexual complementarity, and that we are merely supporting a historical tendency to "privilege" certain activities in determining who gets access to marriage (seen as a gender-neutral institution) under the law.

But as the very *title* of our article reveals, our goal is to show that the debate over civil marriage's definition is ultimately about *what marriage is*, considered as a pre-legal reality that the state has good reasons to track (and that it hurts the common good to obscure). We offer and defend an answer according to which bonds between two men or two women—like those among three or more—simply lack the features essential to marriage: what are denied legal recognition in these cases are not marriages in the relevant sense. To miss or misrepresent these points is to fail to engage our argument at all.

We give a coherent account of marriage as inherently a sexual partnership, one shaped by norms of monogamy and sexual exclusivity. We contend that any view of marriage that would include same-sex partnerships *cannot* defend these norms as a matter of principle rather than sentiment or preference, and we challenge revisionists like Yoshino to show—by arguments—otherwise. If Yoshino could have mustered effective arguments, he would have. But rather than propose an answer to the question *What is marriage?* he assumes an answer that he does not defend or even articulate, and uses it to impute to us groundless aggression: we are, he claims, "declaring war" on people's marriages; our arguments "demean" and "denigrate" those who cannot have biological children of their own.

Then has Yoshino "declared war" on the (according to *Newsweek*) 500,000 polyamorous U.S. households, by failing to support a policy that would ratify their romantic commitments as civil marriages? By this standard, no policy that proposed standards for which arrangements could be legally recognized as marriages—in other words, no marriage policy, period—would pass muster.

Professor Yoshino's rhetoric is thus, to all appearances, designed to exploit caricatures of conservatives as mean-spirited bigots out to thwart those not like themselves. But our argument is either successful or not. If it is successful, pejorative labeling cannot harm it; if it is unsuccessful, a clear explanation of its flaws—for example, by showing that it rests on a false premise or a fallacious inference—gives people all the reason

continued

they require for rejecting it.

Yoshino directs much of his scorn at an analogy we use to defend our view (and the view historically embodied in our law) that marriages, being *comprehensive* interpersonal unions, are consummated and uniquely embodied in coitus—in acts that extend spouses' union of hearts and minds along the biological dimension of their beings, much as various organs unite to form one body: by allowing them to coordinate together toward a biological function (in this case, reproduction) of the whole (in this case, the couple as a unit).

Like any analogy, the analogy of ours that Yoshino criticizes was meant to illustrate a limited point: how a community can derive its structure and defining norms from a certain end, even though it is valuable in itself and not merely as a means to that end. Here's how we put it:

> A baseball team has its characteristic structure largely because of its orientation to winning games; it involves developing and sharing one's athletic skills in the way best suited for honorably winning (among other things, with assiduous practice and good sportsmanship). But such development and sharing are possible and inherently valuable for teammates even when they lose their games.
>
> Just so, marriage has its characteristic structure largely because of its orientation to procreation; it involves developing and sharing one's body and whole self in the way best suited for honorable parenthood—among other things, permanently and exclusively. But such development and sharing, including the bodily union of the generative act, are possible and inherently valuable for spouses even when they do not conceive children.

Now law professors, like philosophers, are familiar enough with analogies to see that they break down: that is what makes *them* analogies and not equations, as we make clear in our article just a few sentences after drawing *this* analogy. One clear difference between marriage and a sport is that the latter is a competitive activity in which having winners and losers is inherent to the practice. Marriage is not. So our point was not to relegate spouses without biological children, or marital acts that (like all spouses' acts most of the time) do not cause conception, to the status of "losers" (who are then "denigrated" or "demeaned").

Professor Yoshino dismisses (without quite rehearsing) another one of our arguments—that only the conjugal view can account for the deep connection between marriage and children—on the ground that this argument relies on studies asserting the superiority of biological parenting without comparing it to same-sex parenting. But we never denied that there are not yet high-quality studies comparing opposite-sex to same-sex (or, for that matter, polyamorous) parenting. Here is what we did say about the connection between marriage understood as a conjugal union, and children:

> We learn something about a relationship from the way it is sealed or embodied in certain activities. Most generically, ordinary friendships center on a union of minds and wills, by which each person comes to know and seek the other's good; thus, friendships are sealed in conversations and common pursuits. Similarly, scholarly relationships are sealed or embodied in joint inquiry, investigation, discovery, and dissemination; sports communities, in practices and games.
>
> If there is some conceptual connection between children and marriage, therefore, we can expect a correlative connection between children and the way that marriages are sealed. That connection is obvious if the conjugal view of marriage is correct. Marriage is a comprehensive union of two sexually complementary persons who seal (consummate or complete) their relationship by the generative act—by the kind of activity that is by its nature fulfilled by the conception of a child. So marriage itself is oriented to and fulfilled by the bearing, rearing, and education of children. The procreative-type act distinctively seals or completes a procreative-type union.

[...]

Given the marital relationship's natural orientation to children, it is not surprising that, according to the best available sociological evidence, children fare best on virtually every indicator of wellbeing when reared by their wedded biological parents. Studies that control for other relevant factors, including poverty and even genetics, suggest that children reared in intact homes fare best on the following indices.

We cite some evidence suggesting that mothers and fathers tend to bring different strengths to the parenting enterprise. But we think that everyone in this debate should support rigorous studies designed to compare directly various parenting arrangements, and executed by teams of sociologists that disagree on the moral questions about sex and marriage, so that all are precommitted to the results. We also expect, however, that few would take the sociological results as decisive on the central issue (what is marriage?), just as we did not in our article. But this raises a question: Does Yoshino deny that children deserve to be raised, wherever possible, by a mother and father—that this is worth promoting as an ideal?

Finally, having ignored our central arguments, made unwarranted linguistic associations, indulged in pejorative labeling, and studiously ignored every challenge we pose, Yoshino ends with a resounding declaration of victory: Even the best argument available against gay civil marriage fails, because it "denies" marriage to

continued

same-sex partners only by "denigrating" and "demeaning" the marriages of many opposite-sex couples. But Yoshino would be warranted in declaring victory only if he had given good reasons for rejecting our actual arguments, and provided his own answer to the central question of what marriage is. He did neither.

http://www.thepublicdiscourse.com/2010/12/2217

QUESTIONS FOR READING

1. What do George, Anderson, and Girgis cite as their "central argument"? What question must be answered in the debate?
2. What argument, according to Yoshino, were Proposition 8 defenders "right not to shine too bright a light on"?
3. What is George, Anderson, and Girgis's account or definition of "marriage"?
4. According to George, Anderson, and Girgis, when do children fare best?
5. According to Yoshino, what argument "declares war on all same-sex marriages"?

QUESTIONS FOR REASONING AND ANALYSIS

1. What do you think the George, Anderson, and Girgis mean by "conjugal view of marriage"? Why is the idea of "conjugal view of marriage" important for their argument?
2. How would you describe the tone of Yoshino's article?
3. What purpose does the analogy of a baseball team and marriage serve in the George, Anderson, and Girgis argument? Have they successfully answered their opponent's criticism of this analogy? Why or why not?
4. What do George, Anderson, and Girgis mean by the term "polyamorous"?
5. Have George, Anderson, and Girgis effectively answered Yoshino? Why or why not?

QUESTIONS FOR REFLECTING AND WRITING

1. Should marriage only be defined as between a man and a woman? Why or why not? Write an essay defending your position.
2. George, Anderson, and Girgis strongly suggest that a major reason why marriage should only be defined as between a man and woman is that marriage leads to biological procreation and child rearing. Do you find any aspect of this argument problematic? Are they making the definition of marriage too narrow? Why or why not?
3. Yoshino mentions Proposition 8 in the opening of his piece. Conduct some additional research on Proposition 8 in California. What are the common arguments for and against Proposition 8? Which arguments are most and least compelling? Why?
4. How might George, Anderson, and Girgis respond to the Nan Hunter piece presented earlier in this chapter?

predicted it would, Dr. Collins would face a conflict between his job and his faith. "There will be a moment of truth for Dr. Collins," Dr. Weissman said.

In a recent interview over French toast at a diner near the agency's sprawling campus here, Dr. Collins rejected any notion that faith and science conflicted in substantial ways. Indeed, he said, science illuminates the work and language of God. And he pointed out that he wrote in his book about God that he supports therapeutic cloning. When his book on personalized medicine comes out early next year, he hopes to move the conversation about his writings back to science.

I certainly agree that religion and science are not incompatible, although some scientists are certainly at war with religion. But that is beside the point. What I find disturbing is Collins's seeming acceptance that religion is the only basis for opposing human cloning. In fact, it is the least of it. Treating human life as a mere commodity, manufactured solely for instrumental use, quality control, and destruction, is a hugely important ethical issue that extends far beyond religion and into important human rights issues, including the intrinsic value of human life, e.g. human exceptionalism.

What I don't understand is where Collins comes down on *when* human life becomes protectable. Based [on] the statements I have seen—and admittedly, I have not done exhaustive research on his views—Collins support of ESCR and therapeutic cloning seem to be reflexive and expedient, rather than deeply considered or philosophically based. In any event, if he hasn't yet, he had better figure that out: It is conceivable that during his tenure he could well face the question of whether to permit gestation of embryos beyond the Petri dish for use in research, indeed, depending on the speed of science, perhaps even the launching of fetal farming in artificial environments.

http://www.firstthings.com/blogs /secondhandsmoke/2009/10/06 /dear-francis-collins-opposition- to-therapeutic-cloning-about-ethics- not-religion

QUESTIONS FOR READING

1. What does Smith find disturbing about Collins's comments?

2. What is a "hugely important ethical issue," according to Smith?

3. According to Smith, what should Collins figure out?

QUESTIONS FOR REASONING AND ANALYSIS

1. Aside from human cloning in general, what is at issue for Smith in this piece?

2. What does Smith infer as the meaning of "human exceptionalism"?

3. Why does Smith begin his argument with the excerpt from *The New York Times*?

QUESTIONS FOR REFLECTING AND WRITING

1. Do you agree with the advice Smith gives Collins at the end of this piece? Why or why not? Write an essay defending your position.

2. What are the major issues associated with the human cloning controversy? Which issues should law and

policy makers prioritize? Why should they prioritize these issues higher than others?

3. Do you agree or disagree that scientists are ethically and morally obligated to conduct research that will ultimately benefit society? Why or why not?

Science and Religion Today Statistical Graphics

The following images were posted on May 28, 2010, to Science and Religion Today, a website and forum devoted to exploring the relationship between science and religion. The data was gathered as part of the 2010 Virginia Commonwealth University Life Survey.

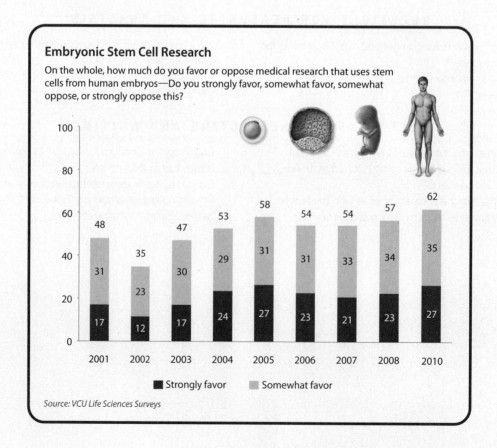

Views of Scientific Consensus Linked with Beliefs About Evolution

From what you've heard or read, do you think the evidence on evolution is widely accepted within the scientific community, or do many scientists have serious doubts about it?

	Widely accepted by scientists	Many scientists have serious doubts	Don't Know	
God directly created life	44%	40%	16%	=100%
Life developed over time, God guided process	68%	24%	8%	=100%
Life developed over time, God did *not* guide process	72%	21%	7%	=100%

Source: VCU Life Sciences Survey 2010

Embryonic Stem Cell Research

On the whole, how much do you favor or oppose medical research that uses stem cells from human embryos—Do you strongly favor, somewhat favor, somewhat oppose, or strongly oppose this?

Year	Strongly favor	Somewhat favor	Total
2001	17	31	48
2002	12	23	35
2003	17	30	47
2004	24	29	53
2005	27	31	58
2006	23	31	54
2007	21	33	54
2008	23	34	57
2010	27	35	62

■ Strongly favor   ■ Somewhat favor

Source: VCU Life Sciences Surveys

1. Does the data in the first chart suggest that most people believe a consensus exists among scientists regarding the origin of life? Why or why not?
2. Over a 10-year span (2001–2010), did you expect to see a more dramatic difference between those who strongly support embryonic stem cell research and those who somewhat support it? Why or why not?
3. What can you conclude from the data presented in both images?

1. Are evolutionism and creationism mutually exclusive? In other words, can a person only believe one or the other regarding the origin of the human species? Why or why not?
2. What is your position on embryonic stem cell research? Do you strongly oppose, somewhat oppose, strongly support, or somewhat support stem cell research? What are the reasons for your position?

website essay

prereading questions } Have you ever heard of "intelligent design"? If not, what do you think it means? If so, what do you already know about intelligent design?

Helping Christians Reconcile God with Science

Amy Sullivan

Amy Sullivan's article, "Helping Christians Reconcile God with Science," appeared on Time.com on May 2, 2009. Sullivan is a staff writer for *Time* magazine.

For many young Christians, the moment they first notice discrepancies in the Biblical tales they've faithfully studied is a rite of passage: e.g., *if Adam and Eve were the first humans, and they had two sons—where did Cain's wife come from?* The revelation that everything in the Bible may not have happened exactly as written can be startling. And when the discovery comes along with scientific evidence of evolution and the actual age of planet Earth, it can prompt a full-blown spiritual crisis.

That's where Francis Collins would like to step in. A renowned geneticist and former director of the Human Genome Project, Collins is also an evangelical Christian who was the keynote speaker at the 2007 National Prayer Breakfast, and he has spent years establishing the compatibility between science and religious belief. And this week he unveiled a new initiative to guide Christians through scientific questions while holding firm to their faith. (See pictures of John 3:16 in pop culture.)

After his best-selling *The Language of God* came out three years ago, Collins began receiving thousands of e-mails—primarily from other Evangelicals—asking questions about how to reconcile scriptural teachings with scientific evidence. "Many of these Christians have been taught that evolution is wrong," Collins explains. "They go to college and get exposed to data, and then they're thrust into personal crises of great intensity. If the church was wrong about the origins of life, was it wrong about everything? Some of them walk away from science or faith—or both."

Collins, 59, who with his mustache and shock of gray hair looks like former U.N. Ambassador John Bolton's cheerful twin, seems genuinely pained by the idea that science could be viewed as a threat to religion, or religion to science. And so he decided to gather a group of theologians and scientists to create the Bio-Logos Foundation in order to foster dialogue between the two sides. The name—combining *bios* (Greek for "life") and *logos* ("the word")—is also what Collins calls his blended theory of evolution and creation, an approach he hopes can replace intelligent design, which he derides as "not a scientific proposal" and "not good theology either."

Through the Washington-based foundation, Collins says he and his colleagues hope to support scholarship that "takes seriously the claims of both faith and science." Its online component, biologos.org, is designed to be a resource for skeptics and nonbelievers who are interested in religious arguments for God's existence. But the primary audience for BioLogos is Collins' own Evangelical community. (See the top 10 religion stories of 2008.)

continued

As he read through the thousands of e-mails he received from readers of his book, the former NIH scientist noticed that there were 25 or so common questions that his mostly Evangelical correspondents raised. How should Christians respond to Darwin? If God created the universe, who or what created God? Does believing in science mean one can't believe in miracles? What is up with Noah's Ark and the flood? The new website offers answers to these vexing questions and, through those responses lays out the BioLogos theory that God chose to create the world by way of evolution. (Collins plans to build on that work by developing a home-schooling curriculum that can serve as an alternative to the literalist creationism materials widely used by many conservative Evangelical parents.)

A large slice of the questions deal with Genesis, the first book in both Christian and Jewish Scriptures, and the text that explains the creation and population of Earth, and well as the relationship between God and man. Some answers are straightforward, as with the mystery of where Cain's wife came from. "The scientific evidence suggests a dramatically larger population at this point in history," conclude Collins and his colleagues. One possible explanation they offer—an idea that was embraced by C.S. Lewis, among others—is that human-like creatures had evolved to the point where they had the mental capacity to reason; God then endowed them to distinguish between good and evil, and in that way they became "in the image of God."

But on other topics, such as whether Adam and Eve were real people or when humans became creatures with souls, BioLogos offers several possible answers—an approach that is either refreshing or unsatisfying, depending on one's need for certainty. "We cannot say that Adam and Eve were formed as acts of special creation," Collins explains. "That is a troubling conclusion for many people."

"Science can't be put together with a literalist interpretation of Genesis," he continues. "For one thing, there are two different versions of the creation story"—in Genesis 1 and 2—"so right from the start, you're already in trouble." Christians should think of Genesis "not as a book about science but about the nature of God and the nature of humans," Collins believes. "Evolution gives us the 'how,' but we need the Bible to understand the 'why' of our creation."

Who Teaches This? You May Be Surprised!

Ken Ham, president of Answers in Genesis, the Creation Museum, and future Ark Encounter

This article was published on Opposingviews.com on May 11, 2009, by Answers in Genesis. Answers in Genesis is a Christianity-defending ministry.

As you read the following paragraphs, see if you can guess which well-known evangelical holds these beliefs. Hints: He is a best-selling author; a well-known scientist; and was a keynote speaker at the U.S. National Prayer Breakfast in 2007.

"Belief in a supernatural creator always leaves open the possibility that human beings are a fully-intended part of creation. If the Creator chooses to interact with creation, he could very well influence the evolutionary process to ensure the arrival of his intended result. . . . Furthermore, an omniscient creator could easily create the universe in such a way that physical and natural laws would result in human evolution. . . .

"God planned for humans to evolve to the point of attaining these characteristics. . . . For example, in order to reflect God's Image by engaging in meaningful relationships, the human brain had to evolve to the point where an understanding of love and relationship could be grasped and lived out. God's intention for humans to have relationships is illustrated in the opening chapters of Genesis, where many fundamental truths about God and humankind are communicated through the imagery of a creation story. After placing Adam in the Garden of Eden, Genesis 2 describes God's decision to provide Adam with a partner. . . . The Image of God also includes moral consciousness and responsibility. Humans did not have a fully formed moral consciousness prior to the time of Adam and Eve. . . . However, general consciousness must have already evolved so that a moral consciousness and the associated responsibility were possible. . . . When Adam and Eve received God's image, they had evolved to where they could understand the difference between right and wrong. It seems that Adam and Eve first demonstrated their new moral prowess when, using their free will, they chose wrong by eating from the forbidden tree of knowledge of good and evil. Adam and Eve then knew the difference between right and wrong in a more personal way than before, having experienced the guilt and shame that accompanied their decision (see Genesis 3:1–13). . . . When Did Humans Receive the Image of God? . . .

"We cannot know the exact time that humans attained God's image. In fact, it may be that the image of God emerged gradually over a period of time. Estimates of the historical time of Adam and Eve are varied. . . . While some literalist interpreters of Genesis argue that God created Adam and Eve in their present form, the evidence of DNA and the fossil record establishes that humans were also participants in the long evolutionary continuum, and God used this process as his means of creation. . . .

"We also do not know if humanity received the image of God by the immediate onset of a relationship with God or by a slower evolutionary process. In either case, this development occurred before the fall of Adam and Eve, since moral responsibility and a broken relationship with God are both involved in the story of the fall. Perhaps God used the evolutionary process to equip humankind with language, free will and culture, and then revealed God's will to individuals or a community so that they might then enter into meaningful relationship with God through obedience, prayer and worship. In this scenario, the evolutionary process is necessary but not sufficient to encompass the biblical teaching on the image of God. . . ."

The person who wrote this is Dr. Francis Collins, the scientist best known for his leadership in the Human Genome project. Dr. Collins is a member of the Bio-Logos team, which is described on its website as:

". . . a team of believing scientists who are committed to promoting a perspective of both theological and scientific soundness, which takes seriously the claims of theism and of evolution, and finds compelling evidence for their compatibility."

The BioLogos website has received a grant from the theologically liberal (though relatively morally conservative) John Templeton Foundation, (By the way, such a foundation would never support an organization like Answers in Genesis that stands uncompromisingly on the authority of God's Word.) The paragraphs above come from the BioLogos website.

An article in *Time* magazine about Collins and his new website stated that after the publication of his book about the human genome project (and his public comments about evolution), Dr. Collins received many emails that asked him numerous questions—many about the Book of Genesis—and the same sorts of questions we receive at Answers in Genesis. Sadly, Collins and his group are destructive to biblical authority and are leading many people astray. The *Time* magazine article stated:

"After his best-selling *The Language of God* came out three years ago, Collins began receiving thousands of e-mails—primarily from other Evangelicals—asking questions about how to reconcile scriptural teachings with scientific evidence.

"'Many of these Christians have been taught that evolution is wrong,' Collins explains. 'They go to college and get exposed to data, and then they're thrust into personal crises of great intensity. If the church was wrong about the origins of life, was it wrong about everything? Some of them walk away from science or faith—or both.'"

Actually we have found exactly the opposite. It is biblical compromisers like Dr. Colllins who have caused people to doubt and disbelieve the Bible—causing many of them to walk away from the church. In fact, in our new book *Already Gone*, we present well-documented research that confirms this phenomenon.

The *Time* magazine article continues:

"Collins . . . decided to gather a group of theologians and scientists to create the BioLogos Foundation in order to foster dialogue between the two sides. The name—combining bios (Greek for "life") and logos ("the word")—is also what Collins calls his blended theory of evolution and creation, an approach he hopes can replace intelligent design, which he derides as "not a scientific proposal" and "not good theology either."

". . . As he read through the thousands of e-mails he received from readers of his book, the former NIH scientist noticed that there were 25 or so common questions that his mostly Evangelical correspondents raised. How should Christians respond to Darwin? If God created the universe, who or what created God? Does believing in science mean one can't believe in miracles? What is up with Noah's Ark and the flood? The new website offers answers to these vexing questions and, through those responses lays out the BioLogos theory that God chose to create the world by way of evolution."

It is sad to note that according to *Time* magazine, "Collins plans to build on that work by developing a home-schooling curriculum that can serve as an alternative to the literalist creationism materials widely used by many conservative Evangelical parents." If the home-schooling movement adopts such a curriculum, it will certainly lose many young people of the next generation that it was attempting to train up for the Lord.

continued

It is also no surprise, as the *Time* magazine article states, that:

"A large slice of the questions deal with Genesis, the first book in both Christian and Jewish Scriptures, and the text that explains the creation and population of Earth, and well as the relationship between God and man. Some answers are straightforward, as with the mystery of where Cain's wife came from. 'The scientific evidence suggests a dramatically larger population at this point in history,' conclude Collins. . . ."

In this era of history, people are asking questions about Genesis. As they recognize that if Genesis is not true, how can they trust any of God's Word? Collins is offering them answers that will only further undermine biblical authority; AiG is giving answers that stand on biblical authority. As a result of this approach, so many people have testified they became Christians or rededi- cated their lives to the Lord.

AiG stands unapologetically on the authority of the Word of God. How we need to pray that Collins and his group will repent of their compromise and return to biblical authority. Sadly, they honor the fallible ideas of men instead of God's infallible Word.

The *Time* magazine article can be found at:

http://www.time.com/time/nation/article/ 0,8599,1895284,00.html

As we have often said over the years, compromising Christians are much more of a problem than the athe- ists in undermining the Bible's authority in the culture. No wonder the church is in big trouble in this nation. Discover more at www.AnswersInGenesis.org

http://www.opposingviews.com/i/you- can-t-believe-in-both-creationism-evolution

QUESTIONS FOR READING

1. Who is Francis Collins?
2. Why was the BioLogos Foundation created?
3. According to Collins, how should Christians think of Genesis?
4. What is Answers in Genesis's view of Collins?
5. Answers in Genesis "stands unapologetically" upon what?

QUESTIONS FOR REASONING AND ANALYSIS

1. Why is the issue of Cain's wife important in this debate?
2. What is meant by "literalist interpretation"? How does "literalist interpretation" play into this debate?
3. Why do you think Answers in Genesis mention the grant the BioLogos website received from the John Templeton Foundation?

QUESTIONS FOR REFLECTING AND WRITING

1. What do you see as the major issue in this debate over these two biblically oriented views of creation and human origins? With which point of view are you inclined to agree? Perhaps neither point of view? Why or why not?
2. Can a person agree with evolution and still call him- or herself a Christian? Why or why not?
3. Why do you think the creation vs. evolution debate receives so much attention? Is that attention deserved? Why or why not?

Jeff Parker

This cartoon by artist Jeff Parker appeared in *Florida Today* in 2005. It makes reference to the Kansas Board of Education hearings, the outcome of which determined that intelligent design must be taught as a viable, alternative explanation to evolution.

Copyright © 2005 by Jeff Parker. www.politicalcartoons.com.

QUESTIONS FOR REASONING AND ANALYSIS

1. What do you see as the argument of Parker's cartoon?
2. What function does the clown serve in the cartoon? Is it important that the clown is placed in between the two cavemen? Why or why not?

3. Is it important that some of the characters (e.g., one caveman, the chimpanzee) appear to be surprised (wide eyes)? Why or why not?

QUESTIONS FOR REFLECTING AND WRITING

1. Conduct additional research on the Kansas Board of Education hearings from 2005. What major issues and themes emerge from these hearings? What is your opinion of the outcome?
2. Should teachers teach only one theory or hypothesis concerning the origins of the universe? How should teachers go about teaching this subject?

3. As a student, how do you wish to learn about the origin of species? How about the origin of the universe?

Censoring Science Won't Make Us Any Safer

Laura K. Donohue

Laura Donohue is an Associate Professor of Law at Georgetown Law, and a faculty affiliate of Georgetown's Center on National Security and the Law. Professor Donohue has held fellowships at Stanford Law School's Center for Constitutional Law, Stanford University's Center for International Security and Cooperation, and Harvard University's John F. Kennedy School of Government. She is the author of numerous articles as well as *Counter-Terrorist Law and Emergency Powers in the United Kingdom 1922–2000* (2001). The following article was published in *The Washington Post* on June 26, 2005.

In 1920, the Irish Republican Army reportedly considered a terrifying new weapon: typhoid-contaminated milk. Reading from an IRA memo he claimed had been captured in a recent raid, Sir Hamar Greenwood described to Parliament the ease with which "fresh and virulent cultures" could be obtained and introduced into milk served to British soldiers. Although the plot would only target the military, the memo expressed concern that the disease might spread to the general population.

Although the IRA never used this weapon, the incident illustrates that poisoning a nation's milk supply with biological agents hardly ranks as a new concept. Yet just two weeks ago, the National Academy of Sciences' journal suspended publication of an article analyzing the vulnerability of the U.S. milk supply to botulinum toxin, because the Department of Health and Human Services warned that information in the article provided a "road map for terrorists."

That approach may sound reasonable, but the effort to suppress scientific information reflects a dangerously outdated attitude. Today, information relating to microbiology is widely and instantly available, from the Internet to high school textbooks to doctoral theses. Our best defense against those who would use it as a weapon is to ensure that our own scientists have better information. That means encouraging publication.

The article in question, written by Stanford University professor Lawrence Wein and graduate student Yifan Liu, describes a theoretical terrorist who obtains a few grams of botulinum toxin on the black market and pours it into an unlocked milk tank. Transferred to giant dairy silos, the toxin contaminates a much larger supply. Because even a millionth of a gram may be enough to kill an adult, hundreds of thousands of people die. (Wein summarized the article in an op-ed he wrote for *The New York Times*.[1]) The scenario is frightening, and it is meant to be—the authors want the dairy industry and its federal regulators to take defensive action.

The national academy's suspension of the article reflects an increasing concern that publication of sensitive data can provide terrorists with a how-to manual, but it also brings to the fore an increasing anxiety in the scientific community that curbing the dissemination of research may impair our ability to counter biological threats. This dilemma reached national prominence in fall 2001, when 9/11 and the anthrax mailings drew attention to another controversial article. This one came from a team of Australian scientists.

Approximately every four years, Australia suffers a mouse infestation. In 1998, scientists in Canberra began examining the feasibility of using a highly contagious disease, mousepox, to alter the rodents' ability to reproduce. Their experiments yielded surprising results. Researchers working with mice naturally resistant to the disease found that combining a gene from the rodent's immune system (interleukin-4) with the pox virus and inserting the pathogen into the animals killed them—all of them. Plus 60 percent of the mice not naturally resistant who had been vaccinated against mousepox.

In February 2001 the American Society for Microbiologists' (ASM) *Journal of Virology* reported the findings. Alarm ensued. The mousepox virus is closely related to smallpox—one of the most dangerous pathogens known to humans. And the rudimentary nature of the experiment demonstrated how even basic, inexpensive microbiology can yield devastating results.

When the anthrax attacks burst into the news seven months later, the mousepox case became a lightning rod for deep-seated fears about biological weapons. *The Economist* reported rumors about the White House pressuring American microbiology journals to restrict publication of similar pieces. Samuel Kaplan, chair of the ASM publications board, convened a meeting of the editors in chief of the ASM's nine primary journals and two review journals. Hoping to head off government censorship, the organization—

while affirming its earlier decision—ordered its peer reviewers to take national security and the society's code of ethics into account.

Not only publications came under pressure, but research itself. In spring 2002 the newly formed Department of Homeland Security developed an information-security policy to prevent certain foreign nationals from gaining access to a range of experimental data. New federal regulations required that particular universities and laboratories submit to unannounced inspections, register their supplies and obtain security clearances. Legislation required that all genetic engineering experiments be cleared by the government.

On the mousepox front, however, important developments were transpiring. Because the Australian research had entered the public domain, scientists around the world began working on the problem. In November 2003, St. Louis University announced an effective medical defense against a pathogen similar to—but even more deadly than—the one created in Australia. This result would undoubtedly not have been achieved, or at least not as quickly, without the attention drawn by the ASM article.

The dissemination of nuclear technology presents an obvious comparison. The 1946 Atomic Energy Act classifies nuclear information "from birth." Strong arguments can be made in favor of such restrictions: The science involved in the construction of the bomb was complex and its application primarily limited to weapons. A short-term monopoly was possible. Secrecy bought the United States time to establish an international nonproliferation regime. And little public good would have been achieved by making the information widely available.

Biological information and the issues surrounding it are different. It is not possible to establish even a limited monopoly over microbiology. The field is too fundamental to the improvement of global public health, and too central to the development of important industries such as pharmaceuticals and plastics, to be isolated. Moreover, the list of diseases that pose a threat ranges from high-end bugs, like smallpox, to common viruses, such as influenza. Where does one draw the line for national security?

Experience suggests that the government errs on the side of caution. In 1951, the Invention Secrecy Act gave the government the authority to suppress any design it deemed detrimental to national defense. Certain areas of research—atomic energy and cryptography—consistently fell within its purview. But the state also placed secrecy orders on aspects of cold fusion, space technology, radar missile systems, citizens band radio voice scramblers, optical engineering and vacuum technology. Such caution, in the microbiology realm, may yield devastating results. It is not in the national interest to stunt research into biological threats.

In fact, the more likely menace comes from naturally occurring diseases. In 1918 a natural outbreak of the flu infected one-fifth of the world's population and 25 percent of the United States'. Within two years it killed more than 650,000 Americans, resulting in a 10-year drop in average lifespan. Despite constant research into emerging strains, the American Lung Association estimates that the flu and related complications kill 36,000 Americans each year. Another 5,000 die annually from food-borne pathogens—an extraordinarily large number of which have no known cure. The science involved in responding to these diseases is incremental, meaning that small steps taken by individual laboratories around the world need to be shared for larger progress to be made.

The idea that scientific freedom strengthens national security is not new. In the early 1980s, a joint Panel on Scientific Communication and National Security concluded security by secrecy was untenable. Its report called instead for security by accomplishment—ensuring strength through advancing research. Ironically, one of the three major institutions participating was the National Academy of Sciences—the body that suspended publication of the milk article earlier this month.

The government has a vested interest in creating a public conversation about ways in which our society is vulnerable to attack. Citizens are entitled to know when their milk, their water, their bridges, their hospitals lack security precautions. If discussion of these issues is censored, the state and private industry come under less pressure to alter behavior; indeed, powerful private interests may actively lobby against having to install expensive protections. And failure to act may be deadly.

Terrorists will obtain knowledge. Our best option is to blunt their efforts to exploit it. That means developing, producing and stockpiling effective vaccines. It means funding research into biosensors—devices that detect the presence of toxic substances in the environment—and creating more effective reporting requirements for early identification of disease outbreaks. And it means strengthening our public health system.

For better or worse, the cat is out of the bag—something brought home to me last weekend when I visited the Tech Museum of Innovation in San Jose. One hands-on exhibit allowed children to transfer genetic material from one species to another. I watched a 4-year-old girl take a red test tube whose contents included a gene that makes certain jellyfish glow green. Using a pipette, she transferred the material to a blue test tube containing bacteria. She cooled the solution, then heated it, allowing the gene to enter the bacteria. Following instructions on a touch-screen computer, she transferred the contents to a petridish, wrote her name on the bottom, and placed the dish in an incubator. The next day, she could log on to a website to view her experiment, and see her bacteria glowing a genetically modified green.

continued

In other words, the pre-kindergartener (with a great deal of help from the museum) had conducted an experiment that echoed the Australian mousepox study. Obviously, this is not something the child could do in her basement. But just as obviously, the state of public knowledge is long past anyone's ability to censor it.

Allowing potentially harmful information to enter the public domain flies in the face of our traditional way of thinking about national security threats. But we have entered a new world. Keeping scientists from sharing information damages our ability to respond to terrorism and to natural disease, which is more likely and just as devastating. Our best hope to head off both threats may well be to stay one step ahead.

_____

1. Actually the description of a theoretical terrorist obtaining a toxin on the black market appeared only in *The New York Times* article, not in the original article that the National Academy of Sciences refused to publish.

QUESTIONS FOR READING

1. What is the occasion for Donohue's article?
2. What other restrictions have been developed by Homeland Security?
3. How is the scientific community reacting to restrictions? What is their concern?
4. What is probably a greater threat than terrorism?
5. Is it possible to censor information on microbiology?

QUESTIONS FOR REASONING AND ANALYSIS

1. What is Donohue's claim? State it as a problem/solution type of argument.
2. To state her claim as a problem/solution type of argument is to suggest that her argument is more practical than philosophical; is that a fair assessment?

Why or why not? What are the two key points of her argument?

3. In paragraph 11, Donohue reminds readers that nuclear information is classified and asserts that it should be. Why does she include this paragraph?

QUESTIONS FOR REFLECTING AND WRITING

1. Donohue reminds readers that scientific knowledge is built up by many contributing a little bit to the knowledge base. And yet a scientific journal suppressed an article. Why? Does Homeland Security have too much power? Have we all become too fearful of terrorists?
2. Has the author convinced you that we are at greater risk by censoring knowledge than by publishing information? Why or why not?

prereading question } Are people taking global warming too seriously?

Global Warming as Religion
You Had to See It Coming

Chuck Colson

Chuck Colson is a conservative Christian writer and speaker as well as former special counsel to President Richard Nixon. This opinion piece was published to *The Christian Post* on December 4, 2009.

Religious freedom is one of the most difficult and vexing issues of our day—whether the subject is Muslim schoolgirls in France or Christian photographers in New Mexico.

And that's before government starts calling just about any sincerely held belief a "religion."

That is essentially what has happened in Britain. In July 2008, Tim Nicholson was let go from his job at a property management firm. According to Nicholson, his dismissal was due to his beliefs about man-made global warming.

Nicholson calls man-made global warming "the most important issue of our time" and believes that "nothing should stand in the way of diverting this catastrophe." This led to "frequent clashes" with his co-workers over his concerns.

For instance, Nicholson, out of concern about excess CO2 emissions, refuses to fly. He objected when the firm's CEO flew someone from London to Ireland to retrieve his Blackberry.

When he was dismissed, Nicholson sued under Britain's Employment Equality act, specifically the part that prohibits discrimination on account of "religion and belief."

"I want more Christian news!"

According to Nicholson, "Belief in man-made climate change is . . . a philosophical belief that reflects my moral and ethical values."

For its part, his former employer countered that "green views were political and based on science, as opposed to religious or philosophical in nature."

In what's being called a "landmark ruling," a British judge ruled for Nicholson, saying that "a belief in man-made climate change . . . is capable, if genuinely held, of being a philosophical belief for the purpose" of laws covering discrimination in employment.

The judge's ruling opens the door to the possibility of employees suing their employers "for failing to account for their green lifestyles, such as providing recycling facilities or offering low-carbon travel."

Theoretically, an employer could say "I need you in Helsinki by tomorrow," to which the employee could reply, "Too much carbon, we'll have to aim for next week, since I'll be going by bicycle, train, and boat."

The possibilities are, as advertisers say, endless. And the upcoming Copenhagen conference will, no doubt, add more "converts" to the faith.

And what of the faith that actually created and nurtured Britain? (That's Christianity.) Let's just say that British officials aren't as solicitous of its practitioners as they are of those belonging to newer arrivals.

For those of us who say that could never happen here, let me remind you of a Supreme Court case defining religion decades ago as "a sincere and meaningful belief which occupies, in the life of its possessor, a place parallel to that filled by God."

And remember that, last year, Al Gore argued that you could have civil disobedience morally justified in order to stop the construction of a coal-fired electric generating plant.

Listen, folks, in today's climate, the earth could soon enough take the place of that archaic idea of an ancient God of the Bible. Please go to ColsonCenter.org for my "Two-Minute Warning."

http://www.christianpost.com/news/globalwarming-as-religion-42124

QUESTIONS FOR READING

1. According to Colson, what is one of the most difficult issues of the day?
2. Why was Tim Nicholson fired from his job?
3. What is Colson's concern over the judge's ruling in the Nicholson case?

QUESTIONS FOR REASONING AND ANALYSIS

1. What is Colson's thesis?
2. Does Colson's argument reflect the slippery slope fallacy? Why or why not?
3. Was Nicholson's claim a valid one? Why or why not?

QUESTIONS FOR REFLECTING AND WRITING

1. Are people justified in going to extremes based on their global warming concerns? Why or why not?
2. Conduct some additional research on the Nicholson case. Do you agree that the judge's decision was justified? Why or why not?

OUR NATIONAL DEBT

$8,200,283,852,2

YOUR *Family share* $89,5

THE NATIONAL DEBT CLOC

competing perspectives on the american economic and financial crisis

chapter 24

Foreclosure. Bailout. Deficit. Recession. Depression. These terms have become all too familiar as our nation's leaders debate how to resolve the economic and financial crisis that began in 2008. This crisis has created a feeling of uncertainty in most Americans, many of whom lost their jobs, their homes, and their hope for the future. In response, the U.S. Congress passed almost $1 trillion of "economic stimulus," but some feared the measure would create more problems than it would solve by increasing deficits and eventually resulting in more taxes. Others feared our nation was on the brink of complete financial collapse, perhaps even worse than the Great Depression of the 1930s. The following selections capture these differing and competing perspectives, addressing, for example, the mortgage-lending debacle as well as President Obama's economic recovery plan for resolving one of the most serious crises in our nation's history.

---

prereading questions

1. What are the answers to the economic and financial crisis, which poses serious potential consequences for both the United States and the rest of the world?

2. What were the major causes of the economic crisis? Is any one party (political or otherwise) or group to blame for the crisis? Should politicians engage in finger-pointing in the midst of catastrophe? Why or why not?

3. Should the federal government bail out failing financial-lending institutions and major corporations? Why or why not?

4. Does President Obama's plan represent the right course of action for addressing the country's economic problems and financial woes? Why or why not?

5. How do you think this crisis will affect you as well as your family and friends in the next 10 to 20 years?

---

websites related to this chapter's topic

AMERICANS UNITED FOR CHANGE
www.americansunitedforchange.com
Website for the grassroots organization Americans United for Change, offering several links and multiple resources.

THE WORLD BANK
www.worldbank.org/html/extdr/financialcrisis
World Bank site addressing the global economic and financial crisis.

RELEVANT WHITE HOUSE LINKS
National Economic Council
www.whitehouse.gov/administration/eop/nec
Council of Economic Advisors
www.whitehouse.gov/administration/eop/cea
White House Agenda—Economy
www.whitehouse.gov/issues/economy

---

newspaper editorial

prereading question } Is technology eliminating many of the jobs for college graduates?

Degrees and Dollars

Paul Krugman

Paul Krugman is an op-ed columnist for *The New York Times* and a professor of economics and international affairs at Princeton University. *The New York Times* published this editorial on March 6, 2011.

It is a truth universally acknowledged that education is the key to economic success. Everyone knows that the jobs of the future will require ever higher levels of skill. That's why, in an appearance Friday with former Florida Gov. Jeb Bush, President Obama declared that "If we want more good news on the jobs front then we've got to make more investments in education."

But what everyone knows is wrong.

The day after the Obama-Bush event, the *Times* published an article about the growing use of software to perform legal research. Computers, it turns out, can quickly analyze millions of documents, cheaply performing a task that used to require armies of lawyers and paralegals. In this case, then, technological progress is actually reducing the demand for highly educated workers.

And legal research isn't an isolated example. As the article points out, software has also been replacing engineers in such tasks as chip design. More broadly, the idea that modern technology eliminates only menial jobs, that well-educated workers are clear winners, may dominate popular discussion, but it's actually decades out of date.

The fact is that since 1990 or so the U.S. job market has been characterized not by a general rise in the demand for skill, but by "hollowing out": both high-wage and low-wage employment have grown rapidly, but medium-wage jobs—the kinds of jobs we count on to support a strong middle class—have lagged behind. And the hole in the middle has been getting wider: many of the high-wage occupations that grew rapidly in the 1990s have seen much slower growth recently, even as growth in low-wage employment has accelerated.

Why is this happening? The belief that education is becoming ever more important rests on the plausible-sounding notion that advances in technology increase job opportunities for those who work with information—loosely speaking, that computers help those who work with their minds, while hurting those who work with their hands.

Some years ago, however, the economists David Autor, Frank Levy and Richard Murnane argued that this was the wrong way to think about it. Computers, they pointed out, excel at routine tasks, "cognitive and manual tasks that can be accomplished by following explicit rules." Therefore, any routine task—a category that includes many white-collar, nonmanual jobs—is in the firing line. Conversely, jobs that can't be carried out by following explicit rules—a category that includes many kinds of manual labor, from truck drivers to janitors—will tend to grow even in the face of technological progress.

And here's the thing: Most of the manual labor still being done in our economy seems to be of the kind that's hard to automate. Notably, with production workers in manufacturing down to about 6 percent of U.S. employment, there aren't many assembly-line jobs left to lose. Meanwhile, quite a lot of white-collar work currently carried out by well-educated, relatively well-paid workers may soon be computerized. Roombas are cute, but robot janitors are a long way off; computerized legal research and computer-aided medical diagnosis are already here.

And then there's globalization. Once, only manufacturing workers needed to worry about competition from overseas, but the combination of computers and telecommunications has made it possible to provide many services at long range. And research by my Princeton colleagues Alan Blinder and Alan Krueger suggests that high-wage jobs performed by highly educated workers are, if anything, more "offshorable" than jobs done by low-paid, less-educated workers. If they're right, growing international trade in services will further hollow out the U.S. job market.

So what does all this say about policy?

Yes, we need to fix American education. In particular, the inequalities Americans face at the starting line—bright children from poor families are less likely to finish college than much less able children of the affluent—aren't just an outrage; they represent a huge waste of the nation's human potential.

But there are things education can't do. In particular, the notion that putting more kids through college can restore the middle-class society we used to have is wishful thinking. It's no longer true that having a college degree guarantees that you'll get a good job, and it's becoming less true with each passing decade.

So if we want a society of broadly shared prosperity, education isn't the answer—we'll have to go about building that society directly. We need to restore the bargaining power that labor has lost over the last 30 years, so that ordinary workers as well as superstars have the power to bargain for good wages. We need to guarantee the essentials, above all health care, to every citizen.

What we can't do is get where we need to go just by giving workers college degrees, which may be no more than tickets to jobs that don't exist or don't pay middle-class wages.

QUESTIONS FOR READING

1. According to Krugman, what is reducing the demand for highly educated workers?
2. What does Krugman mean by "hollowing out"?
3. What argument did Autor, Levy, and Murnane make?
4. According to the author, what can education not do?

QUESTIONS FOR REASONING AND ANALYSIS

1. What is Krugman's thesis or main argument?
2. Why does Krugman contend that if the United States wants to achieve prosperity, then it should restore the bargaining power of labor? Why does he suggest that restoring bargaining power to labor becomes the solution to the problem he discusses?
3. How is Krugman's piece a problem-solution essay?

QUESTIONS FOR REFLECTING AND WRITING

1. In your view, what actions should the United States government take to create jobs? Why do you think these actions will solve the problem?
2. What is your perspective on jobs for college graduates in years to come? Are you concerned about your prospects after graduating college? Why or why not?
3. Do you agree or disagree with Krugman? Why or why not? Write an essay defending your position.

---

newspaper editorial

prereading question } **Is raising taxes on the wealthiest Americans the answer to bringing down the budget deficit?**

Please Raise My Taxes

Reed Hastings

Reed Hastings is the chief executive of Netflix. *The New York Times* published this piece on February 5, 2009.

I'm the chief executive of a publicly traded company and, like my peers, I'm very highly paid. The difference between salaries like mine and those of average Americans creates a lot of tension, and I'd like to offer a suggestion. President Obama should celebrate our success, rather than trying to shame us or cap our pay. But he should also take half of our huge earnings in taxes, instead of the current one-third.

Then, the next time a chief executive earns an eye-popping amount of money, we can cheer that half of it is going to pay for our soldiers, schools and security. Higher taxes on huge pay days can finance opportunity for the next generation of Americans.

Clearly, the efforts over the past few decades to control executive compensation haven't accomplished much. Improved public disclosure was supposed to shame companies into lowering salaries, and it obviously hasn't worked. In 1993, President Bill Clinton changed the tax law to effectively cap executives' salaries at $1 million a year, but that simply drove corporate boards to offer larger bonuses and stock options to attract and keep talent. More recently, "say on pay" proposals would have shareholders opine on their boards' compensation decisions, but "say and pay" won't change the fact that luring a top executive away from another company is never easy or cheap.

The reality is that the boards of public companies hate overpaying for anything, including executives. But picking the wrong chief executive is an enormous disaster, so boards are willing to pay an arm and a leg for already proven talent. Putting limits on the salaries at public companies, or trying to shame them into coming down, won't stop this costly competition for talent.

Of course, it's galling when a chief executive fails and is still handsomely rewarded. But with the concept of "tax, not shame," a shocking $20 million severance package would generate $10 million for the government. That's a far better solution than what we have today, not least because it works with the market rather than against it.

Another advantage is that it would also cover the sometimes huge earnings of hedge fund managers, star athletes, stunning movie stars, venture capitalists and the chief executives of private companies. Surely there is no reason to focus only on executives at publicly traded companies.

This week, President Obama proposed imposing a $500,000 compensation cap on companies seeking a bailout. It's a terrible idea. We all want the taxpayers' money returned, and capping compensation at bailout recipients will just make it that much harder for those boards to hire and hold on to the executives who can lead their companies to compete and thrive.

Perhaps a starting place for "tax, not shame" would be creating a top federal marginal tax rate of 50 percent on all income above $1 million per year. Some will tell you that would reduce the incentive to earn but I don't see that as likely. Besides, half of a giant compensation package is still pretty huge, and most of our motivation is the sheer challenge of the job anyway.

Instead of trying to shame companies and executives, the president should take advantage of our success by using our outsized earnings to pay for the needs of our nation.

http://www.nytimes.com/2009/02/06/opinion/06hastings.html

QUESTIONS FOR READING

1. What efforts have failed in recent years to control executive compensation?
2. What is Hastings "tax, not shame" proposal? What are the advantages he cites of this proposal?
3. According to Hastings, what is the major problem with corporate boards attempting to cap compensation?

QUESTIONS FOR REASONING AND ANALYSIS

1. How is Hastings's piece a problem-solution essay?
2. What is the assumption or warrant behind Hastings's argument that the U.S. government should raise tax rates for corporate executives?
3. Do you think Hastings proposed solution would solve the problem he describes? Why or why not?

QUESTIONS FOR REFLECTING AND WRITING

1. How do you think corporate executives would respond to Hastings's proposal? Why do you think they would respond in a particular way?
2. Should steps be taken to control the levels of salaries for corporate executives? Why or why not?

newspaper editorial

prereading question } **How should a government go about solving the financial crisis?**

Think This Economy Is Bad? Wait for 2012.

Greg Ip

Greg Ip is the U.S. economics editor for *The Economist*. He has also authored such books as *The Little Book of Economics: How the Economy Works in the Real World*. This essay was published in the *Washington Post Outlook* on October 24, 2010.

We're barely two years past the banking crisis, still weathering the mortgage crisis and nervously watching Europe struggle with its sovereign debt crisis. Yet every economic seer has a favorite prediction about what part of the economy the next crisis will come from: Municipal bonds? Hedge funds? Derivatives? The federal debt?

I, for one, have no idea what will cause the next economic disaster. But I do have an idea of when it will begin: 2012.

Yes, an election year. Economic crises have a habit of erupting just when politicians face the voters. The reason is simple: They are born of long-festering problems such as lax lending, excessive deficits or an overvalued

continued

currency, and these are precisely the sort of problems that politicians try to ignore, hide or even double down on during campaign season, hoping to delay the reckoning until after the polls close or a new government takes office. Perversely, this only worsens the underlying imbalances, making the mess worse and the cost to the economy—in lost income and jobs—much higher.

Election-year prevarication has a storied history in the United States. In the summer of 1971, President Richard Nixon imposed wage and price controls in hopes of suppressing inflation pressure until after the 1972 election. He succeeded, but the result was even worse inflation in 1973 and a deep recession starting that fall.

During the 1988 presidential campaign, Vice President George H.W. Bush and Democratic nominee Michael Dukakis largely ignored the mounting losses in the nation's insolvent thrifts for fear of admitting to taxpayers the price of cleaning them up. The delay allowed the losses and the price tag to grow, and the burden of bad loans hamstrung the economy into the early 1990s.

Go back to 1932 for an even more dramatic example: After defeating Herbert Hoover that year, Franklin D. Roosevelt refused during the four-month transition to say whether he'd support the lame-duck administration's policy for fixing the banks and keeping the dollar linked to gold. Depositors fled banks and investors dumped the dollar, resulting in another wave of bank failures that vastly worsened the Depression.

But perhaps the most poignant example of election-year myopia came in 2008. After agreeing to an ad hoc bailout of Bear Stearns that March, then-Treasury Secretary Henry Paulson knew he needed authority and money to deal with such situations. But he didn't ask Congress for either, reasoning that lawmakers would never approve something so contentious just months from a presidential election. (He was probably right.) So when Lehman Brothers foundered that fall, Paulson, with no orderly way to wind the company down, let it fail.

He then proposed the Troubled Assets Relief Program to deal with the resulting chaos, but the House, gripped by an election-year aversion to bailouts, voted it down. The defeat sent markets into a tailspin. Lawmakers changed their minds and passed the TARP, but the intervening panic worsened the economic pain.

Elections are even more of a trigger for crises in other countries. When Greece's national election campaign began in September 2009, the government claimed that the budget deficit was more than 6 percent of gross domestic product, high but manageable. Yet shortly after the socialist government took power, it revealed that the deficit was in fact closer to 12.5 percent. The previous government, it turned out, had been issuing optimistic forecasts and hiding some of its spending.

As foreign investors' confidence in Greece evaporated, interest rates on its debt soared. To avoid default, it was forced to seek a bailout from the International Monetary Fund and the European Union. The Greek economy will probably shrink at least 3 percent both this year and next.

Mexico's financial crises regularly coincide with presidential elections. In early 1982, the government knew that its deficit was too large and that its currency was overvalued. Investors were pulling their money out, draining the nation's foreign currency reserves. Government officials hoped to postpone action until after the July election, and the Federal Reserve helped by making short-term dollar loans to Mexico designed solely to make its reserves appear larger.

"We were trying to buy time until the election and new government. We failed," recalls Ted Truman, a Fed official at the time. Money continued to flee, and a month after the election, Mexico announced it couldn't repay its bank loans, triggering the Latin American debt crisis, a severe recession and what many called the region's "lost decade."

A similar dynamic brought on Mexico's election-year "tequila crisis" of 1994, which forced a massive and sudden devaluation of the peso and required tens of billions of dollars in international assistance.

Even when a government tries to do the right thing, electoral politics make it difficult. During the 1997 Asian financial crisis, South Korea negotiated a $55 billion loan from the International Monetary Fund, the World Bank and others to avoid defaulting on its private bank loans; in return, it promised reforms such as closing weak banks. But confidence evaporated and the currency plunged when the leading opposition candidate in that year's presidential election attacked the agreement.

A similar situation occurred in the election to succeed Brazil's President Fernando Henrique Cardoso, who had brought stability to his country during the 1990s after decades of inflation and default. When it became apparent that his handpicked successor would lose in 2002 to leftist challenger Luiz Inácio Lula da Silva, Brazil's stock markets and currency plunged, and the government lost the ability to issue long-term bonds. Inflation and interest rates shot up, hammering the economy.

These countries actually offer an uplifting lesson: The damage wrought by the crises helped build support for solutions. In Korea in 1997 and Brazil in 2002, populist challengers ultimately embraced their predecessors' reform plans. Greece's socialists campaigned last year promising to raise public salaries, invest in infrastructure and help small businesses. But they are now undertaking painful reforms, such as raising retirement ages and injecting more competition into protected industries such as trucking.

Of course, these countries are relatively young democracies with legacies of economic mismanagement. It couldn't happen here anymore, right? Think again. Yes, this year the United States passed the sweeping Dodd-Frank Act, seeking to make financial crises a thing of the past. But there are countless problems that can develop into disasters (think Foreclosure-Gate). And Dodd-Frank is useless if the next crisis involves our tattered government finances.

Which brings us to 2012.

Let me take a stab at what the next crisis will be. Our deficit, as a share of GDP, is at a peacetime record, and the debt is climbing toward a post–World War II record. Thoughtful economists agree on the response: Combine stimulus for our fragile economy now with a plan to slash the deficit and stabilize the debt when the recovery is more entrenched.

Yet the approaching November midterms have made it impossible to advance a serious proposal for doing that. Congress has been unable to pass a budget, and the government is operating on a short-term "continuing resolution." President Obama's plan for reining in the national debt consists of appointing a bipartisan commission that won't report until after the midterms. Even if the commission can agree on a realistic plan to chop the deficit, the polarized state of Congress suggests slim odds of adoption.

With neither party able to muster the support to get serious about reducing the deficit, both may prefer to kick the problem down the road to after 2012, in hopes that the election hands one of them a clear mandate.

For now, there's enough risk of Japanese-style stagnation and deflation that U.S. interest rates could remain very low for a while yet. But if that risk fades, investors in U.S. Treasury bonds will want to know how we'll get our deficits and debt under control—and could demand higher interest rates to compensate for the uncertainty. By then, though, the 2012 campaign may be upon us. The Republican nominee will assail Obama's fiscal record and promise a determined assault on the debt. Obama will respond by blaming George W. Bush and promising to unveil his own plan once he's reelected. Neither will commit political suicide by specifying which taxes they'll raise or which entitlements they'll cut.

Will investors trust them, or will they start to worry that the endgame is either inflation or default, two tried-and-true ways other countries have escaped their debts? If it's the latter, we'll face a vicious circle of rising interest rates and budget deficits, squeezing the economy and potentially forcing abrupt and painful austerity measures.

And if, instead, the markets continue to give us the benefit of the doubt, relieving our politicians of the need to act: Circle 2016 on your calendar.

http://gregip.wordpress.com/2010/10/24/think-this-economy-is-bad-wait-for-2012/#more-900

QUESTIONS FOR READING

1. According to Ip, why do economic crises erupt in election years?
2. What action did Treasury Secretary Paulson take in 2008?
3. What "uplifting lesson" do the experiences of other countries offer?
4. What does Ip speculate will be the next financial crisis in the United States?

QUESTIONS FOR REASONING AND ANALYSIS

1. What is the meaning of the word "prevarication" as Ip uses it in the fourth paragraph?
2. What does Ip suggest as the relationship between interest rates and the deficit?
3. What does Ip mean by the last sentence of the essay?

QUESTIONS FOR REFLECTING AND WRITING

1. Do you believe the United States is destined for an even more severe economic and financial crisis? Why or why not?
2. Is finger pointing appropriate in the midst of an economic crisis? Why or why not?
3. Conduct some additional research on the recent U.S. financial and economic crisis. In your view, what were the primary causes of this crisis? Write an essay relating the primary causes and effects of the crisis.

The following two cartoons explore the effects of the banking crisis and the bailouts of corporations by the U.S. Congress. The first cartoon, by Rob Tornoe, was posted to the Irvine Housing Blog in October 2010. The second, by Lloyd Dangle, appeared on the Troubletown Blog on May 30, 2009.

© Rob Tornoe. Reprinted by permission of Cagle Cartoons, Inc.

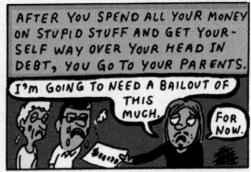

©2009 TROUBLETOWN.com

QUESTIONS FOR REASONING AND ANALYSIS

1. How would you explain the depiction of American corporations in the first cartoon? What is the cartoon's message?

2. What analogy does Dangle use in the second cartoon? Is it effective in conveying the point?

3. What is Dangle saying in the fifth frame of his cartoon?

QUESTIONS FOR REFLECTING AND WRITING

1. Should the U.S. government bail out failing corporations and financial institutions? Why or why not?

2. If you were a member of the U.S. Congress, how would you propose to resolve the financial crisis? Write an

essay detailing the steps you would take to solve the problem.

The United States of Inequality

Introducing the Great Divergence

Timothy Noah

Timothy Noah is a senior writer for Slate.com. This article is the first in a series discussing income inequality. It was posted on September 3, 2010.

In 1915, a statistician at the University of Wisconsin named Willford I. King published *The Wealth and Income of the People of the United States*, the most comprehensive study of its kind to date. The United States was displacing Great Britain as the world's wealthiest nation, but detailed information about its economy was not yet readily available; the federal government wouldn't start collecting such data in any systematic way until the 1930s. One of King's purposes was to reassure the public that all Americans were sharing in the country's newfound wealth.

King was somewhat troubled to find that the richest 1 percent possessed about 15 percent of the nation's income. (A more authoritative subsequent calculation puts the figure slightly higher, at about 18 percent.)

This was the era in which the accumulated wealth of America's richest families—the Rockefellers, the Vanderbilts, the Carnegies—helped prompt creation of the modern income tax, lest disparities in wealth turn the United States into a European-style aristocracy. The socialist movement was at its historic peak, a wave of anarchist bombings was terrorizing the nation's industrialists, and President Woodrow Wilson's attorney general, Alexander Palmer, would soon stage brutal raids on radicals of every stripe. In American history, there has never been a time when class warfare seemed more imminent.

That was when the richest 1 percent accounted for 18 percent of the nation's income. Today, the richest 1 percent account for 24 percent of the nation's income. What caused this to happen? Over the next two weeks, I'll try to answer that question by looking at all potential explanations—race, gender, the computer revolution, immigration, trade, government policies, the decline of labor, compensation policies on Wall Street and in executive suites, and education. Then I'll explain why people who say we don't need to worry about income inequality (there aren't many of them) are wrong.

Income inequality in the United States has not worsened steadily since 1915. It dropped a bit in the late teens, then started climbing again in the 1920s, reaching its peak just before the 1929 crash. The trend then reversed itself. Incomes started to become more equal in the 1930s and then became dramatically more equal in the 1940s. Income distribution remained roughly stable through the postwar economic boom of the 1950s and 1960s. Economic historians Claudia Goldin and Robert Margo have termed this midcentury era the "Great Compression." The deep nostalgia for that period felt by the World War II generation—the era of *Life* magazine and the bowling league—reflects something more than mere sentimentality. Assuming you were white, not of draft age, and Christian, there probably was no better time to belong to America's middle class.

The Great Compression ended in the 1970s. Wages stagnated, inflation raged, and by the decade's end, income inequality had started to rise. Income inequality grew through the 1980s, slackened briefly at the end of the 1990s, and then resumed with a vengeance in the aughts. In his 2007 book *The Conscience of a Liberal*, the Nobel laureate, Princeton economist and *New York Times* columnist Paul Krugman labeled the post-1979 epoch the "Great Divergence."

It's generally understood that we live in a time of growing income inequality, but "the ordinary person is not really aware of how big it is," Krugman told me. During the late 1980s and the late 1990s, the United States experienced two unprecedentedly long periods of sustained economic growth—the "seven fat years" and the "long boom." Yet from 1980 to 2005, *more than 80 percent* of total increase in Americans' income went to the top 1 percent. Economic growth was more sluggish in the aughts, but the decade saw productivity increase by about 20 percent. Yet virtually none of the increase translated into wage growth at middle and lower incomes, an outcome that left many economists scratching their heads.

Here is a snapshot of income distribution during the past 100 years:

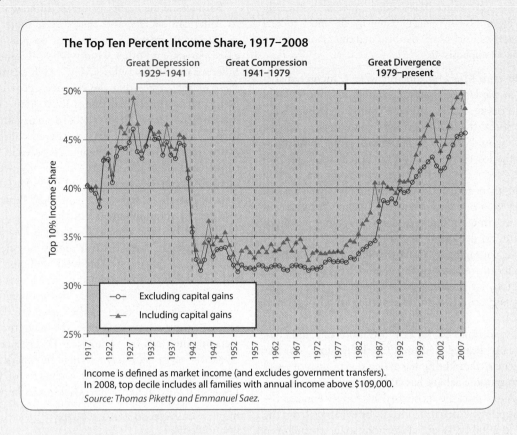

The Top Ten Percent Income Share, 1917–2008

Great Depression 1929–1941 · Great Compression 1941–1979 · Great Divergence 1979–present

— Excluding capital gains
— Including capital gains

Income is defined as market income (and excludes government transfers).
In 2008, top decile includes all families with annual income above $109,000.

Source: Thomas Piketty and Emmanuel Saez.

Why don't Americans pay more attention to growing income disparity? One reason may be our enduring belief in social mobility. Economic inequality is less troubling if you live in a country where any child, no matter how humble his or her origins, can grow up to be president. In a survey of 27 nations conducted from 1998 to 2001, the country where the highest proportion agreed with the statement "people are rewarded for intelligence and skill" was, of course, the United States. (69 percent). But when it comes to *real* as opposed to imagined social mobility, surveys find less in the United States than in much of (what we consider) the class-bound Old World. France, Germany, Sweden, Denmark, Spain—not to mention some newer nations like Canada and Australia—are all places where your chances of rising from the bottom are better than they are in the land of Horatio Alger's *Ragged Dick*.

All my life I've heard Latin America described as a failed society (or collection of failed societies) because of its grotesque maldistribution of wealth. Peasants in rags beg for food outside the high walls of opulent villas, and so on. But according to the Central Intelligence Agency (whose patriotism I hesitate to question), income distribution in the United States is more un-

equal than in Guyana, Nicaragua, and Venezuela, and roughly on par with Uruguay, Argentina, and Ecuador. Income inequality is actually declining in Latin America even as it continues to increase in the United States. Economically speaking, the richest nation on earth is starting to resemble a banana republic. The main difference is that the United States is big enough to maintain geographic distance between the villa-dweller and the beggar. As Ralston Thorpe tells his St. Paul's classmate, the investment banker Sherman McCoy, in Tom Wolfe's 1987 novel *The Bonfire of the Vanities*: "You've got to insulate, insulate, insulate."

In 1915, King wrote, "It is easy to find a man in almost any line of employment who is twice as efficient as another employee,"

but it is very rare to find one who is ten times as efficient. It is common, however, to see one man possessing not ten times but a thousand times the wealth of his neighbor. . . . Is the middle class doomed to extinction and shall we soon find the handful of plutocrats, the modern barons of wealth, lined up squarely in opposition to the propertyless masses with no buffer between to lessen the chances of open battle? With the middle class gone and the laborer condemned to remain a life-

continued

long wage-earner with no hope of attaining wealth or even a competence in his old age, all the conditions are ripe for a crowning class-conflict equaling in intensity and bitterness anything pictured by the most radical follower of Karl Marx. Is this condition soon coming to pass? [emphasis his]

In the end, King concluded it wasn't. Income distribution in the United States, he found, was more equal than in Prussia, France, and the United Kingdom. King was no socialist. Redistributing income to the poor, he wrote, "would merely mean more rapid multiplication of the lowest and least desirable classes," who remained, "from the reproductive standpoint, on the low point of their four-footed ancestors." A Malthusian, he believed in population control. Income inequality in the United States could be addressed by limiting immigration (King deplored "low-standard alien invaders") and by discouraging excessive breeding among the poor ("eugenicists are just beginning to impress upon us the absurd folly of breeding great troops of paupers, defectives and criminals to be a burden upon organized society").

Today, incomes in the U.S. are more unequal than in Germany, France, and the United Kingdom, not less so. Eugenics (thankfully) has fallen out of fashion, and the immigration debate has become (somewhat) more polite. As for income inequality, it's barely entered the national political debate. Indeed, the evidence from the 2000 and 2004 presidential elections suggests that even mild economic populism was a loser for Democrats. (To sample authentic economic populism, click here.)

But income inequality is a topic of huge importance to American society and therefore a subject of large and growing interest to a host of economists, political scientists, and other wonky types. Except for a few Libertarian outliers (whose views we'll examine later), these experts agree that the country's growing income inequality is deeply worrying. Even Alan Greenspan, the former Federal Reserve Board chairman and one-time Ayn Rand acolyte, has registered concern. "This is not the type of thing which a democratic society—a capitalist democratic society—can really accept without addressing," Greenspan said in 2005. Greenspan's Republican-appointed successor, Ben Bernanke, has also fretted about income inequality.

Yet few of these experts have much idea how to reverse the trend. That's because almost no one can agree about what's causing it. This week and next, I will detail and weigh the strengths and weaknesses of various prominent theories as to what has brought about the income inequality boom of the last three decades. At the same time, I'll try to convey the magnitude of its effects on American life. The Great Divergence may represent the most significant change in American society in your lifetime—and it's not a change for the better. Let's see if we can figure out what got us here.

http://www.slate.com/id/2266025/entry/2266026

QUESTIONS FOR READING

1. What prompted the creation of the modern income tax?
2. What was the "Great Compression"?
3. Who labeled the post-1979 epoch the "Great Divergence"?
4. How did King believe income inequality could be addressed in 1915?
5. According to Noah, why is income inequality an important topic?

QUESTIONS FOR REASONING AND ANALYSIS

1. How would you summarize or explain Noah's main point?
2. Why do you think Noah begins his essay with a story about Willford King's 1915 publication?
3. Does Noah convince you, as a reader, of the significance of this problem? Why or why not?

QUESTIONS FOR REFLECTING AND WRITING

1. In your view, is income inequality a serious problem that the United States should address? Why or why not?
2. In essays following this piece, how do you think Noah will advocate for addressing income inequality? Why do you think he will support certain courses of action?
3. Do you think income inequality has affected either you and/or your family? Why or why not?

Glenn Beck is a political commentator and talk show host. His report on the U.S. housing market crash originally aired on the Fox News Channel on June 16, 2009. You can download Beck's commentary from YouTube at www.youtube.com/watch?v=a3g6Yr5S7cg&feature=related.

QUESTIONS FOR REASONING AND ANALYSIS

(Stream the video before answering these questions.)

1. Why does David Buckner choose to use a graph to make his point? Is it an effective technique? Why or why not?

2. What does Prechter mean by "bear market" in his answers to Beck's questions?

3. What purpose do the captions at the bottom of the screen serve? Are these captions effective in communicating the message? Why or why not?

4. If this video makes a claim or argument, what might that claim be?

QUESTIONS FOR REFLECTING AND WRITING

1. Conduct some additional research on the current U.S. housing market. Based on your research, do you think the market will improve? Why or why not?

2. What were the primary causes of the housing crisis in 2008 and 2009? In your view, what steps can be taken to avoid another housing crisis?

3. Glenn Beck is a controversial figure in the American media. In fact, Fox News recently cancelled his program on their network. Does the fact that this report aired on his show affect whether you take it seriously? Why or why not?

prereading question } Is the United States facing another Great Depression?

The Shadow of Depression

Robert J. Samuelson

As a weekly columnist for *The Washington Post,* Robert J. Samuelson writes about economic, political, and social issues. *The Washington Post* published this piece on March 16, 2009.

We live in the shadow of the Great Depression. Americans' gloom does not reflect just 8.1 percent unemployment or the loss of $13 trillion worth of housing and stock market value since mid-2007. There is also an amorphous anxiety that we are falling into a deep economic ravine from which escape will be difficult. These worries may prove ill-founded. But until they do, they promote pessimism and the hoarding of cash, by consumers and companies alike, that further weaken the economy.

Our only frame of reference for this sort of breakdown is the Great Depression. Superficially, the comparison seems absurd. We are a long way from the 1930s, as Christina Romer, head of President Obama's Council of Economic Advisers, noted recently in a useful talk. Unemployment peaked at 25 percent in 1933. At its low point, the economy (gross domestic product) was down 25 percent from its 1929 high. So far, U.S. GDP has dropped only about 2 percent.

What's more, the Depression changed our thinking and institutions. The human misery of economic turmoil has diminished. "American workers [in the 1930s] had painfully few of the social safety nets that today help families," Romer said. Until 1935, there was no federal unemployment insurance. At last count, there were 32 million food stamp recipients and 49 million on Medicaid. These programs didn't exist in the 1930s.

Government also responds more quickly to slumps. Despite many New Deal programs, "fiscal policy"—in effect, deficit spending—was used only modestly in the 1930s, Romer argued. Some of Franklin Roosevelt's extra spending was offset by a tax increase enacted in Herbert Hoover's last year. The federal deficit went from 4.5 percent of GDP in 1933 to 5.9 percent in 1934, not a huge increase.

Contrast that with the present. In fiscal 2009, the budget deficit is projected at 12.3 percent of GDP, up from 3.2 percent in 2008. Some of the increase reflects "automatic stabilizers" (in downturns, government spending increases and taxes decrease); the rest stems from the massive "stimulus program." On top of this, the Federal Reserve has cut its overnight interest rate to about zero and is lending directly in markets where private investors have retreated, including housing.

Government's aggressive actions should reinforce some of the economy's normal mechanisms for recovery. As pent-up demand builds, so will the pressure for more spending. The repayment of loans, lowering debt burdens, sets the stage for more spending. Ditto for the runoff of surplus inventories.

So, are Depression analogies far-fetched, needlessly alarmist? Probably—but not inevitably. Even some Depression scholars, who once dismissed the possibility of a repetition, are less confident.

"Unfortunately, the similarities [between then and now] are growing more striking every day," says economic historian Barry Eichengreen of the University of California at Berkeley. "I never thought I'd say that in my lifetime." Argues economist Gary Richardson of UC Irvine: "This is the first business downturn since the 1930s that looks like the 1930s."

One parallel is that it's worldwide. In the 1930s, the gold standard transmitted the crisis from country to country. Governments raised interest rates to protect their gold reserves. Credit tightened, production and trade suffered, unemployment rose. Now, global investors and banks transmit the crisis. If they suffer losses in one country, they may sell stocks and bonds in other markets to raise cash. Or as they "deleverage"—reduce their own borrowing—they may curtail lending and investing in many countries.

The consequences are the same. In the fourth quarter of 2008, global industrial production fell at a 20 percent annual rate from the third quarter, says the World Bank. International trade may "register its largest decline in 80 years." Developing countries need to borrow at least $270 billion; if they can't, their economies will slow and that will hurt the advanced countries that export to them. It's a vicious circle.

Just as in the 1930s, there's a global implosion of credit. What's also reminiscent of the Depression are quarrels over who's to blame and what should be done. The Obama administration wants bigger stimulus packages from Europe and Japan. Europeans have rebuffed the proposal. The United States has also proposed greater lending by the International Monetary Fund to relieve stresses on poorer countries. Disputes could fuel protectionism and economic nationalism.

No one knows how this epic struggle will end—whether the forces pushing down the global economy will prevail over those trying to pull it up. "Depression" captures a general alarm. The vague fear that something bad is happening, by whatever label, causes consumers and business managers to protect themselves by conserving their cash and slashing their spending. They hope for the best and prepare for the worst.

When people stop worrying about depression, when the shadow lifts, the crisis will be over.

From *The Washington Post*, March 16, 2009, p. A17. © 2009 The Washington Post. All rights reserved. www.washingtonpost.com/wp-dyn/content/article/2009/03/15/AR2009031501946.html

QUESTIONS FOR READING

1. What did the Depression change, according to Samuelson?
2. What differences does he cite between the Depression of the 1930s and the present age? What are some similarities?
3. What does the "vague fear that something bad is happening" cause?

QUESTIONS FOR REASONING AND ANALYSIS

1. In your own words, what is Samuelson's thesis?
2. What does Samuelson mean by the "shadow of the Great Depression"? Why do you think he uses this imagery?
3. What type of evidence does Samuelson typically rely upon for supporting his point? Has he effectively used this evidence? Why or why not?
4. What does Samuelson mean when he states that "disputes could fuel protectionism and economic nationalism"? What is he suggesting might cause "disputes"?

QUESTIONS FOR REFLECTING AND WRITING

1. In your view, are fears of another Great Depression well founded? Why or why not? What evidence supports that we will face another Depression? If fears are unfounded, then what evidence supports that we will *not* face another Great Depression?
2. What are your concerns related to the current economic and financial crisis? Are you, for instance, worried about finding a job after earning your degree? Why or why not?
3. How would you respond to Samuelson? Would you agree with him? Why or why not?

Photos

Design Elements

Design Elements

Try It! feature: (grass) © Eva Serrabassa/ iStockphoto, (stork) © Dick Freder/ iStockphoto, (parasol) © Gary Blakeley/ iStockphoto, (billboard) © Photodisc/ Getty Images, (cow) © Erik de Graaf/ iStockphoto, (temple) © Robert Churchill/ iStockphoto. *Good Advice* feature: (tablet) © Vincenzo Lombardo/Getty Images. *Seeing the Argument* feature: (glasses) © Murat Giray Kaya/iStockphoto. *Did You Know?* feature: (newspapers) © Kyle Maass/iStockphoto, (books) © Viorika Prikhodko/iStockphoto. *Collaborative Exercise* feature: (handshake) © Ben Blankenburg/iStockphoto, (students) © Jacob Wackerhausen/iStockphoto, (hands) © Jacob Wackerhausen/iStockphoto, (cd) © Tatiana Popova/iStockphoto.

Chapter 1

pp. 2–3: © Lars Niki; p. 4 (top): Vanity Fair Cover; March 2010 Hollywood Issue. © Annie Leibovitz/Contact Press Images; p. 4 (bottom): Phrased & Confused - www. phrasedandconfused.co.uk; p. 5 (top): © From Time Magazine, February 7 © 2011 Time Inc. Used under license; p. 5 (bottom): Courtesy of Grand Central Publishing, a division of Hachette Book Group, Inc.; p. 6 (top: left to right): © Ingram Publishing / AGE Fotostock, © Stockdisc/PunchStock, © Comstock Images/ Alamy; p. 6 (bottom): © Digital Vision/Getty Images; p. 9: © Ryan McVay/Getty Images; p. 11: © The McGraw-Hill Companies Inc./ John Flournoy, photographer; p. 12: © Theo Westenberger/Corbis Outline; p. 13 (left): Martha Stewart © 2008 America's Milk Processors/Lowe, NY; p. 13 (right): David Beckham © 2006 America's Milk Processors/ Lowe, NY; p. 14 (top): © PETA.org.uk; p. 14 (bottom): The Bridgeman Art Library/Greek; p. 15: © Irene Fertik; p. 17 (top): Courtesy of www.askleap.com; p. 17 (bottom): © Brand X Pictures; p. 19: Courtesy of Soulforce; p. 22: The McGraw-Hill Companies, Inc./ John Flournoy, photographer; p. 23: © Rich Messina, File/AP Photo; p. 24: Arne Nævra/ Naturbilder.

Chapter 2

pp. 28–29: © Veer; p. 30: Library of Congress Prints and Photographs Division [LC-USZ62- 15984 (b&w film copy neg.)]; p. 32: © Library of Congress Prints and Photographs Division [LC-USZ62-105425 (b&w film copy neg.)]; p. 40: Photo by Hulton Archive/Getty Images.

Chapter 3

pp. 46–47: © BananaStock/PictureQuest; p. 48: © Joshua Roberts/Stringer/Getty Images; p. 50: © Borders Perrin Norrander & Pollinate Media; p. 51: (gun) © Stockbyte/Getty Images, (fetus) © Brand X Pictures/PunchStock; p. 52 (left to right): (blackboard) © Digital Vision/ PunchStock, (graphics) © Ryan McVay/Getty Images, (presentation) © Corbis, (newspaper) © BananaStock / PunchStock, (magazine) © The McGraw-Hill Companies, Inc./John Flournoy, photographer, (protest) The McGraw-Hill Companies, Inc./John Flournoy, photographer, (laptop) © BananaStock/PunchStock, (argument) © BananaStock/PunchStock; p. 53 (top): © Stan Honda/AFP/Getty Images, (left to right) © Royalty-Free/Corbis, © Ingram Publishing / Fotosearch, © Big Cheese Photo / JupiterImages, © Royalty-Free/Corbis; p. 55: (figures) © Ferdinand Daniel/Getty Images, (screen) © Photodisc/Getty Images; p. 56: © Alex Brandon/AP Photo; p. 58 (left to right): (drafting) © Stockbyte/PunchStock, (revising) © Ryan McVay/Getty Images, (editing) © Photodisc Collection/Getty Images, (proofreading) © Photodisc Collection/Getty Images; p. 61: © Last Resort/PhotoDisc/Getty Images; p. 62: The Grand Junction Daily Sentinel, Gretel Daugherty/AP Photo.

Chapter 4

p. 69: Wega Theatre Atmosphere.Sony. © Euro RSCG Buenos Aires, Argentina; p. 72: © Concept & Design: Shibin K.K. www.shibi.in; p. 73 (top): © Jack Star/PhotoLink/Getty Images; p. 73 (bottom): © Worth1000.com; p. 75: © Manny Ceneta/AFP/Getty Images; p. 76 (left): Courtesy of Kevin Hall, http:// www.ovalstickers.org/; p. 76 (right): Photo by Dirck Halstead/Time Life Pictures/Getty Images.

Chapter 5

pp. 84–85: Copyright © 2009 Hearst Communications, Inc. All Rights Reserved; p. 86 (top): © Mark Cunningham/MLB Photos via Getty Images; p. 86 (bottom): © West Plains Daily Quill, Melissa McEntire/ AP Photo; p. 90: Image by Jesus Metropolitan Community Church, www.JesusMCC.org.

Chapter 19

pp. 338–339: © Ryan McVay/Getty Images.

Chapter 20

pp. 354–355: © Clay Good/Zuma Press.

Chapter 21

pp. 378–379: The McGraw-Hill Companies, Inc./Andrew Resek, photographer; **p. 382:** © Stephen Hird/Reuters.

Chapter 22

pp. 394–395: The McGraw-Hill Companies, Inc./Jill Braaten, photographer.

Chapter 23

pp. 410–411: © Comstock Images/PictureQuest; **p. 414 (top):** © Nova Development; **p. 414 (bottom):** McGraw-Hill Companies.

Chapter 24

pp. 424–425: AFP/Getty Images; **p. 437:** © Jose Luis Magana/AP Photo.

Figures/Text

Chapter 1

p. 8: Excerpt from "Audience," www.unc.edu/writingcenter, The Writing Center, The University of North Carolina at Chapel Hill. Reprinted with permission; **pp. 10–11:** Lehigh Valley Live Opinion, "Find the Right Punishment for Teen-Age 'Sexting'" by Express-Times Opinion staff, Jan. 27, 2011. Used with permission. http://www.lehighvalleylive.com/today/index.ssf/2011/01/opinion_find_the_right_punishm.html.

Chapter 2

p. 34: Screen Shot of Jason Mraz's home page, http://jasonmraz.com/index.php. Reprinted by permission of Bill Silva Management. All rights reserved; **p. 39:** *Variety* Screen shot. Copyright © Reed Business Information, a division of Reed Elsevier, Inc.; **p. 41:** "Grim Warning for America's Fast Food Consumers Offered By 'Supersize Me' Mice Research," *Medical News Today*, May 29, 2007. Reprinted by permission of Medical News Today; **pp. 42–43:** "Communication Key to Egypt's Uprising" by Hany Rashwan. Used with permission of *The Lantern*, the student voice of The Ohio State University.

Chapter 3

p. 55: Graph: "The Long-Term Legacy of TV Violence" from *ISR Update*, vol. 1, no. 2 (Spring 2002), p. 7. Reprinted by permission of Institute for Social Research, University of Michigan; **pp. 63–65:** Deborah Tannen, "We Need Higher Quality Outrage," *The Christian Science Monitor*, October 22, 2004, p. 9. Copyright © Deborah Tannen. Reprinted by permission. This article is adapted from *The Argument Culture: Moving from Debate to Dialogue*. New York: Ballantine, 1999. This article first appeared in *The Christian Science Monitor* (www.csmonitor.com).

Chapter 4

pp. 81–82: "How to Argue Effectively" by Dave Barry. Copyright © by David Barry. Reprinted by permission of the author. Dave Barry is a humorist with the Miami Herald; **p. 83:** Miles Haefner, Letter to the Editor, "Better Things to Worry About than Smoking," *Reporter*, May 2, 2006. Reprinted by permission of Reporter, Minnesota State University, Mankato.

Chapter 5

pp. 87–88: David Sadker, "Gender Games," The Washington Post, July 31, 2000. Reprinted by permission of the author. David Sadker is professor emeritus, American University and currently teaching and writing in Tucson, Arizona. He is co-author of *Still Failing at Fairness* (Scribner's 2009); **pp. 89–90:** Mike Alleyway, "Response to Goth's Wan Stamina," *The Chronicle of Higher Education*, Chronicle Forums, posted June 13, 2007. Reprinted by permission of Mike Alleyway.

Chapter 6

pp. 103–104: Editorial, "Ultimately We Control Our Own Privacy Levels on Facebook," *Collegiate Times*, February 19, 2009. Copyright © 2009 Educational Media Company at Virginia Tech Inc. Reprinted with permission.

Chapter 7

pp. 121–123: Excerpts from Gregg Easterbrook, "TV Really Might Cause Autism. A *Slate* Exclusive: Findings from a New Cornell Study," *Slate*, October 16, 2006. Copyright © 2006 by Gregg Easterbrook. Reprinted by permission of the author.

Chapter 8

p. 131: Screen shot from The State News home page: www.statenews.com/index.php/section/opinion. Reprinted by permission of The State News/statenews.com; **pp. 135–136:** "It's Time to Legalize Drugs," by Peter Moskos and Stanford "Neill" Franklin. *The Washington Post*, August 17, 2009. Reprinted by permission of the authors.

Chapter 10

pp. 172–174: "Everybody's Talking" by Joe Navarro. Copyright © 2008 by Joe Navarro. Originally appeared in *The Washington Post* 6/24/08. Reprinted by permission of the author; **p. 174:** "Body Language" by Peter Arkle. Originally published in The Washington Post. Copyright © 2011 by Peter Arkle. Reprinted by permission of the illustrator.

Chapter 15

pp. 274–277: Hugh Graham, "The End of Consumer Culture?" hughgrahamcreative.com, January 30, 2008. Reprinted by permission of the author. The figure is from Grouzet, F. M. E., Kasser, T., Ahuvia, A., et al. (2005). The structure of goal contents across 15 cultures. *Journal of Personality and Social Psychology*, 89: 800–816 (Figure 1, p. 808). Copyright © 2005 by the American Psychological Association. Reprinted with permission; **pp. 278–280:** "Capitalism, Consumerism and Feminism" by Nina Power. Originally appeared in www.newleftproject.org February 25, 2010. Reprinted by permission of the author; **p. 281:** "This or That" Kia Motors Advertisement reprinted by permission of Kia Motors of North America and David & Goliath Advertising Agency. All rights reserved; **pp. 282–283:** "Consumerism is Eating the Future" by Andy Coughlan. Copyright © 2009 Reed Business Information–UK. Distributed by Tribune Media Services; **pp. 284–285:**

"McDonald's Hit by Happy Meal Toy Ban" by Carla Fried. From www.moneywatch.com. November 4, 2010. Reprinted by permission of the YGS Group; **pp. 286–287:** Jeff Howe, "Why the Music Industry Hates *Guitar Hero*, *Wired*, Feb. 23, 2009. Reprinted by permission of Jeff Howe, Contributing Editor, *Wired* magazine. Originally published in *Wired*.

Chapter 16

pp. 293–296: (including graph) Henry Blodgett, "Five Years Later, The Huffington Post (And Online Media) Are Coming of Age," Reprinted by permission of Henry Blodget and *Business Insider*; **pp. 299–300:** "Defending Video Games: Breeding Evil? There's No Solid Evidence That Video Games are Bad for People, and They May Be Positively Good," Copyright © The Economist Newspaper Limited, London, August 4, 2005. By permission of the Economist Newspaper Limited via the Copyright Clearance Center; **pp. 301–303:** "If Technology is Making Us Stupid, It's Not Technology's Fault." Copyright © David Theo Goldberg. Reprinted by permission; **p. 306:** "All Watched Over by Machines of Loving Grace" from *The Pill Versus the Springhill Mine Disaster* by Richard Brautigan. Copyright © 1968 by Richard Brautigan. Reprinted by permission of Houghton Mifflin Harcourt Publishing Company. All rights reserved.

Chapter 17

pp. 310–311: "Arizona Immigration Law Could Lead to Surge in Violent Crime," *America's Voice*, July 12, 2010. Reprinted by permission of America's Voice; **p. 312:** Screen shot with movie review by Christopher Gildemeister. Reprinted by permission of Parents Television Council. http://www.parentstv.org/ptc/publications/moviereviews/ptc/2009/newmoon.asp; **pp. 315–317:** "Do Guns Provide Safety? At What Cost?" by Puneet Narang, MD, et al. http://www.medscape.com/viewarticle/717278. Reprinted by permission of Walters Kluwer Heatlh via Copyright Clearance Center; **pp. 319–320:** "Mall Riots: Why Are Some Americans Becoming Violent Shoppers?" Copyright © 2011 by Seth Sandronsky. Reprinted by permission of the author.

Chapter 23

pp. 412–413: "Dear Francis Collins: Opposition to Therapeutic Cloning About Ethics, Not Religion" by Wesley J. Smith. Reprinted by permission of *First Things*; **pp. 416–418:** "You Can't Believe in Both Creationism and Evolution" Essay by Ken Ham of "Answers in Genesis." Reprinted by permission of *Answers in Genesis.* www.answersingenesis. org. Essay also incorporates several paragraphs of text by Pete Enns, Alister McGrath and Jeff Schloss taken from The BioLogos Foundation website. Reprinted by permission of The BioLogos Foundation, www.biologos.org; **pp. 420–422:** Laura K. Donohue, "Censoring Science Won't Make Us Any Safer," *The Washington Post*, June 26, 2005, p. B5. Reprinted by permission of the author; **pp. 422–423:** "Global Warming as Religion: You Had to See it Coming" by Chuck Colson. From BreakPoint, December 2, 2009. Reprinted with permission of Prison Fellowship, www.breakpoint.org.

Chapter 24

pp. 428–429: "Please Raise My Taxes" by Reed Hastings. *New York Times*, Op-Ed, 2/6/2009. Copyright © 1997–2011 Netflix, Inc. Reproduced by permission of Netflix, Inc. All rights reserved; **pp. 429–431:** Ip, Greg. "Think This Economy is Bad? Wait for 2012." Reprinted by permission of the author; **pp. 434–436:** "The United States of Inequality" by Timothy Noah. From Slate, 9/30/10. Copyright © 2010 The Slate Group. All rights reserved. Used by permission and protected by the Copyright Laws of the United States. The printing, copying, redistribution, or retransmission of the Material without express written permission is prohibited; **pp. 438–439:** "The Shadow of Depressions" by Robert J. Samuelson. From *The Washington Post*, March 16, 2009, p. A17. © 2009 The Washington Post. All rights reserved. Used by permission and protected by the Copyright Laws of the United States. The printing, copying, redistribution, or retransmission of the Material without express written permission is prohibited.